SO-AJL-889

Curr
f

1023
B68
1994
c. 2

DUE DATE

INDEX TO
POETRY
for CHILDREN *and*
YOUNG PEOPLE

1988–1992

/

VOLUMES IN THIS SERIES

INDEX TO
POETRY
for CHILDREN and
YOUNG PEOPLE
1988–1992

A TITLE, SUBJECT, AUTHOR, AND FIRST LINE INDEX

TO POETRY IN COLLECTIONS

FOR CHILDREN AND YOUNG PEOPLE

Compiled by
G. Meredith Blackburn III

THE H.W. WILSON COMPANY • NEW YORK 1994

International Standard Book Number 0–8242–0861–7

Printed in the United States of America

Library of Congress Cataloging-in-Publication Data

Blackburn, G. Meredith.
    Index to poetry for children and young people, 1988–1992:
a title, subject, author, and first line index to poetry in collections for children and young people / compiled by G. Meredith Blackburn III.
        p.   cm.
    Includes bibliographical references.
    ISBN 0–8242–0861–7
    1. Children's poetry—Indexes.   I. Title.
PN1023.B68   1994
016.80881'0083—dc20   94–13171
                                                             CIP

CONTENTS

INTRODUCTION

The *Index to Poetry for Children and Young People: 1988–1992* is a dictionary index—with title, subject, author and first line entries—to 123 collections of poetry for children and young people. Most of the collections were published between 1988 and 1992, inclusive; a few were issued at an earlier date but omitted from earlier editions of the *Index*. In this edition, more than 7,500 poems by approximately 2,000 authors and translators are classified under some 1,500 subjects.

One of a series, this volume is the fourth supplement to the *Index to Poetry for Children and Young People: 1964–1969*. The series was initiated in 1942 with the publication of the *Index to Children's Poetry*, compiled by John E. and Sara W. Brewton. Additional volumes are listed on page ii.

Scope. The carefully-selected books of poetry that are indexed here include collections for the very young child (e.g., books classified as "Easy Books" in *Children's Catalog*, Mother Goose rhymes, etc); collections for the elementary school grades (e.g., the range of collections in class 811 in *Children's Catalog*); and collections suitable for junior and senior high school students (e.g., such collections as are found in class 821.08 in *Junior High School Library Catalog* and in *Senior High School Library Catalog*). In addition to anthologies or collections of poetry by more than one poet, volumes by individual poets (e.g., books by Maya Angelou, Myra Cohn Livingston, X. J. Kennedy) and selections from the works of a single author (e.g., *Rhymes and Verses: Collected Poems for Young People*, Walter De La Mare) are also included. Poems that appear in anthologies that also contain prose selections (e.g., *Children of Promise: African-American Literature and Art for Young People*, edited by Charles Sullivan) are indexed, as well as those that appear in collections of poetry devoted to a single subject (e.g., *American Sports Poems*, compiled by May Swenson and R. R. Knudson). The inclusion of comprehensive collections (e.g., *The Family Read-Aloud Holiday Treasury*, edited by Alice Low, and *Wider Than The Sky: Poems to Grow Up With*, compiled by Scott Elledge) give the index a wide range.

Selection of Collections Included. Selection of the 123 collections indexed here is based on a list of titles voted on by consulting librarians and specialists in various parts of the United States. A comprehensive list of anthologies and volumes of poetry by individual authors was sent to the consultants, their advice secured, and the final selections made. The names of the consultants follow this Introduction.

Entries. Entries are of four basic types: title, subject, author, and reference from first line to title. The addition of collection symbols to title, subject, and author entries makes these complete within themselves, thus obviating the necessity for cross references.

1. TITLE ENTRY. The fullest information is given in this entry. Although the symbols

designating the books in which the poems are to be found are also given in the author and subject entries, the title entry is the only one which gives the full name of the author, when known, and the full name of the translator, if any. References to the title entry have been made both from first lines (e.g., "In and out the bushes, up the ivy." See The chipmunk) and from variant titles (e.g., The chipmunk's day. See The chipmunk).

The title entry includes:

(a) Title, followed by first line in parentheses when needed to distinguish between poems with the same title. If a poem is untitled, the first line is treated as the title.

(b) Variant titles, indented under the main title. When the same poem appears in different books with different titles, one title, generally the one most frequently used, has been chosen as the title entry and all variations have been listed under this title. When a poem appears in a bilingual format, the foreign-language version is listed as the main title and the English-language version as the variant.

(c) Full name of author, when known.

(d) Full name of translator, if any.

(e) Symbols for collections in which the poem is found.

In order to bring together selections from a single source, selections are listed under source titles, as well as individually. An example follows:

> **Alice's** adventures in wonderland, sels. Lewis Carroll
> "How doth the little crocodile".—WhAa
>   The crocodile.—ClI
> The lobster quadrille.—MoR
> "Twinkle, twinkle, little bat."—ClI

All entries subordinated under source titles in this manner are also entered in their own alphabetical position, and identified as to source. An example follows:

> The **lobster** quadrille. From Alice's adventures in wonderland. Lewis
>   Carroll.—MoR

A group title (e.g., Four poems for Roy G Biv) under which several poems appear has been treated as a source title. An example follows:

> **Four** poems for Roy G Biv, complete. Barbara Juster Esbensen
> Prism in the window.—EsW
> A question.—EsW
> Rainbow making, a mystery.—EsW
> Rainbow making, magic.—EsW

2. SUBJECT ENTRY. Entries are listed alphabetically by title under various subject headings. For example, under **Animals** are listed poems about animals in general or in variety, while poems about specific animals are grouped under the names of types of animals, as **Apes and monkeys**. A single poem is often classified under a number of subject headings. The poem Grape Sherbert is listed not only under the heading **Ice cream** but also under **Picnics, Memorial day, Fathers and fatherhood, Graves,** and **Childhood recollections**.

Both *See* and *See also* references have been made freely to and from related subjects. These are filed at the beginning of entries for the subject. Examples follow:

> **Honesty.** See Truthfulness and falsehood
> **Honey.** See also Bees

In order that individual poems or selections from longer poems which have been subordinated to source titles may be classified according to subject and may also be readily identified as to sources, they have been entered under subject headings as follows:

> **United States—History—Civil War**
> "Two months after marching through Boston". From For the Union dead. R. Lowell.—SuC

The subject entry gives under the subject heading:

(a) Title, followed by first line in parentheses when needed to distinguish between poems with the same title.

(b) Last name and initials of author.

(c) Symbols for collections in which the poem is to be found.

3. AUTHOR ENTRY. All titles are listed alphabetically under the name of the author. Titles of selections subordinated under source titles are also entered in their proper alphabetical place and referred to the source title; variant titles are cross-referenced to main titles when necessary.

The author entry gives, under the full name of the author:

(a) Title, followed by first line in parentheses when needed to distinguish between poems with the same title.

(b) Symbols for collections in which the poem is to be found.

(c) Cross references from variant titles to main titles, as needed.

(d) Cross references from titles of selections to source titles.

An example follows.

> **Jarrell, Randall**
> The bat ("A bat is born"). See bats
> Bats.—ElW
>   The bat ("A bat is born").—LaN
> Fly by night, sels.
>   "My nest is in the hollow tree".—LiIf
> "My nest is in the hollow tree". See Fly by night
> Say goodbye to Big Daddy.—KnAs

Where the information is available, a translation is listed under both the name of the original author and the names of the translators, in the latter case with the notation tr. An example follows.

> **Fukao, Sumako**
> Bright house, tr. by Kenneth Rexroth and Ikuko Atsumi.— GoU

> **Rexroth, Kenneth**
> Bright house, tr.—GoU
> A dialogue of watching.—GoU
> Raccoon ("The raccoon wears a black mask").—CoAz

4. FIRST LINE REFERENCES. The first line is always given in quotation marks, even when it is also the title. When the title differs from the first line, reference is made from first line to title. An example follows.

> "The **lark** is but a bumpkin fowl". See The bonny bonny owl

Arrangement. The arrangement is alphabetical. Articles are always retained at the beginning of title and first line, but these articles (in English, in foreign languages, and in dialect) are disregarded in alphabetizing. Such entries are alphabetized by the word following the article, and this word is printed in **boldface** (e.g., The **cat** is filed under **C**; La **belle** dame sans merci, under **B**; and "De **almighty** dollar" under **A**). Abbreviations are filed as spelled (e.g., **Mister** precedes **Mr.**). Contractions are filed as one word (e.g., **I'd** is filed as **Id**). Hyphenated compounds are filed as separate words (e.g., **Bed-time** precedes **Bedtime**). To facilitate quick use, the entries beginning with **O** and **Oh** have been filed together under **Oh**. Likewise, names beginning **Mac** and **Mc** have been filed together as **Mac**. Punctuation within a title or first line has been regularized to facilitate mechanical filing. Where the wording is the same, entries have been arranged in the following order: author, subject, title, first line used as title, first line.

Grades. The books have been graded, and the grades are given in parentheses in the Analysis of Books Indexed and in the Key to Symbols. The grading is only approximate and is provided to indicate in general the grades for which each book is suitable. Open-ended grades (e.g., A child's treasury of poems, k–up) are used to establish a minimum age of readership even though some of the material indexed may appeal to older students as well. A book that is comprehensive in nature and is suitable for a wide range of grades up to and beyond the twelfth is designated (r), reference.

Uses. The *Index to Poetry for Children and Young People* should serve as a practical reference book for all who desire to locate poems for children and young people by subject, author, title, or first line. It should prove especially useful to librarians, teachers in elementary and secondary schools, teachers and students of literature for children and young people, radio and television artists, parents, young people, and children. The variety of subject classifications should be helpful to anyone preparing programs for special occasions, to teachers planning activities around the interests of children and young people, to parents who desire to share poetry, and to anyone searching for poems on any given topic. The Analysis of Books Indexed, which gives in detail the contents of each book, number of poems included, number of authors represented, and number of poems in each group or classification, should prove valuable in the selection of collections for purchase or use. The comprehensiveness of the books indexed insures the usefulness of the *Index* to those interested in poetry from the nursery level through secondary school and beyond.

Acknowledgements. The compiler would like to thank the consultants who cooperated in evaluating lists of books. Grateful recognition is given to John Edmund Brewton and Sara Westbrook Brewton, my grandparents, who were the originators and compilers of the first five volumes in this series and assisted in the preparation of the sixth. Thanks are also due to many publishers who kindly provided copies of their books for indexing, and to Bruce Carrick and Norris Smith of The H. W. Wilson Company, who worked diligently and with much patience throughout this project.

GEORGE MEREDITH BLACKBURN III

CONSULTANTS

Dr. Caroline Feller Bauer
Specialist, Children's Literature
Miami Beach, Florida

Terese Bigelow
Children's and YA Librarian
Wayne County Public Library
Goldsboro, North Carolina

Elizabeth Breting
Director, Children's Services
Kansas City Public Library
Kansas City, Missouri

Laurie Dudley
Special Services Librarian
Abilene Public Library
Abilene, Texas

Evaluation Committee
The Newton Public Schools
Newtonville, Massachusetts

Sally Holmes Holtze
Editor and Critic of Children's
    and YA Literature
New York, New York

Amy Kellman
Coordinator, Children's Services
Carnegie Library of Pittsburgh
Pittsburgh, Pennsylvania

Elizabeth Overmyer
Children's Reference Specialist
Bay Area Library and Information
    System
Oakland, California

Linda Perkins
Supervising Program Librarian
Young People's Services
The Berkeley Public Library
Berkeley, California

Dr. Henrietta M. Smith
Instructor, Children's Literature
School of Library and Information
    Science
University of South Florida
Tampa, Florida

Arrolyn H. Vernon
Librarian Emeritus
Beaver Country Day School
Chestnut Hill, Massachusetts

Caroljean Wagner
Central Library, Children's Room
Milwaukee Public Library
Milwaukee, Wisconsin

ANALYSIS OF BOOKS OF POETRY INDEXED

*Adoff, Arnold. Chocolate Dreams; illustrated by Turi MacCombie. Lothrop 1989 (5–up).

    Contents—49 poems, ungrouped.

Adoff, Arnold. In for Winter, Out for Spring; illustrated by Jerry Pinkney. Harcourt 1991 (k–2).

    Contents—30 poems, ungrouped.

Agard, John, comp. Life Doesn't Frighten Me at All; illustrated by Lo Cole. Holt 1990 (YA). Originally published in England by William Heinemann, Ltd.

    Contents—84 poems by 78 authors grouped as follows: Body talk, 13; Mum Dad me, 12; Did Jesus have a baby sister, 17; Propositions, 11; The lesson, 13; Life doesn't frighten me, 18. Indexed by first lines and authors.

*Angelou, Maya. I Shall Not Be Moved. Random 1990 (YA).

    Contents—33 poems, ungrouped. Table of contents.

*Bauer, Caroline Feller, comp. Halloween: Stories and Poems; illustrated by Peter Sis. Lippincott 1989 (5–up).

    Contents—42 poems by 30 authors, ungrouped. Indexed by authors and titles, table of contents, Read about Halloween booklist, and recipes.

Bauer, Caroline Feller, comp. Windy Day: Stories and Poems; illustrated by Dirk Zimmer. Lippincott 1988 (3–5).

    Contents—29 poems by 28 authors, ungrouped. Indexed by authors and titles, table of contents.

Berry, James. When I Dance; illustrated by Karen Barbour. Harcourt 1991 (YA).

    Contents—59 poems grouped as follows: Teach the making of summer, 9; A toast for everybody who is growin', 8; What we said sitting making fantasies, 4; Body-steadier, 9; One, 8; Barriers, 5; Sunny market song, 11; Pods pop and grin, 5.

PR 4145 Z7 T55 1990

Booth, David, comp. 'Til All the Stars Have Fallen: A Collection of Poems for Children; illustrated by Kady MacDonald Denton. Viking 1990 (3–5).

Contents—76 poems by 63 authors grouped as follows: When your ears sing, 13; In silent snow, 9; Higher than the sun, 15; Everything in its place, 12; All my secrets, 10; Voices on the wind, 11; Whistling in the dark, 6. Indexed by authors and titles.

PS 3552 R848 S57 1992

Bryan, Ashley. Sing to the Sun: Poems and Pictures; illustrated by the author. HarperCollins 1992 (k–up).

Contents—23 poems, ungrouped.

PS 3553 A7674 S76 1989

Carson, Jo. Stories I Ain't Told Nobody Yet: Selections From The People Pieces. Orchard 1989 (7–up).

Contents—50 poems grouped as follows: Prologue, 1; Neighbors and kin, 15; Observations, 7; Relationships, 7; Work, 9; We say of ourselves, 11.

PN 6110 A7 B57 1991

Carter, Anne, comp. Birds, Beasts and Fishes: A Selection of Animal Poems; illustrated by Reg Cartwright. Macmillan 1991 (5–up).

Contents—51 poems by 48 authors, ungrouped. Indexes to first lines and titles.

PL 782 E3 R4 1992

Cassedy, Sylvia and Suetake, Kunihiro, comps. and trs. Red Dragonfly on My Shoulder; illustrated by Molly Bang. HarperCollins 1992 (k–5).

Contents—13 poems by twelve authors, ungrouped. Translator's note, Illustrator's note.

PS 3505 I27 H65 1989

Ciardi, John. The Hopeful Trout and Other Limericks; illustrated by Susan Meddaugh. Houghton 1989 (5–up).

Contents—38 poems grouped as follows: Sometimes even parents win, 7; It came from outer space, 9; He was brave, but not for long, 7; Iron men and wooden ships, 5; Heights made him dizzy, 10.

PR 1195 N64 C58

Clark, Emma Chichester, comp. I Never Saw a Purple Cow and Other Nonsense Rhymes; illustrated by the compiler. Little 1991 (k–3).

Contents—118 poems, ungrouped. Index to first lines.

Cole, Joanna and Calmenson, Stephanie, comps. The Eentsy, Weentsy Spider: Finger Plays and Action Rhymes; illustrated by Allan Tiegreen. Morrow 1991 (Pres–2).

Contents—38 poems, ungrouped. Table of contents.

GR 105.5 M57 1990

Cole, Joanna and Calmenson, Stephanie, comps. Miss Mary Mack and Other Children's Street Rhymes; illustrated by Allan Tiegreen. Morrow 1990 (k–3).

Contents—114 rhymes grouped as follows: Hand-clapping rhymes, 18; Ball-bouncing rhymes, 13; Counting-out rhymes, 29; Just for fun rhymes, 32; Teases and comebacks, 22. Index to first lines.

PS595 A5 Z66 1992

Cole, William, comp. A Zooful of Animals; illustrated by Lynn Munsinger. Houghton 1992 (2–up).

Contents—44 poems by 40 authors, ungrouped.

Nixon

*⚹***Dakos, Kalli.** If You're Not Here, Please Raise Your Hand: Poems About School; illustrated by G. Brian Karas. Four Winds/Macmillan 1990 (4–8).

Contents—38 poems ungrouped. Table of contents.

M 1990 A78 1989

Delacre, Lulu, comp. Arroz Con Leche: Popular Songs and Rhymes from Latin America; illustrated by the compiler. Scholastic 1989 (3–up).

Contents—12 poems ungrouped, in Spanish and English.

PQ 2613 A655 P7313 1962

De Gasztold, Carmen Bernos. Prayers from the Ark; illustrated by Barry Moser. Translated by Rumer Godden. Viking/Penguin 1992 (5–up).

Contents—13 poems ungrouped.

PL 782 E3 D46 1992

Demi, comp. In the Eyes of the Cat: Japanese Poetry for All Seasons; illustrated by the compiler. Translated by Tze-si Huang. Holt 1992 (2–5).

Contents—77 poems by 41 authors grouped as follows: Winter, 13; Spring 22; Summer, 28; Autumn, 14.

PR 6007 E3 P4 1989

De La Mare, Walter. Peacock Pie: A Book of Rhymes; illustrated by Edward Ardizzone. Faber 1989 (5–up).

Contents—92 poems, ungrouped. Table of contents.

PR 6007 E3 A6 2002

De La Mare, Walter. Rhymes and Verses: Collected Poems for Young People; illustrated by Elinore Blaisdell. Holt 1988 (4–up. r).

Contents—343 poems grouped as follows: Green grow the rashes, O, 23; All around about the town, 27; Soldiers, sailors, far Countries, and the sea, 31; All creatures great and small, 57; Fairies, witches, phantoms, 63; Winter and Christmas, 21; Books and stories, 22; Moon and stars, night and dream, 38; Odds and ends, 19; Somewhere, 41; A child's day, 1. Table of contents, indexed by titles and first lines.

PN 6109.97 S36 1988

De Regniers, Beatrice Schenk, comp. Sing a Song of Popcorn: Every Child's Book of Poems; illustrated by nine Caldecott Medal artists. Scholastic 1988 (3–up).

Contents—138 poems by 67 authors grouped as follows: Fun with rhymes, 16; Mostly weather, 28; Spooky poems, 7; Story poems, 5; Mostly animals, 28; Mostly people, 19; Mostly nonsense, 13; Seeing, feeling, thinking, 13; In a few words, 9. Indexed by titles, first lines, and authors. Table of contents.

PS3554 E1755 W39 1988

De Regniers, Beatrice Schenk. The Way I Feel . . . Sometimes; illustrated by Susan Meddaugh. Clarion 1988 (3–up).

Contents—12 poems grouped as follows: Feeling mean, mostly, 5; Feeling better, 3; Feeling wishful, 3; Feeling OK, after all, 1. Table of contents.

PN6109.97 T66 1988

DePaola, Tomie, comp. Tomie DePaola's Book of Poems; illustrated by the compiler. Putnam 1988 (3–up).

    Contents—86 poems by 70 authors ungrouped. Indexed by first lines.

Nixon

Edens, Cooper, comp. The Glorious Mother Goose; illustrated by "The best artists from the past". Atheneum 1988 (k–up).

    Contents—42 Mother Goose rhymes, ungrouped.

PR1175.3 W55 1990

Elledge, Scott, comp. Wider Than the Sky: Poems to Grow Up With. Harper 1990 (5–up, r).

    Contents—220 poems by 121 authors, ungrouped. Indexed by authors and titles. Table of contents.

PS3555 S24 W4 1992

Esbensen, Barbara Juster. Who Shrank My Grandmother's House: Poems of Discovery; illustrated by Eric Beddows. HarperCollins 1992 (2–5).

    Contents—23 poems, ungrouped. Table of contents.

PR9619.3 F38 C68 1990

Fatchen, Max. The Country Mail Is Coming: Poems from Down Under; illustrated by Catharine O'Neill. Little 1987 (5–up).

    Contents—41 poems, ungrouped. Table of contents.

PS3511 I7294 A6 1991

Fisher, Aileen. Always Wondering; illustrated by Joan Sandin. HarperCollins 1991 (7–12).

    Contents—80 poems grouped as follows: Think about people, 20; Suddenly, 16; Such things as these, 17; Whoever planned the world, 27. Table of contents.

Fisher, Aileen. The House of a Mouse; illustrated by Joan Sandin. Harper 1988 (4–8).

    Contents—19 poems, ungrouped.

PS3556 L42268 J69 1988

Fleischman, Paul. Joyful Noise: Poems for Two Voices; illustrated by Eric Beddows. Harper 1988 (5–up).

    Contents—14 poems, ungrouped. Table of contents.

E444 T82 C37 1990

Foster, John, comp. Let's Celebrate: Festival Poems; illustrated by various artists. Oxford 1989 (6–up).

    Contents—84 poems by 41 authors, ungrouped. Table of contents, indexed by titles, authors and first lines.

PS595 N22 S6 1990

Frank, Josette, comp. Snow Toward Evening: A Year in a River Valley; illustrated by Thomas Locker. Dial 1990 (5–up).

    Contents—13 poems by 13 authors, ungrouped.

Glenn, Mel. Back to Class; illustrated with photographs by Michael J. Bernstein. Houghton/Clarion 1988 (7–up).

    Contents—65 poems grouped as follows: Mr. Robert Winograd, English, 5; Mr. Neil Pressman, Fine Arts, 4; Mr. Henry Ashelm, Math, 4; Mr. Joshua Cantor, Physics, 3; Ms. Emily Parsons, History, 4; Ms. Charlotte Kendall, Biology, 3; Mr. Eugene Worthington, Physical Education, 5; Ms. Marilyn Lindowsky, Counselor, 4; Ms. Nadine Sierra, French, 5; Mr. Desmond Klinger, Music, 4; Ms. Yvonne Harmon, Librarian, 4; Mr. John Fletcher, Chemistry, 4; Ms. Phyllis Shaw, Speech, 5; Ms. Joan Gladstone, Special Education, 6; Mr. Ted Sage, Accounting, 5.

Goode, Diane, comp. Diane Goode's American Christmas; illustrated by the compiler. Dutton 1990 (5–up).

   Contents—13 poems by 13 authors, ungrouped, also stories and songs. Table of contents.

Gordon, Ruth, comp. Time Is the Longest Distance: An Anthology of Poems. HarperCollins 1991 (5–up).

   Contents—61 poems by 38 authors, ungrouped. Table of contents. Indexed by authors, first lines, and titles. A Charlotte Zolotow Book.

Gordon, Ruth, comp. Under All Silences, Shades of Love: An Anthology of Poems. Harper 1987 (YA).

   Contents—65 poems by 44 authors, ungrouped. Table of contents. Indexed by authors, first lines, and titles.

Greenfield, Eloise. Night on Neighborhood Street; illustrated by Jan Spivey Gilchrist. Dial 1991 (1–4).

   Contents—17 poems, ungrouped.

Greenfield, Eloise. Under the Sunday Tree; illustrated by Amos Ferguson. Harper 1988 (5–up).

   Contents—20 poems, ungrouped.

Heide, Florence Parry. Grim and Ghastly Goings-on; illustrated by Victoria Chess. Lothrop 1992 (k–5).

   Contents—21 poems, ungrouped.

Hoberman, Mary Ann. Fathers, Mothers, Sisters, Brothers: A Collection of Family Poems; illustrated by Marylin Hafner. Joy Street/Little 1991 (1–4).

   Contents—26 poems, ungrouped. Table of contents.

Hopkins, Lee Bennett, comp. Good Books, Good Times; illustrated by Harvey Stevenson. HarperCollins 1990 (5–8).

   Contents—14 poems by 14 authors, ungrouped.

Hopkins, Lee Bennett, comp. Side by Side: Poems to Read Together; illustrated by Hilary Knight. Simon 1988 (3–up).

   Contents—57 poems by 30 authors, ungrouped. Indexed by authors, first lines, and titles.

Nixon

*Hopkins, **Lee Bennett**, comp. Still as a Star: A Book of Nighttime Poems; illustrated by Karen Milone. Little 1989 (k–3).
Contents—14 poems by 13 authors, ungrouped.

Nixon

*Hopkins, **Lee Bennett**, comp. To the Zoo: Animal Poems; illustrated by John Wallner. Little 1992 (1–4).
Contents—19 poems by 18 authors, ungrouped. Table of contents.

PS3204 H66 1988

Hopkins, **Lee Bennett**, comp. Voyages: Poems by Walt Whitman; illustrated by Charles Mikolaycak. Harcourt 1988 (YA).
Contents—53 poems grouped as follows: Out of the cradle endlessly rocking, 9; You road I enter upon, 14; I mourned, and yet shall mourn, 7; I am the poet of the Body and I am the poet of the Soul, 9; So long, and I hope we shall meet again, 14. Indexed by titles and first lines.

Nixon

*Janeczko, **Paul B.** Brickyard Summer; illustrated by Ken Rush. Orchard 1989 (7–up).
Contents—30 poems, ungrouped. Table of contents.

PS593 N2 M87 1988

Janeczko, **Paul B.**, comp. The Music of What Happens: Poems That Tell Stories. Orchard 1988 (7–up).
Contents—75 poems by 55 authors, ungrouped. Table of contents and index to poets.

PS586.3 P5 1990

Janeczko, **Paul B.**, comp. The Place My Words Are Looking For; illustrated with photographs by various artists. Bradbury 1990 (5–up).
Contents—68 poems by 39 authors, ungrouped. Table of contents and index to authors.

PS586.3 J37 1991

Janeczko, **Paul B.**, comp. Preposterous: Poems of Youth. Orchard 1991 (7–up).
Contents—108 poems by 82 poets, ungrouped. Table of contents and index to authors.

PS3521 E563 F7 1990

Kennedy, **X. J.** Fresh Brats; illustrated by James Watts. McElderry 1990 (5–up).
Contents—42 poems, ungrouped.

Nixon

*Kennedy, **X. J.** Ghastlies, Goops & Pincushions: Nonsense Verse; illustrated by Ron Barrett. McElderry 1989 (4–up).
Contents—62 poems, ungrouped. Table of contents.

PS3521 E563 K58 1991

Kennedy, **X. J.** The Kite That Braved Old Orchard Beach: Year-Round Poems for Young People; illustrated by Marian Young. McElderry 1991 (4–up).
Contents—60 poems grouped as follows: Joys, 7; Growing and dreaming, 10; Family, 5; Friends, 8; Not so ordinary things, 9; Birds, beasts and fish, 9; Times of year, 12. Table of contents.

PN 6109.97 T34 1992

Kennedy, X. J. and Kennedy, Dorothy M., comps. Talking Like the Rain: A Read-to-Me Book of Poems; illustrated by Jane Dyer. Little 1991 (k–2).
> *Contents*—122 poems by 59 authors.

PS 595 S78 A44 1988

Knudson, R. R. and Swenson, May, comps. American Sports Poems. Orchard 1989 (7–up).
> *Contents*—158 poems by 138 authors, ungrouped, informally arranged by sport. Table of contents. Indexed by subjects, authors, and titles.

Nixon

✳ **Knight, Joan.** Tickle-toe Rhymes; illustrated by John Wallner. Orchard 1989 (1–3).
> *Contents*—13 rhymes, ungrouped.

PS 595 C3813 1988

Larrick, Nancy, comp. Cats Are Cats; illustrated by Ed Young. Philomel 1988 (5–up).
> *Contents*—43 poems by 31 authors, ungrouped. Indexed by titles, authors, and first lines.

PN 6110 M43 M54 1990

Larrick, Nancy, comp. Mice Are Nice; illustrated by Ed Young. Philomel 1990 (4–up).
> *Contents*—26 poems by 19 authors, ungrouped. Table of contents, indexed by titles and poets.

Nixon

✳ **Larrick, Nancy,** comp. The Night of the Whippoorwill; illustrated by David Ray. Putnam/Philomel 1992 (4–6).
> *Contents*—34 poems by 25 authors, ungrouped. Indexed by first lines, poets, and titles. Table of contents.

ND 315 L47 L42 1989

Lessac, Frané, comp. Caribbean Canvas; illustrated with paintings by the compiler. Lippincott 1987 (3–6).
> *Contents*—20 poems by 12 authors, ungrouped.

PS 3562 E9465 E27 1991

Lewis, J. Patrick. Earth Verses and Water Rhymes; illustrated by Robert Sabuda. Atheneum 1991 (2–5).
> *Contents*—17 poems, ungrouped.

PS 3562 E9465 H56 1990

Lewis, J. Patrick. A Hippopotamusn't: And Other Animal Verses; illustrated by Victoria Chess. Dial 1990 (5–up).
> *Contents*—35 poems, ungrouped.

PS 3562 E9465 T9 1991

Lewis, J. Patrick. Two-Legged, Four-Legged, No-Legged Rhymes; illustrated by Pamela Paparone. Knopf 1991 (k–2).
> *Contents*—28 poems, ungrouped. Table of contents.

PR 9199.3 L555 H48 1989

Little, Jean. Hey World, Here I Am; illustrated by Sue Truesdell. Harper 1989 (7–up).
> *Contents*—47 poems, ungrouped. Table of contents.

PS 3562 I945 B5 1989

Livingston, Myra Cohn. Birthday Poems; illustrated by Margot Tomes. Holiday House 1989 (3–6).

Contents—24 poems, ungrouped. Table of contents.

PS 586.3 D55 1989

Livingston, Myra Cohn, comp. Dilly Dilly Piccalilli: Poems for the Very Young; illustrated by Eileen Christelow. McElderry 1989 (k–4).

Contents—54 poems by 31 poets, ungrouped. Table of contents, indexed by authors, first lines, and titles.

PS 595 D63 D57 1990

Livingston, Myra Cohn, comp. Dog Poems; illustrated by Leslie Morill. Holiday House 1990 (5–up).

Contents—17 poems by 17 authors, ungrouped. Table of contents.

PS 595 H35 H34 1989

Livingston, Myra Cohn, comp. Halloween Poems; illustrated by Stephen Gammell. Holiday House 1989 (k–up).

Contents—18 poems by 17 authors, ungrouped. Table of contents.

PN 6109.97 I3 1990

Livingston, Myra Cohn, comp. If the Owl Calls Again: A Collection of Owl Poems; illustrated by Antonio Frasconi. McElderry 1990 (5–up).

Contents—71 poems by 62 authors, grouped as follows: Owls in the light, 18; Owls in flight, 15; Owls to delight, 15; Owls of night, 18; Owls to fright, 15. Indexed by authors, translators, first lines, and titles.

PN 6231 L5 L6 1991

Livingston, Myra Cohn, comp. Lots of Limericks; illustrated by Rebecca Perry. McElderry 1991 (k–6).

Contents—210 limericks by 45 authors, grouped as follows: A bundle of birdbrains, 21; Incidents and accidents, 23; Peculiar people, 24; Strange shapes, 19; All in the head, 18; Fabulous foods, 19; Odd numbers and outer space, 20; Flutes and fiddles, 16; Wordplay and puns, 17; Happy holidays, 12; The very end, 21. Indexed by authors, first lines and titles.

Nixon

Livingston, Myra Cohn. My Head Is Red and Other Riddle Rhymes; illustrated by Tere LoPrete. Holiday 1990 (3–up).

Contents—27 riddles, ungrouped.

PS 3562 I945 I8 1992

Livingston, Myra Cohn. I Never Told and Other Poems. McElderry 1992 (4–8).

Contents—42 poems, ungrouped. Table of contents.

Nixon

Livingston, Myra Cohn, comp. Poems for Fathers; illustrated by Robert Casilla. Holiday 1989 (5–up).

Contents—18 poems by 18 authors, ungrouped. Table of contents.

Nixon

Livingston, Myra Cohn, comp. Poems for Grandmothers; illustrated by Patricia Cullen-Clark. Holiday 1990 (5–up).

Contents—18 poems by 18 authors, ungrouped. Table of contents.

Livingston, Myra Cohn, comp. Poems for Mothers; illustrated by Deborah
Kogan Ray. Holiday 1989 (5–up).
  Contents—20 poems by 19 authors, ungrouped. Table of contents.

Nixon

Livingston, Myra Cohn. Remembering and Other Poems. McElderry 1989
(5–up).
  Contents—45 poems, ungrouped. Table of contents.

Nixon

Livingston, Myra Cohn. There Was a Place and Other Poems. McElderry 1988
(5–up).
  Contents—32 poems, ungrouped. Table of contents.

PZ5 F2144 1991

Low, Alice, comp. The Family Read-Aloud Holiday Treasury: illustrated by
Marc Brown. Joy Street/Little 1991 (1–4, r).
  Contents—72 poems by 51 authors grouped as follows: Celebrating
me, 3; New Year's day, 3; Martin Luther King Day, 2; Valentine's day, 5;
President's day, 2; St. Patrick's day, 1; April Fool's day, 1; Passover, 1;
Easter, 4; Earth day, 4; Mother's day, 1; Memorial day, 1; Happy birthday, 4; Father's day, 1; Summer vacation, 6; Canada day, 2; Independence day, 1; Friendship day, 3; Labor day, 1; First day of school, 2;
Grandparent's day, 2; Rosh Ha-shanah, 1; Columbus day, 1; Halloween,
5; Veteran's day, 1; Book week, 3; Thanksgiving, 4; Hanukkah, 1; Christmas, 5; End of year, 1. Table of contents.

Nixon

Mahy, Margaret. Nonstop Nonsense; illustrated by Quentin Blake. McElderry
1989 (3–up).
  Contents—27 poems, ungrouped. Table of contents.

PS3563 A83645 R4 1991

Mathis, Sharon Bell. Red Dog Blue Fly: Football Poems; illustrated by Jan
Spivey Gilchrist. Viking 1991 (5–up).
  Contents—14 poems, ungrouped.

jE PZ2 M2282 PL

McMillan, Bruce. Play Day: A Book of Terse Verse; illustrated with photographs by the poet. Holiday 1991 (k–3).
  Contents—14 poems, ungrouped.

Nixon

Merriam, Eve. Chortles: New and Selected Wordplay Poems; illustrated by
Sheila Hamanaka. Morrow 1989 (7–up).
  Contents—46 poems, ungrouped. Table of contents.

Merriam, Eve. A Poem for a Pickle: Funnybone Verses; illustrated by Sheila
Hamanaka. Morrow 1989 (2–4).
  Contents—28 poems, ungrouped.

PS3525 E639 S58 1992

Merriam, Eve. The Singing Green: New and Selected Poems for All Seasons;
illustrated by Kathleen Collins Howell. Morrow 1992 (5–up).
  Contents—80 poems grouped as follows: Sallies and saunters, 39; The
singing green, 41. Table of contents.

Nixon

✗ **Merriam, Eve.** You Be Good & I'll Be Night: Jump on the Bed Poems; illustrated by Karen Lee Schmidt. Morrow 1988 (k–3)

Contents—28 poems, ungrouped.

PS 586.3 S86 1992

Moore, Lilian, comp. Sunflakes: Poems for Children; illustrated by Jan Ormerod. Clarion 1992 (k–2).

Contents—76 poems by 44 authors grouped as follows: I am very fond of bugs, 5; I like to look in puddles, 7; Me and potato chips, 6; Well, would you, 7; As I was going along, 7; The night is long but fur is deep, 6; Breathing on the window pane in winter, 7; Bright summer lives over the wall, 8; I wonder who is coming, 7; Franks with beans, kings with queens, 6; Oh will you be my wallaby, 4; If sunlight fell like snowflakes, 6. Table of contents; author, title, and first line indexes.

PS 595 B33 A86 1992

Morrison, Lillian, comp. At the Crack of the Bat: Baseball Poems; illustrated by Steve Cieslawski. Hyperion 1992 (3–up).

Contents—44 poems by 33 authors, ungrouped. Table of contents, index to titles and authors.

PS 595 M67 R48 1988

Morrison, Lillian, comp. Rhythm Road: Poems to Move To. Lothrop 1988 (5–up).

Contents—94 poems by 67 authors grouped as follows: The twirl and the swirl, 13; Back through clouds, 17; Wet, wet, wet, 7; Oompah on the tuba, 6; Grasshopper copters whir, 11; Hooray for the show, 9; At the starting line, 11; This old hammer, 7; The rusty spigot sputters, 6; I will remember with my breath, 7. Index to titles, authors, and first lines.

PR 9320.9 N45 C6 1990

Nichols, Grace. Come on into My Tropical Garden: Poems for Children; illustrated by Caroline Blinch. Lippincott 1988 (7–up).

Contents—28 poems, ungrouped. Table of contents.

Nye, Naomi Shihab, comp. This Same Sky: A Collection of Poems from Around the World. Four Winds 1992 (YA).

Contents—163 poems by 132 authors from 68 countries, grouped as follows: Words and silences, 22; Dreams and dreamers, 25; Families, 32; This earth and sky in which we live, 32; Losses, 18; Human mysteries, 33. Notes on contributors, table of contents, indexed by authors, first lines, and titles.

PR 977 I85 1992

Opie, Peter and Opie, Iona, comps. I Saw Esau: The Schoolchild's Pocket Book; illustrated by Maurice Sendak. Candlewick 1992 (k–4, r).

Contents—174 rhymes. Extensive origin notes, introduction by the compilers.

PZ 8.3 O6 Tai 1988

Opie, Peter & Opie, Iona, comps. Tail Feathers from Mother Goose: The Opie Rhyme Book; illustrated by various artists. Little 1988 (k–4).

Contents—65 rhymes, ungrouped. Index to titles.

PS 3566 R36

Plotz, Helen, comp. A Week of Lullabies; illustrated by Marisabina Russo. Greenwillow 1988 (k–3).

    Contents—14 poems by 14 authors, ungrouped.

PS 3566 R36 B4 1990

Prelutsky, Jack. Beneath a Blue Umbrella; illustrated by Garth Williams. Greenwillow 1990 (k–3).

    Contents—28 poems, ungrouped. Table of contents.

PS 595 H8 F67 1991

Prelutsky, Jack, comp. For Laughing Out Loud: Poems to Tickle Your Funnybone; illustrated by Marjorie Priceman. Knopf 1991 (1–5).

    Contents—132 poems by 57 authors, ungrouped. Indexed by authors, titles, and first lines.

PS 586.3 A2 1993

Prelutsky, Jack. Poems of A. Nonny Mouse; illustrated by Henrik Drescher. Knopf 1989 (k–3).

    Contents—68 poems, ungrouped.

PS 3566 R36 T97 1988

Prelutsky, Jack. Tyrannosaurus Was a Beast: Dinosaur Poems; illustrated by Arnold Lobel. Greenwillow 1988 (3–up).

    Contents—14 poems, ungrouped. Table of contents.

PZ5 B445 1990

Sachs, Marilyn and Durrell, Ann, comps. The Big Book for Peace; illustrated by various artists. Dutton 1990 (5–up).

    Contents—8 poems ungrouped. Also stories.

PS 477 S39 1992

Schwartz, Alvin, comp. And the Green Grass Grew All Around: Folk Poetry from Everyone; illustrations by Sue Truesdell. HarperCollins 1992 (3–up).

    Contents—261 rhymes grouped as follows: People, 26; Food, 18; School 15; Teases and taunts, 32; Wishes and warnings, 12; Love and marriage, 23; Work, 1; Stories, 5; Nonsense, 13; Riddles, 15; Fun and games, 41; Rain and shine, 15; A tree, 2; Animals and insects, 15; Other things, 27. Table of contents, notes on origins, index to first lines.

Nixon

✳**Shine, Deborah Slier; Turner, Elizabeth; and Patrick, Denise Lewis**, comps. Make a Joyful Sound: Poems for Children by African American poets; illustrated by Cornelius Van Wright and Ying-Hwa Hu. Checkerboard 1990 (k–4).

    Contents—75 poems by 27 authors. Indexed by authors, first lines, and titles. Also notes about the poets.

PS 3569 I546 T87 1989

Singer, Marilyn. Turtle in July; illustrated by Jerry Pinkney. MacMillan 1990 (3–up).

    Contents—17 poems, ungrouped.

PS 3537 M8693 L3 1990

Smith, William Jay. Laughing Time: Collected Nonsense; illustrated by Fernando Krahn. Farrar 1990 (k–5).

Contents—171 poems grouped as follows: The King of hearts, 1; Laughing time, 33; Puptents and pebbles, 28; Boy Blue's beasts, 38; The old man from Okefenokee, 34; Brooklyn Bridge, 7; Imaginary dialogues, 6; A clutch of clerihews, 6; A nuthatch of nonsense birds, 20; Nonsense cookery, 3; The floor and the ceiling, 15; The King of Spain, 1. Table of contents.

PM 197 E3 D36 1984

Sneve, Virgina Driving Hawk, comp. Dancing Teepees: Poems of American Indian Youth; illustrated by Stephen Gammell. Holiday 1989 (7–up).
Contents—19 poems ungrouped. Table of contents.

PS 3569 O72 F5 1990

Soto, Gary. A Fire in My Hands: A Book of Poems; illustrated by James M. Cardillo. Scholastic 1991 (7–12).
Contents—24 poems ungrouped. Table of contents.

PS 3569 O72 N45 1992

Soto, Gary. Neighborhood Odes; illustrated by David Diaz. Harcourt 1992 (4–6).
Contents—21 poems ungrouped. Table of contents.

BV 265 P74 1992

Stoddard, Sandol, comp. Prayers, Praises, and Thanksgivings; illustrated by Rachel Isadora. Dial 1992 (3–6).
Contents—239 poems grouped as follows: Hello God, Beginnings, 73; Wings of freedom, reaching out; 77; Lord of the dance, the great journey, 89. Index to first lines.

PZ5 C43546 1991

Sullivan, Charles, comp. Children of Promise: African-American Literature and Art for Young People; illustrated with 80 reproductions of paintings and drawings by various artists. Abrams 1991 (4–up, r).
Contents—71 poems by 58 authors ungrouped. Indexed by first lines and authors.

Sullivan, Charles, comp. Imaginary Gardens: American Poetry and Art for Young People; 80 illustrations by various artists. Abrams 1989 (7–up).
Contents—86 poems by 54 authors ungrouped. Indexed by first lines and authors.

PZ8.3 S97 Or 1990

Sutherland, Zena, comp. The Orchard Book of Nursery Rhymes; illustrated by Faith Jaques. Orchard 1990 (k–3).
Contents—77 nursery rhymes ungrouped. Index to first lines.

Watson, Wendy, comp. Wendy Watson's Mother Goose; illustrated by the compiler. Lothrop 1989 (k–3).
Contents—218 rhymes ungrouped. Indexed by first lines and subjects.

PN 6110 A7 C37 1989

Whipple, Laura, comp. Eric Carle's Animals, Animals; illustrated by Eric Carle. Philomel 1989 (3–up).
Contents—59 poems ungrouped. Indexed by first lines. Alphabetical list of animals.

PN 6109.97 C37 1991

Whipple, Laura, comp. Eric Carle's Dragons, Dragons & Other Creatures That
Never Were; illustrated by Eric Carle. Philomel 1991 (3–up).
   Contents—34 poems by 29 authors ungrouped. Indexed by authors
and creatures.

PZ 8.3 W76 Ro 1948

Withers, Carl, comp. A Rocket in My Pocket: The Rhymes and Chants of Young
Americans; illustrated by Susanne Suba. Holt 1977 (k–3).
   Contents—428 rhymes ungrouped. Indexed by first lines.

Worth, Valerie. All the Small Poems; illustrated by Natalie Babbitt. Farrar 1989
(2–4).
   Contents—99 poems grouped as follows: Small poems, 24; More small
poems, 25; Still more small poems, 25; Small poems again, 25. Table of
contents.

PS 3573 0697 A93 1992

Worth, Valerie. At Christmastime; illustrated by Antonio Frasconi. Harpercollins 1992 (1–5).
   Contents—29 poems ungrouped.

Nixon

✳**Yolen, Jane.** Best Witches: Poems for Halloween; illustrated by Elise Prima-
vera. Putnam 1989 (4–up).
   Contents—21 poems ungrouped. Table of contents.

PS 3575 043 B5 1990

Yolen, Jane. Bird Watch: A Book of Poetry; illustrated by Ted Lewin. Philomel
1990 (5–up).
   Contents—17 poems ungrouped.

PS 3575 043 D56 1990

Yolen, Jane. Dinosaur Dances; illustrated by Bruce Degen. Putnam 1990 (7–up).
   Contents—17 poems ungrouped. Table of contents.

j PZ 1 Y785 fa

Yolen, Jane. The Faery Flag: Stories and Poems of Fantasy and the Supernatural. Orchard 1989 (7–up).
   Contents—6 poems ungrouped. Table of contents.

PZ8 Y6 Har 1991

Yolen, Jane. Hark! A Christmas Sampler; illustrated by Tomie DePaola. Putnam
1991 (k–up).
   Contents—46 poems ungrouped. Table of contents.

Yolen, Jane, comp. Street Rhymes Around the World; illustrated by various
artists. Wordsong 1992 (1–2).
   Contents—32 rhymes from 16 countries ungrouped.

KEY TO SYMBOLS FOR BOOKS INDEXED

(handwritten: (Nixon) PS 3551.D66 C49 1989)

AdCd Adoff, A. Chocolate Dreams. Lothrop 1989 (5–up)

(handwritten: Curr PS 3551 D66 I6 1991)

AdIn Adoff, A. In for Winter, Out for Spring. Harcourt 1991 (k–2)

(handwritten: Curr PR 1175.3 L54 1990)

AgL Agard, J., comp. Life Doesn't Frighten Me at All. Holt 1990 (YA)

(handwritten: PS 3551 N464 I17 1990)

AnI Angelou, M. I Shall Not Be Moved. Random 1990 (YA)

(handwritten: O.R./(Nixon) PZ5.H157 1989)

BaH Bauer, C. F., comp. Halloween: Stories and Poems. Lippincott 1989 (5–up)

(handwritten: J 808.8 W725)

BaW Bauer, C. F., comp. Windy Day: Stories and Poems. Lippincott 1988 (3–5)

(handwritten: Curr PR 9265.9 B47 W4 1991)

BeW Berry, J. When I Dance. Harcourt 1991 (YA)

(handwritten: Curr PR 9195.27 T55 1990)

BoT Booth, D. 'Til All the Stars Have Fallen: A Collection of Poems for Children. Viking 1990 (3–5)

(handwritten: Curr PS 3552 R848 S57 1992)

BrS Bryan, A. Sing To the Sun: Poems and Pictures. HarperCollins 1992 (k–up)

(handwritten: Curr PN 6110 A4 B57 1991)

CaB Carter, A., comp. Birds, Beasts, and Fishes: A Selection of Animal Poems. Macmillan 1991 (5–up)

(handwritten: PL 782 E3 R4 1992)

CaR Cassedy, S. and Suetake, K., comps. and trs. Red Dragonfly on My Shoulder. HarperCollins 1992 (k–5)

(handwritten: PS 3553 A7674)

CaS Carson, J. Stories I Ain't Told Nobody Yet: Selections From the People Pieces. Orchard 1989 (7–up)

(handwritten: PS 3505 I27 H65 1989)

CiH Ciardi, J. The Hopeful Trout and Other Limericks. Houghton 1989 (5–up)

(handwritten: Curr PR 1195 N64 C58 1991)

ClI Clark, E. C., comp. I Never Saw a Purple Cow and Other Nonsense Rhymes. Little 1991 (k–3)

(handwritten: Curr PS 595 A5 Z46 1992)

CoAz Cole, W., comp. A Zooful of Animals. Houghton 1992 (2–up)

CoE Cole, J. and Calmenson, S., comps. The Eentsy, Weentsy Spider: Finger Plays and Action Rhymes. Morrow 1991 (k–2)

(handwritten: GR 105.5 M57 1990)

CoM Cole, J. and Calmenson, S., comps. Miss Mary Mack: And Other Children's Street Rhymes. Morrow 1990 (k–3)

(handwritten: (Nixon) PS 3554 A414 I37 1990)

DaI Dakos, K. If You're Not Here, Please Raise Your Hand: Poems About School. Macmillan/Four Winds 1990 (4–8)

(handwritten: M 1990 A78 1989)

DeA Delacre, L., comp. Arroz Con Leche: Popular Songs and Rhymes from Latin America. Scholastic 1989 (3–up)

(handwritten: Curr PL 782 E3 D46 1992)

DeI Demi, comp. In the Eyes of the Cat: Japanese Poetry for All Seasons. Holt 1992 (2–5)

(handwritten: (Nixon) PQ 2613 A655 P7313)

DeP De Gasztold, C. B. Prayers from the Ark. Viking Penguin 1992 (5–up)

(handwritten: Curr PN6109.97 S36 1988)

DeS De Regniers, B. S., comp. Sing a Song of Popcorn. Scholastic 1988 (3–up)

(handwritten: Curr PR 6007 E3 A6 2002)

DeR De La Mare, W. Rhymes and Verses: Collected Poems for Young People. Holt 1988 (4–up)

(handwritten: Curr PN 6109.97 T66 1988)

DeT DePaola, T., comp. Tomie DePaola's Book of Poems. Putnam 1988 (2–5)

(handwritten: PS 3554 E1155 W34 1988)

DeW De Regniers, B. S. The Way I Feel . . . Sometimes. Clarion 1988 (3–up)

(handwritten: ordered)

EdGl Edens, C., comp. The Glorious Mother Goose. Atheneum 1988 (3–up)

(handwritten: Curr PR 1175.3 W55 1990)

ElW Elledge, S., comp. Wider Than the Sky: Poems to Grow Up With. Harper 1990 (5–up, r)

(handwritten: Curr PS 3555 S24 W4 1992)

EsW Esbensen, B. J. Who Shrank My Grandmother's House. HarperCollins 1992 (2–5)

(handwritten: Curr PR 9619.3 F38 C68 1990)

FaCm Fatchen, M. The Country Mail Is Coming. Little Brown 1987 (5–up)

LiHp Livingston, M. C., comp. Halloween Poems. Holiday 1989 (k–up)

LiIf Livingston, M. C., comp. If the Owl Calls Again. McElderry 1990 (5–up)

LiLo Livingston, M. C., comp. Lots of Limericks. McElderry 1991 (k–6)

LiMh Livingston, M. C., My Head Is Red and Other Riddle Rhymes. Holiday 1990 (3–up)

LiNe Livingston, M. C., I Never Told Any Other Poems. McElderry 1992 (4–8)

LiPf Livingston, M. C., comp. Poems for Fathers. Holiday 1989 (5–up)

LiPg Livingston, M. C., comp. Poems for Grandmothers. Holiday 1990 (5–up)

LiPm Livingston, M. C., comp. Poems for Mothers. Holiday 1989 (5–up)

LiR Livingston, M. C. Remembering and Other Poems. McElderry 1989 (5–up)

LiT Livingston, M. C. There Was a Place and Other Poems. McElderry 1988 (5–up)

LoFh Low, A. The Family Read-Aloud Holiday Treasury. Joy Street/Little 1991 (1–4)

MaN Mahy, M. Nonstop Nonsense. McElderry 1989 (3–up)

MaP De La Mare, W. Peacock Pie. Faber 1989 (5–up)

MaR Mathis, S. B. Red Dog Blue Fly: Football Poems. Viking 1991 (3–5)

McP McMillan, B. Play Day: A Book of Terse Verse. Holiday 1991 (k–3)

MeCh Merriam, E. Chortles, New and Selected Wordplay Poems. Morrow 1989 (7–up)

MeP Merriam, E. A Poem For a Pickle: Funnybone Verses. Morrow 1989 (2–4)

MeS Merriam, E. The Singing Green: New and Selected Poems for All Seasons. Morrow 1992 (5–up)

MeY Merriam, E. You Be Good & I'll Be Night. Morrow 1988 (k–3)

MoA Morrison, L., comp. At the Crack of the Bat: Baseball Poems. Hyperion 1992 (3–8)

MoR Morrison, L., comp. Rhythm Road: Poems to Move To. Lothrop 1988 (5–up)

MoS Moore, L., comp. Sunflakes: Poems for Children. Clarion 1992 (k–2)

NiCo Nichols, G. Come on into My Tropical Garden: Poems for Children. Lippincott 1988 (7–up)

NyT Nye, N. S., comp. This Same Sky: A Collection of Poems from Around the World. Four Winds 1992 (YA)

OpI Opie, P. and Opie, I., comps. I Saw Esau: The Schoolchild's Pocket Book. Candlewick 1992 (k–up, r)

OpT Opie, P. and Opie, I., comps. Tail Feathers from Mother Goose: The Opie Rhyme Book. Little 1988 (3–up)

PlW Plotz, H., comp. A Week of Lullabies. Greenwillow 1988 (k–3)

PrBe Prelutsky, J. Beneath a Blue Umbrella. Greenwillow 1988 (k–3)

PrFo Prelutsky, J., comp. For Laughing Out Loud. Poems to Tickle Your Funnybone. Knopf 1991 (1–5)

PrP Prelutsky, J., comp. Poems of A Nonny Mouse. Knopf 1989 (k–3)

PrT Prelutsky, J. Tyrannosaurus Was a Beast: Dinosaur Poems. Greenwillow 1988 (3–up)

SaB Sachs, A. and Sachs, M., comps. The Big Book for Peace. Dutton 1990 (5–up)

ScA Schwartz, A., comp. And the Green Grass Grew All Around: Folk Poetry from Everyone. HarperCollins 1992 (3–up)

SiT Singer, M. Turtle in July. MacMillan 1990 (3–up)

SlM Slier, D., comp. Make a Joyful Sound: Poems for Children by African-American Poets. Checkerboard 1990 (k–4)

SmL Smith, W. J. Laughing Time: Collected Nonsense. Farrar 1990 (k–5)

SoNe Soto, G. Neighborhood Odes. Harcourt 1992 (4–6)

SnD Sneve, V. D. H., comp. Dancing Teepees: Poems of American Indian Youth. Holiday 1989 (7–up)

PS3569.072 F5

SoA   Soto, G. A Fire in My Hands: A Book of Poems. Scholastic 1991 (7–12)

curr BV 265 .P74 1992.

StP   Stoddard, S., comp. Prayers, Praises and Thanksgiving. Dial 1992 (3–6)

curr PZ5 C43546 1991

SuC   Sullivan, C., comp. Children of Promise: African-American Literature and Art for Young People. Abrams 1991 (4–up)

o **SuI**   Sullivan, C., comp. Imaginary Gardens: American Poetry and Art for Young People. Abrams 1989 (7–up)

curr PZ8. 3 S97 Or 1990.

SuO   Sutherland, Z., comp. The Orchard Book of Nursery Rhymes. Orchard 1990 (k–3)

op

WaM   Watson, W., comp. Wendy Watson's Mother Goose. Lothrop 1989 (k–3)

curr PN 6110. A7 C37 1989.

WhAa   Whipple, L., comp. Eric Carle's Animals, Animals. Philomel 1989 (3–up)

curr PN 6109.97 C37 1991.

WhDd   Whipple, L., comp. Eric Carle's Dragons, Dragons & Other Creatures That Never Were. Philomel 1991 (3–up)

PZ8.3 W7 Ro 1948

WiA   Withers, C., comp. A Rocket in My Pocket: The Rhymes and Chants of Young Americans. Holt 1988 (k–3)

curr PS 3573.0697 A93 1992.

WoA   Worth, V. At Christmastime. HarperCollins 1992 (1–5)

o **WoAl**   Worth, V. All the Small Poems. Farrar 1989 (2–4)

op (Nixon) PS3575.043 R471989

YoBe   Yolen, J. Best Witches: Poems for Halloween. Putnam 1989 (4–up)

PS3575 043 B5 /ARC

YoBi   Yolen, J. Bird Watch. Philomel 1990 (5–up)

curr PS3575. 043 B5 1990.

YoDd   Yolen, J. Dinosaur Dances. Putnam 1990 (7–up)

j PZ1 Y785 fa

YoFf   Yolen, J. The Faery Flag: Stories and Poems of Fantasy and the Supernatural. Orchard 1989 (7–up)

curr PZ5. Y6 Har 1991

YoH   Yolen, J., comp. Hark! A Christmas Sampler. Putnam 1991 (k–up)

YoS   o Yolen, J., comp. Street Rhymes Around the World. Wordsong 1992 (1–2)

KEY TO ABBREVIATIONS

ad. adapted
at. attributed
bk. book
comp. compiler, compiled
comps. compilers
ed. edition, editor
eds. editors
il. illustrated, illustrator
ils. illustrators
jt. auth. joint author
jt. auths. joint authors
k kindergarten or preschool grade

pseud. pseudonym
pseuds. pseudonyms
r reference
rev. revised
rev. ed. revised edition
sel. selection
sels. selections
tr. translator
trs. translators
unat. unattributed
wr. at. wrongly attributed

DIRECTIONS FOR USE

The title entry is the main entry and gives the fullest information, including title (with first line in parentheses when needed to distinguish between poems with the same title); variant titles; full name of author; translator; and symbols for collections in which the poem is to be found. Variant titles and titles with variant first lines are also listed in their alphabetical order, with attribution to the main title. If a poem is untitled, the first line is treated as the title.

> **A boy's** head. Miroslav Holub, tr. by Ian Milner.—NyT
> "A **horse** and a flea and three blind mice." Unknown.— CoM—WiA
>   Whoops.—ClI
> **Whoops.** See "A horse and a flea and three blind mice"

Titles of poems are grouped according to subject, in alphabetical order under a subject heading. Each Subject Entry gives the title of the poem, the last name of the author with initials, the first line where needed for identification, the source title for subordinate selections, and the symbols for the collections in which the poem is to be found.

> **Beauty, of nature or art**
>   Afternoon on a hill. E. S.V. Millay.—PrS—SuI
>   "All this time and at all times wait the words of true poems."
>   From Song of myself. W. Whitman.—WoVo

The Author Entry gives the full name of the author, title of poem with its variants (first line in parentheses when needed for identification), and the symbols for the collections in which the poem is to be found. Included under the author entry are references from variant titles and from titles of selections to the source title.

> **Carroll, Lewis** (pseud. of Charles Lutwidge Dodgson)
>   Alice's adventures in wonderland, sels.
>   "How doth the little crocodile."—WhAa
>   The crocodile.—ClI
>   The lobster quadrille.—MoR
>   The crocodile. See Alice's adventures in wonderland—
>   "How doth the little crocodile"
>   "How doth the little crocodile." See Alice's adventures in wonderland
>   The lobster quadrille. See Alice's adventures in wonderland

First lines of poems, enclosed in quotation marks, are listed in their alphabetical order with references to the title entry where all the information may be found. First lines are enclosed in quotation marks even when used as titles.

> "**All** my life I lived in a coconut." See Locked in
> "**All** shall be well." Julian of Norwich.—StP

When the source of a poem is more familiar than the title of the poem, or when only the selections from a longer work are given, such titles are grouped under the same source title. All titles subordinated to source titles also appear as individual entries in their alphabetical order with references to the source title.

"If we shadows have offended." From A midsummer night's dream. William Shakespeare.—WhDh

A midsummer night's dream, sels. William Shakespeare
"If we shadows have offended."—WhDh

INDEX TO POETRY FOR CHILDREN AND YOUNG PEOPLE

A

A. John Travers Moore and Margaret Moore.—DeS
A—**Apple** pie. Walter De La Mare.—DeR
"A B C D". See "Alef beys giml dolid"
"A, b, c, d, e, f, g,". See ABC song
"A. B. C. D. Gol'fish". Unknown.—ClI
"A fe ackee, salt fish bes' friend, an'". See Jamaican alphabet
A is for alpaca. William Jay Smith.—SmL
"A la vibora, vibora". Unknown.—YoS
  "To the sea snake we will play".—YoS
"A, my name is Alice". See Alphabet ball
"A, my name is Anna". See Alphabet ball
A-**tishoo**. Walter De La Mare.—DeR
"A was an apple pie". Mother Goose.—SuO
"A was once an apple pie". Edward Lear.—HoS
Aa couple of doublles. Eve Merriam.—MeCh
Aardvarks
  Mom and Pop Ghastly come up for air. X. J. Kennedy.—KeGh
Aaron, Hank (about)
  Hammerin' Hank. D. R. Martin.—MoA
Aaron. Arnold Adoff.—AdIn
Abby Kramer. Mel Glenn.—GlBc
ABC song. Unknown.—HoS
"An **abhorrent** young person named Plunkett". William Jay Smith.—SmL
"**Abner** from an Alpine height". X. J. Kennedy.—KeFb
The **abominable** baseball bat. X. J. Kennedy.—MoA
Aborigines
  Corroboree ("The clap, clap, clap of the clapsticks beat"). M. Fatchen.—FoLe
  Corroboree ("Hot day dies, cook time comes"). K. Walker.—FoLe
About angels and age. Jean Little.—LiHe
About God. Jean Little.—LiHe
About learning things the hard way. John Ciardi.—CiH
About notebooks. Jean Little.—LiHe
About old people. Jean Little.—LiHe
About poems, sort of. Jean Little.—LiHe
About the teeth of sharks. John Ciardi.—CoAz—PrFo
"**About** them whiskey boys". Jo Carson.—CaS
"**Above** the chorus". Kyoshi, tr. by Sylvia Cassedy and Kunihiro Suetake.—CaR
Abraham Lincoln. Stephen Vincent Benet and Rosemary Carr Benet.—LoFh
Absence
  Distances of longing. F. Abu Khalid.—NyT
  The emeritus. L. Nathan.—JaM
  Family. M. C. Livingston.—LiT
  Help ("Would it help"). M. C. Livingston.—LiT
  His girlfriend. M. C. Livingston.—LiT
  "I see the moon, the moon sees me". Unknown.—WiA
  In retrospect. M. Angelou.—GoU
  "It is so long since my heart has been with yours". E. E. Cummings.—GoU
  Letter. M. C. Livingston.—LiT
  Love story (for Deirdre). A. Henri.—GoU
  Poem ("I loved my friend"). L. Hughes.—DeS—DeT—SlM
  Ratio. L. Morrison.—GoU
  Susan. J. Berry.—BeW
  Western wind. Unknown.—ElW
Absolutely nothing. Florence Parry Heide.—HeG
Abu Khalid, Fawziyya
  Distances of longing, tr. by May Jayyusi.—NyT
  A pearl, tr. by Salwa Jabsheh and John Heath-Stubbs.—NyT
Acceptance
  Winston Hines. M. Glenn.—GlBc
Accidents
  Anthony. J. Shore.—JaPr
  Boy, fifteen, killed by hummingbird. L. Linssen.—JaPr
  The bridge. P. B. Janeczko.—JaB
  Casey Jones. Unknown.—MoR
  "A decrepit old gasman, named Peter". Unknown.—LiLo
  "Help, murder, police". Unknown.—CoM
  "Hie to the market, Jenny come trot". Mother Goose.—WaM
    A wasted journey.—OpT
  "Humpty Dumpty sat on a wall". Mother Goose.—EdGl—SuO—WaM
  I hear the usual thump. A. Adoff.—AdIn
  "I was born three months before I's due". J. Carson.—CaS
  "It's raining, it's pouring". Mother Goose.—CoM—OpI—ScA—WiA
  "Jack and Jill". Mother Goose.—EdGl—SuO—WaM
  Jim Jay ("Do diddle di do"). W. De La Mare.—DeR—MaP
  "Joe, Joe, stumped his toe". Unknown.—WiA
  "A lady who lived in Mont.". Unknown.—LiLo
  Leg broken. S. B. Mathis.—MaR
  My happiness. G. Pape.—JaM
  No question. L. Dangel.—JaPr
  "Oh say, kid". Unknown.—WiA
  The old math, one. A. Adoff.—AdCh
  The optimist. Unknown.—PrFo
  "A peanut sat on a railroad track". Unknown.—KeT—PrP
    "A peanut sat on the railroad track".—WiA
    The peanut song ("Oh, a peanut sat . . .").—CoE
  "Piggy on the railway, picking up stones". Unknown.—OpI
  The pioneers. C. Mortimer.—JaPr
  "Rin Tin Tin swallowed a pin". Unknown.—WiA
  "Rock-a-bye, baby, on the treetop". Mother Goose.—SuO—WaM
  "Said a foolish young lady of Wales". L. Reed.—LiLo
  "Said a lady beyond Pompton Lakes". M. Bishop.—LiLo
  Shakespeare's gone. K. Dakos.—DaI
  Skater in blue. J. Parini.—KnAs
  A story that could be true. W. Stafford.—JaP
  The straw. A. Adoff.—AdCh
  "Teddy on the railroad". Unknown.—WiA

Adoff, Arnold—*Continued*
I raise my voice most high, this night.—AdCh
I will hold your hand.—AdCh
In my horror fantasy chiller.—AdCh
In public, I pick a piece or two from the plate.—
AdCh
In the ending of this evening snow.—AdIn
In the memories of our cookies.—AdCh
In this last class before lunch, I close my eyes.—
AdCh
It is late.—AdIn
Labels.—AdCh
Late past bedtime.—BaW
Let the biter beware.—AdCh
Life in the forest, or, bad news, good news, bad
news.—AdCh
Mathematical metric conversion version.—AdCh
The morning wind from the west.—AdIn
Mouse under the house, mouse in the house.—
AdIn
My brother Aaron runs outside to tell us there is
a severe thunderstorm warning.—AdIn
A nature story.—AdCh
October afternoons we walk around the house.—
AdIn
The old math, one.—AdCh
The old math, two.—AdCh
On Limestone Street.—AdIn
On May Day.—AdIn
On this winter after noon.—AdCh
One night.—AdIn
Out for spring.—AdIn
Point guard.—KnAs
The rain falling on west train tracks, Ohio.—
AdCh
Rescue mission.—AdCh
She was hungry and cold.—AdIn
So dry this July.—AdIn
The straw.—AdCh
Sunday afternoon under a warm blue sky.—AdIn
This house is the center.—AdIn
Those who do not study history are doomed.—
AdCh
Three thirty.—AdCh
Two AM.—AdCh
Volunteers one.—AdIn
Volunteers two.—AdIn
Why did the fireman.—AdCh
Why I always brush.—AdCh
The world is in chaos, the world is in flames.—
AdCh
Wrestling the beast.—KnAs
You are walking along eating.—AdCh
Adolphus. Colin West.—PrFo
"**Adolphus** is despicable". See Adolphus
Adoption
"When Annie was adopted". M. A. Hoberman.—
HoFa
Adventure and adventurers. See also Camping and
hiking; Explorers and exploration; Frontier and
pioneer life; Heroes and heroines; Seafaring life;
Space and space travel
Eldorado. E. A. Poe.—MoR
"I met a dragon face to face". J. Prelutsky.—
HoGo
Kiph. W. De La Mare.—DeR
Seafarer. Unknown.—OpT
The story of your life. B. Bennett.—MoR
"There is a land". L. B. Jacobs.—HoGo
Western wagons. S. V. Benet, and R. C. Benet.—
SuI
The **adventures** of Isabel, sels. Ogden Nash

"Isabel met an enormous bear".—DeS
Advertising
"The codfish lays ten thousand eggs".
Unknown.—PrP
A commercial for spring. E. Merriam.—MeP
Hallowe'en ad (attention witches). G. Tall.—BaH
Sales talk for Annie. M. Bishop.—ElW
Advice
Advice. X. J. Kennedy.—KeGh
Advice on how to sleep well Halloween night. J.
Yolen.—YoBe
Agies's advice. K. Smith.—AgL
All right, do it your way. J. Ciardi.—CiH
The black widow, a cautionary tale. W. J.
Smith.—SmL
C. C. Johnson. M. Glenn.—GlBc
"The day I married, my mother". J. Carson.—CaS
Don't do it my way. F. Landesman.—AgL
Down by the salley gardens. W. B. Yeats.—ElW
Dreams. L. Hughes.—LoFh—SlM
"Every time I get a little headache". J. Carson.—
CaS
A fishy story. E. Merriam.—MeS
The four corners of the universe. Unknown.—
SnD
From the autograph album. Unknown.—MoA
Garden calendar. N. M. Bodecker.—KeT
"Go to bed late". Mother Goose.—WaM
"He is the Way". From For the time being. W. H.
Auden.—StP
"He that would thrive". Mother Goose.—WaM
"Hey black child". U. E. Perkins.—SlM
If ("If you can keep your head when all about
you"). R. Kipling.—ElW
"In the greenhouse lives a wren". Mother
Goose.—WaM
Kick and live. G. W. Porter.—SlM
"Ladies and gentlemen". Unknown.—ScA—WiA
A lesson from golf. E. Guest.—KnAs
Lines for remembering about lids. X. J.
Kennedy.—KeK
Mamma settles the dropout problem. B. Gates.—
SuC
Metaphor for my son. J. Holmes.—SuI
Mother has a talk with me. J. Little.—LiHe
Mother to son. L. Hughes.—DeT—SlM—SuC
Ms. Emily Parsons, history. M. Glenn.—GlBc
Ms. Marilyn Lindowsky, counselor. M. Glenn.—
GlBc
Owl ("The diet of the owl is not"). X. J.
Kennedy.—LiIf
"Said the crab, 'tis not beauty or birth". O.
Herford.—LiLo
"Sara Cynthia Sylvia Stout would not take the
garbage out". S. Silverstein.—ElW
"Say not the struggle nought availeth". A. H.
Clough.—ElW
She should have listened to me. K. Dakos.—DaI
A short story. D. E. Galindo.—NyT
The spider and the fly. M. Howitt.—ElW
To meet Mr. Lincoln. E. Merriam.—DeS
"To sleep easy all night". Mother Goose.—WaM
To the virgins, to make much of time. R.
Herrick.—ElW
"Tomorrow come never". Unknown.—OpI
Two precepts. Unknown.—OpT
Victor Jeffreys. M. Glenn.—GlBc
The vulture. H. Belloc.—CaB—ElW
We must be polite. C. Sandburg.—DeS
"When I was one and twenty". A. E. Housman.—
ElW

Advice—*Continued*
"When land is gone and money spent". Mother
  Goose.—WaM
"When you get married and your husband gets
  cross". Unknown.—WiA
Young soul. I. A. Baraka.—SuC
Zip on "good advice". G. Hyland.—JaPr
Advice. X. J. Kennedy.—KeGh
Advice on how to sleep well Halloween night. Jane
  Yolen.—YoBe
Aelourophile. Eve Merriam.—MeCh
Aelourophobe. Eve Merriam.—MeCh
Aesop
  The ass in the lion's skin, tr. by William Ellery
    Leonard.—CaB
Aesthetic curiosity. A. M. Klein.—BoT
"**Afiya** has fine black skin". See A story about Afiya
"**Afoot** and light-hearted I take to the open road".
  From Song of the open road. Walt Whitman.—
  HoVo
Africa
  Africa. A. Oyewole.—SlM
  Anansi the spider. G. McDermott.—WhDd
  Ancestry. A. Bryan.—BrS
  Cleaned the crocodile's teeth. N. Col.—NyT
  Fishing festival. J. Kenward.—FoLe
  The giraffes ("I think before they saw me the
    giraffes"). R. Fuller.—ElW
  Haiku ("I have looked into"). S. Sanchez.—SlM
  Kwanzaa is. C. McClester.—SlM
  The mask. D. K. Hru.—SlM
  Okolo the leopard warrior. C. Price.—WhDd
  People of gleaming cities, and of the lion's and
    the leopard's brood. S. Bourke.—SuC
  The rhythm of the tomtom. A. Jacinto.—NyT
  What is Africa to me. From Heritage. C.
    Cullen.—SuC
Africa. Abiodun Oyewole.—SlM
"**Africa?** A book one thumbs". See What is Africa to
  me
"**Africa** the Mother of all mothers". See Africa
African-Americans. See also Blacks
  Africa. A. Oyewole.—SlM
  Ailey, Baldwin, Floyd, Killens, and Mayfield. M.
    Angelou.—AnI
  Alabama centennial. N. Madgett.—SuC
  Ancestry. A. Bryan.—BrS
  Aunt Sue's stories. L. Hughes.—SlM
  Black is beautiful. U. E. Perkins.—SlM
  Brothers ("We're related, you and I"). L.
    Hughes.—SlM
  But he was cool or, he even stopped for green
    lights. D. L. Lee.—ElW
  Coleridge Jackson. M. Angelou.—AnI
  Color. L. Hughes.—SlM
  Crown. D. K. Hru.—SlM
  Dance poem. N. Giovanni.—MoR
  A different image. D. Randall.—SuC
  Dream variation. L. Hughes.—DeT—LoFh
  The enlistment of free blacks as Continental
    soldiers. J. Thomas.—SuC
  "Fine black kinfolk". D. K. Hru.—SlM
  For my people. M. Walker.—SuC
  Forgive. M. Angelou.—AnI
  Glory falls. M. Angelou.—AnI
  "Go down, Moses". From Go down, Moses.
    Unknown.—SuC
  Haiku ("I have looked into"). S. Sanchez.—SlM
  Harlem. L. Hughes.—ElW
  "Hey black child". U. E. Perkins.—SlM
  Incident. C. Cullen.—ElW

Integration of the armed services of the United
  States. H. S. Truman.—SuC
Jackie Robinson. L. Clifton.—KnAs—MoA
Ka 'Ba. I. A. Baraka.—SuC
Kwanzaa is. C. McClester.—SlM
Louleen's feelings. X. J. Kennedy.—KeK
Lullaby for a black mother. L. Hughes.—SlM
Martine Provencal. M. Glenn.—GlBc
The mask. D. K. Hru.—SlM
The melting pot. D. Randall.—SuC
Minstrel man. L. Hughes.—SuC
Mother to son. L. Hughes.—DeT—SlM—SuC
"My natural mama". L. Clifton.—LiPm
My people. L. Hughes.—SlM
Nationhood. U. E. Perkins.—SlM
Negro soldier's civil war chant. Unknown.—SuC
The negro speaks of rivers. L. Hughes.—SuC
The new negro. J. E. McCall.—SuC
Old Mag. J. Hollingsworth-Barkley.—JaPr
On being brought from Africa to America. P.
  Wheatley.—SuC
Our grandmothers. M. Angelou.—AnI
People of gleaming cities, and of the lion's and
  the leopard's brood. S. Bourke.—SuC
A protest poem for Rosa Parks. A. Oyewole.—
  SlM
Return of the native. I. A. Baraka.—SuC
"Science". G. Nelson.—SlM
Shadow ("Silhouette"). R. Bruce.—SuC
Southern road. S. A. Brown.—SuC
Sugarfields. B. Mahone.—LiPm
Summertime and the living. R. Hayden.—SuC
Temple for tomorrow. From The negro artist and
  the racial mountain. L. Hughes.—SuC
"They had supposed their formula was fixed".
  From The white troops had their orders but the
  negroes looked like men. G. Brooks.—SuC
They were my people. G. Nichols.—NiCo
To those of my sisters who kept their naturals. G.
  Brooks.—SuC
Tradition. E. Greenfield.—GrU
"Two months after marching through Boston".
  From For the Union dead. R. Lowell.—SuC
"We shall overcome". Z. Horton, and F.
  Hamilton.—LoFh
We wear the mask. P. L. Dunbar.—SuC
What color is black. B. Mahone.—SlM
What is Africa to me. From Heritage. C.
  Cullen.—SuC
The white city. C. McKay.—SuC
"Who can be born black". M. Evans.—SlM
Why are they happy people. M. Angelou.—AnI
Zora. J. Schell.—JaPr
After a bath. Aileen Fisher.—FiA
"**After** a book is finished". See After the end
After a visit to the natural history museum. Laura
  E. Richards.—SuI
After Easter snow. X. J. Kennedy.—KeK
After English class. Jean Little.—LiHe
"**After** I'd bought balloons and". See Waiting at the
  St. Louis Zoo
"**After** its lid". See Pumpkin
"**After** my bath". See After a bath
"**After** my birthday". See Birthday night
"**After** my divorce my world fell apart". See Ms.
  Charlotte Kendall, biology
"**After** she eats". See Cat bath
"**After** spending the summer in Paris". See Gayle
  Buckingham
"**After** surmounting three-score and ten". See My
  71st year
"**After** that tight". See Barefoot

"**After** the ball was over". Unknown.—ScA
"**After** the brilliance". See Beaded braids
"**After** the dark of night". See Daybreak
After the dazzle of day. Walt Whitman.—HoVo
"**After** the dazzle of day is gone". See After the
    dazzle of day
After the end. Aileen Fisher.—FiA
After the last hard freeze in early spring weather.
    Arnold Adoff.—AdIn
"**After** the teacher asked if anyone had". See The
    sacred
"**After** the yellow-white". See Pie
"**After** waiting up". See New Year's eve
"**After** weeks of hard raining". See Wildlife refuge
"**After** work". See Match
Afterglow. Jorge Luis Borges, tr. by Norman
    Thomas Di Giovanni.—GoT
Afternoon
    Afternoon on a hill. E. S. V. Millay.—FrS—SuI
    "The bus weaves its way through the jungle
      home". M. Wayne.—LeCa
    Early dark. E. Coatsworth.—PlW
    Late afternoon. M. C. Livingston.—LiT
    Three o'clock. V. Worth.—WoA
    Three thirty. A. Adoff.—AdCh
    "The winter they bombed Pearl Harbor". W.
      McDonald.—JaPr
Afternoon in March. Jean Little.—LiHe
"**Afternoon**, mid August". See Cicadas
Afternoon on a hill. Edna St. Vincent Millay.—
    FrS—SuI
Afton water. Robert Burns.—ElW
"**Again** and again". Kazue Mizumura.—BaW
"**Again** and again through the day". See Cat
Against idleness and mischief. Isaac Watts.—ElW
Agard, John
    All fool's day.—FoLe
    Checking out me history.—AgL
    Spell to banish a pimple.—AgL
Agard, Yansan
    When ("When tigers don't roar").—AgL
Agatha, Agatha. Mary Ann Hoberman.—HoFa
"**Agatha**, Agatha, honestly, Agatha". See Agatha,
    Agatha
Agatha Ghastly makes light of Auntie. X. J.
    Kennedy.—KeGh
"**Agatha** Goop with a whale of a whoop". See
    Basketball bragging
Age. See Birthdays; Old age; Youth and age
"The **age**". See A different image
Age four and my father. Julia Cunningham.—LiPf
The **age** of reason. Michael Van Walleghen.—JaPr
Agee, James
    A lullaby ("Sleep, child, lie quiet, let be").—GoT
Agies's advice. Ken Smith.—AgL
"**Ah** bar arkh". See Fox's song
"**Ah**, on Thanksgiving day, when from east and
    from west". See The pumpkin
"**Ah** who dydle de". Unknown.—ScA
"**Ah**, would I were a pastrycook". See For Mopsa
"**Ahem**". See Euphemistic
"**Ahoy**, and ahoy". See The changeling
Aiken, Conrad
    The owl ("To whit, to whoo").—LiIf
    "Said an ogre from old Saratoga".—LiLo
Aiken, Joan
    Cat ("Old Mog comes in and sits on the
      newspaper").—LaCc
    John's song.—KeT
    Man and owl.—LiIf
    Rhyme for night.—KeT
    The smile.—LiPg

Ailey, Baldwin, Floyd, Killens, and Mayfield. Maya
    Angelou.—AnI
"**Ain't** no hell on earth". Jo Carson.—CaS
"**Ain't** you terrible". See Father to son
"The **air** is quiet". See The coming of teddy bears
"The **air** was damp". From Song of ships. Virginia
    Schonborg.—LaN
Airplanes and aviators
    The age of reason. M. Van Walleghen.—JaPr
    Dreamers and flyers. J. LaBombard.—JaM
    "The engingines". P. Goodman.—MoR
    First solo. W. McDonald.—MoR
    Jet. J. T. Moore.—MoR
    Metaphor for my son. J. Holmes.—SuI
    "Oh, I have slipped the surly bonds of earth". J.
      G. Magee.—StP
      High flight.—SuI
    Over the field. M. Swenson.—MoR
Airport. X. J. Kennedy.—KeK
Airport in the grass. X. J. Kennedy.—MoR
Aizpuriete, Amanda
    "Do what you like with my face".—NyT
Swami Akhilananda
    "May He Who is the Father in Heaven of the".—
      StP
Akin, Sunay
    Debt, tr. by Yusuf Eradam.—NyT
Al'Adawiyah, Rabi'ah
    "Should I worship Him from fear of hell".—StP
Al-Fayiz, Muhammad
    A sailor's memoirs, tr. by Issa Boullata and
      Naomi Shihab Nye.—NyT
Al-Ghuzzi, Muhammad
    The pen, tr. by May Jayyusi and John
      Heath-Stubbs.—NyT
Al-Harizi, Judah
    A secret kept, tr. by Robert Mezey.—GoU
Al-Maghut, Muhammad
    The orphan, tr. by May Jayyusi and Naomi
      Shihab Nye.—NyT
Al-Mak, Ali
    The gatherer, tr. by Al-Fatih Mahjoub and
      Constance E. Berkley.—NyT
Al-Sa'igh, Yusuf
    Ants, tr. by Diana Der Hovanessian and Salma
      Khadra Jayyusi.—NyT
Alabama
    Alabama centennial. N. Madgett.—SuC
    Daybreak in Alabama. L. Hughes.—SuC
    A long time ago. Unknown.—SuC
Alabama, sels. Julia Fields
    "God save the owls".—LiIf
Alabama centennial. Naomi Madgett.—SuC
Alas. Walter De La Mare.—DeR
Alas, alack. Walter De La Mare.—DeR—MaP
"**Alas**, alas, for Miss Mackay". Mother Goose.—
    WaM
Alaska
    He saved a lot of time by not working. J.
      Ciardi.—CiH
Albatrosses
    The rime of the ancient mariner, complete. S. T.
      Coleridge.—ElW
Aldan, Daisy
    Dawn ("I kindle my light over the whole
      Atlantic"), tr.—NyT
    A whirring.—MoR
Aldis, Dorothy
    The balloon man.—DeT
    Blum.—LiDd
    Brooms.—DeT
    Bursting.—PrFo

Aldis, Dorothy—*Continued*
Every insect.—WhAa
Fireworks ("Pin wheels whirling round").—LoFh
The hungry waves.—DeT
The island.—DeT
Kick a little stone.—KeT
Little.—DeT
The little girl and the turkey.—DeT
My brother.—DeT
No one heard him call.—KeT
The picnic.—HoS
Singing.—DeT
The storm ("In my bed all safe and warm").—DeT
Supper for a lion.—CoAz—HoT
When I was lost.—MoS
"**Alecumjockaby,** blindfold eye". See Blindman's in
"**Alef** beys giml dolid". Unknown.—YoS
"A B C D".—YoS
Alexander, Cecil Frances
"All things bright and beautiful".—StP
Algebra. See Mathematics
"**Algy** met a bear". Unknown.—ClI—PrP—WiA
Ali, Jamal
The bum.—AgL
Ali, Muhammad
"They all must fall".—KnAs
Ali, Muhammad (about)
Black lady in an afro hairdo cheers for Cassius. R. E. Holmes.—KnAs
Alice. William Jay Smith.—SmL
"**Alice,** dear, what ails you". See A frosty night
Alice's adventures in wonderland, sels. Lewis Carroll
Father William.—LiPf
You are old, Father William.—ElW
"How doth the little crocodile".—WhAa
The crocodile.—ClI
The lobster quadrille.—MoR
"Twinkle, twinkle, little bat".—ClI
"The **alien**". Julie Holder.—PrFo
"**All** along the backwater". See Ducks' ditty
"**All** areas were notified". See Calling all cars
"**All** around the butter dish". Unknown.—CoM—WiA
All asleep. Charlotte Pomerantz.—PlW
"**All** at once, the storm". Buson, tr. by Sylvia Cassedy and Kunihiro Suetake.—CaR
"**All** August we thrilled to rumors". See Summer killer
"**All** babies". See Nestlings
"**All** but blind". Walter De La Mare.—DeR—MaP
"**All** day I hear the noise of waters". James Joyce.—ElW
"**All** day long I have been working". See Madonna of the evening flowers
"**All** day my father complained". See Rare rhythms
"**All** day she has slept". See New baby poem (I)
"**All** else". See Winter walk in forest
All eyes. J. Patrick Lewis.—LeA—LiIf
All fool's day. John Agard.—FoLe
"**All** hail, thou truly noble chief". From To Cinque. James M. Whitfield.—SuC
All Hallows' Eve. Ann Bonner.—FoLe
All Hallows' Eve (My mother brings me to visit a Sicilian cemetery). Emanuel Di Pasquale.—LiHp
"**All** hot (the chestnut man). Walter De La Mare.—DeR
All I am. Abiodun Oyewole.—SlM
"**All** I want in this creation's". See Black-eyed Susie
All in a word. Aileen Fisher.—FiA—HoS

"**All** in together". Unknown.—Wia
"**All** is silent". Hsieh Ping-hsin.—StP
All kinds of grands. Lucille Clifton.—LiPg
"**All** my life I lived in a coconut". See Locked in
All my secrets. Marguerite Mack.—BoT
"**All** night". See Sunrise
"**All** night I lay awake beside you". See Marthe away (she is away)
"**All** night they whine upon their ropes and boom". See Nocturne of the wharves
"**All** of us went for Jan's birthday". See Dinosaur birthday
"**All** over the world". See Polyglot
"**All** policeman have big feet". Unknown.—WiA
"**All** praise to Thee, my God, this night". Thomas Ken.—StP
All right, do it your way. John Ciardi.—CiH
"**All** shall be well". Julian of Norwich.—StP
"**All** summer". See Ode to el guitarron
"**All** summer long, your round stone eardrum held". See To a forgetful wishing well
"**All** the fishermen here remember the one". See Fish story
All the fun (for a picture). Walter De La Mare.—DeR
"**All** the girls in our town live a happy life". Unknown.—OpI
"**All** the leaves have turned to cornflakes". See October Saturday
All the way. Walter De La Mare.—DeR
"**All** the way from Adam". See All the way
"**All** things bright and beautiful". Cecil Frances Alexander.—StP
"**All** this hoopla". See Ebonee
"**All** this time and at all times wait the words of true poems". From Song of myself. Walt Whitman.—HoVo
"**All** those years". See A kinsman
"**All** through the night the happy sheep". See The happy sheep
"**All** us girls knew about sin". See Sugar-n-spice, etc
All wet. Tony Johnston.—DeT
"**Alla** en la fuente". Unknown.—DeA
The fountain ("There in the fountain").—DeA
Allen, Marie Louise
First snow ("Snow makes whiteness where it falls").—DeS
Alley cat school. Frank Asch.—LaCc
The **alligator.** Mary MacDonald.—PrFo
Alligator ("If you want to see an alligator"). Grace Nichols.—NiCo
"The **alligator** chased his tale". See The alligator
Alligator on the escalator. Eve Merriam.—DeT
Alligators and crocodiles
The alligator. M. MacDonald.—PrFo
Alligator ("If you want to see an alligator"). G. Nichols.—NiCo
Alligator on the escalator. E. Merriam.—DeT
"A careless zookeeper named Blake". Unknown.—LiLo
Crocodile. W. J. Smith.—SmL
"Crocodile or alligator". C. West.—CoAz
"Did you ever go fishing on a bright sunny day". Unknown.—WiA
"Did you ever go fishing on a bright summer day".—ScA
"Don't call an alligator a long-mouth till you have crossed the river". From Jamaican Caribbean proverbs. Unknown.—BeW
"An eccentric explorer named Hayter". W. J. Smith.—SmL

Alligators and crocodiles—*Continued*

"How doth the little crocodile". From Alice's adventures in wonderland. L. Carroll.—WhAa

The crocodile.—CII

"If you should meet a crocodile". Unknown.—CII—PrP

"Oh, the bullfrog tried to court the alligator". Unknown.—WiA

Allingham, William

The fairies.—ElW

"Four ducks on a pond".—ElW

A swing song.—KeT

Allosaurus. Jack Prelutsky.—PrT

"**Allosaurus** liked to bite". See Allosaurus

"**Allosaurus, stegosaurus**". See The dinosaur dinner

"**Allthegirlsarebunched**". See Crystal Rowe, track star

"De **almighty** dollar". See Dollar horror

"**Almighty** one, in the woods I am blessed". Ludwig Van Beethoven.—StP

Almost a madrigal. Salvatore Quasimodo, tr. by Allen Mandelbaum.—GoT

Almost dancing. Simmerman. Jim.—JaM

Alone ("Alone in a house with no one to talk to"). Sharon Hudson.—BaH

Alone ("I am alone, and lonely"). Jean Little.—LiHe

"**Alone**, along the edge of Granny's field". See She was hungry and cold

"**Alone** in a house with no one to talk to". See Alone

"**Alone** in the night". See Night storm

Alone in winter. J. Patrick Lewis.—LeT

Alone on a broom. Jane Yolen.—YoBe

"**Alone** with none but Thee, my God". Saint Columba.—StP

Along came Ruth. Ford Frick.—MoA

"**Along** the wires". See Song birds

"**Alpha**, beta, gamma, delta". Unknown.—OpI

Alphabet

A. J. T. Moore, and M. Moore.—DeS

A is for alpaca. W. J. Smith.—SmL

"A was an apple pie". Mother Goose.—SuO

"A was once an apple pie". E. Lear.—HoS

ABC song. Unknown.—HoS

"Alpha, beta, gamma, delta". Unknown.—OpI

Alphabet ball. Unknown.—WiA

"A, my name is Alice".—CoM

B is for bats. W. J. Smith.—SmL

C is for cabbages. W. J. Smith.—SmL

Composition ball. Unknown.—WiA

D is for dog. W. J. Smith.—SmL

E is for egg. W. J. Smith.—SmL

"Extra, extra, extra, every Egyptian eats exactly". Unknown.—CoM

F is for frog-boy. W. J. Smith.—SmL

G is for goat. W. J. Smith.—SmL

"Great A, little a". Mother Goose.—WaM

H is for hat. W. J. Smith.—SmL

I is for inkspot. W. J. Smith.—SmL

"I'll go to A". Unknown.—OpI

"It is in the rock, but not in the stone". Unknown.—OpI

J is for jack-in-the-box. W. J. Smith.—SmL

Jamaican alphabet. L. Bennett.—LeCa

A jamboree for j. E. Merriam.—MeS

K is for king. W. J. Smith.—SmL

L is for laundry. W. J. Smith.—SmL

M is for mask. W. J. Smith.—SmL

"M was once a little mouse". E. Lear.—WhAa

N is for needle. W. J. Smith.—SmL

O is for owl. W. J. Smith.—LiIf—SmL

"O was an owl who flew". E. Lear.—LiIf

"O was once a little owl". E. Lear.—LiIf

P is for pirate. W. J. Smith.—SmL

"P with a little o". Mother Goose.—WaM

Q is for queen. W. J. Smith.—SmL

Quibble. E. Merriam.—MeS

R is for reindeer. W. J. Smith.—SmL

"Round and round the rugged rock the ragged rascal ran". Unknown.—ScA—WiA

S is for springs. W. J. Smith.—SmL

T is for tub. W. J. Smith.—SmL

U is for up. W. J. Smith.—SmL

V is for volcano. W. J. Smith.—SmL

W is for well. W. J. Smith.—SmL

"What is it you always see". Unknown.—ScA

"What's in the church". Unknown.—WiA

X is for x. W. J. Smith.—SmL

Y is for yarn. W. J. Smith.—SmL

"YYUR". Unknown.—WiA

Z is for zebu. W. J. Smith.—SmL

Alphabet ball. Unknown.—WiA

"A, my name is Alice".—CoM

"**Already** fallen plum-bloom stars the green". See The poor man's pig

Altazor, sels. Vicente Huidobro, tr. by Eliot Weinberger

"At the horislope of the mountizon".—NyT

"**Although** affirmative goals I sought". See Un-negative

"**Although** I saw you". See Doves

"**Although** it's cold no clothes I wear". See Fish riddle

"**Although** I've been to Kankakee". See Schenectady

"**Although** the wind". Izumi Shikibu, tr. by Jane Hirschfield.—GoT

"**Although** there is". Ono No Komachi, tr. by Jane Hirschfield.—GoT

"**Although** you bash her". See A mosquito in the cabin

Alulvan. Walter De La Mare.—DeR

Alvarez, Leticia Herrera

Country memory, tr. by Judith Infante.—NyT

Alvaro

Green velvet suit.—AgL

"**Always** a new wrinkle". See The story of your life

"**Always** be kind to animals". John Gardner.—CoAz

Always wondering. Aileen Fisher.—FiA

"**Am** I really a sports fan, I ask myself". See The boxing match

"**Amanda** found a flounder". Jack Prelutsky.—PrBe

Ambition

Every chance we got. C. H. Webb.—JaPr

Excelsior. W. Whitman.—HoVo

Getting nowhere. J. Berry.—BeW

"Hast never come to thee an hour". W. Whitman.—HoVo

"He that would thrive". Mother Goose.—WaM

A headstrong boy. G. Cheng.—NyT

In praise of a contented mind. E. Dyer.—ElW (unat.)

Janet DeStasio. M. Glenn.—GlBc

Kyle Quinn. M. Glenn.—GlBc

Ms. Yvonne Harmon, librarian. M. Glenn.—GlBc

Of necessity, Weeb jokes about his height. C. H. Webb.—JaPr

"Somebody said that it couldn't be done". Unknown.—PrFo

Today. J. Little.—LiHe

Wanting to move. V. Mukhopadhyay.—NyT

When I grow up. M. A. Hoberman.—HoFa

The window cleaner. M. Long.—BaW

The world is too much with us. W. Wordsworth.—ElW

Ambition—*Continued*
A young lady from Glitch. T. Kitt.—DeS
"**America,** if you were a basketball court". See Anthem
American Indians. See Indians of the Americas
American Revolution. See United States—History—Revolution
"The **American** Revolution". See Dawn Weinberg
Amichai, Yehuda
Jerusalem, tr. by Stephen Mitchell.—NyT
Wildpeace, tr. by Chana Bloch.—NyT
"**Amidst** the litter". See Christmas scene
Ammons, Archie Randolph
Contingency.—ElW
Mirrorment.—DeS
Spruce woods.—ElW—JaP
World.—ElW
"**Amo,** amas". Unknown.—OpI
Amoeba. Valerie Worth.—WoAl
Amoebas
Amoeba. V. Worth.—WoAl
Among iron fragments. Tuvia Ruebner, tr. by Robert Friend.—GoU
"**Among** iron fragments and rusty dreams". See Among iron fragments
"**Among** the later dinosaurs". See Pachycephalosaurus
"**Among** the taller wood with ivy hung". See The vixen
"**Among** these mountains, do you know". See For Allan, who wanted to see how I wrote a poem
Amphibian. Eve Merriam.—MeCh
The **amphisbaena.** Myra Cohn Livingston.—WhDd
See The amphisbaena
"**An** a so de rain a-fall". See A song for England
Anaconda. Doug Macleod.—CoAz
Analysis of baseball. May Swenson.—KnAs—SuI
"**Anansi**". See Anansi the spider
Anansi the spider. Gerald McDermott.—WhDd
Anatomy. See names of parts of the body, as Hands
Ancestry. See also Heritage
Ancestry. A. Bryan.—BrS
Ching ming. I. Rawnsley.—FoLe
Hamilton Greene. E. L. Masters.—ElW
"Many an underfed cow in the pasture is mother of a bull". From Jamaican Caribbean proverbs. Unknown.—BeW
The mask. D. K. Hru.—SlM
A pearl. F. Abu Khalid.—NyT
They stooped over and came out. Unknown.—GoT
To the ancestors. Unknown.—NyT
Wolf-ancestry. V. Popa.—NyT
"You never see a cow that kicks who doesn't produce a calf that kicks". From Jamaican Caribbean proverbs. Unknown.—BeW
Ancestry. Ashley Bryan.—BrS
And after. Jane Yolen.—YoDd
"**And** after they have sung the song". See Birthday wish
"**And** because". See Playmate
·"**And** children still grow up with longing eyes". See Twilight of the outward life
"**And** dark green this afternoon". See Clouds are black
And even now. Dorothy Livesay.—BoT
"**And** God created great whales, and every living creature that moveth". From Book of Genesis. Bible/Old Testament.—WhAa
"**And** here's a carpet, slightly torn". See The used carpet salesman

"**And** I am standing on this cold kitchen floor". See Two AM
"**And** know that one more robin". See I hear the usual thump
And my heart soars. Chief Dan George.—BoT—LoFh
"**And** now at sunset, ripples flecked with gold". See The wind is from the north
"**And** pretends to be a boy worker on this farm". See Daddy carries his empty basket on his head
And s-s-so to b-b-bed. Max Fatchen.—FaCm
And suddenly it's evening. Salvatore Quasimodo, tr. by Jack Bevan.—GoT
"**And** take a fine walk". See I will hold your hand
"**And** the next I remembered I'm on a table". See The loser
And then. Prince Redcloud.—HoGo
And they met in the middle. John Ciardi.—CiH
"**And** think I feel the unreal yet palpable crunch". See In this last class before lunch, I close my eyes
"**And** this was the way of it, brethren brethren". See Mean to be free
"**And** tomorrow the sun will shine again". See Tomorrow
"**&** we are camping in the romantic land". See Postcards
"**And** we were speaking easily and all the light stayed low". See In judgment of the leaf
"**And** what if you tire". See The home-watcher
"**And** what is so rare as a day in June". From The vision of Sir Launfal. James Russell Lowell.—SuI
"**And** x marks the spot". See X is for x
Andersen, Benny
Goodness, tr. by Alexander Taylor.—NyT
Anderson, Teresa
"I was born in Jacinto Vera", tr.—NyT
Andrade, Jorge Carrera
Life of the cricket, tr. by John Malcolm Brinnin.—NyT
Andre. Gwendolyn Brooks.—SlM
Andrea Pulovsky. Mel Glenn.—GlBc
Andy Battle's and Nod's song. Walter De La Mare.—MaP
Yeo ho.—DeR
Andy Battle's song. From The three royal monkeys. Walter De La Mare.—DeR
Andy Fierstein. Mel Glenn.—GlBc
Angel tunes. Jane Yolen.—YoHa
Angell, Barbara
Fox's song.—SuI
Angelotti, Mike
The last man killed by Indians in Kimble County, Texas.—JaM
Still life.—JaM
Angelou, Maya
Ailey, Baldwin, Floyd, Killens, and Mayfield.—AnI
Born that way.—AnI
Changing.—AnI
Coleridge Jackson.—AnI
Equality.—AnI
"Fightin' was natural".—AnI
Forgive.—AnI
Glory falls.—AnI
Human family.—AnI
"In my Missouri".—AnI
In retrospect.—GoU
Insignificant.—AnI
Is love.—AnI
Known to Eve and me.—AnI

Angelou, Maya—*Continued*
Life doesn't frighten me.—AgL
London.—AnI
Loss of love.—AnI
Love letter.—AnI
Man bigot.—AnI
Many and more.—AnI
Me and my work.—AnI
The new house.—AnI
Nothing much.—AnI
Old folks laugh.—AnI
Our grandmothers.—AnI
"Preacher, don't send me".—AnI
Savior.—AnI
Seven women's blessed assurance.—AnI
Son to mother.—AnI
Televised.—AnI
These yet to be United States.—AnI
They ask why.—AnI
Times Square shoeshine competition.—MoR
Why are they happy people.—AnI
Worker's song.—AnI

Angels
Angel tunes. J. Yolen.—YoHa
Angels. V. Worth.—WoA
"Angels from the realms of glory". J. Montgomery.—YoHa
"En la puerta del cielo". Unknown.—DeA
    "At heaven's gate".—DeA
"Hark, the herald angels sing". C. Wesley.—YoHa
Listening to baseball in the car. G. Mazur.—KnAs
A warning ("If you keep two angels in a cage"). A. Mitchell.—AgL
When angels came to Zimmer. P. Zimmer.—JaM

Angels. Valerie Worth.—WoA
"Angels from the realms of glory". James Montgomery.—YoHa

Anger
"At last I have my anger breathalyser". From What we said sitting making fantasies. J. Berry.—BeW
Be warned. M. Fatchen.—FaCm
The chameleon. J. Gardner.—CoAz
"A dog's bark isn't going to frighten the moon". From Jamaican Caribbean proverbs. Unknown.—BeW
Growing pains. J. Little.—LiHe
Heman. M. Wandor.—AgL
"Jenny got so angry". Unknown.—WiA
"Mary's mad". Unknown.—WiA
Ms. Yvonne Harmon, librarian. M. Glenn.—GlBc
My mother really knew. W. T. Lum.—JaM
A poison tree. W. Blake.—ElW
"Stay mad, stay mad". Unknown.—WiA
"There was a young girl of Asturias". Unknown.—LiLo
"Too bad". Unknown.—ScA
Wars. J. Little.—LiHe
The wind and the moon, complete. G. MacDonald.—BaW

Anglo-Swiss, or a day among the Alps, sels. William Plomer
"Away she flies and he follows".—MoR
"The **angry** hens from Never-when". Michael Rosen.—PrFo

The **animal** fair. See "I went to the animal fair"

Animal tracks
The truth about the abominable footprint. M. Baldwin.—PrFo
Who. L. Moore.—LiDd

Animalimericks, complete. Eve Merriam

Beware ("When a cub, unaware being bare").—MeS
An odd one.—LiLo—MeS
Variety.—MeS

Animals. See also Circus; Fables; also names of classes of the animal kingdom, as Birds; names of animals, as Elephants
The answers. R. Clairmont.—CoAz
As soon as it's fall. A. Fisher.—FiA
Bird song. Unknown.—OpT
The gallows. E. Thomas.—ElW
Good morning. M. Sipe.—DeS
How to tell the wild animals. C. Wells.—CoAz
I had a cat. Unknown.—CII
"I saw a ship a-sailing". Mother Goose.—SuO
I speak, I say, I talk. A. L. Shapiro.—DeT
"I think I could turn and live with animals, they are so placid". From Song of myself. W. Whitman.—HoVo
"I went to the animal fair". Unknown.—HoS—WiA
    The animal fair.—CII
Laughing time. W. J. Smith.—PrFo—SmL
Mr. Zoo. E. Merriam.—MeCh
Names. From The family of man. C. Sandburg.—WhAa
Necks. R. Bennett.—DeS
Old Noah's ark. Unknown.—DeT—HoS—SuI
Part III: Little birds bathe. From A child's day. W. De La Mare.—DeR
The praising cows. J. Yolen.—YoHa
"Quack, said the billy goat". C. Causley.—WhAa
The Quangle Wangle's hat. E. Lear.—CII
River lovers. J. P. Lewis.—LeA
Rodomontade in the menagerie. E. Merriam.—MeCh
Tails. R. Bennett.—DeS
"Three young rats with black felt hats". Mother Goose.—PrP—SuO
    Three young rats.—CII
Ululation. E. Merriam.—MeS
Unstooping. W. De La Mare.—DeR—MaP
Up the hill. W. J. Smith.—LiDd—SmL
Who. L. Moore.—LiDd
Will you. E. Merriam.—HoS
The woman and her pig. Unknown.—OpT
Wouldn't it be funny. P. O'Harris.—CoAz

Animals—Care
"Always be kind to animals". J. Gardner.—CoAz
"Be kind to your web-footed friends". Unknown.—ScA
Be lenient with lobsters. Unknown.—CII
Caring for animals. J. Silkin.—NyT
Cat toys. V. Worth.—WoA
Crumbs. W. De La Mare.—DeR
"Ding dong bell". Mother Goose.—SuO—WaM
"Every time I come to town". Unknown.—WiA
For a bird. M. C. Livingston.—DeS
The frog ("Be kind and tender to the frog"). H. Belloc.—CII—ElW
Glowworm. D. McCord.—MoS
Gracious goodness. M. Piercy.—ElW
"Hurt no living thing". C. G. Rossetti.—DeS—StP—WhAa
"I love little pussy". Mother Goose.—WaM
The lost cat. E. V. Rieu.—LaCc
Mary's lamb. S. J. Hale.—SuI
    "Mary had a little lamb".—EdGl (unat.)—SuO (unat.)—WaM (unat.)
"Old Mother Hubbard". Mother Goose.—EdGl—SuO—WaM

Animals—Care—*Continued*
The personable porcupine. W. G. Howcroft.—CoAz
Rescue ("Bony cat"). V. Schonborg.—LaCc
The rime of the ancient mariner, complete. S. T. Coleridge.—ElW
The runaway. R. Frost.—ElW
She was hungry and cold. A. Adoff.—AdIn
The stray cat. E. Merriam.—LaCc—MeS
The vet. M. C. Livingston.—LiR
Animals—Prehistoric. See Prehistoric animals
Ankylosaurus. Jack Prelutsky.—PrT
"The **ankylosaurus** is showing her leg". See Improper moves
"**Ann**, Ann". See Alas, alack
"**Ann**, upon the stroke of three". See Part XII: Ann, upon the stroke of three
"**Anna** and Frankie went for a ride". Unknown.—ScA
"**Anna** and her adorable brother Alvin ate apples at". See Composition ball
"**Anna** banana". Unknown.—WiA
"**Anna** Banana went out in the rain". Jack Prelutsky.—PrBe
"**Anna** Elise, she jumped with surprise". Mother Goose.—ScA—SuO
Annabel Lee. Edgar Allan Poe.—ElW
Anne Frank. Sheryl L. Nelms.—JaPr
Annette Harrison. Mel Glenn.—GlBc
"**Annie** ate jam". Unknown.—OpI
"**Annie** has run to the mill dam". See Dreamland
Another dad. Edward Archibald Markham.—AgL
Another mountain. Abiodun Oyewole.—SlM
Answer to a child's question. Samuel Taylor Coleridge.—CaB—ElW
The **answers.** Robert Clairmont.—CoAz
The **ant.** Clarence Day.—WhAa
"The **ant** climbs up a trunk". See A short story
"The **ant** is knowing and wise, but". See The ant
Anteater ("The anteater makes a meal of ants"). William Jay Smith.—PrFo—SmL
Anteater ("Imagine overturning"). Valerie Worth.—WoAl
"The **anteater** makes a meal of ants". See Anteater
Anteaters
Anteater ("The anteater makes a meal of ants"). W. J. Smith.—PrFo—SmL
Anteater ("Imagine overturning"). V. Worth.—WoAl
Antelope ("A girl with legs like an antelope"). Kazuko Shiraishi.—AgL
Antelope ("When he takes a bath, the antelope"). William Jay Smith.—SmL
The **antelope** ("When one of us hit"). David Allan Evans.—JaPr
Antelopes
Antelope ("When he takes a bath, the antelope"). W. J. Smith.—SmL
The antelope ("When one of us hit"). D. A. Evans.—JaPr
The gazelle calf. D. H. Lawrence.—CaB
Anthem. Stephen Vincent.—KnAs
Anthony, Brother
The birth of a stone, tr.—NyT
The land of mists, tr.—NyT
Anthony. Jane Shore.—JaPr
The **antimacassar** and the ottoman. William Jay Smith.—SmL
Ants
The ant. C. Day.—WhAa
Anteater ("The anteater makes a meal of ants"). W. J. Smith.—PrFo—SmL

Ants. Y. Al-Sa'igh.—NyT
"The ants go marching one by one". Unknown.—ScA
Dog's song. R. Wallace.—KeT
Failing in the presence of ants. G. Soto.—SoA
Insec' lesson. V. Bloom.—AgL
"Once a grasshoppper (food being scant)". O. Herford.—LiLo
A short story. D. E. Galindo.—NyT
Ants. Yusuf Al-Sa'igh, tr. by Diana Der Hovanessian and Salma Khadra Jayyusi.—NyT
"The **ants** go marching one by one". Unknown.—ScA
"**Ants** look up as I trot by". See Dog's song
"**Anxious**". Miriam Waddington.—BoT
"**Any** cold night I am hiding". See Runaway teen
"**Any** hound a porcupine nudges". See The porcupine
"**Any** magazines". See Help
"**Any** silly little soul". Unknown.—OpI
Anybody home. Aileen Fisher.—LaM
Anyone seen my. Max Fatchen.—PrFo
Anyone wanting a fiery dragon. Max Fatchen.—FaCm
"**Anything** wrong". See King Kong bat
Aohozuki
"Now the pond is still".—CaR
Apache Indians. See Indians of the Americas—Apache
Apartment cats. Thom Gunn.—LaCc
Apartments and apartment life. See also Cities and city life; Houses and dwellings
Apartment cats. T. Gunn.—LaCc
Envying the children of San Francisco. G. Soto.—SoA
Garage apartment. M. C. Livingston.—LiT
Great grandma. L. Morrison.—LiPg
Leak. E. Merriam.—MeS
Apes and monkeys
Be kind to dumb animals. J. Ciardi.—CiH—LiLo
"A clever gorilla named Gus". J. Prelutsky.—PrP
"Eleven yellow monkeys". J. Prelutsky.—PrBe
"Five little monkeys". Unknown.—CoE
"Geat but not naudy". Unknown.—WiA
George's pet. M. Mahy.—MaN
"I know something I won't tell". Mother Goose.—WaM—WiA
Three little monkeys.—PrFo
"I went up one pair of stairs". Unknown.—OpI
Idea. Shiki.—DeI
The isle of Lone. W. De La Mare.—DeR
"John and a chimpanzee". Unknown.—ClI
Little monkey. D. J. Bissett.—HoT
Marching song. From The three royal monkeys. W. De La Mare.—DeR
Monkey ("High on a banyan tree in a row"). W. J. Smith.—SmL
Monkey ("Out of a tree"). Kyotai.—DeI
"Monkey, monkey, bottle of pop". Unknown.—CoM—WiA
"Monkey, monkey, sittin' on a rail". Unknown.—WiA
Monkeys. K. Koettner-Benigni.—NyT
Monkeys on the bed. Unknown.—OpT
Motherhood. M. Swenson.—ElW
"Once upon a time, a monkey drank some wine". Unknown.—WiA
"One little monkey laughed loudly". J. Knight.—KnT
The prayer of the monkey. C. B. De Gasztold.—DeP

Apes and monkeys—*Continued*
  "Said the monkey to the donkey". Unknown.—WiA
    The monkey and the donkey.—ClI
  "Said the monkey to the owl". Unknown.—LiIf
  The ship of Rio. W. De La Mare.—DeR—ElW—MaP
  "Silence in the court". Unknown.—ScA
  We must be polite. C. Sandburg.—DeS
  "When you talk to a monkey". R. Bennett.—DeS
  Winter monkey. Basho.—DeI
"The **apes** yawn and adore their fleas in the sun". See The jaguar
Apologies
  "I beg your pardon". Unknown.—OpI
Apology. Lynn Emanuel.—JaPr
"The **appearance** of my parents". See Mom and Pop Ghastly come up for air
The **apple**. Judah Halevi, tr. by Robert Mezey.—GoU
Apple bobbing. R. H. Marks.—LiHp
The **apple** charm. Walter De La Mare.—DeR
Apple-fall. Walter De La Mare.—DeR
Apple harvest. Unknown.—OpT
"**Apple** on a stick". Unknown.—WiA
Apple scoop. Emilie Glen.—LiPg
Apple tree. Myra Cohn Livingston.—LiR
Apple trees
  Apple-fall. W. De La Mare.—DeR
  Apple harvest. Unknown.—OpT
  Apple tree. M. C. Livingston.—LiR
  Apples ("Way up high in the apple tree"). Unknown.—CoE
  "As I went up the apple tree". Unknown.—CoM
  Hanging. E. Gourlay.—BoT
  "Here's to thee, old apple tree". Mother Goose.—WaM
  In autumn. B. J. Esbensen.—EsW
  The orchard. W. De La Mare.—DeR
  Our tree. M. Chute.—DeS
  The sky is falling. D. Dawber.—BoT
  Zeroing in. D. Dawber.—BoT
Apples. See also Apple trees
  A—Apple pie. W. De La Mare.—DeR
  The apple. J. Halevi.—GoU
  Apple bobbing. R. H. Marks.—LiHp
  The apple charm. W. De La Mare.—DeR
  Apple scoop. E. Glen.—LiPg
  Apples ("Some people say that apples are red"). W. J. Smith.—SmL
  Apples ("Way up high in the apple tree"). Unknown.—CoE
  "Catch him, crow". Mother Goose.—WaM
  Counting-out rhyme. E. Merriam.—MeP
  In autumn. B. J. Esbensen.—EsW
  Lunchbox. V. Worth.—MoS
  Ode to weight lifting. G. Soto.—SoNe
  "Once an apple met an apple". Unknown.—CoM
  "There was an old woman of Ryde". Unknown.—PrP
    "There was a young lady of Ryde".—LiLo
Apples ("Some people say that apples are red"). William Jay Smith.—SmL
Apples ("Way up high in the apple tree"). Unknown.—CoE
"**Apples** and oranges, four for a penny". Unknown.—OpI
"**Apples**, peaches, pumpkin pie". Unknown.—ScA
An **appointment**. Chang Shiang-hua, tr. by Stephen L. Smith and Naomi Shihab Nye.—NyT
"The **approach** to the bar". See Pole vaulter

"**Approaching**, nearing, curious". See Queries to my seventieth year
April
  April. L. Clifton.—LiDd
  "April is a dog's dream". M. Singer.—SiT
  April rain song. L. Hughes.—DeS—ElW—HoS—LiDd—SlM—SuI
  "April showers". Unknown.—WiA
April. Lucille Clifton.—LiDd
April 1st. Ann Bonner.—FoLe
April fool. John Ciardi.—CiH—LiLo
"**April** fool, go to school". Unknown.—WiA
April Fool's Day
  All fool's day. J. Agard.—FoLe
  April 1st. A. Bonner.—FoLe
  April fool. J. Ciardi.—CiH—LiLo
  "April fool, go to school". Unknown.—WiA
  "April fool's gone past". Unknown.—OpI
  "Fool, fool, April fool". Unknown.—OpI
  "I've drowned seventy ants in a pool". A. Story.—LiLo
  "Oh did you hear". S. Silverstein.—DeS
  School dinner menu for 1st of April. W. Magee.—FoLe
"**April** fool's gone past". Unknown.—OpI
"**April** is a dog's dream". Marilyn Singer.—SiT
April rain song. Langston Hughes.—DeS—ElW—HoS—LiDd—SlM—SuI
"**April** showers". Unknown.—WiA
Aquarium. Valerie Worth.—WoAl
Araby. Walter De La Mare.—DeR
Arapaho Indians. See Indians of the Americas—Arapaho
Archers and archery. See also Bows and arrows
  "God is the bow". Unknown.—StP
  The need to win. T. Merton.—KnAs
Arctic regions. See Polar regions
"**Are** aching this October morning, the sun is bright in the pale". See Granny's ninety-two-year-old legs
"**Are** you a camel, a big yellow camel". Unknown.—ScA
Are you a marsupial. John Becker.—CoAz
Are you in there. Max Fatchen.—FaCm
"**Are** you ready when the Lord shall come". Unknown.—StP
"**Are** you the guy". Unknown.—WiA
"**Are** zebras black with broad white stripes". See Zebra
"**Aren't** you fearful you'll trip and fall". See Ice-creepers
Arguments
  Father and son. T. Jastrun.—NyT
  Home ("Yelling, shouting, arguing"). M. C. Livingston.—LiT
  My hard repair job. J. Berry.—BeW
  "My little old man and I fell out". Mother Goose.—WaM
Aridjis, Homero
  "In his room the man watches".—NyT
"**Arise**, arise, arumble". See Defiance
"**Arise**, arise, Domino Decree". Unknown.—OpT
Arithmetic. See Mathematics
Arithmetic, sels. Carl Sandburg
  "Arithmetic is where numbers fly".—DeS
"**Arithmetic** is where numbers fly". From Arithmetic. Carl Sandburg.—DeS
Arithmetrix. Eve Merriam.—MeS
Arjan
  "Even if I have gone astray, I am".—StP
"The **Ark** waits, Lord". See The prayer of the dove

Armenian language
  "Elim, elim, ep elim". Unknown.—YoS
    "Who am I, I am me".—YoS
  "Meg, yergoo, yergunnas". Unknown.—YoS
    "One, two, grow tall".—YoS
Armenian nursery rhymes. See Nursery rhymes—
    Armenian
Armour, Richard
  Numbers game.—MoA
  Pachycephalosaurus.—DeS
  Unsound condition.—KnAs
Arms (limbs)
  Octopus ("Marvel at the"). V. Worth.—WoAl
  The octopus ("Tell me, o octopus, I begs"). O.
    Nash.—CaB—WhAa
Armstrong, Louis B. (about)
  Old Satchmo's gravelly voice. M. B. Tolson.—
    SuC
Arnold Flitterman. Mel Glenn.—GlBc
Around my room. William Jay Smith.—KeT—
  LiDd—SmL
"**Around** the block against the clock". See Health
  fanatic
Around the campfire. Andrew Hudgins.—JaM
"**Around** the campfire we sang hymns". See Around
  the campfire
"**Around** the round path". See "Gyro gyrovoli"
"**Around** their igloo fires with glee". See Narwhal
Arrows. See Bows and arrows
Arroz con leche. Unknown.—DeA
  Rice and milk ("I'm rice and milk, I'd like to be
    wed").—DeA
"**Arroz** con leche, se quiere casar". See Arroz con
  leche
"'**Arry** 'ad an 'awk in an 'atbag". See 'Arry's 'awk
'**Arry's** 'awk. Unknown.—CII
Art and artists. See also Beauty, of nature or art;
  Painting and pictures
  The artist. A. Bryan.—BrS
  Gayle Buckingham. M. Glenn.—GlBc
  The making of dragons. J. Yolen.—YoFf
  Mr. Neil Pressman, fine arts. M. Glenn.—GlBc
  Origami for two. P. Dominick.—MoR
  The picture-book. W. De La Mare.—DeR
  Remodeling the hermit's cabin. F. Chappell.—
    JaM
  Salt and memory, a tribute to Marc Chagall. Z.
    Zelk.—NyT
  The slave and the iron lace. M. Danner.—SuC
  Temple for tomorrow. From The negro artist and
    the racial mountain. L. Hughes.—SuC
  "The unicorn I tried to paint". X. J. Kennedy.—
    KeK
Arthur. Ogden Nash.—LiLo
"**Arthur** drove his truck from Georgia". See Pigeons
  and peanuts for sale
Arthur Mitchell. Marianne Moore.—MoR
The **artist.** Ashley Bryan.—BrS
Artists. See Art and artists
Arymouse, arymouse. Unknown.—CII
"**Arymouse,** arymouse, fly over my head". See
  Arymouse, arymouse
"**As** a beauty I'm not a great star". Anthony
  Euwer.—LiLo
"**As** a leaning". See Shakes and ladders
"**As** a sloop with a sweep of immaculate wing on
  her delicate spine". See Buick
"**As** always". See Gazebo
"**As** Daddy stands me up against the cold back
  door". See The first flakes are falling on our
  heads
"**As** Eenty Feenty Halligolun". Unknown.—OpI

"**As** far as possible, she strove". See Born that way
"**As** I came out of Wiseman's Street". See Not I
As I did rove. Walter De La Mare.—DeR
"**As** I did rove in blinded night". See As I did rove
"**As** I lay awake in the white moonlight". See
  Sleepyhead
"**As** I lie in my bed". See Attic fanatic
As I looked out. Unknown.—CII
"**As** I looked out on Saturday last". See As I looked
  out
"**As** I rowed out to the light house". See The light
  house keeper's white mouse
"**As** I sat in the gloaming". See The voice
"**As** I sat musing by the frozen dyke". See The song
  of soldiers
"**As** I sit looking out of a window of the building".
  See The instruction manual
"**As** I walk along". See Crabs
"**As** I walked out in the streets of Laredo". See The
  cowboy's lament
"**As** I walked out one morning for pleasure". See
  Whoopee ti yi yo, git along, little dogies
"**As** I was going along, along". Mother Goose.—
  MoS
"**As** I was going o'er Tipple Tine". Mother Goose.—
  CII
"**As** I was going out one day". Unknown.—ScA
  "As I went out".—PrP
"**As** I was going over London Bridge". Unknown.—
  OpI
"**As** I was going to Newbury". Mother Goose.—
  WaM
"**As** I was going to St. Ives". Unknown.—ScA
"**As** I was going up Pippen Hill". Mother Goose.—
  OpT—WaM
"**As** I was sitting in my chair". See The perfect
  reactionary
"**As** I was walking". See Master Rabbit
"**As** I was walking all alane". See The twa corbies
"**As** I was walking around the lake". See "As I was
  walking round the lake"
"**As** I was walking round the lake". Unknown.—CII
  "As I was walking around the lake".—PrP
"**As** I went by a dyer's door". See Gypsy
"**As** I went down the Icky Picky Lane".
  Unknown.—CII
"**As** I went out". See "As I was going out one day"
"**As** I went over the water". Mother Goose.—CII
"**As** I went through a field of wheat". Unknown.—
  WiA
"**As** I went to Bonner". Mother Goose.—CII
"**As** I went to the well-head". Walter De La Mare.—
  DeR
"**As** I went up a slippery gap". Unknown.—OpT
"**As** I went up the apple tree". Unknown.—CoM
"**As** I went up the high hill". Unknown.—CII
"**As** I went walking one fine Sunday". See Coati-
  mundi
"**As** if a voice had called, I woke". See The border
  bird
"**As** if the sky could no longer hold its color". See
  The evening light along the sound
"**As** in old". See Beetle
"**As** little Bess was walking home". See The robin
"**As** long as I live". See Me
As Lucy went a-walking. Walter De La Mare.—DeR
"**As** Lucy went a-walking one morning cold and
  fine". See As Lucy went a-walking
"**As** poor old Biddie". See The bird
"**As** puffed up". See First robin
"**As** soon as ever twilight comes". See Part XIII: As
  soon as ever twilight comes

As soon as it's fall. Aileen Fisher.—FiA
"As sure as a vine grows round a rafter".
   Unknown.—ScA
"As sure as a vine grows round a stump".
   Unknown.—ScA
"As the cat". See Poem
"As the fat sheriff who's taken". See Sneaking in the
   state fair
"As the guns thunder". Eve Merriam.—MeS
"As the orange-striped cat". See Nature
"As the sun". See Sphinx
"As the sun came up, a ball of red". See Chinese
   dragon
"As we are so wonderfully done with each other".
   Kenneth Patchen.—GoU
"As we sailed out of London river". See Bonum
   omen
"As we sit". See Remember
"As wet as a fish, as dry as a bone". Unknown.—
   ScA
Asch, Frank
   Alley cat school.—LaCc
   Puddles.—MoS
   The sugar lady.—DeT
   Sunflakes.—DeS—MoS
   Tree ("If only I could stand").—MoS
"**Aserrin,** aserran". Unknown.—DeA
   Sawdust song ("Sawdust sings, sawdust songs").—
   DeA
Ashbery, John
   The instruction manual.—ElW
Ashe, Arthur (about)
   Tennis in the city. F. Higgins.—KnAs
"**Ask** me no questions". Unknown.—WiA
Asleep. Walter De La Mare.—DeR
"**Asleep** he wheezes at his ease". See Roger the dog
Asparagus. Valerie Worth.—WoAl
"The **aspens** and the maples now". See Valentine's
   day
Aspiration. See Ambition
The **ass** in the lion's skin. Aesop, tr. by William
   Ellery Leonard.—CaB
"An **ass** put on a lion's skin and went". See The ass
   in the lion's skin
Asses. See Donkeys
Assiniboin Indians. See Indians of the Americas—
   Assiniboin
Associations. Eve Merriam.—MeS
Astley, Jacob
   "O Lord, Thou knowest how".—StP
Astronomy. See also Moon; Planets; Stars; Sun
   "When I heard the learn'd astronomer". W.
   Whitman.—HoVo
"**At** a city square". See Envying the children of San
   Francisco
"**At** a disco girls cluster and dance me in". See Let
   me rap you my orbital map
"**At** another year". See Birthday on the beach
"**At** dawn the milk truck's bell should be lightly".
   See An appointment
"**At** dusk". See If the owl calls again
"**At** eight I was brilliant with my body". See Black
   hair
"**At** fifteen Jim Calvin made a list". See
   Preposterous
"**At** heaven's gate". See "En la puerta del cielo"
At last. Walter De La Mare.—DeR
"**At** last I have my anger breathalyser". From What
   we said sitting making fantasies. James Berry.—
   BeW
"**At** Michael's party". See Michael's birthday
"**At** midnight". See Worm

"**At** midnight in the alley". See The tomcat
At night. Aileen Fisher.—MoS
"**At** night may I roam". Unknown.—LiIf
"**At** night, my Uncle Rufus". See Night starvation or
   the biter bit
"**At** night when the bats". See B is for bats
"**At** Pina's house". See Country memory
At Plymouth, the first Thanksgiving, 1621. X. J.
   Kennedy.—KeK
"**At** recess". See She should have listened to me
"**At** school they told us". See Saint David's Day
At sea. Eve Merriam.—MeP
"**At** show and tell time yesterday". See April fool
"**At** six o'clock, most people". See Stay with me
At sunrise. Max Fatchen.—FaCm
At sunset. Joseph von Eichendorff.—GoT
"**At** sunset my foot outreached the mounting
   Pacific's". See Swimming in the Pacific
"**At** Tara today in this fateful hour". Saint
   Patrick.—StP
At the beach ("Johnny, Johnny, let go of that crab").
   John Ciardi.—PrFo
"**At** the beach ("Our holiday activities"). Max
   Fatchen.—FaCm
At the beach ("The waves are erasing the
   footprints"). Kemal Ozer, tr. by O. Yalim and
   W. Fielder and Dionis Riggs.—NyT
"**At** the beach (1)". From Beach birthdays. Myra
   Cohn Livingston.—LiBp
"**At** the beach (2)". From Beach birthdays. Myra
   Cohn Livingston.—LiBp
"**At** the crack". See Pull hitter
"**At** the edge of all the ages". See The song of Finis
At the ferry. Vijaya Mukhopadhyay.—NyT
"**At** the fireworks show, rash Randall". X. J.
   Kennedy.—KeFb
"**At** the horislope of the mountizon". From Altazor.
   Vicente Huidobro, tr. by Eliot Weinberger.—
   NyT
At the keyhole. Walter De La Mare.—DeR—MaP
At the New Year. Kenneth Patchen.—GoT
At the piano. Andrew Hudgins.—JaM
At the playground. William Stafford.—JaP—KeT
At the sea side. Robert Louis Stevenson.—KeT—
   LiDd
"**At** the Top Hat Cafe". See Ruth
"**At** the wall". See Playing stickball with Robbie
   Shea
At the waterhole. J. Patrick Lewis.—LeA
At the witch's drugstore. Jane Yolen.—YoBe
At the zoo. Myra Cohn Livingston.—HoT
"**At** Union Station the pigeons flock". See Pigeons
   and popcorn
"**At** winter's end". See Snowman sniffles
Athletes and athletics. See also names of sports, as
   Baseball
   Babe Didrikson. G. Rice.—KnAs
   Ex-basketball player. J. Updike.—KnAs
   The gymnasts. I. Feldman.—KnAs
   Hurdler. G. Butcher.—KnAs
   Idyll. J. Updike.—KnAs
   "I'm going to die". K. Dakos.—DaI
   Instruction. C. Hilberry.—KnAs—MoA
   International ski flying championship, Obersdorf.
   E. Ritchie.—KnAs
   Let's go, Mets. L. Morrison.—KnAs
   The midnight tennis match. T. Lux.—KnAs
   Nine triads. L. Morrison.—KnAs
   The Notre Dame victory march. J. Shea.—KnAs
   Pole vaulter. D. A. Evans.—KnAs
   Prefontaine. C. Ghigna.—KnAs
   Preparedness. F. Lamport.—KnAs

Athletes and athletics.—*Continued*
Pumping iron. D. Ackerman.—KnAs
The rider. N. S. Nye.—JaP
Say goodbye to Big Daddy. R. Jarrell.—KnAs
The standing broad jump. R. Frost.—KnAs
To an athlete dying young. A. E. Housman.—ElW
Uneven parallel bars. P. Gary.—KnAs
Watching gymnasts. R. Francis.—MoR
Atlas. Jane Yolen.—YoFf
Atong. Benilda S. Santos, tr. by Ramon C. Sunico.—NyT
Atong and his goodbye. Benilda S. Santos, tr. by Ramon C. Sunico.—NyT
Atsumi, Ikuko
Bright house, tr.—GoU
Attar, Farid-Uddin
Then from a ruin, tr. by Edward Fitzgerald.—LiIf
"**Attention,** architect". See Message from a mouse, ascending in a rocket
Attic dance. Joan Drew Ritchings.—MoR
Attic fanatic. Lois Simmie.—PrFo
Attire. Eve Merriam.—MeCh
Atwood, Margaret
Snake woman.—BoT
Auden, Wystan Hugh
For the time being, sels.
"He is the Way".—StP
"He is the Way". See For the time being
Audrey Reynolds. Mel Glenn.—GlBc
Auguries of innocence, sels. William Blake
"To see a world in a grain of sand".—StP
August
August ("Buttercup nodded and said goodby"). C. Thaxter.—SuI
August ("The sprinkler twirls"). J. Updike.—ElW
August outing. T. Harvey.—FoLe
Dragonfly. M. Singer.—SiT
In August. G. Soto.—SoA
August ("Buttercup nodded and said goodby"). Celia Thaxter.—SuI
August ("The sprinkler twirls"). John Updike.—ElW
"The **August** bank holiday's here again". See August outing
August 8. Norman Jordan.—SlM
"An **August** night". See Fireflies
August outing. Trevor Harvey.—FoLe
Saint Augustine
"Keep watch, dear Lord, with those who work".—StP
Auks
Word of warning. X. J. Kennedy.—KeGh
"**Aunt** Gilda wears twelve hat pins". See Aunt Gilda's pincushion head
Aunt Gilda's pincushion head. X. J. Kennedy.—KeGh
Aunt Roberta. Eloise Greenfield.—MoS
"**Aunt** Sue has a head full of stories". See Aunt Sue's stories
Aunt Sue's stories. Langston Hughes.—SlM
Aunts
Agatha Ghastly makes light of Auntie. X. J. Kennedy.—KeGh
Aunt Gilda's pincushion head. X. J. Kennedy.—KeGh
Aunt Roberta. E. Greenfield.—MoS
Aunt Sue's stories. L. Hughes.—SlM
"Crocodile or alligator". C. West.—CoAz
Lecture. P. B. Janeczko.—JaB
Maud. M. Swander.—JaM
My yellow straw hat. L. J. Little.—KeT
"Once a grasshoppper (food being scant)". O. Herford.—LiLo

Thank you letter. R. Klein.—FoLe
Austin, Mary
A song of greatness, tr.—SuI
Australia
City to surf. D. Bateson.—FoLe
Corroboree ("The clap, clap, clap of the clapsticks beat"). M. Fatchen.—FoLe
Corroboree ("Hot day dies, cook time comes"). K. Walker.—FoLe
Tree festival. D. Bateson.—FoLe
Authors and authorship. See Writers and writing
Autobiographical note. Vernon Scannell.—JaPr
Autograph album verses
"As sure as a vine grows round a rafter". Unknown.—ScA
"As sure as a vine grows round a stump". Unknown.—ScA
"Can't think". Unknown.—WiA
"Do you love me". Unknown.—WiA
From the autograph album. Unknown.—MoA
"I love you, I love you". Unknown.—LoFh—PrP—ScA—WiA
"I love you little". Unknown.—WiA
"I wish you luck, I wish you joy". Unknown.—CoM—ScA
"If you love me as I love you". Unknown.—WiA
"If you think you are in love". Unknown.—WiA
"It tickles me". Unknown.—WiA
"I've thought and thought and thought in vain". Unknown.—WiA
"Just as the mouse". Unknown.—WiA
"Just as the vine". Unknown.—WiA
"Like your books". Unknown.—WiA
"May your life be bright and sunny". Unknown.—WiA
"My love for you will never fail". Unknown.—WiA
"Pigs like mud". Unknown.—WiA
"Read up and down". Unknown.—ScA—WiA
"Roses are red, violets are blue, grass is green". Unknown.—WiA
"Roses are red, violets are blue, sugar is sweet". Unknown.—WiA
"Roses are red, violets are blue, what you need". Unknown.—WiA
"Some write for pleasure". Unknown.—WiA
"There are gold ships". Unknown.—WiA
"U R 2 good". Unknown.—WiA
"When on this page you look". Unknown.—WiA
"When you are courting". Unknown.—WiA
"When you get married and live on a hill". Unknown.—WiA
"When you get married and your husband gets cross". Unknown.—WiA
"When you get married and your wife has twins". Unknown.—WiA
"When you get old". Unknown.—WiA
"When you see a monkey up a tree". Unknown.—WiA
"When you stand upon the stump". Unknown.—WiA
"You be the ice cream, I'll be the freezer". Unknown.—WiA
Automobiles
"An abhorrent young person named Plunkett". W. J. Smith.—SmL
Buick. K. Shapiro.—MoR
The car. R. Creeley.—MoR
"The cars in Caracas". J. Updike.—MoR
Driving. M. C. Livingston.—MoR
For people who can't open their hoods. J. Daniels.—JaPr

The **babes** in the wood. Unknown.—ElW
Babies. See also Childhood recollections; Children and childhood; Lullabies; Nursery play
All asleep. C. Pomerantz.—PlW
All the way. W. De La Mare.—DeR
"Baby and I". Mother Goose.—PrP—WaM
"Baby, baby, in the tub". Unknown.—CoM
"Baby in a highchair". Unknown.—WiA
The baby-sitter and the baby. E. Merriam.—MeS
Baby's drinking song. J. Kirkup.—MoS
"Baby's heart is lifted up". R. L. Gales.—StP
Bats. R. Jarrell.—ElW
  The bat.—LaN
Brand new baby. B. S. De Regniers.—DeW
Butterfly song. Unknown.—KeT
"Coo, coo, coo". Unknown.—PrP
Dear delight. W. De La Mare.—DeR
Do it yourself. M. Fatchen.—FaCm
Do witches have. J. Yolen.—YoBe
The first shoe. M. Mhac an tSaoi.—NyT
"I wish you luck, I wish you joy". Unknown.—CoM—ScA
Infant sorrow. W. Blake.—ElW
"Jen said, baby, don't you swaller". X. J. Kennedy.—KeFb
"Judge, judge, tell the judge". Unknown.—WiA
The legend of Rosemary. J. Yolen.—YoHa
Long distance call. X. J. Kennedy.—KeGh
Louisa, Louisa. J. Little.—LiHe
Lullaby for a black mother. L. Hughes.—SlM
Misnomer. E. Merriam.—MeCh—PrFo
"Miss Lucy had a baby". Unknown.—CoM—ScA
Monster mothers. F. P. Heide.—HeG
Mother and babe. W. Whitman.—HoVo
Motherhood. M. Swenson.—ElW
My baby brother. M. A. Hoberman.—HoFa
My family tree. E. Merriam.—MeP
Nestlings. J. Yolen.—YoBi
New baby poem (I). E. Greenfield.—GrN
New baby poem (II). E. Greenfield.—GrN
Newborn neurological exam. M. Baron.—JaM
Pacifier. X. J. Kennedy.—KeK
"Que linda manito". Unknown.—DeA
  A pretty little hand ("How pretty, how little").—DeA
Surprise ("A balloon, my Daddy brought for me"). B. Rodriguez.—NyT
Surprise ("I wonder"). A. Fisher.—FiH
"There was a little baby". Unknown.—WiA
Trouble. J. Wright.—JaPr
Trouble with baby. X. J. Kennedy.—KeGh
"Two deep clear eyes". W. De La Mare.—DeR
Baboons. See Apes and monkeys
"**Baby** and I". Mother Goose.—PrP—WaM
"**Baby, baby**". Unknown.—ScA
"**Baby, baby**, in the tub". Unknown.—CoM
Baby chick. Aileen Fisher.—FiA—WhAa
"**Baby** in a highchair". Unknown.—WiA
"**Baby** June". See My family tree
The **baby-sitter** and the baby. Eve Merriam.—MeS
Baby's drinking song. James Kirkup.—MoS
"**Baby's** got a plastic bottle". See The wholly family
"**Baby's** heart is lifted up". R. L. Gales.—StP
Babysitters
About angels and age. J. Little.—LiHe
The baby-sitter and the baby. E. Merriam.—MeS
Guinevere Ghastly sits baby. X. J. Kennedy.—KeGh
Miss McGillicuddy. M. A. Hoberman.—HoFa
"**Back** and forth". See Horses
"**Back** flat on the carpet". See Telephone talk

"**Back** from camp that morning". See What Saundra said about being short
"**Back** in times too poor". See Muscling rocks
"**Back** into your garden beds". See To pumpkins at pumpkin time
"**Back** of the loaf is the snowy flour". M. D. Babcock.—StP
"**Back** through clouds". See Train tune
Back yard. Valerie Worth.—DeT—WoAl
"**Backpacking** Max". See The hiker
Backsides. Deepak Kalha.—AgL
Backyard volcano. X. J. Kennedy.—KeGh
Bacmeister, Rhoda
  Galoshes.—DeS
Bad. Paul B. Janeczko.—JaB
Bad boy's swan song. William Jay Smith.—SmL
"**Bad** chemistry exists between me and Mr. Fletcher". See Arnold Flitterman
"**Bad** I am, but yet thy child". Gerard Manley Hopkins.—StP
Baez, Joan
  Love song to a stranger.—GoU
"**Baffled** by the choreography of the season". See Autumn piece
The **bagel.** David Ignatow.—BaW
Baird, Martha
  Confidence.—LaCc
Bakers and baking
  "Baby and I". Mother Goose.—PrP—WaM
  "Charley, Charley". Mother Goose.—WaM
  Every so often. J. Little.—LiHe
  "Pat-a-cake, pat-a-cake, baker's man". Mother Goose.—EdGl—SuO
    "Patty cake, patty cake".—WaM
  "Round the 4H baked goods sale". X. J. Kennedy.—KeFb
  "Stealthy Steffan stuck a dead". X. J. Kennedy.—KeFb
  Twelve pies. J. Yolen.—YoHa
Baldwin, Michael
  The truth about the abominable footprint.—PrFo
Bali
  Night of the full moon. D. Batson.—FoLe
  Nyepi, the day of yellow rice. T. Millum.—FoLe
"The **ball** dances in". See For Hoyt Wilhelm
The **ball** poem. John Berryman.—KnAs
"**Ball** tight". See Touchdown
Ballad of Birmingham. Dudley Randall.—ElW
Ballad of black and white. William Jay Smith.—SmL
The **ballad** of Jimi. Curtis Knight.—SuC
Ballad of John Henry. Useni Eugene Perkins.—SlM
The **ballad** of old Rocky Nelson. Raymond Souster.—MoA
Ballads
  Ballad of Birmingham. D. Randall.—ElW
  Ballad of black and white. W. J. Smith.—SmL
  The ballad of Jimi. C. Knight.—SuC
  Ballad of John Henry. U. E. Perkins.—SlM
  The ballad of old Rocky Nelson. R. Souster.—MoA
  La belle dame sans merci. J. Keats.—ElW
  Casey at the bat. E. L. Thayer.—ElW—MoA
  The rime of the ancient mariner, complete. S. T. Coleridge.—ElW
Ballads—Traditional
  The best in the land. From John Henry. Unknown.—SuC
  Bonny George Campbell. Unknown.—ElW
  Casey Jones. Unknown.—MoR
  The cowboy's lament. Unknown.—ElW
  "Lully, lulley, lully, lulley". Unknown.—StP

"**Bat**, bat". Mother Goose.—ClI
The **bat** in the bedroom. Robert Crum.—JaM
"A **bat** is born". See Bats
Bateson, David
City to surf.—FoLe
Crown of light festival.—FoLe
Tree festival.—FoLe
Waitangi Day.—FoLe
The **bathers**. Karl Shapiro.—KnAs
Bathing
After a bath. A. Fisher.—FiA
Antelope ("When he takes a bath, the antelope").
W. J. Smith.—SmL
"Baby, baby, in the tub". Unknown.—CoM
Cat bath ("After she eats"). A. Fisher.—FiA
Cat bath ("In the midst"). V. Worth.—LaCc—
WoAl
Cat bath ("She always tries"). A. Fisher.—CoAz
"Charlie, Charlie, in the tub". Unknown.—OpI
Chocolate dreams, six thirty. A. Adoff.—AdCh
Dickery Dean. D. Lee.—KeT
It rained in the park today. J. Thurman.—MoS
"It's hard to lose a friend". Unknown.—PrP
Part III: Little birds bathe. From A child's day.
W. De La Mare.—DeR
"Patience is a virtue". Unknown.—OpI
Playing dirty. M. Fatchen.—FaCm
"Queen, Queen Caroline". Unknown.—KeT—OpI
"Rub a dub dub". Mother Goose.—EdGl—WaM
"Rub a dub dub". Unknown.—WiA
"Sam, Sam, dirty old man". Unknown.—CoM—
OpI
"She fell into the bathtub". Unknown.—PrP
Soap. J. Thurman.—MoS
T is for tub. W. J. Smith.—SmL
"There was a little baby". Unknown.—WiA
"There was a small pig who wept tears". A.
Lobel.—HoS
"Wash and wipe together". Unknown.—WiA
Watering trough. M. Kumin.—JaP
"Who are you, a dirty old man". Mother
Goose.—OpI—WaM
Bats
The abominable baseball bat. X. J. Kennedy.—
MoA
Arymouse, arymouse. Unknown.—ClI
B is for bats. W. J. Smith.—SmL
The bat ("By day the bat is cousin to the mouse").
T. Roethke.—CoAz—DeS—ElW
Bat ("Dark air life looping"). D. H. Lawrence.—
WhAa
The bat ("Lightless, unholy, eldritch thing"). R.
Pitter.—CaB
"Bat, bat". Mother Goose.—ClI
The bat in the bedroom. R. Crum.—JaM
Bats. R. Jarrell.—ElW
The bat.—LaN
Doctor Blair. G. Nichols.—NiCo
The flight of the one-eyed bat. W. J. Smith.—
SmL
King Kong bat. W. J. Smith.—SmL
The sound. Shiki.—DeI
"Tell me, why so pale and wan". X. J.
Kennedy.—KeFb
"Twinkle, twinkle, little bat". From Alice's
adventures in wonderland. L. Carroll.—ClI
Bats. Randall Jarrell.—ElW
The bat.—LaN
Batson, David
Night of the full moon.—FoLe
Battle hymn of the republic, sels. Julia Ward Howe
Mine eyes have seen the glory.—SuC

Battles. See also War
Concord hymn. R. W. Emerson.—ElW
"Joshua fit the battle of Jericho, Jericho".
Unknown.—StP
"Would you hear of an old-time sea fight". W.
Whitman.—SuI
Baumel, Judith
Led by the Hebrew School rabbi.—KnAs
Bay breasted barge bird. William Jay Smith.—SmL
"The **bay** breasted barge bird delights in
depressions". See Bay breasted barge bird
"The **Bay** of Tsunu". Hitomaro Kakinomoto, tr. by
Kenneth Rexroth.—GoU
Baylor, Byrd
"The way to start a day is this". See The way to
start the day
The way to start the day, sels.
"The way to start a day is this".—DeT
"**Be** comforted, you would not have searched".
Blaise Pascal.—StP
"**Be** glad your nose is on your face". Jack
Prelutsky.—PrFo
"**Be** kind and tender to the frog". See The frog
Be kind to dumb animals. John Ciardi.—CiH—
LiLo
"**Be** kind to your web-footed friends". Unknown.—
ScA
Be lenient with lobsters. Unknown.—ClI
"**Be** lenient with lobsters, and even kind to crabs".
See Be lenient with lobsters
"**Be** thy right hand, O God, under my head".
Unknown.—StP
Be warned. Max Fatchen.—FaCm
"**Be** wary of the fairies". See Changelings
Beach birthdays, complete. Myra Cohn Livingston
"At the beach (1)".—LiBp
"At the beach (2)".—LiBp
Beaches. See Shore
The **bead** mat. Walter De La Mare.—DeR
Beaded braids. Ashley Bryan.—BrS
The **beak** of the pelican. J. Patrick Lewis.—LeA
"The **beam**". See Audrey Reynolds
Beans
"Green bean". B. McMillan.—McP
"**Bear** chair". Bruce McMillan.—McP
"A **bear**, however hard he tries". From Teddy bear.
Alan Alexander Milne.—DeT
"The **bear** stands". Unknown.—WhAa
"The **bear** went over the mountain". See Song
without end
Beards
"A beautiful lady named Psyche". Unknown.—
LiLo
"I know a man named Michael Finnegan".
Unknown.—WiA
"There was an old man with a beard". E. Lear.—
ClI—KeT—LiIf—LiLo
"When you see your neighbour's beard on fire,
take some water and wet your own". From
Jamaican Caribbean proverbs. Unknown.—
BeW
Bears
"Algy met a bear". Unknown.—ClI—PrP—WiA
"Bear chair". B. McMillan.—McP
"A bear, however hard he tries". From Teddy
bear. A. A. Milne.—DeT
"The bear stands". Unknown.—WhAa
Bears. A. Fisher.—FiA
Beware ("When a cub, unaware being bare").
From Animalimericks. E. Merriam.—MeS
"A big bare bear". R. Heidbreder.—PrFo
The coming of teddy bears. D. Lee.—KeT

Bears—*Continued*
The common cormorant. Unknown.—ClI
    The cormorant.—CaB (at. to Christopher Isherwood)
Furry bear. A. A. Milne.—DeS
"Fuzzy Wuzzy was a bear". Unknown.—PrP—WiA
    Fuzzy Wuzzy.—ClI
Grandpa bear's lullaby. J. Yolen.—DeS—HoS—MoS
"Isabel met an enormous bear". From The adventures of Isabel. O. Nash.—DeS
March bear. M. Singer.—SiT
"Mary had a little bear". Unknown.—PrP
An old person of Ware. E. Lear.—MoS
"On a trip through Yellowstone". X. J. Kennedy.—KeFb
"One little grizzly grew grumpy". J. Knight.—KnT
"One little panda read music". J. Knight.—KnT
The panda. W. J. Smith.—SmL
Part VI: Thousands of years ago. From A child's day. W. De La Mare.—DeR
Paying through the nose. J. Ciardi.—CiH
Polar bear ("Every time"). L. Blair.—HoT
Polar bear ("The polar bear never makes his bed"). W. J. Smith.—KeT—SmL
Song without end. Unknown.—WiA
Speedy Sam. J. Ciardi.—CiH
"Teddy bear, teddy bear". Unknown.—YoS
"There once was a dancing black bear". J. P. Lewis.—LiLo
Too hot to sleep. S. Marty.—BoT
Wedding bears. J. P. Lewis.—LeT
Who really. W. De La Mare.—DeR
Win some, lose some. J. Ciardi.—CiH
Bears. Aileen Fisher.—FiA
"The **beast** that is most fully dressed". See Lion
"**Beat** the batter". See Shrove Tuesday
"**Beatrix** Potter". William Jay Smith.—SmL
"The **beautiful** boys curve and writhe". See Young wrestlers
"A **beautiful** lady named Psyche". Unknown.—LiLo
"A **beautiful** maiden dressed in sage". See White buffalo woman
Beautiful women. Walt Whitman.—HoVo
Beauty, of nature or art
Afternoon on a hill. E. S. V. Millay.—FrS—SuI
"All this time and at all times wait the words of true poems". From Song of myself. W. Whitman.—HoVo
And my heart soars. Chief D. George.—BoT—LoFh
As I did rove. W. De La Mare.—DeR
"Crowned crane". J. Gleason.—NyT
Cynthia in the snow. G. Brooks.—KeT
Daffodils. W. Wordsworth.—FrS
    "I wandered lonely as a cloud".—ElW
Egrets ("Once as I traveled through a quiet evening). J. Wright.—ElW
Fish ("Look at the fish"). W. J. Smith.—SmL
Flint. C. G. Rossetti.—ElW
"Glory be to God for dappled things". G. M. Hopkins.—StP
"Go to the shine that's on a tree". R. Eberhart.—ElW
"God save the owls". From Alabama. J. Fields.—LiIf
God's world. E. S. V. Millay.—StP
"It's changing here". J. Carson.—CaS
Lines to a nasturtium (a lover muses). A. Spencer.—SuC

"Loveliest of trees, the cherry now". A. E. Housman.—ElW
Music. W. De La Mare.—DeR
My heart leaps up. W. Wordsworth.—ElW
No jewel. W. De La Mare.—DeR
Oliver Johnson comes back to bed the morning after the ice storm and tells his wife why. D. Jauss.—JaM
On New Year's Day, watching it snow. I. Shikibu.—GoT
"Passing and catching overcome the world". From Watching football on TV. H. Nemerov.—KnAs
The pear tree. E. S. V. Millay.—ElW
Pretty is. A. Bryan.—BrS
Sandpipers. H. Nemerov.—ElW
Seashell. V. Worth.—WoAl
The song of the secret. W. De La Mare.—DeR—MaP
"There's a tiresome young man from Bay Shore". M. Bishop.—LiLo
"Thou art the sky and thou art the nest as well". R. Tagore.—StP
Vorobyev Hills. B. Pasternak.—GoT
The world is too much with us. W. Wordsworth.—ElW
Beauty, personal
Abby Kramer. M. Glenn.—GlBc
"After the ball was over". Unknown.—ScA
The apple. J. Halevi.—GoU
"As a beauty I'm not a great star". A. Euwer.—LiLo
Beautiful women. W. Whitman.—HoVo
Black is beautiful. U. E. Perkins.—SlM
The changeling. W. De La Mare.—DeR—MaP
Cheerleader. J. W. Miller.—JaPr
A dialogue of watching. K. Rexroth.—GoU
"During the sermon". W. Kloefkorn.—JaPr
The flower's perfume. A. Bryan.—BrS
Growing old. R. Henderson.—DeT
"He is handsome". Unknown.—ScA
"I want to tell". J. Carson.—CaS
"If you are not handsome at twenty". Mother Goose.—WaM
Lines to a nasturtium (a lover muses). A. Spencer.—SuC
"Little dabs of powder". Unknown.—ScA
"Little soul sister". U. E. Perkins.—SlM
My dress is old. Unknown.—SnD
My people. L. Hughes.—SlM
Now blue October. R. Nathan.—GoU
Sallie. W. De La Mare.—DeR
Saucer hat lady. E. Greenfield.—GrU
A secret kept. J. Al-Harizi.—GoU
The song of the secret. W. De La Mare.—DeR—MaP
The tarantula. R. Whittemore.—ElW
"There was an old lady named Hart". W. J. Smith.—LiLo—SmL
Beauty and the beast, an anniversary. Jane Yolen.—YoFf
"The **beauty** of the trees". See And my heart soars
"**Beaver**, river weaver". See River lovers
Beavers
Beavers in November. M. Singer.—SiT
"One little beaver worked hard as can be". J. Knight.—KnT
Beavers in November. Marilyn Singer.—SiT
Bebe Belinda and Carl Colombus. Adrian Mitchell.—AgL
"**Because** I could not stop for death". Emily Dickinson.—SuI
"**Because** my mouth". See Minstrel man

"**Because** of the steepness". See Mountain brook
"**Because** parrots are chatterers people say they are the only ones who eat up the fruits". From Jamaican Caribbean proverbs. Unknown.—BeW
"**Because** talk in the town". See Why Rosalie did it
Becker, John
Are you a marsupial.—CoAz
"Seven little rabbits".—HoS
Bed in summer. Robert Louis Stevenson.—DeT
Bed mate. Constance Andrea Keremes.—HoS
Bed-time. See Bedtime
Beds
Monkeys on the bed. Unknown.—OpT
Bedtime. See also Lullabies
Absolutely nothing. F. P. Heide.—HeG
The admiration of Willie. G. Brooks.—PlW
Advice on how to sleep well Halloween night. J. Yolen.—YoBe
All asleep. C. Pomerantz.—PlW
All Hallows' Eve. A. Bonner.—FoLe
"All praise to Thee, my God, this night". T. Ken.—StP
And even now. D. Livesay.—BoT
And s-s-so to b-b-bed. M. Fatchen.—FaCm
"Annie ate jam". Unknown.—OpI
Around my room. W. J. Smith.—KeT—LiDd—SmL
Attic fanatic. L. Simmie.—PrFo
The baby-sitter and the baby. E. Merriam.—MeS
Bed in summer. R. L. Stevenson.—DeT
Bed mate. C. A. Keremes.—HoS
Beware of rubber bands. F. P. Heide.—HeG
Birthday night. M. C. Livingston.—LiBp
Blanket hog. P. B. Janeczko.—KeT
Boy reading. J. Holmes.—SuI
The child in the story goes to bed. W. De La Mare.—DeR
Christmas eve night. J. Cotton.—FoLe
"Cold cold shivery cold me in". E. Merriam.—MeY
The coming of teddy bears. D. Lee.—KeT
Counting sheep ("1, 2, my daddy, who"). L. Clifton.—LiPf
Covers. N. Giovanni.—DeT
The dark ("It's always dark"). M. C. Livingston.—KeT
Darnell. E. Greenfield.—GrN
"Diddle diddle dumpling, my son John". Mother Goose.—SuO—WaM
Diddle diddle dumpling.—HoS
Don't be afraid. D. Vogel.—LiPm
"Each night father fills me with dread". E. Gorey.—PrFo
Early dark. E. Coatsworth.—PlW
Fambly time. E. Greenfield.—GrN
"Father, bless me in my body". Unknown.—StP
"Four legs". M. C. Livingston.—LiMh
"From ghoulies and ghosties". Unknown.—LiHp—LoFh
Ghoulies and ghosties.—DeT
"Go to bed late". Mother Goose.—WaM
"Go to bed, Tom". Mother Goose.—WaM
Going into dream. E. Farjeon.—HoSt
Good night ("Father puts the paper down"). A. Fisher.—PlW
Good night ("Goodnight Mommy"). N. Giovanni.—HoS—PlW
"Good night and sweet repose, I hope". Unknown.—OpI
"Good night, sleep tight". Unknown.—PrFo (longer)—ScA—WiA

"Good night, sweet repose, half the bed". Unknown.—OpI—WaM
Goodnight, Juma. E. Greenfield.—GrN
The hammer song. Unknown.—CoE
Hark. W. De La Mare.—DeR
Hide and seek. W. De La Mare.—DeR—MaP
House noises. X. J. Kennedy.—LiPm
The huntsmen. W. De La Mare.—DeR—MaP
"Hush, my dear, lie still and slumber". I. Watts.—StP
I hear my mother's. R. Whitman.—LiPm
"I like to stay up". G. Nichols.—NiCo
"I turn out the light". E. Merriam.—MeY
"In my little bed I lie". Unknown.—StP
In the dark. J. Pridmore.—BaH
In the forest. Unknown.—DeI
It rained in the park today. J. Thurman.—MoS
Ivy. J. Yolen.—YoBe
"Keep a poem in your pocket". B. S. De Regniers.—HoSt—LoFh
"Keep watch, dear Lord, with those who work". Saint Augustine.—StP
A lantern. W. De La Mare.—DeR
Late past bedtime. A. Adoff.—BaW
Lawanda's walk. E. Greenfield.—GrN
Little donkey close your eyes. M. W. Brown.—DeT
Look out. M. Fatchen.—PrFo
Lullaby ("Cat's in the alley"). J. R. Plotz.—PlW
Lullaby ("Near and far, near and far"). M. Hillert.—HoSt
Lullaby ("Sleep, sleep, thou lovely one"). W. De La Mare.—DeR
Lullaby for Suzanne. M. Stillman.—KeT
Lully. W. De La Mare.—DeR
Magic story for falling asleep. N. Willard.—HoSt—MoS
Make believe. H. Behn.—HoSt
Mama's song. D. Chandra.—LiPm
Man and owl. J. Aiken.—LiIf
Many a mickle. W. De La Mare.—DeR—MaP
Maybe. F. P. Heide.—HeG
Moonstruck. A. Fisher.—HoS—HoSt
A mosquito in the cabin. M. Stilborn.—BoT
My family tree. E. Merriam.—MeP
New baby poem (II). E. Greenfield.—GrN
"Nicholas Ned". L. E. Richards.—DeS
Night ("Night is a blanket"). S. Liatsos.—HoSt
"The night creeps in". M. C. Livingston.—LiDd
The night.—KeT
Night fun. J. Viorst.—KeT
Night light. M. C. Livingston.—LiR
Night song. E. Merriam.—LaN
Night starvation or the biter bit. C. Blyton.—PrFo
No bed. W. De La Mare.—DeR
Nobody knows. W. De La Mare.—DeR—MaP
Now all the roads. W. De La Mare.—DeR
"Now I lay me down to sleep, a bag of peanuts at my feet". Unknown.—ScA—WiA
Ode to Pablo's tennis shoes. G. Soto.—SoNe
"O God of light, God of might". D. Adam.—StP
"O Lord, my day's work is over, bless all". Unknown.—StP
"On a still calm night when the bugs begin to bite". Unknown.—OpI
"On Friday night I go backwards to bed". Mother Goose.—WaM
"One little lamb put on records". J. Knight.—KnT
The owl's bedtime story. R. Jarrell.—LiIf
Pacifier. X. J. Kennedy.—KeK

Before the game. Vasko Popa, tr. by Charles Simic.—NyT
Before you fix your next peanut butter sandwich, read this. Florence Parry Heide.—HeG
Beggars
  "Christmas is coming and the geese are getting fat". Mother Goose.—OpI—SuO—WaM
    Christmas is coming.—HoS
  A glass of beer. J. Stephens.—ElW
  Groat nor tester. W. De La Mare.—MaP
  "Hark, hark, the dogs do bark". Mother Goose.—WaM
  "I asked my mother for fifty cents, I asked my father". Unknown.—WiA
  "I had a little moppet". Mother Goose.—WaM
    Little moppet.—OpT
  "Little Tommy Tucker". Mother Goose.—SuO—WaM
    "Little Tom Tucker".—EdGl
  The old soldier. W. De La Mare.—DeR—MaP
  The penny owing. W. De La Mare.—DeR
  Propositions. N. Parra.—AgL
  The three beggars. W. De La Mare.—DeR
  "Who comes here". Mother Goose.—WaM
A **beginning**. Myra Cohn Livingston.—LiT
Beginning a new year means. Ruth Whitman.—LoFh
"The **beginning** of a lizard". See Lizard
Beginning of term. Unknown.—OpI
Beginning on paper. Ruth Krauss.—DeS
Behavior. See also Conduct of life; Manners
  Adolphus. C. West.—PrFo
  Agatha, Agatha. M. A. Hoberman.—HoFa
  The ass in the lion's skin. Aesop.—CaB
  Bad. P. B. Janeczko.—JaB
  Bad boy's swan song. W. J. Smith.—SmL
  Bebe Belinda and Carl Colombus. A. Mitchell.—AgL
  Big and little. W. J. Smith.—SmL
  Books. W. De La Mare.—DeR
  "The boy stood in the supper room". Unknown.—OpI
  Brother. M. A. Hoberman.—DeS—DeT—MoS—PrFo
  Budging line ups. K. Dakos.—DaI
  Cat ("Cats are not at all like people"). W. J. Smith.—LaCc—SmL
  The cheerful child's week. B. S. De Regniers.—DeW
  The churlish child's week. B. S. De Regniers.—DeW
  Co-op-er-ate. B. S. De Regniers.—DeW
  Company manners. E. Merriam.—MeS
  Confession to Mrs. Robert L. Snow. G. Soto.—JaPr
  "Crosspatch". Mother Goose.—WaM
  Cruel boys. G. Soto.—JaM
  The cupboard. W. De La Mare.—DeR—MaP
  "A diller, a dollar". Mother Goose.—SuO—WaM
  "Ding dong bell". Mother Goose.—SuO—WaM
  Disobedience. A. A. Milne.—KeT
  Do you know anyone like him. J. Ciardi.—CiH
  Dog ("Dogs are quite a bit like people"). W. J. Smith.—LiDp—SmL
  "Don't say it, don't say it". Unknown.—ScA
  Don't you remember how sick you are. K. Dakos.—DaI
  Elevation. R. Morgan.—JaM
  "Elsie Marley is grown so fine". Mother Goose.—WaM
  Father to son. A. L. Woods.—SlM
  "Five little monkeys". Unknown.—CoE

The giggles. M. Gardner.—PrFo
Go to the Bahamas. K. Dakos.—DaI
Grump. E. Merriam.—MeS
Halloween, the hydrant dare. G. Roberts.—JaPr
"Heigh ho, heigh ho, I bit the teacher's toe". Unknown.—ScA
Heman. M. Wandor.—AgL
"Here's Sulky Sue". Mother Goose.—WaM
Hoods. P. B. Janeczko.—JaB
"House to let". Unknown.—OpI—WiA
"How dry I am, how wet I'll be". Unknown.—CoM
"I asked my mother for fifty cents, I asked my father". Unknown.—WiA
"I wish you'd speak when you're spoken to". Unknown.—PrP
Improper moves. J. Yolen.—YoDd
"In the dining car, mean Myrt". X. J. Kennedy.—KeFb
"In the pet store Roscoe Rice". X. J. Kennedy.—KeFb
Jackie Grant. M. Glenn.—GlBc
Jimmy Zale. M. Glenn.—GlBc
Jittery Jim. W. J. Smith.—SmL
"A lady was chasing her boy round the room". Unknown.—WiA
Learning. J. Viorst.—PrFo
Lecture. P. B. Janeczko.—JaB
"Little Jack Horner". Mother Goose.—EdGl—SuO—WaM
"Little Polly Flinders". Mother Goose.—SuO—WaM
Mamma settles the dropout problem. B. Gates.—SuC
"Mary had a stick of gum". Unknown.—ScA
"Mary Pary Pinder". Unknown.—OpI
Mean song ("I'm warning you"). B. S. De Regniers.—DeW
Mischief City. T. Jones-Wynne.—BoT
"A mother in old Alabama". W. J. Smith.—SmL
Mother's nerves. X. J. Kennedy.—ElW
"My mommy told me, if I was goody". Unknown.—CoM
"My mother says I'm sickening". J. Prelutsky.—PrFo
"Naughty little Margaret". Unknown.—ScA
The new suit. N. Sanabria de Romero.—NyT
North wind ("Is your father"). M. O'Neill.—BaW
"An obnoxious old person named Hackett". W. J. Smith.—LiLo—SmL
Ode to the Mayor. G. Soto.—SoNe
"On top of Old Smoky, all covered with sand". Unknown.—ScA
The Optileast and the Pessimost. E. Merriam.—MeS
Part XI: Now fie, o fie, how sly a face. From A child's week. W. De La Mare.—DeR
People. W. J. Smith.—SmL
The perfect reactionary. H. Mearns.—PrFo
Pets. D. Pettiward.—CoAz
Pick up your room. M. A. Hoberman.—HoFa
A poison tree. W. Blake.—ElW
"A querulous cook from Pomona". W. J. Smith.—SmL
Reason. J. Miles.—ElW
Resolution. E. Merriam.—MeCh
"Said old peeping Tom of Fort Lee". M. Bishop.—LiLo
Sales talk for Annie. M. Bishop.—ElW
"Sally over the water". Unknown.—WiA
"Sara Cynthia Sylvia Stout would not take the garbage out". S. Silverstein.—ElW

Behavior.—*Continued*
The secret ("We don't mention where he went").
M. C. Livingston.—LiT
Shy. M. A. Hoberman.—HoFa
Silly Sallie. W. De La Mare.—DeR
Sneaky Bill. W. Cole.—PrFo
A song in the front yard. G. Brooks.—ElW
The song of the mischievous dog. D. Thomas.—
DeT
"Sorry, sorry Mrs. Lorry". N. Mellage.—SlM
Spring fever. E. Merriam.—MeS
Sugar-n-spice, etc. R. Quillen.—JaPr
System. R. L. Stevenson.—ElW
"Teacher, could you". K. Dakos.—DaI
"There was a little baby". Unknown.—WiA
"There was a young man on a plain". W. J.
Smith.—SmL
There was an old woman ("There was an old
woman of Bumble Bhosey"). W. De La Mare.—
DeR
This is just to say. W. C. Williams.—ElW
The time we cherry-bombed the toilet at the
River Oaks. C. H. Webb.—JaPr
Together. C. Mamchur.—BoT
"Tom tied a kettle to the tail of a cat".
Unknown.—OpI
"Tonight, tonight, the pillow fight". Unknown.—
WiA
Trouble with baby. X. J. Kennedy.—KeGh
"Two revolting young persons named Gruen". W.
J. Smith.—SmL
The way I really am. B. S. De Regniers.—DeW
"We are the boys of Avenue D". Unknown.—ScA
We real cool. G. Brooks.—AgL—ElW
Weird. J. Viorst.—PrFo
"When Buster Brown was one". Unknown.—WiA
Who's here. E. Merriam.—MeS
Willimae's cornrows. N. Mellage.—SlM
Won't. W. De La Mare.—DeR
Zimmer in grade school. P. Zimmer.—JaPr
Behind bars. Fadwa Tuqan. tr. by Hatem
Hussaini.—NyT
"**Behind** the blinds I sit and watch". See The
window
"**Behind** the window". See Mother
Behn, Harry
Circles ("The things to draw with compasses").—
LiDd
Crickets ("We cannot say that crickets sing").—
WhAa
Follow the leader.—HoS
A friendly mouse.—LaM
Ghosts ("A cold and starry darkness moans").—
BaH—LiIf
Hallowe'en ("Tonight is the night").—LiHp
"A hungry owl hoots", tr.—LiIf
Make believe.—HoSt
The new little boy.—KeT
Tea party.—LiDd
"**Behold** her, single in the field". See The solitary
reaper
"**Behold** the duck". See The duck
"**Behold** the sun". See Roc
"**Behold** the wonders of the mighty deep".
Unknown.—PrP
"**Being** a bee". See Honeybees
"**Being** lost". Karla Kuskin.—HoGo
"**Being** small, I always choose". See Carving
pumpkins with my father
"**Being** to timelessness as it's to time". Edward
Estlin Cummings.—GoU
Belief. See Faith

Believe it or not. Nicolai Kantchev, tr. by Jascha
Kessler and Alexander Shurbanov.—NyT
"**Believe** me, if all those endearing young charms".
Thomas Moore.—ElW
Belinda Enriquez. Mel Glenn.—GlBc
Bell, J. J.
The flying fish.—PrFo
Bell. Valerie Worth.—WoAl
"A **bell** can ring". See Can a can
"**Bell** horses, bell horses". Mother Goose.—WaM
"**Bella** Bella, Bella Coola". See Canadian Indian
place names
"**Bella** had a new umbrella". Eve Merriam.—PrFo
La **belle** dame sans merci. John Keats.—ElW
Belloc, Hilaire
The early morning.—KeT
The elephant ("When people call this beast to
mind").—CII
The frog ("Be kind and tender to the frog").—
CII—ElW
"Jesus Christ, thou child so wise".—StP
The lion ("The lion, the lion, he dwells in the
waste").—CII
Tarantella.—MoR
The vulture.—CaB—ElW
The waterbeetle.—CaB
Bells
Bell. V. Worth.—WoAl
The bells, complete. E. A. Poe.—MoR
"Hear the sledges with the bells". From The bells.
E. A. Poe.—GoA
"I heard the bells on Christmas Day". H. W.
Longfellow.—YoHa
Madonna of the evening flowers. A. Lowell.—
GoU
Part XIX: Sadly, o, sadly, the sweet bells of
Baddeley. From A child's day. W. De La
Mare.—DeR
The **bells**, complete. Edgar Allan Poe.—MoR
The **bells**, sels. Edgar Allan Poe
"Hear the sledges with the bells".—GoA
"The **bells** chime clear". See The christening
"**Below** the hill, the cemetery sits". See All Hallows'
Eve (My mother brings me to visit a Sicilian
cemetery)
"**Below** your nose". Myra Cohn Livingston.—LiMh
"**Beneath** a blue umbrella". Jack Prelutsky.—PrBe
"**Beneath** a shady tree they sat". Unknown.—ScA
"**Beneath** the waters". See Mermaid—undersea
"**Beneath** this stone, a lump of clay". Unknown.—
BaH
Benet, Rosemary Carr. See Benet, Stephen Vincent,
and Benet, Rosemary Carr
Benet, Stephen Vincent, and Benet, Rosemary Carr
Abraham Lincoln.—LoFh
Christopher Columbus.—LoFh
Western wagons.—SuI
Bennani, Ben
The prison cell, tr.—NyT
Bennett, Bruce
The disaster.—MoR
The story of your life.—MoR
Bennett, Louise
Jamaican alphabet.—LeCa
Bennett, Rowena
The gingerbread man.—DeS
Necks.—DeS
The steam shovel.—DeS
Tails.—DeS
"There once was a witch of Willowby Wood". See
The witch of Willowby Wood
"When you talk to a monkey".—DeS

Bennett, Rowena—*Continued*
The witch of Willowby Wood, sels.
"There once was a witch of Willowby
Wood".—DeS
Benoit, Joan (about)
Joan Benoit. R. Ferrarelli.—KnAs
"**Bent** low over the handlebars". See Boy, fifteen,
killed by hummingbird
Berg, Stephen
I hid you, tr.—GoU
Bergin, Thomas G.
Woman, tr.—GoU
Berkley, Constance E.
The gatherer, tr.—NyT
Berries
Berries. W. De La Mare.—DeR—MaP
"Berries red, have no dread". Unknown.—ScA
"Black currant, red currant, raspberry tart".
Unknown.—OpI
Daddy is tall, has shoulders, strong hands. A.
Adoff.—AdIn
"Gooseberry, juiceberry". E. Merriam.—LiDd—
MoS
"H, u, uckle". Unknown.—WiA
Volunteers one. A. Adoff.—AdIn
Berries. Walter De La Mare.—DeR—MaP
"**Berries** red, have no dread". Unknown.—ScA
Berry, James
"At last I have my anger breathalyser". See What
we said sitting making fantasies
Banana and mackerel.—BeW
Banana talk.—BeW
The barkday party.—BeW
Barriers.—BeW
Black kid in a new place.—BeW
Body-steadier.—BeW
Boxer man in a skippin workout.—BeW
Boy alone at noon.—BeW
"Boy is sent for something". See Riddle poems
Breath pon wind.—BeW
City nomad.—BeW
Coming home on my own.—BeW
Cool time rhythm rap.—BeW
Date-beggin sweet word them.—BeW
Different feelings.—BeW
A different kind of Sunday.—BeW
Diggin sing.—BeW
Disco date, 1980.—BeW
The donkey and the man.—BeW
Don't howl.—BeW
Dreaming black boy.—BeW
"Eyes ablaze looking up". See Riddle poems
Flame and water.—AgL
Friday work.—BeW
Getting nowhere.—BeW
Girls can we educate we dads.—BeW
Goodbye now.—BeW
"Hill is my pillow, I have my own bed". See
Riddle poems
Hurricane ("Under low black clouds").—BeW
"I have a three-legged donkey". See What we said
sitting making fantasies
"I want a talking dog wearing a cap". See What
we said sitting making fantasies
"I'd like a great satellite-looking dish". See What
we said sitting making fantasies
"I'd like a white bull with one horn only". See
What we said sitting making fantasies
"I'd like to have a purple pigeon". See What we
said sitting making fantasies
"I'd like to see cats with stubby wings". See What
we said sitting making fantasies

It seems I test people.—BeW
Jamaican song.—BeW
Kept home.—BeW
Leaps of feeling.—BeW
Let me rap you my orbital map.—BeW
Light fabric.—BeW
Listn big brodda dread, na.—BeW
"Little Miss Singer brushes her dress". See Riddle
poems
"Little pools". See Riddle poems
Me go a Granny Yard.—BeW
Mek drum talk, man, for Caribbean
Independence.—BeW
Mum Dad and me.—BeW
"My first solo trial flight, you see". See What we
said sitting making fantasies
My hard repair job.—BeW
Nativity play plan.—BeW
One.—BeW
Pair of hands against football.—BeW
Pods pop and grin.—BeW
Quick ball man, for Michael Holding.—BeW
"Riddle my this, riddle my that". See Riddle
poems
Riddle poems, complete.
"Boy is sent for something".—BeW
"Eyes ablaze looking up".—BeW
"Hill is my pillow, I have my own bed".—
BeW
"Little Miss Singer brushes her dress".—BeW
"Little pools".—BeW
."Riddle my this, riddle my that".—BeW
"Rooms are full, hall is full, but".—BeW
"Waltzing for leaves".—BeW
"What follows king walking, yet stays".—
BeW
"What is vessel of gold sent off".—BeW
"What's hearty as a heart, round as a ring".—
BeW
"Rooms are full, hall is full, but". See Riddle
poems
Scribbled notes picked up by owners, and
rewritten because of bad grammar, bad spelling,
bad writing.—BeW
Seeing Granny.—BeW
Shapes and actions.—BeW
Skateboard flyer.—BeW
Song of the sea and people.—BeW
Spite shots labels.—BeW
A story about Afiya.—BeW
Sunny market song.—BeW
Susan.—BeW
Take away some but leave some.—BeW
Teach the making of summer.—BeW
A toast for everybody who is growin.—BeW
"Waltzing for leaves". See Riddle poems
What do we do with a variation.—BeW
"What follows king walking, yet stays". See Riddle
poems
"What is vessel of gold sent off". See Riddle
poems
What we said sitting making fantasies, complete.
"At last I have my anger breathalyser".—
BeW
"I have a three-legged donkey".—BeW
"I want a talking dog wearing a cap".—BeW
"I'd like a great satellite-looking dish".—BeW
"I'd like a white bull with one horn only".—
BeW
"I'd like to have a purple pigeon".—BeW
"I'd like to see cats with stubby wings".—
BeW

"**Big** rocks into pebbles". See Rocks
Big Saul Fein. X. J. Kennedy.—KeK
"**Big** ships shudder". See Worker's song
Big sister. Mary Ann Hoberman.—HoFa
"The **big** trees exposed to the west wind are losing their leaves". See Reading in the autumn
"A **big** turtle sat on the end of a log". Unknown.—WiA
"**Big** Willie's back from the war". See Right where he left off
"The **biggest**". See Surprise
"The **biggest** funeral this town". See The teenage cocaine dealer considers his death on the street outside a Key West funeral for a much-loved civic leader
The **biggest** questions. Myra Cohn Livingston.—LiNe
"**Bill**, Bill, can't sit still". Unknown.—WiA
Bill Bolling's avalanche. X. J. Kennedy.—KeGh
Billiards and pool
  Clean. L. Newman.—KnAs
"**Bill's** on the hay-wain". See Haymaking
"**Billy** Batter". Dennis Lee.—KeT
"**Billy**, Billy, strong and able". Unknown.—WiA
Billy could ride. James Whitcomb Riley.—KnAs
Billy Ray Smith. Ogden Nash.—KnAs
"**Billy** was born for a horse's back". See Billy could ride
Bingo. Paul B. Janeczko.—JaB—JaP
"The **binocular** owl". See The woods at night
Birch trees
  Birches. R. Frost.—SuI
  Tell me. B. J. Esbensen.—EsW
Birches. Robert Frost.—SuI
The **bird** ("As poor old Biddie"). Walter De La Mare.—DeR
A **bird** ("A bird came down the walk"). Emily Dickinson.—DeS
"A **bird** came down the walk". See A bird
The **bird** of night. Randall Jarrell.—LiIf
  The owl.—LaN
The **bird** set free. Walter De La Mare.—DeR
Bird sighting. X. J. Kennedy.—KeGh
Bird song. Unknown.—OpT
Bird talk. Aileen Fisher.—FiA
Bird watcher. Jane Yolen.—YoBi
"**Birdie**, birdie, in the sky". Unknown.—CoM—ScA
"A **birdie** with a yellow bill". See Time to rise
Birds. See also names of birds, as Sparrows
  Answer to a child's question. S. T. Coleridge.—CaB—ElW
  "As I went to the well-head". W. De La Mare.—DeR
  "At the horislope of the mountizon". From Altazor. V. Huidobro.—NyT
  "Away, you black devils, away". Mother Goose.—WaM
  Bay breasted barge bird. W. J. Smith.—SmL
  Beware ("An ominous bird sang from its branch"). W. De La Mare.—DeR
  The bird ("As poor old Biddie"). W. De La Mare.—DeR
  A bird ("A bird came down the walk"). E. Dickinson.—DeS
  The bird set free. W. De La Mare.—DeR
  Bird sighting. X. J. Kennedy.—KeGh
  Bird song. Unknown.—OpT
  Bird talk. A. Fisher.—FiA
  "Birdie, birdie, in the sky". Unknown.—CoM—ScA
  Birds know. M. C. Livingston.—LiT

"Birds of a feather flock together". Mother Goose.—WaM
  Birds of a feather.—CII
"Blackbird, whistle". Unknown.—ScA
Blizzard birds. J. P. Lewis.—LeA
Bluebirds. Unknown.—CoE
The border bird. W. De La Mare.—DeR
Buddies. E. Greenfield.—GrU
Captive bird. Boethius.—CaB
Carol of the birds. Unknown.—YoHa
The cat heard the cat-bird. J. Ciardi.—LaCc
The catch ("The kingfisher"). Tori.—DeI
Caw. W. De La Mare.—DeR
A charm against a grackle. J. P. Lewis.—LeA
Chit chat. W. J. Smith.—SmL
The cockatoo. J. Gardner.—PrFo
Collector bird. W. J. Smith.—SmL
Common mudlatch. W. J. Smith.—SmL
Contingency. A. R. Ammons.—ElW
"Coo, coo, coo". Unknown.—PrP
Cruel Jenny Wren. Unknown.—ElW
Crumbs. W. De La Mare.—DeR
The dead bird. J. Yolen.—YoBi
The dictionary bird. M. Mahy.—MaN
Dollar bird. W. J. Smith.—SmL
Dressmaking screamer. W. J. Smith.—SmL
"Eat, birds, eat, and make no waste". Mother Goose.—WaM
"The elephant is a graceful bird". Unknown.—CII
"Elim, elim, ep elim". Unknown.—YoS
  "Who am I, I am me".—YoS
"Estaba la paraja pinta". Unknown.—DeA
  The lovely bird ("Cu cu ru, sang the lovely bird").—DeA
Faucet. W. J. Smith.—SmL
The feather. W. De La Mare.—DeR
The flingamango. M. Mahy.—MaN
For a bird. M. C. Livingston.—DeS
Freedom. W. Dissanayake.—NyT
The gallows. E. Thomas.—ElW
Gazinta. E. Merriam.—MeCh
"Go to the shine that's on a tree". R. Eberhart.—ElW
A goldfinch. W. De La Mare.—DeR
Good morrow. T. Heywood.—ElW
Gooloo. S. Silverstein.—PrFo
Gooney bird. W. J. Smith.—SmL
Gracious goodness. M. Piercy.—ElW
Hackle bird. W. J. Smith.—SmL
Hoolie bird. W. J. Smith.—SmL
How birds should die. P. Zimmer.—JaP
"How sadly the bird in his cage". Issa.—WhAa
I hear the usual thump. A. Adoff.—AdIn
"I heard a bird sing". O. Herford.—DeS
I say. M. Fatchen.—FaCm
"If you find a little feather". B. S. De Regniers.—HoT—MoS
Improvisation. K. Perryman.—NyT
"In the woods there was a hole". Unknown.—ScA
"Jaybird a-sitting on a hickory limb". Unknown.—WiA
Jennie Wren. W. De La Mare.—DeR
Joe. D. McCord.—MoS
"The kingfisher". Unknown.—DeI
Kingfisher. E. Farjeon.—MoR
A little bird ("What do you have for breakfast"). A. Fisher.—FiA
"Little Miss Singer brushes her dress". From Riddle poems. J. Berry.—BeW
Little trotty wagtail. J. Clare.—ElW
Lucky little birds. E. Greenfield.—GrU
Macaw. M. C. Livingston.—LiNe

Birthdays

The age of reason. M. Van Walleghen.—JaPr
"At the beach (1)". From Beach birthdays. M. C. Livingston.—LiBp
"At the beach (2)". From Beach birthdays. M. C. Livingston.—LiBp
The barkday party. J. Berry.—BeW
Bicycle birthday. M. C. Livingston.—LiBp
A birthday. C. G. Rossetti.—ElW
Birthday cake ("Chocolate or butter"). M. C. Livingston.—LiBp
Birthday cake ("Ten candles on a birthday cake"). Unknown.—CoE
Birthday clown. M. C. Livingston.—LiBp
The birthday cow. E. Merriam.—WhAa
Birthday night. M. C. Livingston.—LiBp
The birthday of Buddha. J. Kirkup.—FoLe
Birthday on the beach. O. Nash.—KnAs
Birthday wish. M. C. Livingston.—LiBp
Buying a puppy. L. Norris.—LiDp
Dinosaur birthday. M. C. Livingston.—LiBp
"Each, peach, pear, plum". Unknown.—CoM
Earth's birthday. X. J. Kennedy.—KeK
Eight. M. C. Livingston.—LiBp
The end. A. A. Milne.—LoFh
Five ("Is old enough"). M. C. Livingston.—LiBp
For someone on his tenth birthday. J. Ciardi.—LoFh
Four. M. C. Livingston.—LiBp
Goodbye, six, hello, seven. J. Viorst.—LoFh
"Happy birthday to you, you belong in a zoo". Unknown.—CoM
    "Happy birthday to you".—PrFo
The hayride. M. C. Livingston.—LiBp
"I often pause and wonder". Unknown.—PrP
If we didn't have birthdays. Dr. Seuss.—LoFh
Invitation ("My birthday invitation"). M. C. Livingston.—LiBp
Michael's birthday. M. C. Livingston.—LiBp
"Monday's child is fair of face". Mother Goose.—SuO—WaM
"My party dress". From Party dress, party shirt. M. C. Livingston.—LiBp
"My party shirt". From Party dress, party shirt. M. C. Livingston.—LiBp
The new suit. N. Sanabria de Romero.—NyT
Old man moon. A. Fisher.—DeT—FiA
On my birthday. F. Mazhar.—NyT
Party favors. M. C. Livingston.—LiBp
Party prizes. M. C. Livingston.—LiBp
Party table. M. C. Livingston.—LiBp
Pearls. J. Little.—LiHe
Presents ("My friends all gave me presents"). M. C. Livingston.—LiBp
The rose on my cake. K. Kuskin.—KeT
Seven. M. C. Livingston.—LiBp
Six. M. C. Livingston.—LiBp
"When Joan had a birthday". From Birthday secrets. M. C. Livingston.—LiBp
"When my dog had a birthday". From Birthday secrets. M. C. Livingston.—LiBp

Bishop, Elizabeth

The fish ("I caught a tremendous fish").—ElW—KnAs

Bishop, Morris

"Said a lady beyond Pompton Lakes".—LiLo
"Said old peeping Tom of Fort Lee".—LiLo
Sales talk for Annie.—ElW
"There's a tiresome young man from Bay Shore".—LiLo

Bisons. See Buffaloes

Bissett, Donald J.

Little monkey.—HoT
"Bitter batter boop". See The last cry of the damp fly
Bitter waters. Walter De La Mare.—DeR

Black (color)

Black is beautiful. U. E. Perkins.—SlM
"Detestable crow". Basho.—CaR
"Touch black, touch black". Unknown.—WiA
What color is black. B. Mahone.—SlM
"Black as a chimney is his face". See Sooeep
"Black, black, sit on a tack". Unknown.—WiA
"Black bug's blood, black bug's blood". Unknown.—WiA
The black bull. Basho, tr. by Tze-si Huang.—DeI
"The black cat yawns". See Cat
"Black currant, red currant, raspberry tart". Unknown.—OpI
Black dog, red dog. Stephen Dobyns.—JaPr

Black Elk

"Hear me, four quarters of the world".—StP
The life of a man is a circle.—SnD
Black-eyed Susie. Unknown.—SuC
Black hair. Gary Soto.—JaP—SoA
"Black hair". Akiko Yosano, tr. by Kenneth Rexroth.—GoU
"Black hound and blue hound". See Hunting song
Black is beautiful. Useni Eugene Perkins.—SlM
"Black is beautiful and so am I". See Black is beautiful
"Black is the color of". See What color is black
Black kid in a new place. James Berry.—BeW
"The black kitten". See Kitten
"Black lacqueys at the wide-flung door". See Sephina
Black lady in an afro hairdo cheers for Cassius. R. Ernest Holmes.—KnAs
Black patent leather shoes. Karen L. Mitchell.—JaPr
"Black raspberry bushes, blackberries". See Volunteers one
Black river. Myra Cohn Livingston.—LiNe
"Black-smocked smiths, smattered with smoke". See Blacksmiths
"Black snake". See Black river
The black snake. Patricia Hubbell.—HoT
"Black snake, black snake". See The black snake
The black snake wind. Unknown.—BaW
"The black snake wind came to me". See The black snake wind
"Black swallows swooping or gliding". See The skaters
The black turkey gobbler. Unknown.—SnD
"The black turkey gobbler, under the East, the middle of his". See The black turkey gobbler
The black widow, a cautionary tale. William Jay Smith.—SmL
The blackbird. Humbert Wolfe.—DeT
"Blackbird, whistle". Unknown.—ScA

Blackbirds

"As I went over the water". Mother Goose.—ClI
The blackbird. H. Wolfe.—DeT
"Blackbird, whistle". Unknown.—ScA
Blackbirds. W. De La Mare.—DeR
The blackbirds' party. A. Bryan.—BrS
"Colin, Colin, Colin". Unknown.—OpT
The ousel cock. R. Hodgson.—ElW
"Sing a song of sixpence". Mother Goose.—EdGl—SuO—WaM
"There were two blackbirds, sitting on a hill". Unknown.—WiA
Blackbirds. Walter De La Mare.—DeR
The blackbirds' party. Ashley Bryan.—BrS

"**Blackout** in the buildings". See A city ditty
Blacks. See also African-Americans
  Black kid in a new place. J. Berry.—BeW
  Carol of the brown king. L. Hughes.—GoA
  Checking out me history. J. Agard.—AgL
  A different kind of Sunday. J. Berry.—BeW
  Dreaming black boy. J. Berry.—BeW
  How can I lose hope. From Sing a softblack poem. Kwelismith.—SuC
  It seems I test people. J. Berry.—BeW
  Jouvert morning. D. Calder.—FoLe
  King of the band. A. Johnson.—FoLe
  Kinky hair blues. U. Marson.—LeCa
  Martine Provencal. M. Glenn.—GlBc
  Mek drum talk, man, for Caribbean Independence. J. Berry.—BeW
  Mum Dad and me. J. Berry.—BeW
  A story about Afiya. J. Berry.—BeW
  They were my people. G. Nichols.—NiCo
  What do we do with a variation. J. Berry.—BeW
Blacksmiths
  Blacksmiths. Unknown.—MoR
  The slave and the iron lace. M. Danner.—SuC
Blacksmiths. Unknown.—MoR
Blaine, Scott
  Hockey.—KnAs
Blair, Lee
  Polar bear ("Every time").—HoT
"**Blair**, to make his mother screech". X. J. Kennedy.—KeFb
Blake, William
  Auguries of innocence, sels.
    "To see a world in a grain of sand".—StP
  The echoing green.—ElW
  Infant sorrow.—ElW
  "Little lamb, who made thee".—StP
  "Piping down the valleys wild".—DeT
  A poison tree.—ElW
  The tiger ("Tiger, tiger, burning bright").—CaB
    "Tyger, tyger, burning bright".—StP
  "To see a world in a grain of sand". See Auguries of innocence
  "Tyger, tyger, burning bright". See The tiger ("Tiger, tiger, burning bright")
Blanco, Alberto
  Horse by moonlight, tr. by Jennifer Clement.—NyT
  The parakeets ("They talk all day"), tr. by William Stanley Merwin.—NyT
Blanket hog. Paul B. Janeczko.—KeT
Blasing, Randy
  The cucumber, tr.—NyT
"**Blazing** in gold, and". Emily Dickinson.—GoT
"**Bless** the meat". Unknown.—OpI
"**Bless** to me, O God". Unknown.—StP—StP
"**Bless** to us, O God, the earth beneath our feet". Unknown.—StP
"**Bless** you, bless you, burnie-bee". Mother Goose.—WaM
  The messenger.—OpT
"**Blessed** are they that have eyes to see". John Overham.—StP
"**Blessed** be the memory". Unknown.—OpI
"**A blimp** was above me". See In August
Blind
  "All but blind". W. De La Mare.—DeR—MaP
  Lucia. L. Casalinuovo.—NyT
  One time. W. Stafford.—JaP
  "Three blind mice". Mother Goose.—EdGl—WaM
Blindman's in. Walter De La Mare.—DeR
Blizzard birds. J. Patrick Lewis.—LeA

Bloch, Ariel
  Magic, tr.—NyT
  Pride, tr.—NyT
Bloch, Chana
  Magic, tr.—NyT
  Pride, tr.—NyT
  Wildpeace, tr.—NyT
Blocks. See Toys
Bloom, Valerie
  Insec' lesson.—AgL
"**Blooming** gardens are my words". See The gatherer
Blossom, Laurel
  Skate.—KnAs
Blow up. X. J. Kennedy.—LoFh
"**Blow** us up". Myra Cohn Livingston.—LiMh
"**Blow**, wind, blow, and go, mill, go". Mother Goose.—WaM
Blowin' in the wind, sels. Bob Dylan
  How many times.—SuC
Blue (color)
  "Blue shoe". B. McMillan.—McP
  "If you touch blue". Unknown.—WiA
  "Violet picks bluebells". E. Merriam.—MeY
"**Blue** brushes paint". See Indian summer
"**Blue-eyed** beauty". Unknown.—WiA
"**Blue**, gold". See Championship
Blue herons. J. Patrick Lewis.—LeE
Blue jays. See Jays
"**Blue** legs". Myra Cohn Livingston.—LiMh
"**Blue** shoe". Bruce McMillan.—McP
The blue-tail fly, sels. Unknown
  "When I was young, I used to wait".—SuC
Blue whale knowledge. Zolan Quobble.—AgL
Bluebells. Walter De La Mare.—DeR
Bluebirds. Unknown.—CoE
The blues. Langston Hughes.—KeT
Blues for Benny "Kid" Paret. Dave Smith.—KnAs
Bluest whale. J. Patrick Lewis.—LeA
The bluffalo. Jane Yolen.—PrFo
Blum, Eliezer
  Wandering chorus, tr. by Howard Schwartz.—GoT
Blum. Dorothy Aldis.—LiDd
Blunden, Edmund
  The poor man's pig.—CaB
Bly, Robert
  Schoolcrafts's diary, written on the Missouri, 1830.—SuI
Blyton, Carey
  Night starvation or the biter bit.—PrFo
"**Bo-bo-skee**". Unknown.—CoM
"**Bo** elai parpar nechmad". Unknown.—YoS
  "Come to me, nice butterfly".—YoS
Boa constrictors. See Snakes
The boar's head carol. Unknown.—YoHa
"**The boar's** head in hand bear I". See The boar's head carol
"**The boaster** will make out someone else is the liar". From Jamaican Caribbean proverbs. Unknown.—BeW
Boats and boating. See also Canoes and canoeing; Ferries; Ships; Toys
  At sea. E. Merriam.—MeP
  Bonum omen. W. De La Mare.—DeR
  "A bug and a flea". Unknown.—CII—OpI
  "Captain Flea and Sailor Snail". J. Prelutsky.—PrBe
  Choosing craft. M. Swenson.—KnAs
  Eight oars and a coxswain. A. Guiterman.—KnAs
  "Ferry me across the water". C. G. Rossetti.—KeT
  "Four fat goats upon a boat". J. Prelutsky.—PrBe

Boats and boating.—*Continued*
  Fourth of July night. C. Sandburg.—LaN
  "From the boat, while Uncle Sid". X. J. Kennedy.—KeFb
  "Goat boat". B. McMillan.—McP
  Gondola swan. W. J. Smith.—SmL
  Houseboat mouse. C. Sullivan.—SuI
  Iron men and wooden ships. J. Ciardi.—CiH
  John Boatman. Unknown.—OpT
  The jumblies. E. Lear.—DeS—ElW
  "Leaping flying fish". Koson.—CaR
  The light house keeper's white mouse. J. Ciardi.—LaM—MoS
  London fisherman. Unknown.—OpT
  Mindoro. R. C. Sunico.—NyT
  Nod's song. From The three royal monkeys. W. De La Mare.—DeR
  The O. M. O. R. E. W. De La Mare.—DeR
  Overboard. M. Swenson.—MoR
  The owl and the pussy-cat. E. Lear.—ElW—LiDd—LoFh
  Part XVII: Now through the dusk. From A child's day. W. De La Mare.—DeR
  "Protect me, O Lord". Unknown.—StP
  Quack-hunting. W. De La Mare.—DeR
  "Row, row, row". N. M. Bodecker.—LiDd
  "Rub a dub dub". Mother Goose.—EdGl—WaM
  "Rub a dub dub". Unknown.—WiA
  The sailboat race. E. Greenfield.—GrU
  Sailing, sailing. L. Morrison.—KnAs
  The silver penny. W. De La Mare.—DeR
  Song ("I placed my dream in a boat"). C. Meireles.—NyT
  "Sound the bell, sound the bell". Unknown.—ScA
  "Three wise men of Gotham". Mother Goose.—WaM
  Water boatmen. P. Fleischman.—FlJ
  Where go the boats. R. L. Stevenson.—ElW—KeT
  Yacht for sale. A. MacLeish.—KnAs
"The **boats** are ready". See The sailboat race
"**Bob**, Ted, and I (13 apiece) would take off hunting". See Every chance we got
"**Bobbing** for (blub blub) for apples". See Apple bobbing
"**Bobby** Orr's marble". See High stick
"**Bobby** Shaftoe's gone to sea". Mother Goose.—SuO
Bodecker, N. M.
  Bedtime mumble.—PlW
  Cats and dogs.—KeT—LaM—MoS
  A crusty mechanic.—LiLo
  A driver from Deering.—LiLo
  An explorer named Bliss.—LiLo
  First snowflake.—KeT
  Garden calendar.—KeT
  "Good-by my winter suit".—MoS
  "Hello book".—LoFh
  "Hurry, hurry, Mary dear".—KeT
  A lady in Madrid.—LiLo
  "Let's marry, said the cherry".—LiDd
  Lew and Lee, tr.—LaCc
  A man in a tree.—LiLo
  A man of Pennang.—LiLo
  Mr. Slatter.—KeT
  One year.—KeT
  A person in Spain.—LiLo
  A person in Stirling.—LiLo
  Pippin in the evening.—LiPm
  Pitcher McDowell.—LiLo
  The porcupine ("Rebecca Jane").—PrFo
  "Pumpkin, pumpkin, pumpkin bright".—LiHp
  "Row, row, row".—LiDd

  "Sing me a song of teapots and trumpets".—PrFo
  Snowman sniffles.—KeT
  "When skies are low and days are dark".—FrS
  "When you stand on the tip of your nose".—PrFo
Body, Human. See also names of parts of the body, as Hands
  Backsides. D. Kalha.—AgL
  Birthday on the beach. O. Nash.—KnAs
  Black hair. G. Soto.—JaP—SoA
  Body-steadier. J. Berry.—BeW
  "Boots have tongues". Unknown.—PrP
  Boxer man in a skippin workout. J. Berry.—BeW
  Camp Calvary. R. Wallace.—JaPr
  Constipation. R. Wallace.—JaM
  Dodo ("Years they mistook me for you"). H. Carlile.—JaPr
  Miss T. W. De La Mare.—DeR—MaP
  My body. W. J. Smith.—SmL
  My father toured the south. J. Nichols.—KnAs
  On my head. Unknown.—CoE
  Pumping iron. D. Ackerman.—KnAs
  The racer's widow. L. Gluck.—KnAs
  A secret kept. J. Al-Harizi.—GoU
  Spite shots labels. J. Berry.—BeW
  A tree within. O. Paz.—NyT
  Trouble. J. Wright.—JaPr
  "Two deep clear eyes". W. De La Mare.—DeR
  Volunteer worker. T. Perez.—NyT
  When I dance. J. Berry.—BeW
  Young. A. Sexton.—AgL—JaPr
Body-steadier. James Berry.—BeW
Boethius
  Captive bird, tr. by Helen Waddell.—CaB
Bogan, Louise
  Train tune.—MoR
Bogart, Sandra
  "Poems can give you".—BoT
Bogin, George
  Cottontail.—JaM
  The kiss ("Come into the hall with me, George").—JaM
  Martha Nelson speaks.—JaM
"The **bogus-boo**". James Reeves.—BaH
"**Boita** and Goitie sat on de coib". Unknown.—WiA
Bolat, Salih
  My share, tr. by Yusuf Eradam.—NyT
"The **bomb** dropped a year ago". See Nicholas Townshend
Bombs and bombing
  Ballad of Birmingham. D. Randall.—ElW
  "A bicycle rider named Crockett". W. J. Smith.—SmL
Boncho
  The mole's work, tr. by Tze-si Huang.—DeI
"The **bone-deep** chill of early fall". See Fog
Bones
  At the keyhole. W. De La Mare.—DeR—MaP
  Bones. W. De La Mare.—PrFo
  Edward Jones. S. Mandlsohn.—PrFo
  Flies. V. Worth.—WoAl
  The fossilot. J. Yolen.—YoBe
  "Hannah Bantry in the pantry". Mother Goose.—WaM
  Iguanodon. J. Prelutsky.—PrT
  Mr. Glump. F. P. Heide.—HeG
  "Old Mother Hubbard". Mother Goose.—EdGl—SuO—WaM
  "Violetta is in the pantry". Unknown.—ScA
Bones. Walter De La Mare.—PrFo
Bonfire. Paul B. Janeczko.—JaB
Bonner, Ann
  All Hallows' Eve.—FoLe

Bonner, Ann—*Continued*
April 1st.—FoLe
December ("This is the month").—FoLe
Dipa, the lamp.—FoLe
February 14th.—FoLe
The harvest queen.—FoLe
On midsummer's eve.—FoLe
Saint Swithin's Day.—FoLe
Shrove Tuesday.—FoLe
The **bonny**, bonny owl. Sir Walter Scott.—LiIf
Bonny George Campbell. Unknown.—ElW
Bonny sailor boy. Unknown.—OpT
Bontemps, Arna
Nocturne of the wharves.—SuC
Southern mansion.—SuC
Bonum omen. Walter De La Mare.—DeR
"**Bony** cat". See Rescue
Boo hoo. Arnold Spilka.—PrFo
Boogie chant and dance. Unknown.—MoR
"A **book** fell out the window". See Shakespeare's
gone
Book lice. Paul Fleischman.—FlJ
Book of Genesis, sels. Bible/Old Testament
"And God created great whales, and every living
creature that moveth".—WhAa
Book of Job, sels. Bible/Old Testament
Leviathan.—WhDd
The **book** of numbers, sels. Bible/Old Testament
"The Lord bless us, and keep us".—StP
The **book** of psalms, sels. Bible/Old Testament
"Let the heavens rejoice, and let the earth be
glad".—StP
"Let the words of my mouth and the".—StP
"The Lord is my shepherd, I shall not want".—
StP
    Psalm 23.—SuC
"O give thanks unto the Lord".—StP
Psalm 104.—StP
"Where can I go then from your spirit".—StP
Books. Walter De La Mare.—DeR
Books and reading
About notebooks. J. Little.—LiHe
After the end. A. Fisher.—FiA
And then. P. Redcloud.—HoGo
Andy Fierstein. M. Glenn.—GlBc
Anne Frank. S. L. Nelms.—JaPr
Be warned. M. Fatchen.—FaCm
"Being lost". K. Kuskin.—HoGo
Belinda Enriquez. M. Glenn.—GlBc
Book lice. P. Fleischman.—FlJ
Books. W. De La Mare.—DeR
"Books fall open". D. McCord.—HoGo
Books to the ceiling. A. Lobel.—HoGo
The bookworm ("I'm tired, oh, tired of books,
said Jack"). W. De La Mare.—DeR—MaP
Boy reading. J. Holmes.—SuI
"By hook or by crook". Unknown.—OpI
"Closed, I am a mystery". M. C. Livingston.—
LiMh
Companion. D. Manjush.—NyT
Condensed version. J. Little.—LiHe
Dancing on a rainbow. K. Dakos.—DaI
Dictionary. W. J. Smith.—SmL
"Don't steal this book, my little lad".
Unknown.—ScA
    "Do not steal this book, my lad".—OpI
The dunce. W. De La Mare.—DeR—MaP
The flying pen. E. Merriam.—MeS
"Give me a book". M. C. Livingston.—HoGo
"Give me books, give me wings". M. C.
Livingston.—LiNe

"Going home with her books through the snow".
W. Tripp.—LiLo
"Good books, good times". L. B. Hopkins.—
HoGo
"Hello book". N. M. Bodecker.—LoFh
I hear my mother's. R. Whitman.—LiPm
"I left my book in Hawaii". K. Dakos.—DaI
"I met a dragon face to face". J. Prelutsky.—
HoGo
"I'd like a story". X. J. Kennedy.—HoGo
"If any man should see this book". Unknown.—
OpI
"If my name you wish to see". Unknown.—OpI
"If this book should chance to roam".
Unknown.—OpI—WiA
"If you have got a funnybone". J. Prelutsky.—
PrFo
Janet DeStasio. M. Glenn.—GlBc
The king of hearts. W. J. Smith.—SmL
The King of Spain. W. J. Smith.—SmL
Learning to read. From Sketches of southern life.
F. E. W. Harper.—SuC
Library. V. Worth.—WoAl
"My daughter got divorced". J. Carson.—CaS
"My mother". V. Worth.—LiPm
A new song for Old Smoky. E. Merriam.—MeP
Ode to my library. G. Soto.—SoNe
"On a day in summer". A. Fisher.—HoGo
The orphan. M. Al-Maghut.—NyT
Part XII: Ann, upon the stroke of three. From A
child's day. W. De La Mare.—DeR
Photograph of Managua. From Nicaragua libre. J.
Jordan.—AgL
The picture-book. W. De La Mare.—DeR
Reading, fall. M. C. Livingston.—LiR
Reading, spring. M. C. Livingston.—LiR
Reading, summer. M. C. Livingston.—LiR
Reading, winter. M. C. Livingston.—LiR
"The reason I like chocolate". N. Giovanni.—
LoFh
Shakespeare's gone. K. Dakos.—DaI
Shut not your doors. W. Whitman.—HoVo
"Steal not this book for fear of shame".
Unknown.—OpI
Summer cooler. X. J. Kennedy.—KeK
Summer doings. W. Cole.—HoGo
Surprise ("The biggest"). B. McLoughland.—
HoGo
"There is a land". L. B. Jacobs.—HoGo
"There is no frigate like a book". E. Dickinson.—
DeT—ElW
"This book is mine". M. C. Livingston.—LiNe
"This book is one thing". Unknown.—OpI
Thou reader. W. Whitman.—HoVo
"Thoughts that were put into words". K.
Kuskin.—JaP
"What if". I. J. Glaser.—HoGo
When mother reads aloud. Unknown.—SuI
"Who folds a leaf down". Unknown.—OpI
Worlds I know. M. C. Livingston.—DeT
"**Books** fall open". David McCord.—HoGo
Books to the ceiling. Arnold Lobel.—HoGo
"**Books** to the ceiling, books to the sky". See Books
to the ceiling
The **bookworm** ("I'm tired, oh, tired of books, said
Jack"). Walter De La Mare.—DeR—MaP
"**Boom**, boom, ain't it great to be crazy".
Unknown.—ScA
Booman. Unknown.—OpT
Booth, Philip
Household.—JaPr

Boots and shoes
Black patent leather shoes. K. L. Mitchell.—JaPr
"Blue shoe". B. McMillan.—McP
The bottoms of my sneaks are green. A. Adoff.—AdIn
"Cobbler, cobbler, mend my shoe". Mother Goose.—WaM
"Do ghouls". L. Moore.—PrFo
"En la puerta del cielo". Unknown.—DeA
　"At heaven's gate".—DeA
The first shoe. M. Mhac an tSaoi.—NyT
Galoshes. R. Bacmeister.—DeS
How to treat shoes. X. J. Kennedy.—KeGh
Ice-creepers. E. Merriam.—MeS
"Leatherty patch". From Two dancing songs. Unknown.—OpT
The lost shoe. W. De La Mare.—DeR—MaP
"My shoes are new and squeaky shoes". Unknown.—PrP
"Nebuchadnezzar the King of the Jews". Unknown.—OpI
Ode to Pablo's tennis shoes. G. Soto.—SoNe
"Old lady Fry". Unknown.—WiA
Postcards of the hanging. A. Hudgins.—JaM
"Sheila, into Dad's right shoe". X. J. Kennedy.—KeFb
"Shoe a little horse". Mother Goose.—WaM
Shoes. V. Worth.—WoAl
Sticky situation. X. J. Kennedy.—LiLo
"There once was a centipede neat". Unknown.—LiLo
"There was an old man from Peru". Unknown.—ScA
　An old man from Peru.—PrFo
　Old man of Peru.—DeS
"There was an old woman who lived in a shoe". Mother Goose.—EdGl—SuI—SuO—WaM
Times Square shoeshine competition. M. Angelou.—MoR
"**Boots** have tongues". Unknown.—PrP

The **border** bird. Walter De La Mare.—DeR

Boredom
Arnold Flitterman. M. Glenn.—GlBc
The bookworm ("I'm tired, oh, tired of books, said Jack"). W. De La Mare.—DeR—MaP
Hank and Peg. W. Burt.—JaPr
Ho hum. J. Ciardi.—CiH
I once dressed up. R. Fisher.—BaH
Keeping busy is better than nothing. J. Ciardi.—CiH—LiLo
A man in a tree. N. M. Bodecker.—LiLo
"Moods and tenses". Unknown.—OpI
The pioneers. C. Mortimer.—JaPr
Pooh. W. De La Mare.—DeR
"There was a girl named Mary Lou". Unknown.—ScA
"There was an old man with a gong". E. Lear.—LiLo
Tired Tim. W. De La Mare.—DeR—MaP
Turtle ("The turtle"). V. Worth.—WoAl
Whodunnit. E. Merriam.—MeCh
The wind is calling me away. K. Dakos.—DaI

Borges, Jorge Luis
Afterglow, tr. by Norman Thomas Di Giovanni.—GoT

Born that way. Maya Angelou.—AnI

Borum, Paul
Grass ("The grass is strangely tall to me"), tr.—NyT
Lizard ("The beginning of a lizard"), tr.—NyT
"A train is passing".—NyT

"A **Boston** boy went out to Yuma". Unknown.—LiLo
Botany. See Plants and planting; Science
Bottom of the ninth haiku. R. Gerry Fabian.—MoA
The **bottoms** of my sneaks are green. Arnold Adoff.—AdIn
Boullata, Issa
A sailor's memoirs, tr.—NyT
"**Bounce** me". Myra Cohn Livingston.—LiMh
"**Bouncie**, bouncie, ballie". Unknown.—CoM—ScA
Bouquet of roses ("A bouquet of roses"). See "Traigo un ramillete"
Bourinot, Arthur S.
Paul Bunyan.—BoT
Bourke, Sharon
People of gleaming cities, and of the lion's and the leopard's brood.—SuC
Bourne, Daniel
Father and son, tr.—NyT
"**Bow-wow,** says the dog". Mother Goose.—SuO
"**Bow** wow wow". Mother Goose.—WaM
"**Bowing** such lean". See Mantis
"**Bowlerman** bowlerman". See Quick ball man, for Michael Holding
Bowling
Bowling alley. M. Van Walleghen.—JaPr
Genuine poem, found on a blackboard in a bowling alley in Story City, Iowa. T. Kooser.—KnAs
Hook. F. Skloot.—KnAs
Bowling alley. Michael Van Walleghen.—JaPr
Bows and arrows
"God is the bow". Unknown.—StP
"Little Dick was so quick". Unknown.—WiA
Boxer man in a skippin workout. James Berry.—BeW
Boxers and boxing
Black lady in an afro hairdo cheers for Cassius. R. E. Holmes.—KnAs
Blues for Benny "Kid" Paret. D. Smith.—KnAs
Boxer man in a skippin workout. J. Berry.—BeW
The boxing match. D. Ignatow.—KnAs
"Fightin' was natural". M. Angelou.—AnI
Kangaroo. W. J. Smith.—SmL
The loser. C. Bukowski.—KnAs
The seventh round. J. Merrill.—KnAs
Shadowboxing. J. Tate.—KnAs
"They all must fall". M. Ali.—KnAs
Boxes
Ornaments. V. Worth.—WoA
What shall I pack in the box marked summer. B. Katz.—LoFh
Wrappings. V. Worth.—WoA
"The **boxes** break". See Ornaments
Boxing. See Boxers and boxing
The **boxing** match. David Ignatow.—KnAs
Boy alone at noon. James Berry.—BeW
"A **boy** and a bird can be buddies". See Buddies
Boy at the window. Richard Wilbur.—ElW
"A **boy** called Jack, as I've been told". See Books
Boy, fifteen, killed by hummingbird. Linda Linssen.—JaPr
"The **boy** had been alone for fifteen days". See Keeping the horses
"**Boy** is sent for something". From Riddle poems. James Berry.—BeW
Boy reading. John Holmes.—SuI
"The **boy** stood in the supper room". Unknown.—OpI
"The **boy** stood on the burning deck". Unknown.—PrFo—WiA
"A **boy** told me". See The rider

"The **boy** waits on the top step, his hand on the door". See Black dog, red dog
Boys and boyhood. See also Babies; Childhood recollections
Adolphus. C. West.—PrFo
The age of reason. M. Van Walleghen.—JaPr
The antelope ("When one of us hit"). D. A. Evans.—JaPr
Apology. L. Emanuel.—JaPr
Atong and his goodbye. B. S. Santos.—NyT
Autobiographical note. V. Scannell.—JaPr
Bad boy's swan song. W. J. Smith.—SmL
The ball poem. J. Berryman.—KnAs
"A barefoot boy with shoes on". Unknown.—ScA
Big and little. W. J. Smith.—SmL
Billy could ride. J. W. Riley.—KnAs
Boy alone at noon. J. Berry.—BeW
A boy's head. M. Holub.—NyT
Boys' night out. M. Vinz.—JaPr
A boy's song. J. Hogg.—ElW
Breath pon wind. J. Berry.—BeW
The bridge. P. B. Janeczko.—JaB
A brief reversal, 1941. H. Scott.—JaPr
Buddies. E. Greenfield.—GrU
Camp Calvary. R. Wallace.—JaPr
Catch ("Two boys uncoached are tossing a poem together"). R. Francis.—KnAs
Cheerleader. J. W. Miller.—JaPr
Circus dreams. X. J. Kennedy.—KeK
Collecting things. X. J. Kennedy.—KeK
Confession to Mrs. Robert L. Snow. G. Soto.—JaPr
Cool time rhythm rap. J. Berry.—BeW
Cruel boys. G. Soto.—JaM
The cry guy. K. Dakos.—DaI
Daddy. M. C. Livingston.—LiPf
Dancers. P. B. Janeczko.—JaB
"Ding dong bell". Mother Goose.—SuO—WaM
Dinosaur department. M. Fatchen.—FaCm
Disobedience. A. A. Milne.—KeT
"During the sermon". W. Kloefkorn.—JaPr
Eagle rock. G. Hewitt.—JaPr
Economics. R. Wrigley.—JaPr
Every chance we got. C. H. Webb.—JaPr
First job. J. Daniels.—JaPr
"First time at third". J. Sweeney.—MoA
Firsts. P. B. Janeczko.—JaB
Fishing. L. Dangel.—JaPr
"For his mother's mudpack, Brent". X. J. Kennedy.—KeFb
For someone on his tenth birthday. J. Ciardi.—LoFh
A friendly mouse. H. Behn.—LaM
Gaining yardage. L. Dangel.—JaPr
"Georgie Porgie, pudding and pie". Mother Goose.—SuO—WaM
Ginger. Unknown.—OpT
"Girls are dandy". Unknown.—WiA
Halloween, the hydrant dare. G. Roberts.—JaPr
Hank and Peg. W. Burt.—JaPr
Harry the hawk. M. Mahy.—MaN
"He is handsome". Unknown.—ScA
A headstrong boy. G. Cheng.—NyT
Heaven. G. Soto.—SoA
Heman. M. Wandor.—AgL
"Higgledy-Piggledy keeps his room tidy". M. C. Livingston.—PrFo
High school. G. Roberts.—JaPr
Hitchhiking with a friend and a book that explains the Pacific Ocean. G. Soto.—SoA
Hoods. P. B. Janeczko.—JaB
How I learned English. G. Dianikian.—JaM

Howie Kell suspends all lust to contemplate the universe. R. Torreson.—JaPr
I like it when. R. Margolis.—LiPf
Jennie Wren. W. De La Mare.—DeR
Jody Walker, the first voice. P. Ruffin.—JaPr
Jump. J. Carson.—JaPr
The kiss ("The kiss started when I danced"). P. B. Janeczko.—JaB
Let me rap you my orbital map. J. Berry.—BeW
Liberty. R. Ikan.—JaPr
"Little Boy Blue, come blow your horn". Mother Goose.—EdGl—SuO—WaM
Little boy blues. E. Greenfield.—GrN
"Little Jack Horner". Mother Goose.—EdGl—SuO—WaM
Michael's birthday. M. C. Livingston.—LiBp
Mull. J. Kay.—AgL
Muscling rocks. R. Morgan.—JaPr
"My mother is a Russian". Unknown.—ScA
The new kid. M. Makley.—MoA
No bed. W. De La Mare.—DeR
Not quite Kinsey. G. Hyland.—JaPr
Ode to pomegranates. G. Soto.—SoNe
Ode to weight lifting. G. Soto.—SoNe
Of necessity, Weeb jokes about his height. C. H. Webb.—JaPr
"O tan-faced prairie-boy". W. Whitman.—HoVo
One for one. J. Heynen.—JaPr
Orphanage boy. R. P. Warren.—JaPr
Part XI: Now fie, o fie, how sly a face. From A child's day. W. De La Mare.—DeR
Preposterous. J. Hall.—JaPr
The purpose of altar boys. A. Rios.—JaPr
The quartette. W. De La Mare.—DeR—MaP
Raymond. P. B. Janeczko.—JaB
Ronnie Schwinck. D. A. Evans.—JaPr
The sad story of a little boy that cried. Unknown.—PrFo
Scribbled notes picked up by owners, and rewritten because of bad grammar, bad spelling, bad writing. J. Berry.—BeW
The sea body. W. De La Mare.—MaP
Shaking. R. Morgan.—JaPr
Smoke. E. Pankey.—JaPr
Sneaking in the state fair. K. Fitzpatrick.—MoR
Spider ("Spider always wore sunglasses"). P. B. Janeczko.—JaB
The Strand Theatre. T. Cader.—JaPr
Summer killer. T. A. Broughton.—JaM
Swinging the river. C. H. Webb.—JaPr
Target practice. G. Soto.—JaPr
That girl. G. Soto.—SoA
Their names. G. Hyland.—JaPr
"There was a boy, ye knew him well, ye cliffs". From The prelude. W. Wordsworth.—LiIf
Thieves. P. B. Janeczko.—JaB
The time we cherry-bombed the toilet at the River Oaks. C. H. Webb.—JaPr
To impress the girl next door. R. Koertge.—JaPr
Tom cat. A. Turner.—LaCc
Trick or treating at age eight. L. Rosenberg.—LiHp
Walking with Jackie, sitting with a dog. G. Soto.—JaPr
"We are the boys of Avenue D". Unknown.—ScA
We heard Wally wail. J. Prelutsky.—JaP
We real cool. G. Brooks.—AgL—ElW
What Johnny told me. J. Ciardi.—KeT
"Who to trade stamps with". X. J. Kennedy.—KeK
Why can't a girl be the leader of the boys. K. Dakos.—DaI

Boys and boyhood.—*Continued*
"Willie, Willie wheezer". Unknown.—ScA
The yes and the no, Redondo. G. Pape.—JaPr
Young wrestlers. G. Butcher.—KnAs
Zimmer in grade school. P. Zimmer.—JaPr
"Boys and girls come out to play". Mother Goose
"The boys chase the girls". See Why can't a girl be
    the leader of the boys
A **boy's** head. Miroslav Holub, tr. by Ian Milner.—
    NyT
Boys' night out. Mark Vinz.—JaPr
A **boy's** song. James Hogg.—ElW
Brachiosaurus. Jack Prelutsky.—PrT
"Brachiosaurus had little to do". See Brachiosaurus
"Bracken on the hillside". See November
Bracker, Milton
The home-watcher.—MoA
Tomorrow ("Hoorah, hooray").—MoA
Wamby or the nostalgic record book.—MoA
Bragging in the barnyard. J. Patrick Lewis.—LeA
Brahmendra, Sadasiva
"O mind, move in the Supreme Being".—StP
Brain drain. Max Fatchen.—FaCm
"The brain is wider than the sky". Emily
    Dickinson.—ElW
Brains
Brain drain. M. Fatchen.—FaCm
Braithwaite, William Stanley
Rhapsody.—SlM
Braley, Berton
"Young Frankenstein's robot invention".—LiLo
Brand, Dionne
Fisherman.—BoT
Hurricane ("Shut the windows").—BoT
Brand new baby. Beatrice Schenk De Regniers.—
    DeW
"Brass buttons, blue coat". Unknown.—WiA
Brathwaite, Edward
Caliban limbo.—LeCa
South ("But today I recapture the islands'").—
    LeCa
The **brave** ones. Eloise Greenfield.—GrU
Braves. X. J. Kennedy.—KeK
Bread
"Back of the loaf is the snowy flour". M. D.
    Babcock.—StP
Circles ("Two loaves of bread are very well"). M.
    Mahy.—MaN
Every so often. J. Little.—LiHe
"Stealthy Steffan stuck a dead". X. J. Kennedy.—
    KeFb
Bread and cherries. Walter De La Mare.—DeR—
    MaP
Break dance. Grace Nichols.—AgL
"Break, kid, you get one chance". See Clean
"Break master neck but nuh break master law".
    Unknown.—LeCa
"Breakers at high tide shoot". See World
Breakfast
Crunchy. M. Fatchen.—FaCm
A little bird ("What do you have for breakfast").
    A. Fisher.—FiA
Mummy slept late and daddy fixed breakfast. J.
    Ciardi.—LiPf—PrFo
"There was a young pig who, in bed". A. Lobel.—
    LiLo
"Breaking the silence". See The frog
Breath and breathing
The breath of death (the cigarette). L. Sissay.—
    AgL
Dolphins. K. Pokereu.—AgL
Dragon smoke. L. Moore.—DeS—DeT

The frost pane. D. McCord.—MoS
"Light as a feather". Unknown.—ScA
Night practice. M. Swenson.—MoR
Norman Norton's nostrils. C. West.—PrFo
"A small boy, while learning to swim". E.
    Gordon.—LiLo
The **breath** of death (the cigarette). Lemn Sissay.—
    AgL
Breath pon wind. James Berry.—BeW
"Breathe and blow". See Dragon smoke
Breeze, Jean Binta
Natural high.—AgL
"The breeze at dawn has secrets to tell you". See 91
"Brenda pushed in front of Ted". See Budging line
    ups
Brent Sorensen. Mel Glenn.—GlBc
Brickyard. Paul B. Janeczko.—JaB
Brides and bridegrooms. See Weddings
The **bridge.** Paul B. Janeczko.—JaB
"A bridge engineer, Mister Crumpett". Unknown.—
    LiLo
"The bridge says, come across, try me, see how".
    See Potomac town in February
Bridges
The bridge. P. B. Janeczko.—JaB
"A bridge engineer, Mister Crumpett".
    Unknown.—LiLo
Brooklyn Bridge, a jump-rope rhyme. W. J.
    Smith.—SmL
"I stood on the bridge at midnight". Unknown.—
    WiA
Queensboro Bridge. M. C. Livingston.—LiNe
"Bridges are for going over water". See Over and
    under
A **brief** note to the bag lady, ma sister. Yusuf
    Eradam.—NyT
A **brief** reversal, 1941. Herbert Scott.—JaPr
Bright house. Sumako Fukao, tr. by Kenneth
    Rexroth and Ikuko Atsumi.—GoU
A **bright** idea. X. J. Kennedy.—LiLo
"A bright mountaintop". See V is for volcano
"Bright sun, hot sun, oh, to be". See Gone
"Bring an old towel, said Pa". See Buying a puppy
"Bring another straw, cock-sparrow". See Mrs.
    Sparrow
"Bring Daddy home". Mother Goose.—WaM
"Bring me all of your dreams". See The dream
    keeper
Brinnin, John Malcolm
Life of the cricket, tr.—NyT
"Broke is not sissy-footing around". Jo Carson.—
    CaS
Broken mirror. Zuiryu, tr. by Tze-si Huang.—DeI
Bronco busting, event #1. May Swenson.—KnAs—
    MoR
"Brooding he stands". See All hot (the chestnut
    man)
The **brook.** Alfred Tennyson.—ElW
Brooke, Rupert
The fish, sels.
    The fish ("In a cool curving world he lies").—
        CaB
The fish ("In a cool curving world he lies"). See
    The fish
Brooklyn Bridge, a jump-rope rhyme. William Jay
    Smith.—SmL
"Brooklyn Bridge, Brooklyn Bridge". See Brooklyn
    Bridge, a jump-rope rhyme
Brooks, Gwendolyn
The admiration of Willie.—PlW
Andre.—SlM
Building.—SuC

Brooks, Gwendolyn—*Continued*
Computer.—JaP
Cynthia in the snow.—KeT
Gang girls.—JaPr
Keziah.—LiDd
A little girl's poem.—JaP
Marie Lucille.—KeT
Narcissa.—ElW
Old Mary.—SuC
Pete at the zoo.—HoT—KeT
Pete at the zoo.—KeT
Rudolph is tired of the city.—SlM
A song in the front yard.—ElW
Strong men, riding horses.—SuC
"They had supposed their formula was fixed". See
    The white troops had their orders but the
    negroes looked like men
Timmy and Tawanda.—SlM
To Don at Salaam.—SlM
To the young who want to die.—SuC
To those of my sisters who kept their naturals.—
    SuC
Tommy.—HoS—SlM
Vern.—LiDp
We real cool.—AgL—ElW
A welcome song for Laini Nzinga.—SlM
The white troops had their orders but the negroes
    looked like men, sels.
        "They had supposed their formula was
            fixed".—SuC

Brooms
Brooms. D. Aldis.—DeT
Jim Whitehead. M. C. Livingston.—LiR
"Waltzing for leaves". From Riddle poems. J.
    Berry.—BeW
Brooms. Dorothy Aldis.—DeT
Brother. Mary Ann Hoberman.—DeS—DeT—
    MoS—PrFo
"Brother Pete". Eve Merriam.—MeP
Brotherhood
"Farewell, my younger brother". Unknown.—SnD
Frankie Dempster. M. Glenn.—GlBc
"A leaf for hand in hand". W. Whitman.—HoVo
"Walk together children". From Walk together
    children. Unknown.—SuC
"What do you seek so pensive and silent". From
    Starting from Paumanok. W. Whitman.—HoVo
Brothers ("Raymond slowed"). Paul B. Janeczko.—
    JaB
Brothers ("We're related, you and I"). Langston
    Hughes.—SlM
Brothers and sisters
Aaron. A. Adoff.—AdIn
Ancestry. A. Bryan.—BrS
Basketball. N. Giovanni.—DeT
Bed mate. C. A. Keremes.—HoS
Big sister. M. A. Hoberman.—HoFa
Blanket hog. P. B. Janeczko.—KeT
"Bouncie, bouncie, ballie". Unknown.—CoM—
    ScA
Brand new baby. B. S. De Regniers.—DeW
Breath pon wind. J. Berry.—BeW
A brief note to the bag lady, ma sister. Y.
    Eradam.—NyT
Brother. M. A. Hoberman.—DeS—DeT—MoS—
    PrFo
"Brother Pete". E. Merriam.—MeP
Brothers ("Raymond slowed"). P. B. Janeczko.—
    JaB
Brother's snacks. X. J. Kennedy.—KeGh
"The bus weaves its way through the jungle
    home". M. Wayne.—LeCa

Changelings. X. J. Kennedy.—KeGh
"Did Jesus have a baby sister". D. Previn.—AgL
Doll. M. C. Livingston.—KeT
Early love. H. Scott.—JaM
Esme on her brother's bicycle. R. Hoban.—JaP
Evening dawn. H. Scott.—JaPr
Family. M. C. Livingston.—LiT
"First it bit my behind". B. L. Polisar.—PrFo
Guinevere Ghastly sits baby. X. J. Kennedy.—
    KeGh
Half-whole-step. M. A. Hoberman.—HoFa
A Halloween problem. S. Stone.—LiHp
The house on Buder Street. G. Gildner.—JaPr
"I am the youngest, so they call". A. Adoff.—
    AdIn
"I had a little brother". Unknown.—PrP—WiA
An important conversation. B. S. De Regniers.—
    DeW
"In the sort of paint that glows". X. J.
    Kennedy.—KeFb
Incident on beggar's night. J. P. Lewis.—LiHp
Jephson Gardens. D. J. Enright.—ElW
John Wesley. Unknown.—OpT
Karen. E. Greenfield.—GrN
Keziah. G. Brooks.—LiDd
Late for breakfast. M. Dawson.—KeT
Listn big brodda dread, na. J. Berry.—BeW
Little. D. Aldis.—DeT
The little sister store. M. A. Hoberman.—HoFa
"Little soul sister". U. E. Perkins.—SlM
"Little tree". E. E. Cummings.—ElW—GoA
Mima. W. De La Mare.—MaP
Must and May. W. De La Mare.—MaP
My baby brother. M. A. Hoberman.—HoFa
My big brothers. M. A. Hoberman.—HoFa
My brother. D. Aldis.—DeT
My brother Bert. T. Hughes.—ElW
"My brother Estes". J. Carson.—CaS
My sister. M. Mahy.—LiLo—MaN
Ode to mi parque. G. Soto.—SoNe
Ode to the Mayor. G. Soto.—SoNe
Patches of sky. D. Greger.—SuI
Peak and Puke. W. De La Mare.—DeR—MaP
Rescue ("Sunday, beginning the week late"). E.
    Trethewey.—JaPr
Rites of passage. D. Laux.—JaPr
Saturday fielding practice. L. Morrison.—LiPf
The secret ("We don't mention where he went").
    M. C. Livingston.—LiT
Sister ("You said red hair made you"). M.
    Lowery.—JaPr
Sister ("Younger than they"). H. R. Coursen.—
    JaPr
"Sister Ann". E. Merriam.—MeP
"Sister has a blister". X. J. Kennedy.—KeGh
"Sister has a boyfriend". Unknown.—ScA
Sisters. P. B. Janeczko.—JaB
"A small boy, while learning to swim". E.
    Gordon.—LiLo
Smart remark. J. Little.—BoT—LiHe
Smoke. E. Pankey.—JaPr
Some things don't make any sense at all. J.
    Viorst.—DeT
Susannah and the daisies. J. Little.—LiHe
Taste the air. A. Bryan.—BrS
The twa brothers. Unknown.—ElW
We are seven. W. Wordsworth.—ElW
Weird. J. Viorst.—PrFo
A welcome song for Laini Nzinga. G. Brooks.—
    SlM
Wheels. J. Daniels.—JaPr

Brothers and sisters—*Continued*
"When Annie was adopted". M. A. Hoberman.—HoFa
"Willie built a guillotine". W. E. Engel.—PrFo
"The winter they bombed Pearl Harbor". W. McDonald.—JaPr
Zeroing in. D. Dawber.—BoT
"**Brothers** and sisters have I none". Unknown.—OpI
Brother's snacks. X. J. Kennedy.—KeGh
Broughton, T. Alan
Summer killer.—JaM
"**Brow-bone**". See "Pandebeen"
"**Brow-brinker**". Unknown.—WiA
Brown, Clarence
"Take from my palms, to soothe your heart", tr.—GoU
Brown, Margaret Wise
"Dear Father".—PlW
Little donkey close your eyes.—DeT
Song of summer.—MoS
Song of the bugs.—MoS
Brown, Sterling A.
Southern road.—SuC
Strong men.—SuC
"**Brown** and furry". See The caterpillar
"**Brown** crown". Bruce McMillan.—McP
Brown girl, blonde okie. Gary Soto.—SoA
"The **brown** owl sits in the ivy bush". See The great brown owl
"**Brown** owls come here in the blue evening". Unknown.—LiIf
"**Brown** sugar nights". See Honeycomb days
Browne, Jane Euphemia
The great brown owl.—LiIf
Brownies. See Fairies
Browning, Elizabeth Barrett
"How do I love thee, let me count the ways".—ElW
Pan.—WhDd
Browning, Robert
"Hamelin Town's in Brunswick". See The pied piper of Hamelin
The pied piper of Hamelin, complete.—ElW
The pied piper of Hamelin, sels.
"Hamelin Town's in Brunswick".—CaB
Pippa passes, sels.
"The year's at the spring".—ElW—StP
"The year's at the spring". See Pippa passes
Brownjohn, Alan
"Little ostriches". See Ostrich
Ostrich, sels.
"Little ostriches".—HoT
Brownout. Tony Perez.—NyT
Bruce, Richard
Shadow ("Silhouette").—SuC
"**Brutus** adsum jam forte". Unknown.—OpI
Bryan, Ashley
Ancestry.—BrS
The artist.—BrS
Beaded braids.—BrS
Big questions.—BrS
The blackbirds' party.—BrS
Do good.—BrS
The flower's perfume.—BrS
Full moon ("Night on the verandah").—BrS
Good flower blues.—BrS
Granny ("Granny had a way with fruit trees").—BrS
Grape pickers.—BrS
The hurricane ("I cried to the wind").—BrS
Leaving.—BrS
Mama's bouquets.—BrS

My dad.—BrS
Pretty is.—BrS
Rain coming.—BrS
Song ("Sing to the sun").—BrS
Storyteller ("Emerald").—BrS
Sweet talk.—BrS
Taste the air.—BrS
Village voices.—BrS
Vine leaves.—BrS
"**Bubble, bubble**". See The water midden's song
"**Bubble,** said the kettle". Unknown.—PrP
Bubbles
"Bubble, said the kettle". Unknown.—PrP
Bubbles. C. Sandburg.—DeT
Silly Billy. M. Fatchen.—FaCm
Soap bubble. V. Worth.—WoAl
Bubbles. Carl Sandburg.—DeT
The **buckle.** Walter De La Mare.—DeR
Buckley, Christopher
White ("1964 and I'm parked").—JaM
Buddhism
The birthday of Buddha. J. Kirkup.—FoLe
Doll funerals. J. Kirkup.—FoLe
The visitors. B. Wade.—FoLe
Buddies. Eloise Greenfield.—GrU
Buddy's dream. Eloise Greenfield.—GrN
Budging line ups. Kalli Dakos.—DaI
Budianta, Eka
Family portrait, tr. by E. U. Kratz.—NyT
Budney, Blossom
A kiss is round.—MoS
"**Budoom-a** budoom-a budoom-a ba-dap". See Mek drum talk, man, for Caribbean Independence
Buffalo dusk. Carl Sandburg.—CaB—DeS—ElW
Buffaloes
Buffalo dusk. C. Sandburg.—CaB—DeS—ElW
The flower-fed buffaloes. V. Lindsay.—CaB
"Great spirit". From Warrior nation trilogy. L. Henson.—SuI
"I rise, I rise". Unknown.—SnD
Water buffalo. W. J. Smith.—SmL
White buffalo woman. J. Bierhorst.—WhDd
"The **buffaloes** are gone". See Buffalo dusk
"A **bug** and a flea". Unknown.—ClI—OpI
"A **bug** sat in a silver flower". Karla Kuskin.—PrFo
Bugles
The splendor falls. A. Tennyson.—ElW
Bugs. See Insects
Bugs. Karla Kuskin.—LiDd—MoS
Buick. Karl Shapiro.—MoR
"**Build** me my tomb, the raven said". See The raven's tomb
Build-on rhymes
"As I was going to St. Ives". Unknown.—ScA
Bird song. Unknown.—OpT
The green grass grows all around. Unknown.—WiA
"Hush, little baby, don't say a word". Mother Goose.—SuO
Hush, little baby.—KeT
I had a cat. Unknown.—ClI
"I had a little dog, his name was Ball". Unknown.—WiA
"I went downtown". Unknown.—KeT—OpI—ScA—WiA
"Mama, Mama, have you heard". Unknown.—ScA
Old Obadiah. Unknown.—WiA
Poor old lady. Unknown.—ElW—HoS
"There was a crooked man". Mother Goose.—DeS—EdGl—SuO—WaM

Build-on rhymes—_Continued_
There's a hole in the middle of the sea. Unknown.—WiA
"This is the house that Jack built". Mother Goose.—SuO
The house that Jack built.—HoS
"Three young rats with black felt hats". Mother Goose.—PrP—SuO
Three young rats.—CII
The twelve days of Christmas ("On the first day of Christmas"). Unknown.—YoHa
"The first day of Christmas".—SuO
What is this here. Unknown.—WiA
The woman and her pig. Unknown.—OpT

Builders and building
Beavers in November. M. Singer.—SiT
Braves. X. J. Kennedy.—KeK
Building. G. Brooks.—SuC
Remodeling the hermit's cabin. F. Chappell.—JaM
Skyscraper. C. Sandburg.—SuI
To a giraffe. P. Hubbell.—HoT
To raise a chimney. G. Young.—JaM

Building. Gwendolyn Brooks.—SuC

Buildings. See names of kinds of buildings, as Houses

Bukowski, Charles
The loser.—KnAs

"Bulbs strung along". See Christmas lights

Bull dog. Cole Porter.—KnAs

"Bull dog, bull dog, bow, wow, wow, Eli Yale". See Bull dog

Bullhead in autumn. Marilyn Singer.—SiT

Bullhead in spring. Marilyn Singer.—SiT

Bullhead in summer. Marilyn Singer.—SiT

Bullhead in winter. Marilyn Singer.—SiT

The **bum.** Jamal Ali.—AgL

"Bumblebee, bumblebee". Unknown.—CoM

"Bump, bump, bumpity bump". See Mr. Glump

Bunches of grapes. Walter De La Mare.—DeR

"Bunches of grapes, says Timothy". See Bunches of grapes

"Bundled, eyes watering against the glare". See Winter yard

Bunyan, John
Upon the snail.—CaB

Bunyip. Jenny Wagner.—WhDd

Burge, Maureen
Disillusion.—AgL

Burgess, Clinton Brooks
"Said Mrs. Isosceles Tri".—LiLo
"Said Rev. Rectangular Square".—LiLo

Burgess, Gelett
"I wish that my room had a floor".—LiLo—PrFo
"I'd rather have fingers than toes".—LiLo
The purple cow.—CII—KeT

Burials. See Funerals

Buried treasure. Aileen Fisher.—FiA

"The Burlington will now no more". See The California Zephyr

Burness, Don
A man never cries, tr.—NyT
The rhythm of the tomtom, tr.—NyT

Burning bright. Lillian Morrison.—JaP

Burns, Joan M.
"I am here, Lord".—StP
"Let my thoughts and words please you, Lord".—StP

Burns, Robert
Afton water.—ElW
"Some hae meat and canna eat".—StP

"Burpod, Grooben, Blug, and Krodspit". See Friends I'm going to invite to dinner (if they don't eat me first)

Bursting. Dorothy Aldis.—PrFo

Burt, William
Hank and Peg.—JaPr
Mamaw and Frank.—JaPr

"Burt, Burt, lost his shirt". Unknown.—WiA

Burton, Richard
Roc.—WhDd

Bury me in a free land, sels. Frances E. W. Harper
"Make me a grave where'er you will".—SuC

Bus depot reunion. David Allan Evans.—JaPr

"The bus weaves its way through the jungle home". Marcus Wayne.—LeCa

Buses
Bus depot reunion. D. A. Evans.—JaPr
Byes. M. Redoles.—AgL
"A clever gorilla named Gus". J. Prelutsky.—PrP
A driver from Deering. N. M. Bodecker.—LiLo
"In bright yellow coats". M. C. Livingston.—LiMh
Jittery Jim. W. J. Smith.—SmL
"Mary had a little lamb, its fleece was white as snow". Unknown.—WiA
Punch, boys, punch. Unknown.—OpT
Stay with me. G. K. Hongo.—JaPr
"The wheels on the bus". Unknown.—CoE

"Bushel of wheat, bushel of barley". Unknown.—ScA—WiA

"The business man the acquirer vast". See My legacy

Buson
"All at once, the storm".—CaR
Conversation.—DeS
The deer on the mountain, tr. by Tze-si Huang.—DeI
Foxes ("The foxes"), tr. by Tze-si Huang.—DeI
The mouse ("A mouse is"), tr. by Tze-si Huang.—DeI
The pheasant, tr. by Tze-si Huang.—DeI
The reader, tr. by Tze-si Huang.—DeI
Unseen till now, tr. by Tze-si Huang.—DeI
Weasel, tr. by Tze-si Huang.—DeI

Busy ("Busy, busy, busy, busy"). Phyllis Halloran.—WhAa

Busy ("Little gray cuckoos"). Basho, tr. by Tze-si Huang.—DeI

"Busy, busy, busy, busy". See Busy

Busy summer. Aileen Fisher.—DeT

Busza, Andrzej
Oh, oh, should they take away my stove, my inexhaustible ode to joy, tr.—NyT

But he was cool or, he even stopped for green lights. Don L. Lee.—ElW

"But how can his reindeer fly without wings". See Questions on Christmas eve

"But I am the mulberry girl". See Daddy is tall, has shoulders, strong hands

But I dunno. Unknown.—CII

"But I have shrugged and tried to shift". See Atlas

"But of course you were". See Nothing much

But then. Aileen Fisher.—FiA

"But there are these candies, neatly sweetly". See I love my mom, I love my pop, I love my dog, I love my sheep

"But these fall days are for the gathering of". See I know that summer is the famous growing season

"But today I recapture the islands'". See South

But why not. Max Fatchen.—FaCm

Butcher, Grace
  Hurdler.—KnAs
  Motorcycle racer thinks of quitting.—KnAs
  Young wrestlers.—KnAs
Butter
  "Betty Botter bought some butter". Mother
    Goose.—PrP—SuO
  "Come, butter, come". Mother Goose.—WaM
  "Donkey, donkey, do not bray". Mother Goose.—
    WaM
"**Buttercup** nodded and said goodby". See August
Butterflies
  "Bo elai parpar nechmad". Unknown.—YoS
    "Come to me, nice butterfly".—YoS
  "Butterflies dancing through falling snow".
    Demaru.—WhAa
  Butterfly ("I had to leave the winter of my life").
    A. Oyewole.—SlM
  Butterfly ("Of living creatures most I prize"). W.
    J. Smith.—SmL
  Butterfly ("What is a butterfly, at best"). B.
    Franklin.—WhAa
  Butterfly song. Unknown.—KeT
  Butterfly wings. A. Fisher.—FiA
  "Butting, tumbling cat". Kikaku.—CaR
  The caterpillar ("Brown and furry"). C. G.
    Rossetti.—DeS—DeT—ElW
  Chrysalis diary. P. Fleischman.—FlJ
  Dreams of flowers. Reikan.—DeI
  Flying crooked. R. Graves.—CaB
  "I get high on butterflies". J. Roseblatt.—BoT
  Korean butterfly dance. J. Kirkup.—FoLe
  On May Day. A. Adoff.—AdIn
  "Polly saw a butterfly". J. Prelutsky.—PrBe
  The reader. Buson.—DeI
  We chased butterflies. Plenty-Coups.—SnD
  Your world. G. D. Johnson.—SlM
"**Butterflies** dancing through falling snow".
  Demaru.—WhAa
Butterfly ("I had to leave the winter of my life").
  Abiodun Oyewole.—SlM
Butterfly ("Of living creatures most I prize").
  William Jay Smith.—SmL
Butterfly ("What is a butterfly, at best"). Benjamin
  Franklin.—WhAa
"The **butterfly**, a cabbage white". See Flying crooked
"**Butterfly**, butterfly, butterfly, butterfly". See
  Butterfly song
Butterfly song. Unknown. tr. by Frances
  Densmore.—KeT
Butterfly wings. Aileen Fisher.—FiA
"**Butting**, tumbling cat". Kikaku, tr. by Sylvia
  Cassedy and Kunihiro Suetake.—CaR
"**Button** to the chin". Unknown.—ScA
Buttons
  "Button to the chin". Unknown.—ScA
  "Rich man, poor man, beggar man, thief".
    Unknown.—CoM
Buying a puppy. Leslie Norris.—LiDp
Buying and selling. See Markets and marketing;
  Peddlers and vendors; Shops and shopkeepers
"The **buzzard** and the owl". See Six birds
"**By** day the bat is cousin to the mouse". See The
  bat
"**By** day the skyscraper looms in the smoke and sun
  and has a soul". See Skyscraper
"**By** flat tink". See Bell
By Frazier Creek Falls. Gary Snyder.—ElW
"**By** hook or by crook". Unknown.—OpI
By myself. Eloise Greenfield.—SlM
"**By** pen or by paint". Unknown.—OpI

"**By** spaceships full of extraterrestrial space". See I
  believe in the theory that says we were visited
  long ago
"**By** the aid of my quill". Unknown.—OpI
"**By** the rude bridge that arched the flood". See
  Concord hymn
By the sea. Eve Merriam.—MeS
"**By** the shape of the beak, if not the size". See
  Faucet
By the shores of Pago Pago. Eve Merriam.—MeCh
"**By** twos we flocked". See Matinees
"**By** what sends". See Children's rhymes
"**Bye**, baby bunting". Mother Goose.—SuO—WaM
"**Bye**, fly". See So long, see you later
Byes. Mauricio Redoles.—AgL
Byrne, Patricia Alanah
  Overture, tr.—NyT
Byron, Lord (George Gordon Byron)
  "When we two parted".—ElW

C

C. C. Johnson. Mel Glenn.—GlBc
C is for cabbages. William Jay Smith.—SmL
Cabbages
  C is for cabbages. W. J. Smith.—SmL
  Skunk cabbage slaw. X. J. Kennedy.—KeGh
"**Cackle**, cackle, Mother Goose". Mother Goose.—
  WaM
Cacophony. Eve Merriam.—MeCh
Cader, Teresa
  The Strand Theatre.—JaPr
Caesar, Julius (about)
  "Brutus adsum jam forte". Unknown.—OpI
  "Julius Caesar made a law". Unknown.—OpI
  "Julius Caesar said with a smile". Unknown.—
    OpI
  "Julius Caesar, the Roman geezer". Unknown.—
    OpI
"**Caesar** is my king". See Louisa Jones sings a praise
  to Caesar
The **cage.** Savitri Hensman.—AgL
Cake and sack. Walter De La Mare.—DeR—MaP
Cakes and cookies
  Birthday cake ("Chocolate or butter"). M. C.
    Livingston.—LiBp
  Birthday cake ("Ten candles on a birthday cake").
    Unknown.—CoE
  Birthday wish. M. C. Livingston.—LiBp
  The case of the crumbled cookies. X. J.
    Kennedy.—KeGh
  Chocolate dreams, one. A. Adoff.—AdCh
  Chocolate dreams, five. A. Adoff.—AdCh
  "The fiddler and his wife". Mother Goose.—WaM
  The gingerbread man. R. Bennett.—DeS
  In the memories of our cookies. A. Adoff.—AdCh
  "Mother made a seedy cake". Unknown.—OpI
  "Pat-a-cake, pat-a-cake, baker's man". Mother
    Goose.—EdGl—SuO
    "Patty cake, patty cake".—WaM
  The remarkable cake. M. Mahy.—MaN
  "Smiling girls, rosy boys". Mother Goose.—WaM
    Pedlar's song .—OpT
  What the little girl said. V. Lindsay.—DeT
    "The moon's the north wind's cooky".—LiDd
  You are walking along eating. A. Adoff.—AdCh
Calder, Dave
  Jouvert morning.—FoLe
Caleb's desk is a mess. Kalli Dakos.—DaI
Calgary. Myra Cohn Livingston.—LiNe

Caliban limbo. Edward Brathwaite.—LeCa
"**Calico** ban". From Calico pie. Edward Lear.—LaM
Calico pie, complete. Edward Lear.—ClI—LiDd
Calico pie, sels. Edward Lear
  "Calico ban".—LaM
"**Calico** pie, the little birds fly". See Calico pie, complete
California
  Monte Rio, California. Z. Rogow.—GoT
  Morning at Malibu. M. C. Livingston.—LiNe
The **California** Zephyr. Ernest Kroll.—MoR
"**Call** a tiger Master he'll still eat you". From Jamaican Caribbean proverbs. Unknown.—BeW
"**Call** John the boatman". See John Boatman
"**Call** the cows home". See Thunder
"**Call** the doctors, call the nurses, give me a breath of". See Call the periods, call the commas
Call the periods, call the commas. Kalli Dakos.—DaI
Calligraphy. Jane Yolen.—YoBi
Calling all cars. Max Fatchen.—FaCm
"**Calmly** in the twilight made". See Muted
Camara, Helder
  "Lord, isn't your creation wasteful".—StP
The **camel** ("The camel has a single hump"). Ogden Nash.—DeS
Camel ("The camel is a long legged humpbacked beast"). William Jay Smith.—SmL
Camel ("The camel's a mammal"). Maxine W. Kumin.—HoT
"The **camel** has a single hump". See The camel
"The **camel** is a long legged humpbacked beast". See Camel
Camels
  "Are you a camel, a big yellow camel". Unknown.—ScA
  The camel ("The camel has a single hump"). O. Nash.—DeS
  Camel ("The camel is a long legged humpbacked beast"). W. J. Smith.—SmL
  Camel ("The camel's a mammal"). M. W. Kumin.—HoT
  Camels of the Kings. L. Norris.—CaB
  Commissariat camels. R. Kipling.—WhAa
  How to tell a camel. J. P. Lewis.—KeT—LeA
  We three camels. J. Yolen.—YoHa
"The **camel's** a mammal". See Camel
Camels of the Kings. Leslie Norris.—CaB
"**Camel's** oil". See At the witch's drugstore
"The **camels**, the Kings' camels, haie-aie". See Camels of the Kings
Camp Calvary. Ronald Wallace.—JaPr
Campana, Dino
  Autumn garden, tr. by Carlo L. Golino.—GoT
Campbell, Alison
  A short note on schoolgirls.—AgL
Camping and hiking
  The hiker. E. Merriam.—MeCh
  My marshmallows. X. J. Kennedy.—KeK
  Stories ("Circling by the fire"). J. P. Lewis.—LeT—LiDp
  The tent. W. De La Mare.—DeR
Can a can. Eve Merriam.—MeP
"**Can** anybody tell me, please". See Help
"**Can** you Con". See Constantinople
"**Can** you count". Unknown.—WiA
"**Can** you see". See O say
Canada
  Calgary. M. C. Livingston.—LiNe
  Canadian Indian place names. M. Zola.—BoT

  Niagara, Canadian Horseshoe Falls. M. C. Livingston.—LiNe
  Remembrance Day ("To some"). J. Kitching.—FoLe
  So I'm proud. J. Little.—LiHe
  "There once was a boy of Quebec". R. Kipling.—LiLo
  "There was an old woman from Winnipeg". W. J. Smith.—SmL
Canada goose. Marilyn Singer.—SiT
Canadian Indian place names. Meguido Zola.—BoT
The **canal** bank. James Stephens.—LiIf
Canapes a la poste. William Jay Smith.—SmL
Canaries
  Cat whiskered Catbird. W. J. Smith.—SmL
  Our canary. L. Simmie.—PrFo
Cancion tonta. Federico Garcia Lorca.—DeT
  Silly song ("Mama").—DeT
Candle. Myra Cohn Livingston.—LiNe
"**Candle**, candle, burning clear". See The house of dream
"**Candle** lank and lean and pale". See To bed
Candles
  Birthday cake ("Ten candles on a birthday cake"). Unknown.—CoE
  Candle. M. C. Livingston.—LiNe
  Hanukkah candles. M. Hillert.—HoS
  The house of dream. W. De La Mare.—DeR
  In the discreet splendor. A. L. Strauss.—GoT
  "Jack be nimble, Jack be quick". Mother Goose.—EdGl—SuO—WaM
  "Little Nancy Etticoat". Mother Goose.—WaM
  No one. L. Moore.—KeT
  To bed. W. De La Mare.—DeR
Candy
  Candy cane. V. Worth.—WoA
  Chips, one. A. Adoff.—AdCh
  Chocolate rabbit. X. J. Kennedy.—KeK
  The cupboard. W. De La Mare.—DeR—MaP
  Her she bar. A. Adoff.—AdCh
  "Hippity hop to the barber shop". Mother Goose.—CoM—WaM—WiA
  Honeycomb days. J. P. Lewis.—LeE
  I love my mom, I love my pop, I love my dog, I love my sheep. A. Adoff.—AdCh
  I raise my voice most high, this night. A. Adoff.—AdCh
  "I'm sticky". M. C. Livingston.—LiMh
  Let the biter beware. A. Adoff.—AdCh
  Life in the forest, or, bad news, good news, bad news. A. Adoff.—AdCh
  The magic house. J. Yolen.—LiHp—YoBe
  My marshmallows. X. J. Kennedy.—KeK
  A nature story. A. Adoff.—AdCh
  Ode to la pinata. G. Soto.—SoNe
  "Old man Moses, sick in bed". Unknown.—ScA
  Patience. B. Katz.—LoFh
  "Peter's Pop kept a lollipop shop". Unknown.—OpI
  Rescue mission. A. Adoff.—AdCh
  Sweets. V. Worth.—WoAl
  "Tom Teeple ate a steeple". Unknown.—WiA
  Valentine hearts. M. C. Livingston.—LiR
  The world is in chaos, the world is in flames. A. Adoff.—AdCh
Candy cane. Valerie Worth.—WoA
Cane, Melville
  Snow toward evening.—FrS
Cannibals
  "A certain young man of great gumption". Unknown.—LiLo

Canoes and canoeing
    Lullaby ("The long canoe"). R. Hillyer.—SuI
    "The Milky Way is a sail". Unknown.—LaN
    "My little son". Makah.—SnD
    Summer night, canoeing. B. J. Esbensen.—EsW
Canseco, Jose (about)
    Jose Canseco. Unknown.—MoA
"Can't curl, but can swim". See The tortoise and the hedgehog
"Can't stop watching you". See Crown
"Can't think". Unknown.—WiA
Cantwell, Billie Lou
    Code blue.—JaPr
"**Captain** Flea and Sailor Snail". Jack Prelutsky.—PrBe
Captain Lean. Walter De La Mare.—DeR
Captain Molly. William Collins.—SuI
"A **captain,** retired from the Navy". William Jay Smith.—SmL
Captive bird. Boethius, tr. by Helen Waddell.—CaB
The **car.** Robert Creeley.—MoR
"**Car** coughing moves with". See The car
Caracola ("Me han traido una caracola"). Federico Garcia Lorca.—DeT
    Snail ("They have brought me a snail").—DeT
The **cardinal.** Jane Yolen.—YoBi
"A **cardinal** is perched upon a bat". See World champions
Cardinals (birds)
    The cardinal. J. Yolen.—YoBi
Careful, mouse. Aileen Fisher.—FiH
"**Careless** and still". See The rabbit hunter
"A **careless** zookeeper named Blake". Unknown.—LiLo
Caribbean islands
    Banana and mackerel. J. Berry.—BeW
    Banana talk. J. Berry.—BeW
    "Because parrots are chatterers people say they are the only ones who eat up the fruits". From Jamaican Caribbean proverbs. Unknown.—BeW
    "Befoh yu marry keep two yeye opn, afta yu marry shet one". From Jamaican Caribbean proverbs. Unknown.—BeW
    "The boaster will make out someone else is the liar". From Jamaican Caribbean proverbs. Unknown.—BeW
    "Break master neck but nuh break master law". Unknown.—LeCa
    "The bus weaves its way through the jungle home". M. Wayne.—LeCa
    "Call a tiger Master he'll still eat you". From Jamaican Caribbean proverbs. Unknown.—BeW
    A different kind of Sunday. J. Berry.—BeW
    "A dog's bark isn't going to frighten the moon". From Jamaican Caribbean proverbs. Unknown.—BeW
    "The donkey says the world isn't level ground". From Jamaican Caribbean proverbs. Unknown.—BeW
    "Don't call an alligator a long-mouth till you have crossed the river". From Jamaican Caribbean proverbs. Unknown.—BeW
    "Don't wait until you hear the drum beat before you grind your axe". From Jamaican Caribbean proverbs. Unknown.—BeW
    "Every family has its deformity". From Jamaican Caribbean proverbs. Unknown.—BeW
    "Good boy is a fool's nickname". From Jamaican Caribbean proverbs. Unknown.—BeW
    "The great fool is as proud as a dog with two tails". From Jamaican Caribbean proverbs. Unknown.—BeW
    Haiti, skin diving. J. Shore.—KnAS
    "He is a clever man who drives away hunger by just working his jaws". From Jamaican Caribbean proverbs. Unknown.—BeW
    The hymn tunes. E. Lucie-Smith.—LeCa
    "If nightingale sings too sweetly, jealousy will kill its mother". From Jamaican Caribbean proverbs. Unknown.—BeW
    "If you back a monkey he'll fight a tiger". From Jamaican Caribbean proverbs. Unknown.—BeW
    Ilan' life. S. J. Wallace.—LeCa
    Jamaican alphabet. L. Bennett.—LeCa
    Jamaican song. J. Berry.—BeW
    Jouvert morning. D. Calder.—FoLe
    King of the band. A. Johnson.—FoLe
    "A little axe can cut down a big tree". From Jamaican Caribbean proverbs. Unknown.—BeW
    "The man who is all honey, flies are going to eat him up". From Jamaican Caribbean proverbs. Unknown.—BeW
    "Many an underfed cow in the pasture is mother of a bull". From Jamaican Caribbean proverbs. Unknown.—BeW
    Market women. D. Myrie.—LeCa
    Mek drum talk, man, for Caribbean Independence. J. Berry.—BeW
    "The mosquito often goes to the village for syrup but doesn't always get it". From Jamaican Caribbean proverbs. Unknown.—BeW
    "The needle makes clothes yet the needle itself is naked". From Jamaican Caribbean proverbs. Unknown.—BeW
    An old Jamaican woman thinks about the hereafter. A. L. Hendricks.—LeCa
    "The peacock hides its leg when its tail gets praises". From Jamaican Caribbean proverbs. Unknown.—BeW
    "The rich and the poor do not meet". From Jamaican Caribbean proverbs. Unknown.—BeW
    Sea school. B. Howes.—LeCa
    "Sickness come di gallop, but e tek e own time fo walk' way". Unknown.—LeCa
    The song of the banana man. E. Jones.—LeCa
    Song of the sea and people. J. Berry.—BeW
    South ("But today I recapture the islands'"). E. Brathwaite.—LeCa
    "When you see your neighbour's beard on fire, take some water and wet your own". From Jamaican Caribbean proverbs. Unknown.—BeW
    "You live in de cement house, and no worry de hurricane". Unknown.—LeCa
    "You never see a cow that kicks who doesn't produce a calf that kicks". From Jamaican Caribbean proverbs. Unknown.—BeW
Caring for animals. Jon Silkin.—NyT
Carlile, Henry
    Dodo ("Years they mistook me for you").—JaPr
    Fish story.—KnAs
"**Carmencita** loves Patrick". See Little song
Carmi, T.
    Don't be afraid, tr.—LiPm
Carnival in Rio. James Kirkup.—FoLe
Carol of the birds. Unknown.—YoHa
Carol of the brown king. Langston Hughes.—GoA
"**Carolina** sphinx moths". See Requiem

Cassedy, Sylvia—*Continued*
"Red dragonfly on", tr.—CaR
"**Casting** the body's vest aside". From The garden. Andrew Marvell.—StP
"A **castle** has". See Having
Castro, Tania Diaz
The wall, tr. by Pablo Medina and Carolina Hospital.—NyT
Cat ("Again and again through the day"). Jibananda Das, tr. by Lila Ray.—NyT
Cat ("The black cat yawns"). Mary Britton Miller.—KeT
"The **cat**". See A cat may look at a King
Cat ("Cats are not at all like people"). William Jay Smith.—LaCc—SmL
The **cat** ("Flourishing his head around"). Kusatao, tr. by Tze-si Huang.—DeI
Cat ("I prefer"). Marilyn Singer.—SiT
Cat ("Old Mog comes in and sits on the newspaper"). Joan Aiken.—LaCc
Cat ("The spotted cat hops"). Valerie Worth.—WoAl
"**Cat**". Eleanor Farjeon.—LaCc
Cat and mouse game. Patricia Hubbell.—LaM
"The **cat** asleep by the side of the fire". See The cat sat asleep
Cat at night. Adrien Stoutenburg.—LaCc
Cat at the cream. Unknown.—CaB
Cat bath ("After she eats"). Aileen Fisher.—FiA
Cat bath ("In the midst"). Valerie Worth.—LaCc—WoAl
Cat bath ("She always tries"). Aileen Fisher.—CoAz
A **cat** came fiddling. Mother Goose.—CII
"A **cat** came fiddling out of a barn". See A cat came fiddling
Cat cat. Eve Merriam.—LaCc
"**Cat** cat cat on the bed". See Cat cat
"The **cat** goes out". See Our cat
The **cat** heard the cat-bird. John Ciardi.—LaCc
"**Cat,** if you go outdoors you must walk in the snow". See On a night of snow
"The **cat** in moonlight". See Cat at night
Cat in moonlight. Douglas Gibson.—DeT—LaCc
A **cat** is. Adrien Stoutenburg.—MoS
Cat kisses. Bobbi Katz.—Det
A **cat** may look at a King. Laura E. Richards.—WhAa
"A **cat** may look at a king". Unknown.—OpI
"The **cat** ran over the roof with a lump of raw liver". Unknown.—WiA
The **cat** sat asleep. Mother Goose.—CII
  "The **cat** sat asleep by the side of the fire".—WaM
"The **cat** sat asleep by the side of the fire". See The cat sat asleep
"The **cat** she walks on padded claws". See Earth folk
"The **cat**, the cat". See I can't go back to school
Cat toys. Valerie Worth.—WoA
"The **cat** was once a weaver". See What the gray cat sings
Cat whiskered Catbird. William Jay Smith.—SmL
The **cat** who aspired to higher things. X. J. Kennedy.—LaM
Catalogue, sels. Rosalie Moore
Cats sleep fat.—LaCc
The **cataract** of Lodore, sels. Robert Southey
"From its sources which well".—MoR
The **catch** ("Happy to have these fish"). Raymond Carver.—KnAs
The **catch** ("The kingfisher"). Tori, tr. by Tze-si Huang.—DeI
Catch ("Two boys uncoached are tossing a poem together"). Robert Francis.—KnAs

"**Catch** him, crow". Mother Goose.—WaM
The **caterpillar** ("Brown and furry"). Christina Georgina Rossetti.—DeS—DeT—ElW
Caterpillar ("The feet of the"). Valerie Worth.—WoAl
Caterpillars
The caterpillar ("Brown and furry"). C. G. Rossetti.—DeS—DeT—ElW
Caterpillar ("The feet of the"). V. Worth.—WoAl
Caterpillars. A. Fisher.—KeT
Chrysalis diary. P. Fleischman.—FlJ
Lasiocampidae. M. C. Livingston.—LiNe
"Little Arabella Miller". Unknown.—PrP
My opinion. M. Shannon.—WhAa
"Patter pitter caterpillar". J. Prelutsky.—PrBe
The shriving. J. Carter.—JaM
Song of summer. M. W. Brown.—MoS
The tickle rhyme. I. Serraillier.—MoS
Unseen till now. Buson.—DeI
Caterpillars. Aileen Fisher.—KeT
"**Catfish**, Mudcat, Ducky, Coot". See The song of Snohomish
Catherine. Karla Kuskin.—HoS
"**Catherine** said, I'll think I'll bake". See Catherine
Cats
Aelourophile. E. Merriam.—MeCh
Aelourophobe. E. Merriam.—MeCh
Alley cat school. F. Asch.—LaCc
Apartment cats. T. Gunn.—LaCc
"As Eenty Feenty Halligolun". Unknown.—OpI
At night. A. Fisher.—MoS
Back yard. V. Worth.—DeT—WoAl
Bartholo. J. P. Lewis.—LeT
"Butting, tumbling cat". Kikaku.—CaR
Careful, mouse. A. Fisher.—FiH
"Cat". E. Farjeon.—LaCc
Cat ("Again and again through the day"). J. Das.—NyT
Cat ("The black cat yawns"). M. B. Miller.—KeT
Cat ("Cats are not at all like people"). W. J. Smith.—LaCc—SmL
The cat ("Flourishing his head around"). Kusatao.—DeI
Cat ("I prefer"). M. Singer.—SiT
Cat ("Old Mog comes in and sits on the newspaper"). J. Aiken.—LaCc
Cat ("The spotted cat hops"). V. Worth.—WoAl
Cat and mouse game. P. Hubbell.—LaM
Cat at night. A. Stoutenburg.—LaCc
Cat at the cream. Unknown.—CaB
Cat bath ("After she eats"). A. Fisher.—FiA
Cat bath ("In the midst"). V. Worth.—LaCc—WoAl
Cat bath ("She always tries"). A. Fisher.—CoAz
A cat came fiddling. Mother Goose.—CII
Cat cat. E. Merriam.—LaCc
The cat heard the cat-bird. J. Ciardi.—LaCc
Cat in moonlight. D. Gibson.—DeT—LaCc
A cat is. A. Stoutenburg.—MoS
Cat kisses. B. Katz.—Det
A cat may look at a King. L. E. Richards.—WhAa
The cat sat asleep. Mother Goose.—CII
  "The cat asleep by the side of the fire".—WaM
Cat toys. V. Worth.—WoA
The cat who aspired to higher things. X. J. Kennedy.—LaM
Cats ("Cats sleep"). E. Farjeon.—ElW
Cats ("Cats walk neatly"). R. Francis.—MoR
Cats and dogs. N. M. Bodecker.—KeT—LaM—MoS
The cat's eye. Yorie.—DeI

Cats—*Continued*
"Wind is a cat". E. R. Fuller.—BaW
The winter cat. Yaso.—DeI
The world is much. J. P. Lewis.—LeE
"A young man from old Terre Haute". W. J. Smith.—SmL
Cats ("Cats sleep"). Eleanor Farjeon.—ElW
Cats ("Cats walk neatly"). Robert Francis.—MoR
Cats and dogs. N. M. Bodecker.—KeT—LaM—MoS
"Cats are not at all like people". See Cat
The cat's eye. Yorie, tr. by Tze-si Huang.—DeI
"Cat's in the alley". See Lullaby
The cats of Kilkenny ("There were once . . ."). See "There once were two cats of Kilkenny"
"Cats purr". See I speak, I say, I talk
"Cats sleep". See Cats
Cats sleep fat. From Catalogue. Rosalie Moore.—LaCc
"Cats sleep fat and walk thin". See Cats sleep fat
The cat's song. Unknown.—CaB
"Cats walk neatly". See Cats
Cattle
The birthday cow. E. Merriam.—WhAa
The black bull. Basho.—DeI
"Charley Warley had a cow". Mother Goose.—WaM
Cow ("The cow"). V. Worth.—WoAl
The cow ("The cow is of the bovine ilk"). O. Nash.—CaB
Cow ("Cows are not supposed to fly"). W. J. Smith.—SmL
The cow ("The friendly cow all red and white"). R. L. Stevenson.—ElW—KeT
Cow ("I approve of June"). M. Singer.—SiT
Cow's complaint. G. Nichols.—NiCo
The cow's moo. Issa.—DeI
"Four stiff-standers". Unknown.—CaB—ScA
"I had a cow that gave such milk". Unknown.—WiA
I had a little cow. Mother Goose.—ClI
"I went to Wisconsin". J. Prelutsky.—PrBe
"I'd like a white bull with one horn only". From What we said sitting making fantasies. J. Berry.—BeW
A kitten's thought. O. Herford.—ElW
"Many an underfed cow in the pasture is mother of a bull". From Jamaican Caribbean proverbs. Unknown.—BeW
"Milk white moon, put the cows to sleep". C. Sandburg.—SuI
November calf. J. Kenyon.—ElW
"Oh, the cow kicked Nelly in the belly in the barn". Unknown.—ScA
Old man and the cow. E. Lear.—DeS
    There was an old man who said.—ClI
One cow, two moos. J. P. Lewis.—LeT
The pasture. R. Frost.—KeT
The prayer of the ox. C. B. De Gasztold.—DeP
The purple cow. G. Burgess.—ClI—KeT
"Then let us sing merrily, merrily now". Mother Goose.—WaM
"There once was a man who said, how". Unknown.—LiLo
"There was a piper had a cow". Mother Goose.—ClI
"They strolled down the lane together". Unknown.—PrP
Thunder. W. De La Mare.—DeR
To the snow. Unknown.—OpI
"Two-legs sat on three-legs by four-legs". Unknown.—WiA

Whoopee ti yi yo, git along, little dogies. Unknown.—SuI
"You never see a cow that kicks who doesn't produce a calf that kicks". From Jamaican Caribbean proverbs. Unknown.—BeW
Young calves. Banko.—DeI
Caught. Gaston Dubois.—KnAs
Causley, Charles
"The owl looked out of the ivy bush".—LiIf
"Quack, said the billy goat".—WhAa
Cavalry crossing a ford. Walt Whitman.—ElW
Caves
Speedy Sam. J. Ciardi.—CiH
Caw. Walter De La Mare.—DeR
"Cease your chatter". Unknown.—OpI
Cedering, Siv
Suppose ("Suppose I were as clever as a bird").—JaP
"When it is snowing".—JaP
Celebration. Alonzo Lopez.—DeT
Celestial. Michael Pettit.—JaM
"Celia sat beside the seaside". Unknown.—PrP
Cellars
Cat and mouse game. P. Hubbell.—LaM
John Mouldy. W. De La Mare.—DeR
"Popeye went down in the cellar". Unknown.—WiA
"Where was Moses when the light went out, down in the cellar". Unknown.—WiA
"Celui-ci a vu un lievre". Unknown.—YoS
"This one saw a hare".—YoS
Cemeteries. See Graves
At last. W. De La Mare.—DeR
The witch ("Weary went the old witch"). W. De La Mare.—DeR
The centaurs. James Stephens.—WhDd
"A centipede was happy quite". Unknown.—PrP
Centipedes
"A centipede was happy quite". Unknown.—PrP
"A mathematician named Lynch". Unknown.—LiLo
Sticky situation. X. J. Kennedy.—LiLo
Subway centipede. W. J. Smith.—SmL
"There once was a centipede neat". Unknown.—LiLo
Cerberus. N. B. Taylor.—WhDd
"Certain acts survive, I recall". See A victory
"A certain person wondered why". See They ask why
"A certain young fellow, named Bobbie". Unknown.—LiLo
"A certain young man of great gumption". Unknown.—LiLo
Chacon, Barbara
"Coils the robot", tr.—NyT
Chagall, Marc (about)
Salt and memory, a tribute to Marc Chagall. Z. Zelk.—NyT
The chair. Florence Parry Heide.—HeG
Chairs
The antimacassar and the ottoman. W. J. Smith.—SmL
"Bear chair". B. McMillan.—McP
The chair. F. P. Heide.—HeG
Chairs. V. Worth.—WoAl
The difference. M. C. Livingston.—LiNe
"I spent the first years of my life". J. Carson.—CaS
"No neck". M. C. Livingston.—LiMh
The perfect reactionary. H. Mearns.—PrFo
S is for springs. W. J. Smith.—SmL

Chairs—*Continued*
"Said Noble Aaron to Aaron Barron". Mother Goose.—WaM
The table and the chair. E. Lear.—LiDd
Chairs. Valerie Worth.—WoAl
"A **chair's** a piece of furniture". See The chair
"**Chairs** seem to". See Chairs
Chakravarti, Nirendranath
The garden of a child.—NyT
Chamberlain, Wilt (about)
Wilt Chamberlain. R. R. Knudson.—KnAs
The **chameleon.** John Gardner.—CoAz
"A **chameleon,** when he's feeling blue". See Variety
Championship. Sharon Bell Mathis.—MaR
Chandra, Deborah
Daddy's gone.—LiPf
Garuda.—WhDd
Jack.—LiHp
Mama's song.—LiPm
The owl ("Your eyes, a searching yellow light").—LiIf
Sleeping Simon.—LiDp
Sphinx.—WhDd
The thief.—LiIf
"**Chang** McTang McQuarter Cat". John Ciardi.—LaCc
Change
"Believe me, if all those endearing young charms". T. Moore.—ElW
Buffalo dusk. C. Sandburg.—CaB—DeS—ElW
The chameleon. J. Gardner.—CoAz
Changing. M. Angelou.—AnI
Chrysalis diary. P. Fleischman.—FlJ
The closing of the rodeo. W. J. Smith.—KnAs
Clothes ("My mother keeps on telling me"). E. Jennings.—AgL
A different image. D. Randall.—SuC
Dust of snow. R. Frost.—ElW
Fence. V. Worth.—WoAl
From the most distant time. L. Wu-ti.—GoT
The garden of a child. N. Chakravarti.—NyT
How many times. From Blowin' in the wind. B. Dylan.—SuC
I love you it's true. C. Stewart.—AgL
In August. G. Soto.—SoA
Inside. K. Chiha.—NyT
Journey of the Magi. T. S. Eliot.—ElW
Long ago days. M. C. Livingston.—LiT
Love ("I believed"). T. Karpowicz.—NyT
Marie Lucille. G. Brooks.—KeT
Mum Dad and me. J. Berry.—BeW
The new negro. J. E. McCall.—SuC
"The night will never stay". E. Farjeon.—ElW
Pail. V. Worth.—WoAl
Polo ponies practicing. W. Stevens.—KnAs
The Red Stockings. G. Ellard.—MoA
Sea timeless song. G. Nichols.—NiCo
Sisters. P. B. Janeczko.—JaB
Taking down the space-trolley. X. J. Kennedy.—KeK
"There are some things I want to know about". J. Carson.—CaS
To the thawing wind. R. Frost.—ElW
Variety. From Animalimericks. E. Merriam.—MeS
Winner ("Mrs. Macey worked behind"). P. B. Janeczko.—JaB
"Wrinkles in the lake". From Diary of a woodcutter. F. Rifka.—NyT
Yesterday. J. Little.—LiHe
The **changeling.** Walter De La Mare.—DeR—MaP
Changelings. X. J. Kennedy.—KeGh

Changing. Maya Angelou.—AnI
Chanticleer. See "Oh my pretty cock, oh my handsome cock"
Chants
Bull dog. C. Porter.—KnAs
Cheers. E. Merriam.—MeS
"Gilly, gilly, gilly, gilly". Unknown.—ScA
"I scream, you scream". Unknown.—OpI—ScA—WiA
"Kum by yah, my Lord". Unknown.—StP
"Ladies and gentlemen". Unknown.—ScA—WiA
"Left, left". Unknown.—ScA
Marching chant. Unknown.—WiA
"The moon shines bright and the stars give a light". Unknown.—OpI
"Mrs. Sue, Mrs. Sue". Unknown.—ScA
"My father left me, as he was able". Unknown.—ScA
Negro soldier's civil war chant. Unknown.—SuC
The Notre Dame victory march. J. Shea.—KnAs
"Oh my, I want a piece of pie". Unknown.—ScA
"Ooo-ah, wanna piece of pie".—CoM
"Pease porridge hot, pease porridge cold". Unknown.—ScA
"Strawberry shortcake". Unknown.—ScA
"Two, four, six, eight". Unknown.—WiA
"Who put the overalls in Mrs. Murphy's chowder". Unknown.—ScA
Endless chant.—WiA
"Yankees, Yankees". Unknown.—MoA
Chapman, John
"Oh, the Lord is good to me".—StP
Chappell, Fred
Cleaning the well.—JaPr
Remodeling the hermit's cabin.—JaM
Character. See Conduct of life
Charity. See also Gifts and giving; Sympathy
"Christmas is coming and the geese are getting fat". Mother Goose.—OpI—SuO—WaM
Christmas is coming.—HoS
The fairy-pedlar's song. From Crossings. W. De La Mare.—DeR
Lob-lie-by-the-fire. W. De La Mare.—DeR
The penny owing. W. De La Mare.—DeR
The pilgrim. W. De La Mare.—DeR
The three beggars. W. De La Mare.—DeR
Charlene Cottier. Mel Glenn.—GlBc
Charles, Dorthi
Getting dirty.—KeT
"**Charles** the First and Ikey Mo". See Woe
"**Charles** the First walked and talked". Unknown.—OpI
"**Charles** the Second, so they tell". See Oak apple day
"**Charley** Barley, butter and eggs". Mother Goose.—WaM
"**Charley,** Charley". Mother Goose.—WaM
"**Charley** Warley had a cow". Mother Goose.—WaM
"**Charlie** Chaplin sat on a pin". Unknown.—ScA
"**Charlie** Chaplin went to France". Unknown.—WiA
"**Charlie,** Charlie, in the tub". Unknown.—OpI
"**Charlie** Chuck". Unknown.—WiA
"**Charlie** McCarthy sat on a pin". Unknown.—WiA
A **charm** against a grackle. J. Patrick Lewis.—LeA
A **charm** for the trees. J. Patrick Lewis.—LeE
Charms
The apple charm. W. De La Mare.—DeR
Arymouse, arymouse. Unknown.—ClI
"Bat, bat". Mother Goose.—ClI
Bewitched. W. De La Mare.—DeR—MaP

Charms—*Continued*
"Blow, wind, blow, and go, mill, go". Mother Goose.—WaM
A charm against a grackle. J. P. Lewis.—LeA
A charm for the trees. J. P. Lewis.—LeE
"Come, butter, come". Mother Goose.—WaM
Curses. M. P. Hearn.—BaH
Dragon ("A dragon named Ernest Belflour"). W. J. Smith.—SmL
"Hiccup, hiccup, go away". Mother Goose.—WaM
"Hiccup, snickup". Unknown.—ScA—WiA
"Ladybug, ladybug, fly away home". Mother Goose.—ScA—WiA
    "Ladybird, ladybird".—WaM
    To the ladybird ("Ladybird, ladybird").—OpI
Magic wands. J. Yolen.—PrBe
Nine charms against the hunter. D. Wagoner.—KnAs
Prayer ("Owl"). Unknown.—LiIf
"Rain, rain, go away". Mother Goose.—DeS—EdGl—WiA
"Rain, rain, go to Spain". Unknown.—ScA
"Snow, snow faster". Mother Goose.—ScA—WaM
Spell to banish a pimple. J. Agard.—AgL
Spells. J. Yolen.—YoBe
To the rain. Unknown.—OpI
To the snail. Unknown.—OpI
To the snow. Unknown.—OpI
The witch ("Weary went the old witch"). W. De La Mare.—DeR
The witch's cauldron. J. Yolen.—YoBe
"You can't catch me". Unknown.—WiA
The **chatelaine**. Unknown.—OpT
Chaves, Raquel
Pitcher, tr.—NyT
Checking out me history. John Agard.—AgL
"**Cheer**, cheer for old Notre Dame". See The Notre Dame victory march
The **cheerful** child's week. Beatrice Schenk De Regniers.—DeW
"The **cheerful** cricket, when he sings". See Cricket
Cheerily man. Unknown.—MoR
Cheerleader. Jim Wayne Miller.—JaPr
Cheerleaders. Sharon Bell Mathis.—MaR
Cheers. Eve Merriam.—MeS
Cheese
"Green cheese, yellow laces". Mother Goose.—WaM
"There was a man dressed all in cheese". A. Lobel.—PrFo
"The underwater wibbles". J. Prelutsky.—JaP
Welsh rabbit. Unknown.—OpT
Chemistry
Arnold Flitterman. M. Glenn.—GlBc
Cheng, Gu
Far and close, tr. by Edward Morin.—NyT
A headstrong boy, tr. by Donald Finkel.—NyT
Cherries and cherry trees
Blow up. X. J. Kennedy.—LoFh
Bread and cherries. W. De La Mare.—DeR—MaP
Let's be merry. C. G. Rossetti.—KeT
"Loveliest of trees, the cherry now". A. E. Housman.—ElW
"**Cherries**, ripe cherries". See Bread and cherries
"A **cherry** pip". See Bedtime mumble
"**Chester** Lester Kirkenby Dale". See Chester's undoing
Chester's undoing. Julie Holder.—PrFo
Chesterton, Gilbert Keith
"Elder Father, though thine eyes".—StP

"The snail does the holy".—StP
Chestnuts and chestnut trees
All hot (the chestnut man). W. De La Mare.—DeR
The chestnuts are falling. L. Moore.—MoR
The **chestnuts** are falling. Lilian Moore.—MoR
Cheung Chau festival. Jean Kenward.—FoLe
Cheyenne Indians. See Indians of the Americas—Cheyenne
Chicago
"Chicken in the car". Unknown.—WiA
    "A chicken in the car".—ScA
    Chicago.—CoM
Chicago. See "Chicken in the car"
"**Chick,** chick, chatterman". Unknown.—WiA
Chicken. Walter De La Mare.—DeR—MaP
"A **chicken** in the car". See "Chicken in the car"
"**Chicken** in the car". Unknown.—WiA
    "A chicken in the car".—ScA
    Chicago.—CoM
The **chicken** poem. Don Welch.—JaM
Chickens
"The angry hens from Never-when". M. Rosen.—PrFo
Baby chick. A. Fisher.—FiA—WhAa
"The barnyard fowls that lay our eggs". Unknown.—PrP
Bragging in the barnyard. J. P. Lewis.—LeA
But I dunno. Unknown.—ClI
Chicken. W. De La Mare.—DeR—MaP
"Chicken in the car". Unknown.—WiA
    "A chicken in the car".—ScA
    Chicago.—CoM
The chicken poem. D. Welch.—JaM
The chickens. Unknown.—KeT
Chook-chook-chook. Unknown.—CoE
Cock, cock, cock, cock. Unknown.—ClI
"The codfish lays ten thousand eggs". Unknown.—PrP
"Down in the henhouse on my knees". Unknown.—WiA
E is for egg. W. J. Smith.—SmL
Egg. V. Worth.—WoAl
"The farm is in a flurry". J. Prelutsky.—PrP
Five little chickens. Unknown.—HoS
Grace. W. De La Mare.—DeR
Hen. W. J. Smith.—SmL
The hens. E. M. Roberts.—LiDd
"Hickety pickety, my black hen". Mother Goose.—SuO—WaM
The Hirdy Dirdy. Unknown.—OpT
Horn-rimmed hen. W. J. Smith.—SmL
How to trick a chicken. J. P. Lewis.—LeA
"I had a little hen". Mother Goose.—ClI
"I went down to my garden patch". Unknown.—WiA
"If a rooster crows when he goes to bed". Unknown.—WhAa—WiA
Killing chickens. B. Weigl.—JaPr
Life. A. Kreymborg.—CoAz
Mother hen. Seibi.—DeI
My old hen. Unknown.—KeT
"Oh my pretty cock, oh my handsome cock". Mother Goose.—WaM
    Chanticleer.—OpT
"The old hen sat on turkey eggs". Unknown.—WiA
The prayer of the cock. C. B. De Gasztold.—DeP
The red hen. J. S. Tippett.—WhAa
Roosters. E. Coatsworth.—WhAs
"Whistling girls and crowing hens". Unknown.—WiA

Childhood recollections—*Continued*
Wolf-ancestry. V. Popa.—NyT
Yellow sonnet. P. Zimmer.—JaP
Young. A. Sexton.—AgL—JaPr
Zora. J. Schell.—JaPr
Children and childhood. See also Boys and boyhood;
    Girls and girlhood
Agatha, Agatha. M. A. Hoberman.—HoFa
Andre. G. Brooks.—SlM
Answer to a child's question. S. T. Coleridge.—
    CaB—ElW
An appointment. C. Shiang-hua.—NyT
Are you in there. M. Fatchen.—FaCm
The babes in the wood. Unknown.—ElW
Believe it or not. N. Kantchev.—NyT
Big questions. A. Bryan.—BrS
Black hair. G. Soto.—JaP—SoA
Body-steadier. J. Berry.—BeW
Books. W. De La Mare.—DeR
"Boys and girls come out to play". Mother Goose.
Budging line ups. K. Dakos.—DaI
But why not. M. Fatchen.—FaCm
The cheerful child's week. B. S. De Regniers.—
    DeW
"Childhood is the only lasting flower". R. D.
    Eterovic.—NyT
The children's hour. H. W. Longfellow.—SuI
Children's rhymes. L. Hughes.—SuC
Chore boy. J. Thomas.—LiPm
The christening ("The bells chime clear"). W. De
    La Mare.—DeR
The churlish child's week. B. S. De Regniers.—
    DeW
Closet. M. C. Livingston.—LiNe
Constipation. R. Wallace.—JaM
Dance poem. N. Giovanni.—MoR
"Days were as great as lakes". D. Vogel.—GoT
Digging for China. R. Wilbur.—SuI
Don't be afraid. D. Vogel.—LiPm
Drawing by Ronnie C., grade one. Lechlitner.
    Ruth.—GoT
Dreaming black boy. J. Berry.—BeW
Elevation. R. Morgan.—JaM
Envoy. W. De La Mare.—DeR
Envying the children of San Francisco. G. Soto.—
    SoA
"Every time it rained, mean Merl's". X. J.
    Kennedy.—KeFb
Excuse. M. C. Livingston.—LiT
The fastest belt in town. G. Nichols.—NiCo
Father to son. A. L. Woods.—SlM
February 14th. A. Bonner.—FoLe
"Fill your children with kindness". Unknown.—
    StP
"First a daughter, then a son". Unknown.—ScA
Free time. J. Thomas.—LiPm
Friends. B. J. Esbensen.—EsW
The funeral. W. De La Mare.—DeR
The game ("Plastic soldiers march on the floor").
    M. C. Livingston.—SaB
    The game ("Plastic soldiers on the floor").—
      LiNe
Gathering strength. L. Dangel.—JaM
Getting dirty. D. Charles.—KeT
A gift horse. A. Hashmi.—NyT
Hallowe'en indignation meeting. M. Fishback.—
    DeT
Hanging fire. A. Lorde.—AgL
Hapless. W. De La Mare.—DeR—MaP
Hark. W. De La Mare.—DeR
The haunted child. M. Mahy.—MaN
He was so little. J. Little.—LiHe

Help ("Any magazines"). M. Fatchen.—FaCm
"Hey black child". U. E. Perkins.—SlM
Home ("Yelling, shouting, arguing"). M. C.
    Livingston.—LiT
How to play night baseball. J. Holden.—MoA
How to sell things. G. Soto.—SoA
I could never convince any of the other members.
    A. Adoff.—AdCh
I eat kids yum yum. D. Lee.—KeT
"I know a boy". E. Merriam.—MeY
If we had lunch at the White House. K. Dakos.—
    DaI
In the middle. M. C. Livingston.—LiT
J.T. never will be ten. K. Dakos.—DaI
"Jack and Jill". Mother Goose.—EdGl—SuO—
    WaM
Jocelyn Ridley. M. Glenn.—GlBc
Knoxville, Tennessee. N. Giovanni.—DeS—SlM
Late afternoon. M. C. Livingston.—LiT
Lawanda's walk. E. Greenfield.—GrN
Leap and dance. Unknown.—HoS
Lemonade stand. M. C. Livingston.—KeT
Let's dress up. M. A. Hoberman.—KeT
The lifeguard. J. Dickey.—KnAs
The little bird ("My dear Daddie bought a
    mansion"). W. De La Mare.—DeR—MaP
A little girl's poem. G. Brooks.—JaP
Louleen's feelings. X. J. Kennedy.—KeK
A lullaby ("Sleep, child, lie quiet, let be"). J.
    Agee.—GoT
"Me, myself, and I". Unknown.—PrP—WiA
Mischief City. T. Jones-Wynne.—BoT
"Monday's child is fair of face". Mother Goose.—
    SuO—WaM
"Monday's child is red and spotty". C.
    McNaughton.—PrFo
Ms. Joan Gladstone, special education. M.
    Glenn.—GlBc
My father. M. A. Hoberman.—HoFa
"My mother says I'm sickening". J. Prelutsky.—
    PrFo
Nationhood. U. E. Perkins.—SlM
Neighborhood street. E. Greenfield.—GrN
Nerissa. E. Greenfield.—GrN
The new suit. N. Sanabria de Romero.—NyT
Ode to el guitarron. G. Soto.—SoNe
Ode to fireworks. G. Soto.—SoNe
Ode to La Llorona. G. Soto.—SoNe
Ode to la pinata. G. Soto.—SoNe
Ode to los chicharrones. G. Soto.—SoNe
Ode to Los Raspados. G. Soto.—SoNe
Ode to my library. G. Soto.—SoNe
Ode to Pablo's tennis shoes. G. Soto.—SoNe
Ode to the Mayor. G. Soto.—SoNe
"Oh, policeman, policeman". Unknown.—ScA
Old Mag. J. Hollingsworth-Barkley.—JaPr
On Mother's day. A. Fisher.—FiA—FoLe
"One little kid took a limo". J. Knight.—KnT
One, two, three, four m-o-t-h-e-r. F. Holman.—
    LiPm
An only child. M. A. Hoberman.—HoFa
Oranges ("The first time I walked"). G. Soto.—
    JaM—SoA
Papa loves baby. S. Smith.—ElW
The parent. O. Nash.—PrFo
Part I: I sang a song to Rosamund Rose. From A
    child's day. W. De La Mare.—DeR
The party's over. R. Edwards.—FoLe
Piano recital. M. C. Livingston.—LiR
Pick up your room. M. A. Hoberman.—HoFa
Playmate ("And because"). K. Wilson.—JaPr

Children and childhood.—*Continued*

Poor grandma. G. Nichols.—NiCo

"Pumpkin neba bear watermelan". Unknown.—LeCa

Puzzle. M. C. Livingston.—LiR

The question ("People always say to me"). K. Kuskin.—LiDd

The rain falling on west train tracks, Ohio. A. Adoff.—AdCh

Rules. K. Kuskin.—PrFo

Runaway teen. W. Stafford.—JaPr

Running. R. Wilbur.—KnAs

Sales talk for Annie. M. Bishop.—ElW

"Sea shell". M. C. Livingston.—LiT

The seller. E. Greenfield.—GrN

Sephina. W. De La Mare.—DeR

Shy. M. A. Hoberman.—HoFa

Silly Billy. M. Fatchen.—FaCm

Skater in blue. J. Parini.—KnAs

Skating in Pleasant Hill, Ohio. K. Iddings.—KnAs

Small wants. B. Padhi.—NyT

Sometimes even parents win. J. Ciardi.—CiH—LiLo

The straw. A. Adoff.—AdCh

System. R. L. Stevenson.—ElW

Taking down the space-trolley. X. J. Kennedy.—KeK

Televised. M. Angelou.—AnI

There was a man. P. Janowitz.—JaP

There was an old woman ("There was an old woman of Bumble Bhosey"). W. De La Mare.—DeR

"There was an old woman who lived in a shoe". Mother Goose.—EdGl—SuI—SuO—WaM

These yet to be United States. M. Angelou.—AnI

Things ("Went to the corner"). E. Greenfield.—SlM

This place. E. Greenfield.—GrU

Three thirty. A. Adoff.—AdCh

Thrum drew a small map. S. Musgrave.—BoT

Tide talk. M. Fatchen.—FaCm

Timmy and Tawanda. G. Brooks.—SlM

Tired Tim. W. De La Mare.—DeR—MaP

A toast for everybody who is growin. J. Berry.—BeW

Together. C. Mamchur.—BoT

The truants. W. De La Mare.—DeR—MaP

Victory banquet. S. B. Mathis.—MaR

Vistasp. G. Patel.—NyT

"Walk together children". From Walk together children. Unknown.—SuC

The way I really am. B. S. De Regniers.—DeW

We are seven. W. Wordsworth.—ElW

Were you ever fat like me. K. Dakos.—DaI

"When Buster Brown was one". Unknown.—WiA

Won't. W. De La Mare.—DeR

Working with mother. M. C. Livingston.—KeT—LiPm—LiR

Zora. J. Schell.—JaPr

"**Children** aren't happy with nothing to ignore". See The parent

"**Children,** children, please beware". See Milehigh Jeff the giant hare

Children lost. Max Fatchen.—FaCm

"**Children,** when was". See Napoleon

The **children's** hour. Henry Wadsworth Longfellow.—SuI

Children's rhymes. Langston Hughes.—SuC

A **child's** day, complete. Walter De La Mare
Part I: I sang a song to Rosamund Rose.—DeR
Part II: Softly, drowsily.—DeR
Part III: Little birds bathe.—DeR

Part IV: The queen of Arabia, Uanjinee.—DeR

Part V: England over.—DeR

Part VI: Thousands of years ago.—DeR

Part VII: When safe in to the fields Ann got.—DeR

Part VIII: When she was in her garden.—DeR

Part IX: There was an old woman who lived in the Fens.—DeR

Part X: This little morsel of morsels here.—DeR

Part XI: Now fie, o fie, how sly a face.—DeR

Part XII: Ann, upon the stroke of three.—DeR

Part XIII: As soon as ever twilight comes.—DeR

Part XIV: Now, dear me.—DeR

Part XV: Now, my dear, for gracious sake.—DeR

Part XVI: The king in slumber when he lies down.—DeR

Part XVII: Now through the dusk.—DeR

Part XVIII: He squats by the fire.—DeR

Part XIX: Sadly, o, sadly, the sweet bells of Baddeley.—DeR

Part XX: This brief day now over.—DeR

A **child's** dream. Frances Cornford.—ElW

Chimera. Penelope Scambly Schott.—WhDd

Chimes. See Bells

"**Chimney** squirrels". John Goldthwaite.—PrFo

Chimney sweeps
"Eaper Weaper, chimney sweeper". Unknown.—OpI
Sooeep. W. De La Mare.—DeR—MaP

Chimneys
"Chimney squirrels". J. Goldthwaite.—PrFo
"A flea and a fly in a flue". Unknown.—LiLo
A fly and a flea.—CII
"A fly and a flea flew up in a flue".—WiA
To raise a chimney. G. Young.—JaM

China
Cheung Chau festival. J. Kenward.—FoLe
Ching ming. I. Rawnsley.—FoLe
Digging for China. R. Wilbur.—SuI

Chinaware. See Tableware

Chinese dragon. Unknown.—WhDd

"A **Chinese** dragon's in the street". See Dragon dance

Chinese language
"Xiao Ming, Xiao Ming". Unknown.—YoS
"Little Ming, Little Ming".—YoS
"Xiao pi qiu, xiang jiao li". Unknown.—YoS
"A little ball, a banana, a pear".—YoS

Chinese New Year. Unknown.—LoFh

Chinese nursery rhymes. See Nursery rhymes—Chinese

Ch'ing, Liu Ch'ang
Snow on Lotus Mountain, tr. by Kenneth Rexroth.—GoT

Ching ming. Irene Rawnsley.—FoLe

The **chipmunk.** Randall Jarrell.—MoR
The chipmunk's day.—ElW

Chipmunks
The chipmunk. R. Jarrell.—MoR
The chipmunk's day.—ElW
Sunday afternoon under a warm blue sky. A. Adoff.—AdIn

The **chipmunk's** day. See The chipmunk

Chippewa Indians. See Indians of the Americas—Chippewa

Chips, one. Arnold Adoff.—AdCh

Chips, two. Arnold Adoff.—AdCh

Chips, three. Arnold Adoff.—AdCh

Chisoku
"The face of the dragonfly".—WhAa

Chit chat. William Jay Smith.—SmL

Chivalry. See Knights and knighthood

Choco cheers. Arnold Adoff.—AdCh
Chocolate
  Chips, one. A. Adoff.—AdCh
  Chips, two. A. Adoff.—AdCh
  Chips, three. A. Adoff.—AdCh
  Choco cheers. A. Adoff.—AdCh
  Chocolate dreams and chocolate schemes. A. Adoff.—AdCh
  Chocolate dreams, one. A. Adoff.—AdCh
  Chocolate dreams, two. A. Adoff.—AdCh
  Chocolate dreams, three. A. Adoff.—AdCh
  Chocolate dreams, four. A. Adoff.—AdCh
  Chocolate moose. W. J. Smith.—SmL
  Chocolate rabbit. X. J. Kennedy.—KeK
  Facing Pennsylvania. A. Adoff.—AdCh
  Her she bar. A. Adoff.—AdCh
  I could never convince any of the other members. A. Adoff.—AdCh
  I don't mean to say I am Martian, Morkian. A. Adoff.—AdCh
  I love my mom, I love my pop, I love my dog, I love my sheep. A. Adoff.—AdCh
  I meet sweet Sue for a walk on a cold and sunny afternoon. A. Adoff.—AdCh
  In public, I pick a piece or two from the plate. A. Adoff.—AdCh
  In this last class before lunch, I close my eyes. A. Adoff.—AdCh
  Mathematical metric conversion version. A. Adoff.—AdCh
  A nature story. A. Adoff.—AdCh
  The old math, two. A. Adoff.—AdCh
  Patience. B. Katz.—LoFh
  Why did the fireman. A. Adoff.—AdCh
  You are walking along eating. A. Adoff.—AdCh
Chocolate dreams and chocolate schemes. Arnold Adoff.—AdCh
Chocolate dreams, one. Arnold Adoff.—AdCh
Chocolate dreams, two. Arnold Adoff.—AdCh
Chocolate dreams, three. Arnold Adoff.—AdCh
Chocolate dreams, four. Arnold Adoff.—AdCh
Chocolate dreams, five. Arnold Adoff.—AdCh
Chocolate dreams, six thirty. Arnold Adoff.—AdCh
"**Chocolate** Easter bunny". See Patience
Chocolate moose. William Jay Smith.—SmL
"**Chocolate** or butter". See Birthday cake
Chocolate rabbit. X. J. Kennedy.—KeK
"**Chocolate** sun". See Chocolate dreams, two
"**Chomp**". See The ultimate product
Chook-chook-chook. Unknown.—CoE
"**Chook,** chook, chook-chook-chook". See Chook-chook-chook
Choosing
  "All around the butter dish". Unknown.—CoM—WiA
  "Birds of a feather flock together". Mother Goose.—WaM
    Birds of a feather.—ClI
  "Birds of a feather flock together, and so do pigs". Unknown.—OpI
  "Come times sometimes". J. Carson.—CaS
  "The day I married, my mother". J. Carson.—CaS
  "Don't talk to me about no options, I'm poor". J. Carson.—CaS
  Evan King. M. Glenn.—GlBc
  "I used to work down". J. Carson.—CaS
  "Ickle, ockle, blue bockle". Mother Goose.—WaM
  "I'd rather have fingers than toes". G. Burgess.—LiLo
  In the middle. M. C. Livingston.—LiT
  Lullaby for Suzanne. M. Stillman.—KeT
  The making of dragons. J. Yolen.—YoFf

"A matron well known in Montclair". W. J. Smith.—LiLo—SmL
The ousel cock. R. Hodgson.—ElW
Pets. D. Pettiward.—CoAz
"A robin and a robin's son". Mother Goose.—ClI—WaM
Runaway teen. W. Stafford.—JaPr
"Sally, Sally Waters, sprinkle in the pan". Mother Goose.—WaM
Shoes. V. Worth.—WoAl
So I'm proud. J. Little.—LiHe
Tube time. E. Merriam.—KeT—MeS
The wraggle taggle gypsies. Unknown.—ElW
Choosing craft. May Swenson.—KnAs
Choosing up rhymes. See Counting-out rhymes
"**Chopped** for". See Tree fire
Chore boy. Jim Thomas.—LiPm
Chou, Shen
  Reading in the autumn.—SuI
Choudhurry, Nurunnessa
  The sun witness.—AgL
The **chow** hound. John Ciardi.—CiH
Chowdhury, Kabir
  On my birthday, tr.—NyT
  Poetry was like this, tr.—NyT
The **christening** ("The bells chime clear"). Walter De La Mare.—DeR
The **christening** ("What shall I call"). Alan Alexander Milne.—LaM
Christenings
  The christening ("The bells chime clear"). W. De La Mare.—DeR
Christianity. See also Jesus Christ (about)
  On being brought from Africa to America. P. Wheatley.—SuC
Christmas. See also Christmas carols; Christmas trees; Santa Claus
  Angel tunes. J. Yolen.—YoHa
  Candy cane. V. Worth.—WoA
  Carol of the brown king. L. Hughes.—GoA
  Cat toys. V. Worth.—WoA
  Christmas. M. Chute.—LoFh
  "Christmas comes but once a year". Mother Goose.—WaM
  Christmas dinner. V. Worth.—WoA
  Christmas eve. V. Worth.—WoA
  Christmas eve night. J. Cotton.—FoLe
  Christmas eve rhyme. C. MacCullers.—GoA
  "Christmas is coming and the geese are getting fat". Mother Goose.—OpI—SuO—WaM
    Christmas is coming.—HoS
  Christmas lights. V. Worth.—WoAl
  A Christmas lullaby. M. Hillert.—PlW
  Christmas morning. V. Worth.—WoA
  Christmas mouse. A. Fisher.—FiA—FiH
  Christmas night. V. Worth.—WoA
  Christmas scene. V. Worth.—LiPg
  Christmas wish. T. Johnston.—LiPf
  Counting sheep ("I am a poor shepherd"). J. Yolen.—YoHa
  Creche. V. Worth.—WoA
  Crown of light festival. D. Bateson.—FoLe
  Day before Christmas. M. Chute.—DeS
  December ("I like days"). A. Fisher.—FiA—GoA
  December ("This is the month"). A. Bonner.—FoLe
  Decorations. V. Worth.—WoA
  "Do rabbits have Christmas". A. Fisher.—FiA
  Doll. M. C. Livingston.—KeT
  Early December. V. Worth.—WoA
  Emily Jane. L. E. Richards.—ElW
  "Knock at the knocker". Unknown.—OpI

Chute, Marchette—*Continued*
Our tree.—DeS
The swing ("The wind blows strong and the swing rides free").—BaW
Thanksgiving ("I'm glad that I was good today").—LoFh
Weather ("It is a windy day").—DeS

Ciardi, John
About learning things the hard way.—CiH
About the teeth of sharks.—CoAz—PrFo
All right, do it your way.—CiH
And they met in the middle.—CiH
April fool.—CiH—LiLo
At the beach ("Johnny, Johnny, let go of that crab").—PrFo
Be kind to dumb animals.—CiH—LiLo
The cat heard the cat-bird.—LaCc
"Chang McTang McQuarter Cat".—LaCc
The chow hound.—CiH
Do you know anyone like him.—CiH
The dollar dog.—LiDp
The elephant boy.—CiH
The fast fiddler.—CiH
For someone on his tenth birthday.—LoFh
Friendship ("There once were two backcountry geezers").—CiH
Goodbye please.—CiH
The Halloween house.—CiH—LiLo
He saved a lot of time by not working.—CiH
He was brave, but not for long.—CiH
Heights made him dizzy.—CiH
Ho hum.—CiH
Home sweet home.—CiH
The hopeful trout, poor fish.—CiH
How to tell a tiger.—PrFo
How to tell the top of a hill.—DeS
I am home, said the turtle.—CoAz
I wouldn't.—KeT—LaM—MoS
Iron men and wooden ships.—CiH
It came from outer space.—CiH—LiLo
Keeping busy is better than nothing.—CiH—LiLo
The light house keeper's white mouse.—LaM—MoS
Like a fire eating dragon.—CiH
Mummy slept late and daddy fixed breakfast.—LiPf—PrFo
The music master.—CiH
My cat, Mrs. Lick-a-chin.—DeS—LaCc
The mystery ("There was a young fellow named Chet").—CiH
Paying through the nose.—CiH
The poor boy was wrong.—CiH
Rest in peace.—CiH
Serves him right.—CiH
Some cook.—PrFo
Sometimes even parents win.—CiH—LiLo
"Sometimes running".—MoR
Speedy Sam.—CiH
Stop squirming.—CiH
That fish was just too fussy.—CiH
There once was an owl.—LiIf
There seems to be a problem.—CiH
"There was a young fellow named Shear".—LiLo
They had a point to make.—CiH
The thingamajig.—CiH
The thinker.—CiH—LiLo
What Johnny told me.—KeT
When you are there at all, that is.—CiH
Willis C. Sick.—CiH
Win some, lose some.—CiH
Wouldn't you.—MoS
The **cicada**. Basho, tr. by Tze-si Huang.—DeI

Cicadas. Paul Fleischman.—FlJ
"The **cicadas** sing". Ono No Komachi, tr. by Jane Hirschfield.—GoT
"**Cinderella** dressed in yella". Unknown.—ScA
"**Cinderella**, dressed in yellow". Unknown.—WiA
"**Cinnamon** shoot". See "Pimpolla de canela"
"**Cinquain**". See On being introduced to you
"**Ciranda**, cirandinha". Unknown.—YoS
"Circle, little circle".—YoS
"**Circle**, little circle". See "Ciranda, cirandinha"
"**Circle** me Lord". David Adam.—StP
"**Circled** by trees, ringed with the faded folding chairs". See The tennis
Circles
Circles ("I am speaking of circles"). M. C. Livingston.—JaP—LiT
Circles ("The things to draw with compasses"). H. Behn.—LiDd
A kiss is round. B. Budney.—MoS
The life of a man is a circle. Black Elk.—SnD
Circles ("I am speaking of circles"). Myra Cohn Livingston.—JaP—LiT
Circles ("The things to draw with compasses"). Harry Behn.—LiDd
Circles ("Two loaves of bread are very well"). Margaret Mahy.—MaN
"**Circling** by the fire". See Stories
Circular compositions
Endless dialogue. Unknown.—WiA
Endless riddle. Unknown.—WiA
"I know a man named Michael Finnegan". Unknown.—WiA
A southern circular saying. Unknown.—WiA
Story without end. Unknown.—WiA
"Who put the overalls in Mrs. Murphy's chowder". Unknown.—ScA
Endless chant.—WiA
Circus. See also Clowns
Circus clown. M. C. Livingston.—LiNe
Circus dreams. X. J. Kennedy.—KeK
A circus garland. R. Field.—ElW
The circus, or one view of it. T. Spencer.—MoR
Circus time. E. Merriam.—MeS
Forty performing bananas. J. Prelutsky.—PrFo
"Loose and limber". A. Lobel.—PrFo
Two performing elephants. D. H. Lawrence.—CaB
Circus clown. Myra Cohn Livingston.—LiNe
Circus dreams. X. J. Kennedy.—KeK
A **circus** garland. Rachel Field.—ElW
"The **circus** is coming to town". See Circus time
The **circus**, or one view of it. Theodore Spencer.—MoR
Circus time. Eve Merriam.—MeS
Cities and city life. See also names of cities, as New York
Alley cat school. F. Asch.—LaCc
Bay breasted barge bird. W. J. Smith.—SmL
Bread and cherries. W. De La Mare.—DeR—MaP
Breath pon wind. J. Berry.—BeW
Brickyard. P. B. Janeczko.—JaB
Cacophony. E. Merriam.—MeCh
"The cars in Caracas". J. Updike.—MoR
A city ditty. E. Merriam.—MeP
City lights. R. Field.—DeT
The city mouse and the garden mouse. C. G. Rossetti.—LaM
City nomad. J. Berry.—BeW
City rain. V. Schonborg.—LaN
City to surf. D. Bateson.—FoLe
Cool time rhythm rap. J. Berry.—BeW
The country mouse and the city mouse. R. S. Sharpe.—ElW

Clean. Lance Newman.—KnAs
Cleaned the crocodile's teeth. Nyabuk Col, tr. by
   Terese Svoboda.—NyT
Cleaning the well. Fred Chappell.—JaPr
Cleanliness. See also Bathing
   Cat bath ("She always tries"). A. Fisher.—CoAz
   Dickery Dean. D. Lee.—KeT
   "Every morning". G. Swede.—BoT
   "A lady who lives there close to me". J. Carson.—
      CaS
   "Little Polly Flinders". Mother Goose.—SuO—
      WaM
   Marguerite. Unknown.—PrFo
   A mouse and her house. A. Fisher.—FiH
   Part III: Little birds bathe. From A child's day.
      W. De La Mare.—DeR
   Pig ("Pigs are always awfully dirty"). W. J.
      Smith.—SmL
   Raccoon ("The raccoon wears a black mask"). K.
      Rexroth.—CoAz
   "Sam, Sam, dirty old man". Unknown.—CoM—
      OpI
   "Shirt dirt". B. McMillan.—McP
   Spell to banish a pimple. J. Agard.—AgL
   "There was a young lady of Crete". Unknown.—
      LiLo—PrP
      A young lady of Crete.—PrFo
   "Who are you, a dirty old man". Mother
      Goose.—OpI—WaM
A **clear** midnight. Walt Whitman.—HoVo
"**Clearers** of thornbush". See To the ancestors
Clement, Jennifer
   Horse by moonlight, tr.—NyT
Clemente, Roberto (about)
   The great one. T. Clark.—MoA
Clergy
   At the piano. A. Hudgins.—JaM
Clerihews
   "Beatrix Potter". W. J. Smith.—SmL
   "Edmund Clerihew Bentley". W. J. Smith.—SmL
   "Lady Hester Stanhope". W. J. Smith.—SmL
   "Sir Walter Raleigh". W. J. Smith.—SmL
   "What difference did it make to Longfellow". W.
      J. Smith.—SmL
   "William Penn". W. J. Smith.—SmL
"**Cleveland** and them hung out in that Watts cafe
   used". See Poetry lesson number one
"**Clever** Clem went out of doors". See Dinosaur
   department
"A **clever** gorilla named Gus". Jack Prelutsky.—PrP
"**Click**, clack". See Traveling
"**Clifford**, we've grown too far apart". See Postcards
   of the hanging
Clifton, Lucille
   All kinds of grands.—LiPg
   April.—LiDd
   Counting sheep ("1, 2, my daddy, who").—LiPf
   The 1st.—ElW
   Good times.—ElW
   Jackie Robinson.—KnAs—MoA
   "Love rejected".—SuC
   "My natural mama".—LiPm
   September.—SlM
   "Still it was nice".—ElW
Climbing
   Another mountain. A. Oyewole.—SlM
   Apple tree. M. C. Livingston.—LiR
   Birches. R. Frost.—SuI
   Companions. Unknown.—OpT
   How to tell the top of a hill. J. Ciardi.—DeS
   Shakes and ladders. M. Fatchen.—FaCm
   Sneaking in the state fair. K. Fitzpatrick.—MoR

"There was a young lady from Woosester".
   Unknown.—LiLo
"**Clinging** to our stucco wall". See Snails
Clobber the lobber. Felicia Lamport.—MoR
Clock. Valerie Worth.—KeT—WoAl
"The **clock** stands still". Unknown.—WiA
Clocks and watches
   Clock. V. Worth.—KeT—WoAl
   "The clock stands still". Unknown.—WiA
   Cogs and gears and wheels and springs. J.
      Sweeney.—MoS
   "Hickory dickory dock". Mother Goose.—EdGl—
      SuO—WaM
   "Hickory dickory dock". Unknown.—WiA
   "Round as a doughnut". Unknown.—WiA
   "A silly young fellow named Ben". J. Prelutsky.—
      LiLo—PrP
   Time. B. J. Esbensen.—EsW
   The watch ("I wakened on my hot, hard bed"). F.
      Cornford.—MoR
   "What's hearty as a heart, round as a ring". From
      Riddle poems. J. Berry.—BeW
"The **clod** of earth in his shovel". See Tending the
   garden
"**Close** by". See Telephone poles
Close to home. Frank Steele.—JaM
"**Close** your eyes". See Pussy willows
"**Closed**, I am a mystery". Myra Cohn Livingston.—
   LiMh
"**Closed**, it sleeps". See Safety pin
"A **closed** window looks down". See Ka 'Ba
Closet. Myra Cohn Livingston.—LiNe
The **closing** of the rodeo. William Jay Smith.—
   KnAs
Clothes ("I like new clothes"). Jean Little.—LiHe
Clothes ("My mother keeps on telling me").
   Elizabeth Jennings.—AgL
"The **clothes** that get clean". See L is for laundry
Clothespins. Stuart Dybek.—KnAs
Clothing and dress. See also names of clothing, as
   Boots and shoes
   And they met in the middle. J. Ciardi.—CiH
   Around my room. W. J. Smith.—KeT—LiDd—
      SmL
   As soon as it's fall. A. Fisher.—FiA
   Attire. E. Merriam.—MeCh
   "Beneath this stone, a lump of clay". Unknown.—
      BaH
   Beware ("When a cub, unaware being bare").
      From Animalimericks. E. Merriam.—MeS
   "Blue legs". M. C. Livingston.—LiMh
   The buckle. W. De La Mare.—DeR
   Butterfly ("What is a butterfly, at best"). B.
      Franklin.—WhAa
   "Button to the chin". Unknown.—ScA
   Chester's undoing. J. Holder.—PrFo
   Child in a blue linen dress. H. Sorrells.—JaM
   Circus clown. M. C. Livingston.—LiNe
   Clothes ("I like new clothes"). J. Little.—LiHe
   Clothes ("My mother keeps on telling me"). E.
      Jennings.—AgL
   The coat. D. Lee.—KeT
   Coat hangers. V. Worth.—WoAl
   "Daisy and Lily". From Waltz. E. Sitwell.—MoR
   "Dicky, Dicky Dout". Unknown.—OpI
   "Diddle diddle dumpling, my son John". Mother
      Goose.—SuO—WaM
      Diddle diddle dumpling.—HoS
   Dress code, a sedimental journey. J. Yolen.—
      YoDd
   Dressing a baby. Unknown.—OpT
   The Easter parade. W. J. Smith.—LoFh—SmL

Clothing and dress.—*Continued*
Enigma sartorial. L. W. Rhu.—WhAa
The flower's perfume. A. Bryan.—BrS
Furry bear. A. A. Milne.—DeS
Green velvet suit. Alvaro.—AgL
A Halloween problem. S. Stone.—LiHp
The happy sheep. W. Thorley.—CoAz
"Hector Protector was dressed all in green".
  Mother Goose.—SuO
How to trick a chicken. J. P. Lewis.—LeA
Hunting. J. Sheedy.—KnAs
I can't go back to school. M. P. Hearn.—JaP
I once dressed up. R. Fisher.—BaH
"I see London". Unknown.—CoM
"I'm a little Hindoo". Unknown.—WiA
Itinerant. E. Merriam.—MeCh
Jacob and Joseph. Unknown.—OpT
Jim-jam pyjamas. G. Wilson.—CoAz
John Wesley. Unknown.—OpT
"Left foot, right foot". Mother Goose.—WaM
Let's dress up. M. A. Hoberman.—KeT
Letter from a witch named Flo. J. Yolen.—YoBe
"Little Miss Donnet". Mother Goose.—WaM
"Little Miss Lily, you're dreadfully silly". Mother
  Goose.—WaM
"Little Polly Flinders". Mother Goose.—SuO—
  WaM
The man in red. E. Greenfield.—GrU
Marvin Pickett. M. Glenn.—KnAs
"A matron well known in Montclair". W. J.
  Smith.—LiLo—SmL
"Miss Mary Mack, Mack, Mack". Unknown.—
  CoM
"The morns are meeker than they were". E.
  Dickinson.—SuI
    Autumn.—DeT
My body. W. J. Smith.—SmL
My dress is old. Unknown.—SnD
"My party dress". From Party dress, party shirt.
  M. C. Livingston.—LiBp
"My party shirt". From Party dress, party shirt.
  M. C. Livingston.—LiBp
"My Scottish great granduncle Milt's". X. J.
  Kennedy.—KeGh
A new dress. R. Dallas.—NyT
New jacket. M. A. Hoberman.—HoFa
The new suit. N. Sanabria de Romero.—NyT
"A nip for new". Unknown.—OpI
Notions. E. Merriam.—MeCh
Ode to a day in the country. G. Soto.—SoNe
"One little piggy wore leggings". J. Knight.—KnT
"Paddy O'Flynn had no breeches to wear".
  Unknown.—WiA
"The panteater". W. Cole.—JaP
Part IV: The queen of Arabia, Uanjinee. From A
  child's day. W. De La Mare.—DeR
Part XIII: As soon as ever twilight comes. From
  A child's day. W. De La Mare.—DeR
Part XVI: The king in slumber when he lies
  down. From A child's day. W. De La Mare.—
  DeR
Penguin ("I think it must be very nice"). W. J.
  Smith.—SmL
Polar bear ("Every time"). L. Blair.—HoT
Rags. V. Worth.—WoAl
"Red stockings, blue stockings". Mother Goose.—
  WaM
The reluctant hero or barefoot in the snow. M.
  Mahy.—MaN
A story about Afiya. J. Berry.—BeW
"There once was a person of Benin". C.
  Monkhouse.—LiLo

"There she goes, there she goes". Unknown.—
  ScA—WiA
"There was a man dressed all in cheese". A.
  Lobel.—PrFo
"There was a young man of Bengal". Unknown.—
  LiLo—PrP
    There was a young man.—ClI
"There was an old man of the Cape". R. L.
  Stevenson.—LiLo
"There was an old man of Toulon". W. J.
  Smith.—SmL
The three foxes. A. A. Milne.—DeT
"A thrifty young fellow of Shoreham".
  Unknown.—LiLo
"Tra-la-la-boom-de-ay". Unknown.—CoM
Uncle Fred. M. Fatchen.—FaCm
"Victor wore a velvet cape". J. Prelutsky.—PrBe
"We each wore half a horse". J. Prelutsky.—FoLe
"We're all jolly boys". Mother Goose.—WaM
"What difference did it make to Longfellow". W.
  J. Smith.—SmL
Whiskers meets Polly. M. Stillman.—KeT
"The **cloud** tonight". See Summer full moon
Clouds
Clouds ("Don't trust the wind"). B. J. Esbensen.—
  EsW
Clouds ("White sheep, white sheep"). C. G.
  Rossetti.—DeS
Clouds ("Wonder where they come from"). A.
  Fisher.—FiA
Clouds are black. A. Adoff.—AdIn
The dark and falling summer. D. Schwartz.—
  GoT—SuI
Dragon smoke. L. Moore.—DeS—DeT
First solo. W. McDonald.—MoR
Listening to baseball in the car. G. Mazur.—KnAs
The sky is vast. P. Khadun.—NyT
Song ("Don't you ever"). Unknown.—DeT
Summer full moon. J. Kirkup.—LaN
Thunder. W. De La Mare.—DeR
"When the clouds". Mother Goose.—WaM
Clouds ("Don't trust the wind"). Barbara Juster
  Esbensen.—EsW
Clouds ("White sheep, white sheep"). Christina
  Georgina Rossetti.—DeS
Clouds ("Wonder where they come from"). Aileen
  Fisher.—FiA
Clouds are black. Arnold Adoff.—AdIn
"**Clouds** are flying over the moon". See What all the
  owls know
"**Clouds** of flies when the hot dogs are done". See
  Volunteers two
Clouds on the sea. Ruth Dallas.—NyT
Clough, Arthur Hugh
"Say not the struggle nought availeth".—ElW
"A **clown** came to Pat's party". See Birthday clown
Clowns
Birthday clown. M. C. Livingston.—LiBp
Circus clown. M. C. Livingston.—LiNe
Co-op-er-ate. Beatrice Schenk De Regniers.—DeW
Coach. Sharon Bell Mathis.—MaR
"The **coach** has taught her how to swing". See
  Instruction
Coal
First foot. I. Serraillier.—FoLe
Coals. Walter De La Mare.—DeR
The **coat.** Dennis Lee.—KeT
Coat hangers. Valerie Worth.—WoAl
Coati-mundi. William Jay Smith.—SmL
Coatsworth, Elizabeth
Early dark.—PlW
Mountain brook.—FrS

Coatsworth, Elizabeth—*Continued*
The mouse ("I heard a mouse").—LaM
On a night of snow.—LaCc
The open door.—KeT—LaCc
Rain poem.—DeS
Rhyme.—MoS
Roosters.—WhAs
"Sing a song of kittens".—LaCc
The swallows.—KeT
"Violets, daffodils".—KeT
"**Cobalt** and umber and ultramarine". See The paint box
"**Cobbler,** cobbler, mend my shoe". Mother Goose.—WaM
Cobblers
At the keyhole. W. De La Mare.—DeR—MaP
"Cobbler, cobbler, mend my shoe". Mother Goose.—WaM
"En la puerta del cielo". Unknown.—DeA
"At heaven's gate".—DeA
"The **Cobbles** live in the house next door". See Neighbors
Cobwebs
No jewel. W. De La Mare.—DeR
Precious. M. Fatchen.—FaCm
Spider web. M. C. Livingston.—LiT
"**Cock-a-doodle-doo**". Mother Goose.—SuO—WaM
Cock, cock, cock, cock. Unknown.—CII
"A **cock** it was, in the stable yard". See Pigs
The **cockatoo.** John Gardner.—PrFo
"The **cockatoo** is widely known". See The cockatoo
"**Cockatoos** are talkative". See I say
"**Cockbendy's** lying sick". See The cure
Cockles and mussels. Unknown.—ElW
"A **cockroach** hasn't many friends". See Just friends
Cockroaches
Just friends. M. Fatchen.—FaCm
Cocks. See Chickens
"**Cocks** crowing". See Early country village morning
Coconuts
"Boy is sent for something". From Riddle poems. J. Berry.—BeW
Drinking water coconut. G. Nichols.—NiCo
Locked in. I. Leckius.—NyT
Code blue. Billie Lou Cantwell.—JaPr
"The **codfish** lays ten thousand eggs". Unknown.—PrP
Coelophysis. Jack Prelutsky.—PrT
"**Coelophysis** was a hunter". See Coelophysis
"**Coffee** spice chocolate ackee". See Sunny market song
Coffeepot face. Aileen Fisher.—FiA
Cogs and gears and wheels and springs. Jacqueline Sweeney.—MoS
Cohen, J. M.
Vorobyev Hills, tr.—GoT
"**Coils** the robot". Floria Herrero Pinto, tr. by Barbara Chacon.—NyT
Coins. Valerie Worth.—WoAl
"**Coins** are pleasant". See Coins
Col, Nyabuk
Cleaned the crocodile's teeth, tr. by Terese Svoboda.—NyT
Cold
Chrysalis diary. P. Fleischman.—FlJ
"Cold cold shivery cold me in". E. Merriam.—MeY
December ("I like days"). A. Fisher.—FiA—GoA
Dragon smoke. L. Moore.—DeS—DeT
"An Eskimo sleeps in his white bearskin". Unknown.—PrP
A frosty night. R. Graves.—ElW

"The **gnomes** of Nome". X. J. Kennedy.—KeGh
Grandmother in winter. X. J. Kennedy.—LiPg
Hot milk. X. J. Kennedy.—KeK
It's great when you get in. E. O'Neill.—KnAs
"The more it snows". A. A. Milne.—DeS
Mrs. Burns' lullaby. Unknown.—OpT
"The north wind doth blow". Mother Goose.—DeS—SuO—WaM
"The sodden moss sinks underfoot when we cross half-frozen bays and". A. Debeljak.—NyT
"There once was a boy of Quebec". R. Kipling.—LiLo
"When icicles hang by the wall". From Love's labour's lost. W. Shakespeare.—LiIf
Winter.—ElW
Windigo spirit. K. Stange.—BoT
Winter monkey. Basho.—DeI
Winter pause, Mt. Liberty, N.H. M. Robbins.—MoR
"**Cold** and raw the north winds blow". Mother Goose.—WaM
"A **cold** and starry darkness moans". See Ghosts
"**Cold** cold shivery cold me in". Eve Merriam.—MeY
"A **cold** coming we had of it". See Journey of the Magi
"A **cold** day, though only October". See October
"**Cold** meat, mutton pies". Unknown.—OpI
"**Cold** told me, November 13". See Chrysalis diary
Cole, William
Banananananananana.—PrFo
Here comes the band.—DeS
"My zoo is open to all".—CoAz
News story.—PrFo
"The panteater".—JaP
Piggy.—PrFo
Sneaky Bill.—PrFo
Some sights sometimes seen and seldom seen.—KeT
Summer doings.—HoGo
Thorny.—CoAz
Coleman, Wanda
Poetry lesson number one.—JaPr
Coleridge, Samuel Taylor
Answer to a child's question.—CaB—ElW
"He prayeth best, who loveth best". See The rime of the ancient mariner
The rime of the ancient mariner, complete.—ElW
The rime of the ancient mariner, sels.—ElW
"He prayeth best, who loveth best".—StP
Coleridge Jackson. Maya Angelou.—AnI
"**Coleridge** Jackson had nothing". See Coleridge Jackson
"**Colin,** Colin, Colin". Unknown.—OpT
Collecting. See Hobbies
Collecting things. X. J. Kennedy.—KeK
Collector bird. William Jay Smith.—SmL
"The **collector,** I am told, exists". See Collector bird
"A **collegiate** damsel named Breeze". Unknown.—LiLo
Collins, Billy
High stick.—KnAs
Collins, William
Captain Molly.—SuI
Color. Langston Hughes.—SlM
Colorado
Rocky Mountains, Colorado. M. C. Livingston.—LiNe
Colors
Apples ("Some people say that apples are red"). W. J. Smith.—SmL
"Black, black, sit on a tack". Unknown.—WiA

Conduct of life.—*Continued*
Strong men, riding horses. G. Brooks.—SuC
Stronger lessons. W. Whitman.—HoVo
Sun is shining. B. Marley.—AgL
The sun witness. N. Choudhurry.—AgL
Take away some but leave some. J. Berry.—BeW
"Teach me, Father, how to be". E. Markham.—StP
"Teach me, my God and King". G. Herbert.—StP
"They furnish shade to others". Unknown.—StP
"This train don't carry no gamblers, this train". Unknown.—StP
"'Tis the gift to be simple". Unknown.—StP
"To all this there are rules, the players must". From Watching football on TV. H. Nemerov.—KnAs
To the field goal kicker in a slump. L. Pastan.—KnAs
To you. W. Whitman.—HoVo
Try, try again. T. H. Palmer.—SuI
Un-negative. E. Merriam.—MeCh
A warbler. W. De La Mare.—DeR
"Wash and wipe together". Unknown.—WiA
We must be polite. C. Sandburg.—DeS
Weather ("Whether the weather be fine"). Unknown.—SuI
What do we do with a variation. J. Berry.—BeW
What happens. E. Fried.—AgL
"A wise old owl lived in an oak". Mother Goose.—LiIf
A wise old owl (". . . sat in an oak").—ClI
Young soul. I. A. Baraka.—SuC
Zinnias. V. Worth.—WoAl
"The **conductor,** when he receives a fare". See Punch, boys, punch
Confederate States of America. See United States—History—Civil War
Confession to Mrs. Robert L. Snow. Gary Soto.—JaPr
Confidence. Martha Baird.—LaCc
Conkling, Hilda
Dandelion ("O little soldier with the golden helmet").—DeT
Gift ("This is mint and here are three pinks").—LiPm
Little snail.—DeS
Connell, Charles
"Doctor Who, I am forced to admit".—LiLo
Conscience. See also Duty
Roscoe. P. B. Janeczko.—JaB
Conservation
For forest. G. Nichols.—NiCo
"**Consider** the penguin". See Enigma sartorial
"The **constant** cry against an old order". See Polo ponies practicing
Constantinople. Unknown.—CoM
Constellations. See also Milky Way
Constipation. Ronald Wallace.—JaM
"A **contentious** old person named Reagan". William Jay Smith.—SmL
Contentment. See also Discontent
"As we are so wonderfully done with each other". K. Patchen.—GoU
"Cold cold shivery cold me in". E. Merriam.—MeY
The country mouse and the city mouse. R. S. Sharpe.—ElW
Haunted ("The rabbit in his burrow keeps"). W. De La Mare.—DeR
I dream of a place. W. De La Mare.—DeR

"I think I could turn and live with animals, they are so placid". From Song of myself. W. Whitman.—HoVo
In praise of a contented mind. E. Dyer.—ElW (unat.)
Looking around, believing. G. Soto.—SoA
Ode to los chicharrones. G. Soto.—SoNe
"Often we are foolish". Unknown.—ScA
The old man's comforts and how he gained them. R. Southey.—ElW
On a cat ageing. A. Gray.—CaB
Part XII: Ann, upon the stroke of three. From A child's day. W. De La Mare.—DeR
South ("Today's cool asphalt . . . where had the cars gone"). T. Gunn.—ElW
Worms and the wind. C. Sandburg.—CaB
Contingency. Archie Randolph Ammons.—ElW
"**Continually,** a bell rings in my heart". See Wanting to move
"The **convent** yard seems larger than before". See The mad nun
Conversation
Bird watcher. J. Yolen.—YoBi
Conversation. Buson.—DeS
Endless dialogue. Unknown.—WiA
Grandmother. S. Shirazie.—NyT
"I have just hung up, why did he telephone". M. Quoist.—StP
An important conversation. B. S. De Regniers.—DeW
"Mississippi said to Missouri". Unknown.—WiA
Owls talking. D. McCord.—LiIf
"Said Arlene Francis to Granville Hicks". W. J. Smith.—SmL
"Said Dorothy Hughes to Helen Hocking". W. J. Smith.—SmL
"Said General Shoup to Adja Yunkers". W. J. Smith.—SmL
"Said Justice Douglas to Douglass Cater". W. J. Smith.—SmL
"Said Marcia Brown to Carlos Baker". W. J. Smith.—SmL
"Said Ogden Nash to Phyllis McGinley". W. J. Smith.—SmL
The sugar lady. F. Asch.—DeT
The telephone. R. Frost.—SuI
A token of unspoken. E. Merriam.—MeCh
A true account of talking to the sun at Fire Island. F. O'Hara.—ElW
"What's your name". Unknown.—OpI
Conversation. Buson.—DeS
"**Coo,** ah, coo". Unknown.—SnD
"**Coo,** coo, coo". Unknown.—PrP
"**Coo-oo,** coo-oo". See Pigeon and wren
Cook, Iona
"My mouth is a horse's mouth", tr.—NyT
Cook, Stanley
Easter.—FoLe
Hallowe'en ("Hallowe'en, they say").—FoLe
The lord mayor's parade.—FoLe
Mothering Sunday.—FoLe
Ramadan.—FoLe
"Ramadan".—FoLe
St. David's Day ("The land returns from winter").—FoLe
"**Cook** in a dudgeon, aggrieved against the boss". See Whodunnit
Cookies. See Cakes and cookies
Cooks and cooking. See also names of foods, as Cakes and cookies
Alas, alack. W. De La Mare.—DeR—MaP
All right, do it your way. J. Ciardi.—CiH

Cooks and cooking.—*Continued*
Apple scoop. E. Glen.—LiPg
Berries. W. De La Mare.—DeR—MaP
"Betty Botter bought some butter". Mother Goose.—PrP—SuO
Canapes a la poste. W. J. Smith.—SmL
Catherine. K. Kuskin.—HoS
Chocolate dreams and chocolate schemes. A. Adoff.—AdCh
Chocolate dreams, five. A. Adoff.—AdCh
Chocolate moose. W. J. Smith.—SmL
"The day I married, my mother". J. Carson.—CaS
"Five little monsters". E. Merriam.—HoS
The gingerbread grandma. J. C. Thomas.—LiPg
Hot and cold tin can surprise. W. J. Smith.—SmL
"It was a Saturday and my mother was cooking". J. Carson.—CaS
"It's not me". J. Carson.—CaS
A lady in Madrid. N. M. Bodecker.—LiLo
Licorice. J. P. Duggan.—BoT
"Mix a pancake". C. G. Rossetti.—LiDd
Molly Mock Turtle. W. J. Smith.—SmL
"Mother made a seedy cake". Unknown.—OpI
Mummy slept late and daddy fixed breakfast. J. Ciardi.—LiPf—PrFo
"My mother made a chocolate cake". Unknown.—WiA
Ode to La Tortilla. G. Soto.—SoNe
"Oh dear me". Unknown.—OpI
"On Christmas Eve I turned the spit". Mother Goose.—WaM
The Paignton Christmas pudding. J. Yolen.—YoHa
The pancake collector. J. Prelutsky.—PrFo
Pie. V. Worth.—WoAl
"The Queen of Hearts". Mother Goose.—EdGl—SuO
"A querulous cook from Pomona". W. J. Smith.—SmL
Recipe for a hippopotamus sandwich. S. Silverstein.—PrFo
Recipe for Thanksgiving Day soup. D. Farmiloe.—BoT
The remarkable cake. M. Mahy.—MaN
Rhinoceros stew. M. Luton.—PrFo
Ruth. P. B. Janeczko.—JaB
"Said Arlene Francis to Granville Hicks". W. J. Smith.—SmL
"Snowflake souffle". X. J. Kennedy.—PrFo
Some cook. J. Ciardi.—PrFo
The spaghetti nut. J. Prelutsky.—DeS
"There was an old lady of Rye". Unknown.—LiLo
"Up the ladder and down the wall". Unknown.—OpI
"Wake up, Jacob". Unknown.—WiA
What you don't know about food. F. P. Heide.—HeG
When it's Thanksgiving. A. Fisher.—FiA
"While, unwatched, the soup pot boils". X. J. Kennedy.—KeFb
"Who put the overalls in Mrs. Murphy's chowder". Unknown.—ScA
Endless chant.—WiA
"With wild mushrooms Madge had found". X. J. Kennedy.—KeFb
Cool time rhythm rap. James Berry.—BeW
Coons. See Raccoons
Cooper, Harriet
October nights.—BoT
Copycat. J. Patrick Lewis.—LeT
The **coquette.** Walter De La Mare.—DeR

Corbett, Pie
Scarecrow Christmas.—FoLe
Corkett, Anne
November ("Snow and night").—BoT
This I know.—BoT
Unicorn ("Unicorn, unicorn").—BoT
The **cormorant.** See The common cormorant
Corn and cornfields
"Corn knee high". Unknown.—ScA
Fields of corn. S. Reavin.—MoS
The harvest queen. A. Bonner.—FoLe
My brother Aaron runs outside to tell us there is a severe thunderstorm warning. A. Adoff.—AdIn
Nicely, nicely. Unknown.—SnD
Quetzalcoatl. T. Johnston.—WhDd
Song of the Osage woman. M. C. Livingston.—LiR
Storm bringer. J. Yolen.—YoBi
"**Corn** knee high". Unknown.—ScA
The **corner.** Walter De La Mare.—DeR
Cornfields. See Corn and cornfields
Cornford, Frances
A child's dream.—ElW
The watch ("I wakened on my hot, hard bed").—MoR
Cornish, Sam
Generations.—JaPr
Sam's world.—LiPm
Corroboree ("The clap, clap, clap of the clapsticks beat"). Max Fatchen.—FoLe
Corroboree ("Hot day dies, cook time comes"). Kath Walker.—FoLe
Corso, Gregory
The runaway girl.—JaPr
Corwin, Norman
"The heart of man has four chambers, and each is filled with".—GoT
Corythosaurus. Jack Prelutsky.—[rT
"**Corythosaurus** long ago". See Corythosaurus
Cotton, John
Christmas eve night.—FoLe
A week to Christmas.—FoLe
Cotton
Roll the cotton down. Unknown.—SuC
Cotton bottomed menace. X. J. Kennedy.—KeK
Cottontail. George Bogin.—JaM
Couch, Helen F., and Barefield, Sam S.
"Thanks for today, God, for all of it".—StP
Counting. See also Counting-out rhymes
Blue herons. J. P. Lewis.—LeE
Counting. L. B. Hopkins.—HoS
"Eins, zwei, polizei". Unknown.—YoS
"One, two, police".—YoS
"I one my mother". Unknown.—OpI
"One for anger". Unknown.—ScA
"One for the money". Mother Goose.—ScA—WaM
"One I love, two I love". Mother Goose.—WaM—WiA
"One, two, buckle my shoe". Mother Goose.—SuO
Counting. Lee Bennett Hopkins.—HoS
Counting-out rhyme. Eve Merriam.—MeP
Counting-out rhymes
"Acka, bacca, soda cracka". Unknown.—CoM—WiA
"Ade milo sti milia". Unknown.—YoS
"Go, apple, to the apple tree".—YoS
"Alef beys giml dolid". Unknown.—YoS
"A B C D".—YoS

Counting-out rhymes—*Continued*

"All around the butter dish". Unknown.—CoM—WiA

"Apples, peaches, pumpkin pie". Unknown.—ScA

"As Eenty Feenty Halligolun". Unknown.—OpI

"As I went down the Icky Picky Lane". Unknown.—CoM

"Bumblebee, bumblebee". Unknown.—CoM

"Celui-ci a vu un lievre". Unknown.—YoS
  "This one saw a hare".—YoS

Counting. L. B. Hopkins.—HoS

Counting-out rhyme. E. Merriam.—MeP

Counting sheep ("1, 2, my daddy, who"). L. Clifton.—LiPf

"Don't give me the dishcloth wet". Unknown.—CoM

"Each, peach, pear, plum". Unknown.—CoM

"Eena, meena, dippa deena". Unknown.—CoM

"Eenie, meenie, minie, mo". Unknown.—SuI

"Eenie, meenie, minie, mo, catch a thief". Unknown.—WiA

"Eenie, meenie, minie, mo, catch a tiger". Unknown.—WiA

"Eeny, meeny, miney, mo". Unknown.—ScA

"Eeny, meeny, pasadini". Unknown.—CoM

"Eggs and ham". Unknown.—YoS

"Eggs, butter, cheese, bread". Unknown.—OpI

"Eins, zwei, polizei". Unknown.—YoS
  "One, two, police".—YoS

"Elim, elim, ep elim". Unknown.—YoS
  "Who am I, I am me".—YoS

"Engine, engine number nine". Unknown.—CoM—ScA

"First in a carriage". Mother Goose.—WaM

Great big ball. Unknown.—CoE

"Hello, hello, hello, sir". Unknown.—CoM—WiA

"Here's your fortune, here's your fame". Unknown.—CoM

"Hik sprik, sprouw". Unknown.—YoS
  "Hikkup-ikkup sprew".—YoS

"Hinx, minx, the old witch winks". Unknown.—OpI

"Hunter on the horse, fox on the run". E. Merriam.—MeY

"Ink, a-bink, a bottle of ink". Unknown.—WiA

"Intery, mintery, cutery, corn". Unknown.—CoM
  "Hinty, minty, cuty, corn".—SuI

"Intie, mintie, tootsie, lala". Unknown.—ScA

"Meg, yergoo, yergunnas". Unknown.—YoS
  "One, two, grow tall".—YoS

"Monkey, monkey, bottle of beer". Unknown.—ScA

"Monkey, monkey, bottle of pop". Unknown.—CoM—WiA

"My mother and your mother". Unknown.—CoM—WiA
  "My mother, your mother".—ScA

"Na zlatom cryeltse sidelly". Unknown.—YoS
  "On a golden step sat".—YoS

"Ocka, bocka, soda crocka". Unknown.—CoM

"Old Mother Ink". Unknown.—CoM

"Once an apple met an apple". Unknown.—CoM

"One-ery, ore-ery, ickery Ann". Unknown.—SuI

"One potato, two potato". Unknown.—CoM—SuI—WiA

"One, two, sky blue". Unknown.—CoM

"One, two, three a-nation". Unknown.—CoM—YoS

"One, two, three, four, five, I caught a fish alive". Unknown.—WiA

"1, 2, 3, 4, 5, 6, 7". Unknown.—ScA

"One, two, three, four, five, six, seven, all good children go to heaven". Unknown.—OpI

"1, 2, 3, look out for me". Unknown.—ScA

"One, two, three, mother caught a flea". Unknown.—CoM

"One, two, three, one, two, three". Unknown.—CoM

"One, two, three, the bumblebee". Unknown.—CoM

"Onery, twoery". Mother Goose.—OpI

"Out goes the rat". Unknown.—SuI—WiA

"Peach, plum, have a stick". Unknown.—CoM

"Raz, dva, tree, chiteery, pyat". Unknown.—YoS
  "1, 2, 3, 4, 5".—YoS

"Rood wit blauw". Unknown.—YoS
  "Red white blue".—YoS

"Skoe min hest". Unknown.—YoS
  "Shoe my horse".—YoS

"The sky is blue, how old are you". Unknown.—CoM

"Tarzan, Tarzan, in a tree". Unknown.—CoM

"Ten little apples on ten apple trees". E. Merriam.—MeY

"When I went up the apple tree". Unknown.—ScA

"Wire, briar, limberlock". Unknown.—ScA

"Xiao pi qiu, xiang jiao li". Unknown.—YoS
  "A little ball, a banana, a pear".—YoS

"Yellow cornmeal". Unknown.—ScA

Counting sheep ("I am a poor shepherd"). Jane Yolen.—YoHa

Counting sheep ("1, 2, my daddy, who"). Lucille Clifton.—LiPf

Countries. See names of countries, as Mexico

Country. See Country life

Country calendar. Eve Merriam.—MeS

Country life. See also Farm life; Village life

Afternoon on a hill. E. S. V. Millay.—FrS—SuI

"As I was going to Newbury". Mother Goose.—WaM

"As I went up the high hill". Unknown.—ClI

August ("Buttercup nodded and said goodby"). C. Thaxter.—SuI

Bird song. Unknown.—OpT

The bookworm ("I'm tired, oh, tired of books, said Jack"). W. De La Mare.—DeR—MaP

Childhood. J. Joubert.—NyT

Country calendar. E. Merriam.—MeS

The country mouse and the city mouse. R. S. Sharpe.—ElW

Coyotes ("You never see them"). M. C. Livingston.—LiR

Crickets ("Creak creak a wicker rocker"). E. Merriam.—MeP

Daisies. V. Worth.—WoAl

A dream of paradise in the shadow of war. M. Niazi.—NyT

Fishing. L. Dangel.—JaPr

Friday work. J. Berry.—BeW

Friendship ("There once were two backcountry geezers"). J. Ciardi.—CiH

Hares at play. J. Clare.—CaB

The harvest moon ("The flame red moon, the harvest moon"). T. Hughes.—LaN

The hayride. M. C. Livingston.—LiBp

The Hirdy Dirdy. Unknown.—OpT

Holidays (for a picture). W. De La Mare.—DeR

"I lived off old 42". J. Carson.—CaS

"I spent the first years of my life". J. Carson.—CaS

In the country. A. Fisher.—FiA

In these dissenting times. A. Walker.—ElW

Cow ("The cow"). Valerie Worth.—WoAl See Cow

The cow ("The cow is of the bovine ilk"). Ogden Nash.—CaB

Cow ("Cows are not supposed to fly"). William Jay Smith.—SmL

The cow ("The friendly cow all red and white"). Robert Louis Stevenson.—ElW—KeT

Cow ("I approve of June"). Marilyn Singer.—SiT

"The cow is of the bovine ilk". See The cow

"Coward, cowardy custard". Unknown.—OpI—ScA

"Cowardy, cowardy custard".—WiA

"Cowardy, cowardy custard". See "Coward, cowardy custard"

Cowboys

    Bronco busting, event #1. M. Swenson.—KnAs—MoR

    The closing of the rodeo. W. J. Smith.—KnAs

    The cowboy's lament. Unknown.—ElW

    Whoopee ti yi yo, git along, little dogies. Unknown.—SuI

The cowboy's lament. Unknown.—ElW

Cowper, William

    "God moves in a mysterious way".—ElW

"Cows are not supposed to fly". See Cow

Cow's complaint. Grace Nichols.—NiCo

The cow's moo. Issa, tr. by Tze-si Huang.—DeI

Cox, Palmer

    The mouse's lullaby.—KeT

Coyotes

    Coyotes ("The coyotes are howling"). J. Whyte.—BoT

    Coyotes ("You never see them"). M. C. Livingston.—LiR

Coyotes ("The coyotes are howling"). Jon Whyte.—BoT

Coyotes ("You never see them"). Myra Cohn Livingston.—LiR

"The coyotes are howling". See Coyotes

A cozy little house. Aileen Fisher.—FiH

Crab. Valerie Worth.—WoAl

Crab dance. Grace Nichols.—NiCo

Crabbe, George

    His mother's wedding ring.—GoU

Crabs

    At the beach ("Johnny, Johnny, let go of that crab"). J. Ciardi.—PrFo

    Crab. V. Worth.—WoAl

    Crab dance. G. Nichols.—NiCo

    Crabs. Seishi.—DeI

    "Said the crab, 'tis not beauty or birth". O. Herford.—LiLo

Crabs. Seishi, tr. by Tze-si Huang.—DeI

"Crackers, meringues, and pink blomonge". See The feast

Crane, Nathalia

    Spooks.—BaH

Crane, Stephen

    "In Heaven".—StP

Cranes (birds)

    "Crowned crane". J. Gleason.—NyT

    My dame. Unknown.—ClI

Craveirinha, Jose

    A man never cries, tr. by Don Burness.—NyT

"The craving of Samuel Rouse for clearance to create". See The slave and the iron lace

Crazed. Walter De La Mare.—DeR

"Creak creak a wicker rocker". See Crickets

"Creating God, your fingers trace". Jeffery Rowthorn.—StP

Creation

    All I am. A. Oyewole.—SlM

"All things bright and beautiful". C. F. Alexander.—StP

"And God created great whales, and every living creature that moveth". From Book of Genesis. Bible/Old Testament.—WhAa

"Creator, you who dwell at the ends of the earth". Unknown.—StP

"God made you". Unknown.—CoM

"God of all power, ruler of the universe". Unknown.—StP

Howie Kell suspends all lust to contemplate the universe. R. Torreson.—JaPr

"I celebrate myself, and sing myself". From Song of myself. W. Whitman.—HoVo

"Little lamb, who made thee". W. Blake.—StP

"Lord, you made the world and everything in it, you". F. Kaan.—StP

Mayflies. P. Fleischman.—FlJ

"Oh, the Lord looked down from his window in the sky". Unknown.—StP

"Once upon a time, she said". J. Yolen.—YoFf

The ousel cock. R. Hodgson.—ElW

The penguin ("The penguin isn't meat, fish or bird"). R. Yanez.—NyT

Six birds. J. P. Lewis.—LeA

Sky tales of the Assiniboin Indians. M. C. Livingston.—LiR

Song of creation. Unknown.—GoT

They stooped over and came out. Unknown.—GoT

The tiger ("Tiger, tiger, burning bright"). W. Blake.—CaB

    "Tyger, tyger, burning bright".—StP

"When God gave out noses". Unknown.—ScA

Wise. A. Fisher.—FiA

Creativity

    About poems, sort of. J. Little.—LiHe

    "All this time and at all times wait the words of true poems". From Song of myself. W. Whitman.—HoVo

    The artist. A. Bryan.—BrS

    Blum. D. Aldis.—LiDd

    Busy summer. A. Fisher.—DeT

    Daybreak in Alabama. L. Hughes.—SuC

    Excelsior. W. Whitman.—HoVo

    The flying pen. E. Merriam.—MeS

    "Hast never come to thee an hour". W. Whitman.—HoVo

    The making of dragons. J. Yolen.—YoFf

    "Once I got a postcard from the Fiji Islands". J. Kaplinski.—NyT

    "Out of the cradle endlessly rocking". W. Whitman.—HoVo

    The paint box. E. V. Rieu.—ElW

    Poetry ("I too, dislike it, there are things that are important"). M. Moore.—SuI

    Poets to come. W. Whitman.—HoVo

    Portmanteaux. E. Merriam.—MeCh

    Temple for tomorrow. From The negro artist and the racial mountain. L. Hughes.—SuC

    Thrum drew a small map. S. Musgrave.—BoT

    To rich givers. W. Whitman.—HoVo

    "The unicorn I tried to paint". X. J. Kennedy.—KeK

"Creator, you who dwell at the ends of the earth". Unknown.—StP

Creche. Valerie Worth.—WoA

Cree Indians. See Indians of the Americas—Cree

Creeley, Robert

    The car.—MoR

"Crescendo". See Starry night I

"The **crested** newt creep up the trees". See Blizzard
  birds
"A **crew** took part of the big tree away". See
  Mountain tambourine
"**Crick,** crack". Eve Merriam.—BaW
Cricket (sport)
  Quick ball man, for Michael Holding. J. Berry.—
    BeW
Cricket ("The cheerful cricket, when he sings"). X.
  J. Kennedy.—KeK
The **cricket** ("In a sorrowful voice"). Basho, tr. by
  Tze-si Huang.—DeI
Crickets
  "Above the chorus". Kyoshi.—CaR
  Cricket ("The cheerful cricket, when he sings"). X.
    J. Kennedy.—KeK
  The cricket ("In a sorrowful voice"). Basho.—DeI
  Crickets ("Crickets talk"). V. Worth.—WoAl
  Crickets ("They tell"). M. C. Livingston.—LiNe
  Crickets ("We cannot say that crickets sing"). H.
    Behn.—WhAa
  First job. J. Daniels.—JaPr
  Halloween concert ("It's cold, said the cricket").
    A. Fisher.—FiA
  House crickets. P. Fleischman.—FlJ
  Joyful crickets. Issa.—DeI
  Life of the cricket. J. C. Andrade.—NyT
  On the grasshopper and cricket. J. Keats.—ElW
  Singing. D. Aldis.—DeT
  Wicked witch's travels. X. J. Kennedy.—KeGh
Crickets ("Creak creak a wicker rocker"). Eve
  Merriam.—MeP
Crickets ("Crickets talk"). Valerie Worth.—WoAl
Crickets ("They tell"). Myra Cohn Livingston.—
  LiNe
Crickets ("We cannot say that crickets sing"). Harry
  Behn.—WhAa
"**Crickets** talk". See Crickets
"**Cried** a man on the Salisbury Plain". Myra Cohn
  Livingston.—LiLo
"**Cries** a sheep to a ship on the Amazon". J. Patrick
  Lewis.—LiLo
Crime and criminals. See also Murder; Thieves
  Autumnal equinox. E. E. Wilson.—JaM
  The babes in the wood. Unknown.—ElW
  Calling all cars. M. Fatchen.—FaCm
  The case of the crumbled cookies. X. J.
    Kennedy.—KeGh
  The dog poisoner. K. Wilson.—JaM
  Macavity, the mystery cat. T. S. Eliot.—ElW
  Reach for the sky. Unknown.—ScA
  "Rusty nail, went to jail". Unknown.—WiA
  Summer killer. T. A. Broughton.—JaM
  Whodunnit. E. Merriam.—MeCh
"**Crime** in the kitchen, calling all cars". See The case
  of the crumbled cookies
Crocodile. William Jay Smith.—SmL
The **crocodile.** See "How doth the little crocodile"
"**Crocodile** or alligator". Colin West.—CoAz
"The **crocodile** wept bitter tears". See Crocodile
Crocodiles. See Alligators and crocodiles
Crocuses
  O dear me. W. De La Mare.—DeR
"**Cross** my heart and hope to die". Unknown.—ScA
"**Cross** your fingers, cross your eyes". See How to
  spell
The **crossing** of Mary of Scotland. William Jay
  Smith.—SmL
"**Crossing** that". See Wise men
Crossing the park. Howard Moss.—SuI
"**Crossing** the park to see a painting". See Crossing
  the park

Crossings, sels. Walter De La Mare
  The fairy-pedlar's song.—DeR
"**Crosspatch**". Mother Goose.—WaM
The **crow** ("A crow"). Santoka, tr. by Tze-si
  Huang.—DeI See The crow
Crow ("Jump-Johnny Peacoat"). J. Patrick Lewis.—
  LeT
Crow call. Jane Yolen.—YoBi
"**Crow,** crow, get out of my sight". See To the crow
Crow Indians. See Indians of the Americas—Crow
"**Crow** on the fence". Unknown.—CaB
Crowd. Eve Merriam.—MeCh
Crowds
  Crowd. E. Merriam.—MeCh
Crown. Dakari Kamau Hru.—SlM
Crown of light festival. David Bateson.—FoLe
"**Crowned** crane". Judith Gleason.—NyT
Crows
  "Away, you black devils, away". Mother Goose.—
    WaM
  But I dunno. Unknown.—ClI
  The crow ("A crow"). Santoka.—DeI
  Crow ("Jump-Johnny Peacoat"). J. P. Lewis.—
    LeT
  Crow call. J. Yolen.—YoBi
  "Crow on the fence". Unknown.—CaB
  Crows. V. Worth.—SuI—WoAl
  A desolate scene. Basho.—DeI
  "Detestable crow". Basho.—CaR
  Dust of snow. R. Frost.—ElW
  Fox and crow. W. J. Smith.—SmL
  Rainbow crow. N. Van Laan.—WhDd
  6:15 A.M. M. C. Livingston.—LiNe
  "There once was a scarecrow named Joel". D.
    McCord.—LiLo
  "There was an old crow". Mother Goose.—WaM
  To the crow. Unknown.—OpI
  The twa corbies. Unknown.—CaB
Crows. Valerie Worth.—SuI—WoAl
"The **crows** are cawing". See Coming and going
Crucifixion. See Easter
Cruel boys. Gary Soto.—JaM
Cruel Jenny Wren. Unknown.—ElW
Cruelty
  The antelope ("When one of us hit"). D. A.
    Evans.—JaPr
  At the piano. A. Hudgins.—JaM
  Coleridge Jackson. M. Angelou.—AnI
  The gallows. E. Thomas.—ElW
  In the spring. J. Hall.—JaM
  Jennie Wren. W. De La Mare.—DeR
  Sister ("Younger than they"). H. R. Coursen.—
    JaPr
Cruikshank, Alfred M.
  I love the sea.—SlM
Crum, Robert
  The bat in the bedroom.—JaM
"A **crumbling** churchyard, the sea, and the moon".
  See The visitor
Crumbs. Walter De La Mare.—DeR
Crume, Vic
  The haunted house ("Not a window was
    broken").—BaH
Crunchy. Max Fatchen.—FaCm
"**Crusty** corn bread". Eve Merriam.—MeY
A **crusty** mechanic. N. M. Bodecker.—LiLo
Cruz, Victor Hernandez
  Sonsito.—MoR
"**Cry,** baby, cry". Unknown.—CoM—OpI—ScA—
  WiA
The **cry** guy. Kalli Dakos.—DaI

Crying
The baby-sitter and the baby. E. Merriam.—MeS
Boo hoo. A. Spilka.—PrFo
"Cry, baby, cry". Unknown.—CoM—OpI—ScA—WiA
The cry guy. K. Dakos.—DaI
"An impressionable lady in Wales". E. Gorey.—LiLo
"Laugh before you eat". Unknown.—WiA
A man never cries. J. Craveirinha.—NyT
New baby poem (I). E. Greenfield.—GrN
The playmate ("Weep no more, nor grieve, nor sigh"). W. De La Mare.—DeR
The sad story of a little boy that cried. Unknown.—PrFo
A small discovery. J. A. Emanuel.—DeT—LiDd
Why ("Why do you weep, Mother, why do you weep"). W. De La Mare.—DeR
Wicked thoughts. J. Viorst.—PrFo
Crystal Rowe, track star. Mel Glenn.—MoR
Crystal's waltz. Myra Cohn Livingston.—LiR
"**Cub** tub". Bruce McMillan.—McP
The **cuckoo**. Basho, tr. by Tze-si Huang.—DeI
Cuckoos
Busy ("Little gray cuckoos"). Basho.—DeI
The cuckoo. Basho.—DeI
Riddling song. Unknown.—OpT
The **cucumber**. Nazim Hikmet, tr. by Randy Blasing and Mutlu Konuk.—NyT
Cuernavaca. Aline Pettersson, tr. by Judith Infante.—NyT
Cullen, Countee
Heritage, sels.
What is Africa to me.—SuC
Incident.—ElW
Under the mistletoe.—SlM
What is Africa to me. See Heritage
The **culture** of the vulture. J. Patrick Lewis.—LeA
Cummings, Edward Estlin
"Being to timelessness as it's to time".—GoU
"I carry your heart with me (I carry it in)".—GoU
"I thank you God for most this amazing".—StP
"In just-spring".—ElW
"It is so long since my heart has been with yours".—GoU
"Jimmie's got a goil".—MoR
"L(a".—MoR
"Little tree".—ElW—GoA
"Maggie and Milly and Molly and May".—SuI
"Maggie and Millie . . .".—ElW
"Off a pane the".—MoR
"O purple finch".—ElW
"Since feeling is first".—ElW
"Somewhere I have never travelled, gladly beyond".—GoU
"Whippoorwill this".—MoR
"Who knows if the moon's".—DeS
Cunliffe, John
Prince Rama comes to Longsight.—FoLe
Cunningham, Julia
Age four and my father.—LiPf
Carousel.—JaP
A short long story.—JaP
The **cupboard**. Walter De La Mare.—DeR—MaP
The **cure**. Unknown.—OpT
Curiosity
Always wondering. A. Fisher.—FiA
Elevation. R. Morgan.—JaM
Inquisitiveness. C. West.—AgL
"Mind your own business". Unknown.—ScA
"**Curious** fly". Unknown.—PrP
"**Curly** locks, curly locks". Mother Goose.—EdGl

Currie, Robert
Poem ("If I write").—JaP
"**Curried** goat and rabbit stew". See Victory banquet
Curses
La belle dame sans merci. J. Keats.—ElW
Curses. M. P. Hearn.—BaH
A glass of beer. J. Stephens.—ElW
The Lady of Shalott. A. Tennyson.—ElW
The rime of the ancient mariner, complete. S. T. Coleridge.—ElW
"Will-o'-the-wisp". W. De La Mare.—DeR
The word. P. B. Janeczko.—JaB
Curses. Michael Patrick Hearn.—BaH
"The **curtains** of the solemn night". See Daybreak
"**Customers** flood the Inn's restaurant". See Monte Rio, California
"**Cut** your nails on Monday, cut for health". Unknown.—WiA
Cymbeline, sels. William Shakespeare
"Fear no more the heat o' the sun".—ElW
Cynthia in the snow. Gwendolyn Brooks.—KeT
Czaykowski, Bogdan
Oh, oh, should they take away my stove, my inexhaustible ode to joy, tr.—NyT

D

D is for dog. William Jay Smith.—SmL
Daby, Toolsy
The labourer.—NyT
Dacey, Philip
Jill, afterwards.—JaM
"**Dad** gave me a string of pearls for my birthday". See Pearls
Daddy. Myra Cohn Livingston.—LiPf
Daddy carries his empty basket on his head. Arnold Adoff.—AdIn
Daddy fell into the pond. Alfred Noyes.—LiPf
"**Daddy** fixed the breakfast". See Mummy slept late and daddy fixed breakfast
"**Daddy**, how does an elephant feel". See Questions, quistions and quoshtions
Daddy is tall, has shoulders, strong hands. Arnold Adoff.—AdIn
"**Daddy** made Evangeline and me". See Elevation
"**Daddy**, you are gone away". See Christmas wish
Daddy's gone. Deborah Chandra.—LiPf
Dadu
"Glory to thee, glory to thee, O Lord".—StP
Daffodils
Daffodils. W. Wordsworth.—FrS
"I wandered lonely as a cloud".—ElW
"Daffy-down-dilly is new come to town". Mother Goose.—SuO
"Daffy-down-dilly has just come to town".—ScA
To daffodils. R. Herrick.—ElW
Daffodils. William Wordsworth.—FrS
"I wandered lonely as a cloud".—ElW
"**Daffy-down-dilly** has just come to town". See "Daffy-down-dilly is new come to town"
"**Daffy-down-dilly** is new come to town". Mother Goose.—SuO
"Daffy-down-dilly has just come to town".—ScA
Daiches, David
To Kate, skating better than her date.—KnAs
"**Dainty** Miss Apathy". See Pooh
Daisies
Daisies. V. Worth.—WoAl
Summer daisies. M. C. Livingston.—LiNe

Daisies—*Continued*
Susannah and the daisies. J. Little.—LiHe
Daisies. Valerie Worth.—WoAl
"**Daisy** and Lily". From Waltz. Edith Sitwell.—MoR
Dakos, Kalli
Budging line ups.—DaI
Caleb's desk is a mess.—DaI
Call the periods, call the commas.—DaI
The cry guy.—DaI
Dancing on a rainbow.—DaI
A day in school.—DaI
Don't you remember how sick you are.—DaI
Go to the Bahamas.—DaI
Happy hiccup to you.—DaI
I brought a worm.—DaI
I have no time to visit with King Arthur.—DaI
"I left my book in Hawaii".—DaI
I won the prize.—DaI
If we had lunch at the White House.—DaI
If you're not here, please raise your hand.—DaI
"I'm going to die".—DaI
"I'm in another dimension".—DaI
"Is your head on nice and tight".—DaI
It's gross to kiss.—DaI
It's inside my sister's lunch.—DaI
J.T. never will be ten.—DaI
A late assignment.—DaI
A lifetime in third grade.—DaI
Math is brewing and I'm in trouble.—DaI
The mighty eye.—DaI
My homework isn't done.—DaI
Poor substitute.—DaI
Shakespeare's gone.—DaI
She should have listened to me.—DaI
"Teacher, could you".—DaI
A teacher's lament.—DaI
There's a cobra in the bathroom.—DaI
They don't do math in Texas.—DaI
Were you ever fat like me.—DaI
Why can't a girl be the leader of the boys.—DaI
The wind is calling me away.—DaI
You can do better.—DaI
Dakota Indians. See Indians of the Americas—Dakota
Dallas, Ruth
Clouds on the sea.—NyT
A new dress.—NyT
Dame Hickory. Walter De La Mare.—DeR
"**Dame** Hickory, Dame Hickory". See Dame Hickory
"**Dame** Trot and her cat". Mother Goose.—ClI
Damn Yankees, sels. Jerry Ross and Richard Adler Heart.—KnAs
Dams
"On the dam, Neil spied a wheel". X. J. Kennedy.—KeFb
"**Dana** went to catch a fish". See To catch a fish
Dance calls. Unknown.—MoR
Dance of the mushrooms. J. Patrick Lewis.—LeE
Dance poem. Nikki Giovanni.—MoR
Dancers. Paul B. Janeczko.—JaB
Dances and dancing
Almost dancing. Simmerman. Jim.—JaM
And after. J. Yolen.—YoDd
Arthur Mitchell. M. Moore.—MoR
Attic dance. J. D. Ritchings.—MoR
Boogie chant and dance. Unknown.—MoR
Boys' night out. M. Vinz.—JaPr
Break dance. G. Nichols.—AgL
Caliban limbo. E. Brathwaite.—LeCa
Carnival in Rio. J. Kirkup.—FoLe
Celebration. A. Lopez.—DeT

"Charlie Chaplin went to France". Unknown.—WiA
Cleaned the crocodile's teeth. N. Col.—NyT
"Come dance a jig". Mother Goose.—WaM
Corroboree ("The clap, clap, clap of the clapsticks beat"). M. Fatchen.—FoLe
Corroboree ("Hot day dies, cook time comes"). K. Walker.—FoLe
Crab dance. G. Nichols.—NiCo
Crystal's waltz. M. C. Livingston.—LiR
Dance calls. Unknown.—MoR
Dance of the mushrooms. J. P. Lewis.—LeE
Dance poem. N. Giovanni.—MoR
Dancers. P. B. Janeczko.—JaB
Dinosaur dances. J. Yolen.—YoDd
Dinosaur waltz. J. Yolen.—YoDd
Disco date, 1980. J. Berry.—BeW
"Disco dino dancing". J. Yolen.—YoDd
Dragon dance. M. Fatchen.—FoLe
Dream boogie. L. Hughes.—MoR
Dream variation. L. Hughes.—DeT—LoFh
"Drexel on the ballroom floor". X. J. Kennedy.—KeFb
The fairies dancing. W. De La Mare.—DeR
A fishy square dance. E. Merriam.—MeCh
The flingamango. M. Mahy.—MaN
The ghost dance, August, 1976. D. Jauss.—JaM
Halloween concert ("Elbows bent, tireless"). B. J. Esbensen.—LiHp
The harlot's house. O. Wilde.—ElW
"I danced in the morning". S. Carter.—StP
"I throw myself to the left". Unknown.—WhAa
Improper moves. J. Yolen.—YoDd
"It rains and it pours". A. Lobel.—LiDd
"Jimmie's got a goil". E. E. Cummings.—MoR
Jouvert morning. D. Calder.—FoLe
Juke box love song. L. Hughes.—JaPr
Kearney Park. G. Soto.—SoA
Kick line. J. Yolen.—YoDd
King of the band. A. Johnson.—FoLe
Klassical dub. L. K. Johnson.—AgL
Korean butterfly dance. J. Kirkup.—FoLe
"Ladies and gentlemen". Unknown.—ScA—WiA
"Leatherty patch". From Two dancing songs. Unknown.—OpT
"Left foot, right foot". Mother Goose.—WaM
Lion dance. T. Millum.—FoLe
The lobster quadrille. From Alice's adventures in wonderland. L. Carroll.—MoR
Martha Graham. J. Laughlin.—MoR
May day ("Twirl your ribbons"). J. Kenward.—FoLe
Melmillo. W. De La Mare.—DeR—MaP
Mrs. A. Hulas. J. Yolen.—YoDd
My dad. A. Bryan.—BrS
My papa's waltz. T. Roethke.—ElW
Mystery ("One Friday night"). P. B. Janeczko.—JaB
Off the ground. W. De La Mare.—DeR—MaP
"Oh dear mother, what a rose I be". From Two dancing songs. Unknown.—OpT
"One, two, three, four, Charlie Chaplin". Unknown.—CoM
Partners ("Some dinosaurs dance lightly"). J. Yolen.—YoDd
The rural dance about the Maypole. Unknown.—MoR
The sea body. W. De La Mare.—MaP
"Slip past the window". From Nightdances. J. Skofield.—LaN
Song for a banjo dance. L. Hughes.—SuC

Dances and dancing—*Continued*

The song of the jellicles. T. S. Eliot.—DeT—LaCc—SuI

Sonsito. V. H. Cruz.—MoR

Square dance. J. Yolen.—YoDd

The stranger ("A little after twilight"). W. De La Mare.—DeR

Tarantella. H. Belloc.—MoR

"There was a roof over our heads". A. Rios.—SuI

Twinkle toes triceratops. J. Yolen.—YoDd

Tyrannosaurus ("He strides onto the dance floor"). J. Yolen.—YoDd

"Uncle Dick". E. Merriam.—MeP

"Unless you lead me, Lord, I cannot dance". Mechtild of Magdeburg.—StP

Wallflower. J. Yolen.—YoDd

When I dance. J. Berry.—BeW

"When the allosaurus". J. Yolen.—YoDd

Dancing on a rainbow. Kalli Dakos.—DaI

"**Dancing** teepees". Calvin O'John.—SnD

Dandelion ("O little soldier with the golden helmet"). Hilda Conkling.—DeT

Dandelion ("Out of green space"). Valerie Worth.—WoAl

Dandelion ("These lions, each by a daisy queen"). Sacheverell Sitwell.—ElW

Dandelions

Dandelion ("O little soldier with the golden helmet"). H. Conkling.—DeT

Dandelion ("Out of green space"). V. Worth.—WoAl

Dandelion ("These lions, each by a daisy queen"). S. Sitwell.—ElW

Dangel, Leo

Fishing.—JaPr

Gaining yardage.—JaPr

Gathering strength.—JaM

The love nest.—JaPr

The new lady barber at Ralph's Barber Shop.—JaM

No question.—JaPr

"**Daniel** was a naughty man". Unknown.—ScA

Daniels, Jim

Baseball cards #1.—JaP

First job.—JaPr

For people who can't open their hoods.—JaPr

Speech class, for Joe.—JaP

Wheels.—JaPr

Daniels, Kate

The playhouse.—JaPr

Daniels, Shirley

Drums of my father.—BoT

Danish language

"Hik sprik, sprouw". Unknown.—YoS

"Hikkup-ikkup sprew".—YoS

"Pandebeen". Unknown.—YoS

"Brow-bone".—YoS

"Rood wit blauw". Unknown.—YoS

"Red white blue".—YoS

"Skoe min hest". Unknown.—YoS

"Shoe my horse".—YoS

Danish nursery rhymes. See Nursery rhymes—Danish

Danner, Margaret

The slave and the iron lace.—SuC

"**Danny** dawdles". See Spring fever

"A **daring** young lady of Guam". Unknown.—LiLo

The **dark** ("It's always dark"). Myra Cohn Livingston.—KeT

The **dark** ("There are six little houses up on the hill"). Elizabeth Madox Roberts.—LaN

"**Dark** air life looping". See Bat

The **dark** and falling summer. Delmore Schwartz.—GoT—SuI

"**Dark-browed** sailor, tell me now". See Araby

"**Dark** brown is the river". See Where go the boats

"**Dark,** dark this mind, if ever in vain it rove". See Divine delight

"**Dark** is soft, like fur". See Rhyme for night

"A **dark** theme keeps me here". See In evening air

Darkness

Brownout. T. Perez.—NyT

The dark ("It's always dark"). M. C. Livingston.—KeT

The dark and falling summer. D. Schwartz.—GoT—SuI

The evening light along the sound. S. Santos.—GoT

Fireflies ("Fireflies on night canvas"). Q. Troupe.—SlM

Grass ("The grass is strangely tall to me"). T. Kristensen.—NyT

Hark. W. De La Mare.—DeR

In evening air. T. Roethke.—GoT

In the dark. J. Pridmore.—BaH

In this deep darkness. N. Zach.—GoT

Nightfall ("One by one"). B. J. Esbensen.—EsW

No one heard him call. D. Aldis.—KeT

Objectivity. M. Jamal.—AgL

Panther ("I am as black as coal is black"). J. P. Lewis.—LeT

The prayer of the glow-worm. C. B. De Gasztold.—DeP

Rhyme for night. J. Aiken.—KeT

The sound. Shiki.—DeI

Stopping by woods on a snowy evening. R. Frost.—DeS—DeT—ElW—SuI

"The way I must enter". I. Shikibu.—GoT

"Where was Moses when the light went out, in the dark". Unknown.—WiA

"**Darkness** has lured you out". See Beech, to owl

Darnell. Eloise Greenfield.—GrN

Darwish, Ali

Or.—NyT

Darwish, Mahmud

The prison cell, tr. by Ben Bennani.—NyT

Das, Jibananda

Cat ("Again and again through the day"), tr. by Lila Ray.—NyT

Date-beggin sweet word them. James Berry.—BeW

Dating (social)

Annette Harrison. M. Glenn.—GlBc

C. C. Johnson. M. Glenn.—GlBc

Charlene Cottier. M. Glenn.—GlBc

Date-beggin sweet word them. J. Berry.—BeW

Disco date, 1980. J. Berry.—BeW

I meet sweet Sue for a walk on a cold and sunny afternoon. A. Adoff.—AdCh

The kiss ("The kiss started when I danced"). P. B. Janeczko.—JaB

Kristin Leibowitz. M. Glenn.—GlBc

Mother has a talk with me. J. Little.—LiHe

"My girl friend is a lulu". Unknown.—WiA

Oranges ("The first time I walked"). G. Soto.—JaM—SoA

Regina Kelsey. M. Glenn.—GlBc

"Sister has a boyfriend". Unknown.—ScA

To Kate, skating better than her date. D. Daiches.—KnAs

Valerie O'Neill. M. Glenn.—GlBc

Willy nilly. E. Merriam.—MeP

"The **daughter** of the farrier". See A rash stipulation

Daughters

About poems, sort of. J. Little.—LiHe

Daughters—*Continued*
Autumn with a daughter who's just catching on. G. Soto.—SoA
The comb. W. De La Mare.—DeR
Eating bread. G. Soto.—SoA
Evening walk. G. Soto.—SoA
A frosty night. R. Graves.—ElW
Full circle. W. De La Mare.—DeR
Mosquitoes. J. Little.—LiHe
Mother has a talk with me. J. Little.—LiHe
"My daughter got divorced". J. Carson.—CaS
My father's words. C. Lewis.—LiPf
Rare rhythms. S. London.—JaM
Sometimes even parents win. J. Ciardi.—CiH—LiLo
Where we could go. G. Soto.—SoA
Working with mother. M. C. Livingston.—KeT—LiPm—LiR
The writer. R. Wilbur.—SuI
"**Dave**, dear Dave". See Teach the making of summer
"**Dave** Dirt came to dinner". Kit Wright.—PrFo
David, King of Israel (about)
King David. W. De La Mare.—DeR—MaP
"**David** asks for his dessert". See Dinnertime
David's mouse. Patricia Hubbell.—LaM
Davies, Mary Carolyn
A New Year ("Here's a clean year").—FrS
Dawber, Diane
The sky is falling.—BoT
Tinkering.—BoT
Zeroing in.—BoT
Dawn. See also Morning
"At the horislope of the mountizon". From Altazor. V. Huidobro.—NyT
The black turkey gobbler. Unknown.—SnD
The child in the story awakes. W. De La Mare.—DeR
Dawn ("I kindle my light over the whole Atlantic"). E. Sodergran.—NyT
Dawn ("The little kitten's face"). Unknown.—DeI
Daybreak ("After the dark of night"). W. De La Mare.—DeR
Daybreak ("The curtains of the solemn night"). W. De La Mare.—DeR
Early country village morning. G. Nichols.—NiCo
The early morning. H. Belloc.—KeT
Enlightenment. M. Horovitz.—AgL
Grass ("The grass is strangely tall to me"). T. Kristensen.—NyT
"Let me get up early on this summer morning". E. Guillevic.—GoT
Little fish. Basho.—DeI
Moon's ending. S. Teasdale.—GoT
91. J.-U.-D. Rumi.—GoT
Now day is breaking. S. Quasimodo.—GoT
"The owl hooted". Unknown.—LiIf
Recuerdo. E. S. V. Millay.—ElW
Song, the owl. A. Tennyson.—LiIf
The owl.—ElW
The sun ("The sun is a glowing spider"). G. Nichols.—NiCo
Sunrise. B. J. Esbensen.—EsW
"Thou dawnest beautifully in the horizon". Unknown.—StP
"Watching the moon". I. Shikibu.—GoT
Dawn ("I kindle my light over the whole Atlantic"). Edith Sodergran, tr. by Daisy Aldan and Leif Sjoberg.—NyT
Dawn ("The little kitten's face"). Unknown, tr. by Tze-si Huang.—DeI
Dawn Weinberg. Mel Glenn.—GlBc

Dawson, Hester Jewell
October ("The high fly ball").—MoA
Dawson, Mary
Late for breakfast.—KeT
Day, Clarence
The ant.—WhAa
Day. See also Afternoon; Bedtime; Dawn; Evening; Morning; Night
Bed in summer. R. L. Stevenson.—DeT
"Days were as great as lakes". D. Vogel.—GoT
"Let me get up early on this summer morning". E. Guillevic.—GoT
"There". Unknown.—GoT
Day before Christmas. Marchette Chute.—DeS
"The **day** Dad said". See The word
Day-dream. Samarendra Sengupta, tr. by Lila Ray.—NyT
"The **day** I married, my mother". Jo Carson.—CaS
A **day** in school. Kalli Dakos.—DaI
"The **day** is hot and icky and the sun sticks to my skin". Eloise Greenfield.—MoS
"The **day** is so pretty". See Duet
"The **day**? Memorial.". See Grape sherbert
"The **day** my father and Jack Grimes". See Dreamers and flyers
Daybreak. See Dawn
Daybreak ("After the dark of night"). Walter De La Mare.—DeR
Daybreak ("The curtains of the solemn night"). Walter De La Mare.—DeR
Daybreak in Alabama. Langston Hughes.—SuC
"**Daylight** is drifting". See Dusk
Days. See Days of the week
"The **days** are filled with air, a cloud". See Eating bread
"The **days** are short". See January
Days of the week
The cheerful child's week. B. S. De Regniers.—DeW
The churlish child's week. B. S. De Regniers.—DeW
"Cut your nails on Monday, cut for health". Unknown.—WiA
"Here we go round the mulberry bush". Mother Goose.—EdGl—SuO—WaM
"Monday's child is fair of face". Mother Goose.—SuO—WaM
"Monday's child is red and spotty". C. McNaughton.—PrFo
"Sneeze on Monday, sneeze for danger". Unknown.—WiA
Someday. E. Merriam.—MeS
There are days. B. S. De Regniers.—DeW
A week to Christmas. J. Cotton.—FoLe
The white wind. J. P. Lewis.—LeE
Days of the week—Friday
"Friday night's dream". Mother Goose.—WaM
Friday the thirteenth. A. Adoff.—AdCh
Friday work. J. Berry.—BeW
"On Friday night I go backwards to bed". Mother Goose.—WaM
Days of the week—Saturday
Bingo. P. B. Janeczko.—JaB—JaP
"Sally go round the sun". Mother Goose.—WaM
The tennis. E. B. White.—KnAs
Days of the week—Sunday
"It used to be only Sunday afternoons". From Watching football on TV. H. Nemerov.—KnAs
Mothering Sunday. S. Cook.—FoLe
Ode to mi parque. G. Soto.—SoNe
Sunday afternoon under a warm blue sky. A. Adoff.—AdIn

De La Mare, Walter—*Continued*

Daybreak ("The curtains of the solemn night").—DeR
Dear delight.—DeR
Divine delight.—DeR
Done for.—DeR
The double.—DeR
"Down-adown-derry".—DeR
Dream song.—DeR—MaP
Dreamland.—DeR
Ducks.—DeR
The dunce.—DeR—MaP
The dwarf.—DeR
Earth folk.—DeR—MaP
Echo ("Seven sweet notes").—DeR
Echo ("Who called, I said, and the words").—DeR
Echoes.—DeR
Eden.—DeR
Eeka, neeka.—DeR
The enchanted hill.—DeR
The Englishman.—DeR
Envoy.—DeR
Esmeralda (for a picture).—DeR
Ever.—DeR
The fairies dancing.—DeR
The fairy in winter.—DeR
The fairy-pedlar's song. See Crossings
The feast.—DeR
The feather.—DeR
The fiddlers.—DeR
The fire.—DeR
Five eyes.—DeR—MaP
Five of us.—DeR
The fleeting.—DeR
The flower.—DeR
The fly.—DeR
Fol dol do.—DeR
For Mopsa.—DeR
The four brothers.—DeR
Foxes ("Old Dr. Cox's").—DeR
Full circle.—DeR
Full moon ("One night as Dick lay fast asleep").—DeR—MaP
The funeral.—DeR
The gage.—DeR
The garden (for a picture).—DeR
Gaze now.—DeR
The ghost chase.—DeR
A goldfinch.—DeR
Gone ("Bright sun, hot sun, oh, to be").—DeR
Gone ("Where's the Queen of Sheba").—DeR
Grace.—DeR
The grey wolf.—DeR
Grim.—DeR—MaP
Groat nor tester.—MaP
Hapless.—DeR—MaP
The hare ("In the black furrow of a field").—DeR
The harebell.—DeR
Hark.—DeR
Harvest (for a picture).—DeR
Haunted ("From out the wood I watched them shine").—DeR
Haunted ("The rabbit in his burrow keeps").—DeR
Haymaking.—DeR
Here today.—DeR
Hi.—DeR
Hide and seek.—DeR—MaP
High.—DeR
Holidays (for a picture).—DeR
The holly.—DeR
The honey robbers.—DeR—MaP

The horn.—DeR
The horseman ("I heard a horseman").—DeR—MaP
The horseman ("There was a horseman rode so fast").—DeR—MaP
The house ("A lane at the end of Old Pilgrim Street").—DeR
The house of dream.—DeR
The hunt.—DeR
The huntsmen.—DeR—MaP
I can't abear.—DeR—MaP
I dream of a place.—DeR
I met at eve.—DeR
"I saw three witches".—DeR
Ice.—DeR
In the dying of daylight.—DeR
Innocency.—DeR
The isle of Lone.—DeR
Jennie Wren.—DeR
Jim Jay ("Do diddle di do").—DeR—MaP
John Mouldy.—DeR
The journey ("Heart-sick of his journey was the Wanderer").—DeR
The journey ("When the high road").—DeR
King David.—DeR—MaP
Kings.—DeR
Kings and queens.—DeR—MaP
Kiph.—DeR
Known of old.—DeR
The lamplighter.—DeR
A lantern.—DeR
Late ("Three small men in a small house").—MaP
Listen.—DeR
The little bird ("My dear Daddie bought a mansion").—DeR—MaP
The little creature.—DeR
The little green orchard.—DeR—MaP
The little old cupid.—DeR—MaP
The little salamander.—DeR
The little shop (for a picture).—DeR
Lob-lie-by-the-fire.—DeR
Logs.—DeR
Lone.—DeR
Longlegs.—DeR—MaP
The lost shoe.—DeR—MaP
Lovelocks.—DeR
Lullaby ("Sleep, sleep, thou lovely one").—DeR
Lully.—DeR
The magnifying glass ("With this round glass").—DeR
Many a mickle.—DeR—MaP
March hares.—DeR
Marching song. See The three royal monkeys
Mary.—DeR
Master Rabbit.—DeR
Me ("As long as I live").—DeR
Melmillo.—DeR—MaP
Mermaids ("Leagues, leagues over").—DeR
The mermaids ("Sand, sand, hills of sand").—DeR
The miller and his son.—DeR
Mima.—DeR—MaP
"Misericordia".—DeR
Miss Cherry.—DeR
Miss T.—DeR—MaP
Missel thrush.—DeR
Mistletoe.—DeR—MaP
The mocking fairy.—DeR—MaP
The mother bird.—DeR
Mr. Alacadacca's.—MaP
Mr. Punch (for a picture).—DeR
Mrs. Earth.—DeR—MaP

De La Mare, Walter—*Continued*
The song of the mad prince.—DeR—ElW—MaP
The song of the secret.—DeR—MaP
Sooeep.—DeR—MaP
Sorcery.—DeR
Stars ("If to the heavens you lift your eyes").—DeR
The storm ("First there were two of us, then there were three of us").—DeR
The stranger ("In the nook of a wood where a pool freshed with dew").—DeR
The stranger ("A little after twilight").—DeR
Strangers.—DeR
Summer evening.—DeR—MaP
Sunk Lyonesse.—DeR
The sunken garden.—DeR
Supper ("Her pinched grey body").—DeR
Supper ("I supped where bloomed the red red rose").—DeR
The supper ("A wolf he pricks with eyes of fire").—DeR
Suppose ("Suppose, and suppose that a wild little horse of magic").—DeR
Tartary.—DeR
The tent.—DeR
Thames.—DeR
Then.—DeR—MaP
Then as now.—DeR
"There sate good Queen Bess, oh".—DeR
There was an old woman ("There was an old woman of Bumble Bhosey").—DeR
They told me.—DeR
The thief at Robin's castle.—DeR—MaP
The three beggars.—DeR
The three royal monkeys, sels.
   Andy Battle's song.—DeR
   Marching song.—DeR
   Nod's song.—DeR
   The water midden's song.—DeR
The thrush.—DeR
Thunder.—DeR
Tillie.—DeR—MaP
"Tiny Eenanennika".—DeR
Tired Tim.—DeR—MaP
Tit for tat.—DeR—MaP
To bed.—DeR
Tom's little dog.—DeR
Trees ("Of all the trees in England").—DeR—MaP
The truants.—DeR—MaP
"Two deep clear eyes".—DeR
Under the rose (the song of the wanderer).—DeR
The unfinished dream.—DeR
The universe.—DeR
Unstooping.—DeR—MaP
Up and down.—DeR—MaP
The voice.—DeR
Voices.—DeR
Wanderers.—DeR—MaP
A warbler.—DeR
The water midden's song. See The three royal monkeys
Where ("Houses, houses, oh, I know").—DeR
Where ("Monkeys in a forest").—DeR
White ("Once a miller, and he would say").—DeR
Who really.—DeR
Why ("Why do you weep, Mother, why do you weep").—DeR
A widow's weeds.—DeR—MaP
Wild are the waves.—DeR
Will ever.—DeR—MaP
"Will-o'-the-wisp".—DeR

The wind ("The wind, yes, I hear it, goes wandering by").—DeR
The window ("Behind the blinds I sit and watch").—DeR—MaP
Winter ("Green mistletoe").—DeR
The witch ("Weary went the old witch").—DeR
Won't.—DeR
Yeo ho. See Andy Battle's and Nod's song
De-min, Xu
The moon rises slowly over the ocean, tr. by Edward Morin and Dennis Ding.—NyT
De Paola, Tomie
The secret place.—DeT
De Regniers, Beatrice Schenk
Brand new baby.—DeW
The cheerful child's week.—DeW
The churlish child's week.—DeW
Co-op-er-ate.—DeW
"Did you ever have a dog".—MoS
I wish.—DeW
"If we walked on our hands".—DeS
"If you find a little feather".—HoT—MoS
An important conversation.—DeW
"Keep a poem in your pocket".—HoSt—LoFh
Mean song ("I'm warning you").—DeW
Queen of the world (or king).—DeW
There are days.—DeW
"This big cat".—MoS
The way I really am.—DeW
"What if".—DeW
When I tell you I'm scared.—DeW
De Souza, Eunice
Sweet sixteen.—AgL
The **deacon's** masterpiece, or, the wonderful one-hoss shay. Oliver Wendell Holmes.—ElW
The **dead** bird. Jane Yolen.—YoBi
"The **dead** crab". See Crab
Dear delight. Walter De La Mare.—DeR
"**Dear** Father". Margaret Wise Brown.—PlW
"**Dear** Father, hear and bless". Unknown.—StP
"**Dear** God". See The prayer of the little ducks
"**Dear** God". Irene Wells.—StP
"**Dear** God, give me time". See The prayer of the ox
"**Dear** God, it is I, the elephant". See The prayer of the elephant
"**Dear** God, why have you made me so ugly". See The prayer of the monkey
"**Dear** God, would you take your light". See The prayer of the glow-worm
"**Dear** Lord my God". Madeleine L'Engle.—StP
"**Dear** Lord, you are the Truth, when I keep". Henri J. Nouwen.—StP
"**Dear** Mayor". See Ode to the Mayor
"**Dear** reader, prythee, stay, and look". See The picture-book
"**Dear** Santa Claus". Jack Prelutsky.—LoFh
"**Dear** Sirs". See Letter from a witch named Flo
Dearmer, Geoffrey
The giraffe ("Hide of a leopard and hide of a deer").—CoAz
Death. See also Grief; Immortality; Laments
After the dazzle of day. W. Whitman.—HoVo
Ailey, Baldwin, Floyd, Killens, and Mayfield. M. Angelou.—AnI
Annabel Lee. E. A. Poe.—ElW
Anthony. J. Shore.—JaPr
At last. W. De La Mare.—DeR
At sunset. J. von Eichendorff.—GoT
At the ferry. V. Mukhopadhyay.—NyT
Autumnal equinox. E. E. Wilson.—JaM
The babes in the wood. Unknown.—ElW

Death.—*Continued*

Ballad of Birmingham. D. Randall.—ElW
The ballad of Jimi. C. Knight.—SuC
"Because I could not stop for death". E. Dickinson.—SuI
The bird ("As poor old Biddie"). W. De La Mare.—DeR
Blues for Benny "Kid" Paret. D. Smith.—KnAs
Boy, fifteen, killed by hummingbird. L. Linssen.—JaPr
The breath of death (the cigarette). L. Sissay.—AgL
The bridge. P. B. Janeczko.—JaB
Brothers ("Raymond slowed"). P. B. Janeczko.—JaB
Captain Lean. W. De La Mare.—DeR
Celestial. M. Pettit.—JaM
"Charlie Chuck". Unknown.—WiA
Children lost. M. Fatchen.—FaCm
Cleaning the well. F. Chappell.—JaPr
A clear midnight. W. Whitman.—HoVo
Cockles and mussels. Unknown.—ElW
Code blue. B. L. Cantwell.—JaPr
Come up from the fields father. W. Whitman.—HoVo
The cowboy's lament. Unknown.—ElW
Crab. V. Worth.—WoAl
The dead bird. J. Yolen.—YoBi
"Did you ever have a dog". B. S. De Regniers.—MoS
"Did you ever think". Unknown.—CoM
The dog poisoner. K. Wilson.—JaM
"Down-adown-derry". W. De La Mare.—DeR
Early love. H. Scott.—JaM
Elegy for the girl who died in the dump at Ford's Gulch. J. Johnson.—JaPr
The emeritus. L. Nathan.—JaM
Euphemistic. E. Merriam.—MeCh
The evening light along the sound. S. Santos.—GoT
"Farewell, my younger brother". Unknown.—SnD
"Fear no more the heat o' the sun". From Cymbeline. W. Shakespeare.—ElW
Fireworks ("The Fourth of July's"). M. C. Livingston.—LiR
For Mugs. M. C. Livingston.—LiDp
For the death of Vince Lombardi. J. Dickey.—KnAs
Forgotten. C. Rylant.—JaP
Gambler. E. Stuckey.—AgL
"Garth, from off the garden wall". X. J. Kennedy.—KeFb
Gliding o'er all. W. Whitman.—HoVo
"Good-bye my fancy". W. Whitman.—HoVo
A grandfather's last letter. N. Dubie.—JaM
The great one. T. Clark.—MoA
How birds should die. P. Zimmer.—JaP
"How's mama". J. Carson.—CaS
"I am asking you to come back home". J. Carson.—CaS
"I kept on past". A. MacNeacail.—AgL
If our dogs outlived us. D. Hines.—JaM
"I'm going to die". K. Dakos.—DaI
J.T. never will be ten. K. Dakos.—DaI
Jasmine. K. Hong Ryou.—NyT
John Mouldy. W. De La Mare.—DeR
Killing chickens. B. Weigl.—JaPr
Kings and queens. W. De La Mare.—DeR—MaP
The Lady of Shalott. A. Tennyson.—ElW
The last man killed by Indians in Kimble County, Texas. M. Angelotti.—JaM
"Lully, lulley, lully, lulley". Unknown.—StP

Marching song. From The three royal monkeys. W. De La Mare.—DeR
Married love. Kuan Tao Sheng.—GoU
Maud. M. Swander.—JaM
Me ("As long as I live"). W. De La Mare.—DeR
The memory of horses. R. Jacobsen.—NyT
The mermaid. W. B. Yeats.—AgL
The monument. P. B. Janeczko.—JaB
Moon's ending. S. Teasdale.—GoT
"Mother, we are cold". Unknown.—SnD
Mountain bride. R. Morgan.—JaM
Music. W. De La Mare.—DeR
My city. J. W. Johnson.—SuC
"My father died a month ago". Mother Goose.—WaM
My great grand uncle. T. Ray.—NyT
My legacy. W. Whitman.—HoVo
"My life closed twice before its close". E. Dickinson.—SuI
Napoleon. M. Holub.—NyT
Never be as fast as I have been, the jockey Tony DeSpirito dead at thirty-nine. R. Hahn.—KnAs
Nine charms against the hunter. D. Wagoner.—KnAs
"No labor-saving machine". W. Whitman.—HoVo
No, love is not dead. R. Desnos.—GoU
Nobody knows. W. De La Mare.—DeR—MaP
Nocturne ("A long arm embossed with gold slides from the tree tops"). L.-P. Fargue.—GoT
Now lift me close. W. Whitman.—HoVo
"O Lord, support us all the day long, until". Unknown.—StP
"O purple finch". E. E. Cummings.—ElW
Old folks laugh. M. Angelou.—AnI
The old king. W. De La Mare.—DeR
One for one. J. Heynen.—JaPr
Our grandmothers. M. Angelou.—AnI
"Out of the cradle endlessly rocking". W. Whitman.—HoVo
Part XIX: Sadly, o, sadly, the sweet bells of Baddeley. From A child's day. W. De La Mare.—DeR
The pedlar. W. De La Mare.—DeR
The penny owing. W. De La Mare.—DeR
The pioneers. C. Mortimer.—JaPr
Playmate ("And because"). K. Wilson.—JaPr
Please to remember ("Here am I"). W. De La Mare.—DeR
Poem ("I loved my friend"). L. Hughes.—DeS—DeT—SlM
Poem III. From Twenty-one love poems. A. Rich.—GoU
Postcards of the hanging. A. Hudgins.—JaM
Queries to my seventieth year. W. Whitman.—HoVo
The rabbit hunter. R. Frost.—KnAs
The racer's widow. L. Gluck.—KnAs
The raven. E. A. Poe.—SuI
The raven's tomb. W. De La Mare.—DeR
Relationship. M. C. Livingston.—LiT
Requiem. P. Fleischman.—FlJ
"Rin Tin Tin swallowed a pin". Unknown.—WiA
Sam's three wishes or life's little whirligig. W. De La Mare.—DeR
Say goodbye to Big Daddy. R. Jarrell.—KnAs
The sea gull's eye. R. Hoban.—JaP
Secrets ("I doubt that you remember her, except"). R. Pack.—JaM
Setting the traps. D. Jauss.—JaPr
A short long story. J. Cunningham.—JaP
Skater in blue. J. Parini.—KnAs
Sleep, grandmother. M. Van Doren.—SuI

Death.—*Continued*
"The sodden moss sinks underfoot when we cross half-frozen bays and". A. Debeljak.—NyT
Something left to say. K. Soniat.—JaM
Song ("When I am dead, my dearest"). C. G. Rossetti.—ElW
The song of Finis. W. De La Mare.—DeR—MaP
Sorcery. W. De La Mare.—DeR
Still life. M. Angelotti.—JaM
Stopping by woods on a snowy evening. R. Frost.—DeS—DeT—ElW—SuI
Sunk Lyonesse. W. De La Mare.—DeR
The teenage cocaine dealer considers his death on the street outside a Key West funeral for a much-loved civic leader. J. Hall.—JaPr
That summer. H. Scott.—JaPr
Then as now. W. De La Mare.—DeR
"There was a little girl". Unknown.—WiA
"There was a young fellow named Hall". Unknown.—LiLo
"There was an old woman of Ryde". Unknown.—PrP
   "There was a young lady of Ryde".—LiLo
"There's a certain slant of light". E. Dickinson.—GoT—SuI
They told me. W. De La Mare.—DeR
To an athlete dying young. A. E. Housman.—ElW
To daffodils. R. Herrick.—ElW
To the young who want to die. G. Brooks.—SuC
The twa brothers. Unknown.—ElW
The twa corbies. Unknown.—CaB
Twilight of the outward life. H. von Hofmannsthal.—GoT
"Used to be just fine with me". J. Carson.—CaS
The watch ("I wakened on my hot, hard bed"). F. Cornford.—MoR
We are seven. W. Wordsworth.—ElW
We real cool. G. Brooks.—AgL—ElW
"When howitzers began". H. Carruth.—MoR
"When lilacs last in the dooryard bloom'd". W. Whitman.—HoVo
The white rose, Sophie Scholl, 1921-1943. E. Mumford.—JaM
"Willis Comfort did not outlive". J. Carson.—CaS
Windigo spirit. K. Stange.—BoT
"The winter they bombed Pearl Harbor". W. McDonald.—JaPr
You better be ready. J. Lane.—BoT

Debeljak, Ales
"The sodden moss sinks underfoot when we cross half-frozen bays and".—NyT

Debt. Sunay Akin, tr. by Yusuf Eradam.—NyT

Deceit
The flattered flying fish. E. V. Rieu.—ElW
A poison tree. W. Blake.—ElW
The spider and the fly. M. Howitt.—ElW
The walrus and the carpenter. From Through the looking-glass. L. Carroll.—DeT—ElW—HoS

December
Cat ("I prefer"). M. Singer.—SiT
Crown of light festival. D. Bateson.—FoLe
December ("I like days"). A. Fisher.—FiA—GoA
December ("Round slice of moon, December night"). F. Newman.—BoT
December ("This is the month"). A. Bonner.—FoLe
Early December. V. Worth.—WoA
"I heard a bird sing". O. Herford.—DeS
Oranges ("The first time I walked"). G. Soto.—JaM—SoA
Suddenly. A. Fisher.—FiA

December ("I like days"). Aileen Fisher.—FiA—GoA
December ("Round slice of moon, December night"). Fran Newman.—BoT
December ("This is the month"). Ann Bonner.—FoLe
Deciduous. Eve Merriam.—MeS
"**Deciduous** deciduous". See Deciduous
Deck the halls. Unknown.—YoHa
"**Deck** the halls with boughs of holly". See Deck the halls
Decorations. Valerie Worth.—WoA
"A **decrepit** old gasman, named Peter". Unknown.—LiLo
Dedicated to F.W. Ernest Hemingway.—KnAs
"**Deep** in dark". See Penguins
"**Deep** peace of the running wave to you". Fiona McLeod.—StP
Deer
Alone in winter. J. P. Lewis.—LeT
The deer on the mountain. Buson.—DeI
The fallow deer at the lonely house. T. Hardy.—ElW
In the forest. Unknown.—DeI
January deer. M. Singer.—SiT
Just once. M. C. Livingston.—LiNe
"Night deepens". O. N. Komachi.—GoT
R is for reindeer. W. J. Smith.—SmL
"There is a young reindeer named Donder". J. P. Lewis.—LiLo
"Used to be just fine with me". J. Carson.—CaS
The wapiti. O. Nash.—KeT
Deer mouse ("Get get get get get"). Marilyn Singer.—SiT
Deer mouse ("Who tells the little deer mouse"). Aileen Fisher.—FiH
The **deer** on the mountain. Buson, tr. by Tze-si Huang.—DeI
Defeat. See Failure
Defiance. Unknown.—OpT
Degli Sposi. Rika Lesser.—GoU
Deidre Spector. Mel Glenn.—GlBc
Deinonychus. Jack Prelutsky.—PrT
"**Deinonychus** was named for its terrible claw". See Deinonychus
"**Dem** tell me". See Checking out me history
Demaru
"Butterflies dancing through falling snow".—WhAa
Dennis, Clarence James
Growing up ("Little Tommy Tadpole began to weep and wail").—CoAz
Dennis Finch. Mel Glenn.—GlBc
Densmore, Frances
Butterfly song, tr.—KeT
The **dental** history of Flossie Fly. X. J. Kennedy.—KeGh
Dentists
"Daniel was a naughty man". Unknown.—ScA
The dental history of Flossie Fly. X. J. Kennedy.—KeGh
A war baby looks back. J. Holden.—JaPr
Why I always brush. A. Adoff.—AdCh
Der Hovanessian, Diana
Ants, tr.—NyT
The question mark, tr.—NyT
"**Descend**, silent spirit". See Prayer to the snowy owl
Descent. Eve Merriam.—MeCh
Desert baseball. J. Patrick Lewis.—LeT
Deserted farm. Mark Vinz.—JaP
Deserts
Desert baseball. J. P. Lewis.—LeT

Deserts—*Continued*
Ozymandias. P. B. Shelley.—ElW
Desnos, Robert
No, love is not dead, tr. by Bill Zavatsky.—GoU
The owls ("The owls take a broad view"), tr. by John Mole.—LiIf
"**Desolate** and lone". See Lost
A **desolate** scene. Basho, tr. by Tze-si Huang.—DeI
Despair
Alas. W. De La Mare.—DeR
"Although there is". O. N. Komachi.—GoT
As I did rove. W. De La Mare.—DeR
Baseball's sad lexicon. F. P. Adams.—MoA
The blues. L. Hughes.—KeT
Captive bird. Boethius.—CaB
Championship. S. B. Mathis.—MaR
The dunce. W. De La Mare.—DeR—MaP
February 14. M. C. Livingston.—LiT
Footpath. S. Ngatho.—NyT
Hapless. W. De La Mare.—DeR—MaP
Help ("Would it help"). M. C. Livingston.—LiT
Home ("Yelling, shouting, arguing"). M. C. Livingston.—LiT
If sometimes blue. A. L. Woods.—SlM
The labourer. T. Daby.—NyT
Lost ("Desolate and lone"). C. Sandburg.—LaN
"Misericordia". W. De La Mare.—DeR
My father's leaving. I. Sadoff.—JaPr
The Optileast and the Pessimost. E. Merriam.—MeS
The playmate ("Weep no more, nor grieve, nor sigh"). W. De La Mare.—DeR
The prayer of the monkey. C. B. De Gasztold.—DeP
The raven. E. A. Poe.—SuI
Scraping the world away. C. H. Webster.—AgL
The slave auction. F. E. W. Harper.—SuC
Stay with me. G. K. Hongo.—JaPr
There was a pig. From Sylvie and Bruno. L. Carroll.—ClI
"There's a certain slant of light". E. Dickinson.—GoT—SuI
Tired Tim. W. De La Mare.—DeR—MaP
"Twilight". I. Shikibu.—GoT
The watch ("I wakened on my hot, hard bed"). F. Cornford.—MoR
Who's here. E. Merriam.—MeS
"Year that trembled and reel'd beneath me". W. Whitman.—HoVo
DeSpirito, Tony (about)
Never be as fast as I have been, the jockey Tony DeSpirito dead at thirty-nine. R. Hahn.—KnAs
Desserts
"Bananas and cream". D. McCord.—DeT—LiDd
Chocolate dreams and chocolate schemes. A. Adoff.—AdCh
Chocolate dreams, one. A. Adoff.—AdCh
Chocolate moose. W. J. Smith.—SmL
"For water-ices, cheap but good". A. Laing.—StP
Friday the thirteenth. A. Adoff.—AdCh
I will hold your hand. A. Adoff.—AdCh
"The Queen of Hearts". Mother Goose.—EdGl—SuO
"**Detestable** crow". Basho, tr. by Sylvia Cassedy and Kunihiro Suetake.—CaR
Deutsch, Babette
"Put out my eyes, and I can see you still", tr.—GoU
Devi, Shyamasree
The ship's whistle, tr.—NyT
Devil
"Did you eever, iver, over". Unknown.—WiA

A gardener. Unknown.—OpT
"Oh, little devil". Unknown.—CoM
There was a knight. Unknown.—ElW
Dew
Dew. L. Suryadi.—NyT
The foggy dew. Unknown.—ElW
Dew. Linus Suryadi, tr. by John H. McGlynn.—NyT
"**Dew** adorns the morning world". See Dew
Di, Xue
The mushroom river, tr. by Ping Wang and Gale Nelson.—NyT
"My mouth is a horse's mouth". See Remembering
Remembering, sels.
"My mouth is a horse's mouth".—NyT
Di Giovanni, Norman Thomas
Afterglow, tr.—GoT
Di Pasquale, Emanuel
All Hallows' Eve (My mother brings me to visit a Sicilian cemetery).—LiHp
Father's magic.—LiPf
"In the early morning".—LiPg
Louisa Jones sings a praise to Caesar.—LiDp
"My mother and I".—LiPm
The owl takes off at Upper Black Eddy, Pa.—LiIf
A **dialogue** of watching. Kenneth Rexroth.—GoU
"**Diamonds**, hearts, kings and aces". Marcus Wayne.—LeCa
Diana Marvin. Mel Glenn.—GlBc
Dianikian, Gregory
How I learned English.—JaM
Diary of a woodcutter, sels. Fuad Rifka, tr. by Shirley Kaufman
"Wrinkles in the lake".—NyT
Dickens, Charles
"God bless us, every one".—StP
Dickery Dean. Dennis Lee.—KeT
"**Dickery**, dickery, dare". Mother Goose.—ClI
Dickey, James
For the death of Vince Lombardi.—KnAs
In the pocket.—KnAs—MoR
The lifeguard.—KnAs
Dickinson, Emily
Autumn. See "The morns are meeker than they were"
"Because I could not stop for death".—SuI
"Bee, I'm expecting you".—WhAa
Letter to bee.—KeT
A bird ("A bird came down the walk").—DeS
"Blazing in gold, and".—GoT
"The brain is wider than the sky".—ElW
"I never saw a moor".—SuI
"I'm nobody, who are you".—ElW
Letter to bee. See "Bee, I'm expecting you"
"The morns are meeker than they were".—SuI
Autumn.—DeT
"My life closed twice before its close".—SuI
"A narrow fellow in the grass".—ElW
"Our share of night to bear".—GoT
"A slash of blue, a sweep of gray".—GoT
"There is no frigate like a book".—DeT—ElW
"There's a certain slant of light".—GoT—SuI
"Wild nights, wild nights".—GoU
Yellow man, purple man.—KeT
"**Dicky**, Dicky Dout". Unknown.—OpI
Dictionary. William Jay Smith.—SmL
The **dictionary** bird. Margaret Mahy.—MaN
"A **dictionary's** where you can look things up". See Dictionary
"**Did** he say I said you said she said that". Unknown.—WiA

"**Did** I dream the owl or was it really there". See Beware

"**Did** I ever tell you that Mrs. McCave". See Too many Daves

"**Did** I tell you". See Canada goose

"**Did** Jesus have a baby sister". Dory Previn.—AgL

"**Did** you eever, iver, over". Unknown.—WiA

"**Did** you ever ever ever". Unknown.—WiA

"**Did** you ever go fishing on a bright summer day". See "Did you ever go fishing on a bright sunny day"

"**Did** you ever go fishing on a bright sunny day". Unknown.—WiA

"Did you ever go fishing on a bright summer day".—ScA

"**Did** you ever have a dog". Beatrice Schenk De Regniers.—MoS

"**Did** you ever hear about Elephant Bill". See Elephant Bill and Jackrabbit Jack

"**Did** you ever hear such a noise and clamor". Unknown.—WiA

"**Did** you ever see the devil". See A gardener

"**Did** you ever think". Unknown.—CoM

"**Did** you see my wife". Mother Goose.—WaM

Diddle diddle dumpling. See "Diddle diddle dumpling, my son John"

"**Diddle** diddle dumpling, my son John". Mother Goose.—SuO—WaM

Diddle diddle dumpling.—HoS

"**Diddlety** diddlety dumpty". Mother Goose.—WaM

Didrikson, Babe (about)
Babe Didrikson. G. Rice.—KnAs

"The **diet** of the owl is not". See Owl

Diets and dieting
"I would reduce". Unknown.—ScA
"Jack Sprat could eat no fat". Mother Goose.—EdGl—SuO—WaM

The **difference**. Myra Cohn Livingston.—LiNe

Different dads. X. J. Kennedy.—KeK—LiPf

A **different** door. X. J. Kennedy.—LaCc

Different feelings. James Berry.—BeW

A **different** image. Dudley Randall.—SuC

A **different** kind of Sunday. James Berry.—BeW

"**Different** people have different 'pinions". Unknown.—OpI

"**Dig** your starting holes deep". From To James. Frank Horne.—SuC

The **digger** wasp. Paul Fleischman.—FlJ

Diggin sing. James Berry.—BeW

Digging for China. Richard Wilbur.—SuI

"**Dignified** and thin". See Unitas

"**Dill**, paprika, onion, clove". See A charm against a grackle

"A **diller**, a dollar". Mother Goose.—SuO—WaM

"**Dilly** dilly piccalilli". Clyde Watson.—LiDd

"**Dimpleton** the simpleton". Dennis Lee.—CoAz

Dina Harper. Mel Glenn.—GlBc

Ding, Dennis
The moon rises slowly over the ocean, tr.—NyT

"**Ding** dong bell". Mother Goose.—SuO—WaM

"**Ding,** dong, darrow". Unknown.—ClI

"**Ding** dong for Booman". See Booman

"**Dingty** diddlety". Mother Goose.—WaM

Dinner table rhymes, complete. Unknown
"Here's good bread and cheese and porter".—OpT
"Little Popsie-Wopsie".—OpT
"Please, Lord, send summat good to eat".—OpT

Dinnertime. Mary Ann Hoberman.—HoFa

Dinosaur birthday. Myra Cohn Livingston.—LiBp

Dinosaur dances. Jane Yolen.—YoDd

Dinosaur department. Max Fatchen.—FaCm

The **dinosaur** dinner. Dennis Lee.—BoT

Dinosaur hard rock band. Jane Yolen.—YoDd

Dinosaur waltz. Jane Yolen.—YoDd

Dinosaurs. See Prehistoric animals

"**Dinosaurs**". See Absolutely nothing

Dinosaurs ("Dinosaurs do not count"). Valerie Worth.—WoAl

Dinosaurs ("Diplodocus"). Grace Nichols.—NiCo

"The **dinosaurs** did not remain". See Brain drain

"**Dinosaurs** do not count". See Dinosaurs

The **dinosore**. Jane Yolen.—PrFo

Dipa, the lamp. Ann Bonner.—FoLe

"**Diplodocus**". See Dinosaurs

Diplodocus. Jack Prelutsky.—PrT

"**Diplodocus** plodded along on the trail". See Diplodocus

"**Dirdum** drum". See The cat's song

Direction. Alonzo Lopez.—AgL

Directions
Compass. V. Worth.—WoAl
"East, west, north, south". Unknown.—WiA
The four brothers. W. De La Mare.—DeR
The four corners of the universe. Unknown.—SnD
Points of the compass. E. Merriam.—MeS

Dirges. See Laments

"A **dirty** cloud of sheep". See Ode to a day in the country

"**Dis** is a dreadful bad bass bounce". See Klassical dub

Disappointment. See Failure

The **disaster**. Bruce Bennett.—MoR

Disasters. See also Shipwrecks
The disaster. B. Bennett.—MoR
Wind's foam. A. Mahmud.—NyT

"A **discerning** young lamb of Long Sutton". Myra Cohn Livingston.—LiLo

Disco date, 1980. James Berry.—BeW

"**Disco** dino dancing". Jane Yolen.—YoDd

Discontent. See also Contentment
"Oh that I were". Mother Goose.—WaM

"A **discovery**". Yaku.—WhAa
Haiku.—DeT

Disease. See Sickness

The **disgruntled** husband. Unknown.—OpT

Dishes. See Tableware

Dishman, Nelda
Trees ("The trees share their shade with").—LoFh

Dishonesty. See Truthfulness and falsehood

Disillusion. Maureen Burge.—AgL

Dislikes. See Likes and dislikes

Disobedience. Alan Alexander Milne.—KeT

Dissanayake, Wimal
Freedom.—NyT

Distance
Distances of longing. F. Abu Khalid.—NyT
Family portrait. E. Budianta.—NyT
Far and close. G. Cheng.—NyT
Great grandma. L. Morrison.—LiPg
"I didn't go to the moon, I went much further". From The Glass Menagerie. T. Williams.—GoT
"Living here". Unknown.—GoU

Distances of longing. Fawziyya Abu Khalid, tr. by May Jayyusi.—NyT

Distributing the harvest. Brian Moses.—FoLe

Ditlevsen, Tove
Divorce.—AgL

Ditto marks or, how do you amuse a muse. Eve Merriam.—MeCh

Divali ("Ravana's gone"). Judith Nicholls.—FoLe

Divali ("Winter stalks us"). David Harmer.—FoLe

Divine delight. Walter De La Mare.—DeR

Diving. See Swimming and diving

Divorce

Circles ("I am speaking of circles"). M. C. Livingston.—JaP—LiT

Deidre Spector. M. Glenn.—GlBc

Divorce. T. Ditlevsen.—AgL

Excuse. M. C. Livingston.—LiT

Father ("I look for you on every street"). M. C. Livingston.—LiT

Garage apartment. M. C. Livingston.—LiT

The gift ("When I was five my father kidnapped me"). M. Jarman.—JaM

His girlfriend. M. C. Livingston.—LiT

"I cannot remember all the times he hit me". J. Carson.—CaS

In the middle. M. C. Livingston.—LiT

Invitation ("Listen, I've a big surprise"). M. C. Livingston.—KeT—LiT

Letter. M. C. Livingston.—LiT

Long ago days. M. C. Livingston.—LiT

Ms. Charlotte Kendall, biology. M. Glenn.—GlBc

"My daughter got divorced". J. Carson.—CaS

My father. M. A. Hoberman.—HoFa

My father's leaving. I. Sadoff.—JaPr

New Dad. M. C. Livingston.—LiT

Nicholas Townshed. M. Glenn.—GlBc

Divorce. Tove Ditlevsen.—AgL

Dixon, Zuhur

Overture, tr. by Patricia Alanah Byrne and Salma Khadra Jayyusi.—NyT

"Do alley cats go". See Alley cat school

"Do diddle di do". See Jim Jay

"Do ghouls". Lilian Moore.—PrFo

"Do go to bed, they're saying". See And s-s-so to b-b-bed

Do good. Ashley Bryan.—BrS

"Do it this way do it your way". See Don't do it my way

Do it yourself. Max Fatchen.—FaCm

"Do not forget, Lord". See The prayer of the cock

"Do not jump on ancient uncles". See Rules

"Do not steal this book, my lad". See "Don't steal this book, my little lad"

"Do rabbits have Christmas". Aileen Fisher.—FiA

"Do skyscrapers ever grow tired". See Skyscrapers

"Do what you like with my face". Amanda Aizpuriete, tr. by Inguna Jansone.—NyT

Do witches have. Jane Yolen.—YoBe

"Do witches have babies". See Do witches have

"Do you always act polite". See Chimera

"Do you ask what the birds say, the sparrow, the dove". See Answer to a child's question

"Do you carrot all for me". Unknown.—WiA

"Do you ever think about grass". See Grass

Do you know anyone like him. John Ciardi.—CiH

"Do you know, do you know". See Under the snow

"Do you know where a mouse". See A cozy little house

"Do you like to shine all the time". See Talking to the sun

"Do you love me". Unknown.—WiA

"Do you remember an Inn". See Tarantella

"Do your ears hang low". Unknown.—ScA

"Dobbin's in stable, pigs are in sty". See Holidays (for a picture)

Dobyns, Stephen

Black dog, red dog.—JaPr

"Doctor Bell fell down the well". Unknown.—PrP

Doctor Blair. Grace Nichols.—NiCo

"Doctor Blair is the name of a bat". See Doctor Blair

"Doctor Foster went to Gloucester". Mother Goose.—SuO—WaM

"**Doctor** Who, I am forced to admit". Charles Connell.—LiLo

Doctors

"Doctor Bell fell down the well". Unknown.—PrP

"Doctor Foster went to Gloucester". Mother Goose.—SuO—WaM

"I do not like thee, Doctor Fell". Mother Goose.—OpI—SuO—WaM

"Old man Moses, sick in bed". Unknown.—ScA

"One, two, three, a-nation, doctor, doctor". Unknown.—WiA

"To the medicine man's house they have led me". Unknown.—LiIf

The vet. M. C. Livingston.—LiR

The dodo ("The mournful dodo lay in bed"). Peter Wesley-Smith.—PrFo

Dodo ("Years they mistook me for you"). Henry Carlile.—JaPr

Dodos

The dodo ("The mournful dodo lay in bed"). P. Wesley-Smith.—PrFo

Dodo ("Years they mistook me for you"). H. Carlile.—JaPr

Dodos. X. J. Kennedy.—KeK

Dodos. X. J. Kennedy.—KeK

"**Does** an owl appreciate". See Aesthetic curiosity

"**Does** he love me". Unknown.—WiA

"**Does** it all add up". See Mr. Ted Sage, accounting

"**Does** your shirt shop stock short socks with spots". Unknown.—WiA

Dog ("Dogs are quite a bit like people"). William Jay Smith.—LiDp—SmL

Dog ("Under a maple tree"). Valerie Worth.—JaP—WoAl

The dog (as seen by the cat). Oliver Herford.—ElW

"**Dog** caught a rye straw". Unknown.—WiA

Dog days. Julia Fields.—LiDp

"**The dog** is black or white or brown". See The dog (as seen by the cat)

"**Dog** means dog". See Blum

The dog poisoner. Keith Wilson.—JaM

Dogs

All hot (the chestnut man). W. De La Mare.—DeR

"April is a dog's dream". M. Singer.—SiT

Autumn ("The puppy"). Issa.—DeI

The bandog. W. De La Mare.—DeR—MaP

The barkday party. J. Berry.—BeW

Big black dog. C. Michael.—CoAz

"Bow wow wow". Mother Goose.—WaM

Buying a puppy. L. Norris.—LiDp

Cats and dogs. N. M. Bodecker.—KeT—LaM—MoS

Cerberus. N. B. Taylor.—WhDd

Chihuahua. B. MacLoughland.—LiDp

A child's dream. F. Cornford.—ElW

The chow hound. J. Ciardi.—CiH

"Come hither, little puppy dog". Mother Goose.—WaM

D is for dog. W. J. Smith.—SmL

"Did you ever have a dog". B. S. De Regniers.—MoS

"Ding, dong, darrow". Unknown.—ClI

Dog ("Dogs are quite a bit like people"). W. J. Smith.—LiDp—SmL

Dog ("Under a maple tree"). V. Worth.—JaP—WoAl

The dog (as seen by the cat). O. Herford.—ElW

"Dog caught a rye straw". Unknown.—WiA

Dog days. J. Fields.—LiDp

The dog poisoner. K. Wilson.—JaM

Dogs. M. Chute.—DeS

Dogs—*Continued*

"A dog's bark isn't going to frighten the moon". From Jamaican Caribbean proverbs. Unknown.—BeW

Dog's song. R. Wallace.—KeT

The dollar dog. J. Ciardi.—LiDp

Dumb dog. J. Ridland.—LiDp

"Every time I come to town". Unknown.—WiA

"Eyes ablaze looking up". From Riddle poems. J. Berry.—BeW

For Mugs. M. C. Livingston.—LiDp

The fox and the hounds. G. Swede.—BoT

The gage. W. De La Mare.—DeR

George Bernard Shaw's opus 1. G. B. Shaw.—OpT

Hank and Peg. W. Burt.—JaPr

Happy as a dog's tail. A. Swir.—NyT

"High noon! A hot sun". Hajime.—CaR

How to sell things. G. Soto.—SoA

Hunting song. J. Yolen.—LiDp

"I had a dog whose name was Buff". Mother Goose.—WaM

I had a little dog. Mother Goose.—CII

"I had a little dog, his name was Ball". Unknown.—WiA

"I have a dog". Unknown.—ScA

"I once had a dog". Unknown.—WiA

"I want a talking dog wearing a cap". From What we said sitting making fantasies. J. Berry.—BeW

If our dogs outlived us. D. Hines.—JaM

"In downtown Philadelphia". J. Prelutsky.—PrBe

"I've got a dog as thin as a rail". Unknown.—CII—PrP

    "I have a dog as thin as a rail".—ScA

"Leg over leg". Mother Goose.—CII—WaM

A lesson ("He made fun of my Pekingese"). X. J. Kennedy.—KeK

Lost ("It's quiet"). R. H. Marks.—LiDp

Lost dog. M. C. Livingston.—LiT

Louisa Jones sings a praise to Caesar. E. Di Pasquale.—LiDp

Maud. M. Swander.—JaM

Mike and Major. C. Rylant.—JaP

"Mother doesn't want a dog". J. Viorst.—WhAa

My dog ("Here's what we think of, Gov and I"). F. Holman.—LiDp

My dog ("His nose is short and scrubby"). M. Chute.—SuI

My dog ("My dog is such a gentle soul"). M. Fatchen.—PrFo

My puppy. A. Fisher.—FiA

Napoleon. M. Holub.—NyT

Newborn puppy. A. W. Paul.—LiDp

Ode to mi perrito. G. Soto.—SoNe

Old hound. V. Worth.—LiDp

"Old Mother Hubbard". Mother Goose.—EdGl—SuO—WaM

Orphanage boy. R. P. Warren.—JaPr

Padiddle. J. P. Lewis.—LeT

A personal experience. O. Herford.—LiLo

"Poor dog Bright". Unknown.—CII

The porcupine ("Any hound a porcupine nudges"). O. Nash.—PrFo

The prayer of the dog. C. B. De Gasztold.—DeP

Puppy ("Summer is a long yellow gown"). J. P. Lewis.—LeE

Puppy ("Under the willow"). Issa.—DeI

"Rin Tin Tin swallowed a pin". Unknown.—WiA

Roger the dog. T. Hughes.—ElW

Rover. E. Merriam.—MeP

She was hungry and cold. A. Adoff.—AdIn

Sleeping Simon. D. Chandra.—LiDp

Something strange. M. C. Livingston.—LiNe

The song of the mischievous dog. D. Thomas.—DeT

Stories ("Circling by the fire"). J. P. Lewis.—LeT—LiDp

The tables turned. X. J. Kennedy.—KeK

The tale of a dog. J. H. Lambert.—CoAz

"There was a little dog and he had a little tail". Unknown.—PrP

    There was a little dog (". . . and he had a tail").—CII

"There was a small maiden named Maggie". Unknown.—LiLo—PrP

    There was a young maiden (". . . called Maggie").—CII

"To sup like a pup". D. Baruch.—MoS

Tom's little dog. W. De La Mare.—DeR

"Two little dogs". Mother Goose.—CII—WaM

Vern. G. Brooks.—LiDp

The vet. M. C. Livingston.—LiR

Walking Big Bo. X. J. Kennedy.—KeK—LiDp

Wiggle waggle, wiggle waggle. Unknown.—CII

Dogs. Marchette Chute.—DeS

"**Dogs** are quite a bit like people". See Dog

"A **dog's** bark isn't going to frighten the moon". From Jamaican Caribbean proverbs. Unknown.—BeW

"The **dogs** I know". See Dogs

Dog's song. Robert Wallace.—KeT

Doherty, Berlie

    Idh Mubarak.—FoLe

"**Doing** nothing at all". See Nothing at all

Doll. Myra Cohn Livingston.—KeT

The **doll** festival. James Kirkup.—FoLe

Doll funerals. James Kirkup.—FoLe

Dollar bird. William Jay Smith.—SmL

"The **dollar** bird lives". See Dollar bird

The **dollar** dog. John Ciardi.—LiDp

"A **dollar** dog is all mixed up". See The dollar dog

Dollar horror. Brother Resistance.—AgL

Dolls

"A bear, however hard he tries". From Teddy bear. A. A. Milne.—DeT

Doll. M. C. Livingston.—KeT

The doll festival. J. Kirkup.—FoLe

Doll funerals. J. Kirkup.—FoLe

Emily Jane. L. E. Richards.—ElW

A gift horse. A. Hashmi.—NyT

"I had a little moppet". Mother Goose.—WaM

    Little moppet.—OpT

Ms. Nadine Sierra, French. M. Glenn.—GlBc

Paper doll. G. Morfin.—NyT

The playhouse. K. Daniels.—JaPr

Sister ("Younger than they"). H. R. Coursen.—JaPr

"Trit trot to market to buy a penny doll". Mother Goose.—WaM

"**Dolly** Dimple walks like this". Unknown.—WiA

Dolphin. J. Patrick Lewis.—LeT

Dolphins. Kembi Pokereu.—AgL

Dolphins and porpoises

Dolphin. J. P. Lewis.—LeT

Dolphins. K. Pokereu.—AgL

"**Dolphins,** dolphins". See Dolphins

The **dome** of night. Claudia Lewis.—LaN

Dominick, Pieter

    Origami for two.—MoR

Don Larsen's perfect game. Paul Goodman.—KnAs

Done for. Walter De La Mare.—DeR

Donkey. Eloise Greenfield.—GrU

The **donkey** and the man. James Berry.—BeW

"**Donkey**, donkey, do not bray". Mother Goose.—
WaM
"**Donkey**, donkey, old and gray". Mother Goose.—
WaM
"The **donkey** is an ani-mule". See Jack A.
"The **donkey** says the world isn't level ground".
From Jamaican Caribbean proverbs.
Unknown.—BeW
"**Donkey** walks on four legs". Unknown.—OpI
"**Donkey** want water". See Do good
Donkeys
The ass in the lion's skin. Aesop.—CaB
Do good. A. Bryan.—BrS
Donkey. E. Greenfield.—GrU
The donkey and the man. J. Berry.—BeW
"Donkey, donkey, do not bray". Mother Goose.—
WaM
"Donkey, donkey, old and gray". Mother
Goose.—WaM
"The donkey says the world isn't level ground".
From Jamaican Caribbean proverbs.
Unknown.—BeW
"Donkey walks on four legs". Unknown.—OpI
The donkey's song. J. Yolen.—YoHa
"Far over the hills, a good way off". Unknown.—
WiA
"I have a three-legged donkey". From What we
said sitting making fantasies. J. Berry.—BeW
"If I had a donkey that wouldn't go". Mother
Goose.—WaM
Jack A. J. P. Lewis.—LeA
"My mother bought a donkey, she thought it was
a cow". Unknown.—WiA
Nicholas Nye. W. De La Mare.—DeR—MaP
The prayer of the donkey. C. B. De Gasztold.—
DeP
A prayer to go to paradise with the donkeys. F.
Jammes.—CaB
"Said the monkey to the donkey". Unknown.—
WiA
    The monkey and the donkey.—ClI
Up in the North. Unknown.—ClI
"Whoa, mule, whoa". Unknown.—WiA
The **donkey's** song. Jane Yolen.—YoHa
Donnybrook at Riverfront Stadium. Lillian
Morrison.—MoA
Don't be afraid. David Vogel, tr. by T. Carmi.—
LiPm
"**Don't** be afraid, my child, those are". See Don't be
afraid
"**Don't** call an alligator a long-mouth till you have
crossed the river". From Jamaican Caribbean
proverbs. Unknown.—BeW
"**Don't** care was made to care". Unknown.—OpI
Don't come out. Raizan, tr. by Tze-si Huang.—DeI
Don't do it my way. Fran Landesman.—AgL
"**Don't** give me the dishcloth wet". Unknown.—
CoM
"**Don't** go anywhere without me". See 2195 In the
arc of your mallet
Don't howl. James Berry.—BeW
"**Don't** say it, don't say it". Unknown.—ScA
"**Don't** shoo the morning flies away". Han Yu, tr. by
Kenneth O. Hanson.—GoT
"**Don't** steal this book, my little lad". Unknown.—
ScA
    "Do not steal this book, my lad".—OpI
"**Don't** talk to me about no options, I'm poor". Jo
Carson.—CaS
"**Don't** tell me the cat ate your math sheet". See A
teacher's lament
"**Don't** trust the wind". See Clouds

"**Don't** wait until you hear the drum beat before you
grind your axe". From Jamaican Caribbean
proverbs. Unknown.—BeW
"**Don't** waste your time in looking for". See Long
gone
"**Don't** worry if your job is small". Unknown.—
PrP—ScA   .
"**Don't** you ever". See Song
"**Don't** you feel sorry". See Moles
Don't you remember how sick you are. Kalli
Dakos.—DaI
"**Don't** you think it's probable". See Little talk
Doomsday
"Are you ready when the Lord shall come".
Unknown.—StP
Mine eyes have seen the glory. From Battle hymn
of the republic. J. W. Howe.—SuC
"Oh, when the saints". Unknown.—StP
Door. Valerie Worth.—WoAl
"A **door**". See The poem as a door
Doors
At the keyhole. W. De La Mare.—DeR—MaP
A different door. X. J. Kennedy.—LaCc
Door. V. Worth.—WoAl
Doors. B. J. Esbensen.—EsW
From a very little sphinx. E. S. V. Millay.—DeS
Granny ("We've a great big knocker"). P.
Hubbell.—MoS
I hear the usual thump. A. Adoff.—AdIn
"Lock the dairy door, lock the dairy door".
Mother Goose.—WaM
The open door. E. Coatsworth.—KeT—LaCc
Overture. Z. Dixon.—NyT
The poem as a door. E. Merriam.—MeS
Secret door. M. C. Livingston.—DeT
Some one. W. De La Mare.—DeR—DeS—KeT—
LiDd—MaP
"There was a young lady of Norway". E. Lear.—
LiLo
"There was an old man who said, well". E.
Lear.—LiLo
"Where was Moses when the light went out,
behind the door". Unknown.—WiA
Doors. Barbara Juster Esbensen.—EsW
"**Dot** a dot dot, dot a dot dot". See Weather
The **double**. Walter De La Mare.—DeR
"**Double** bubble gum bubbles double". Unknown.—
WiA
"The **double** moon". See River moons
Doubt
Journey of the Magi. T. S. Eliot.—ElW
Douglass, Frederick
I have had two masters. See Narrative of the life
of Frederick Douglass
Narrative of the life of Frederick Douglass, sels.
I have had two masters.—SuC
Douskey, Franz
Babe and Lou.—KnAs
Douthwaite, Gina
Five haiku.—FoLe
Dove, Rita
Grape sherbert.—JaM
Doves. See Pigeons
Doves. Masahito, tr. by Tze-si Huang.—DeI
"**Down** a deep well a grasshopper fell". See The
grasshopper
"**Down-adown-derry**". Walter De La Mare.—DeR
Down and up. Max Fatchen.—FaCm
"**Down** by the docks". See Night fog
"**Down** by the ocean, down by the sea".
Unknown.—ScA

"**Down** by the river where the green grass grows".
   Unknown.—ScA
Down by the salley gardens. William Butler Yeats.—
   ElW
"**Down** by the salley gardens my love and I did
   meet". See Down by the salley gardens
"**Down** dere in Stratford". See The bum
"**Down** from the hills, they come". See Market
   women
"**Down** in the cellar where the green toads hop". See
   Cat and mouse game
"**Down** in the henhouse on my knees". Unknown.—
   WiA
"**Down** in the hollow". Aileen Fisher.—FiA
"**Down** the hill of Ludgate". See Up and down
"**Down** the Mississippi". Unknown.—WiA
"**Down** the mountainside Bill Bolling". See Bill
   Bolling's avalanche
"**Downhill** I came, hungry, and yet not starved". See
   The owl
"**Dr.** King was a man". See Martin Luther King, Jr.
Dragon ("A dragon named Ernest Belflour").
   William Jay Smith.—SmL
Dragon ("Let me tell you about me"). Karla
   Kuskin.—WhDd
Dragon ("Oh, tongue, give sound to joy and sing").
   Anne McCaffrey.—WhDd
Dragon dance. Max Fatchen.—FoLe
Dragon flies. See Dragonflies
"A **dragon** named Ernest Belflour". See Dragon
Dragon smoke. Lilian Moore.—DeS—DeT
Dragonflies
   Arthur Mitchell. M. Moore.—MoR
   Dragonfly. M. Singer.—SiT
   Dragonflyer. J. P. Lewis.—LeA
   "The face of the dragonfly". Chisoku.—WhAa
   "Like magic". J. Ryder.—JaP
   The red dragonfly. Basho.—DeI
   "Red dragonfly on". Soseki.—CaR
   Round mirrors. Issa.—DeI
Dragonfly. Marilyn Singer.—SiT
Dragonflyer. J. Patrick Lewis.—LeA
"**Dragonflyer**, dragonflyer". See Dragonflyer
Dragons
   Anyone wanting a fiery dragon. M. Fatchen.—
     FaCm
   Chinese dragon. Unknown.—WhDd
   Dragon ("A dragon named Ernest Belflour"). W. J.
     Smith.—SmL
   Dragon ("Let me tell you about me"). K.
     Kuskin.—WhDd
   Dragon ("Oh, tongue, give sound to joy and
     sing"). A. McCaffrey.—WhDd
   Dragon dance. M. Fatchen.—FoLe
   Dragon smoke. L. Moore.—DeS—DeT
   The dragon's lament. T. Harvey.—FoLe
   "I met a dragon face to face". J. Prelutsky.—
     HoGo
   Like a fire eating dragon. J. Ciardi.—CiH
   The making of dragons. J. Yolen.—YoFf
   Paper dragons. S. A. Schmeltz.—BaW
   The toaster. W. J. Smith.—SmL
The dragon's lament. Trevor Harvey.—FoLe
Drake, Barbara
   The photograph.—KnAs
Drawing. See Painting and pictures
Drawing by Ronnie C., grade one. Lechlitner.
   Ruth.—GoT
The **dreadful** drawkcab. Eve Merriam.—MeS
The **dream** ("If everyone has the same dream").
   Steven Kellogg.—SaB

The **dream** ("My arms"). Myra Cohn Livingston.—
   LiNe
Dream boogie. Langston Hughes.—MoR
The **dream** keeper. Langston Hughes.—SlM
A **dream** of paradise in the shadow of war. Muneer
   Niazi, tr. by Daud Kamal.—NyT
Dream song. Walter De La Mare.—DeR—MaP
Dream variation. Langston Hughes.—DeT—LoFh
Dream voyage to the center of the subway. Eve
   Merriam.—MeS
Dreamers and flyers. Joan LaBombard.—JaM
Dreaming black boy. James Berry.—BeW
Dreamland. Walter De La Mare.—DeR
Dreams. See also Ideals; Visions
   Afterglow. J. L. Borges.—GoT
   Afton water. R. Burns.—ElW
   Andre. G. Brooks.—SlM
   Asleep. W. De La Mare.—DeR
   Ballad of black and white. W. J. Smith.—SmL
   La belle dame sans merci. J. Keats.—ElW
   Beware ("Did I dream the owl or was it really
     there"). M. Robinson.—LiIf
   Bewitched. W. De La Mare.—DeR—MaP
   Brothers ("Raymond slowed"). P. B. Janeczko.—
     JaB
   Buddy's dream. E. Greenfield.—GrN
   A child's dream. F. Cornford.—ElW
   Chocolate dreams and chocolate schemes. A.
     Adoff.—AdCh
   Chocolate dreams, one. A. Adoff.—AdCh
   Chocolate dreams, two. A. Adoff.—AdCh
   Chocolate dreams, three. A. Adoff.—AdCh
   Circus dreams. X. J. Kennedy.—KeK
   Day-dream. S. Sengupta.—NyT
   The dream ("If everyone has the same dream"). S.
     Kellogg.—SaB
   The dream ("My arms"). M. C. Livingston.—
     LiNe
   The dream keeper. L. Hughes.—SlM
   A dream of paradise in the shadow of war. M.
     Niazi.—NyT
   Dream song. W. De La Mare.—DeR—MaP
   Dream variation. L. Hughes.—DeT—LoFh
   Dream voyage to the center of the subway. E.
     Merriam.—MeS
   Dreamland. W. De La Mare.—DeR
   Dreams. L. Hughes.—LoFh—SlM
   Dreams of flowers. Reikan.—DeI
   "During the sermon". W. Kloefkorn.—JaPr
   Ever. W. De La Mare.—DeR
   Fat girl with baton. B. H. Baber.—JaPr
   "Friday night's dream". Mother Goose.—WaM
   Friday the thirteenth. A. Adoff.—AdCh
   Going into dream. E. Farjeon.—HoSt
   Grandmother, rocking. E. Merriam.—MeS
   Grandpa bear's lullaby. J. Yolen.—DeS—HoS—
     MoS
   Grass ("The grass is strangely tall to me"). T.
     Kristensen.—NyT
   Harlem. L. Hughes.—ElW
   He wishes for the cloths of heaven. W. B.
     Yeats.—ElW
   A headstrong boy. G. Cheng.—NyT
   Hide and seek. W. De La Mare.—DeR—MaP
   Hot dreams. E. Greenfield.—GrU
   The house of dream. W. De La Mare.—DeR
   I dream of a place. W. De La Mare.—DeR
   I dream'd in a dream. W. Whitman.—HoVo
   I hid you. M. Radnoti.—GoU
   I swim an ocean in my sleep. N. Farber.—HoSt

Drowning—*Continued*
"An old couple living in Gloucester". Unknown.—LiLo
The silver penny. W. De La Mare.—DeR
Skater in blue. J. Parini.—KnAs
That summer. H. Scott.—JaPr
Drugs. See Drugs and drug use
Drugs and drug use
Lacey Paget. M. Glenn.—GlBc
The seller. E. Greenfield.—GrN
The teenage cocaine dealer considers his death on the street outside a Key West funeral for a much-loved civic leader. J. Hall.—JaPr
"**Drum** drum gong drum". See Lion dance
Drummers and drums
Drums of my father. S. Daniels.—BoT
Mek drum talk, man, for Caribbean Independence. J. Berry.—BeW
The rhythm of the tomtom. A. Jacinto.—NyT
Drummond de Andrade, Carlos
Souvenir of the ancient world, tr. by Mark Strand.—NyT
"**Drums** beat". See The lord mayor's parade
Drums of my father. Shirley Daniels.—BoT
A **drunken** egotist. Eddie Linden.—AgL
Dryads. See Fairies
Du Bois, William Edward Burghardt
"Lord of the springtime, father of flower".—StP
"O God, teach us to know that failure is as much".—StP
Dubie, Norman
A grandfather's last letter.—JaM
The huts at Esquimaux.—JaM
Dubois, Gaston
Caught.—KnAs
Insanity.—KnAs
The **duck** ("Behold the duck"). Ogden Nash.—DeS—WhAa
"**Duck**". See Calligraphy
Duck ("When the neat white"). Valerie Worth.—WoAl
The **duck** and the kangaroo. Edward Lear.—CaB
The **duck** billed platypus. Arnold Sundgaard.—WhAa
"The **duck** billed platypus isn't easy to imagine". See The duck billed platypus
"The **duck** is whiter than whey is". See Quack
"**Duck** truck". Bruce McMillan.—McP
Ducks
"Be kind to your web-footed friends". Unknown.—ScA
Calligraphy. J. Yolen.—YoBi
"Charlie Chuck". Unknown.—WiA
The duck ("Behold the duck"). O. Nash.—DeS—WhAa
Duck ("When the neat white"). V. Worth.—WoAl
The duck and the kangaroo. E. Lear.—CaB
"Duck truck". B. McMillan.—McP
Ducks. W. De La Mare.—DeR
Ducks' ditty. K. Grahame.—ElW
The little duck. Joso.—DeI
"The Milky Way is the wild duck's way". Unknown.—LaN
A misspent youth. X. J. Kennedy.—KeGh
The prayer of the little ducks. C. B. De Gasztold.—DeS—StP
Quack. W. De La Mare.—DeR
Quack-hunting. W. De La Mare.—DeR
"Six little ducks". Unknown.—CoE
Twilight. Shiki.—DeI
Ducks. Walter De La Mare.—DeR
Ducks' ditty. Kenneth Grahame.—ElW

Duet. Ruth Krauss.—MoR
"**Duff-duff** rides companion Cranky". See The donkey and the man
Duggan, John Paul
Licorice.—BoT
Dumas, Henry
My little boy.—AgL
Dumb dog. John Ridland.—LiDp
Dumdum, Simeon
For Genevieve, five years old.—NyT
Why there are no cats in the forest.—NyT
"**Dumpitydoodledum** big bow wow". See George Bernard Shaw's opus 1
Dunbar, Paul Laurence
We wear the mask.—SuC
The **dunce.** Walter De La Mare.—DeR—MaP
Dunce song 6. Mark Van Doren.—DeT
Dunn, Stephen
Basketball, a retrospective.—KnAs
Outfielder.—MoA
The sacred.—JaM
"**Durban**, Birmingham". See Question and answer
"**During** the sermon". William Kloefkorn.—JaPr
"**During** the third mile". See Joan Benoit
Durston, Georgia Roberts
The wolf.—KeT
Dusk ("Daylight is drifting"). Eve Merriam.—MeCh
Dusk ("The moon is red in the foggy sky"). Paul Verlaine, tr. by C. F. MacIntyre.—GoT
Dust
Mote. X. J. Kennedy.—KeK
Old spider web. M. C. Livingston.—LiNe
"**Dust** and ashes". See The prayer of the owl
"**Dust** mote in a sunbeam". See Mote
Dust of snow. Robert Frost.—ElW
"**Dust** settles on the spider's web". See Old spider web
Duty. See also Conduct of life
"Let us have faith that right makes might". From The Gettysburg address. A. Lincoln.—StP
The **dwarf.** Walter De La Mare.—DeR
Dwarfs
The dwarf. W. De La Mare.—DeR
The isle of Lone. W. De La Mare.—DeR
Narnian suite. C. S. Lewis.—MoR
Dwellings. See Houses and dwellings
Dybek, Stuart
Clothespins.—KnAs
Dyer, Edward
In praise of a contented mind.—ElW (unat.)
Dylan, Bob
Blowin' in the wind, sels.
How many times.—SuC
How many times. See Blowin' in the wind

E

E is for egg. William Jay Smith.—SmL
"'**E** was the greatest man on earth". See The greatest man on earth
"**Each** day the first day". Dag Hammarskjold.—StP
"**Each** night father fills me with dread". Edward Gorey.—PrFo
"**Each** of us is alone on the heart of the earth". See And suddenly it's evening
"**Each**, peach, pear, plum". Unknown.—CoM
"**Each** sixth chick sat on a stick". Unknown.—WiA
"**Each** time we eat". Unknown.—StP

"**Each** year brings rookies and makes veterans".
From Watching football on TV. Howard
Nemerov.—KnAs
The **eagle** ("He clasps the crag with crooked
hands"). Alfred Tennyson.—CaB—ElW
The **eagle** ("The sun's rays"). Unknown.—WhAa
Eagle flight. Alonzo Lopez.—DeT
Eagle rock. Geof Hewitt.—JaPr
"An **eagle** wings gracefully". See Eagle flight
Eagles
  The eagle ("He clasps the crag with crooked
    hands"). A. Tennyson.—CaB—ElW
  The eagle ("The sun's rays"). Unknown.—WhAa
  Eagle flight. A. Lopez.—DeT
  Executive Eagle. W. J. Smith.—SmL
  Golden eagle. J. P. Lewis.—LeT
  I watched an eagle soar. V. D. H. Sneve.—SnD
"**Eaper** Weaper, chimney sweeper". Unknown.—OpI
Early country village morning. Grace Nichols.—
  NiCo
Early dark. Elizabeth Coatsworth.—PlW
"**Early** dawn". See Little fish
"**Early** dawn, the violets tilt". See The mole's work
Early December. Valerie Worth.—WoA
"**Early** in the morning, let's go to the country".
  Unknown.—WiA
Early love. Herbert Scott.—JaM
Early March. Zack Rogow.—GoT
The **early** morning. Hilaire Belloc.—KeT
Ears
  "Do your ears hang low". Unknown.—ScA
  "Queen Regina". E. Merriam.—MeP
  "There was a young fellow named Shear". J.
    Ciardi.—LiLo
  "There was a young man of Devizes".
    Unknown.—LiLo
Earth (planet). See World
"**Earth** and water air". See Martha Graham
Earth folk. Walter De La Mare.—DeR—MaP
"The **earth** rotates". See The teacher
"**Earth** rounded". See Source
"The **earth**, they say". See The spinning earth
Earth's birthday. X. J. Kennedy.—KeK
Earthworks Group
  Thinking green.—LoFh
Earthworms. Valerie Worth.—WoAl
"**East**, west, north, south". Unknown.—WiA
"The **east** wind is up". See Father Wolf's midnight
  song
Easter
  After Easter snow. X. J. Kennedy.—KeK
  Easter. S. Cook.—FoLe
  Easter morning. A. Fisher.—FiA
  The Easter parade. W. J. Smith.—LoFh—SmL
  Easter's coming. A. Fisher.—HoS
  Jouvert morning. D. Calder.—FoLe
  Palm Sunday. B. Wade.—FoLe
  Patience. B. Katz.—LoFh
  The sun on Easter day. N. Farber.—LoFh
  Time for rabbits. A. Fisher.—FiA
Easter. Stanley Cook.—FoLe
Easter morning. Aileen Fisher.—FiA
The **Easter** parade. William Jay Smith.—LoFh—
  SmL
Easter's coming. Aileen Fisher.—HoS
Eastwick, Ivy O.
  Halloween ("The sky was yellow").—HoS
  Thanksgiving ("Thank you").—FoLe—LoFh
"**Eat**, birds, eat, and make no waste". Mother
  Goose.—WaM
"**Eat** fresh fried fish free at the fish fry".
  Unknown.—WiA

"**Eat** it, it's good for you". Mary Ann Hoberman.—
  HoFa
"**Eat** your banana, Annie dear". See Sales talk for
  Annie
Eating. See Food and eating
Eating bread. Gary Soto.—SoA
Eberhart, Richard
  "Go to the shine that's on a tree".—ElW
Ebonee. Sharon Bell Mathis.—MaR
The **eccentric**. Unknown.—OpT
"An **eccentric** explorer named Hayter". William Jay
  Smith.—SmL
Echo ("Seven sweet notes"). Walter De La Mare.—
  DeR
Echo ("Who called, I said, and the words"). Walter
  De La Mare.—DeR
Echoes
  Echo ("Seven sweet notes"). W. De La Mare.—
    DeR
  Echo ("Who called, I said, and the words"). W.
    De La Mare.—DeR
  Echoes. W. De La Mare.—DeR
  "Sound the bell, sound the bell". Unknown.—ScA
  The splendor falls. A. Tennyson.—ElW
Echoes. Walter De La Mare.—DeR
The **echoing** green. William Blake.—ElW
Eclipses
  "There was a young man of St. Kitts".
    Unknown.—LiLo
Ecology
  Blue whale knowledge. Z. Quobble.—AgL
  "Oh my good Lord, I am not a young man
    anymore". J. Carson.—CaS
  Thinking green. Earthworks Group.—LoFh
Economics. Robert Wrigley.—JaPr
"**Ed**, Ed, big head". Unknown.—WiA
"**Eddie** the spaghetti nut". See The spaghetti nut
Eden, Garden of
  Eden. W. De La Mare.—DeR
Eden. Walter De La Mare.—DeR
Edey, Marion
  Is it possicle.—PrFo
"**Edmund** Clerihew Bentley". William Jay Smith.—
  SmL
Edward Jones. Sol Mandlsohn.—PrFo
"**Edward** MacDermott". See Mail king
Edwards, Richard
  The party's over.—FoLe
Eeka, neeka. Walter De La Mare.—DeR
"**Eeka**, Neeka, Leeka, Lee". See Eeka, neeka
Eels
  Eels. S. Milligan.—PrFo
  Electric eel. X. J. Kennedy.—WhAa
  "Ignatz Pigfats". X. J. Kennedy.—KeGh
  Remembering Oscar eel. J. P. Lewis.—LeA
  Sea thing. M. Fatchen.—FaCm
  "Sheldon the selfish shellfish". X. J. Kennedy.—
    KeGh
  "To the bowl of champagne punch". X. J.
    Kennedy.—KeFb
Eels. Spike Milligan.—PrFo
"**Eena**, meena, dippa deena". Unknown.—CoM
"**Eenie**, meenie, minie, mo". Unknown.—SuI
"**Eenie**, meenie, minie, mo, catch a thief".
  Unknown.—WiA
"**Eenie**, meenie, minie, mo, catch a tiger".
  Unknown.—WiA
"The **eentsy**, weentsy spider". Unknown.—CoE
"**Eeny**, meeny, miney, mo". Unknown.—ScA
"**Eeny**, meeny, pasadini". Unknown.—CoM
Egg. Valerie Worth.—WoAl
Eggs. See also Birds—Eggs and nests

Elephants—*Continued*
  Way down south.—CII
  We must be polite. C. Sandburg.—DeS
"The **elephants** are coming one by one".
    Unknown.—ScA
"An **elephant's** nose". See The handiest nose
The **elephant's** trunk. Alice Wilkins.—SuI
Eletelephony. Laura E. Richards.—DeS—SuI
Elevation. Robert Morgan.—JaM
"**Eleven** yellow monkeys". Jack Prelutsky.—PrBe
"**Elim**, elim, ep elim". Unknown.—YoS
  "Who am I, I am me".—YoS
Eliot, Thomas Stearns
  Journey of the Magi.—ElW
  Macavity, the mystery cat.—ElW
  The song of the jellicles.—DeT—LaCc—SuI
"**Elise**, I have your valentine with the red shoes, I
    have". See A grandfather's last letter
Elizabeth I, Queen of England (about)
  The fiddlers. W. De La Mare.—DeR
  "There sate good Queen Bess, oh". W. De La
    Mare.—DeR
Ellard, George
  The Red Stockings.—MoA
Elliot West. Mel Glenn.—GlBc
Elm trees
  Rare rhythms. S. London.—JaM
Elsa Wertman. Edgar Lee Masters.—ElW
"**Elsie** Marley is grown so fine". Mother Goose.—
    WaM
Elves. See Fairies
Emanuel, James A.
  A small discovery.—DeT—LiDd
Emanuel, Lynn
  Apology.—JaPr
"**Emerald**". See Storyteller
"An **emerald** is green as grass". See Flint
The **emeritus**. Leonard Nathan.—JaM
Emerson, Ralph Waldo
  Concord hymn.—ElW
Emigration. See Immigration and emigration
"**Emily** and I got talking and we decided". See
    Louisa's liberation
"**Emily** Bronte, how did you do it". See Janet
    DeStasio
Emily Jane. Laura E. Richards.—ElW
Emin, Gevorg
  The question mark, tr. by Diana Der
    Hovanessian.—NyT
"**En** la puerta del cielo". Unknown.—DeA
  "At heaven's gate".—DeA
The **enchanted** hill. Walter De La Mare.—DeR
Enchantment. See also Charms; Magic
  As Lucy went a-walking. W. De La Mare.—DeR
  La belle dame sans merci. J. Keats.—ElW
  Bewitched. W. De La Mare.—DeR—MaP
  The changeling. W. De La Mare.—DeR—MaP
  The coquette. W. De La Mare.—DeR
  The enchanted hill. W. De La Mare.—DeR
  The hairy toe. Unknown.—BaH
  The house ("A lane at the end of Old Pilgrim
    Street"). W. De La Mare.—DeR
  The journey ("Heart-sick of his journey was the
    Wanderer"). W. De La Mare.—DeR
  Little bush. E. M. Roberts.—LiDd
  Nowel. W. De La Mare.—DeR
  Pigs. W. De La Mare.—DeR
  The princess and the frog. S. C. Field.—BaH
  The rime of the ancient mariner, complete. S. T.
    Coleridge.—ElW
  The sleeping beauty. W. De La Mare.—DeR

  Song of enchantment. W. De La Mare.—DeR—
    MaP
  Tillie. W. De La Mare.—DeR—MaP
  The witch ("Weary went the old witch"). W. De
    La Mare.—DeR
Enchantment. Joanne Ryder.—JaP
The **end**. Alan Alexander Milne.—LoFh
"The **end** of autumn". See A desolate scene
End of winter. Eve Merriam.—MoA
Endless chant. See "Who put the overalls in Mrs.
    Murphy's chowder"
Endless compositions. See Circular compositions
Endless dialogue. Unknown.—WiA
Endless riddle. Unknown.—WiA
Enemies. Charlotte Zolotow.—SaB
Energy. Torei, tr. by Tze-si Huang.—DeI
Engaged. Jean Little.—LiHe
Engel, William E.
  "Willie built a guillotine".—PrFo
"**Engine**, engine number nine". Unknown.—CoM—
    ScA
"The **engingines**". Paul Goodman.—MoR
England
  Banana and mackerel. J. Berry.—BeW
  A different kind of Sunday. J. Berry.—BeW
  Distributing the harvest. B. Moses.—FoLe
  The dragon's lament. T. Harvey.—FoLe
  Eden. W. De La Mare.—DeR
  The Englishman. W. De La Mare.—DeR
  The holly. W. De La Mare.—DeR
  May day ("Oak and ivy, sycamore, ash, what shall
    we leave by the cottage door"). J. Nicholls.—
    FoLe
  May day ("Twirl your ribbons"). J. Kenward.—
    FoLe
  Mothering Sunday. S. Cook.—FoLe
  On midsummer's eve. A. Bonner.—FoLe
  Part VI: Thousands of years ago. From A child's
    day. W. De La Mare.—DeR
  Prince Rama comes to Longsight. J. Cunliffe.—
    FoLe
  Saint Swithin's Day. A. Bonner.—FoLe
  A song for England. A. Salkey.—AgL
  Trees ("Of all the trees in England"). W. De La
    Mare.—DeR—MaP
England—History
  "Charles the First walked and talked".
    Unknown.—OpI
  Kings. W. De La Mare.—DeR
  Kings and queens. W. De La Mare.—DeR—MaP
  Oak apple day. R. Wilson.—FoLe
  Part VI: Thousands of years ago. From A child's
    day. W. De La Mare.—DeR
  Please to remember ("He comes to see us every
    year"). G. Holloway.—FoLe
  Remember. D. Ward.—FoLe
  Remembrance Day ("Poppies, oh, miss"). J.
    Nicholls.—FoLe
"**England** over". See Part V: England over
The **Englishman**. Walter De La Mare.—DeR
Enigma sartorial. Lucy W. Rhu.—WhAa
Enlightenment. Michael Horovitz.—AgL
The **enlistment** of free blacks as Continental
    soldiers. John Thomas.—SuC
Enos Slaughter. Jim Lavella Havelin.—KnAs
Enright, Dennis Joseph
  Jephson Gardens.—ElW
Envoi, Washington Square Park. Myra Cohn
    Livingston.—LiR
Envoy. Walter De La Mare.—DeR
Envy. See also Jealousy
  The bird set free. W. De La Mare.—DeR

Envy.—*Continued*
But I dunno. Unknown.—CII
Camp Calvary. R. Wallace.—JaPr
Economics. R. Wrigley.—JaPr
Envying the children of San Francisco. G. Soto.—SoA
The flying fish. J. J. Bell.—PrFo
Green with envy. E. Merriam.—MeCh
"Have mercy on me, o beneficent one". Unknown.—StP
High school. G. Roberts.—JaPr
"I raised a great hullabaloo". Unknown.—CII
"I think I could turn and live with animals, they are so placid". From Song of myself. W. Whitman.—HoVo
Jim-jam pyjamas. G. Wilson.—CoAz
Kinky hair blues. U. Marson.—LeCa
Listn big brodda dread, na. J. Berry.—BeW
Louleen's feelings. X. J. Kennedy.—KeK
Maisie's lament. X. J. Kennedy.—KeK
A new dress. R. Dallas.—NyT
"One little piggy wore leggings". J. Knight.—KnT
Others. M. C. Livingston.—LiT
The owl ("Your eyes, a searching yellow light"). D. Chandra.—LiIf
The paragon. B. Katz.—JaP
The playhouse. K. Daniels.—JaPr
A song in the front yard. G. Brooks.—ElW
A toast for everybody who is growin. J. Berry.—BeW
Envying the children of San Francisco. Gary Soto.—SoA
Epictetus
"May we, O God, keep ourselves modest".—StP
"An **epicure,** dining at Crewe". Unknown.—LiLo
Epiphany. See Magi
An **epitaph** on a robin redbreast. Samuel Rogers.—CaB
Epitaphs
"Beneath this stone, a lump of clay". Unknown.—BaH
"Blessed be the memory". Unknown.—OpI
An epitaph on a robin redbreast. S. Rogers.—CaB
"Here lies". Unknown.—BaH
"Here lies the body of our Anna". Unknown.—BaH
"It was a cough". Unknown.—BaH
"Just plant a watermelon on my grave". Unknown.—ScA
"Let this be my last word". R. Tagore.—StP
My legacy. W. Whitman.—HoVo
Rest in peace. J. Ciardi.—CiH
"So died John So". Unknown.—BaH
"Under this sod lies a great bucking horse". Unknown.—ScA
"Underneath this pile of stones". Unknown.—BaH
"Willis Comfort did not outlive". J. Carson.—CaS
Equality. Maya Angelou.—AnI
Eradam, Yusuf
A brief note to the bag lady, ma sister.—NyT
Debt, tr.—NyT
My share, tr.—NyT
Eraser. Eve Merriam.—MeS
"**Ere** my heart beats too coldly and faintly". See The truants
Erikson, Joan
"You, neighbor God, if in the long night", tr.—StP
Esbensen, Barbara Juster
Clouds ("Don't trust the wind").—EsW
Doors.—EsW

Four poems for Roy G Biv, sels.
Prism in the window.—EsW
A question ("If I shine").—EsW
Rainbow making, a mystery.—EsW
Rainbow making, magic.—EsW
Friends.—EsW
Geode.—EsW
Halloween concert ("Elbows bent, tireless").—LiHp
Homework.—EsW
In autumn.—EsW
Lullaby for a rainy night.—EsW
The Milky Way.—LaN
My cat ("My cat is asleep, white paws").—EsW
Nightfall ("One by one").—EsW
Old photograph album, grandfather.—EsW
Pencils.—EsW
Prism in the window. See Four poems for Roy G Biv
A question ("If I shine"). See Four poems for Roy G Biv
Rainbow making, a mystery. See Four poems for Roy G Biv
Rainbow making, magic. See Four poems for Roy G Biv
The rescue ("Rain poured down, the house").—EsW
Sand dollar.—EsW
Sparrow dreaming.—EsW
Summer night, canoeing.—EsW
Sunrise.—EsW
Tell me.—EsW
Time.—EsW
Two ways to look at kites.—BaW
"What a moonstruck".—LiIf
Escalators
Alligator on the escalator. E. Merriam.—DeT
Escapes
Birds know. M. C. Livingston.—LiT
Hoods. P. B. Janeczko.—JaB
Eskimo. See Indians of the Americas—Eskimo
"An **Eskimo** sleeps in his white bearskin". Unknown.—PrP
"**Eskimos** in Manitoba". See Recital
Esme on her brother's bicycle. Russell Hoban.—JaP
Esmeralda (for a picture). Walter De La Mare.—DeR
Espy, Willard R.
"My TV came down with a chill".—KeT
"**Estaba** la paraja pinta". Unknown.—DeA
The lovely bird ("Cu cu ru, sang the lovely bird").—DeA
"**Eternal** God". Masao Takenaka.—StP
Eternity. See also Infinity
"To see a world in a grain of sand". From Auguries of innocence. W. Blake.—StP
Eterovic, Ramon Diaz
"Childhood is the only lasting flower".—NyT
"**Eugene,** said Claire". See Out of the city
Euphemistic. Eve Merriam.—MeCh
Euwer, Anthony
"As a beauty I'm not a great star".—LiLo
"No matter how grouchy you're feeling".—LiLo
Evan King. Mel Glenn.—GlBc
Evans, David Allan
The antelope ("When one of us hit").—JaPr
Bus depot reunion.—JaPr
Mrs. Perkins.—JaPr
Pole vaulter.—KnAs
Ronnie Schwinck.—JaPr
Evans, Mari
Marrow of my bone.—SuC

Evans, Mari—*Continued*
  Spectrum.—SuC
  "Where have you gone".—SuC
  "Who can be born black".—SlM
Eve. See Adam and Eve
"Even earlier yet this listening thrush". See The
  thrush
"Even if I have gone astray, I am". Arjan.—StP
"Even the moon lies". See Long Beach, February
"Even the quiet blue". See Macaw
"Even the sun-clouds this morning cannot manage
  such skirts". See Poppies in October
Evening. See also Night
  The accompaniment. W. De La Mare.—DeR
  After the dazzle of day. W. Whitman.—HoVo
  Afterglow. J. L. Borges.—GoT
  "Although there is". O. N. Komachi.—GoT
  And suddenly it's evening. S. Quasimodo.—GoT
  At sunset. J. von Eichendorff.—GoT
  Bad boy's swan song. W. J. Smith.—SmL
  Bed in summer. R. L. Stevenson.—DeT
  Before the end of this falling day. A. Adoff.—
    AdIn
  Beware ("An ominous bird sang from its branch").
    W. De La Mare.—DeR
  "Blazing in gold, and". E. Dickinson.—GoT
  "Brown owls come here in the blue evening".
    Unknown.—LiIf
  Celestial. M. Pettit.—JaM
  The children's hour. H. W. Longfellow.—SuI
  "The cicadas sing". O. N. Komachi.—GoT
  Coals. W. De La Mare.—DeR
  The dark and falling summer. D. Schwartz.—
    GoT—SuI
  Dipa, the lamp. A. Bonner.—FoLe
  A dream of paradise in the shadow of war. M.
    Niazi.—NyT
  Dream song. W. De La Mare.—DeR—MaP
  Dream variation. L. Hughes.—DeT—LoFh
  Dusk ("Daylight is drifting"). E. Merriam.—MeCh
  Dusk ("The moon is red in the foggy sky"). P.
    Verlaine.—GoT
  Enchantment. J. Ryder.—JaP
  Evening. I. Manger.—GoT
  Evening comes. L. S. Yin.—GoT
  Evening dawn. H. Scott.—JaPr
  The evening light along the sound. S. Santos.—
    GoT
  Fambly time. E. Greenfield.—GrN
  Fireflies ("An August night"). J. P. Lewis.—LeT
  Fireflies ("Fireflies at twilight"). M. A.
    Hoberman.—DeS
  Fireflies in the garden. R. Frost.—ElW
  "The fireflies wink and glow". R. Hillyer.—GoT
  Five of us. W. De La Mare.—DeR
  Foxes ("The foxes"). Buson.—DeI
  Gnats. Unknown.—DeI
  Grasshopper ("Silence stilled the meadow"). J. P.
    Lewis.—LeE
  Hares at play. J. Clare.—CaB
  Harvest (for a picture). W. De La Mare.—DeR
  The hens. E. M. Roberts.—LiDd
  Hits and runs. C. Sandburg.—KnAs
  Holidays (for a picture). W. De La Mare.—DeR
  Home ("Between the sunset and the eucalyptus
    tree"). N. Aziz.—NyT
  How to play night baseball. J. Holden.—MoA
  In evening air. T. Roethke.—GoT
  In the dying of daylight. W. De La Mare.—DeR
  In this deep darkness. N. Zach.—GoT
  Jasmine. K. Hong Ryou.—NyT
  The labourer. T. Daby.—NyT

The lamplighter. W. De La Mare.—DeR
Little donkey close your eyes. M. W. Brown.—
  DeT
Madonna of the evening flowers. A. Lowell.—
  GoU
"Milk white moon, put the cows to sleep". C.
  Sandburg.—SuI
Mindoro. R. C. Sunico.—NyT
The moon rises slowly over the ocean. X.
  De-min.—NyT
Muted. P. Verlaine.—GoU
Night heron. F. Frost.—CaB
Nightfall ("The last light fails, that shallow pool of
  day"). W. De La Mare.—DeR
No bed. W. De La Mare.—DeR
Now silent falls. W. De La Mare.—DeR
On midsummer's eve. A. Bonner.—FoLe
One night. A. Adoff.—AdIn
One time. W. Stafford.—JaP
An open arc. S. Quasimodo.—GoT
The orchard. W. De La Mare.—DeR
The owl on the aerial. C. Short.—LiIf
The owl takes off at Upper Black Eddy, Pa. E. Di
  Pasquale.—LiIf
The pheasant. Buson.—DeI
Quack-hunting. W. De La Mare.—DeR
Questioning faces. R. Frost.—LiIf
The quiet enemy. W. De La Mare.—DeR
The river. C. Zolotow.—FrS
The ruin. W. De La Mare.—DeR—MaP
VI. P. Verlaine.—GoT
"Smitty on the railroad, picking up sticks".
  Unknown.—WiA
Snow ("No breath of wind"). W. De La Mare.—
  DeR—MaP
Snow on Lotus Mountain. L. C. Ch'ing.—GoT
Snow toward evening. M. Cane.—FrS
The song of shadows. W. De La Mare.—DeR—
  MaP
"Song of the moon". N. Farber.—HoSt
"Star light, star bright". Mother Goose.—WaM—
  WiA
    First star.—HoS
Stopping by woods on a snowy evening. R.
  Frost.—DeS—DeT—ElW—SuI
Summer evening. W. De La Mare.—DeR—MaP
The sunken garden. W. De La Mare.—DeR
Supper ("Her pinched grey body"). W. De La
  Mare.—DeR
Supper ("I supped where bloomed the red red
  rose"). W. De La Mare.—DeR
Taking turns. N. Farber.—KeT
"There came a gray owl at sunset". Unknown.—
  LiIf
This evening. Z. Landau.—GoT
This I know. A. Corkett.—BoT
"This is my rock". D. McCord.—KeT—LiDd
"Thoughts that were put into words". K.
  Kuskin.—JaP
"Twilight". I. Shikibu.—GoT
Twilight. Shiki.—DeI
Twilight of the outward life. H. von
  Hofmannsthal.—GoT
The voice. W. De La Mare.—DeR
Voices. W. De La Mare.—DeR
Wandering chorus. E. Blum.—GoT
"Wee Willie Winkie runs through the town".
  Mother Goose.—EdGl—SuO—WaM
    Wee Willie Winkie.—HoS
The wind is from the north. R. Hillyer.—GoT
Winter dusk. V. Worth.—WoA

Eyes—*Continued*
Goldfish ("I have four fish with poppy eyes"). A. Fisher.—MoS
The great brown owl. J. E. Browne.—LiIf
Haiku ("I have looked into"). S. Sanchez.—SlM
"I love that black-eyed boy". Unknown.—ScA
Lights in the dark. E. Merriam.—MeP
"Lincoln". M. C. Livingston.—LiR
"Little pools". From Riddle poems. J. Berry.—BeW
A long overdue poem to my eyes. J. Meiling.—AgL
"Margaret, Margaret, has big eyes". Unknown.—WiA
The midnight snack. J. Merrill.—ElW
The mighty eye. K. Dakos.—DaI
O is for owl. W. J. Smith.—LiIf—SmL
The old stone house. W. De La Mare.—DeR—MaP
The portrait of a warrior. W. De La Mare.—DeR
The prayer of the owl. C. B. De Gasztold.—DeP—LiIf
The rabbit ("When they said the time to hide was mine"). E. M. Roberts.—ElW
Ronnie Schwinck. D. A. Evans.—JaPr
Round mirrors. Issa.—DeI
The sea gull's eye. R. Hoban.—JaP
Snake eyes. Kyoshi.—DeI
"Somewhere I have never travelled, gladly beyond". E. E. Cummings.—GoU
True. L. Moore.—LaCc
The yes and the no, Redondo. G. Pape.—JaPr
"Eyes ablaze looking up". From Riddle poems. James Berry.—BeW
Ezekiel, Nissim
Songs for Nandu Bhende, sels.
Touching.—AgL
Touching. See Songs for Nandu Bhende

F

"F for Finny". See Finis
F is for frog-boy. William Jay Smith.—SmL
Fabian, R. Gerry
Bottom of the ninth haiku.—MoA
Pull hitter.—MoA
The **fable** of the golden pear. Eve Merriam.—MeS
Fables
The ass in the lion's skin. Aesop.—CaB
The country mouse and the city mouse. R. S. Sharpe.—ElW
The fable of the golden pear. E. Merriam.—MeS
The flattered flying fish. E. V. Rieu.—ElW
The spider and the fly. M. Howitt.—ElW
"The **face** of the dragonfly". Chisoku.—WhAa
Face play. Unknown.—OpT
Head.—WiA
Faces
"As a beauty I'm not a great star". A. Euwer.—LiLo
The bat ("By day the bat is cousin to the mouse"). T. Roethke.—CoAz—DeS—ElW
"Be glad your nose is on your face". J. Prelutsky.—PrFo
Be kind to dumb animals. J. Ciardi.—CiH—LiLo
Between ebb and flow. F. Tuqan.—NyT
"Brow-brinker". Unknown.—WiA
But then. A. Fisher.—FiA
Coffeepot face. A. Fisher.—FiA
Crazed. W. De La Mare.—DeR

A different image. D. Randall.—SuC
"Do what you like with my face". A. Aizpuriete.—NyT
"Do you carrot all for me". Unknown.—WiA
Enemies. C. Zolotow.—SaB
Face play. Unknown.—OpT
Head.—WiA
"For his mother's mudpack, Brent". X. J. Kennedy.—KeFb
"Grace, Grace, dressed in lace". Unknown.—WiA
High stick. B. Collins.—KnAs
In the dying of daylight. W. De La Mare.—DeR
"Little dabs of powder". Unknown.—ScA
"Little seed inside a prune". Unknown.—ScA
"Lovely face, majestic face, face of". Unknown.—StP
M is for mask. W. J. Smith.—SmL
Mr. Robert Winograd, English. M. Glenn.—GlBc
My mother's face. L. Rosenberg.—LiPm
"No matter how grouchy you're feeling". A. Euwer.—LiLo
"Pandebeen". Unknown.—YoS
"Brow-bone".—YoS
People. W. J. Smith.—SmL
The prayer of the monkey. C. B. De Gasztold.—DeP
Relatives. M. A. Hoberman.—HoFa
"Roses are red, violets are blue, a face like yours". Unknown.—ScA
"Roses are red, violets are blue, if I looked like you". Unknown.—CoM
"Sister has a blister". X. J. Kennedy.—KeGh
Sour. Issa.—DeI
Spell to banish a pimple. J. Agard.—AgL
There was a sound of airy seasons passing. S. Quasimodo.—GoT
"There was an old lady named Hart". W. J. Smith.—LiLo—SmL
The thingamajig. J. Ciardi.—CiH
Toward myself. L. Goldberg.—GoT
Yawn. S. O. Huigan.—BoT
Facing Pennsylvania. Arnold Adoff.—AdCh
"The **fact** that we". See Monkeys
Factories
Brickyard. P. B. Janeczko.—JaB
Today is Labor Day. J. Foster.—FoLe
"A **faggot**, a faggot, go fetch for the fire, son". See The grey wolf
Failing in the presence of ants. Gary Soto.—SoA
Failure
Casey at the bat. E. L. Thayer.—ElW—MoA
Circles ("I am speaking of circles"). M. C. Livingston.—JaP—LiT
Garrett Chandler. M. Glenn.—GlBc
Getting nowhere. J. Berry.—BeW
A hot property. R. Wallace.—JaP
A lesson from golf. E. Guest.—KnAs
A lifetime in third grade. K. Dakos.—DaI
Mr. John Fletcher, chemistry. M. Glenn.—GlBc
"O God, teach us to know that failure is as much". W. E. B. Du Bois.—StP
Old Mary. G. Brooks.—SuC
"**Fair** daffodils, we weep to see". See To daffodils
Fairchild, B. H.
For Junior Gilliam.—MoA
Fairies
A-tishoo. W. De La Mare.—DeR
Advice on how to sleep well Halloween night. J. Yolen.—YoBe
At the keyhole. W. De La Mare.—DeR—MaP
The bees' song. W. De La Mare.—DeR—MaP
La belle dame sans merci. J. Keats.—ElW

Faith—*Continued*
 "Lord, thou art the Hindu, the Moslem, the Turk". G. Singh.—StP
 "May He Who is the Father in Heaven of the". Swami Akhilananda.—StP
 "May I follow a life of compassion in pity for". A. Schweitzer.—StP
 "O Great Spirit, whose voice I hear in the wind". Unknown.—StP
 "O my soul's healer, keep me at evening". Unknown.—StP
 "Oh, you gotta get a glory". Unknown.—StP
 The old man's comforts and how he gained them. R. Southey.—ElW
 The pilgrim. W. De La Mare.—DeR
 The purpose of altar boys. A. Rios.—JaPr
 Savior. M. Angelou.—AnI
 "Should I worship Him from fear of hell". R. Al'Adawiyah.—StP
 "The snow is deep on the ground". K. Patchen.—GoU
 They told me. W. De La Mare.—DeR
 Thought. W. Whitman.—HoVo
 "To believe in God". J. Pintauro.—StP
 "What can I give him". C. G. Rossetti.—StP
 "When bad things happen to me, God". I. Wells.—StP
 "When you walk that lonesome valley". Unknown.—StP
 "Where can I go then from your spirit". From The book of psalms. Bible/Old Testament.—StP
 The world is in chaos, the world is in flames. A. Adoff.—AdCh
 "The year's at the spring". From Pippa passes. R. Browning.—ElW—StP
Falco, Liber
 "I was born in Jacinto Vera".—NyT
Fall. See Autumn
Fall. Aileen Fisher.—FiA
"Falling-off has a wobble-trouble". See Body-steadier
The **fallow** deer at the lonely house. Thomas Hardy.—ElW
Falsehood. See Truthfulness and falsehood
Fambly time. Eloise Greenfield.—GrN
Fame
 Famous. N. S. Nye.—JaP
 "I'm nobody, who are you". E. Dickinson.—ElW
 The teenage cocaine dealer considers his death on the street outside a Key West funeral for a much-loved civic leader. J. Hall.—JaPr
 "Fame was a claim of Uncle Ed's". Ogden Nash.—PrFo
Family. See Children and childhood; Home and family life; Married life; Relatives
Family. Myra Cohn Livingston.—LiT
Family genius. X. J. Kennedy.—KeGh
The family of man, sels. Carl Sandburg
 Names.—WhAa
Family portrait. Eka Budianta, tr. by E. U. Kratz.—NyT
Famous. Naomi Shihab Nye.—JaP
"Fanaticism, no, writing is exciting". See Baseball and writing
"The fanciest dive that ever was dove". See Fancy dive
Fancy dive. Shel Silverstein.—KnAs
Fantasti-cat. J. Patrick Lewis.—LeT
Far and close. Gu Cheng, tr. by Edward Morin.—NyT
Far away. David McCord.—HoS

"Far away, and long ago". See The song of seven
"Far away in Nanga-noon". See Marching song
"Far enough down is China, somebody said". See Digging for China
"Far from the loud sea beaches". See A visit from the sea
"Far from the trouble and toil of town". See Old man platypus
"Far over the hills, a good way off". Unknown.—WiA
"Far star". See Her she bar
"Far to the west". Unknown.—SnD
"Faraway and faint". See The wild goose
Farber, Norma
 Guardian owl.—LiIf
 I swim an ocean in my sleep.—HoSt
 Manhattan lullaby ("Lulled by rumble, babble, beep").—KeT
 "Song of the moon".—HoSt
 The sun on Easter day.—LoFh
 Taking turns.—KeT
"Farewell, my younger brother". Unknown.—SnD
Farewells. See also Parting
 "Farewell, my younger brother". Unknown.—SnD
 "Good-by my winter suit". N. M. Bodecker.—MoS
 "Good-bye my fancy". W. Whitman.—HoVo
 The great one. T. Clark.—MoA
 Say goodbye to Big Daddy. R. Jarrell.—KnAs
 September garden. M. C. Livingston.—LiNe
Fargue, Leon-Paul
 Nocturne ("A long arm embossed with gold slides from the tree tops"), tr. by Kenneth Rexroth.—GoT
Farjeon, Eleanor
 "Cat".—LaCc
 Cats ("Cats sleep").—ElW
 Going into dream.—HoSt
 Kingfisher.—MoR
 The London owl.—LiIf
 "Morning has broken".—StP
 "Mrs. Peck Pigeon".—DeS
 "The night will never stay".—ElW
 Oh, hark.—LiIf
 Pegasus.—WhDd
 Poetry ("What is poetry, who knows").—ElW
 The witch, the witch. See "The witch, the witch, don't let her get you"
 "The witch, the witch, don't let her get you".—BaH
 The witch, the witch.—LoFh
Farm animals. See names of farm animals, as cattle
"The farm is in a flurry". Jack Prelutsky.—PrP
Farm life. See also Country life; Fields; Harvests and harvesting; also names of farm products, as Wheat
 Apple scoop. E. Glen.—LiPg
 Autumnal equinox. E. E. Wilson.—JaM
 Bragging in the barnyard. J. P. Lewis.—LeA
 Celestial. M. Pettit.—JaM
 Chicken. W. De La Mare.—DeR—MaP
 The chicken poem. D. Welch.—JaM
 Chore boy. J. Thomas.—LiPm
 The courtship. G. E. Lyone.—JaM
 Daddy carries his empty basket on his head. A. Adoff.—AdIn
 Daybreak ("After the dark of night"). W. De La Mare.—DeR
 Deserted farm. M. Vinz.—JaP
 "Dimpleton the simpleton". D. Lee.—CoAz
 "Elsie Marley is grown so fine". Mother Goose.—WaM

Farm life.—*Continued*
"The farm is in a flurry". J. Prelutsky.—PrP
Farmer, farmer. J. P. Lewis.—LeT
Fence. V. Worth.—WoAl
A fox jumped up. Unknown.—ClI
Gate gossip. M. Fatchen.—FaCm
Gathering strength. L. Dangel.—JaM
Hay for the horses. G. Snyder.—ElW
"Hay is for horses". Mother Goose.—WaM
Haymaking. W. De La Mare.—DeR
He saved a lot of time by not working. J. Ciardi.—CiH
The hens. E. M. Roberts.—LiDd
How to trick a chicken. J. P. Lewis.—LeA
"Hushabye baby, they're gone to milk". Mother Goose.—WaM
I know that summer is the famous growing season. A. Adoff.—AdIn
Improvisation. K. Perryman.—NyT
"I've worked this place". J. Carson.—CaS
Jonathan's farm. M. Waddington.—BoT
Killing chickens. B. Weigl.—JaPr
The labourer. T. Daby.—NyT
Lineage. M. Walker.—LiPg
A long time ago. Unknown.—SuC
"Mary went down to Grandpa's farm". Unknown.—ClI—WiA
The milker. M. Fatchen.—FaCm
Mr. Finney's turnip. Unknown.—HoS
My brother Aaron runs outside to tell us there is a severe thunderstorm warning. A. Adoff.—AdIn
November calf. J. Kenyon.—ElW
"Oh farmer, poor farmer, you're surely". J. Prelutsky.—PrBe
"Oh, the cow kicked Nelly in the belly in the barn". Unknown.—ScA
Oliver Johnson comes back to bed the morning after the ice storm and tells his wife why. D. Jauss.—JaM
"Once there lived a little man". Unknown.—ClI
"One for the pigeon". Mother Goose.—WaM
"Over on the hill there's a big red bull". Unknown.—WiA
The pasture. R. Frost.—KeT
Puppy ("Summer is a long yellow gown"). J. P. Lewis.—LeE
The purpose of poetry. J. Carter.—JaM
She was hungry and cold. A. Adoff.—AdIn
The sheaves. E. A. Robinson.—SuI
The song of the banana man. E. Jones.—LeCa
Sparrow ("Year we worked"). Ewondo-Beti.—NyT
Storm bringer. J. Yolen.—YoBi
"Suky you shall be my wife". Mother Goose.—KeT
Summer evening. W. De La Mare.—DeR—MaP
"There was a young farmer of Leeds". Unknown.—LiLo—SuO
    A young farmer of Leeds.—DeS
"They strolled down the lane together". Unknown.—PrP
"This is the house that Jack built". Mother Goose.—SuO
    The house that Jack built.—HoS
"Three blind mice". Mother Goose.—EdGl—WaM
Thunder. W. De La Mare.—DeR
Tractor. V. Worth.—WoAl
A victory. R. T. Smith.—JaM
Vine leaves. A. Bryan.—BrS
Weights, in memory of my mother, Miriam Murray nee Arnall. L. Murray.—NyT

"We've ploughed our land". Mother Goose.—WaM
"A **farm** team pitcher, McDowell". See Pitcher McDowell
"The **farmer**". See Vine leaves
Farmer, farmer. J. Patrick Lewis.—LeT
"**Farmer** Howe milked the cow". See Farmer, farmer
"A **farmer** in Knox, Ind.". Unknown.—LiLo
A **farmer** went trotting. Mother Goose.—ClI
"A **farmer** went trotting upon his grey mare". See A farmer went trotting
Farmers. See Farm life
Farmiloe, Dorothy
    Recipe for Thanksgiving Day soup.—BoT
Farms and farming. See Farm life
Fast break. Edward Hirsch.—KnAs
The **fast** fiddler. John Ciardi.—CiH
Fast food. Eve Merriam.—MeS
The **fastest** belt in town. Grace Nichols.—NiCo
"**Fat** and Skinny had a race". Unknown.—WiA
"**Fat** bat". Bruce McMillan.—McP
The **fat** black woman's motto on her bedroom door. Grace Nichols.—AgL
"**Fat,** fat, the water rat". Unknown.—ScA
Fat girl with baton. Bob Henry Baber.—JaPr
"**Fat** is". See A fat poem
A **fat** poem. Grace Nichols.—AgL
Fatchen, Max
    And s-s-so to b-b-bed.—FaCm
    Anyone seen my.—PrFo
    Anyone wanting a fiery dragon.—FaCm
    Are you in there.—FaCm
    At sunrise.—FaCm
    At the beach ("Our holiday activities").—FaCm
    Be warned.—FaCm
    Big mouth.—FaCm
    Brain drain.—FaCm
    But why not.—FaCm
    Calling all cars.—FaCm
    Children lost.—FaCm
    Corroboree ("The clap, clap, clap of the clapsticks beat").—FoLe
    Crunchy.—FaCm
    Dinosaur department.—FaCm
    Do it yourself.—FaCm
    Down and up.—FaCm
    Dragon dance.—FoLe
    Gate gossip.—FaCm
    Help ("Any magazines").—FaCm
    Here, puss.—FaCm
    I say.—FaCm
    In a whirl.—FaCm
    Iron man.—FaCm
    Is this yours.—FaCm
    Just friends.—FaCm
    Look out.—PrFo
    The milker.—FaCm
    My dog ("My dog is such a gentle soul").—PrFo
    Ouch.—FaCm
    Playing dirty.—FaCm
    Precious.—FaCm
    Sea thing.—FaCm
    Shakes and ladders.—FaCm
    Silhouettes.—FaCm
    Silly Billy.—FaCm
    Strictly for the birds.—FaCm
    Summer mail.—FaCm
    "There was a young fellow called Hugh".—LiLo
    Thud.—FaCm
    Tide talk.—FaCm
    Uncle Fred.—FaCm
    Whoa.—FaCm

Fatchen, Max—*Continued*
  Who's there.—FaCm
  Windy work.—FaCm
  Wish you were here.—FaCm
  You rang.—FaCm
Fate
  Hapless. W. De La Mare.—DeR—MaP
  Here today. W. De La Mare.—DeR
  Lizard ("The beginning of a lizard"). B. Povlsen.—NyT
  Mathematics of love. M. Hamburger.—GoU
  Nocturne ("If the deep wood is haunted, it is I"). R. Hillyer.—GoU
  On destiny. S. Tanikawa.—NyT
  1246. J.-U.-D. Rumi.—GoU
  "Passing and catching overcome the world". From Watching football on TV. H. Nemerov.—KnAs
  Somewhere. W. De La Mare.—DeR
  The wall. T. D. Castro.—NyT
Father ("I look for you on every street"). Myra Cohn Livingston.—LiT
Father ("My old father walks through"). Tadeusz Rozewicz.—AgL
"Father". See A small discovery
Father and I in the woods. David McCord.—LiPf
"Father and I went down to camp". See The soldier's camp
"Father and mother and Uncle Jan". See Knee ride
Father and son. Tomasz Jastrun, tr. by Daniel Bourne.—NyT
"Father, bless me in my body". Unknown.—StP
"Father has a workshop". See The workshop
"Father, hold my hand". See The white rose, Sophie Scholl, 1921-1943
"Father, may I go to war". Unknown.—WiA
"Father, may I so live the life of love". Unknown.—StP
"A father once said to his son". Unknown.—LiLo
"Father puts the paper down". See Good night
"Father said, heh, heh, I'll fix her". See A social mixer
Father to son. Alfred L. Woods.—SlM
Father William. From Alice's adventures in wonderland. Lewis Carroll.—LiPf
  You are old, Father William.—ElW
Father Wolf's midnight song. Jane Yolen.—LaN
Fathers and fatherhood
  Age four and my father. J. Cunningham.—LiPf
  The age of reason. M. Van Walleghen.—JaPr
  Another dad. E. A. Markham.—AgL
  At the piano. A. Hudgins.—JaM
  Autumn with a daughter who's just catching on. G. Soto.—SoA
  "Bring Daddy home". Mother Goose.—WaM
  "Brothers and sisters have I none". Unknown.—OpI
  Carousel. J. Cunningham.—JaP
  Carving pumpkins with my father. L. Rosenberg.—LiPf
  Charlene Cottier. M. Glenn.—GlBc
  The children's hour. H. W. Longfellow.—SuI
  Christmas night. V. Worth.—WoA
  Christmas wish. T. Johnston.—LiPf
  Daddy. M. C. Livingston.—LiPf
  Daddy carries his empty basket on his head. A. Adoff.—AdIn
  Daddy fell into the pond. A. Noyes.—LiPf
  Daddy is tall, has shoulders, strong hands. A. Adoff.—AdIn
  Daddy's gone. D. Chandra.—LiPf
  Dennis Finch. M. Glenn.—GlBc
  Different dads. X. J. Kennedy.—KeK—LiPf

"Down-adown-derry". W. De La Mare.—DeR
Dream boogie. L. Hughes.—MoR
Dreamers and flyers. J. LaBombard.—JaM
"Each night father fills me with dread". E. Gorey.—PrFo
Eating bread. G. Soto.—SoA
Evening walk. G. Soto.—SoA
Every so often. J. Little.—LiHe
Family. M. C. Livingston.—LiT
Father ("I look for you on every street"). M. C. Livingston.—LiT
Father ("My old father walks through"). T. Rozewicz.—AgL
Father and I in the woods. D. McCord.—LiPf
Father and son. T. Jastrun.—NyT
"A father once said to his son". Unknown.—LiLo
Father's magic. E. Di Pasquale.—LiPf
Father's story. E. M. Roberts.—SuI
The first flakes are falling on our heads. A. Adoff.—AdIn
Forgotten. C. Rylant.—JaP
Four generations. M. A. Hoberman.—HoFa
The gift ("When I was five my father kidnapped me"). M. Jarman.—JaM
Girls can we educate us dads. J. Berry.—BeW
Grape sherbert. R. Dove.—JaM
Hook. F. Skloot.—KnAs
Hunting. J. Sheedy.—KnAs
"Hush, little baby, don't say a word". Mother Goose.—SuO
  Hush, little baby.—KeT
I like it when. R. Margolis.—LiPf
In the kitchen. J. Joubert.—NyT
Iron man. M. Fatchen.—FaCm
"I've worked this place". J. Carson.—CaS
"John Smith and his son, John Smith". W. Stevens.—ElW—KeT
Keeping the horses. R. Scheele.—JaM
Leg broken. S. B. Mathis.—MaR
Letter from my son. S. Sarkar.—NyT
Love don't mean. E. Greenfield.—SlM
"Mama, Mama, have you heard". Unknown.—ScA
Metaphor for my son. J. Holmes.—SuI
The midnight snack. J. Merrill.—ElW
The miller and his son. W. De La Mare.—DeR
The monument. P. B. Janeczko.—JaB
Mr. Desmond Klinger, music. M. Glenn.—GlBc
Mr. Joshua Cantor. M. Glenn.—GlBc
Mr. Neil Pressman, fine arts. M. Glenn.—GlBc
Mummy slept late and daddy fixed breakfast. J. Ciardi.—LiPf—PrFo
My dad. A. Bryan.—BrS
My dad said. M. Wiley, and I. McMillan.—FoLe
My daddy is a cool dude. K. Fufuka.—SlM
My father. M. A. Hoberman.—HoFa
My father toured the south. J. Nichols.—KnAs
My father's fortune. H. Scott.—JaPr
My father's leaving. I. Sadoff.—JaPr
My father's words. C. Lewis.—LiPf
My happiness. G. Pape.—JaM
My Jose. M. Robinson.—LiPf
"My little son". Makah.—SnD
My mother really knew. W. Lum.—JaM
My papa's waltz. T. Roethke.—ElW
Mystery ("One Friday night"). P. B. Janeczko.—JaB
New Dad. M. C. Livingston.—LiT
October Saturday. B. Katz.—JaP
Ode to Los Raspados. G. Soto.—SoNe
Ode to mi perrito. G. Soto.—SoNe
On this, a holy night. K. Bezner.—JaPr

Fathers and fatherhood—*Continued*
Papa is a bear. J. P. Lewis.—LiPf
Papa loves baby. S. Smith.—ElW
Pearls. J. Little.—LiHe
Petrified minute. Z. Zelk.—NyT
Poem for my son. B. Padhi.—NyT
Questions, quistions and quoshtions. S. Milligan.—PrFo
Rare rhythms. S. London.—JaM
Saturday fielding practice. L. Morrison.—LiPf
Secrets ("I doubt that you remember her, except"). R. Pack.—JaM
A short long story. J. Cunningham.—JaP
Small wants. B. Padhi.—NyT
Snowstorm. K. B. Winnick.—LiPf
"Step in the dirt". Unknown.—WiA
Still life. M. Angelotti.—JaM
Sundays. P. B. Janeczko.—JaB
Tableau. K. Wilson.—JaPr
Tennis in the city. F. Higgins.—KnAs
"There was a place". M. C. Livingston.—LiT
Those winter Sundays. R. Hayden.—ElW
"Thou art my father, who is my mother". Unknown.—StP
Thud. M. Fatchen.—FaCm
The volleyball match. B. Pearlman.—KnAs
Walking. A. Fisher.—FiA
"When I married, I caught up". J. Holmes.—SuI
Whistler's father. X. J. Kennedy.—KeGh
White on white. C. E. Hemp.—JaP
Winner ("What I remember most"). G. Fehler.—MoA
The word. P. B. Janeczko.—JaB
The workshop. A. Fisher.—FiA
You rang. M. Fatchen.—FaCm
"**Father's** legs are very long". See Walking
Father's magic. Emanuel Di Pasquale.—LiPf
Father's story. Elizabeth Madox Roberts.—SuI
"**Fatty**, fatty, boom a latty". Unknown.—PrP
Faucet. William Jay Smith.—SmL
Fear
Alone ("Alone in a house with no one to talk to"). S. Hudson.—BaH
Anaconda. D. Macleod.—CoAz
And s-s-so to b-b-bed. M. Fatchen.—FaCm
"Anxious". M. Waddington.—BoT
At the keyhole. W. De La Mare.—DeR—MaP
Attic fanatic. L. Simmie.—PrFo
The bat ("By day the bat is cousin to the mouse"). T. Roethke.—CoAz—DeS—ElW
Be kind to dumb animals. J. Ciardi.—CiH—LiLo
Big black dog. C. Michael.—CoAz
Boy at the window. R. Wilbur.—ElW
The cage. S. Hensman.—AgL
"Coward, cowardy custard". Unknown.—OpI—ScA
   "Cowardy, cowardy custard".—WiA
Darnell. E. Greenfield.—GrN
Don't be afraid. D. Vogel.—LiPm
"Each night father fills me with dread". E. Gorey.—PrFo
Forbidden sounds. E. James.—BaH
"Four and twenty tailors". Mother Goose.—ClI
George. D. Randall.—SuC
The Halloween house. J. Ciardi.—CiH—LiLo
Hanging fire. A. Lorde.—AgL
Hark. W. De La Mare.—DeR
"He drank enough". From Snake. D. H. Lawrence.—MoR
Help ("Can anybody tell me, please"). J. Prelutsky.—PrFo
In the dark. J. Pridmore.—BaH

In the dark of night. A. Fisher.—LaM
Jack. D. Chandra.—LiHp
Knock, knock. J. Yolen.—YoBe
Life doesn't frighten me. M. Angelou.—AgL
"Little Miss Muffet". Mother Goose.—EdGl—SuO—WaM
Look out. M. Fatchen.—PrFo
The mad nun. D. Giola.—JaPr
Mallory Wade. M. Glenn.—GlBc
The mighty eye. K. Dakos.—DaI
"The monster in my closet". F. P. Heide.—HeG
Motorcycle racer thinks of quitting. G. Butcher.—KnAs
"A mouse in her room woke Miss Dowd". Unknown.—LiLo
   A mouse in her room.—ClI—KeT—PrFo
"A narrow fellow in the grass". E. Dickinson.—ElW
No one heard him call. D. Aldis.—KeT
No question. L. Dangel.—JaPr
Ode to La Llorona. G. Soto.—SoNe
Outhouse blues. S. L. Nelms.—JaM
Owl of night. M. C. Livingston.—LiR
Owls ("They stare at you"). L. Clark.—LiIf
Patricia Lampert. M. Glenn.—GlBc
The phantom ("Upstairs in the large closet, child"). W. De La Mare.—DeR
Poem at thirty. S. Sanchez.—SuC
The runaway. R. Frost.—ElW
Scary things. J. Holder.—BaH
Screaming. D. MacLeod.—PrFo
The sick-room. R. A. Simpson.—NyT
"A skeleton once in Khartoum". Unknown.—LiLo
Snake, complete ("A snake came to my water-trough"). D. H. Lawrence.—ElW
The snoffle. F. P. Heide.—HeG
"Something is there". L. Moore.—BaH
Something strange. M. C. Livingston.—LiNe
Summer killer. T. A. Broughton.—JaM
"There came a gray owl at sunset". Unknown.—LiIf
"There once was a scarecrow named Joel". D. McCord.—LiLo
Under the stairs. D. Lister.—BaH
Very much afraid. Unknown.—LiIf
"When bad things happen to me, God". I. Wells.—StP
When I tell you I'm scared. B. S. De Regniers.—DeW
"When you walk that lonesome valley". Unknown.—StP
Whooo. L. Moore.—LiIf
"A wolf". Unknown.—LiIf
"**Fear** is a golden chain around my throat". See Motorcycle racer thinks of quitting
"**Fear** no more the heat o' the sun". From Cymbeline. William Shakespeare.—ElW
The **feast**. Walter De La Mare.—DeR
The **feather**. Walter De La Mare.—DeR
"A **feather**, a feather". See The feather
Feathers
"Cackle, cackle, Mother Goose". Mother Goose.—WaM
"If you find a little feather". B. S. De Regniers.—HoT—MoS
Macaw. M. C. Livingston.—LiNe
Our canary. L. Simmie.—PrFo
"Snow, snow faster". Mother Goose.—ScA—WaM
February
Long Beach, February. M. C. Livingston.—LiR

February—*Continued*
Potomac town in February. C. Sandburg.—LiDd
"When skies are low and days are dark". N. M. Bodecker.—FrS
February 14. Myra Cohn Livingston.—LiT
February 14th. Ann Bonner.—FoLe
"**February** night". See Barn owl
"**Feed** it, it will grow high". Unknown.—ScA
"The **feel** of that leather baby". See Watching the Jets lose to Buffalo at Shea
"**Feeling** thirsty". See Drinking water coconut
Feelings. See also specific emotional states as Fear, Happiness
"Always be kind to animals". J. Gardner.—CoAz
Annette Harrison. M. Glenn.—GlBc
Brand new baby. B. S. De Regniers.—DeW
Different feelings. J. Berry.—BeW
"The first time ever I saw your face". E. MacColl.—GoU
Flame and water. J. Berry.—AgL
Granny's ninety-two-year-old legs. A. Adoff.—AdIn
"He drank enough". From Snake. D. H. Lawrence.—MoR
"I wake up". M. Rosen.—AgL
If sometimes blue. A. L. Woods.—SlM
The lightning. M. Swenson.—SuI
Loneliness. V. Usherwood.—AgL
Marrow of my bone. M. Evans.—SuC
Me I am. Unknown.—LoFh
Mean song ("I'm warning you"). B. S. De Regniers.—DeW
Mercedes Lugo. M. Glenn.—GlBc
The new house. M. Angelou.—AnI
"Poems can give you". S. Bogart.—BoT
Poetry ("What is poetry, who knows"). E. Farjeon.—ElW
Shapes and actions. J. Berry.—BeW
"Since feeling is first". E. E. Cummings.—ElW
Snake, complete ("A snake came to my water-trough"). D. H. Lawrence.—ElW
Spectrum. M. Evans.—SuC
The tale of a dog. J. H. Lambert.—CoAz
Teach the making of summer. J. Berry.—BeW
There are days. B. S. De Regniers.—DeW
"There are times when I can't move". R. Juarroz.—NyT
"There's a certain slant of light". E. Dickinson.—GoT—SuI
This place. E. Greenfield.—GrU
To the tune "Glittering sword hits". Liu Yii Hsi.—GoU
Touching. From Songs for Nandu Bhende. N. Ezekiel.—AgL
We wear the mask. P. L. Dunbar.—SuC
When I dance. J. Berry.—BeW
When I was lost. D. Aldis.—MoS
"Where is a poem". E. Merriam.—MeS
The white city. C. McKay.—SuC
Feet
"All policeman have big feet". Unknown.—WiA
Barefoot. V. Worth.—WoAl
"**Feet** seat". B. McMillan.—McP
The first shoe. M. Mhac an tSaoi.—NyT
Marguerite. Unknown.—PrFo
Neet people. L. Simmie.—PrFo
Nightingale's feet. Issa.—DeI
The pettitoes. Unknown.—CII
The reluctant hero or barefoot in the snow. M. Mahy.—MaN
"Said Noble Aaron to Aaron Barron". Mother Goose.—WaM

Sticky situation. X. J. Kennedy.—LiLo
Swan ("Over the mirror"). J. Yolen.—YoBi
"There once was a centipede neat". Unknown.—LiLo
"There was an old woman from Winnipeg". W. J. Smith.—SmL
The truth about the abominable footprint. M. Baldwin.—PrFo
"You're a poet". Unknown.—WiA
"The **feet** of the". See Caterpillar
"**Feet** seat". Bruce McMillan.—McP
Fehler, Gene
Nolan Ryan.—MoA
Winner ("What I remember most").—MoA
Feldman, Irving
The gymnasts.—KnAs
This evening, tr.—GoT
"A **fellow** named Percival Stein". R. H. Marks.—LiLo
Fence. Valerie Worth.—WoAl
Fences
Fence. V. Worth.—WoAl
"The pickety fence". D. McCord.—HoS
Precious. M. Fatchen.—FaCm
Ferlinghetti, Lawrence
Baseball canto.—KnAs
Ferrarelli, Rina
Joan Benoit.—KnAs
Ferrer de Arrellaga, Renee
Pitcher, tr. by Raquel Chaves and Naomi Shihab Nye.—NyT
Ferries
At the ferry. V. Mukhopadhyay.—NyT
"Ferry me across the water". C. G. Rossetti.—KeT
John Boatman. Unknown.—OpT
Recuerdo. E. S. V. Millay.—ElW
"**Ferry** me across the water". Christina Georgina Rossetti.—KeT
Festival. John Kitching.—FoLe
"**Fetch** bouquets of bittersweet". See Setting the Thanksgiving table
"**Few** and faint a bird's small notes". See Noon
Fichman, Yaakov
"On the shores of Lake Kinneret".—StP
"**Fiddle**-de-dee, fiddle-de-dee". Mother Goose.—WaM
Fiddle faddle. Eve Merriam.—MeS
"The **fiddler** and his wife". Mother Goose.—WaM
The **fiddlers.** Walter De La Mare.—DeR
Fiddlers and fiddling
"Ah who dydle de". Unknown.—ScA
A cat came fiddling. Mother Goose.—CII
The cat sat asleep. Mother Goose.—CII
"The cat asleep by the side of the fire".—WaM
The fast fiddler. J. Ciardi.—CiH
The fiddlers. W. De La Mare.—DeR
"Friendly Fredrick Fuddlestone". A. Lobel.—PrFo
"Got a cornstalk fiddle". Unknown.—WiA
"John, come sell thy fiddle". Mother Goose.—WaM
"Now just who, muses Uncle Bill Biddle". X. J. Kennedy.—KeGh—LiLo
"Old King Cole was a merry old soul". Mother Goose.—EdGl—SuO—WaM
The old tailor. W. De La Mare.—DeR
"There was an old man of the Isles". E. Lear.—LiLo
Field, Edward
The sleeper.—KnAs
Sonja Henie Sonnet.—KnAs

Field, Eugene
  Wynken, Blynken, and Nod.—ElW
Field, Rachel
  A circus garland.—ElW
  City lights.—DeT
  "I'd like to be a lighthouse".—LiDd
  "If once you have slept on an island".—LoFh
  Manhattan lullaby ("Now lighted windows climb the dark").—KeT
  Skyscrapers.—HoSt
  "Something told the wild geese".—FrS
Field, Susan Cohen
  The princess and the frog.—BaH
Field in the wind. Floris Clark McLaren.—BoT
Fielder, W.
  At the beach ("The waves are erasing the footprints"), tr.—NyT
Fields, Julia
  Alabama, sels.
    "God save the owls".—LiIf
  Dog days.—LiDp
  "God save the owls". See Alabama
  Mom is wow.—LiPm
Fields
  Afternoon on a hill. E. S. V. Millay.—FrS—SuI
  At sunrise. M. Fatchen.—FaCm
  "Away, you black devils, away". Mother Goose.—WaM
  Field in the wind. F. C. McLaren.—BoT
  The hare ("In the black furrow of a field"). W. De La Mare.—DeR
  Hayfield. A. Fisher.—FiA
  The island. D. Aldis.—DeT
  The meadow-bout fields. Unknown.—OpT
  Silent noon. D. G. Rossetti.—GoU
  "Three gray geese in the green grass grazing". Unknown.—WiA
    Three gray geese (". . . in a green field grazing") .—ClI
Fields of corn. Sam Reavin.—MoS
"The **5th** black law student". See You've got to learn the white man's game
"**Fightin'** was natural". Maya Angelou.—AnI
Fights
  "Are you the guy". Unknown.—WiA
  At the piano. A. Hudgins.—JaM
  Bebe Belinda and Carl Colombus. A. Mitchell.—AgL
  Dawn Weinberg. M. Glenn.—GlBc
  "Did you ever hear such a noise and clamor". Unknown.—WiA
  Donnybrook at Riverfront Stadium. L. Morrison.—MoA
  "Fightin' was natural". M. Angelou.—AnI
  Flame and water. J. Berry.—AgL
  The grease monkey and the powder puff. W. J. Smith.—SmL
  Hector Velasquez. M. Glenn.—GlBc
  Heman. M. Wandor.—AgL
  "Here stands a fist". Unknown.—OpI
  How it was. G. Hyland.—JaPr
  "Jaybird a-sitting on a hickory limb". Unknown.—WiA
  "The lion and the unicorn". Mother Goose.—EdGl
  The loser. C. Bukowski.—KnAs
  Lunchbox. V. Worth.—MoS
  The madhouse. J. Carter.—JaM
  My big brothers. M. A. Hoberman.—HoFa
  "My mother and your mother". Unknown.—CoM—WiA
    "My mother, your mother".—ScA

No question. L. Dangel.—JaPr
"One bright morning in the middle of the night". Unknown.—WiA
"One fine day in the middle of the night". Unknown.—BaH—OpI
"Punch and Judy fought for a pie". Unknown.—PrFo
Reach for the sky. Unknown.—ScA
"The robin and the wren". Unknown.—CaB—ClI
Ronnie Schwinck. D. A. Evans.—JaPr
Roosters. E. Coatsworth.—WhAs
"See my pinky". Unknown.—ScA
The tables turned. X. J. Kennedy.—KeK
"There once were two cats of Kilkenny". Unknown.—LiLo
  The cats of Kilkenny ("There were once . . .").—ElW—LaCc
"**Fill** your children with kindness". Unknown.—StP
Finches
  Finches. Ho-o.—DeI
  Winter finch. J. Yolen.—YoBi
Finches. Ho-o, tr. by Tze-si Huang.—DeI
"**Finders** keepers". Unknown.—CoM—WiA
Finding a lucky number. Gary Soto.—JaM—SoA
Finding a way. Myra Cohn Livingston.—LiT
"**Fine** black kinfolk". Dakari Kamau Hru.—SlM
"The **finest** animal I know". See Water buffalo
Finger-play poems. See Nursery play
Fingerprint. Harry Thurston.—BoT
Fingers
  "Cut your nails on Monday, cut for health". Unknown.—WiA
  "Here is the beehive, where are the bees". Unknown.—WiA
    The beehive.—CoE
  Names for the fingers. Unknown.—OpT
  Octopus ("Marvel at the"). V. Worth.—WoAl
  Ten little fingers. Unknown.—CoE
  "Where is Thumbkin". Unknown.—CoE
  Whoops, Johnny. Unknown.—CoE
Finis. Unknown.—OpI
The **finish.** David Hoffman.—KnAs
Finkel, Donald
  A headstrong boy, tr.—NyT
  Interview with a winner.—KnAs
The **fir** tree. Jane Yolen.—YoHa
Fire
  "Arise, arise, Domino Decree". Unknown.—OpT
  "The boy stood on the burning deck". Unknown.—PrFo—WiA
  The brave ones. E. Greenfield.—GrU
  "Bubble, said the kettle". Unknown.—PrP
  Candle. M. C. Livingston.—LiNe
  Coals. W. De La Mare.—DeR
  "Feed it, it will grow high". Unknown.—ScA
  The fire. W. De La Mare.—DeR
  "Fire, fire". Unknown.—WiA
  Five haiku. G. Douthwaite.—FoLe
  Flint. C. G. Rossetti.—ElW
  "Ladybug, ladybug, fly away home". Mother Goose.—ScA—WiA
    "Ladybird, ladybird".—WaM
    To the ladybird ("Ladybird, ladybird").—OpI
  Logs. W. De La Mare.—DeR
  "My head is red". M. C. Livingston.—LiMh
  Part XVI: The king in slumber when he lies down. From A child's day. W. De La Mare.—DeR
  The phoenix. P. Fleischman.—WhDd
  Please to remember ("He comes to see us every year"). G. Holloway.—FoLe
  Remember. D. Ward.—FoLe

Fire—*Continued*

"Rooms are full, hall is full, but". From Riddle poems. J. Berry.—BeW

Small town fireworks. X. J. Kennedy.—KeK

Smoke. E. Pankey.—JaPr

Tree fire. V. Worth.—WoA

"When you see your neighbour's beard on fire, take some water and wet your own". From Jamaican Caribbean proverbs. Unknown.—BeW

"Where the sun shone white hot, Cass". X. J. Kennedy.—KeFb

Wiggle waggle, wiggle waggle. Unknown.—ClI

Yule log. J. Yolen.—YoHa

The **fire**. Walter De La Mare.—DeR

"The **fire** crackles in the kitchen range, and big". See In the kitchen

"**Fire, fire**". Unknown.—WiA

"**Fire, fire**, said Obediah". Unknown.—YoS

Fireflies

Fireflies ("An August night"). J. P. Lewis.—LeT

Fireflies ("Fireflies at twilight"). M. A. Hoberman.—DeS

Fireflies ("Fireflies on night canvas"). Q. Troupe.—SlM

Fireflies ("In the soft dark night"). A. Fisher.—FiA

Fireflies ("Light, light"). P. Fleischman.—FlJ

Fireflies in the garden. R. Frost.—ElW

Firefly. E. M. Roberts.—DeS—LiDd—StP—WhAa

"The firefly is a funny bug". Unknown.—PrP
 "The firefly is a funny bird".—ScA

"I think". From Firefly. Li Po.—DeS

Meteor. Basho.—DeI

One night. A. Adoff.—AdIn

The prayer of the glow-worm. C. B. De Gasztold.—DeP

Song of summer. M. W. Brown.—MoS

Fireflies ("An August night"). J. Patrick Lewis.—LeT

Fireflies ("Fireflies at twilight"). Mary Ann Hoberman.—DeS

Fireflies ("Fireflies on night canvas"). Quincy Troupe.—SlM

Fireflies ("In the soft dark night"). Aileen Fisher.—FiA

Fireflies ("Light, light"). Paul Fleischman.—FlJ

"**Fireflies** at twilight". See Fireflies

Fireflies in the garden. Robert Frost.—ElW

"**Fireflies** on night canvas". See Fireflies

"The **fireflies** wink and glow". Robert Hillyer.—GoT

Firefly, sels. Li Po

"I think".—DeS

Firefly. Elizabeth Madox Roberts.—DeS—LiDd—StP—WhAa

"The **firefly** is a funny bird". See "The firefly is a funny bug"

"The **firefly** is a funny bug". Unknown.—PrP
 "The firefly is a funny bird".—ScA

Firewood. See Wood

Fireworks

"At the fireworks show, rash Randall". X. J. Kennedy.—KeFb

Dragon dance. M. Fatchen.—FoLe

Fireworks ("First a far thud"). V. Worth.—MoR—WoAl

Fireworks ("The Fourth of July's"). M. C. Livingston.—LiR

Fireworks ("Pin wheels whirling round"). D. Aldis.—LoFh

The Fourth. S. Silverstein.—MoR

Fourth of July ("Hurrah for the Fourth of July"). M. C. Livingston.—LiLo

Fourth of July night. C. Sandburg.—LaN

"I've got a rocket". Unknown.—WiA

Ode to fireworks. G. Soto.—SoNe

Skywriting I. E. Merriam.—MeS

Small town fireworks. X. J. Kennedy.—KeK

The time we cherry-bombed the toilet at the River Oaks. C. H. Webb.—JaPr

Fireworks ("First a far thud"). Valerie Worth.—MoR—WoAl

Fireworks ("The Fourth of July's"). Myra Cohn Livingston.—LiR

Fireworks ("Pin wheels whirling round"). Dorothy Aldis.—LoFh

"**Fireworks**". See Skywriting I

Fireworks 2. Eve Merriam.—MeS

"**First**". See The chestnuts are falling

The **1st**. Lucille Clifton.—ElW

"**First** a daughter, then a son". Unknown.—ScA

"**First** a far thud". See Fireworks

"The **first** black woman". See Old Mag

"**First** come I, my name is Jowett". Unknown.—OpI

"**First** day, Jackie and I walking in leaves". See Cruel boys

"The **first** day of Christmas". See The twelve days of Christmas ("On the first day of Christmas")

First day of school. Aileen Fisher.—FiA

"**First**, feel, then feel, then". See Young soul

The **first** flakes are falling on our heads. Arnold Adoff.—AdIn

First flight. Myra Cohn Livingston.—LiNe

First foot. Ian Serraillier.—FoLe

First green heron. Gary Margolis.—KnAs

"**First**, Hansel and Gretel try to follow". See Life in the forest, or, bad news, good news, bad news

"The **first** hazelnut trundles down from above". See The squirrel

"**First** in a carriage". Mother Goose.—WaM

"**First** is worst". Unknown.—WiA

"**First** it bit my behind". Barry Louis Polisar.—PrFo

First job. Jim Daniels.—JaPr

"The **first** letter in my name". Unknown.—ScA

"**First** of all". See Festival

First one awake. X. J. Kennedy.—KeK

First robin. Jane Yolen.—YoBi

"The **first** runner reached us". See The finish

The **first** shoe. Maire Mhac an tSaoi, tr. by Brendan O'Hehir.—NyT

First sight. Philip Larkin.—CaB—ElW

First snow ("Snow makes whiteness where it falls"). Marie Louise Allen.—DeS

First snow ("When autumn stills"). Aileen Fisher.—FiH

First snowfall. Aileen Fisher.—FiH

First snowflake. N. M. Bodecker.—KeT

First solo. Walter McDonald.—MoR

First star. See "Star light, star bright"

The **first** Thanksgiving. Jack Prelutsky.—LoFh

"**First** there were two of us, then there were three of us". See The storm

"**First** time at third". Jacqueline Sweeney.—MoA

"The **first** time ever I saw Johnny Spain was". See Johnny Spain's white heifer

"The **first** time ever I saw your face". Ewan MacColl.—GoU

"The **first** time I sat in a restaurant". Jo Carson.—CaS

"The **first** time I walked". See Oranges

"A **flamingo**". J. Patrick Lewis.—LeA
"The **flamingo** lingers". See Flamingo
Flamingos
    "A flamingo". J. P. Lewis.—LeA
    Flamingo. V. Worth.—WoAl
Flanders, Michael
    The walrus.—CaB—PrFo
    "What fun to be".—WhAa
"**Flashing** neon night". J. W. Hackett.—LaN
"**Flat** blonde seeds big". See Watchdogs
The **flattered** flying fish. Emile Victor Rieu.—ElW
"A **flea** and a fly in a flue". Unknown.—LiLo
    A fly and a flea.—ClI
    "A fly and a flea flew up in a flue".—WiA
"A **flea** on a pooch doesn't care". See Home sweet
    home
Fleas
    "A bug and a flea". Unknown.—ClI—OpI
    "A flea and a fly in a flue". Unknown.—LiLo
        A fly and a flea.—ClI
        "A fly and a flea flew up in a flue".—WiA
    Fleas. V. Worth.—WoAl
    Home sweet home. J. Ciardi.—CiH
    "A horse and a flea and three blind mice".
        Unknown.—CoM—WiA
        Whoops.—ClI
    "I've got a dog as thin as a rail". Unknown.—
        ClI—PrP
        "I have a dog as thin as a rail".—ScA
    "Oh dear me". Unknown.—OpI
    "One, two, three, mother caught a flea".
        Unknown.—CoM
    "Some people say that fleas are black".
        Unknown.—ScA
Fleas. Valerie Worth.—WoAl
The **fleeting**. Walter De La Mare.—DeR
Fleischman, Paul
    Book lice.—FlJ
    Chrysalis diary.—FlJ
    Cicadas.—FlJ
    The digger wasp.—FlJ
    Fireflies ("Light, light").—FlJ
    Grasshoppers.—FlJ
    Honeybees.—FlJ
    House crickets.—FlJ
    Mayflies.—FlJ
    The moth's serenade.—FlJ
    Owls ("Sun's down, sky's dark").—LiIf
    The passenger pigeon.—JaP
    The phoenix.—WhDd
    Requiem.—FlJ
    Water boatmen.—FlJ
    Water striders.—FlJ
    Whirligig beetles.—FlJ
Fletcher, John Gould
    The skaters ("Black swallows swooping or
        gliding").—KnAs
"A **flicker** of blue". See Kingfisher
Flies
    "Curious fly". Unknown.—PrP
    The dental history of Flossie Fly. X. J.
        Kennedy.—KeGh
    "Don't shoo the morning flies away". H. Yu.—
        GoT
    "Fiddle-de-dee, fiddle-de-dee". Mother Goose.—
        WaM
    "A flea and a fly in a flue". Unknown.—LiLo
        A fly and a flea.—ClI
        "A fly and a flea flew up in a flue".—WiA
    Flies. V. Worth.—WoAl
    The fly. W. De La Mare.—DeR

"The fly made a visit to the grocery store".
    Unknown.—PrP
Gus. P. B. Janeczko.—JaB
The last cry of the damp fly. D. Lee.—PrFo
Little fly. Unknown.—ClI
"Nellie Bligh caught a fly". Unknown.—OpI
"Off a pane the". E. E. Cummings.—MoR
"Oh, don't strike the fly". Issa.—CaR
The spider and the fly. M. Howitt.—ElW
"There was a young lady of Ealing". Unknown.—
    LiLo
U is for up. W. J. Smith.—SmL
Flies. Valerie Worth.—WoAl
"**Flies** forever". Unknown.—ScA
"**Flies** wear". See Flies
Flight. See also Airplanes and aviators
    "Abner from an Alpine height". X. J. Kennedy.—
        KeFb
    Alone on a broom. J. Yolen.—YoBe
    Barn owl. M. Singer.—SiT
    The bat ("By day the bat is cousin to the mouse").
        T. Roethke.—CoAz—DeS—ElW
    Bat ("Dark air life looping"). D. H. Lawrence.—
        WhAa
    The beak of the pelican. J. P. Lewis.—LeA
    Calgary. M. C. Livingston.—LiNe
    Canada goose. M. Singer.—SiT
    Chrysalis diary. P. Fleischman.—FlJ
    Dragonfly. M. Singer.—SiT
    The dream ("My arms"). M. C. Livingston.—
        LiNe
    The eagle ("He clasps the crag with crooked
        hands"). A. Tennyson.—CaB—ElW
    Eagle flight. A. Lopez.—DeT
    Fireflies ("Light, light"). P. Fleischman.—FlJ
    First flight. M. C. Livingston.—LiNe
    First solo. W. McDonald.—MoR
    Flight of the long-haired yak. W. J. Smith.—SmL
    The flight of the one-eyed bat. W. J. Smith.—
        SmL
    Flying crooked. R. Graves.—CaB
    "Flying-man, flying-man". Mother Goose.—SuO
    The flying squirrel. J. Gardner.—WhAa
    Flying west. M. C. Livingston.—LiNe
    Golden eagle. J. P. Lewis.—LeT
    Goose-wing chariot. Unknown.—OpT
    Gull. W. J. Smith.—SmL
    Harry the hawk. M. Mahy.—MaN
    Hazard's optimism. W. Meredith.—KnAs
    Heights made him dizzy. J. Ciardi.—CiH
    High. W. De La Mare.—DeR
    Hitchhiker. D. McCord.—LiIf
    I am flying. J. Prelutsky.—BaW
    "I get high on butterflies". J. Roseblatt.—BoT
    "I'd like to see cats with stubby wings". From
        What we said sitting making fantasies. J.
        Berry.—BeW
    If the owl calls again. J. Haines.—LiIf
    International ski flying championship, Obersdorf.
        E. Ritchie.—KnAs
    Kite. V. Worth.—WoAl
    Little people's express. X. J. Kennedy.—KeGh
    The manoeuvre. W. C. Williams.—CaB
    "My first solo trial flight, you see". From What
        we said sitting making fantasies. J. Berry.—
        BeW
    Night flight over Kansas. M. C. Livingston.—
        LiNe
    Of wings. P. Redcloud.—HoT
    "Oh, I have slipped the surly bonds of earth". J.
        G. Magee.—StP
        High flight.—SuI

Fol dol do. Walter De La Mare.—DeR
"Fol, dol, do, and a south wind a-blowing o". See
  Fol dol do
Folk poetry. See Autograph album verses; Ballads—
  Traditional; Counting-out rhymes; Jump-rope
  rhymes; Mother Goose
"The folk who live in Backward town". Mary Ann
  Hoberman.—DeS
Folklore. See Fairy tales; Superstitions
Follen, Eliza Lee
  The three little kittens.—HoS
    "Three little kittens, they lost their
      mittens".—SuO (unat.)
    "Three little kittens lost their mittens".—
      EdGl (unat.)—WaM (unat.)
  "Three little kittens lost their mittens". See The
    three little kittens
  "Three little kittens, they lost their mittens". See
    The three little kittens
"Follow the fellow-phant". See Rules for the
  elephant parade
Follow the leader. Harry Behn.—HoS
"Follow the leader away in a row". See Follow the
  leader
"Fondle me". See Marrow of my bone
Food and eating. See also Cooks and cooking; also
  names of Food, as Cakes and cookies; also
  names of meals as Breakfast
  "Annie ate jam". Unknown.—OpI
  Anteater ("The anteater makes a meal of ants").
    W. J. Smith.—PrFo—SmL
  Anteater ("Imagine overturning"). V. Worth.—
    WoAl
  "Baby's heart is lifted up". R. L. Gales.—StP
  "Back of the loaf is the snowy flour". M. D.
    Babcock.—StP
  Banana and mackerel. J. Berry.—BeW
  Banana man. G. Nichols.—NiCo
  "Bananas and cream". D. McCord.—DeT—LiDd
  "Beef and bacon's out of season". Unknown.—
    WiA
  Before you fix your next peanut butter sandwich,
    read this. F. P. Heide.—HeG
  "Beneath a blue umbrella". J. Prelutsky.—PrBe
  Big sister. M. A. Hoberman.—HoFa
  "Bless the meat". Unknown.—OpI
  The boar's head carol. Unknown.—YoHa
  "The boy stood in the supper room".
    Unknown.—OpI
  "The boy stood on the burning deck".
    Unknown.—PrFo—WiA
  "Brother Pete". E. Merriam.—MeP
  Brother's snacks. X. J. Kennedy.—KeGh
  Cake and sack. W. De La Mare.—DeR—MaP
  Chips, three. A. Adoff.—AdCh
  Chocolate dreams, one. A. Adoff.—AdCh
  Chocolate dreams, two. A. Adoff.—AdCh
  Christmas dinner. V. Worth.—WoA
  Circles ("I am speaking of circles"). M. C.
    Livingston.—JaP—LiT
  "Cold meat, mutton pies". Unknown.—OpI
  The country mouse and the city mouse. R. S.
    Sharpe.—ElW
  Crunchy. M. Fatchen.—FaCm
  "Crusty corn bread". E. Merriam.—MeY
  Dinnertime. M. A. Hoberman.—HoFa
  Do good. A. Bryan.—BrS
  "Down the Mississippi". Unknown.—WiA
  "Each time we eat". Unknown.—StP
  "Eat it, it's good for you". M. A. Hoberman.—
    HoFa
  "An epicure, dining at Crewe". Unknown.—LiLo

Fast food. E. Merriam.—MeS
The feast. W. De La Mare.—DeR
"The fiddler and his wife". Mother Goose.—WaM
"For red mouthwash, rotten Ross". X. J.
  Kennedy.—KeFb
"For water-ices, cheap but good". A. Laing.—StP
A funny old person. Unknown.—ClI
Garbage delight. D. Lee.—PrFo
The gingerbread grandma. J. C. Thomas.—LiPg
Giraffe ("When I invite the giraffe to dine"). W.
  J. Smith.—SmL
"Give me a good digestion, Lord". T. H. B.
  Webb.—StP
"God is great". Unknown.—StP
Grace. W. De La Mare.—DeR
"Hannah Bantry in the pantry". Mother Goose.—
  WaM
"Heavenly Father, bless us". Unknown.—StP
"Here I stand all fat and chunky". Unknown.—
  ScA
"Here's good bread and cheese and porter". From
  Dinner table rhymes. Unknown.—OpT
"Hiccup, hiccup, go away". Mother Goose.—
  WaM
The hopeful trout, poor fish. J. Ciardi.—CiH
House crickets. P. Fleischman.—FlJ
Hungry Jake. F. P. Heide.—HeG
I don't mean to say I am Martian, Morkian. A.
  Adoff.—AdCh
"I eat my peas with honey". Unknown.—ScA—
  WiA
"I know a washerwoman, she knows me".
  Unknown.—OpI
I know that summer is the famous growing
  season. A. Adoff.—AdIn
I love my mom, I love my pop, I love my dog,
  I love my sheep. A. Adoff.—AdCh
"I passed by his garden, and marked, with one
  eye". From Through the looking glass. L.
  Carroll.—LiIf
"I raised a great hullabaloo". Unknown.—ClI
"I says, you says". Unknown.—WiA
"I was my mother's darling child". Unknown.—
  ScA
"I would reduce". Unknown.—ScA
If I were a. K. Kuskin.—DeS
If we had lunch at the White House. K. Dakos.—
  DaI
"In her lunchbox Lena packs". X. J. Kennedy.—
  KeFb
In my horror fantasy chiller. A. Adoff.—AdCh
In public, I pick a piece or two from the plate. A.
  Adoff.—AdCh
In the memories of our cookies. A. Adoff.—AdCh
In this last class before lunch, I close my eyes. A.
  Adoff.—AdCh
Italian noodles. X. J. Kennedy.—KeGh
"It's not me". J. Carson.—CaS
"Jack Sprat could eat no fat". Mother Goose.—
  EdGl—SuO—WaM
"Jelly in the bowl". Unknown.—WiA
"Jellyfish stew". J. Prelutsky.—PrFo
Labels. A. Adoff.—AdCh
"Lay the cloth, knife and fork". Unknown.—OpI
Leek soup. X. J. Kennedy.—KeGh
Let the biter beware. A. Adoff.—AdCh
"Let us in peace eat the food". Unknown.—StP
Life in the forest, or, bad news, good news, bad
  news. A. Adoff.—AdCh
Like a fire eating dragon. J. Ciardi.—CiH
"Listen". L. Moore.—SuI
Little Dimity. W. J. Smith.—SmL

Food and eating.—*Continued*
"There was a young prince in Bombay". W. Parke.—LiLo
"There was an old man from Peru". Unknown.—ScA
    An old man from Peru.—PrFo
    Old man of Peru.—DeS
"There was an old man from the coast". W. J. Smith.—SmL
"There was an old man from the Rhine". Unknown.—LiLo
"There was an old person from Queens". W. J. Smith.—SmL
"There was an old person of Dean". E. Lear.—LiLo
"There was an old person of Leeds". Unknown.—LiLo
"They tell of a hunter named Shephard". Unknown.—LiLo
Those who do not study history are doomed. A. Adoff.—AdCh
"Through the teeth". Unknown.—ScA—WiA
The tiger ("A tiger going for a stroll"). E. Lucie-Smith.—CoAz
To a tuna. X. J. Kennedy.—KeK
To pumpkins at pumpkin time. G. Tall.—BaH
"To sleep easy all night". Mother Goose.—WaM
"To sup like a pup". D. Baruch.—MoS
"Tomatoes, lettuce". Unknown.—ScA
Two fat sausages. Unknown.—CoE
    "Two little sausages".—ScA
The ultimate product. E. Merriam.—MeCh
"The underwater wibbles". J. Prelutsky.—JaP
Unexpected summer soup. M. Mahy.—MaN
Victory banquet. S. B. Mathis.—MaR
"Violetta is in the pantry". Unknown.—ScA
A vote for vanilla. E. Merriam.—MeS
The vulture. H. Belloc.—CaB—ElW
"We thank thee, Lord, for happy hearts". Unknown.—StP
Welcome here. Unknown.—GoA
Welsh rabbit. Unknown.—OpT
What I like. M. Mahy.—MaN
What you don't know about food. F. P. Heide.—HeG
Wicked witch's kitchen. X. J. Kennedy.—BaH—LiHp
"Wine and cakes for gentlemen". Mother Goose.—WaM
Witch goes shopping. L. Moore.—LoFh—PrFo
Witch pizza. J. Yolen.—YoBe
"With wild mushrooms Madge had found". X. J. Kennedy.—KeFb
"You know the other day we went over at George's get some eggs". J. Carson.—CaS
"Fool, fool, April fool". Unknown.—OpI
Fools
"April fool's gone past". Unknown.—OpI
"Good boy is a fool's nickname". From Jamaican Caribbean proverbs. Unknown.—BeW
"The great fool is as proud as a dog with two tails". From Jamaican Caribbean proverbs. Unknown.—BeW
"Simple Simon met a pieman". Mother Goose.—EdGl—SuO—WaM
"Three wise men of Gotham". Mother Goose.—WaM
Football
Billy Ray Smith. O. Nash.—KnAs
Bull dog. C. Porter.—KnAs
Championship. S. B. Mathis.—MaR
Cheerleaders. S. B. Mathis.—MaR

Cheers. E. Merriam.—MeS
Coach. S. B. Mathis.—MaR
Cousins. S. B. Mathis.—MaR
Dedicated to F.W. E. Hemingway.—KnAs
"Each year brings rookies and makes veterans". From Watching football on TV. H. Nemerov.—KnAs
Ebonee. S. B. Mathis.—MaR
Football ("The game was ended, and the noise at last had died away, and"). W. Mason.—KnAs
Football ("Now they're ready, now they're waiting"). F. S. Fitzgerald.—KnAs
Football ("You twist"). S. B. Mathis.—MaR
For the death of Vince Lombardi. J. Dickey.—KnAs
Gaining yardage. L. Dangel.—JaPr
In the pocket. J. Dickey.—KnAs—MoR
Insanity. G. Dubois.—KnAs
"It used to be only Sunday afternoons". From Watching football on TV. H. Nemerov.—KnAs
Leg broken. S. B. Mathis.—MaR
Marvin Pickett. M. Glenn.—KnAs
Monster man. S. B. Mathis.—MaR
"Passing and catching overcome the world". From Watching football on TV. H. Nemerov.—KnAs
Playoff pizza. S. B. Mathis.—MaR
"Priam on one side sending forth eleven". From Watching football on TV. H. Nemerov.—KnAs
Quarterback. S. B. Mathis.—MaR
Red dog blue fly. S. B. Mathis.—MaR
Say goodbye to Big Daddy. R. Jarrell.—KnAs
The sleeper. E. Field.—KnAs
"To all this there are rules, the players must". From Watching football on TV. H. Nemerov.—KnAs
To the field goal kicker in a slump. L. Pastan.—KnAs
"Totemic scarabs, exoskeletal". From Watching football on TV. H. Nemerov.—KnAs
Touchdown. S. B. Mathis.—MaR
Trophy. S. B. Mathis.—MaR
Unitas. E. Gold.—KnAs
Victory banquet. S. B. Mathis.—MaR
Watching the Jets lose to Buffalo at Shea. M. Swenson.—KnAs
"We watch all afternoon, we are enthralled". From Watching football on TV. H. Nemerov.—KnAs
You've got to learn the white man's game. M. M. Smith.—KnAs
Football ("The game was ended, and the noise at last had died away, and"). Walt Mason.—KnAs
Football ("Now they're ready, now they're waiting"). F. Scott Fitzgerald.—KnAs
Football ("You twist"). Sharon Bell Mathis.—MaR
"The **football** coach coached tennis in the spring". See In the spring
Foote, Samuel
The great Panjandrum.—OpT
Footpath. Stella Ngatho.—NyT
Footprints
At the beach ("The waves are erasing the footprints"). K. Ozer.—NyT
Snow stitches. A. Fisher.—FiH
"**Footprints** I make". See Song of the Osage woman
"**For** a ballclub to win in the National League". See Tinker to Evers
For a bird. Myra Cohn Livingston.—DeS
"**For** all that has been, thanks". Dag Hammarskjold.—StP
"**For** all that makes for ugliness in our world". Edmund Jones.—StP

For Allan, who wanted to see how I wrote a poem. Robert Frost.—HoS
"**For** breakfast I had ice cream". See Piggy
"**For** cities and towns, factories and farms, flowers". Unknown.—StP
"**For** every cup and plateful". Unknown.—StP
"**For** every sip the hen says grace". See Grace
For forest. Grace Nichols.—NiCo
For Genevieve, five years old. Simeon Dumdum.—NyT
"**For** his mother's mudpack, Brent". X. J. Kennedy.—KeFb
For Hoyt Wilhelm. Joel Oppenheimer.—KnAs
"**For** I will consider my cat Jeoffrey". From Jubilate agno. Christopher Smart.—StP
For Junior Gilliam. B. H. Fairchild.—MoA
"**For,** lo, the winter is past". See Lo, the winter is past
"**For** lunch". See Sundays
"**For** Maria". See Ode to weddings
For Mopsa. Walter De La Mare.—DeR
For Mugs. Myra Cohn Livingston.—LiDp
"**For** my dog's birthday party". See The barkday party
For my people. Margaret Walker.—SuC
"**For** my people everywhere singing their slave songs repeatedly, their". See For my people
"**For** peace sake". Cedric McClester.—SIM
For people who can't open their hoods. Jim Daniels.—JaPr
"**For** red mouthwash, rotten Ross". X. J. Kennedy.—KeFb
For someone on his tenth birthday. John Ciardi.—LoFh
For the death of Vince Lombardi. James Dickey.—KnAs
"**For** the sky, blue, but the six year old". See Drawing by Ronnie C., grade one
For the time being, sels. Wystan Hugh Auden
"He is the Way".—StP
For the Union dead, sels. Robert Lowell
"Two months after marching through Boston".—SuC
"**For** the witch's tv show". See Silly questions
"**For** those who want the recipe". See Licorice
"**For** us a handshake was a duel". See Shaking
"**For** water-ices, cheap but good". Allan Laing.—StP
"**For** weeks". See The yellow tulip
"**For** years I've watched the corners for signs". See Blues for Benny "Kid" Paret
Forbidden sounds. Eric James.—BaH
"**Forest** could keep secrets". See For forest
Forests and forestry. See also Trees
The accompaniment. W. De La Mare.—DeR
"Almighty one, in the woods I am blessed". L. V. Beethoven.—StP
Alone in winter. J. P. Lewis.—LeT
The babes in the wood. Unknown.—ElW
Bitter waters. W. De La Mare.—DeR
Father and I in the woods. D. McCord.—LiPf
For forest. G. Nichols.—NiCo
In the forest. Unknown.—DeI
"In the woods there was a hole". Unknown.—ScA
Little bush. E. M. Roberts.—LiDd
Paul Bunyan. A. S. Bourinot.—BoT
The pigs and the charcoal-burner. W. De La Mare.—DeR—MaP
"The sodden moss sinks underfoot when we cross half-frozen bays and". A. Debeljak.—NyT
Spell of the moon. L. Norris.—LiIf
Spruce woods. A. R. Ammons.—ElW—JaP

Stopping by woods on a snowy evening. R. Frost.—DeS—DeT—ElW—SuI
"There are some things I want to know about". J. Carson.—CaS
"There was a boy, ye knew him well, ye cliffs". From The prelude. W. Wordsworth.—LiIf
Vorobyev Hills. B. Pasternak.—GoT
Who. L. Moore.—LiDd
Forgetfulness
Buried treasure. A. Fisher.—FiA
Forgotten. C. Rylant.—JaP
"I left my book in Hawaii". K. Dakos.—DaI
It's inside my sister's lunch. K. Dakos.—DaI
The owls ("The owls take a broad view"). R. Desnos.—LiIf
Song ("When I am dead, my dearest"). C. G. Rossetti.—ElW
A teacher's lament. K. Dakos.—DaI
"There was an old man of Khartoum". Unknown.—LiLo
The thinker. J. Ciardi.—CiH—LiLo
Tray. M. C. Livingston.—LiBp
Forgive. Maya Angelou.—AnI
Forgiveness. See also Charity; Kindness
"Bad I am, but yet thy child". G. M. Hopkins.—StP
"For all that makes for ugliness in our world". E. Jones.—StP
Forgive. M. Angelou.—AnI
"God of all power, ruler of the universe". Unknown.—StP
Growing pains. J. Little.—LiHe
I wish. B. S. De Regniers.—DeW
"In Heaven". S. Crane.—StP
My homework isn't done. K. Dakos.—DaI
Old folks laugh. M. Angelou.—AnI
"Our Father in heaven". D. Williams.—StP
This is just to say. W. C. Williams.—ElW
"Two pterodactyls". J. Yolen.—YoDd
"**Forgot** my homework". See Excuse
Forgotten. Cynthia Rylant.—JaP
Forks. See Tableware
"**Fortune** teller, fortune teller". Unknown.—ScA
Fortune telling
"Cut your nails on Monday, cut for health". Unknown.—WiA
"Does he love me". Unknown.—WiA
"Fortune teller, fortune teller". Unknown.—ScA
"Gypsy, gypsy, please tell me". Unknown.—WiA
"How many children will we have". Unknown.—WiA
"Monday's child is fair of face". Mother Goose.—SuO—WaM
"One for anger". Unknown.—ScA
"Rich man, poor man, beggar man, thief". Unknown.—CoM
"Where will we get married". Unknown.—WiA
"Whom shall I marry". Unknown.—WiA
Forty performing bananas. Jack Prelutsky.—PrFo
"**Forty** years we courted". Jo Carson.—CaS
The **fossilot.** Jane Yolen.—YoBe
Fossils
Dinosaur hard rock band. J. Yolen.—YoDd
Dinosaur waltz. J. Yolen.—YoDd
Dress code, a sedimental journey. J. Yolen.—YoDd
The fossilot. J. Yolen.—YoBe
Iguanodon. J. Prelutsky.—PrT
Seismosaurus. J. Prelutsky.—PrT
Square dance. J. Yolen.—YoDd
Valuables. X. J. Kennedy.—KeK

Foster, John
Today is Labor Day.—FoLe
Foster, Stephen Collins
My old Kentucky home, sels.
"The sun shines bright in the old Kentucky home".—SuC
"The sun shines bright in the old Kentucky home". See My old Kentucky home
The **fountain** ("There in the fountain"). See "Alla en la fuente"
"**Four**". See Chocolate dreams, four
Four. Myra Cohn Livingston.—LiBp
#4. Doughtry Long.—SlM
"**Four** and twenty tailors". Mother Goose.—ClI
The **four** brothers. Walter De La Mare.—DeR
The **four** corners of the universe. Unknown.—SnD
"**Four** ducks on a pond". William Allingham.—ElW
"**Four** fat goats upon a boat". Jack Prelutsky.—PrBe
"**Four** furry seals, four funny fat seals". Jack Prelutsky.—CoAz
Four generations. Mary Ann Hoberman.—HoFa
The **four** horses. James Reeves.—KeT
"**Four** hundred and forty-four flies". See Specs
400 meter freestyle. Maxine Kumin.—KnAs
"**Four** legs". Myra Cohn Livingston.—LiMh
"**Four** more days and we are free". Unknown.—WiA
Four poems for Roy G Biv, complete. Barbara Juster Esbensen
Prism in the window.—EsW
A question ("If I shine").—EsW
Rainbow making, a mystery.—EsW
Rainbow making, magic.—EsW
Four seasons. Unknown.—DeS
"**Four** stiff-standers". Unknown.—CaB—ScA
"**Four** stories". See Brickyard
The **Fourth**. Shel Silverstein.—MoR
Fourth of July
"Corn knee high". Unknown.—ScA
Fireworks ("The Fourth of July's"). M. C. Livingston.—LiR
The Fourth. S. Silverstein.—MoR
Fourth of July ("Hurrah for the Fourth of July"). M. C. Livingston.—LiLo
The Fourth of July ("On the Fourth of July, yes"). J. Kenward.—FoLe
Fourth of July night. C. Sandburg.—LaN
"I asked my mother for fifty cents". Unknown.—CoM—OpI—WiA
"I asked my mother for fifteen cents".—WaM
Independence day. P. Gross.—FoLe
"I've got a rocket". Unknown.—WiA
Ode to fireworks. G. Soto.—SoNe
Fourth of July ("Hurrah for the Fourth of July"). Myra Cohn Livingston.—LiLo
The **Fourth** of July ("On the Fourth of July, yes"). Jean Kenward.—FoLe
Fourth of July night. Carl Sandburg.—LaN
"The **Fourth** of July's". See Fireworks
"The **fox**". See The fox and the hounds
Fox and crow. William Jay Smith.—SmL
The **fox** and the hounds. George Swede.—BoT
A **fox** jumped up. Unknown.—ClI
"A **fox** jumped up one winter's night". See A fox jumped up
Foxes
Fox and crow. W. J. Smith.—SmL
The fox and the hounds. G. Swede.—BoT
A fox jumped up. Unknown.—ClI
Foxes ("The foxes"). Buson.—DeI
Foxes ("A litter of little black foxes, and later"). M. A. Hoberman.—DeS
Foxes ("Old Dr. Cox's"). W. De La Mare.—DeR

Fox's song. B. Angell.—SuI
The ghost chase. W. De La Mare.—DeR
The hunt. W. De La Mare.—DeR
The red fox. J. P. Lewis.—LeE
The spun gold fox. P. Hubbell.—LaN
"The tail of a fox will show no matter how hard he tries to hide it". Unknown.—WhAa
The three foxes. A. A. Milne.—DeT
The vixen. J. Clare.—CaB
Foxes ("The foxes"). Buson, tr. by Tze-si Huang.—DeI See Foxes
Foxes ("A litter of little black foxes, and later"). Mary Ann Hoberman.—DeS
Foxes ("Old Dr. Cox's"). Walter De La Mare.—DeR
Fox's song. Barbara Angell.—SuI
"**Fragrant** roundness". See Pitcher
Francis, J. G.
"An elephant sat on some kegs".—LiLo
Francis, Robert
The base stealer.—MoA
Catch ("Two boys uncoached are tossing a poem together").—KnAs
Cats ("Cats walk neatly").—MoR
Coming and going.—KeT
His running, my running.—KnAs
"The mouse whose name is time".—KeT
Watching gymnasts.—MoR
Francis of Assisi, Saint
"O high and glorious God".—StP
"Praised be my Lord God for all his creatures".—StP
"**Frank**, Frank". Unknown.—WiA
Frankie Dempster. Mel Glenn.—GlBc
Franklin, Benjamin
Butterfly ("What is a butterfly, at best").—WhAa
Fraser, Marjorie Frost
Spring ("To tangled grass I cling").—SuI
"**Free** at las', free at las'". See I thank God I'm free at las'
Free offer. X. J. Kennedy.—KeGh
Free time. Jim Thomas.—LiPm
Freedom
Afternoon in March. J. Little.—LiHe
Alabama centennial. N. Madgett.—SuC
The bird set free. W. De La Mare.—DeR
Captive bird. Boethius.—CaB
Children's rhymes. L. Hughes.—SuC
For my people. M. Walker.—SuC
The Fourth of July ("On the Fourth of July, yes"). J. Kenward.—FoLe
Freedom. W. Dissanayake.—NyT
The funeral of Martin Luther King, Jr. N. Giovanni.—SuC
"Go down, Moses". From Go down, Moses. Unknown.—SuC
Harriet Tubman. E. Greenfield.—SlM
"How sadly the bird in his cage". Issa.—WhAa
"I say whatever tastes sweet to the most perfect person, that". From Says. W. Whitman.—HoVo
I thank God I'm free at las'. Unknown.—SuC
I'm a parrot. G. Nichols.—NiCo
The little salamander. W. De La Mare.—DeR
Mean to be free. Unknown.—SuC
Mek drum talk, man, for Caribbean Independence. J. Berry.—BeW
The pit ponies. L. Norris.—NyT
The prayer of the goat. C. B. De Gasztold.—DeP
The prison cell. M. Darwish.—NyT
Runagate runagate. R. Hayden.—SuC
"The runaway slave came to my house and stopt outside". From Song of myself. W. Whitman.—HoVo

The **frog** ("Be kind and tender to the frog"). Hilaire Belloc.—ClI—ElW
The **frog** ("Breaking the silence"). Basho, tr. by Tze-si Huang.—DeI
"The **frog**". See Energy
"The **frog**". See Sour
Frog ("The spotted frog"). Valerie Worth.—WoAl
"**Frog-boy** dives in". See F is for frog-boy
"A **froggie** sat on a lily pad". Unknown.—PrP
"**Froggy** Boggy". Unknown.—PrP
"The **frogs** and the serpents each had a football team". See Cheers
Frogs and toads
  "B, u, hippity". Unknown.—WiA
  "A big turtle sat on the end of a log". Unknown.—WiA
  Cheers. E. Merriam.—MeS
  "A discovery". Yaku.—WhAa
      Haiku.—DeT
  Energy. Torei.—DeI
  F is for frog-boy. W. J. Smith.—SmL
  The frog ("Be kind and tender to the frog"). H. Belloc.—ClI—ElW
  The frog ("Breaking the silence"). Basho.—DeI
  Frog ("The spotted frog"). V. Worth.—WoAl
  "A froggie sat on a lily pad". Unknown.—PrP
  "Froggy Boggy". Unknown.—PrP
  Growing up ("Little Tommy Tadpole began to weep and wail"). C. J. Dennis.—CoAz
  Half moon. F. Garcia Lorca.—LaN
  "I went down to the lily pond". Unknown.—WiA
  "I'm nobody, who are you". E. Dickinson.—ElW
  Kick and live. G. W. Porter.—SlM
  "Little frog among". Gaki.—CaR
      Haiku.—DeT
  "Oh, the bullfrog tried to court the alligator". Unknown.—WiA
  The petal. Ryukyo.—DeI
  The princess and the frog. S. C. Field.—BaH
  "Raising frogs for profit". Unknown.—PrFo
  "Red bug, yellow bug, little blue". J. Prelutsky.—PrBe
  Snake song. J. P. Lewis.—LeA
  The song of Mr. Toad. From The wind in the willows. K. Grahame.—CoAz
  Sour. Issa.—DeI
  Toad. V. Worth.—WoAl
  "Way down yonder on the Piankatank". Unknown.—WiA
  What a wonderful bird. Unknown.—ClI
From a very little sphinx. Edna St. Vincent Millay.—DeS
"**From** breakfast on through all the day". See The Land of Nod
"**From** coast to coast some like to fly". See Roller coasters
"**From** dawn until dusk". See Executive Eagle
"**From** friendly Squanto, wise in all things wild". See At Plymouth, the first Thanksgiving, 1621
"**From** ghoulies and ghosties". Unknown.—LiHp—LoFh
  Ghoulies and ghosties.—DeT
"**From** height of noon, remote and still". See The enchanted hill
From her office. R. H. Marks.—LiPg
"**From** his cradle in the glamourie". See Peak and Puke
"**From** its sources which well". From The cataract of Lodore. Robert Southey.—MoR
"**From** my front door there's a path to the moon". See A path to the moon
"**From** my head to my feet". Rudolf Steiner.—StP

"**From** Number Nine, Penwiper Mews". Edward Gorey.—LiLo
"**From** out the wood I watched them shine". See Haunted
"**From** silly devotions". Saint Teresa of Avila.—StP
From the autograph album. Unknown.—MoA
"**From** the boat, while Uncle Sid". X. J. Kennedy.—KeFb
"**From** the high jump of Olympic fame". See Babe Didrikson
From the Japanese. Eve Merriam.—MeS
"**From** the moment of her hatching". See Twinkle toes triceratops
From the most distant time. Liang Wu-ti, tr. by Kenneth Rexroth.—GoT
"**From** the mountains we come". From Warrior nation trilogy. Lance Henson.—SuI
"**From** the orphanage All came to". See Orphanage boy
"**From** warlocks, witches and wurricoes". Unknown.—StP
"**From** zoo keepers' pails Gail steals". X. J. Kennedy.—KeFb
Frontier and pioneer life. See also Cowboys
  "Dancing teepees". C. O'John.—SnD
  The ghost dance, August, 1976. D. Jauss.—JaM
  The last man killed by Indians in Kimble County, Texas. M. Angelotti.—JaM
  Schoolcrafts's diary, written on the Missouri, 1830. R. Bly.—SuI
  "There was a roof over our heads". A. Rios.—SuI
  Western wagons. S. V. Benet, and R. C. Benet.—SuI
Frost, Frances
  Night heron.—CaB
Frost, Richard
  The standing broad jump.—KnAs
Frost, Robert
  Birches.—SuI
  Dust of snow.—ElW
  Fireflies in the garden.—ElW
  For Allan, who wanted to see how I wrote a poem.—HoS
  Mending wall.—SuI
  The pasture.—KeT
  Questioning faces.—LiIf
  The rabbit hunter.—KnAs
  The runaway.—ElW
  Stopping by woods on a snowy evening.—DeS—DeT—ElW—SuI
  The telephone.—SuI
  To the thawing wind.—ElW
  Tree at my window.—ElW
Frost
  Frost. V. Worth.—WoAl
  The frost pane. D. McCord.—MoS
  Requiem. P. Fleischman.—FlJ
Frost. Valerie Worth.—WoAl
The **frost** pane. David McCord.—MoS
A **frosty** night. Robert Graves.—ElW
Fruit. See also names of fruits, as Blueberries
  Granny ("Granny had a way with fruit trees"). A. Bryan.—BrS
  "In his room the man watches". H. Aridjis.—NyT
  Mango. G. Nichols.—NiCo
  "Una mexicana". Unknown.—YoS
  Ode to pomegranates. G. Soto.—SoNe
  Riddle. G. Nichols.—NiCo
  "Upon the hill there is a yellow house". Unknown.—WiA
"**Fudge**, fudge, tell the judge". Unknown.—ScA

Fufuka, Karama
  Big Mama.—SlM
  My daddy is a cool dude.—SlM
  Parades.—SlM
  "Pretty brown baby".—SlM
  Summer vacation.—SlM
Fukao, Sumako
  Bright house, tr. by Kenneth Rexroth and Ikuko
    Atsumi.—GoU
"**Full**-blown blooms the dewsprung morning". See
  Summer solstice
Full circle. Walter De La Mare.—DeR
"The **full** moon". See Broken mirror
Full moon ("Night on the verandah"). Ashley
  Bryan.—BrS
Full moon ("One night as Dick lay fast asleep").
  Walter De La Mare.—DeR—MaP
Fuller, Ethel Romig
  "Wind is a cat".—BaW
Fuller, Roy
  The giraffes ("I think before they saw me the
    giraffes").—ElW
"**Fun** run". Bruce McMillan.—McP
The **funeral**. Walter De La Mare.—DeR
The **funeral** of Martin Luther King, Jr. Nikki
  Giovanni.—SuC
Funerals. See also Death; Grief
  Booman. Unknown.—OpT
  "Did you ever think". Unknown.—CoM
  Doll funerals. J. Kirkup.—FoLe
  The funeral. W. De La Mare.—DeR
  The funeral of Martin Luther King, Jr. N.
    Giovanni.—SuC
  In these dissenting times. A. Walker.—ElW
  "Now, George is sick". J. Carson.—CaS
  Playmate ("And because"). K. Wilson.—JaPr
  The teenage cocaine dealer considers his death on
    the street outside a Key West funeral for a
    much-loved civic leader. J. Hall.—JaPr
Funny glasses. Myra Cohn Livingston.—LiBp
A **funny** man. Natalie Joan.—DeS
A **funny** old person. Unknown.—CII
"A **funny** old person of Slough". See A funny old
  person
"A **furious** man in a tree". See A man in a tree
Furry bear. Alan Alexander Milne.—DeS
Fuzzy Wuzzy. See "Fuzzy Wuzzy was a bear"
"**Fuzzy** Wuzzy was a bear". Unknown.—PrP—WiA
  Fuzzy Wuzzy.—CII
Fyleman, Rose
  Mice ("I think mice").—DeS—LaM
  Wanted.—LaM
  What they said, tr.—DeS

G

G is for goat. William Jay Smith.—SmL
Gab. Eve Merriam.—MeCh
The **gage.** Walter De La Mare.—DeR
"**Gaily** bedight". See Eldorado
Gaining yardage. Leo Dangel.—JaPr
Gaki
  Haiku. See "Little frog among"
  "Little frog among".—CaR
    Haiku.—DeT
Gales, R. L.
  "Baby's heart is lifted up".—StP
Galindo, David Escobar
  A short story, tr. by Jorge D. Piche.—NyT

Gallagher, Tess
  Women's tug of war at Lough Arrow.—KnAs
"The **gallant** Welsh of all degrees". See Welsh rabbit
"**Galloping** pony". Kyorai, tr. by Sylvia Cassedy and
  Kunihiro Suetake.—CaR—WhAa
The **gallows.** Edward Thomas.—ElW
Galoshes. Rhoda Bacmeister.—DeS
Gambler. Elma Stuckey.—AgL
Gamblers and gambling
  Bingo. P. B. Janeczko.—JaB—JaP
  "Diamonds, hearts, kings and aces". M. Wayne.—
    LeCa
  Gambler. E. Stuckey.—AgL
  Off the ground. W. De La Mare.—DeR—MaP
  "There was a story about my daddy's daddy". J.
    Carson.—CaS
"The **game** ends in the air". See What the diamond
  does is hold it all in
The **game** ("Plastic soldiers march on the floor").
  Myra Cohn Livingston.—SaB
The **game** ("Plastic soldiers on the floor").—LiNe
The **game** ("Plastic soldiers on the floor"). See The
  game ("Plastic soldiers march on the floor")
"The **game** was ended, and the noise at last had
  died away, and". See Football
Games. See also Nursery play; Singing games; also
  names of games, as Baseball
  Apple bobbing. R. H. Marks.—LiHp
  Before the game. V. Popa.—NyT
  Blindman's in. W. De La Mare.—DeR
  Cat and mouse game. P. Hubbell.—LaM
  "Ciranda, cirandinha". Unknown.—YoS
  "Circle, little circle".—YoS
  Composition ball. Unknown.—WiA
  Elegy for the girl who died in the dump at Ford's
    Gulch. J. Johnson.—JaPr
  "Extra, extra, extra, every Egyptian eats exactly".
    Unknown.—CoM
  "First is worst". Unknown.—WiA
  Follow the leader. H. Behn.—HoS
  Funny glasses. M. C. Livingston.—LiBp
  The game ("Plastic soldiers march on the floor").
    M. C. Livingston.—SaB
    The game ("Plastic soldiers on the floor").—
    LiNe
  Hey, bug. L. Moore.—MoS
  Hug o' war. S. Silverstein.—MoS
  "I made you look, I made you look".
    Unknown.—WiA
  "I win one game". Unknown.—ScA
  "I'm the king of the castle". Mother Goose.—
    WaM
  Jacks. V. Worth.—WoAl
  Love ("Too close"). C. S. Muth.—MoR
  "Mademoiselle". Unknown.—OpI
  Muscling rocks. R. Morgan.—JaPr
  "Number one, touch your tongue". Unknown.—
    CoM
  Party prizes. M. C. Livingston.—LiBp
  "Pinning the tail on the donkey". M. C.
    Livingston.—LiBp
  Playing stickball with Robbie Shea. M.
    Lukeman.—MoA
  The sleeper. E. Field.—KnAs
  Song, take who takes you. F. Gardner.—KnAs
  Tray. M. C. Livingston.—LiBp
  The volleyball match. B. Pearlman.—KnAs
  You've got to learn the white man's game. M. M.
    Smith.—KnAs
The **games** of night. Nancy Willard.—JaP
Gandhi, Mahatma
  "I am a man of peace, I believe in peace".—StP

Gandhi, Mahatma—*Continued*
"Ganesha, Ganesh". Myra Cohn Livingston.—WhDd
Gang girls. Gwendolyn Brooks.—JaPr
"**Gang** girls are sweet exotics". See Gang girls
Garage apartment. Myra Cohn Livingston.—LiT
Garbage
    Bay breasted barge bird. W. J. Smith.—SmL
    Cacophony. E. Merriam.—MeCh
    Garbage ("The stained"). V. Worth.—WoAl
    Garbage ("We hauled trash that summer, the three of us"). E. Trethewey.—JaM
    Garbage delight. D. Lee.—PrFo
    The raccoon ("The raccoon wears a mask at night"). P. Johnson.—CoAz
    "Sara Cynthia Sylvia Stout would not take the garbage out". S. Silverstein.—ElW
    The term. W. C. Williams.—BaW
Garbage ("The stained"). Valerie Worth.—WoAl
Garbage ("We hauled trash that summer, the three of us"). Eric Trethewey.—JaM
Garbage delight. Dennis Lee.—PrFo
"**Garbage** truck". See Cacophony
Garcia Lorca, Federico
    Cancion tonta.—DeT
        Silly song ("Mama").—DeT
    Caracola ("Me han traido una caracola").—DeT
        Snail ("They have brought me a snail").—DeT
    Half moon.—LaN
    Silly song ("Mama"). See Cancion tonta
    Snail ("They have brought me a snail"). See Caracola ("Me han traido una caracola")
A **garden**. Aileen Fisher.—FiA
Garden calendar. N. M. Bodecker.—KeT
The **garden** (for a picture). Walter De La Mare.—DeR
The **garden** of a child. Nirendranath Chakravarti.—NyT
"**Garden** soil". See Earthworms
The **garden**, sels. Andrew Marvell
    "Casting the body's vest aside".—StP
A **gardener**. Unknown.—OpT
Gardeners. See Gardens and gardening
Gardens and gardening
    Autumn garden. D. Campana.—GoT
    The city mouse and the garden mouse. C. G. Rossetti.—LaM
    "Come on into my tropical garden". G. Nichols.—NiCo
    Cotton bottomed menace. X. J. Kennedy.—KeK
    A garden. A. Fisher.—FiA
    Garden calendar. N. M. Bodecker.—KeT
    The garden (for a picture). W. De La Mare.—DeR
    The garden of a child. N. Chakravarti.—NyT
    A gardener. Unknown.—OpT
    The gatherer. A. Al-Mak.—NyT
    Granny ("Granny had a way with fruit trees"). A. Bryan.—BrS
    House of spring. M. Soseki.—NyT
    "I will give you the key". A. Lobel.—MoS
    "I'd like a great satellite-looking dish". From What we said sitting making fantasies. J. Berry.—BeW
    The little old cupid. W. De La Mare.—DeR—MaP
    Madonna of the evening flowers. A. Lowell.—GoU
    Mama's bouquets. A. Bryan.—BrS
    "Mary, Mary, quite contrary". Mother Goose.—EdGl—SuO
        "Mistress Mary".—WaM

My old hen. Unknown.—KeT
Night garden with ladies. D. Stein.—GoT
On New Year's Day, watching it snow. I. Shikibu.—GoT
"On the shores of Lake Kinneret". Y. Fichman.—StP
"One little bunny grew carrots". J. Knight.—KnT
Package of trees. A. Fisher.—FiA
Part VIII: When she was in her garden. From A child's day. W. De La Mare.—DeR
Po's garden. R. Young.—JaP
Seeds ("The seeds I sowed"). W. De La Mare.—DeR
September garden. M. C. Livingston.—LiNe
Some rabbits. Unknown.—ClI
Souvenir of the ancient world. C. Drummond de Andrade.—NyT
The sunken garden. W. De La Mare.—DeR
Supper ("I supped where bloomed the red red rose"). W. De La Mare.—DeR
Tending the garden. E. Pankey.—JaM
"There was an old person of Leeds". Unknown.—LiLo
"This season our tunnips was red". D. McCord.—LiLo
Tommy. G. Brooks.—HoS—SlM
Vine leaves. A. Bryan.—BrS
Watchdogs. J. Thomas.—LiHp
A widow's weeds. W. De La Mare.—DeR—MaP
"You know the other day we went over at George's get some eggs". J. Carson.—CaS
"**Gardens**, fields". See Snow
Gardner, Fred
    Song, take who takes you.—KnAs
Gardner, John
    "Always be kind to animals".—CoAz
    The barracuda ("Slowly, slowly he cruises").—WhAa
    The chameleon.—CoAz
    The cockatoo.—PrFo
    The flying squirrel.—WhAa
    The lizard ("The lizard is a timid thing").—WhAa
    The owl ("In broad daylight").—LiIf
    The tiger ("The tiger is a perfect saint").—PrFo
    The yeti.—WhDd
Gardner, Martin
    The giggles.—PrFo
Gardner Todd. Mel Glenn.—GlBc
"**The gargoyle**". See History
Garrett Chandler. Mel Glenn.—GlBc
Garter snake. Unknown, tr. by Tze-si Huang.—DeI
"**The garter** snake". See Garter snake
"**Garth**, from off the garden wall". X. J. Kennedy.—KeFb
Garuda. Deborah Chandra.—WhDd
Gary, Patricia
    Uneven parallel bars.—KnAs
Gate gossip. Max Fatchen.—FaCm
Gates, Betty
    Mamma settles the dropout problem.—SuC
Gates
    "En la puerta del cielo". Unknown.—DeA
        "At heaven's gate".—DeA
    Gate gossip. M. Fatchen.—FaCm
    Just once. M. C. Livingston.—LiNe
    "A man went hunting at Ryegate". Mother Goose.—WaM
"**Gather** ye rosebuds while ye may". See To the virgins, to make much of time
The **gatherer**. Ali Al-Mak, tr. by Al-Fatih Mahjoub and Constance E. Berkley.—NyT
Gathering strength. Leo Dangel.—JaM

Girls and girlhood.—*Continued*
  Pooh. W. De La Mare.—DeR
  Queenie. L. B. Jacobs.—DeT
  Regina Kelsey. M. Glenn.—GlBc
  Rites of passage. D. Laux.—JaPr
  The runaway girl. G. Corso.—JaPr
  Secrets ("She slits empty feed sacks"). L.
    Schandelmeier.—JaPr
  A short note on schoolgirls. A. Campbell.—AgL
  A short story. D. E. Galindo.—NyT
  Silly Sallie. W. De La Mare.—DeR
  Sister ("You said red hair made you"). M.
    Lowery.—JaPr
  Snake woman. M. Atwood.—BoT
  A song in the front yard. G. Brooks.—ElW
  A story about Afiya. J. Berry.—BeW
  The Strand Theatre. T. Cader.—JaPr
  Sugar-n-spice, etc. R. Quillen.—JaPr
  Summer. J. Mahapatra.—NyT
  The sun witness. N. Choudhurry.—AgL
  "Susie, Susie Sauerkraut". Unknown.—ScA
  Sweet sixteen. E. De Souza.—AgL
  Sweet talk. A. Bryan.—BrS
  The telling tree. L. Peavy.—JaPr
  "There is a girl on our street". Unknown.—ScA
  They ask why. M. Angelou.—AnI
  "Tiny Eenanennika". W. De La Mare.—DeR
  To the virgins, to make much of time. R.
    Herrick.—ElW
  Trouble. J. Wright.—JaPr
  What the little girl did. R. McGough.—AgL
  "When Tonya's friends come to spend the night".
    E. Greenfield.—GrN
  "Whistling girls and crowing hens". Unknown.—
    WiA
  Why can't a girl be the leader of the boys. K.
    Dakos.—DaI
  Wicked thoughts. J. Viorst.—PrFo
  Willimae's cornrows. N. Mellage.—SlM
  Woman. U. Saba.—GoU
  Young. A. Sexton.—AgL—JaPr
"**Girls** are dandy". Unknown.—WiA
Girls can, too. Lee Bennett Hopkins.—SlM
Girls can we educate we dads. James Berry.—BeW
"The **girls** wake, stretch, and pad up to the door".
  See Apartment cats
"**Give** a thing, take it back". Unknown.—OpI
"**Give** it to him". See The seventh round
"**Give** me a book". Myra Cohn Livingston.—HoGo
"**Give** me a good digestion, Lord". Thomas H. B.
  Webb.—StP
"**Give** me books, give me wings". Myra Cohn
  Livingston.—LiNe
"**Give** me my scallop shell of quiet". Sir Walter
  Raleigh.—StP
"**Give** me water". Myra Cohn Livingston.—LiMh
"**Give** me your tired, your poor, she says". See
  Statue of Liberty
"**Give** to us eyes". Unknown.—StP
"**Give** us a pure heart". Dag Hammarskjold.—StP
"**Give** us courage, gaiety and the quiet mind".
  Robert Louis Stevenson.—StP
"**Give** us grateful hearts, our Father". Unknown.—
  StP
Giving. See Gifts and giving
Glaser, Isabel Joshlin
  "What if".—HoGo
Glass
  The frost pane. D. McCord.—MoS
  "In the antique glass shop, Knute". X. J.
    Kennedy.—KeFb
"**Glass** covers windows". See Covers

Glass eye Harry Coote. Paul B. Janeczko.—JaB
"**Glass** eye Harry Coote lost it". See Glass eye Harry
  Coote
The **Glass** Menagerie, sels. Tennessee Williams
  "I didn't go to the moon, I went much further".—
  GoT
A **glass** of beer. James Stephens.—ElW
Gleason, Judith
  "Crowned crane".—NyT
  Sparrow ("Year we worked"), tr.—NyT
  To the ancestors, tr.—NyT
Glen, Emilie
  Apple scoop.—LiPg
  Neck please.—LiPg
"**Glenda,** in an everglade". X. J. Kennedy.—KeFb
Glenn, Mel
  Abby Kramer.—GlBc
  Andrea Pulovsky.—GlBc
  Andy Fierstein.—GlBc
  Annette Harrison.—GlBc
  Arnold Flitterman.—GlBc
  Audrey Reynolds.—GlBc
  Belinda Enriquez.—GlBc
  Bertha Robbins.—GlBc
  Brent Sorensen.—GlBc
  C. C. Johnson.—GlBc
  Charlene Cottier.—GlBc
  Claud St. Jules.—GlBc
  Crystal Rowe, track star.—MoR
  Dawn Weinberg.—GlBc
  Deidre Spector.—GlBc
  Dennis Finch.—GlBc
  Diana Marvin.—GlBc
  Dina Harper.—GlBc
  Elliot West.—GlBc
  Evan King.—GlBc
  Frankie Dempster.—GlBc
  Gardner Todd.—GlBc
  Garrett Chandler.—GlBc
  Gayle Buckingham.—GlBc
  Greg Hoffman.—MoR
  Hector Velasquez.—GlBc
  Herby Wall.—GlBc
  Jackie Grant.—GlBc
  Jaime Milagros.—GlBc
  Janet DeStasio.—GlBc
  Jimmy Zale.—GlBc
  Jocelyn Ridley.—GlBc
  Jonathan Sobel.—GlBc
  Kristin Leibowitz.—GlBc
  Kumar Ragnath.—GlBc
  Kwang Chin Ho.—GlBc
  Kyle Quinn.—GlBc
  Lacey Paget.—GlBc
  Luanne Sheridan.—GlBc
  Mallory Wade.—GlBc
  Martine Provencal.—GlBc
  Marvin Pickett.—KnAs
  Mercedes Lugo.—GlBc
  Mr. Desmond Klinger, music.—GlBc
  Mr. Eugene Worthington, physical education.—
    GlBc
  Mr. Henry Axhelm, math.—GlBc
  Mr. John Fletcher, chemistry.—GlBc
  Mr. Joshua Cantor.—GlBc
  Mr. Neil Pressman, fine arts.—GlBc
  Mr. Robert Winograd, English.—GlBc
  Mr. Ted Sage, accounting.—GlBc
  Ms. Charlotte Kendall, biology.—GlBc
  Ms. Emily Parsons, history.—GlBc
  Ms. Joan Gladstone, special education.—GlBc
  Ms. Marilyn Lindowsky, counselor.—GlBc

Glenn, Mel—*Continued*
Ms. Nadine Sierra, French.—GlBc
Ms. Phyllis Shaw, speech.—GlBc
Ms. Yvonne Harmon, librarian.—GlBc
Nicholas Townshed.—GlBc
Patricia Lampert.—GlBc
Regina Kelsey.—GlBc
T. C. Tyler.—GlBc
Tammy Yarbrough.—GlBc
Toni Vingelli.—GlBc
Valerie O'Neill.—GlBc
Victor Jeffreys.—GlBc
Warren Christopher.—GlBc
Winston Hines.—GlBc
Gliding o'er all. Walt Whitman.—HoVo
"**Gliding** o'er all, through all". See Gliding o'er all
"A **glimmer**". See Rigmarole
"**Globb's** a tiny creature who". See Before you fix your next peanut butter sandwich, read this
"**Glory** be to God for dappled things". Gerard Manley Hopkins.—StP
Glory falls. Maya Angelou.—AnI
"**Glory** falls around us". See Glory falls
"**Glory** to thee, glory to thee, O Lord". Dadu.—StP
"The **glossy**". See Wreaths
Glowworm. David McCord.—MoS
Glowworms. See Fireflies
Gluck, Louise
The racer's widow.—KnAs
Glue
Hughbert and the glue. K. Kuskin.—PrFo
"Sheila, into Dad's right shoe". X. J. Kennedy.—KeFb
Gluttony
"Annie ate jam". Unknown.—OpI
"The boy stood in the supper room". Unknown.—OpI
"A discerning young lamb of Long Sutton". M. C. Livingston.—LiLo
Hungry Jake. F. P. Heide.—HeG
"Lord be praised, my belly's raised". Unknown.—OpI
"Mary ate some marmalade". Unknown.—ScA
"Mary had a little lamb, a little pork, a little ham". Unknown.—ScA
Part XI: Now fie, o fie, how sly a face. From A child's day. W. De La Mare.—DeR
Piggy. W. Cole.—PrFo
Sneaky Bill. W. Cole.—PrFo
"There was a fat lady from Eye". Unknown.—LiLo
"There was a young lady named Perkins". Unknown.—LiLo
The **gnat** and the gnu. Oliver Herford.—LiLo
Gnats
The gnat and the gnu. O. Herford.—LiLo
Gnats. Unknown.—DeI
Gnats. Unknown, tr. by Tze-si Huang.—DeI
Gnomes. See Fairies
"The **gnomes** of Nome". X. J. Kennedy.—KeGh
Gnus
The gnat and the gnu. O. Herford.—LiLo
"**Go,** apple, to the apple tree". See "Ade milo sti milia"
"**Go** down, Moses". From Go down, Moses. Unknown.—SuC
Go down, Moses, sels. Unknown
"Go down, Moses".—SuC
"**Go,** my son, and shut the shutter". Unknown.—PrP
"**Go** tell it on the mountain". Unknown.—LoFh
"**Go** to bed, Juma". See Goodnight, Juma

"**Go** to bed late". Mother Goose.—WaM
"**Go** to bed, Tom". Mother Goose.—WaM
Go to the Bahamas. Kalli Dakos.—DaI
"**Go** to the shine that's on a tree". Richard Eberhart.—ElW
"**Go** well and safely". Unknown.—StP
"**Goat** boat". Bruce McMillan.—McP
Goats
A bright idea. X. J. Kennedy.—LiLo
"Four fat goats upon a boat". J. Prelutsky.—PrBe
G is for goat. W. J. Smith.—SmL
"Goat boat". B. McMillan.—McP
"Mary went down to Grandpa's farm". Unknown.—CII—WiA
"The night was dark and stormy". Unknown.—ScA
Ode to Senor Leal's goat. G. Soto.—SoNe
Old Hogan's goat. Unknown.—CoAz
The prayer of the goat. C. B. De Gasztold.—DeP
"A sheep and a goat were going to the pasture". Unknown.—WiA
"There was a man, now please take note". Unknown.—PrP
The **goblin.** Jack Prelutsky.—KeT
Goblins. See Fairies
God. See also Faith
About God. J. Little.—LiHe
"All praise to Thee, my God, this night". T. Ken.—StP
"All things bright and beautiful". C. F. Alexander.—StP
"Almighty one, in the woods I am blessed". L. V. Beethoven.—StP
"Alone with none but Thee, my God". Saint Columba.—StP
"Are you ready when the Lord shall come". Unknown.—StP
"At Tara today in this fateful hour". Saint Patrick.—StP
"Back of the loaf is the snowy flour". M. D. Babcock.—StP
"Bad I am, but yet thy child". G. M. Hopkins.—StP
"Be comforted, you would not have searched". B. Pascal.—StP
Bertha Robbins. M. Glenn.—GlBc
"Bless to me, O God". Unknown.—StP—StP
"Blessed are they that have eyes to see". J. Overham.—StP
"A child said, what is the grass, fetching it". W. Whitman.—StP
"Circle me Lord". D. Adam.—StP
"Creating God, your fingers trace". J. Rowthorn.—StP
"Creator, you who dwell at the ends of the earth". Unknown.—StP
"Dear Lord, you are the Truth, when I keep". H. J. Nouwen.—StP
"Each time we eat". Unknown.—StP
"Elder Father, though thine eyes". G. K. Chesterton.—StP
"Even if I have gone astray, I am". Arjan.—StP
"Everyone to his own". A. Silesius.—StP
"Fill your children with kindness". Unknown.—StP
"For all that makes for ugliness in our world". E. Jones.—StP
"For every cup and plateful". Unknown.—StP
"For I will consider my cat Jeoffry". From Jubilate agno. C. Smart.—StP
"From warlocks, witches and wurricoes". Unknown.—StP

God.—*Continued*

"Give me a good digestion, Lord". T. H. B. Webb.—StP

"Give us a pure heart". D. Hammarskjold.—StP

"Glory be to God for dappled things". G. M. Hopkins.—StP

"God before me, God behind me". Unknown.—StP

"God grows weary of great kingdoms". R. Tagore.—StP

"God is Father and Mother". Unknown.—StP

"God is, I know that". Unknown.—StP

"God is light". Unknown.—StP

"God is love, and love enfolds us". T. Rees.—StP

"God is love and we are his children". Unknown.—StP

"God is the bow". Unknown.—StP

"God moves in a mysterious way". W. Cowper.—ElW

"God of all power, ruler of the universe". Unknown.—StP

"Good for good is only fair". Unknown.—StP

"Goodness is stronger than evil". D. Tutu.—StP

"Great and merciful God". A. O'Grady.—StP

A hardware store as proof of the existence of God. N. Willard.—JaP

"He is the Way". From For the time being. W. H. Auden.—StP

"He prayeth best, who loveth best". From The rime of the ancient mariner. S. T. Coleridge.—StP

"Hear me, four quarters of the world". Black Elk.—StP

"Holy, holy, holy Lord, God of power and might". Unknown.—StP

"I am a man of peace, I believe in peace". M. Gandhi.—StP

"I am happy because you have accepted me". Unknown.—StP

"I arise today". Saint Patrick.—StP

"I believe that life is given us so we may". H. Keller.—StP

"I have a secret joy in Thee, my God". A. MacLean.—StP

"I see something of God each hour of the twenty four". W. Whitman.—StP

I thank God I'm free at las'. Unknown.—SuC

"In Heaven". S. Crane.—StP

"In the church". E. Greenfield.—GrN

"In the name of God". Unknown.—StP

"In the one you are never alone". D. Hammarskjold.—StP

"In Tsegihi". Unknown.—StP

"It is a comely fashion to be glad". Socrates.—StP

"Keep us, O Lord, as the apple of your eye". Unknown.—StP

"Let nothing disturb you". Saint Teresa of Avila.—StP

"Let the heavens rejoice, and let the earth be glad". From The book of psalms. Bible/Old Testament.—StP

"Let this be my last word". R. Tagore.—StP

"Let us in peace eat the food". Unknown.—StP

"Let us praise and thank God for all great and". Unknown.—StP

"Little lamb, who made thee". W. Blake.—StP

"Lord all power is yours". D. Adam.—StP

"The Lord is my shepherd, I shall not want". From The book of psalms. Bible/Old Testament.—StP
     Psalm 23.—SuC

"Lord most giving and resourceful". Unknown.—StP

"Lord of the springtime, father of flower". W. E. B. Du Bois.—StP

"The Lord reigneth, the Lord hath reigned". Unknown.—StP

"Lord, thou art the Hindu, the Moslem, the Turk". G. Singh.—StP

"Lord, Thou mighty river, all knowing, all seeing". G. Nanak.—StP

"Lord, you made the world and everything in it, you". F. Kaan.—StP

"Lovely face, majestic face, face of". Unknown.—StP

"May He Who is the Father in Heaven of the". Swami Akhilananda.—StP

"May the road rise to meet you". Unknown.—StP

Mine eyes have seen the glory. From Battle hymn of the republic. J. W. Howe.—SuC

"My fingers like to say hello". L. W. Johnson.—StP

Names. From The family of man. C. Sandburg.—WhAa

"O God, teach us to know that failure is as much". W. E. B. Du Bois.—StP

"O God that bringest all things to pass". Pindar.—StP

"O God, who hast made all things beautiful". Unknown.—StP

"O Great Spirit, whose voice I hear in the wind". Unknown.—StP

"O high and glorious God". Saint Francis of Assisi.—StP

"Oh, I have slipped the surly bonds of earth". J. G. Magee.—StP
     High flight.—SuI

"O Lord, grant us to love Thee, grant that we may love". Mohammed.—StP

"O mind, move in the Supreme Being". S. Brahmendra.—StP

"O our mother the earth, O our father the sky". Unknown.—StP

"Oh, the Lord looked down from his window in the sky". Unknown.—StP

"On the shores of Lake Kinneret". Y. Fichman.—StP

The origin of baseball. K. Patchen.—KnAs

"Our Father in heaven". D. Williams.—StP

"Our Father in heaven". From The gospel according to Matthew. Bible/New Testament.—StP

"Our Pacific islands are yours, O Lord". B. Narokobi.—StP

Psalm 104. From The book of psalms. Bible/Old Testament.—StP

Queen's prayer. Liliuokalani, queen of Hawaii.—StP

The sacred. S. Dunn.—JaM

Savior. M. Angelou.—AnI

"Should I worship Him from fear of hell". R. Al'Adawiyah.—StP

"The snail does the holy". G. K. Chesterton.—StP

"The snow is deep on the ground". K. Patchen.—GoU

"The soul that you have given me, O God". Unknown.—StP

"Teach me, my God and King". G. Herbert.—StP

"There is a mother's heart in the heart". A. MacLean.—StP

"This morning, God". Unknown.—StP

"Thou art my father, who is my mother". Unknown.—StP

God.—*Continued*
"Thou dawnest beautifully in the horizon". Unknown.—StP
"Thou that hast given so much to me". G. Herbert.—StP
The tiger ("Tiger, tiger, burning bright"). W. Blake.—CaB
   "Tyger, tyger, burning bright".—StP
"To believe in God". J. Pintauro.—StP
"Unless you lead me, Lord, I cannot dance". Mechtild of Magdeburg.—StP
"What are you, God". I. Wells.—StP
What Tomas said in a pub. J. Stephens.—ElW
"When bad things happen to me, God". I. Wells.—StP
"When God gave out noses". Unknown.—ScA
"Where can I go then from your spirit". From The book of psalms. Bible/Old Testament.—StP
"Wisdom of serpent be thine". Unknown.—StP
Wise. A. Fisher.—FiA
"You are to me, O Lord". Unknown.—StP
"You, neighbor God, if in the long night". R. M. Rilke.—StP
"God be here, God be there". Mother Goose.—WaM
"God before me, God behind me". Unknown.—StP
"God bless all those that I love". Unknown.—StP
"God bless us, every one". Charles Dickens.—StP
"God grows weary of great kingdoms". Rabindranath Tagore.—StP
"God is Father and Mother". Unknown.—StP
"God is great". Unknown.—StP
"God is, I know that". Unknown.—StP
"God is light". Unknown.—StP
"God is love, and love enfolds us". Timothy Rees.—StP
"God is love and we are his children". Unknown.—StP
"God is the bow". Unknown.—StP
"God made you". Unknown.—CoM
"God moves in a mysterious way". William Cowper.—ElW
"God of all power, ruler of the universe". Unknown.—StP
"God save the owls". From Alabama. Julia Fields.—LiIf
Godden, Rumer
Noah's prayer, tr.—DeP
The prayer of the cat, tr.—DeP
The prayer of the cock, tr.—DeP
The prayer of the dog, tr.—DeP
The prayer of the donkey, tr.—DeP
The prayer of the dove, tr.—DeP
The prayer of the elephant, tr.—DeP
The prayer of the glow-worm, tr.—DeP
The prayer of the goat, tr.—DeP
The prayer of the little pig, tr.—DeP
The prayer of the monkey, tr.—DeP
The prayer of the owl, tr.—DeP—LiIf
The prayer of the ox, tr.—DeP
Gods and goddesses
Atlas. J. Yolen.—YoFf
"Ganesha, Ganesh". M. C. Livingston.—WhDd
Garuda. D. Chandra.—WhDd
Hymn to Cynthia. B. Jonson.—ElW
Pan. E. B. Browning.—WhDd
Quetzalcoatl. T. Johnston.—WhDd
The song of wandering Aengus. W. B. Yeats.—ElW—GoU
They told me. W. De La Mare.—DeR
God's world. Edna St. Vincent Millay.—StP

"Goes around". See Grandpa in March
"Going backward". See In the pocket
"Going home with her books through the snow". Wallace Tripp.—LiLo
Going into dream. Eleanor Farjeon.—HoSt
Gold, Edward
Unitas.—KnAs
Gold (color). See Yellow (color)
Gold (metal)
"Jason Johnson left New Jersey". J. Prelutsky.—PrBe
"Gold locks, and black locks". See The barber's
Goldberg, Leah
"I have not seen you, even in dream". See Love songs from an ancient book
Love songs from an ancient book, sels.
   "I have not seen you, even in dream".—GoT
This night, tr. by Robert Friend.—GoT
Toward myself, tr. by Robert Friend.—GoT
Golden eagle. J. Patrick Lewis.—LeT
The golden stair. Jane Yolen.—YoFf
A goldfinch. Walter De La Mare.—DeR
"The goldfinch". See Winter finch
Goldfish
"A. B. C. D. Gol'fish". Unknown.—ClI
Aquarium. V. Worth.—WoAl
Goldfish ("Goldfish flash past, keeping busy"). X. J. Kennedy.—KeK
Goldfish ("I have four fish with poppy eyes"). A. Fisher.—MoS
Goldfish ("Goldfish flash past, keeping busy"). X. J. Kennedy.—KeK
Goldfish ("I have four fish with poppy eyes"). Aileen Fisher.—MoS
"Goldfish flash". See Aquarium
"Goldfish flash past, keeping busy". See Goldfish
Goldthwaite, John
"Chimney squirrels".—PrFo
Golf
Babe Didrikson. G. Rice.—KnAs
First green heron. G. Margolis.—KnAs
A history of golf, sort of. T. L. Hirsch.—KnAs
A lesson from golf. E. Guest.—KnAs
Golino, Carlo L.
Autumn garden, tr.—GoT
Gomei
"The mud snail".—DeI
Gondola swan. William Jay Smith.—SmL
Gone ("Bright sun, hot sun, oh, to be"). Walter De La Mare.—DeR
Gone ("Where's the Queen of Sheba"). Walter De La Mare.—DeR
"Gone the snowdrop, comes the crocus". See Come, gone
"Gonna lay down my sword and shield". Unknown.—StP
"Good at something, I practiced till I broke". See The standing broad jump
"Good books, good times". Lee Bennett Hopkins.—HoGo
"Good boy is a fool's nickname". From Jamaican Caribbean proverbs. Unknown.—BeW
"Good-by my winter suit". N. M. Bodecker.—MoS
"Good-bye my fancy". Walt Whitman.—HoVo
Good flower blues. Ashley Bryan.—BrS
"Good for good is only fair". Unknown.—StP
"Good Lord, help me to win if I may". Unknown.—StP
Good morning. Muriel Sipe.—DeS
"Good morning, class, I'm glad to see". See If you're not here, please raise your hand
"Good morning, daddy". See Dream boogie

Good-morning poems. See Wake-up poems
Good morrow. Thomas Heywood.—ElW
"Good morrow to you, Valentine". Mother Goose.—WaM
"Good news to tell". See The corner
Good night ("Father puts the paper down"). Aileen Fisher.—PlW
Good night ("Goodnight Mommy"). Nikki Giovanni.—HoS—PlW
"Good night and sweet repose, I hope". Unknown.—OpI
Good-night poems. See Bedtime; Lullabies
"Good night, sleep tight". Unknown.—PrFo (longer)—ScA—WiA
"Good night, sweet repose, half the bed". Unknown.—OpI—WaM
A **good** play. Robert Louis Stevenson.—DeT
Good times. Lucille Clifton.—ElW
Goodbye now. James Berry.—BeW
Goodbye please. John Ciardi.—CiH
Goodbye, six, hello, seven. Judith Viorst.—LoFh
"Goodbye to the summer". See September garden
Goodman, Paul
Don Larsen's perfect game.—KnAs
"The enginegines".—MoR
Surfers at Santa Cruz.—KnAs
Goodness. See Conduct of life
Goodness. Benny Andersen, tr. by Alexander Taylor.—NyT
"Goodness gracious, save my soul, hang me on". Unknown.—WiA
"Goodness gracious, save my soul, lead me to". Unknown.—WiA
"Goodness is stronger than evil". Desmond Tutu.—StP
Goodnight, Juma. Eloise Greenfield.—GrN
"Goodnight Mommy". See Good night
Goodrich, Samuel
"Higglety, pigglety, pop".—ClI—ScA (unat.)—SuO (unat.)
Gooloo. Shel Silverstein.—PrFo
"The **gooloo** bird". See Gooloo
Gooney bird. William Jay Smith.—SmL
Goose-wing chariot. Unknown.—OpT
"Gooseberry, juiceberry". Eve Merriam.—LiDd—MoS
"Goosey goosey gander". Mother Goose.—EdGl—SuO—WaM
Gordon, Elizabeth
"A small boy, while learning to swim".—LiLo
"There was an old maid of Berlin".—LiLo
Gorey, Edward
"Each night father fills me with dread".—PrFo
"From Number Nine, Penwiper Mews".—LiLo
"An impressionable lady in Wales".—LiLo
Gorillas. See Apes and monkeys
The **gospel** according to Matthew, sels. Bible/New Testament
"Our Father in heaven".—StP
Gossip
"Ain't no hell on earth". J. Carson.—CaS
"Did he say I said you said she said that". Unknown.—WiA
Gab. E. Merriam.—MeCh
Gate gossip. M. Fatchen.—FaCm
Johnny Spain's white heifer. H. Carruth.—JaM
"Tattletale, tattletale". Unknown.—ScA—WiA
"There is a girl on our street". Unknown.—ScA
Why Rosalie did it. J. W. Miller.—JaM
"You know Lou Beal". J. Carson.—CaS
"Got a cornstalk fiddle". Unknown.—WiA

Gourlay, Elizabeth
Hanging.—BoT
"A gourmet challenged me to eat". See Rattlesnake meat
Government
"Oh my good Lord, I am not a young man anymore". J. Carson.—CaS
"One day". J. Carson.—CaS
Grace. Walter De La Mare.—DeR
"Grace, Grace, dressed in lace". Unknown.—WiA
The **graceful** elephant ("One elephant balanced gracefully"). See "Un elefante se balanceaba"
Gracious goodness. Marge Piercy.—ElW
Graham, Al
Casey's daughter at the bat.—KnAs
"A Martian named Harrison Harris".—LiLo
Graham, Harry
Grandpapa.—PrFo
Graham, Martha (about)
Martha Graham. J. Laughlin.—MoR
Grahame, Kenneth
Ducks' ditty.—ElW
The song of Mr. Toad. See The wind in the willows
The wind in the willows, sels.
The song of Mr. Toad.—CoAz
The **grammatical** witch. Jane Yolen.—YoBe
Grand Canyon
Grand Canyon east, from the air. M. C. Livingston.—LiR
Grand Canyon east, from the air. Myra Cohn Livingston.—LiR
"Grandest of canyons". See Ocean
"Grandfather, grandfather, show your delight". From Grannies and grandpas. Unknown.—OpT
Grandfathers
Code blue. B. L. Cantwell.—JaPr
The difference. M. C. Livingston.—LiNe
Direction. A. Lopez.—AgL
Driving lesson. M. Pettit.—JaM
"Grandfather, grandfather, show your delight". From Grannies and grandpas. Unknown.—OpT
A grandfather's last letter. N. Dubie.—JaM
Grandmas and grandpas. M. A. Hoberman.—HoFa
Grandpa in March. A. Adoff.—MoS
Grandpapa. H. Graham.—PrFo
Indian summer. J. P. Lewis.—LeE
Indian trail. B. Guernsey.—JaPr
Jonathan Sobel. M. Glenn.—GlBc
Killing chickens. B. Weigl.—JaPr
"Mother, we are cold". Unknown.—SnD
Neck please. E. Glen.—LiPg
Old photograph album, grandfather. B. J. Esbensen.—EsW
"Old Uncle Luke, he thinks he's cute". From Grannies and grandpas. Unknown.—OpT
Remembering ice. X. J. Kennedy.—KeK
The smile. J. Aiken.—LiPg
Some things about grandpas. A. Low.—LoFh
Thanksgiving day, complete. L. M. Child.—FoLe—SuI
Wolf-ancestry. V. Popa.—NyT
"Grandfather's chair". See The difference
A **grandfather's** last letter. Norman Dubie.—JaM
"Grandfathers watch you". See Some things about grandpas
"Grandma is Grandma". See Once upon a time
Grandmas and grandpas. Mary Ann Hoberman.—HoFa
Grandma's spectacles. Unknown.—CoE
Grandmother. Sameeneh Shirazie.—NyT

"Grandmother". See I watched an eagle soar
Grandmother in winter. X. J. Kennedy.—LiPg
Grandmother Ostrich. William Jay Smith.—SmL
"Grandmother Ostrich goes to bed". See Grandmother Ostrich
Grandmother, rocking. Eve Merriam.—MeS
"Grandmother works at a Penney's store". See Working
Grandmothers
   All kinds of grands. L. Clifton.—LiPg
   Apple scoop. E. Glen.—LiPg
   Basket. M. C. Livingston.—LiPg
   Big Mama. K. Fufuka.—SlM
   Childhood. J. Joubert.—NyT
   Christmas scene. V. Worth.—LiPg
   "Come up an' see yer grannie". From Grannies and grandpas. Unknown.—OpT
   The cupboard. W. De La Mare.—DeR—MaP
   "Dave Dirt came to dinner". K. Wright.—PrFo
   The difference. M. C. Livingston.—LiNe
   Door. V. Worth.—WoAl
   Explaining. D. B. Axelrod.—JaPr
   Fingerprint. H. Thurston.—BoT
   #4. D. Long.—SlM
   From her office. R. H. Marks.—LiPg
   The gingerbread grandma. J. C. Thomas.—LiPg
   Grandmas and grandpas. M. A. Hoberman.—HoFa
   Grandma's spectacles. Unknown.—CoE
   Grandmother. S. Shirazie.—NyT
   Grandmother in winter. X. J. Kennedy.—LiPg
   Grandmother, rocking. E. Merriam.—MeS
   Grandmothers. D. McCord.—LiPg
   Granny ("Granny had a way with fruit trees"). A. Bryan.—BrS
   Granny ("We've a great big knocker"). P. Hubbell.—MoS
   "Granny, Granny, please comb my hair". G. Nichols.—NiCo
   Granny's ninety-two-year-old legs. A. Adoff.—AdIn
   Great grandma. L. Morrison.—LiPg
   Growing old. R. Henderson.—DeT
   Her hands. A. W. Paul.—LiPg
   Hot milk. X. J. Kennedy.—KeK
   If our dogs outlived us. D. Hines.—JaM
   "In the early morning". E. Di Pasquale.—LiPg
   In the mirror. M. Robinson.—LiPg
   Interlude. M. C. Livingston.—LiT
   Lineage. M. Walker.—LiPg
   The little creature. W. De La Mare.—DeR
   Lizard ("A lean lizard"). G. Nichols.—NiCo
   Martine Provencal. M. Glenn.—GlBc
   The mask. D. K. Hru.—SlM
   Neck please. E. Glen.—LiPg
   New Year's advice from my Cornish grandmother. X. J. Kennedy.—KeK
   "Old Uncle Luke, he thinks he's cute". From Grannies and grandpas. Unknown.—OpT
   Once upon a time. T. Johnston.—LiPg
   Our grandmothers. M. Angelou.—AnI
   Po's garden. R. Young.—JaP
   Ruthless rhyme. J. A. Lindon.—PrFo
   Seashell. V. Worth.—WoAl
   Seeing Granny. J. Berry.—BeW
   Sleep, grandmother. M. Van Doren.—SuI
   The smile. J. Aiken.—LiPg
   Storyteller ("Emerald"). A. Bryan.—BrS
   Thanksgiving day, complete. L. M. Child.—FoLe—SuI
   A victory. R. T. Smith.—JaM
   Welcome, Florence. J. Steinbergh.—LiPg

Willimae's cornrows. N. Mellage.—SlM
   Working. A. Story.—LiPg
Grandmothers. David McCord.—LiPg
"Grandmothers are kind". See Grandmothers
"Grandmother's basket". See Basket
Grandpa bear's lullaby. Jane Yolen.—DeS—HoS—MoS
Grandpa in March. Arnold Adoff.—MoS
Grandpapa. Harry Graham.—PrFo
"Grandpapa fell down a drain". See Grandpapa
Grandparents. See Grandfathers; Grandmothers
Grannies and grandpas, complete. Unknown
   "Come up an' see yer grannie".—OpT
   "Grandfather, grandfather, show your delight".—OpT
   "Old Uncle Luke, he thinks he's cute".—OpT
Granny ("Granny had a way with fruit trees"). Ashley Bryan.—BrS
Granny ("We've a great big knocker"). Patricia Hubbell.—MoS
"Granny, Granny, please comb my hair". Grace Nichols.—NiCo
"Granny had a way with fruit trees". See Granny
"Granny Smith, Gravenstein". See Counting-out rhyme
Granny's ninety-two-year-old legs. Arnold Adoff.—AdIn
Grant, Eddie
   Electric Avenue.—AgL
Grape pickers. Ashley Bryan.—BrS
"Grape pickers singing". See Grape pickers
Grape sherbert. Rita Dove.—JaM
"The grapes hang green upon the vine". Unknown.—ScA
Grass
   Airport in the grass. X. J. Kennedy.—MoR
   Barefoot. V. Worth.—WoAl
   The bottoms of my sneaks are green. A. Adoff.—AdIn
   "A child said, what is the grass, fetching it". W. Whitman.—StP
   Grass ("Do you ever think about grass"). A. Fisher.—FiA
   Grass ("The grass is strangely tall to me"). T. Kristensen.—NyT
   Grass ("Grass on the lawn"). V. Worth.—WoAl
   "Grass glass". B. McMillan.—McP
   The green grass grows all around. Unknown.—WiA
   "In Heaven". S. Crane.—StP
   "In storm-tossed grassland". Miyoshi.—CaR
   "In the woods there was a hole". Unknown.—ScA
   Spring ("To tangled grass I cling"). M. F. Fraser.—SuI
   "There was a young farmer of Leeds". Unknown.—LiLo—SuO
      A young farmer of Leeds.—DeS
Grass ("Do you ever think about grass"). Aileen Fisher.—FiA
Grass ("The grass is strangely tall to me"). Tom Kristensen, tr. by Paul Borum.—NyT
Grass ("Grass on the lawn"). Valerie Worth.—WoAl
"Grass glass". Bruce McMillan.—McP
"The grass is running in the wind". See Field in the wind
"The grass is strangely tall to me". See Grass
"Grass on the lawn". See Grass
The grasshopper ("Down a deep well a grasshopper fell"). David McCord.—LiDd
Grasshopper ("Silence stilled the meadow"). J. Patrick Lewis.—LeE

The **grasshopper** ("There was a little grasshopper"). Unknown.—CoE
"**Grasshopper** copters whir". See Airport in the grass
Grasshoppers
Airport in the grass. X. J. Kennedy.—MoR
The grasshopper ("Down a deep well a grasshopper fell"). D. McCord.—LiDd
Grasshopper ("Silence stilled the meadow"). J. P. Lewis.—LeE
The grasshopper ("There was a little grasshopper"). Unknown.—CoE
Grasshoppers. P. Fleischman.—FlJ
"Little Miss Tuckett". Mother Goose.—CII
On the grasshopper and cricket. J. Keats.—ElW
"Once a grasshoppper (food being scant)". O. Herford.—LiLo
"Way down south where bananas grow". Unknown.—PrP—WiA
　Way down south.—CII
Grasshoppers. Paul Fleischman.—FlJ
Gratitude. See Thankfulness
Graves, Robert
Flying crooked.—CaB
A frosty night.—ElW
The pumpkin ("You may not believe it, for hardly could I").—DeS
Graves. See also Epitaphs
All Hallows' Eve (My mother brings me to visit a Sicilian cemetery). E. Di Pasquale.—LiHp
At last. W. De La Mare.—DeR
Ching ming. I. Rawnsley.—FoLe
Ghosts ("A cold and starry darkness moans"). H. Behn.—BaH—LiIf
Grape sherbert. R. Dove.—JaM
"Make me a grave where'er you will". From Bury me in a free land. F. E. W. Harper.—SuC
The raven's tomb. W. De La Mare.—DeR
Spooks. N. Crane.—BaH
Tending the garden. E. Pankey.—JaM
To the young who want to die. G. Brooks.—SuC
Tombmates. J. Yolen.—YoBe
"Wailed a ghost in a graveyard at Kew". M. C. Livingston.—LiHp—LiLo
You better be ready. J. Lane.—BoT
Graveyards. See Graves
Gray, Alexander
On a cat ageing.—CaB
"**Gray** and blue". Myra Cohn Livingston.—LiMh
"**Gray** squirrel, red squirrel". See Red and gray in city park
The **grease** monkey and the powder puff. William Jay Smith.—SmL
"The **grease** monkey said to the powder puff". See The grease monkey and the powder puff
"**Great** A, little a". Mother Goose.—WaM
"**Great** and merciful God". Alison O'Grady.—StP
Great are the myths, sels. Walt Whitman
"Great is today, and beautiful".—HoVo
Great Aso. Tatsuji Miyoshi, tr. by Edith Marcombe Shiffert and Yuki Sawa.—NyT
Great big ball. Unknown.—CoE See Great big ball
"**Great** big gawky Gumbo Cole". See Big Gumbo
"A **great** big molicepan". Unknown.—WiA
Great blue heron. Jane Yolen.—YoBi
Great Britain. See England
The **great** brown owl. Jane Euphemia Browne.—LiIf
"The **great** fool is as proud as a dog with two tails". From Jamaican Caribbean proverbs. Unknown.—BeW
"**Great** gobs of greedy beasts are flung". See The culture of the vulture
Great grandma. Lillian Morrison.—LiPg

"The **great** horned owl". See Careful, mouse
"**Great** is today, and beautiful". From Great are the myths. Walt Whitman.—HoVo
The **great** one. Tom Clark.—MoA
The **great** Panjandrum. Samuel Foote.—OpT
"**Great** spirit". From Warrior nation trilogy. Lance Henson.—SuI
"**Great** Spirit, help me never to judge". Unknown.—StP
The **greatest** man on earth. Unknown.—WiA
Greed
Medals and money, a re-evaluation. B. Lamblin.—KnAs
"**Greedy** snowslide". Unknown, tr. by Lawrence Millman.—NyT
Greek language
"Ade milo sti milia". Unknown.—YoS
　"Go, apple, to the apple tree".—YoS
"Alpha, beta, gamma, delta". Unknown.—OpI
"Gyro gyrovoli". Unknown.—YoS
　"Around the round path".—YoS
Greek nursery rhymes. See Nursery rhymes—Greek
Green (color)
The bottoms of my sneaks are green. A. Adoff.—AdIn
Green with envy. E. Merriam.—MeCh
"Hector Protector was dressed all in green". Mother Goose.—SuO
"Little frog among". Gaki.—CaR
　Haiku.—DeT
"**Green** bean". Bruce McMillan.—McP
"**Green** cheese, yellow laces". Mother Goose.—WaM
"**Green** face". See November acorn
The **green** grass grows all around. Unknown.—WiA
"**Green** mistletoe". See Winter
Green velvet suit. Alvaro.—AgL
Green with envy. Eve Merriam.—MeCh
"**Green**, yellow, or red". See H is for hat
Greenaway, Kate
"Jump, jump, jump".—HoS
　The little jumping girls.—LoFh
The little jumping girls. See "Jump, jump, jump"
Greenfield, Eloise
Aunt Roberta.—MoS
The brave ones.—GrU
Buddies.—GrU
Buddy's dream.—GrN
By myself.—SlM
Darnell.—GrN
"The day is hot and icky and the sun sticks to my skin".—MoS
Donkey.—GrU
Fambly time.—GrN
Gazebo.—GrU
Goodnight, Juma.—GrN
Harriet Tubman.—SlM
Hot dreams.—GrU
"The house with the wooden windows".—GrN
"In the church".—GrN
Karen.—GrN
Lawanda's walk.—GrN
Lessie.—MoS
Little boy blues.—GrN
Love don't mean.—SlM
Lucky little birds.—GrU
The man in red.—GrU
The meeting.—GrN
Neighborhood street.—GrN
Nerissa.—GrN
New baby poem (I).—GrN
New baby poem (II).—GrN
Night on neighborhood street.—GrN

Greenfield, Eloise—*Continued*
  The sailboat race.—GrU
  Saucer hat lady.—GrU
  The seller.—GrN
  Song of the water lilies.—GrU
  That kind of day.—GrU
  Things ("Went to the corner").—SlM
  This place.—GrU
  Thoughts.—GrU
  To catch a fish ("It takes more than a wish").—GrU
  To friendship.—GrU
  Tradition.—GrU
  The tree ("It graces our yard").—GrU
  Under the Sunday tree.—GrU
  Wedding day.—GrU
  "When the tourists come to town".—GrU
  "When Tonya's friends come to spend the night".—GrN
Greenland
  Greenland's history, or the history of the Danes on Greenland. S. Holm.—NyT
Greenland's history, or the history of the Danes on Greenland. Sven Holm, tr. by Paula Hostrup-Jessen.—NyT
Greenwald, Roger
  The memory of horses, tr.—NyT
Greetings. See also Wake-up poems
  Grandmother. S. Shirazie.—NyT
  "Hello, hello, Bill". Unknown.—CoM
  "Hello, hello, hello, sir". Unknown.—CoM—WiA
  "My zoo is open to all". W. Cole.—CoAz
  "One misty, moisty morning". Mother Goose.—MoS—SuO—WaM
  Shaking. R. Morgan.—JaPr
  "We wish you a merry Christmas". Unknown.—YoHa
  A welcome song for Laini Nzinga. G. Brooks.—SlM
"Greg has trained a pig that grunts". X. J. Kennedy.—KeFb
Greg Hoffman. Mel Glenn.—MoR
Greger, Debora
  Patches of sky.—SuI
"Gregory Griggs, Gregory Griggs". Mother Goose.—SuO
Gregory's house. David Huddle.—JaPr
"Gretchen has taken Freddy's chair". See Poor substitute
"Grey goose and gander". See Goose-wing chariot
The **grey** wolf. Walter De La Mare.—DeR
Grief. See also Laments; Melancholy
  Bonny George Campbell. Unknown.—ElW
  Come up from the fields father. W. Whitman.—HoVo
  Crocodile. W. J. Smith.—SmL
  The emeritus. L. Nathan.—JaM
  The monument. P. B. Janeczko.—JaB
  The raven. E. A. Poe.—SuI
  The thief at Robin's castle. W. De La Mare.—DeR—MaP
  "When we two parted". Lord Byron.—ElW
The **griffin.** Arnold Sundgaard.—WhDd
Grilikhes, Alexandra
  The statue.—MoR
"Grill me some bones, said the cobbler". See At the keyhole
Grim. Walter De La Mare.—DeR—MaP
Grist mills. See Millers and mills
Groat nor tester. Walter De La Mare.—MaP
Grocery stores. See also Shops and shopkeepers

"The fly made a visit to the grocery store". Unknown.—PrP
I could never convince any of the other members. A. Adoff.—AdCh
No grosser grocer. X. J. Kennedy.—KeGh
A supermarket in Guadalajara, Mexico. D. Levertov.—MoR
Witch goes shopping. L. Moore.—LoFh—PrFo
Grool. Florence Parry Heide.—HeG
Gross, Philip
  Idh al-fitr.—FoLe
  Independence day.—FoLe
Grosvenor, Kali
  Who am I.—SlM
Ground hog day. Lilian Moore.—DeT
"Ground hog sleeps". See Ground hog day
Groundhog Day
  Ground hog day. L. Moore.—DeT
  Groundhog Day. M. Pomeroy.—CoAz
Groundhog Day. Marnie Pomeroy.—CoAz
Groundhogs. See Woodchucks
Growing. Aileen Fisher.—FiA
Growing old. Rose Henderson.—DeT
Growing pains. Jean Little.—LiHe
Growing up. See also Childhood recollections; Children and childhood
  Aaron. A. Adoff.—AdIn
  About angels and age. J. Little.—LiHe
  Almost a madrigal. S. Quasimodo.—GoT
  Atong and his goodbye. B. S. Santos.—NyT
  Autumnal equinox. E. E. Wilson.—JaM
  "Aw, lemme tell you". J. Carson.—CaS
  Bad. P. B. Janeczko.—JaB
  The ball poem. J. Berryman.—KnAs
  Basketball. N. Giovanni.—DeT
  Big sister. M. A. Hoberman.—HoFa
  Black kid in a new place. J. Berry.—BeW
  Born that way. M. Angelou.—AnI
  Breath pon wind. J. Berry.—BeW
  Brown girl, blonde okie. G. Soto.—SoA
  Camp Calvary. R. Wallace.—JaPr
  Charlene Cottier. M. Glenn.—GlBc
  The christening ("The bells chime clear"). W. De La Mare.—DeR
  Companion. D. Manjush.—NyT
  Cool time rhythm rap. J. Berry.—BeW
  The corner. W. De La Mare.—DeR
  Dawn Weinberg. M. Glenn.—GlBc
  "Days were as great as lakes". D. Vogel.—GoT
  Deidre Spector. M. Glenn.—GlBc
  Dennis Finch. M. Glenn.—GlBc
  Dodo ("Years they mistook me for you"). H. Carlile.—JaPr
  "Don't worry if your job is small". Unknown.—PrP—ScA
  Dreaming black boy. J. Berry.—BeW
  Driving lesson. M. Pettit.—JaM
  Eagle rock. G. Hewitt.—JaPr
  Elegy for the girl who died in the dump at Ford's Gulch. J. Johnson.—JaPr
  Elliot West. M. Glenn.—GlBc
  The end. A. A. Milne.—LoFh
  Evan King. M. Glenn.—GlBc
  Ex-basketball player. J. Updike.—KnAs
  Firsts. P. B. Janeczko.—JaB
  Five ("Is old enough"). M. C. Livingston.—LiBp
  For Genevieve, five years old. S. Dumdum.—NyT
  For the death of Vince Lombardi. J. Dickey.—KnAs
  Four. M. C. Livingston.—LiBp
  Frankie Dempster. M. Glenn.—GlBc

Growing up.—*Continued*

Full circle. W. De La Mare.—DeR
Garbage ("We hauled trash that summer, the three of us"). E. Trethewey.—JaM
The garden of a child. N. Chakravarti.—NyT
Generation gap. X. J. Kennedy.—KeK
Generations. S. Cornish.—JaPr
The gift ("When I was five my father kidnapped me"). M. Jarman.—JaM
Girls can we educate we dads. J. Berry.—BeW
Good times. L. Clifton.—ElW
Goodbye, six, hello, seven. J. Viorst.—LoFh
Grass ("The grass is strangely tall to me"). T. Kristensen.—NyT
"Great is today, and beautiful". From Great are the myths. W. Whitman.—HoVo
Growing. A. Fisher.—FiA
Growing pains. J. Little.—LiHe
Growing up ("Little Tommy Tadpole began to weep and wail"). C. J. Dennis.—CoAz
Growing up ("When I grow up"). A. Fisher.—FiA
Hanging fire. A. Lorde.—AgL
He was so little. J. Little.—LiHe
"Hey black child". U. E. Perkins.—SlM
Hey world, here I am. J. Little.—LiHe
High school. G. Roberts.—JaPr
The house on Buder Street. G. Gildner.—JaPr
"I am young". R. Walker.—StP
I like it when. R. Margolis.—LiPf
If ("If you can keep your head when all about you"). R. Kipling.—ElW
"If you are not handsome at twenty". Mother Goose.—WaM
In my horror fantasy chiller. A. Adoff.—AdCh
Industrial childhood. S. Stevenson.—NyT
Innocency. W. De La Mare.—DeR
Instruction. C. Hilberry.—KnAs—MoA
Interlude. M. C. Livingston.—LiT
Jaime Milagros. M. Glenn.—GlBc
Jim. J. Holden.—JaPr
Jody Walker, the first voice. P. Ruffin.—JaPr
Kristin Leibowitz. M. Glenn.—GlBc
Kyle Quinn. M. Glenn.—GlBc
Lanky Hank Farrow. H. Witt.—KnAs
Louisa's liberation. J. Little.—LiHe
A lullaby ("Sleep, child, lie quiet, let be"). J. Agee.—GoT
Mamaw and Frank. W. Burt.—JaPr
Mamma settles the dropout problem. B. Gates.—SuC
A man never cries. J. Craveirinha.—NyT
Marvin Pickett. M. Glenn.—KnAs
Matinees. K. Soniat.—JaPr
Mr. Desmond Klinger, music. M. Glenn.—GlBc
Mrs. Krikorian. S. Olds.—JaPr
Ms. Nadine Sierra, French. M. Glenn.—GlBc
Ms. Yvonne Harmon, librarian. M. Glenn.—GlBc
My father's leaving. I. Sadoff.—JaPr
"My little son". Makah.—SnD
"My mouth is a horse's mouth". From Remembering. X. Di.—NyT
Nicholas Townshed. M. Glenn.—GlBc
Nocturne ("A long arm embossed with gold slides from the tree tops"). L.-P. Fargue.—GoT
Ode to weddings. G. Soto.—SoNe
Of necessity, Weeb jokes about his height. C. H. Webb.—JaPr
Oh calendar. J. P. Lewis.—LoFh
On destiny. S. Tanikawa.—NyT
Orphanage boy. R. P. Warren.—JaPr
Plans. M. Kumin.—KeT
Poem at thirty. S. Sanchez.—SuC

The question ("People always say to me"). K. Kuskin.—LiDd
The question mark. G. Emin.—NyT
Raymond. P. B. Janeczko.—JaB
Regina Kelsey. M. Glenn.—GlBc
Rescue ("Sunday, beginning the week late"). E. Trethewey.—JaPr
Rites of passage. D. Laux.—JaPr
Runaway teen. W. Stafford.—JaPr
Saturday fielding practice. L. Morrison.—LiPf
Say nay. E. Merriam.—MeS
Secrets ("She slits empty feed sacks"). L. Schandelmeier.—JaPr
Setting the traps. D. Jauss.—JaPr
Seven. M. C. Livingston.—LiBp
A short note on schoolgirls. A. Campbell.—AgL
The shriving. J. Carter.—JaM
Six. M. C. Livingston.—LiBp
The sleeper. E. Field.—KnAs
Small wants. B. Padhi.—NyT
A song in the front yard. G. Brooks.—ElW
"Starting from fish-shape Paumanok where I was born". From Starting from Paumanok. W. Whitman.—HoVo
Still life. M. Angelotti.—JaM
The Strand Theatre. T. Cader.—JaPr
Stronger lessons. W. Whitman.—HoVo
Summer. J. Mahapatra.—NyT
Sweet sixteen. E. De Souza.—AgL
Teaching numbers. G. Soto.—SoA
To the young who want to die. G. Brooks.—SuC
A toast for everybody who is growin. J. Berry.—BeW
Toward myself. L. Goldberg.—GoT
Trick or treating at age eight. L. Rosenberg.—LiHp
A war baby looks back. J. Holden.—JaPr
We chased butterflies. Plenty-Coups.—SnD
What Saundra said about being short. J. Hall.—JaM
Wheels. J. Daniels.—JaPr
When I grow up. M. A. Hoberman.—HoFa
"When I was one and twenty". A. E. Housman.—ElW
White ("1964 and I'm parked"). C. Buckley.—JaM
Why there are no cats in the forest. S. Dumdum.—NyT
The window cleaner. M. Long.—BaW
Woman. U. Saba.—GoU
The world's so big. A. Fisher.—FiA
The writer. R. Wilbur.—SuI
Yesterday. J. Little.—LiHe
Young. A. Sexton.—AgL—JaPr
Young soul. I. A. Baraka.—SuC

Growing up ("Little Tommy Tadpole began to weep and wail"). Clarence James Dennis.—CoAz

Growing up ("When I grow up"). Aileen Fisher.—FiA

"**Grown** folks are wise". See The admiration of Willie

Grump. Eve Merriam.—MeS

"**Grump** grump grump grump". See Grump

Guardian owl. Norma Farber.—LiIf

Guernsey, Bruce
Indian trail.—JaPr

"**Guess** what I've got inside my fist". Eve Merriam.—MeY

Guest, Edgar
A lesson from golf.—KnAs

Guillevic, Eugene
"Let me get up early on this summer morning".—
GoT
Guilt
The rime of the ancient mariner, complete. S. T.
Coleridge.—ElW
"The **guinea-fowl** chick says it is there". See
"Icipyolopyolo ca bana ba nkanga apo"
Guinea pigs
"There was a little guinea-pig". Unknown.—CII
Guinevere Ghastly sits baby. X. J. Kennedy.—KeGh
"**Guinevere**, where's brother Peter". See Guinevere
Ghastly sits baby
Guitars
Ode to el guitarron. G. Soto.—SoNe
Guiterman, Arthur
Eight oars and a coxswain.—KnAs
Habits of the hippopotamus.—PrFo
In praise of llamas.—CoAz
What the gray cat sings.—LaCc
Gull. William Jay Smith.—SmL
Gulls
"The air was damp". From Song of ships. V.
Schonborg.—LaN
Gull. W. J. Smith.—SmL
Ocean diners. J. P. Lewis.—LeT
The sea gull's eye. R. Hoban.—JaP
To the seagull. Unknown.—OpI
A visit from the sea. R. L. Stevenson.—CaB
"The **gun** full swing the swimmer catapults and".
See 400 meter freestyle
Gunn, Thom
Apartment cats.—LaCc
South ("Today's cool asphalt . . . where had the
cars gone").—ElW
Guns. See also Hunters and hunting
"As I went up a slippery gap". Unknown.—OpT
Every chance we got. C. H. Webb.—JaPr
"Long, slim, slick fellow". Unknown.—WiA
Target practice. G. Soto.—JaPr
"**Guns** and rifles". See The biggest questions
Gus. Paul B. Janeczko.—JaB
"**Gus** was slow". See Gus
Guy Fawkes Day
Five haiku. G. Douthwaite.—FoLe
"Guy, guy, guy". Unknown.—OpI
Please to remember ("He comes to see us every
year"). G. Holloway.—FoLe
"Please to remember the fifth of November".
Unknown.—OpI
Remember. D. Ward.—FoLe
"**Guy,** guy, guy". Unknown.—OpI
The **gymnasts.** Irving Feldman.—KnAs
Gymnasts and gymnastics
The gymnasts. I. Feldman.—KnAs
Uneven parallel bars. P. Gary.—KnAs
Gypsies
Gypsy. Unknown.—OpT
"Gypsy, gypsy, please tell me". Unknown.—WiA
Tinker man. Unknown.—MoR
The wraggle taggle gypsies. Unknown.—ElW
Gypsy. Unknown.—OpT
"**Gypsy,** gypsy, please tell me". Unknown.—WiA
"**Gyro** gyrovoli". Unknown.—YoS
"Around the round path".—YoS

H

H is for hat. William Jay Smith.—SmL
"**H,** u, uckle". Unknown.—WiA

Habits
The breath of death (the cigarette). L. Sissay.—
AgL
"Said old peeping Tom of Fort Lee". M.
Bishop.—LiLo
"There was a young girl of Asturias".
Unknown.—LiLo
Habits of the hippopotamus. Arthur Guiterman.—
PrFo
Hackett, J. W.
"Flashing neon night".—LaN
Hackle bird. William Jay Smith.—SmL
"**Had** I the heavens' embroidered cloths". See He
wishes for the cloths of heaven
Hahn, Robert
Never be as fast as I have been, the jockey Tony
DeSpirito dead at thirty-nine.—KnAs
Haiku
"Above the chorus". Kyoshi.—CaR
"All at once, the storm". Buson.—CaR
Bottom of the ninth haiku. R. G. Fabian.—MoA
"Butting, tumbling cat". Kikaku.—CaR
"Detestable crow". Basho.—CaR
"A discovery". Yaku.—WhAa
Haiku.—DeT
The doll festival. J. Kirkup.—FoLe
Five haiku. G. Douthwaite.—FoLe
"Galloping pony". Kyorai.—CaR—WhAa
Haiku ("I have looked into"). S. Sanchez.—SlM
"High noon! A hot sun". Hajime.—CaR
"A hungry owl hoots". Joso.—LiIf
"In storm-tossed grassland". Miyoshi.—CaR
"Leaping flying fish". Koson.—CaR
"Little frog among". Gaki.—CaR
Haiku.—DeT
"Now the pond is still". Aohozuki.—CaR
"Oh, don't strike the fly". Issa.—CaR
"On the dewy trunk". Kyoshi.—CaR
Rain, a haiku sequence. M. C. Livingston.—LiR
"Red dragonfly on". Soseki.—CaR
Haiku. See "A discovery"
Haiku ("I have looked into"). Sonia Sanchez.—SlM
Haiku. See "Little frog among"
Hail
Hail. S. Barry.—MoA
The hare ("The hail comes beating down").
Unknown.—DeI
Hail. Scott Barry.—MoA
"The **hail** comes beating down". See The hare
"**Hail** the way I see it". See Hail
Haines, John
If the owl calls again.—LiIf
Prayer to the snowy owl.—LiIf
Hair
The barber's. W. De La Mare.—DeR—MaP
Beaded braids. A. Bryan.—BrS
"Black hair". A. Yosano.—GoU
The comb. W. De La Mare.—DeR
Combing the hair. Unknown.—OpT
Crown. D. K. Hru.—SlM
"Curly locks, curly locks". Mother Goose.—EdGl
"During the sermon". W. Kloefkorn.—JaPr
"Fuzzy Wuzzy was a bear". Unknown.—PrP—
WiA
Fuzzy Wuzzy.—CII
The golden stair. J. Yolen.—YoFf
"Granny, Granny, please comb my hair". G.
Nichols.—NiCo
"I'd rather have fingers than toes". G. Burgess.—
LiLo
In the ending of this evening snow. A. Adoff.—
AdIn

Hair—*Continued*
In the mirror. M. Robinson.—LiPg
"Johnny on the woodpile". Unknown.—WiA
Kinky hair blues. U. Marson.—LeCa
Lovelocks. W. De La Mare.—DeR
Mima. W. De La Mare.—DeR—MaP
Once upon a time. T. Johnston.—LiPg
A person in Stirling. N. M. Bodecker.—LiLo
A personal experience. O. Herford.—LiLo
"Queen, Queen Caroline". Unknown.—KeT—OpI
The rain falling on west train tracks, Ohio. A. Adoff.—AdCh
"Riddle me, riddle me, what is that". Unknown.—WiA
Ruthless rhyme. J. A. Lindon.—PrFo
Sam's world. S. Cornish.—LiPm
The stars streaming in the sky. Unknown.—SnD
"There was a girl named Mary Lou". Unknown.—ScA
"There was a young lady of Firle". E. Lear.—LiLo
"This morning I will not". H. Kakinomoto.—GoU
To those of my sisters who kept their naturals. G. Brooks.—SuC
Willimae's cornrows. N. Mellage.—SlM
Yak ("The long haired yak has long black hair"). W. J. Smith.—SmL
"**Hair** the color of pencil shavings". See Raymond
The **hairy** toe. Unknown.—BaH
Haiti, skin diving. Jane Shore.—KnAS
Hajime
"High noon! A hot sun".—CaR
Hakotun, Moshe
"When I walk through thy woods".—StP
Hale, Sarah Josepha
"Mary had a little lamb". See Mary's lamb
Mary's lamb.—SuI
  "Mary had a little lamb".—EdGl (unat.)—SuO (unat.)—WaM (unat.)
Halevi, Judah
The apple, tr. by Robert Mezey.—GoU
"**Half** a pint of porter". Unknown.—OpI
Half moon. Federico Garcia Lorca.—LaN
Half-whole-step. Mary Ann Hoberman.—HoFa
Hall, Jim
In the spring.—JaM
Preposterous.—JaPr
The teenage cocaine dealer considers his death on the street outside a Key West funeral for a much-loved civic leader.—JaPr
What Saundra said about being short.—JaM
Halloran, Phyllis
Busy ("Busy, busy, busy, busy").—WhAa
Halloween
Advice on how to sleep well Halloween night. J. Yolen.—YoBe
All Hallows' Eve. A. Bonner.—FoLe
All Hallows' Eve (My mother brings me to visit a Sicilian cemetery). E. Di Pasquale.—LiHp
Alone on a broom. J. Yolen.—YoBe
Apple bobbing. R. H. Marks.—LiHp
Carving pumpkins with my father. L. Rosenberg.—LiPf
Ghosts ("A cold and starry darkness moans"). H. Behn.—BaH—LiIf
Hallowe'en ("Hallowe'en, they say"). S. Cook.—FoLe
Halloween ("Hooting howling hissing witches"). P. J. Perry.—BaH
Hallowe'en ("It's a black plastic bin bag"). D. Ward.—FoLe

Halloween ("The sky was yellow"). I. O. Eastwick.—HoS
Hallowe'en ("Tonight is the night"). H. Behn.—LiHp
Hallowe'en ad (attention witches). G. Tall.—BaH
Halloween concert ("Elbows bent, tireless"). B. J. Esbensen.—LiHp
Halloween concert ("It's cold, said the cricket"). A. Fisher.—FiA
The Halloween house. J. Ciardi.—CiH—LiLo
Hallowe'en indignation meeting. M. Fishback.—DeT
A Halloween problem. S. Stone.—LiHp
Halloween, the hydrant dare. G. Roberts.—JaPr
Incident on beggar's night. J. P. Lewis.—LiHp
Jack. D. Chandra.—LiHp
"Look at that". L. Moore.—HoS
The magic house. J. Yolen.—LiHp—YoBe
Next day. V. Worth.—LiHp
October nights. H. Cooper.—BoT
Pumpkin ("After its lid"). V. Worth.—BaH—WoAl
"Pumpkin, pumpkin, pumpkin bright". N. M. Bodecker.—LiHp
Skeleton. L. Bartlett.—LiHp
"This is the night of Halloween". Unknown.—OpI
Trick or treating at age eight. L. Rosenberg.—LiHp
Watchdogs. J. Thomas.—LiHp
"We three". L. Moore.—LiHp
Wicked witch's kitchen. X. J. Kennedy.—BaH—LiHp
Hallowe'en ("Hallowe'en, they say"). Stanley Cook.—FoLe
Halloween ("Hooting howling hissing witches"). Phyllis J. Perry.—BaH
Hallowe'en ("It's a black plastic bin bag"). David Ward.—FoLe
Halloween ("The sky was yellow"). Ivy O. Eastwick.—HoS
Hallowe'en ("Tonight is the night"). Harry Behn.—LiHp
Hallowe'en ad (attention witches). Grace Tall.—BaH
Halloween concert ("Elbows bent, tireless"). Barbara Juster Esbensen.—LiHp
Halloween concert ("It's cold, said the cricket"). Aileen Fisher.—FiA
The **Halloween** house. John Ciardi.—CiH—LiLo
Hallowe'en indignation meeting. Margaret Fishback.—DeT
A **Halloween** problem. Sandra Stone.—LiHp
Halloween, the hydrant dare. George Roberts.—JaPr
"**Hallowe'en,** they say". See Hallowe'en
Hamburger, Michael
Mathematics of love.—GoU
"**Hamelin** Town's in Brunswick". See The pied piper of Hamelin, complete
"**Hamelin** Town's in Brunswick". From The pied piper of Hamelin. Robert Browning.—CaB
Hamill, Sam
"Once I got a postcard from the Fiji Islands", tr.—NyT
Hamilton, Frank. See Horton, Zilphia, and Hamilton, Frank
Hamilton Greene. Edgar Lee Masters.—ElW
Hammarskjold, Dag
"Each day the first day".—StP
"For all that has been, thanks".—StP
"Give us a pure heart".—StP
"In the one you are never alone".—StP
The **hammer** song. Unknown.—CoE
Hammerin' Hank. D. Roger Martin.—MoA

Hammerstein, Oscar
Ol' man river. See Show Boat
Show Boat, sels.
    Ol' man river.—SuC
"A **handful** of wind that I caught with a kite". See
    What shall I pack in the box marked summer
Handicapped. See Blind; Insanity
The **handiest** nose. Aileen Fisher.—HoS
Hands
Building. G. Brooks.—SuC
Her hands. A. W. Paul.—LiPg
"I see a star". A. Lopez.—LiPm
If my right hand. Z. Mandela.—AgL
"A leaf for hand in hand". W. Whitman.—HoVo
Lines for remembering about lids. X. J.
    Kennedy.—KeK
"My fingers like to say hello". L. W. Johnson.—
    StP
Pair of hands against football. J. Berry.—BeW
"Que linda manito". Unknown.—DeA
    A pretty little hand ("How pretty, how
    little").—DeA
Secret hand. E. Merriam.—MeS
Shaking. R. Morgan.—JaPr
A sprig of rosemary. A. Lowell.—GoU
"This is the church". Unknown.—WiA
"**Hands** off the tablecloth". See Company manners
"A **handsome** young noble of Spain". Unknown.—
    LiLo
Hanging. Elizabeth Gourlay.—BoT
Hanging fire. Audre Lorde.—AgL
Hangings. See Lynchings; Suicide
"**Hangy** Bangy cut my throat". Unknown.—OpI
Hank and Peg. William Burt.—JaPr
"**Hannah** Bantry in the pantry". Mother Goose.—
    WaM
Hanson, Kenneth O.
"Come morning", tr.—GoT
"Don't shoo the morning flies away", tr.—GoT
Hanukkah
Hanukkah candles. M. Hillert.—HoS
Light the festival candles. A. Fisher.—FoLe
Hanukkah candles. Margaret Hillert.—HoS
Hapless. Walter De La Mare.—DeR—MaP
"**Hapless**, hapless, I must be". See Hapless
Happiness
Afternoon on a hill. E. S. V. Millay.—FrS—SuI
And my heart soars. Chief D. George.—BoT—
    LoFh
"April is a dog's dream". M. Singer.—SiT
"As we are so wonderfully done with each other".
    K. Patchen.—GoU
Atong. B. S. Santos.—NyT
The ballad of old Rocky Nelson. R. Souster.—
    MoA
"Being to timelessness as it's to time". E. E.
    Cummings.—GoU
"Billy Batter". D. Lee.—KeT
A birthday. C. G. Rossetti.—ElW
Black-eyed Susie. Unknown.—SuC
Crocodile. W. J. Smith.—SmL
Daffodils. W. Wordsworth.—FrS
    "I wandered lonely as a cloud".—ElW
Dancing on a rainbow. K. Dakos.—DaI
"The fireflies wink and glow". R. Hillyer.—GoT
God's world. E. S. V. Millay.—StP
"Good books, good times". L. B. Hopkins.—
    HoGo
Good flower blues. A. Bryan.—BrS
"Great is today, and beautiful". From Great are
    the myths. W. Whitman.—HoVo
Happy as a dog's tail. A. Swir.—NyT

Happy thought. R. L. Stevenson.—HoS
Heaven. G. Soto.—SoA
"Hey ho, nobody home". Mother Goose.—WaM
"I am happy because you have accepted me".
    Unknown.—StP
I have ten legs. A. Swir.—NyT
I raise my voice most high, this night. A. Adoff.—
    AdCh
"If you're happy and you know it". Unknown.—
    CoE
I'm glad. Unknown.—LoFh
"In old Minako Wada's house". B. Leithauser.—
    ElW
"It is a comely fashion to be glad". Socrates.—StP
Jaime Milagros. M. Glenn.—GlBc
Looking around, believing. G. Soto.—SoA
Memories. W. Whitman.—HoVo
Miss Cherry. W. De La Mare.—DeR
My happiness. G. Pape.—JaM
My heart leaps up. W. Wordsworth.—ElW
My own day. J. Little.—LiHe—LoFh
On being introduced to you. E. Merriam.—MeS
The Optileast and the Pessimost. E. Merriam.—
    MeS
Parades. K. Fufuka.—SlM
"Piping down the valleys wild". W. Blake.—DeT
Playoff pizza. S. B. Mathis.—MaR
The poem as a door. E. Merriam.—MeS
Portrait, my wife. J. Holmes.—GoU
Prayer ("Owl"). Unknown.—LiIf
Pretty is. A. Bryan.—BrS
The quartette. W. De La Mare.—DeR—MaP
"The reason I like chocolate". N. Giovanni.—
    LoFh
Recuerdo. E. S. V. Millay.—ElW
Relationship. M. C. Livingston.—LiT
Rhapsody. W. S. Braithwaite.—SlM
Running. R. Wilbur.—KnAs
Song ("Sing to the sun"). A. Bryan.—BrS
Song ("When your boyfriend writes you a letter").
    R. Krauss.—MoR
The story of your life. B. Bennett.—MoR
The sun ("I told the sun that I was glad"). J.
    Drinkwater.—LiDd
The swing ("How do you like to go up in a
    swing"). R. L. Stevenson.—DeS—HoS—KeT—
    LiDd
"Take me out to the ball game". J. Norworth.—
    KnAs—MoA
Thanksgiving ("I'm glad that I was good today").
    M. Chute.—LoFh
To soar in freedom and in fullness of power. W.
    Whitman.—HoVo
Tomorrow ("And tomorrow the sun will shine
    again"). J. H. Mackay.—GoT
Walking with Jackie, sitting with a dog. G.
    Soto.—JaPr
Winter poem. N. Giovanni.—SlM
"The year's at the spring". From Pippa passes. R.
    Browning.—ElW—StP
Happy as a dog's tail. Anna Swir, tr. by Czeslaw
    Milosz and Leonard Nathan.—NyT
"**Happy** as something unimportant". See Happy as a
    dog's tail
"**Happy** birthday to you". See "Happy birthday to
    you, you belong in a zoo"
"**Happy** birthday to you, you belong in a zoo".
    Unknown.—CoM
"Happy birthday to you".—PrFo
Happy hiccup to you. Kalli Dakos.—DaI
"**Happy** mooday to you". See The birthday cow
"**Happy**, she sings a daylong song". See Bluest whale

The **happy** sheep. Wilfred Thorley.—CoAz
"**Happy** that this is another". See Where we could go
Happy thought. Robert Louis Stevenson.—HoS
"**Happy** to have these fish". See The catch
A **hardware** store as proof of the existence of God. Nancy Willard.—JaP
Hardy, Thomas
    The fallow deer at the lonely house.—ElW
    Snow in the suburbs.—ElW
    Under the waterfall.—ElW
The **hare** ("The hail comes beating down"). Unknown, tr. by Tze-si Huang.—DeI
The **hare** ("In the black furrow of a field"). Walter De La Mare.—DeR
The **harebell**. Walter De La Mare.—DeR
Hares. See Rabbits
Hares at play. John Clare.—CaB
Hark. Walter De La Mare.—DeR
"**Hark**, hark, the dogs do bark". Mother Goose.—WaM
"**Hark**, is that a horn I hear". See The horn
"**Hark**, the herald angels shout". Unknown.—ScA
"**Hark**, the herald angels sing". Charles Wesley.—YoHa
Harlem
    Harlem. L. Hughes.—ElW
    Harlem night song. L. Hughes.—LaN
    Juke box love song. L. Hughes.—JaPr
    Return of the native. I. A. Baraka.—SuC
Harlem. Langston Hughes.—ElW
"**Harlem** is vicious". See Return of the native
Harlem night song. Langston Hughes.—LaN
The **harlot's** house. Oscar Wilde.—ElW
Harmer, David
    Divali ("Winter stalks us").—FoLe
"**Harnessed** and zipped on a bright". See Hazard's optimism
Harper, Frances E. W.
    Bury me in a free land, sels.
        "Make me a grave where'er you will".—SuC
    Learning to read. See Sketches of southern life
    "Make me a grave where'er you will". See Bury me in a free land
    Sketches of southern life, sels.
        Learning to read.—SuC
    The slave auction.—SuC
Harper, Michael S.
    Makin jump shots.—KnAs
"**Harriet**, by magic force". Eve Merriam.—MeY
Harriet Tubman. Eloise Greenfield.—SlM
"**Harriet** Tubman didn't take no stuff". See Harriet Tubman
Harris, William J.
    An historic moment.—HoGo
Harrison, Robert L.
    The baseball card dealer.—MoA
Harry the hawk. Margaret Mahy.—MaN
"**Harry** the hawk on his magic trapeze". See Harry the hawk
Harte, Bret
    What the engines said (the joining of the Union Pacific and Central Pacific Railroads, May 10, 1869).—SuI
Harvest (for a picture). Walter De La Mare.—DeR
The **harvest** moon ("The flame red moon, the harvest moon"). Ted Hughes.—LaN
Harvest moon ("She comes in silence"). Jean Kenward.—FoLe
The **harvest** queen. Ann Bonner.—FoLe
Harvests and harvesting
    Apple harvest. Unknown.—OpT

Distributing the harvest. B. Moses.—FoLe
"**Farewell**, my younger brother". Unknown.—SnD
Grape pickers. A. Bryan.—BrS
Harvest (for a picture). W. De La Mare.—DeR
Harvest moon ("She comes in silence"). J. Kenward.—FoLe
The harvest queen. A. Bonner.—FoLe
I know that summer is the famous growing season. A. Adoff.—AdIn
Harvey, Trevor
    August outing.—FoLe
    The dragon's lament.—FoLe
"**Has** anybody seen my Mopser". See The bandog
"**Has** anybody seen my mouse". See Missing
Hashmi, Alamgir
    A gift horse.—NyT
"**Hast** never come to thee an hour". Walt Whitman.—HoVo
"**Hast** thou, in fancy, trodden where lie". See Santa Claus
Hate
    Co-op-er-ate. B. S. De Regniers.—DeW
    Extinguished. J. Little.—LiHe
    "For peace sake". C. McClester.—SlM
    Glory falls. M. Angelou.—AnI
    "Higgledy-Piggledy keeps his room tidy". M. C. Livingston.—PrFo
    Mean song ("Snickles and podes"). E. Merriam.—MeS
    "Nobody loves me". Unknown.—OpI—ScA
    The paragon. B. Katz.—JaP
    Ronnie Schwinck. D. A. Evans.—JaPr
    "Roses are red, violets are blue, do you hate me". Unknown.—CoM
    "There's someone I know". J. Prelutsky.—DeS
    "We are the boys of Avenue D". Unknown.—ScA
    The white city. C. McKay.—SuC
    Wicked thoughts. J. Viorst.—PrFo
Hats
    Aunt Gilda's pincushion head. X. J. Kennedy.—KeGh
    "Christopher Columbus, what do you think of that". Unknown.—WiA
    H is for hat. W. J. Smith.—SmL
    Hats. W. J. Smith.—SmL
    Mr. Slatter. N. M. Bodecker.—KeT
    My hat. Unknown.—CoE
    My yellow straw hat. L. J. Little.—KeT
    The Quangle Wangle's hat. E. Lear.—ClI
    Saucer hat lady. E. Greenfield.—GrU
    "There was a man who always wore". Unknown.—OpI
    "There was, in the village of Patton". Unknown.—LiLo
    Visiting. Unknown.—OpT
    While you were chasing a hat. L. Moore.—BaW
Hats. William Jay Smith.—SmL
"**Hats** with heads". From Some things go together. Charlotte Zolotow.—MoS
"**Haul** all together". See Cheerily man
Haunted ("From out the wood I watched them shine"). Walter De La Mare.—DeR
Haunted ("The rabbit in his burrow keeps"). Walter De La Mare.—DeR
The **haunted** child. Margaret Mahy.—MaN
Haunted house ("Its echoes"). Valerie Worth.—JaP—WoAl
The **haunted** house ("Not a window was broken"). Vic Crume.—BaH
"**Have** a mango". See Mango
"**Have** mercy on me, o beneficent one". Unknown.—StP

"**Have** you been catching of fish, Tom Noddy". See Tit for tat
"**Have** you come upon a doe". See Alone in winter
"**Have** you ever, ever, ever". Unknown.—CoM
"**Have** you ever in your life seen a possum play possum". See Opossum
"**Have** you ever seen". See Mrs. A. Hulas
"**Have** you got a sister". Unknown.—OpI
"**Have** you heard her yipping". See The red fox
"**Have** you heard of the wonderful one-hoss shay". See The deacon's masterpiece, or, the wonderful one-hoss shay
"**Have** you learn'd lessons only of those who admired you". See Stronger lessons
"**Have** you not seen the famed Mr. Bickerstaff". See Mr. Bickerstaff
Havelin, Jim Lavella
Enos Slaughter.—KnAs
Having. William Jay Smith.—SmL
Hawaii
The Hongo Store, 29 miles volcano, Hilo, Hawaii. G. K. Hongo.—JaM
"I left my book in Hawaii". K. Dakos.—DaI
Hawks
'Arry's 'awk. Unknown.—Cll
Harry the hawk. M. Mahy.—MaN
Hay
Hay for the horses. G. Snyder.—ElW
Hayfield. A. Fisher.—FiA
Haymaking. W. De La Mare.—DeR
The hayride. M. C. Livingston.—LiBp
Hay for the horses. Gary Snyder.—ElW
"**Hay** is for horses". Mother Goose.—WaM
Hayden, Robert
Runagate runagate.—SuC
Summertime and the living.—SuC
Those winter Sundays.—ElW
Hayfield. Aileen Fisher.—FiA
Haymaking. Walter De La Mare.—DeR
The **hayride**. Myra Cohn Livingston.—LiBp
Hazard's optimism. William Meredith.—KnAs
"**Hazel**". See Sisters
Hazo, Samuel
In the Lebanese mountains, tr.—NyT
"**He** blinks upon the hearth-rug". See On a cat ageing
"**He** came, striding". See Paul Bunyan
"**He** clasps the crag with crooked hands". See The eagle
"**He** comes". See Okolo the leopard warrior
"**He** comes to see us every year". See Please to remember
"**He** could help us out". See Tennis in the city
"**He** could not be captured". See Pegasus
"**He** couldn't use his driver any better on the tee". See A lesson from golf
"**He** cries all the way when we go to the vet". See The vet
"**He** drank enough". From Snake. David Herbert Lawrence.—MoR
"**He** had a name". See Generations
"**He** had driven half the night". See Hay for the horses
"**He** had this idea about the hill". See Jill, afterwards
"**He** has trained the owl to wake him". See Man and owl
"**He** is a clever man who drives away hunger by just working his jaws". From Jamaican Caribbean proverbs. Unknown.—BeW
"**He** is dark and wiry". See Fisherman
"**He** is gone now, he is dead". See For Mugs

"**He** is handsome". Unknown.—ScA
"**He** is the Way". From For the time being. Wystan Hugh Auden.—StP
"**He** kept six butterflies chained in the yard". See The eccentric
"**He** learned economics in the shade". See Economics
"**He** lies stiffly awake". See Darnell
"**He** lived so recklessly that". See Gambler
"**He** loved to scare". See Remembering Oscar eel
"**He** made fun of my Pekingese". See A lesson
"**He** makes the deep to boil like a pot, he makes the sea". See Leviathan
"**He** perches in the dusty tamarind tree". See Garuda
"**He** prayeth best, who loveth best". From The rime of the ancient mariner. Samuel Taylor Coleridge.—StP
"**He** put down his pen". See Lamento
"**He** quickly steps over the air". See Hurdler
He saved a lot of time by not working. John Ciardi.—CiH
"**He** says when he comes in a bar". See Meeting my best friend from the eighth grade
"**He** says, with a frown". See K is for king
"**He** scans the world with calm and fearless eyes". See The new negro
"**He** squats by the fire". See Part XVIII: He squats by the fire
"**He** stands". Myra Cohn Livingston.—LiMh
"**He** stands with his forefeet on the drum". See Two performing elephants
"**He** strides onto the dance floor". See Tyrannosaurus
"**He** that loves glass without g". Unknown.—OpI
"**He** that would thrive". Mother Goose.—WaM
"**He** thinks he's a fierce wolf, growling". See Chihuahua
"**He** threw a white pea". See Nolan Ryan
"**He** thrust his joy against the weight of the sea". See The surfer
"**He** waltzes into the lane". See Makin jump shots
"**He** was a druggist. The storefront building". See The shriving
"**He** was a rat, and she was a rat". Unknown.—Cll
He was brave, but not for long. John Ciardi.—CiH
"**He** was praying before the lamp". See Vistasp
"**He** was skinny". See Hank and Peg
"**He** was sleeping when bear". See Too hot to sleep
He was so little. Jean Little.—LiHe
"**He** was so little he had to sit on a book". See He was so little
"**He** wears striped jim-jam pyjamas". See Jim-jam pyjamas
"**He** went down to the woodshed". See No one heard him call
"**He** went out of the room in which he was praying, he spent there". See Or
He wishes for the cloths of heaven. William Butler Yeats.—ElW
"**He** wore old Oregon on his chest". See Prefontaine
"**He** would". See Divorce
Head. See Face play
"**Head** and body of a cock". See Basilisk/cockatrice
"A **head** or tail, which does he lack". See The hippo
Heads
The amphisbaena. M. C. Livingston.—WhDd
"As I was going out one day". Unknown.—ScA
"As I went out".—PrP
A boy's head. M. Holub.—NyT
"Charles the First walked and talked". Unknown.—OpI

Heads—*Continued*
Face play. Unknown.—OpT
    Head.—WiA
"Fame was a claim of Uncle Ed's". O. Nash.—PrFo
"From Number Nine, Penwiper Mews". E. Gorey.—LiLo
"Is your head on nice and tight". K. Dakos.—DaI
"Nicholas Ned". L. E. Richards.—DeS
"There was an old person of Dutton". E. Lear.—LiLo
What is this here. Unknown.—WiA
A **headstrong** boy. Gu Cheng, tr. by Donald Finkel.—NyT
Healing. Yannis Ritsos, tr. by Edmund Keeley.—NyT
Health fanatic. John Cooper Clarke.—AgL
"**Hear** me, four quarters of the world". Black Elk.—StP
"**Hear** the sledges with the bells". See The bells, complete
"**Hear** the sledges with the bells". From The bells. Edgar Allan Poe.—GoA
Hearing. See Sounds
"**Hearing**, hearing, hearing". See Spring poem
"**Hearken**, now the hermit bee". See The quiet enemy
Hearn, Emily
Courage.—BoT
My friend.—BoT
Hearn, Michael Patrick
Curses.—BaH
I can't go back to school.—JaP
Heart. From Damn Yankees. Jerry Ross and Richard Adler.—KnAs
"The **heart** of man has four chambers, and each is filled with". Norman Corwin.—GoT
"**Heart-sick** of his journey was the Wanderer". See The journey
Heat
"The day is hot and icky and the sun sticks to my skin". E. Greenfield.—MoS
"High noon! A hot sun". Hajime.—CaR
"John Poole left Sedalia". J. Prelutsky.—PrBe
Ode to el molcajete. G. Soto.—SoNe
Turtle in July. M. Singer.—SiT
Heath-Stubbs, John
A pearl, tr.—NyT
The pen, tr.—NyT
Heaven
"Don't steal this book, my little lad". Unknown.—ScA
    "Do not steal this book, my lad".—OpI
"En la puerta del cielo". Unknown.—DeA
    "At heaven's gate".—DeA
"I have looked". A. L. Hendricks.—LeCa
"In Heaven". S. Crane.—StP
An old Jamaican woman thinks about the hereafter. A. L. Hendricks.—LeCa
"1, 2, 3, 4, 5, 6, 7". Unknown.—ScA
A prayer to go to paradise with the donkeys. F. Jammes.—CaB
"Preacher, don't send me". M. Angelou.—AnI
"There was a fellow". Unknown.—ScA
"This train don't carry no gamblers, this train". Unknown.—StP
Heaven. Gary Soto.—SoA
"**Heavenly** Father, bless us". Unknown.—StP
"**Heaven's** in the basement". Miles Davis Landesman.—AgL
"**Heavy** footed trot o'mus". See Amphibian
"**Heavy** heavy hot". See Turtle in July

"**Heavy** on the shoulders". See The owl takes off at Upper Black Eddy, Pa
Hebrew language
"Bo elai parpar nechmad". Unknown.—YoS
"Come to me, nice butterfly".—YoS
Hebrew nursery rhymes. See Nursery rhymes—Hebrew
"**Hector** Protector was dressed all in green". Mother Goose.—SuO
Hector Velasquez. Mel Glenn.—GlBc
Hedgehogs
The tortoise and the hedgehog. R. Kipling.—WhAa
Heidbreder, Robert
"A big bare bear".—PrFo
"Here comes the witch".—BoT
Heide, Florence Parry
Absolutely nothing.—HeG
Before you fix your next peanut butter sandwich, read this.—HeG
Beware of rubber bands.—HeG
The chair.—HeG
A friendly warning.—HeG
Friends I'm going to invite to dinner (if they don't eat me first).—HeG
Grool.—HeG
Hungry Jake.—HeG
Interesting facts about monsters.—HeG
Maybe.—HeG
"The monster in my closet".—HeG
Monster mothers.—HeG
Mr. Glump.—HeG
Rocks ("Big rocks into pebbles").—DeS
The sign.—HeG
The silent type.—HeG
"Sir Samuel Squinn".—HeG
The snake ("This is a snake, perhaps you've read of it").—HeG
The snoffle.—HeG
Spinach.—HeG
What you don't know about food.—HeG
The worst thing and the best thing.—HeG
"**Heigh** ho, heigh ho, I bit the teacher's toe". Unknown.—ScA
"**Heigh** ho, heigh ho, it's off to school we go". Unknown.—ScA
Heights made him dizzy. John Ciardi.—CiH
Hejinian, Lyn
"A man comes in, his suit is crumpled", tr.—NyT
Hell
Cerberus. N. B. Taylor.—WhDd
"**Hello** and goodbye". Mary Ann Hoberman.—LiDd
"**Hello, Bill**". Unknown.—WiA
"**Hello** book". N. M. Bodecker.—LoFh
"**Hello**, hello, Bill". Unknown.—CoM
"**Hello**, hello, hello, sir". Unknown.—CoM—WiA
"**Hello**, hello, who's calling, please". Eve Merriam.—MeY
"**Hello** little sister". See A welcome song for Laini Nzinga
Help ("Any magazines"). Max Fatchen.—FaCm
Help ("Can anybody tell me, please"). Jack Prelutsky.—PrFo
Help ("Would it help"). Myra Cohn Livingston.—LiT
"**Help**, murder, police". Unknown.—CoM
Heman. Michelene Wandor.—AgL
Hemingway, Ernest
Dedicated to F.W.—KnAs
"**Hemlock** and pine". See Evergreen
Hemp, Christine E.
White on white.—JaP

Hen. William Jay Smith.—SmL
"Hen, cock, cock, cock, cock". See Cock, cock, cock, cock
Henderson, Rose
Growing old.—DeT
Hendricks, A. L.
"I have looked".—LeCa
An old Jamaican woman thinks about the hereafter.—LeCa
Hendrix, Jimi (about)
The ballad of Jimi. C. Knight.—SuC
Henie, Sonja (about)
Sonja Henie Sonnet. E. Field.—KnAs
Henri, Adrian
Love story (for Deirdre).—GoU
"Henry Small stopped talking". See The monument
The **hens**. Elizabeth Madox Roberts.—LiDd
Hensman, Savitri
The cage.—AgL
Henson, Lance
"From the mountains we come". See Warrior nation trilogy
"Great spirit". See Warrior nation trilogy
"Oh ghost that follows me". See Warrior nation trilogy
Warrior nation trilogy, complete.
"From the mountains we come".—SuI
"Great spirit".—SuI
"Oh ghost that follows me".—SuI
"Her daddy's out of work". See Nerissa
"Her eyes in sleep". Unknown, tr. by William Stanley Merwin and J. Moussaieff Masson.—GoU
"Her eyes the glowworm lend thee". See The night piece, to Julia
"Her hand in my hand". See Dunce song 6
Her hands. Ann Whitford Paul.—LiPg
"Her name is on the tip". See Liberty
"Her name was Ayo". See Ayo
"Her pinched grey body". See Supper
Her she bar. Arnold Adoff.—AdCh
Heraud, Javier
Autumn and the sea, tr. by Naomi Lindstrom.—NyT
Herbert, George
"Teach me, my God and King".—StP
"Thou that hast given so much to me".—StP
Herbs
Gift ("This is mint and here are three pinks"). H. Conkling.—LiPm
The legend of Rosemary. J. Yolen.—YoHa
A sprig of rosemary. A. Lowell.—GoU
The tarragon vinegar song. M. Mahy.—MaN
Herby Wall. Mel Glenn.—GlBc
"Here am I". See Please to remember
"Here am I". Mother Goose.—WaM
"Here are crocuses, white, gold, grey". See O dear me
"Here are grandma's spectacles". See Grandma's spectacles
"Here are mother's knives and forks". Unknown.—CoE
"Here come real stars to fill the upper skies". See Fireflies in the garden
"Here come tiger down the track". See Subway
"Here comes a bunny". See Song of summer
"Here comes teacher, and she is yellin'". Unknown.—ScA
"Here comes teacher with a great big stick". Unknown.—ScA
Here comes the band. William Cole.—DeS
"Here comes the bride". Unknown.—ScA—WiA

"Here comes the cow". See The cow's moo
"Here comes the witch". Robert Heidbreder.—BoT
"Here I stand all fat and chunky". Unknown.—ScA
"Here, in Malibu Beach". See Morning at Malibu
"Here in this library". See Kumar Ragnath
"Here is a list". See Sweets
"Here is a sea-legged sailor". See The picture
"Here is daddy's hayrake". Unknown.—WiA
"Here is not good enough". See Father and son
"Here is the beehive, where are the bees". Unknown.—WiA
The beehive.—CoE
"Here is the church". Unknown.—CoE
"Here is the tree full of light". See Winter forest on Market Street
"Here let's jump rope together, here". See Picnic to the earth
"Here lies". Unknown.—BaH
"Here lies the body of our Anna". Unknown.—BaH
Here, puss. Max Fatchen.—FaCm
Here she is. Mary Britton Miller.—HoT
"Here stands a fist". Unknown.—OpI
Here today. Walter De La Mare.—DeR
"Here today and gone tomorrow". See Here today
"Here we are, back again". See Beginning of term
"Here we come a-wassailing". Unknown.—YoHa
"Here we go round the mulberry bush". Mother Goose.—EdGl—SuO—WaM
"Here's a clean year". See A New Year
"Here's a cup". Unknown.—CoE
"Here's a curmudgeon". See Who's here
"Here's a picture". See Long ago days
"Here's a riddle". Myra Cohn Livingston.—LiMh
"Here's all the fun of the fair, come buy". See All the fun (for a picture)
"Here's good bread and cheese and porter". From Dinner table rhymes. Unknown.—OpT
"Here's Scrawny toolin along". See How it was
"Here's Sulky Sue". Mother Goose.—WaM
"Here's to July". See To July
"Here's to thee, old apple tree". Mother Goose.—WaM
"Here's what we think of, Gov and I". See My dog
"Here's your fortune, here's your fame". Unknown.—CoM
Herford, Oliver
The dog (as seen by the cat).—ElW
The gnat and the gnu.—LiLo
"I heard a bird sing".—DeS
A kitten's thought.—ElW
"Once a grasshoppper (food being scant)".—LiLo
A personal experience.—LiLo
The provident puffin.—LiLo
"Said the condor, in tones of despair".—LiLo
"Said the crab, 'tis not beauty or birth".—LiLo
The unfortunate giraffe.—LiLo
Heritage
Africa. A. Oyewole.—SlM
Ancestry. A. Bryan.—BrS
And after. J. Yolen.—YoDd
Antelope ("A girl with legs like an antelope"). K. Shiraishi.—AgL
Aunt Sue's stories. L. Hughes.—SlM
Brothers ("We're related, you and I"). L. Hughes.—SlM
Carol of the brown king. L. Hughes.—GoA
Casey's daughter at the bat. A. Graham.—KnAs
Chihuahua. B. MacLoughland.—LiDp
Concord hymn. R. W. Emerson.—ElW
The digger wasp. P. Fleischman.—FlJ
Direction. A. Lopez.—AgL
Dreamers and flyers. J. LaBombard.—JaM

Heritage—*Continued*
 Drums of my father. S. Daniels.—BoT
 The ghost dance, August, 1976. D. Jauss.—JaM
 Haiku ("I have looked into"). S. Sanchez.—SlM
 Houses. M. B. Miller.—DeS
 "I am asking you to come back home". J.
  Carson.—CaS
 "I want to know when you get to be from a
  place". J. Carson.—CaS
 "The Indians". R. Sosa.—NyT
 Ka 'Ba. I. A. Baraka.—SuC
 A kinsman. J. W. Miller.—JaM
 Kwanzaa is. C. McClester.—SlM
 Lineage. M. Walker.—LiPg
 The little creature. W. De La Mare.—DeR
 Martine Provencal. M. Glenn.—GlBc
 The mask. D. K. Hru.—SlM
 Mek drum talk, man, for Caribbean
  Independence. J. Berry.—BeW
 Mother to son. L. Hughes.—DeT—SlM—SuC
 Mum Dad and me. J. Berry.—BeW
 "My father died a month ago". Mother Goose.—
  WaM
 "My moccasins have not walked". D. Redbird.—
  BoT
 My people. L. Hughes.—SlM
 Nationhood. U. E. Perkins.—SlM
 The negro speaks of rivers. L. Hughes.—SuC
 "No labor-saving machine". W. Whitman.—HoVo
 A pearl. F. Abu Khalid.—NyT
 People of gleaming cities, and of the lion's and
  the leopard's brood. S. Bourke.—SuC
 Prince Rama comes to Longsight. J. Cunliffe.—
  FoLe
 "Pumpkin neba bear watermelan". Unknown.—
  LeCa
 The rhythm of the tomtom. A. Jacinto.—NyT
 A song of greatness. Unknown.—SuI
 The statue. A. Grilikhes.—MoR
 Strong men. S. A. Brown.—SuC
 Sugarfields. B. Mahone.—LiPm
 "There are times when I can't move". R.
  Juarroz.—NyT
 They stooped over and came out. Unknown.—
  GoT
 They were my people. G. Nichols.—NiCo
 Tradition. E. Greenfield.—GrU
 Warren Christopher. M. Glenn.—GlBc
 "We shall overcome". Z. Horton, and F.
  Hamilton.—LoFh
 What color is black. B. Mahone.—SlM
 What is Africa to me. From Heritage. C.
  Cullen.—SuC
 Where mountain lion lay down with deer. L. M.
  Silko.—SuI
 "Who are you, a dirty old man". Mother
  Goose.—OpI—WaM
 "Who can be born black". M. Evans.—SlM
Heritage, sels. Countee Cullen
 What is Africa to me.—SuC
Hermits
 Black dog, red dog. S. Dobyns.—JaPr
 Remodeling the hermit's cabin. F. Chappell.—
  JaM
Heroes and heroines. See also names of heroes, as
  Washington, George
 Ailey, Baldwin, Floyd, Killens, and Mayfield. M.
  Angelou.—AnI
 "All hail, thou truly noble chief". From To
  Cinque. J. M. Whitfield.—SuC
 Babe and Lou. F. Douskey.—KnAs
 Babe Ruth. D. Runyon.—KnAs

 Ballad of John Henry. U. E. Perkins.—SlM
 Barbara Frietchie. J. G. Whittier.—ElW
 Black hair. G. Soto.—SoA
 Captain Molly. W. Collins.—SuI
 Casey at the bat. E. L. Thayer.—ElW—MoA
 Casey Jones. Unknown.—MoR
 Checking out me history. J. Agard.—AgL
 Exercise in preparation for a pindaric ode to Carl
  Hubbell. D. Schwartz.—KnAs
 Hammerin' Hank. D. R. Martin.—MoA
 Harriet Tubman. E. Greenfield.—SlM
 Jabberwocky. From Through the looking glass. L.
  Carroll.—ElW
 Jackie Robinson. L. Clifton.—KnAs—MoA
 Jody Walker, the first voice. P. Ruffin.—JaPr
 "Joshua fit the battle of Jericho, Jericho".
  Unknown.—StP
 The kid. K. Bezner.—KnAs
 "The kite that braved old Orchard Beach". X. J.
  Kennedy.—KeK
 Martin Luther King, Jr. U. E. Perkins.—SlM
 Paul Bunyan. A. S. Bourinot.—BoT
 Paul Revere's ride. H. W. Longfellow.—ElW—SuI
 The prince. W. De La Mare.—DeR
 Soccer at the Meadowlands. D. Ackerman.—KnAs
 The song of Mr. Toad. From The wind in the
  willows. K. Grahame.—CoAz
 Unitas. E. Gold.—KnAs
 "Would you hear of an old-time sea fight". W.
  Whitman.—SuI
Heroism. See Courage; Heroes and heroines
Heron. Valerie Worth.—WoAl
Herons
 Blue herons. J. P. Lewis.—LeE
 First green heron. G. Margolis.—KnAs
 Great blue heron. J. Yolen.—YoBi
 Heron. V. Worth.—WoAl
 Night heron. F. Frost.—CaB
 Ravens. Unknown.—DeI
 Same and different. Unknown.—DeI
"The herons on the snow". See Same and different
Herrick, Robert
 "May all who share".—StP
 The night piece, to Julia.—ElW
 To daffodils.—ElW
 To the virgins, to make much of time.—ElW
"The herring loves the merry moonlight". From
  Fishermen's songs. Unknown.—OpT
"He's a lionhearted man". See Mr. Zoo
"He's brown as water". See Ode to mi perrito
"He's decked out in white and green". See Cousins
"He's got the little boy blues". See Little boy blues
"He's no Apollo Belvedere". See Babe Ruth
"He's smarter than the tabby". See The lion
"He's white". See Ode to mi gato
Hewison, R.J.P.
 "A scientist living at Staines".—LiLo
Hewitt, Geof
 Eagle rock.—JaPr
"Hey black child". Useni Eugene Perkins.—SlM
Hey, bug. Lilian Moore.—MoS
"Hey, bug, stay". See Hey, bug
"Hey diddle diddle, the cat and the fiddle". Mother
  Goose.—EdGl—SuO—WaM
Hey diddle doubt. Mother Goose.—ClI
"Hey diddle doubt, my candle's out". See Hey
  diddle doubt
"Hey ding a ding". See The silly song
"Hey ho, nobody home". Mother Goose.—WaM
"Hey, it's gonna be all right". See Gardner Todd
"Hey man, after first period, I'm history". See
  Andrea Pulovsky

"Hey, this little kid gets roller skates". See 74th street
"Hey, tuna fish, you know, I wish". See To a tuna
Hey world, here I am. Jean Little.—LiHe
Heynen, Jim
　One for one.—JaPr
Heywood, Thomas
　Good morrow.—ElW
Hi. Walter De La Mare.—DeR
"Hi, handsome hunting man". See Hi
"Hi kid, says lavender". See Valentine hearts
"Hi-tiddley-i-ti, brown bread". Unknown.—OpI
Hibernation
　Grandpa bear's lullaby. J. Yolen.—DeS—HoS—MoS
　March bear. M. Singer.—SiT
　Timber rattlesnake. M. Singer.—SiT
"Hiccup, hiccup". See Happy hiccup to you
"Hiccup, hiccup, go away". Mother Goose.—WaM
"Hiccup, snickup". Unknown.—ScA—WiA
Hiccups
　Happy hiccup to you. K. Dakos.—DaI
　"Hiccup, hiccup, go away". Mother Goose.—WaM
　"Hiccup, snickup". Unknown.—ScA—WiA
　"Hik sprik, sprouw". Unknown.—YoS
　　"Hikkup-ikkup sprew".—YoS
"Hickety pickety, my black hen". Mother Goose.—SuO—WaM
"Hickory dickory dock". Mother Goose.—EdGl—SuO—WaM
"Hickory dickory dock". Unknown.—WiA
"Hidden away". See Mouseways
Hide and seek. Walter De La Mare.—DeR—MaP
"Hide and seek, says the wind". See Hide and seek
"Hide of a leopard and hide of a deer". See The giraffe
Hideout. Aileen Fisher.—DeT
Hiding
　Closet. M. C. Livingston.—LiNe
　I never told. M. C. Livingston.—LiNe
Hiding our love. Carolyn Kizer.—GoU
"Hie to the market, Jenny come trot". Mother Goose.—WaM
　A wasted journey.—OpT
Higgins, Frank
　Tennis in the city.—KnAs
"Higgledy-Piggledy keeps his room tidy". Myra Cohn Livingston.—PrFo
"Higglety, pigglety, pop". Samuel Goodrich.—ClI—ScA (unat.)—SuO (unat.)
High. Walter De La Mare.—DeR
High flight. See "Oh, I have slipped the surly bonds of earth"
"The high fly ball". See October
"High in the flowering catalpa trees". See Fox and crow
"High noon! A hot sun". Hajime, tr. by Sylvia Cassedy and Kunihiro Suetake.—CaR
"High on a banyan tree in a row". See Monkey
"High on the tree one apple alone". See Hanging
High school. George Roberts.—JaPr
High stick. Billy Collins.—KnAs
"High up on the ceiling". See U is for up
"High upon Highlands". See Bonny George Campbell
"Higher than a house". Mother Goose.—WaM
Highways. See Roads and streets
"El hijo del conde". Unknown.—DeA
　The count's son ("The son of the count").—DeA
"Hik sprik, sprouw". Unknown.—YoS
　"Hikkup-ikkup sprew".—YoS

The hiker. Eve Merriam.—MeCh
Hiking. See Camping and hiking
"Hiking in the Scythian hills". See Sir John Mandeville's report on the griffin
"Hikkup-ikkup sprew". See "Hik sprik, sprouw"
Hikmet, Nazim
　The cucumber, tr. by Randy Blasing and Mutlu Konuk.—NyT
Hilberry, Conrad
　Instruction.—KnAs—MoA
The hill. Eve Merriam.—MeS
"Hill is my pillow, I have my own bed". From Riddle poems. James Berry.—BeW
Hillert, Margaret
　A Christmas lullaby.—PlW
　Hanukkah candles.—HoS
　Lullaby ("Near and far, near and far").—HoSt
　Puzzled.—JaP
Hillman, Brenda
　Ophelia.—JaM
Hills. See Mountains
Hillyer, Robert
　"The fireflies wink and glow".—GoT
　Lullaby ("The long canoe").—SuI
　Nocturne ("If the deep wood is haunted, it is I").—GoU
　The wind is from the north.—GoT
Hinduism
　Dipa, the lamp. A. Bonner.—FoLe
　Divali ("Ravana's gone"). J. Nicholls.—FoLe
　Divali ("Winter stalks us"). D. Harmer.—FoLe
　Prince Rama comes to Longsight. J. Cunliffe.—FoLe
Hines, Debra
　If our dogs outlived us.—JaM
"Hinty, minty, cuty, corn". See "Intery, mintery, cutery, corn"
"Hinx, minx, the old witch winks". Unknown.—OpI
"Hippety hop, goes the kangaroo". See Up the hill
"Hippity hop to the barber shop". Mother Goose.—CoM—WaM—WiA
The hippo. Theodore Roethke.—HoT
"A hippo sandwich is easy to make". See Recipe for a hippopotamus sandwich
The hippocamp. Arnold Sundgaard.—WhDd
The hippogriff. Arnold Sundgaard.—WhDd
The hippopot. J. Patrick Lewis.—LeT See The hippopot
Hippopotami
　Amphibian. E. Merriam.—MeCh
　"Beneath a blue umbrella". J. Prelutsky.—PrBe
　Habits of the hippopotamus. A. Guiterman.—PrFo
　The hippo. T. Roethke.—HoT
　The hippopot. J. P. Lewis.—LeT
　Hippopotamus. W. J. Smith.—SmL
　A hippopotamusn't. J. P. Lewis.—LeA
　"One little hippo brought a blanket". J. Knight.—KnT
　Recipe for a hippopotamus sandwich. S. Silverstein.—PrFo
　"What fun to be". M. Flanders.—WhAa
Hippopotamus. William Jay Smith.—SmL
"The hippopotamus, hippo for short". See Hippopotamus
"The hippopotamus is strong". See Habits of the hippopotamus
A hippopotamusn't. J. Patrick Lewis.—LeA
"A hippopotamusn't sit". See A hippopotamusn't
The Hirdy Dirdy. Unknown.—OpT
"The Hirdy Dirdy cam' hame frae the hill, hungry, hungry". See The Hirdy Dirdy

Hirsch, Edward
Fast break.—KnAs
Hirsch, Thomas L.
A history of golf, sort of.—KnAs
Hirschfield, Jane
"Although the wind", tr.—GoT
"Although there is", tr.—GoT
"The cicadas sing", tr.—GoT
"Night deepens", tr.—GoT
On New Year's Day, watching it snow, tr.—GoT
"Twilight", tr.—GoT
"Watching the moon", tr.—GoT
"The way I must enter", tr.—GoT
"**His** angle-rod made of a sturdy oak". See An Indian giant's fishing tackle
"**His** brow is seamed with line and scar". See The portrait of a warrior
His girlfriend. Myra Cohn Livingston.—LiT
"**His** head is so white it shines". See Cleaned the crocodile's teeth
"**His** headstone said". See The funeral of Martin Luther King, Jr.
"**His** lips look like cherries". See Maisie's lament
His mother's wedding ring. George Crabbe.—GoU
"**His** nose is short and scrubby". See My dog
His running, my running. Robert Francis.—KnAs
"**His** swift". See Woodpecker
"**His** tan and golden self". See Known to Eve and me
An **historic** moment. William J. Harris.—HoGo
History. See also Explorers and exploration; Frontier and pioneer life; also names of countries, as United States—History
Baseball canto. L. Ferlinghetti.—KnAs
Checking out me history. J. Agard.—AgL
Garrett Chandler. M. Glenn.—GlBc
Greenland's history, or the history of the Danes on Greenland. S. Holm.—NyT
History. P. B. Janeczko.—JaB
The little shop (for a picture). W. De La Mare.—DeR
Playing dirty. M. Fatchen.—FaCm
Those who do not study history are doomed. A. Adoff.—AdCh
Waitangi Day. D. Bateson.—FoLe
History. Paul B. Janeczko.—JaB
A **history** of golf, sort of. Thomas L. Hirsch.—KnAs
"**Hit**". See Insanity
Hitchhiker. David McCord.—LiIf
Hitchhiking with a friend and a book that explains the Pacific Ocean. Gary Soto.—SoA
"**Hithery**, hethery, I love best". See The four brothers
Hits and runs. Carl Sandburg.—KnAs
Hitting. Unknown.—MoA
"**Ho**, ho, ho, ho". See Caw
Ho-o
Finches, tr. by Tze-si Huang.—DeI
Ho hum. John Ciardi.—CiH
Hoban, Russell
Esme on her brother's bicycle.—JaP
Old Man Ocean.—KeT—LiDd
The sea gull's eye.—JaP
Summer goes.—LoFh
Hobbies
Aquarium. V. Worth.—WoAl
The baseball card dealer. R. L. Harrison.—MoA
"A certain young fellow, named Bobbie". Unknown.—LiLo
Collecting things. X. J. Kennedy.—KeK
My brother Bert. T. Hughes.—ElW
My great grand uncle. T. Ray.—NyT

The pancake collector. J. Prelutsky.—PrFo
"Who to trade stamps with". X. J. Kennedy.—KeK
The workshop. A. Fisher.—FiA
Hobbits. See Fairies
Hoberman, Mary Ann
Agatha, Agatha.—HoFa
Big sister.—HoFa
Brother.—DeS—DeT—MoS—PrFo
"Cousins are cozy".—HoFa
Dinnertime.—HoFa
"Eat it, it's good for you".—HoFa
Fireflies ("Fireflies at twilight").—DeS
"The folk who live in Backward town".—DeS
Four generations.—HoFa
Foxes ("A litter of little black foxes, and later").—DeS
Giraffes ("Giraffes, I like them").—WhAa
Grandmas and grandpas.—HoFa
Half-whole-step.—HoFa
"Hello and goodbye".—LiDd
"How far".—LiDd
Let's dress up.—KeT
The little sister store.—HoFa
Meg's egg.—MoS
Miss McGillicuddy.—HoFa
Mosquito ("O Mrs. Mosquito, quit biting me, please").—PrFo
My baby brother.—HoFa
My big brothers.—HoFa
My father.—HoFa
My uncle.—HoFa
Neighbors.—LoFh
New jacket.—HoFa
"Nuts to you and nuts to me".—PrFo
An only child.—HoFa
"Our family comes from 'round the world".—HoFa
Pick up your room.—HoFa
Relatives.—HoFa
Rhinoceros ("I often wonder whether").—WhAa
Shy.—HoFa
Sick days.—HoFa
Sometimes.—HoFa
Vacation.—HoFa—LoFh
"What is a family".—HoFa
"When Annie was adopted".—HoFa
When I grow up.—HoFa
Whenever.—MoS
Hockey
High stick. B. Collins.—KnAs
Hockey. S. Blaine.—KnAs
"There's this that I like about hockey, my lad". J. Kieran.—KnAs
Hockey. Scott Blaine.—KnAs
Hoddley, poddley. Mother Goose.—ClI
"**Hoddley,** poddley, puddle and frogs". See Hoddley, poddley
Hodgson, Ralph
The ousel cock.—ElW
Hoffman, David
The finish.—KnAs
Hofmannsthal, Hugo von
Twilight of the outward life, tr. by Peter Viereck.—GoT
Hogg, James
A boy's song.—ElW
Hogs. See Pigs
"**Hold** fast to dreams". See Dreams
Holden, Jonathan
How to play night baseball.—MoA
Jim.—JaPr

Holden, Jonathan—*Continued*
A war baby looks back.—JaPr
Holder, Julie
"The alien".—PrFo
Chester's undoing.—PrFo
Scary things.—BaH
Holes
At the sea side. R. L. Stevenson.—KeT—LiDd
Digging for China. R. Wilbur.—SuI
Holes. T. Wynne-Jones.—BoT
Holes. Tim Wynne-Jones.—BoT
"**Holes** are shy and dull and round". See Holes
Holi. Irene Rawnsley.—FoLe
Holidays. See also names of holidays, as Christmas
All fool's day. J. Agard.—FoLe
April 1st. A. Bonner.—FoLe
August outing. T. Harvey.—FoLe
Carnival in Rio. J. Kirkup.—FoLe
Cheung Chau festival. J. Kenward.—FoLe
Ching ming. I. Rawnsley.—FoLe
Corroboree ("The clap, clap, clap of the clapsticks beat"). M. Fatchen.—FoLe
Corroboree ("Hot day dies, cook time comes"). K. Walker.—FoLe
Distributing the harvest. B. Moses.—FoLe
Divali ("Ravana's gone"). J. Nicholls.—FoLe
Divali ("Winter stalks us"). D. Harmer.—FoLe
The doll festival. J. Kirkup.—FoLe
Doll funerals. J. Kirkup.—FoLe
Festival. J. Kitching.—FoLe
Fishing festival. J. Kenward.—FoLe
Holi. I. Rawnsley.—FoLe
Holidays (for a picture). W. De La Mare.—DeR
"I often pause and wonder". Unknown.—PrP
Idh al-fitr. P. Gross.—FoLe
Idh Mubarak. B. Doherty.—FoLe
Jouvert morning. D. Calder.—FoLe
King of the band. A. Johnson.—FoLe
Kwanzaa is. C. McClester.—SlM
Light the festival candles. A. Fisher.—FoLe
Mardi Gras. J. Kenward.—FoLe
May day ("Oak and ivy, sycamore, ash, what shall we leave by the cottage door"). J. Nicholls.—FoLe
May day ("Twirl your ribbons"). J. Kenward.—FoLe
Mela. J. Kenward.—FoLe
My dad said. M. Wiley, and I. McMillan.—FoLe
Night of the full moon. D. Batson.—FoLe
Nyepi, the day of yellow rice. T. Millum.—FoLe
Oak apple day. R. Wilson.—FoLe
Ode to la pinata. G. Soto.—SoNe
On midsummer's eve. A. Bonner.—FoLe
On Mother's day. A. Fisher.—FiA—FoLe
Once upon a great holiday. A. Wilkinson.—FoLe
Prince Rama comes to Longsight. J. Cunliffe.—FoLe
"Ramadan". S. Cook.—FoLe
Ramadan. S. Cook.—FoLe
Remember. D. Ward.—FoLe
Remembrance Day ("Poppies, oh, miss"). J. Nicholls.—FoLe
Shrove Tuesday. A. Bonner.—FoLe
"St. Thomas's Day is past and gone". Mother Goose.—WaM
To pumpkins at pumpkin time. G. Tall.—BaH
Tree festival. D. Bateson.—FoLe
The visitors. B. Wade.—FoLe
Waitangi Day. D. Bateson.—FoLe
Holidays (for a picture). Walter De La Mare.—DeR
Hollander, John
What all the owls know.—LiIf

Hollingsworth-Barkley, Joyce
Old Mag.—JaPr
Hollo, Anselm
Bicycles, tr.—NyT
Holloway, Geoffrey
Please to remember ("He comes to see us every year").—FoLe
The **holly**. Walter De La Mare.—DeR
"The **holly** and the ivy". Unknown.—YoHa
"**Holly** dark, pale mistletoe". See Nowel
Holly trees
The holly. W. De La Mare.—DeR
"The holly and the ivy". Unknown.—YoHa
Hollyhocks. Valerie Worth.—WoAl
"**Hollyhocks** stand in clumps". See Hollyhocks
Holm, Sven
Greenland's history, or the history of the Danes on Greenland, tr. by Paula Hostrup-Jessen.—NyT
Holman, Felice
Humming bird.—JaP
My dog ("Here's what we think of, Gov and I").—LiDp
Night sounds.—HoSt—LaN
One, two, three, four m-o-t-h-e-r.—LiPm
The poem that got away.—JaP
Sails, gulls, sky, sea.—BaW
Holmes, John
Boy reading.—SuI
Metaphor for my son.—SuI
Portrait, my wife.—GoU
"When I married, I caught up".—SuI
Holmes, Oliver Wendell
The deacon's masterpiece, or, the wonderful one-hoss shay.—ElW
Holmes, R. Ernest
Black lady in an afro hairdo cheers for Cassius.—KnAs
Holub, Miroslav
A boy's head, tr. by Ian Milner.—NyT
Napoleon, tr. by Kaca Polackova.—NyT
The teacher.—AgL
"Holy, holy, holy Lord, God of power and might". Unknown.—StP
Home ("Between the sunset and the eucalyptus tree"). Nasima Aziz.—NyT
Home ("Yelling, shouting, arguing"). Myra Cohn Livingston.—LiT
Home and family life
Aaron. A. Adoff.—AdIn
The admiration of Willie. G. Brooks.—PlW
After the last hard freeze in early spring weather. A. Adoff.—AdIn
An appointment. C. Shiang-hua.—NyT
Are you in there. M. Fatchen.—FaCm
Around my room. W. J. Smith.—KeT—LiDd—SmL
August outing. T. Harvey.—FoLe
Back yard. V. Worth.—DeT—WoAl
Bingo. P. B. Janeczko.—JaB—JaP
The birthday of Buddha. J. Kirkup.—FoLe
Breath pon wind. J. Berry.—BeW
Brother. M. A. Hoberman.—DeS—DeT—MoS—PrFo
But why not. M. Fatchen.—FaCm
By the shores of Pago Pago. E. Merriam.—MeCh
The cat sat asleep. Mother Goose.—ClI
   "The cat asleep by the side of the fire".—WaM
Childhood. J. Joubert.—NyT
Chore boy. J. Thomas.—LiPm
Christmas dinner. V. Worth.—WoA

Home and family life—*Continued*

Circles ("I am speaking of circles"). M. C. Livingston.—JaP—LiT

Closet. M. C. Livingston.—LiNe

Cogs and gears and wheels and springs. J. Sweeney.—MoS

Coleridge Jackson. M. Angelou.—AnI

"Come times sometimes". J. Carson.—CaS

"Creating God, your fingers trace". J. Rowthorn.—StP

"Crosspatch". Mother Goose.—WaM

Daddy is tall, has shoulders, strong hands. A. Adoff.—AdIn

Daddy's gone. D. Chandra.—LiPf

"Dancing teepees". C. O'John.—SnD

Dawn Weinberg. M. Glenn.—GlBc

Deidre Spector. M. Glenn.—GlBc

Different dads. X. J. Kennedy.—KeK—LiPf

Dinnertime. M. A. Hoberman.—HoFa

Divorce. T. Ditlevsen.—AgL

Doll. M. C. Livingston.—KeT

"Down by the ocean, down by the sea". Unknown.—ScA

Eating bread. G. Soto.—SoA

Enchantment. J. Ryder.—JaP

"Every family has its deformity". From Jamaican Caribbean proverbs. Unknown.—BeW

Every so often. J. Little.—LiHe

Excuse. M. C. Livingston.—LiT

Fambly time. E. Greenfield.—GrN

Family. M. C. Livingston.—LiT

Family portrait. E. Budianta.—NyT

Father's story. E. M. Roberts.—SuI

February 14. M. C. Livingston.—LiT

The first flakes are falling on our heads. A. Adoff.—AdIn

First job. J. Daniels.—JaPr

Forgotten. C. Rylant.—JaP

Frankie Dempster. M. Glenn.—GlBc

Garage apartment. M. C. Livingston.—LiT

Good night ("Father puts the paper down"). A. Fisher.—PlW

Good times. L. Clifton.—ElW

Hanging fire. A. Lorde.—AgL

Help ("Would it help"). M. C. Livingston.—LiT

His girlfriend. M. C. Livingston.—LiT

Home ("Between the sunset and the eucalyptus tree"). N. Aziz.—NyT

Home ("Yelling, shouting, arguing"). M. C. Livingston.—LiT

The home-watcher. M. Bracker.—MoA

The house on Buder Street. G. Gildner.—JaPr

Household. P. Booth.—JaPr

Howie Kell suspends all lust to contemplate the universe. R. Torreson.—JaPr

"I am the youngest, so they call". A. Adoff.—AdIn

I know that summer is the famous growing season. A. Adoff.—AdIn

I love. B. Zephaniah.—AgL

"I want a talking dog wearing a cap". From What we said sitting making fantasies. J. Berry.—BeW

"I want to know when you get to be from a place". J. Carson.—CaS

"I went to my father's garden". Unknown.—OpI

If sometimes blue. A. L. Woods.—SlM

"I'll tell my own daddy, when he comes home". Mother Goose.—WaM

An important conversation. B. S. De Regniers.—DeW

In my horror fantasy chiller. A. Adoff.—AdCh

In the kitchen. J. Joubert.—NyT

In the middle. M. C. Livingston.—LiT

Indian trail. B. Guernsey.—JaPr

Interlude. M. C. Livingston.—LiT

Invitation ("Listen, I've a big surprise"). M. C. Livingston.—KeT—LiT

Jim. J. Holden.—JaPr

Jimmy Zale. M. Glenn.—GlBc

June, mourning doves. M. C. Livingston.—LiT

Karen. E. Greenfield.—GrN

Keziah. G. Brooks.—LiDd

The king of cats sends a postcard to his wife. N. Willard.—LaCc

Kitchen table. M. C. Livingston.—LiR

Knoxville, Tennessee. N. Giovanni.—DeS—SlM

Lacey Paget. M. Glenn.—GlBc

"A lady was chasing her boy round the room". Unknown.—WiA

"A lady who lives there close to me". J. Carson.—CaS

Late afternoon. M. C. Livingston.—LiT

Late for breakfast. M. Dawson.—KeT

Late past bedtime. A. Adoff.—BaW

Leaving. A. Bryan.—BrS

Let's be merry. C. G. Rossetti.—KeT

The little bird ("My dear Daddie bought a mansion"). W. De La Mare.—DeR—MaP

Long ago days. M. C. Livingston.—LiT

Love ("Wish they'd kiss each other"). M. C. Livingston.—LiT

Love don't mean. E. Greenfield.—SlM

Lullaby ("Cat's in the alley"). J. R. Plotz.—PlW

Mama's bouquets. A. Bryan.—BrS

Mamaw and Frank. W. Burt.—JaPr

Menu. E. Merriam.—MeP

Mima. W. De La Mare.—DeR—MaP

Mom and Pop Ghastly come up for air. X. J. Kennedy.—KeGh

Mosquitoes. J. Little.—LiHe

"Mother, mother, bless my soul". X. J. Kennedy.—KeFb

Mother's nerves. X. J. Kennedy.—ElW

The mouse, the frog, and the little red hen. Unknown.—HoS

"Mr. Willowby's Christmas tree". R. Barry.—GoA

Mummy slept late and daddy fixed breakfast. J. Ciardi.—LiPf—PrFo

My brother Bert. T. Hughes.—ElW

"My brother Estes". J. Carson.—CaS

My father's leaving. I. Sadoff.—JaPr

My happiness. G. Pape.—JaM

My Jose. M. Robinson.—LiPf

My mother really knew. W. T. Lum.—JaM

"My mother works in a bakery". Unknown.—CoM

My papa's waltz. T. Roethke.—ElW

Natural high. J. B. Breeze.—AgL

Neck please. E. Glen.—LiPg

Nerissa. E. Greenfield.—GrN

Nicholas Townshed. M. Glenn.—GlBc

No one heard him call. D. Aldis.—KeT

October afternoons we walk around the house. A. Adoff.—AdIn

October Saturday. B. Katz.—JaP

Ode to fireworks. G. Soto.—SoNe

Ode to mi gato. G. Soto.—SoNe

Ode to mi parque. G. Soto.—SoNe

Ode to the Mayor. G. Soto.—SoNe

Ode to weddings. G. Soto.—SoNe

"Oh, policeman, policeman". Unknown.—ScA

An old Jamaican woman thinks about the hereafter. A. L. Hendricks.—LeCa

Home and family life—*Continued*
Old Mag. J. Hollingsworth-Barkley.—JaPr
Olive Street. M. C. Livingston.—LiT
On Mother's day. A. Fisher.—FiA—FoLe
On this, a holy night. K. Bezner.—JaPr
Once upon a great holiday. A. Wilkinson.—FoLe
One o'clock. K. Pyle.—LaCc
An only child. M. A. Hoberman.—HoFa
Others. M. C. Livingston.—LiT
"Our family comes from 'round the world". M. A. Hoberman.—HoFa
Papa is a bear. J. P. Lewis.—LiPf
Papa loves baby. S. Smith.—ElW
The parent. O. Nash.—PrFo
Part XIV: Now, dear me. From A child's day. W. De La Mare.—DeR
Part XVIII: He squats by the fire. From A child's day. W. De La Mare.—DeR
The party's over. R. Edwards.—FoLe
Pets. D. Pettiward.—CoAz
Piggy-back. L. Hughes.—KeT
Poem for my son. B. Padhi.—NyT
Poetry was like this. A. Mahmud.—NyT
Porches. V. Worth.—WoAl
The prayer of the dog. C. B. De Gasztold.—DeP
"Quick, quick". Unknown.—OpI
Recipe for Thanksgiving Day soup. D. Farmiloe.—BoT
Relationship. M. C. Livingston.—LiT
The rescue ("Rain poured down, the house"). B. J. Esbensen.—EsW
"Rowsty dowt". Mother Goose.—WaM
The runaway girl. G. Corso.—JaPr
"Sally over the water". Unknown.—WiA
The shriving. J. Carter.—JaM
Small wants. B. Padhi.—NyT
Smart remark. J. Little.—BoT—LiHe
A social mixer. X. J. Kennedy.—PrFo
Some things don't make any sense at all. J. Viorst.—DeT
Sometimes even parents win. J. Ciardi.—CiH—LiLo
Souvenir of the ancient world. C. Drummond de Andrade.—NyT
Spells. J. Yolen.—YoBe
Stories ("Circling by the fire"). J. P. Lewis.—LeT—LiDp
Summer evening. W. De La Mare.—DeR—MaP
Summer mama. A. Keiter.—JaPr
System. R. L. Stevenson.—ElW
"There was an old woman who lived in a shoe". Mother Goose.—EdGl—SuI—SuO—WaM
This evening. Z. Landau.—GoT
This house is the center. A. Adoff.—AdIn
Those winter Sundays. R. Hayden.—ElW
Timmy and Tawanda. G. Brooks.—SIM
Two week car trip. X. J. Kennedy.—KeK
Under the Sunday tree. E. Greenfield.—GrU
Vacation. M. A. Hoberman.—HoFa—LoFh
Warren Christopher. M. Glenn.—GlBc
Wars. J. Little.—LiHe
Weird. J. Viorst.—PrFo
"What is a family". M. A. Hoberman.—HoFa
"When Annie was adopted". M. A. Hoberman.—HoFa
"When I married, I caught up". J. Holmes.—SuI
"When I was a chicken". Unknown.—OpI
When mother reads aloud. Unknown.—SuI
Where would you be. K. Kuskin.—LaN
"Who are you, a dirty old man". Mother Goose.—OpI—WaM
The wholly family. E. Merriam.—MeS

"With her one string ukelele". X. J. Kennedy.—KeFb
Won't. W. De La Mare.—DeR
Working parents. J. Little.—LiHe
Wouldn't it be queer. A. Fisher.—FiH
Zip on "good advice". G. Hyland.—JaPr
Zora. J. Schell.—JaPr
Home sweet home. John Ciardi.—CiH
"**Home** to me is not a house". See Associations
The **home-watcher**. Milton Bracker.—MoA
Homelessness
A brief note to the bag lady, ma sister. Y. Eradam.—NyT
City nomad. J. Berry.—BeW
"The **homes** of our". See Houses
Homesickness
Leaving. A. Bryan.—BrS
"My brother Estes". J. Carson.—CaS
Olive Street. M. C. Livingston.—LiT
Strangers. W. De La Mare.—DeR
"The sun shines bright in the old Kentucky home". From My old Kentucky home. S. C. Foster.—SuC
Homework. Barbara Juster Esbensen.—EsW
"**Hominy**, succotash, raccoon, moose". See Where do these words come from
Homosexuality
Victor Jeffreys. M. Glenn.—GlBc
"An **honest** old man of Pennang". See A man of Pennang
Honesty. See Truthfulness and falsehood
Honey. See also Bees
The honey robbers. W. De La Mare.—DeR—MaP
Honeycomb. V. Worth.—WoAl
"**Honey** hued beauty, you are". See Black lady in an afro hairdo cheers for Cassius
The **honey** robbers. Walter De La Mare.—DeR—MaP
Honeybees. Paul Fleischman.—FlJ
Honeycomb. Valerie Worth.—WoAl
Honeycomb days. J. Patrick Lewis.—LeE
Hong Ryou, Kyongjoo
Jasmine.—NyT
Hongo, Garrett Kaoru
The Hongo Store, 29 miles volcano, Hilo, Hawaii.—JaM
Stay with me.—JaPr
The **Hongo** Store, 29 miles volcano, Hilo, Hawaii. Garrett Kaoru Hongo.—JaM
Hood, Thomas
The song of the shirt, sels.
"Work, work, work".—MoR
"Work, work, work". See The song of the shirt
Hoods. Paul B. Janeczko.—JaB
Hook. Floyd Skloot.—KnAs
"A **hook** shot kisses the rim and". See Fast break
Hoolie bird. William Jay Smith.—SmL
"The **hoolie** bird now is almost extinct". See Hoolie bird
"**Hoorah**, hooray". See Tomorrow
"**Hooting** howling hissing witches". See Halloween
"**Hop** on one foot". Eve Merriam.—MeY
Hope
Ailey, Baldwin, Floyd, Killens, and Mayfield. M. Angelou.—AnI
At the beach ("The waves are erasing the footprints"). K. Ozer.—NyT
"Bobby Shaftoe's gone to sea". Mother Goose.—SuO
Dragon ("Oh, tongue, give sound to joy and sing"). A. McCaffrey.—WhDd

Hope—*Continued*

The dream ("If everyone has the same dream"). S. Kellogg.—SaB

Dreams. L. Hughes.—LoFh—SlM

For my people. M. Walker.—SuC

Heart. From Damn Yankees. J. Ross, and R. Adler.—KnAs

Hope. L. Hughes.—SlM

The hopeful trout, poor fish. J. Ciardi.—CiH

"Hoping is knowing that there is love". Unknown.—StP

How can I lose hope. From Sing a softblack poem. Kwelismith.—SuC

I dream'd in a dream. W. Whitman.—HoVo

"I heard a bird sing". O. Herford.—DeS

Kristin Leibowitz. M. Glenn.—GlBc

Kwang Chin Ho. M. Glenn.—GlBc

"A leaf for hand in hand". W. Whitman.—HoVo

A little girl's poem. G. Brooks.—JaP

Mother to son. L. Hughes.—DeT—SlM—SuC

My life story. L. Nguyen.—NyT

October ("The high fly ball"). H. J. Dawson.—MoA

Poor Miss ("Lone and alone she lies"). W. De La Mare.—DeR—MaP

The prayer of the dove. C. B. De Gasztold.—DeP

Remembrance Day ("To some"). J. Kitching.—FoLe

"Say not the struggle nought availeth". A. H. Clough.—ElW

Summertime and the living. R. Hayden.—SuC

Sun is shining. B. Marley.—AgL

Surprise ("I feel like the ground in winter"). J. Little.—LiHe

Televised. M. Angelou.—AnI

A warbler. W. De La Mare.—DeR

Hope. Langston Hughes.—SlM

The hopeful trout, poor fish. John Ciardi.—CiH

Hopi Indians. See Indians of the Americas—Hopi

"Hoping is knowing that there is love". Unknown.—StP

Hopkins, Gerard Manley

"Bad I am, but yet thy child".—StP

"Glory be to God for dappled things".—StP

Inversnaid.—MoR

The windhover.—CaB

Hopkins, John Henry, Jr.

"We three kings of Orient are".—YoHa (unat.)

Hopkins, Lee Bennett

Counting.—HoS

Girls can, too.—SlM

"Good books, good times".—HoGo

Munching peaches.—HoS

Seal at the zoo.—HoT

This tooth.—KeT

To the zoo.—HoT—SlM

The horn. Walter De La Mare.—DeR

"The horn on our pickup truck stayed stuck". X. J. Kennedy.—KeGh

Horn-rimmed hen. William Jay Smith.—SmL

"The horn-rimmed hen". See Horn-rimmed hen

Horne, Frank

"Dig your starting holes deep". See To James

To James, sels.

"Dig your starting holes deep".—SuC

Hornets. See Wasps

Horovitz, Michael

Enlightenment.—AgL

Horse. Valerie Worth.—WoAl

"A horse and a flea and three blind mice". Unknown.—CoM—WiA

Whoops.—CII

Horse by moonlight. Alberto Blanco, tr. by Jennifer Clement.—NyT

"A horse escaped from the circus". See Horse by moonlight

"The horse in the field". See Shadows

Horseback. Carolyn Kizer.—KnAs

The horseman ("I heard a horseman"). Walter De La Mare.—DeR—MaP

The horseman ("There was a horseman rode so fast"). Walter De La Mare.—DeR—MaP

Horses. See also Rides and riding—Horse

Bronco busting, event #1. M. Swenson.—KnAs—MoR

Crunchy. M. Fatchen.—FaCm

The four horses. J. Reeves.—KeT

"Galloping pony". Kyorai.—CaR—WhAa

A gift horse. A. Hashmi.—NyT

"A gigantic beauty of a stallion, fresh and responsive to my caresses". From Song of myself. W. Whitman.—SuI

Stallion.—KnAs

Great Aso. T. Miyoshi.—NyT

"Harriet, by magic force". E. Merriam.—MeY

The hippocamp. A. Sundgaard.—WhDd

Horse. V. Worth.—WoAl

"A horse and a flea and three blind mice". Unknown.—CoM—WiA

Whoops.—CII

Horse by moonlight. A. Blanco.—NyT

Horses ("Back and forth"). A. Fisher.—FiA

Horses ("The huntsman rides a black horse"). Unknown.—OpT

The horses ("It has turned to snow in the night"). M. Kumin.—JaP

"I am the Turquoise Woman's son". Unknown.—StP

"I had a little colt". Unknown.—WiA

"I will not change my horse with any that treads". From King Henry V. W. Shakespeare.—WhAa

In the mist. Seisensui.—DeI

Innocence. Issa.—DeI

Keeping the horses. R. Scheele.—JaM

The meadow-bout fields. Unknown.—OpT

Morning horses. Basho.—DeI

Mother horse. Issa.—DeI

A mother.—DeS

"Oh, I had a horse, his name was Bill". Unknown.—ScA

An old grey horse. Unknown.—CII

Pegasus. E. Farjeon.—WhDd

The pit ponies. L. Norris.—NyT

Raw carrots. V. Worth.—WoAl

Reverie. W. De La Mare.—DeR

The runaway. R. Frost.—ElW

"See, see, what shall I see". Mother Goose.—WaM

"Shoe a little horse". Mother Goose.—WaM

"There was a story about my daddy's daddy". J. Carson.—CaS

Tiny Tony and his pony. C. West.—PrFo

"Under this sod lies a great bucking horse". Unknown.—ScA

Watering trough. M. Kumin.—JaP

Horses ("Back and forth"). Aileen Fisher.—FiA

Horses ("The huntsman rides a black horse"). Unknown.—OpT

The horses ("It has turned to snow in the night"). Maxine Kumin.—JaP

"Horses are standing in rain". See Great Aso

"Horses in front of me". See Merry-go-round

Horton, Zilphia, and Hamilton, Frank

"We shall overcome".—LoFh

Houses and dwellings—*Continued*
"There was an old woman who lived in a shoe".
Mother Goose.—EdGl—SuI—SuO—WaM
This house is the center. A. Adoff.—AdIn
"This is the house that Jack built". Mother
Goose.—SuO
The house that Jack built.—HoS
Thorny. W. Cole.—CoAz
Tree house. S. Silverstein.—DeS
Wanted. R. Fyleman.—LaM
Where ("Houses, houses, oh, I know"). W. De La
Mare.—DeR
"You live in de cement house, and no worry de
hurricane". Unknown.—LeCa
"**Houses**, houses, oh, I know". See Where
"**Houses** veil". See Twelfth night
Housman, Alfred Edward
"Loveliest of trees, the cherry now".—ElW
To an athlete dying young.—ElW
"When I was one and twenty".—ElW
"**How** absurd, said the gnat to the gnu". See The
gnat and the gnu
How birds should die. Paul Zimmer.—JaP
"**How** can he wrench away". See Barriers
How can I lose hope. From Sing a softblack poem.
Kwelismith.—SuC
"**How** can I sit through one more day". See The
wind is calling me away
"**How** can I write a composition". See Luanne
Sheridan
"**How** can it be". See Rainbow making, a mystery
"**How** cool a tent". See The tent
"**How** cool the young calves seem". See Young
calves
"**How** did you get here". See Yellow weed
"**How** do I love thee, let me count the ways".
Elizabeth Barrett Browning.—ElW
"**How** do squirrels remember". See Buried treasure
"**How** do you amuse". See Ditto marks or, how do
you amuse a muse
"**How** do you carry". See Pockets
"**How** do you like to go up in a swing". See The
swing
"**How** does". See Rain
"**How** does it know". See The seed
"**How** does the plain". See Frost
"**How** doth the little busy bee". See Against idleness
and mischief
"**How** doth the little crocodile". From Alice's
adventures in wonderland. Lewis Carroll.—
WhAa
The crocodile.—ClI
"**How** dry I am, how wet I'll be". Unknown.—CoM
"**How** far". Mary Ann Hoberman.—LiDd
"**How** far, today". See Far away
How I learned English. Gregory Dianikian.—JaM
How I went truant from school to visit a river.
Mary Oliver.—JaPr
How it was. Gary Hyland.—JaPr
"**How** large unto the tiny fly". See The fly
"**How** long since I've spent a whole night". See Love
song to a stranger
"**How** lucky". See Giraffe
"**How** many children will we have". Unknown.—
WiA
How many times. From Blowin' in the wind. Bob
Dylan.—SuC
"**How** many times can a man turn his head". See
How many times
"**How** much wood could a woodchuck chuck". See
"How much wood would a woodchuck chuck"

"**How** much wood would a woodchuck chuck".
Unknown.—KeT—PrP—SuO—WiA
Woodchuck.—SuI
"**How** much wood could a woodchuck chuck".—
OpI
"**How** odd it would be if ever a tapir". See Tapir
"**How** rewarding to know Mr. Smith". See Mr.
Smith
"**How** sadly the bird in his cage". Issa.—WhAa
"**How** strange that we can begin at any time". See
Looking around, believing
"**How** suddenly each tiny seed". See Popping
popcorn
"**How** sweet the silent backward tracings". See
Memories
How the rhinoceros got his nose. J. Patrick Lewis.—
LeA
"**How** thin and sharp is the moon tonight". See
Winter moon
How things work. Gary Soto.—SoA
How to live in a howdah. X. J. Kennedy.—KeGh
How to play night baseball. Jonathan Holden.—
MoA
How to sell things. Gary Soto.—SoA
How to spell. Jane Yolen.—YoBe
How to tell a camel. J. Patrick Lewis.—KeT—LeA
How to tell a tiger. John Ciardi.—PrFo
How to tell the top of a hill. John Ciardi.—DeS
How to tell the wild animals. Carolyn Wells.—CoAz
How to treat shoes. X. J. Kennedy.—KeGh
How to trick a chicken. J. Patrick Lewis.—LeA
"**How** visibly". See Unseen till now
"**How** will you dress for the costume ball". See
Attire
"**How** would it be". See Butterfly wings
Howcroft, Wilbur G.
The personable porcupine.—CoAz
Howe, Julia Ward
Battle hymn of the republic, sels.
Mine eyes have seen the glory.—SuC
Mine eyes have seen the glory. See Battle hymn of
the republic
Howes, Barbara
Out fishing.—KnAs
Petrified minute, tr.—NyT
Salt and memory, a tribute to Marc Chagall, tr.—
NyT
Sea school.—LeCa
Howie Kell suspends all lust to contemplate the
universe. Rodney Torreson.—JaPr
Howitt, Mary
The spider and the fly.—ElW
"**How's** mama". Jo Carson.—CaS
Hru, Dakari Kamau
Crown.—SlM
"Fine black kinfolk".—SlM
John Coltrane ditty.—SlM
The mask.—SlM
Huang, Tze-si
Autumn ("The puppy"), tr.—DeI
The black bull, tr.—DeI
Broken mirror, tr.—DeI
Busy ("Little gray cuckoos"), tr.—DeI
The cat ("Flourishing his head around"), tr.—DeI
The catch ("The kingfisher"), tr.—DeI
The cat's eye, tr.—DeI
The cicada, tr.—DeI
The cow's moo, tr.—DeI
Crabs, tr.—DeI
The cricket ("In a sorrowful voice"), tr.—DeI
The crow ("A crow"), tr.—DeI
The cuckoo, tr.—DeI

Hughes, Ted—*Continued*
Skunk ("Skunk's footfall plods padded").—CoAz
Huidobro, Vicente
Altazor, sels.
  "At the horislope of the mountizon".—NyT
"At the horislope of the mountizon". See Altazor
Huigan, Sean O.
The visitor ("One night").—BoT
Yawn.—BoT
Human body. See Body, human
Human family. Maya Angelou.—AnI
Human race. See also World
Afterglow. J. L. Borges.—GoT
And suddenly it's evening. S. Quasimodo.—GoT
At the ferry. V. Mukhopadhyay.—NyT
At the New Year. K. Patchen.—GoT
Babel. W. De La Mare.—DeR
Between ebb and flow. F. Tuqan.—NyT
"The brain is wider than the sky". E. Dickinson.—ElW
Building. G. Brooks.—SuC
By Frazier Creek Falls. G. Snyder.—ElW
Computer. G. Brooks.—JaP
Divine delight. W. De La Mare.—DeR
Dodos. X. J. Kennedy.—KeK
The dog (as seen by the cat). O. Herford.—ElW
Excelsior. W. Whitman.—HoVo
Failing in the presence of ants. G. Soto.—SoA
"For peace sake". C. McClester.—SlM
Haunted ("The rabbit in his burrow keeps"). W. De La Mare.—DeR
"The heart of man has four chambers, and each is filled with". N. Corwin.—GoT
Human family. M. Angelou.—AnI
"I am created in the image of God". E. Tapia.—StP
"I am the poet of the body and I am the poet of the soul". From Song of myself. W. Whitman.—HoVo
I believe in the theory that says we were visited long ago. A. Adoff.—AdCh
"I say whatever tastes sweet to the most perfect person, that". From Says. W. Whitman.—HoVo
I speak, I say, I talk. A. L. Shapiro.—DeT
"I think I could turn and live with animals, they are so placid". From Song of myself. W. Whitman.—HoVo
"If you think". Lottemoos.—AgL
Insec' lesson. V. Bloom.—AgL
"John and a chimpanzee". Unknown.—ClI
"A leaf for hand in hand". W. Whitman.—HoVo
"Let us dedicate ourselves to what the Greeks". R. Kennedy.—StP
"Let us praise and thank God for all great and". Unknown.—StP
Lizard ("The beginning of a lizard"). B. Povlsen.—NyT
Locations and times. W. Whitman.—HoVo
"Lord, you made the world and everything in it, you". F. Kaan.—StP
Methuselah. E. Merriam.—MeS
Monkeys. K. Koettner-Benigni.—NyT
Names. From The family of man. C. Sandburg.—WhAa
"One thought ever at the fore". W. Whitman.—HoVo
"Our family comes from 'round the world". M. A. Hoberman.—HoFa
Poets to come. W. Whitman.—HoVo
Song of the queen bee. E. B. White.—ElW
Stronger lessons. W. Whitman.—HoVo
The tarantula. R. Whittemore.—ElW

Then as now. W. De La Mare.—DeR
Thought. W. Whitman.—HoVo
Tit for tat. W. De La Mare.—DeR—MaP
Ululation. E. Merriam.—MeS
Under this sky. Z. Hyder.—NyT
Unstooping. W. De La Mare.—DeR—MaP
Wanting to move. V. Mukhopadhyay.—NyT
The waterbeetle. H. Belloc.—CaB
Wouldn't it be funny. P. O'Harris.—CoAz
Humility
Kumar Ragnath. M. Glenn.—GlBc
"'Tis the gift to be simple". Unknown.—StP
Humming bird. Felice Holman.—JaP
"A **hummingbird** hums". See Sparrow
Hummingbirds
Boy, fifteen, killed by hummingbird. L. Linssen.—JaPr
Humming bird. F. Holman.—JaP
Ruby-throated hummingbird. E. Merriam.—MeS
Yummyhummingbird. J. P. Lewis.—LeA
Humor
Nerissa. E. Greenfield.—GrN
Preposterous. J. Hall.—JaPr
Humpty Dumpty. Unknown.—PrFo
"**Humpty** Dumpty sat on a wall. . . ". See Humpty Dumpty
"**Humpty** Dumpty sat on a wall". Mother Goose.—EdGl—SuO—WaM
"**Humpty** Dumpty sat on a wall". Unknown.—WiA
"A **hundred** points of flame". See Prince Rama comes to Longsight
"A **hundred** thousand years have passed". See Drums of my father
"**Hundreds** of flowers". See House of spring
"**Hundreds** of starlings". See Father's magic
Hunger
Brother's snacks. X. J. Kennedy.—KeGh
The feast. W. De La Mare.—DeR
"The fiddler and his wife". Mother Goose.—WaM
"Hannah Bantry in the pantry". Mother Goose.—WaM
"He is a clever man who drives away hunger by just working his jaws". From Jamaican Caribbean proverbs. Unknown.—BeW
The Hirdy Dirdy. Unknown.—OpT
I could never convince any of the other members. A. Adoff.—AdCh
"In a glacier Horace Hind". X. J. Kennedy.—KeFb
In this last class before lunch, I close my eyes. A. Adoff.—AdCh
Mary. W. De La Mare.—DeR
The mouse ("I heard a mouse"). E. Coatsworth.—LaM
The ogre. W. De La Mare.—DeR
"Old Mother Hubbard". Mother Goose.—EdGl—SuO—WaM
Parsnips. J. Little.—LiHe
Part X: This little morsel of morsels here. From A child's day. W. De La Mare.—DeR
Part XI: Now fie, o fie, how sly a face. From A child's day. W. De La Mare.—DeR
A professor called Chesterton. W. S. Gilbert.—LiLo
Propositions. N. Parra.—AgL
"Rumpty-iddity, row row row". Mother Goose.—WaM
The supper ("A wolf he pricks with eyes of fire"). W. De La Mare.—DeR
Supper for a lion. D. Aldis.—CoAz—HoT
Hungry Jake. Florence Parry Heide.—HeG

I

"I am a poor shepherd". See Counting sheep
"I am a pretty little Dutch girl". Unknown.—CoM
"I'm a pretty little Dutch girl".—ScA
"I am a secret scientist". See Chocolate dreams, three
"I am a tidy sort of ghost". See Tombmates
"I am alone, and lonely". See Alone
"I am as black as coal is black". See Panther
"I am asking you to come back home". Jo Carson.—CaS
"I am created in the image of God". Elizabeth Tapia.—StP
"I am drawing a picture". See Friends
I am flying. Jack Prelutsky.—BaW
"I am flying, I am flying". See I am flying
"I am fourteen". See Hanging fire
"I am glad daylong for the gift of song". See Rhapsody
"I am happy because you have accepted me". Unknown.—StP
"I am here, Lord". Joan M. Burns.—StP
I am home, said the turtle. John Ciardi.—CoAz
"I am home, said the turtle, as it pulled in its head". See I am home, said the turtle
"I am Jack Jingle, the very first one". See Jack Jingle
"I am leaving this house as soon as I can". See The antimacassar and the ottoman
"I am like Jojon, the farmhand from Tegal". See Family portrait
"I am looking for a book". See The flying pen
"I am me". See Me
"I am not, I am". See A hot property
"I am of old and young, of the foolish as much as the wise". From Song of myself. Walt Whitman.—SuI
"I am phoenix". See The phoenix
"I am queen of the world today". See Queen of the world (or king)
"I am sitting". See The muddy puddle
"I am small". Unknown.—StP
"I am so little and grey". See The prayer of the mouse
"I am sorry to hear that any prejudice should take place in any of the southern". See The enlistment of free blacks as Continental soldiers
"I am speaking of circles". See Circles
"I am the astronomer of". See In autumn
"I am the only me I am who qualifies as me". See Me I am
"I am the pirate". See The necklace
"I am the poet of the body and I am the poet of the soul". From Song of myself. Walt Whitman.—HoVo
"I am the rain". Grace Nichols.—NiCo
"I am the sister of him". See Little
"I am the Turquoise Woman's son". Unknown.—StP
"I am the youngest, so they call". Arnold Adoff.—AdIn
"I am throwing hard again". See In my meanest daydream
"I am very fond of bugs". See Bugs
"I am young". Robbie Walker.—StP
"I approve of June". See Cow
"I arise today". Saint Patrick.—StP
"I ask sometimes why these small animals". See Caring for animals
"I asked a cock blackbird". See The ousel cock
"I asked my mother for fifteen cents". See "I asked my mother for fifty cents"

"I asked my mother for fifty cents". Unknown.—CoM—OpI—WiA
"I asked my mother for fifteen cents".—WaM
"I asked my mother for fifty cents, I asked my father". Unknown.—WiA
"I beg your pardon". Unknown.—OpI
I believe in the theory that says we were visited long ago. Arnold Adoff.—AdCh
"I believe that life is given us so we may". Helen Keller.—StP
"I believed". See Love
"I bought a box of biscuits, a box of mixed biscuits and a biscuit mixer". Unknown.—WiA
"I bought a wooden whistle". Unknown.—WiA
"I bought me a parrot in Trinidad". See Parrot (from Trinidad)
"I bring back a shell so I can always hear". See Souvenir
I brought a worm. Kalli Dakos.—DaI
"I built a house". See Sand house
"I built my house, I built my walls". Unknown.—OpI
"I came in just in time for supper". See Mosquitoes
"I came into oxygen". See Martha Nelson speaks
"I can clear my name". See Confession to Mrs. Robert L. Snow
"I can get through a doorway without any key". See The wind
"I can read the pictures". See Worlds I know
"I can remember coming home". See Summer mama
"I cannot give you the squeak". See The madhouse
"I cannot remember all the times he hit me". Jo Carson.—CaS
"I cannot see your face". See A sprig of rosemary
"I cannot tell you how it was". See May
I can't abear. Walter De La Mare.—DeR—MaP
"I can't abear a butcher". See I can't abear
I can't go back to school. Michael Patrick Hearn.—JaP
"I can't go visit a snowbird". See Winter birds
"I can't turn cartwheels, I've tried and tried". See Cartwheels
"I carried a king". See We three camels
"I carry your heart with me (I carry it in)". Edward Estlin Cummings.—GoU
"I caught a tremendous fish". See The fish
"I caught this morning morning's minion, kingdom". See The windhover
"I celebrate myself, and sing myself". From Song of myself. Walt Whitman.—HoVo
"I climb the black rock mountain". See Where mountain lion lay down with deer
"I climbed down to the stream and looked back". See To raise a chimney
"I closed my eyes". See Secret hand
"I come from haunts of coot and hern". See The brook
"I could eat it". See Snow
I could never convince any of the other members. Arnold Adoff.—AdCh
"I could take the Harlem night". See Juke box love song
"I crack the stone egg". See Geode
"I cried to the wind". See The hurricane
"I curtseyed to the dovecote". See The double
"I cut my hair last week". See The golden stair
"I danced in the morning". Sidney Carter.—StP
"I did my best". See You can do better
"I did not know she'd take it so". See Under the mistletoe

"I have not so much emulated the birds that musically sing". See To soar in freedom and in fullness of power

I have ten legs. Anna Swir, tr. by Czeslaw Milosz and Leonard Nathan.—NyT

"I have ten little fingers". See Ten little fingers

"I have to fight fierce dragons". See In my horror fantasy chiller

I hear America singing. Walt Whitman.—HoVo

"I hear America singing, the varied carols I hear". See I hear America singing

"I hear eating". See Night fun

I hear my mother's. Ruth Whitman.—LiPm

I hear the usual thump. Arnold Adoff.—AdIn

"I hear you say I say I say after every word I say I say". Unknown.—WiA

"I heard a bird sing". Oliver Herford.—DeS

"I heard a horseman". See The horseman

"I heard a little child beneath the stars". See The universe

"I heard a mouse". See The mouse

"I heard along the early hills". See The fairies dancing

"I heard the bells on Christmas Day". Henry Wadsworth Longfellow.—YoHa

"I heard the preacher man ask". See Bertha Robbins

I hid you. Miklos Radnoti, tr. by Stephen Polgar and Stephen Berg and S. J. Marks.—GoU

"I hid you for a long time". See I hid you

"I hide behind simple things so you'll find me". See The meaning of simplicity

"I hope when you're yourself and twice my age". See Metaphor for my son

I is for inkspot. William Jay Smith.—SmL

"I jiggled it". See This tooth

"I kept on past". Aonghas MacNeacail.—AgL

"I kindle my light over the whole Atlantic". See Dawn

"I know a boy". Eve Merriam.—MeY

"I know a girl". See The canal bank

"I know a little cupboard". See The cupboard

"I know a man". See The artist

"I know a man, his name is Mister". Unknown.—WiA

"I know a man named Michael Finnegan". Unknown.—WiA

"I know a place, in the ivy on a tree". See The bird's nest

"I know a pool where nightshade preens". See Crazed

"I know a secret". Unknown.—WiA

"I know a shortcut". See Shortcut

"I know a washerwoman, she knows me". Unknown.—OpI

"I know a young girl who can speak". See A warning

"I know something I won't tell". Mother Goose.—WaM—WiA

Three little monkeys.—PrFo

I know that summer is the famous growing season. Arnold Adoff.—AdIn

"I know there seems to be". See The poet speaks

"I know you are, but what am I". Unknown.—CoM

"I learned two things". See Riding lesson

"I left Atong by the schoolyard". See Atong

"I left my book in Hawaii". Kalli Dakos.—DaI

"I like". See Night creature

"I like coffee, I like tea". Unknown.—WiA

"I like days". See December

"I like fall". Aileen Fisher.—FiA

"I like it sometimes when we meet". See I like it when

I like it when. Richard Margolis.—LiPf

"I like it when it's mizzly". Aileen Fisher.—MoS

"I like my long hair free, let it blow". See In the ending of this evening snow

"I like myself, I think I'm grand". Unknown.—CoM—WiA

"I like new clothes". See Clothes

"I like our gate". See Gate gossip

"I like that boy". See February 14th

"I like this book, said the king of hearts". See The king of hearts

"I like this book, said the King of Spain". See The King of Spain

"I like to". See Seal at the zoo

"I like to be the first one up". See First one awake

"I like to look in puddles". See Puddles

"I like to see a thunder storm". See Rhyme

"I like to see parades". See Parades

"I like to see the wind". See Hayfield

"I like to see you lean back in your chair". See To Don at Salaam

"I like to shuffle in my socks". See Agatha Ghastly makes light of Auntie

"I like to stay up". Grace Nichols.—NiCo

"I like to stay with grandmother". See Interlude

"I lived off old 42". Jo Carson.—CaS

"I look for you on every street". See Father

"I look in the mirror, and what do I see". See The mirror

"I look out of my high up window". See Kept home

"I look over my shoulder". See Gathering strength

"I looked past my coaches". See Leg broken

I love. Benjamin Zephaniah.—AgL

"I love beginning with". See Tinkering

"I love little pussy". Mother Goose.—WaM

"I love me mother and me mother love me". See I love

I love my mom, I love my pop, I love my dog, I love my sheep. Arnold Adoff.—AdCh

"I love my wife and I love my baby". Unknown.—WiA

"I love my wife, I love my baby". Unknown.—CoM

"I love noodles, give me oodles". See Oodles of noodles

"I love that black-eyed boy". Unknown.—ScA

"I love the first page of a new notebook". See About notebooks

I love the sea. Alfred M. Cruikshank.—SlM

"I love the sea, the rippling sea". See I love the sea

"I love to do my homework". Unknown.—PrFo

"I love to see". See Bartholo

"I love you, I like you". See Love

"I love you, I love you". Unknown.—LoFh—PrP—ScA—WiA

I love you it's true. Carole Stewart.—AgL

"I love you it's true but is there anything in that". See I love you it's true

"I love you little". Unknown.—WiA

"I loved my friend". See Poem

"I loved swimming until it became a nightmare for". See Medals and money, a re-evaluation

"I made a sand castle". See Mine

"I made believe fly". See Make believe

"I made my dog a valentine". Jack Prelutsky.—LoFh

"I made you look, I made you look". Unknown.—WiA

I meet sweet Sue for a walk on a cold and sunny afternoon. Arnold Adoff.—AdCh

"I met a dragon face to face". Jack Prelutsky.—HoGo

"I shall write of the old men I knew". See In these dissenting times

"I shear sheep in all sorts of shapes". See Sheepshape

"I should worry, I should care". Unknown.—WiA "Me no worry, me no care".—CoM

"I shrink in my skin". See The mighty eye

"I sing and shout about time". See Out for spring

"I slept with fourteen strange". See Coming home on my own

"I slit a sheet". Unknown.—OpI

"I sneezed a sneeze into the air". See Ode to a sneeze

"I sometimes think I'd rather crow". See But I dunno

"I sought my soul". Unknown.—StP

I speak, I say, I talk. Arnold L. Shapiro.—DeT

"I spent the first years of my life". Jo Carson.—CaS

"I spied John Mouldy in his cellar". See John Mouldy

"I splash in the ocean". See Ancestry

"I stand beside the sea and cast". See Caught

"I stand in the center". See Thoughts

"I start no". See Son to mother

"I stood guard outside the scarred stall". See The time we cherry-bombed the toilet at the River Oaks

"I stood on the bridge at midnight". Unknown.—WiA

"I stopped to pick up the bagel". See The bagel

"I supped where bloomed the red red rose". See Supper

"I swapped me a horse and got me a cow". Unknown.—ScA

I swim an ocean in my sleep. Norma Farber.—HoSt

"I swung and swung at empty air". See The abominable baseball bat

"I teach five classes a day". See Mr. Henry Axhelm, math

"I teach music, hardly noteworthy". See Mr. Desmond Klinger, music

"I tell you, even rocks crack". See Pride

I thank God I'm free at las'. Unknown.—SuC

"I thank you God for most this amazing". Edward Estlin Cummings.—StP

"I think". From Firefly. Li Po.—DeS

"I think before they saw me the giraffes". See The giraffes

"I think I could turn and live with animals, they are so placid". From Song of myself. Walt Whitman.—HoVo

"I think it must be very nice". See Penguin

"I think mice". See Mice

"I think of all the adults in my life". See Jocelyn Ridley

"I think people in the room are watching". See In public, I pick a piece or two from the plate

"I think people wonder". See In the country

"I think that many owls say who-o". See Owls talking

"I thought I'd take my rat to school". Colin McNaughton.—PrFo

"I thought I'd win the spelling bee". See Bananananananananana

"I threw my mother-in-law out". Jo Carson.—CaS

"I throw myself to the left". Unknown.—WhAa

"I told the sun that I was glad". See The sun

I told you so. Jean Little.—LiHe

"I too, dislike it, there are things that are important". See Poetry

"I took a sip of lemon pop". See Puzzled

"I took a trip around the world". See Geography jump rope

"I took the pail for water when the sun was high". See The star in the pail

"I turn out the light". Eve Merriam.—MeY

"I turned on the TV". See Tube time

"I used to believe that story". See A man never cries

"I used to drop my pocket money". See Debt

"I used to like Stopping by woods on a snowy evening'". See After English class

"I used to think". See Snow color

"I used to work down". Jo Carson.—CaS

"I wake to light". See Prism in the window

"I wake up". Michael Rosen.—AgL

"I wake up in your bed, I know I have been dreaming". See Poem II

"I wakened on my hot, hard bed". See The watch

"I walk among men with tall bones". See Clouds on the sea

"I wandered lonely as a cloud". See Daffodils

"I wandered lonely as a cloud". See Daffodils

"I want a talking dog wearing a cap". From What we said sitting making fantasies. James Berry.—BeW

"I want to flood you with unrest". See Sappho to Eranna

"I want to have a talk with you, Katharine, my mother said". See Mother has a talk with me

"I want to know when you get to be from a place". Jo Carson.—CaS

"I want to tell". Jo Carson.—CaS

I want you to meet. David McCord.—DeS

"I wanted to be a doctor". See Mr. John Fletcher, chemistry

"I was a peasant girl from Germany". See Elsa Wertman

"I was angry with my friend". See A poison tree

"I was asking for something specific and perfect for my city". See Mannahatta

"I was born in a". See Book lice

"I was born in Jacinto Vera". Liber Falco, tr. by Teresa Anderson.—NyT

"I was born three months before I's due". Jo Carson.—CaS

"I was born woman". See Lucia

"I was climbing up the sliding board". See Mosquito

"I was cradle and crib". See The donkey's song

"I was directed by my grandfather". See Direction

"I was going great till tenth grade". See Of necessity, Weeb jokes about his height

"I was hating her hotly, fiercely". See Extinguished

"I was in the garden". Unknown.—OpI

"I was my mother's darling child". Unknown.—ScA

"I was once the snake woman". See Snake woman

"I was reading". See And then

"I was shipwrecked on a pillbox". See Seafarer

"I was the only child of Frances Harris of Virginia". See Hamilton Greene

I was there. Marilyn Sachs.—SaB

"I was there when Captain Noah built his ark". See One more time

"I washed my hands in water". Unknown.—WiA

I watched an eagle soar. Virginia Driving Hawk Sneve.—SnD

"I watched the Lady Caroline". See Lovelocks

"I went down to Johnny's house". Unknown.—WiA

"I went down to my garden patch". See My old hen

"I went down to my garden patch". Unknown.—WiA

"I went down to the lily pond". Unknown.—WiA

"**Ickle,** ockle, blue bockle". Mother Goose.—WaM
"**I'd** like a great satellite-looking dish". From What we said sitting making fantasies. James Berry.—BeW
"**I'd** like a little farm". See Jonathan's farm
"**I'd** like a story". X. J. Kennedy.—HoGo
"**I'd** like a white bull with one horn only". From What we said sitting making fantasies. James Berry.—BeW
"**I'd** like to be a lighthouse". Rachel Field.—LiDd
"**I'd** like to have a purple pigeon". From What we said sitting making fantasies. James Berry.—BeW
"**I'd** like to know what hit the dodo bird". See Dodos
"**I'd** like to look". See Anybody home
"**I'd** like to see cats with stubby wings". From What we said sitting making fantasies. James Berry.—BeW
"**I'd** like to see rabbits". See Moonstruck
"**I'd** like you for a friend". See Finding a way
"**I'd** rather be loved, and love, than be Shakespeare". See Portrait, my wife
"**I'd** rather have fingers than toes". Gelett Burgess.—LiLo
"**Idaho** Rose, dressed in polka dot clothes". Jack Prelutsky.—PrBe
Iddings, Kathleen
   Skating in Pleasant Hill, Ohio.—KnAs
Idea. Shiki, tr. by Tze-si Huang.—DeI
Ideals. See also Ambition; Conduct of life; Dreams
   I dream'd in a dream. W. Whitman.—HoVo
   In praise of a contented mind. E. Dyer.—ElW (unat.)
   The King of Yvetot. W. M. Thackeray.—ElW
Idh al-fitr. Philip Gross.—FoLe
Idh Mubarak. Berlie Doherty.—FoLe
Idleness. See Laziness
Idyll. John Updike.—KnAs
If ("If you"). Karla Kuskin.—LaCc
If ("If you can keep your head when all about you"). Rudyard Kipling.—ElW
"**If** a rooster crows when he goes to bed". Unknown.—WhAa—WiA
"**If** a train leaves Union Station". See The old math, one
"**If** all the world and love were young". See The nymph's reply to the shepherd
"**If** any man should see this book". Unknown.—OpI
"**If** at first you don't succeed". See From the autograph album
"**If** butterflies". See Dreams of flowers
"**If** ever there were a time for her". See The emeritus
"**If** ever you should go by chance". See How to tell the wild animals
"**If** everyone has the same dream". See The dream
"**If** he slipped should she slip". Unknown.—WiA
"**If** I". See Wouldn't you
"**If** I could chop wood". See Karate
"**If** I could go anywhere". See Travel plans
"**If** I had a donkey that wouldn't go". Mother Goose.—WaM
"**If** I had you for a teacher". Unknown.—ScA
"**If** I lived at the time". See To meet Mr. Lincoln
"**If** I remember correctly". See London
"**If** I shine". See A question
If I were a. Karla Kuskin.—DeS
"**If** I were a bear". See Furry bear
"**If** I were a sandwich". See If I were a
"**If** I were a snail". Kazue Mizumura.—MoS
"**If** I were a tree". See Open house

"**If** I were Lord of Tartary". See Tartary
If I were smaller than I am, sels. Jacqueline Sweeney
   "If I were smaller than I am, small as a turtle".—MoS
"**If** I were smaller than I am, small as a turtle". From If I were smaller than I am. Jacqueline Sweeney.—MoS
"**If** I write". See Poem
"**If** I'd as much money as I could spend". Mother Goose.—WaM
"**If** ifs and ans". Unknown.—OpI
"**If** my name you wish to see". Unknown.—OpI
If my right hand. Zinzi Mandela.—AgL
"**If** my right hand was white". See If my right hand
"**If** nightingale sings too sweetly, jealousy will kill its mother". From Jamaican Caribbean proverbs. Unknown.—BeW
"**If** once you have slept on an island". Rachel Field.—LoFh
"**If** only I could stand". See Tree
"**If** only it were still simple". See The making of dragons
If our dogs outlived us. Debra Hines.—JaM
"**If** people ask me". See Politeness
"**If** Peter Piper picked a peck of pickled peppers". See "Peter Piper picked a peck of pickled peppers"
If sometimes blue. Alfred L. Woods.—SlM
"**If** sunlight fell like snowflakes". See Sunflakes
"**If** the deep wood is haunted, it is I". See Nocturne
"**If** the lady of the house". Unknown.—WiA
If the owl calls again. John Haines.—LiIf
"**If** there's any". See Co-op-er-ate
"**If** this book should chance to roam". Unknown.—OpI—WiA
"**If** to the heavens you lift your eyes". See Stars
If we didn't have birthdays. Dr. Seuss.—LoFh
"**If** we didn't have birthdays, you wouldn't be you". See If we didn't have birthdays
If we had lunch at the White House. Kalli Dakos.—DaI
"**If** we meet a gorilla". See We must be polite
"**If** we shadows have offended". From A midsummer night's dream. William Shakespeare.—WhDd
"**If** we walked on our hands". Beatrice Schenk De Regniers.—DeS
"**If** we were a rock 'n' roll band". See Rock 'n' roll band
"**If** we were invited". See If we had lunch at the White House
"**If** wishes were horses". Mother Goose.—WaM
"**If** you". See If
"**If** you and your folks like me and my folks". Unknown.—WiA
"**If** you are an honest child". See Knees
"**If** you are knightly on your daily way". See Serendipity
"**If** you are not handsome at twenty". Mother Goose.—WaM
"**If** you back a monkey he'll fight a tiger". From Jamaican Caribbean proverbs. Unknown.—BeW
"**If** you can keep your head when all about you". See If
"**If** you don't come". See All my secrets
"**If** you find a little feather". Beatrice Schenk De Regniers.—HoT—MoS
"**If** you have got a funnybone". Jack Prelutsky.—PrFo
"**If** you hear a dinosaur". See Who's there

Imagination—*Continued*

Narcissa. G. Brooks.—ElW

The north wind ("Once, when I was young I knew the wind"). J. Lysyk. G. Soto.—BoT

Ode to my library. G. Soto.—SoNe

A path to the moon. B. P. Nichol.—BoT

Pegasus. E. Farjeon.—WhDd

Poetry ("I too, dislike it, there are things that are important"). M. Moore.—SuI

The prison cell. M. Darwish.—NyT

Salt and memory, a tribute to Marc Chagall. Z. Zelk.—NyT

A short long story. J. Cunningham.—JaP

Sir John Mandeville's report on the griffin. J. Yolen.—LiDd

Song ("I placed my dream in a boat"). C. Meireles.—NyT

A story that could be true. W. Stafford.—JaP

"There is no frigate like a book". E. Dickinson.—DeT—ElW

"Think of the ocean". S. Swayne.—BoT

"This book is mine". M. C. Livingston.—LiNe

Transformations. T. Rozewicz.—NyT

Tree ("If only I could stand"). F. Asch.—MoS

The universe. W. De La Mare.—DeR

Valentine for Ernest Mann. N. S. Nye.—JaP

What the little girl said. V. Lindsay.—DeT

"The moon's the north wind's cooky".—LiDd

When I tell you I'm scared. B. S. De Regniers.—DeW

A whirring. D. Aldan.—MoR

"Who knows if the moon's". E. E. Cummings.—DeS

Worlds I know. M. C. Livingston.—DeT

"**Imagine** overturning". See Anteater

Immigration and emigration

Black kid in a new place. J. Berry.—BeW

#4. D. Long.—SlM

How I learned English. G. Dianikian.—JaM

Kwang Chin Ho. M. Glenn.—GlBc

Mull. J. Kay.—AgL

Mum Dad and me. J. Berry.—BeW

Statue of Liberty. M. C. Livingston.—LiNe

"When I first came to this land". Unknown.—ScA

Immortality

At the beach ("The waves are erasing the footprints"). K. Ozer.—NyT

"Because I could not stop for death". E. Dickinson.—SuI

The brook. A. Tennyson.—ElW

"Casting the body's vest aside". From The garden. A. Marvell.—StP

Dedicated to F.W. E. Hemingway.—KnAs

"Each year brings rookies and makes veterans". From Watching football on TV. H. Nemerov.—KnAs

The phoenix. P. Fleischman.—WhDd

To an athlete dying young. A. E. Housman.—ElW

We are seven. W. Wordsworth.—ElW

Impatience. See Patience

An **important** conversation. Beatrice Schenk De Regniers.—DeW

"An **impressionable** lady in Wales". Edward Gorey.—LiLo

Improper moves. Jane Yolen.—YoDd

Improvisation. Kevin Perryman.—NyT

"**In** a borrowed field they dig in their feet". See Women's tug of war at Lough Arrow

"**In** a cool curving world he lies". See The fish

"**In** a cottage in Fife". Mother Goose.—SuO

"**In** a dense wood, a drear wood". See Bitter waters

"**In** a glacier Horace Hind". X. J. Kennedy.—KeFb

"**In** a Mississippi valley". Jack Prelutsky.—PrBe

"**In** a raindrop on a windowpane". See Places to hide a secret message

"**In** a shoe box stuffed in an old nylon stocking". See The meadow mouse

"**In** a snug little cot lived a fat little mouse". See The country mouse and the city mouse

"**In** a sorrowful voice". See The cricket

"**In** a stable of boats I lie still". See The lifeguard

"**In** a storm". See Storm

"**In** a tub one fine day". See T is for tub

In a whirl. Max Fatchen.—FaCm

"**In** all Tipperary there wasn't one fairy". See Little people's express

"**In** an oak there liv'd an owl". Mother Goose.—LiIf

"**In** and out the bushes, up the ivy". See The chipmunk

"**In** April, when these orchards blow". See Blackbirds

"**In** art class I gasped at the easel". X. J. Kennedy.—KeGh

In August. Gary Soto.—SoA

"**In** autumn". See Bullhead in autumn

In autumn. Barbara Juster Esbensen.—EsW

"**In** black leather jackets". See Hoods

"**In** bright yellow coats". Myra Cohn Livingston.—LiMh

"**In** broad daylight". See The owl

"**In** Central Park I saw Uncle Jack". Unknown.—WiA

"**In** Daddy's day there were such things". See Icebox

"**In** downtown Philadelphia". Jack Prelutsky.—PrBe

"**In** dresser drawers, collector kids". See Collecting things

"**In** drowsy fit". See Coals

"**In** Dublin's fair city, where the girls are so pretty". See Cockles and mussels

In evening air. Theodore Roethke.—GoT

"**In** February when few gusty flakes". See Groundhog Day

"**In** grade school I wondered". See Zimmer in grade school

"**In** grandmother's". See Po's garden

"**In** Hans' old mill his three black cats". See Five eyes

"**In** Harry's Discounts Men and Boys". See Hunting

"**In** Heaven". Stephen Crane.—StP

"**In** her dreams". See Hot dreams

"**In** her lunchbox Lena packs". X. J. Kennedy.—KeFb

"**In** her room at the prow of the house". See The writer

"**In** high school we danced the lindy white-style". See Sonja Henie Sonnet

"**In** his final World Series, Pete Rose". See The last baseball samurai

"**In** his room the man watches". Homero Aridjis, tr. by Eliot Weinberger.—NyT

"**In** it there is a space-ship". See A boy's head

"**In** January". See Carols

"**In** Japan, so many memorial ceremonies". See Doll funerals

In judgment of the leaf. Kenneth Patchen.—GoU

"**In** just-spring". Edward Estlin Cummings.—ElW

"**In** Lapland the Lapps". See R is for reindeer

"**In** marble halls as white as milk". Unknown.—CaB—OpT

"**In** March, kites bite the wind". See Paper dragons

In memoriam John Coltrane. Michael Stillman.—MoR

"**In** moving slow he has no peer". See The sloth

In these dissenting times. Alice Walker.—ElW
In this deep darkness. Natan Zach, tr. by Peter
    Everwine and Shula Starkman.—GoT
"In this deep heavy darkness". See In this deep
    darkness
"In this grave picture mortal man may see". See
    Innocency
"In this jungle". Myra Cohn Livingston.—HoT
"In this kind of wind". See Almost dancing
In this last class before lunch, I close my eyes.
    Arnold Adoff.—AdCh
"In this library". See Andy Fierstein
"In this room". See No one
"In this squalid, dirty dooryard". See The pear tree
"In this water, clear as air". See The pool in the
    rock
"In those deep mountain ravines". See The birth of
    a stone
"In time of silver rain". Langston Hughes.—FrS
"In Tsegihi". Unknown.—StP
"In winter". See Bullhead in winter
"In winter fields". See Scarecrow Christmas
"In winter I get up at night". See Bed in summer
"In words, in books". See Jewelry
Inca Indians. See Indians of the Americas—Inca
Incident. Countee Cullen.—ElW
Incident on beggar's night. J. Patrick Lewis.—LiHp
Independence day. See Fourth of July
Independence day. Philip Gross.—FoLe
India
    Dipa, the lamp. A. Bonner.—FoLe
    Divali ("Ravana's gone"). J. Nicholls.—FoLe
    Divali ("Winter stalks us"). D. Harmer.—FoLe
    "Ganesha, Ganesh". M. C. Livingston.—WhDd
    Garuda. D. Chandra.—WhDd
    Holi. I. Rawnsley.—FoLe
An Indian giant's fishing tackle. Unknown.—OpT
"Indian, Indian, lived in a tent". Unknown.—WiA
Indian summer. See Autumn
Indian summer. J. Patrick Lewis.—LeE
Indian trail. Bruce Guernsey.—JaPr
"The Indians". Roberto Sosa, tr. by Jim Lindsey.—
    NyT
Indians of the Americas
    And my heart soars. Chief D. George.—BoT—
        LoFh
    At Plymouth, the first Thanksgiving, 1621. X. J.
        Kennedy.—KeK
    Braves. X. J. Kennedy.—KeK
    Canadian Indian place names. M. Zola.—BoT
    Drums of my father. S. Daniels.—BoT
    The flower-fed buffaloes. V. Lindsay.—CaB
    The four corners of the universe. Unknown.—
        SnD
    The ghost dance, August, 1976. D. Jauss.—JaM
    An Indian giant's fishing tackle. Unknown.—OpT
    "The Indians". R. Sosa.—NyT
    Kansas visit. M. C. Livingston.—LiNe
    The last man killed by Indians in Kimble County,
        Texas. M. Angelotti.—JaM
    Long, long ago. A. Nowlan.—BoT
    "Mother, we are cold". Unknown.—SnD
    "My horse, fly like a bird". V. D. H. Sneve.—SnD
    "My moccasins have not walked". D. Redbird.—
        BoT
    Rainbow crow. N. Van Laan.—WhDd
    Schoolcrafts's diary, written on the Missouri,
        1830. R. Bly.—SuI
    Story without end. Unknown.—WiA
    "Tbl". V. D. H. Sneve.—SnD
    "There came a gray owl at sunset". Unknown.—
        LiIf

Where do these words come from. C.
    Pomerantz.—DeS
Where mountain lion lay down with deer. L. M.
    Silko.—SuI
White buffalo woman. J. Bierhorst.—WhDd
Indians of the Americas—Acoma
    Butterfly song. Unknown.—KeT
Indians of the Americas—Apache
    The black turkey gobbler. Unknown.—SnD
Indians of the Americas—Arapaho
    "Our father, hear us, and our grandfather, I
        mention also". Unknown.—StP
Indians of the Americas—Assiniboin
    Sky tales of the Assiniboin Indians. M. C.
        Livingston.—LiR
Indians of the Americas—Aztec
    "Lord most giving and resourceful". Unknown.—
        StP
Indians of the Americas—Cheyenne
    "From the mountains we come". From Warrior
        nation trilogy. L. Henson.—SuI
    "Great spirit". From Warrior nation trilogy. L.
        Henson.—SuI
    "Huchdjeho niochdzi". Unknown.—YoS
        "Come, ye wood rats, here to me".—YoS
    "Oh ghost that follows me". From Warrior nation
        trilogy. L. Henson.—SuI
Indians of the Americas—Chippewa
    It is I, the little owl. Unknown.—LiIf
    A song of greatness. Unknown.—SuI
    Very much afraid. Unknown.—LiIf
Indians of the Americas—Cree
    Windigo spirit. K. Stange.—BoT
Indians of the Americas—Crow
    We chased butterflies. Plenty-Coups.—SnD
Indians of the Americas—Dakota
    "Far to the west". Unknown.—SnD
    "O Great Spirit, whose voice I hear in the wind".
        Unknown.—StP
Indians of the Americas—Eskimo
    "An Eskimo sleeps in his white bearskin".
        Unknown.—PrP
    Magic words. Unknown.—SuI
    "My little son". Makah.—SnD
    Narwhal. X. J. Kennedy.—WhAa
Indians of the Americas—Hopi
    The owl ("The owl hooted and told of").
        Unknown.—LaN
    "Puva, puva, puva". Unknown.—SnD
    "There". Unknown.—GoT
Indians of the Americas—Inca
    "Creator, you who dwell at the ends of the earth".
        Unknown.—StP
    "With rejoicing mouth". Unknown.—StP
Indians of the Americas—Iroquois
    Law of the great peace. Unknown.—SaB
Indians of the Americas—Kekchi
    "Thou art my father, who is my mother".
        Unknown.—StP
Indians of the Americas—Navajo
    "Dancing teepees". C. O'John.—SnD
    "Farewell, my younger brother". Unknown.—SnD
    "I am the Turquoise Woman's son". Unknown.—
        StP
    "In Tsegihi". Unknown.—StP
Indians of the Americas—Nootka
    Song ("Don't you ever"). Unknown.—DeT
Indians of the Americas—Omaha
    "Sun, moon, stars". Unknown.—SnD
Indians of the Americas—Osage
    "I rise, I rise". Unknown.—SnD

Insults—*Continued*

"Coward, cowardy custard". Unknown.—OpI—ScA

"Cowardy, cowardy custard".—WiA

"Cry, baby, cry". Unknown.—CoM—OpI—ScA—WiA

"Dicky, Dicky Dout". Unknown.—OpI

"Donkey walks on four legs". Unknown.—OpI

"Don't call an alligator a long-mouth till you have crossed the river". From Jamaican Caribbean proverbs. Unknown.—BeW

"Don't care was made to care". Unknown.—OpI

"Don't worry if your job is small". Unknown.—PrP—ScA

"Eight and eight are sixteen". Unknown.—WiA

"Every party needs a pooper". Unknown.—CoM

"Fat, fat, the water rat". Unknown.—ScA

"Fatty, fatty, boom a latty". Unknown.—PrP

The frog ("Be kind and tender to the frog"). H. Belloc.—CII—ElW

"God made you". Unknown.—CoM

"Good boy is a fool's nickname". From Jamaican Caribbean proverbs. Unknown.—BeW

Goodbye please. J. Ciardi.—CiH

"Happy birthday to you, you belong in a zoo". Unknown.—CoM

"Happy birthday to you".—PrFo

"Have you got a sister". Unknown.—OpI

"He that loves glass without g". Unknown.—OpI

"I beg your pardon". Unknown.—OpI

"I know you are, but what am I". Unknown.—CoM

"I love you, I love you". Unknown.—LoFh—PrP—ScA—WiA

"I saw you in the ocean". Unknown.—CoM

"I see London". Unknown.—CoM

"I went up one pair of stairs". Unknown.—OpI

"I wouldn't be you". Unknown.—OpI

"I'm rubber and you're glue". Unknown.—CoM—WiA

"Je suis". Unknown.— OpI

"Kindergarten baby". Unknown.—CoM

"Liar, liar, lick spit". Unknown.—OpI

"Liar, liar, pants on fire". Unknown.—CoM—ScA

"Made you look". Unknown.—CoM

"Made you stare". Unknown.—CoM

"Maggie Meek, the tail of a leek". Unknown.—WiA

Marguerite. Unknown.—PrFo

"Me no know". Unknown.—WiA

Mean song ("Snickles and podes"). E. Merriam.—MeS

"Monkey see, monkey do". Unknown.—WiA

"Red, white, and blue, I don't speak to you". Unknown.—OpI

"Robert, Bedobert, Hadobert, Gofobert". Unknown.—ScA

"Robinson one". Unknown.—OpI

"Roses are red, cabbages are green". Unknown.—ScA

"Roses are red, violets are black". Unknown.—CoM—ScA

"Roses are red, violets are blue, a face like yours". Unknown.—ScA

"Roses are red, violets are blue, do you hate me". Unknown.—CoM

"Roses are red, violets are blue, grass is green". Unknown.—WiA

"Roses are red, violets are blue, if I looked like you". Unknown.—CoM

"Roses are red, violets are blue, what you need". Unknown.—WiA

"Rusty nail, went to jail". Unknown.—WiA

"Sha-ame, sha-ame". Unknown.—CoM—WiA

"Shame, shame".—ScA

"Silence in the court". Unknown.—ScA

"Sit on your thumb". Unknown.—OpI

"Skinny bone, skinny bone". Unknown.—ScA

"Smarty, smarty, smarty". Unknown.—WiA

"Stare, stare like a bear". Unknown.—ScA

"Sticks and stones". Unknown.—CoM—OpI—ScA—WiA

Sweet like a crow. M. Ondaatje.—NyT

"Tattletale, tattletale". Unknown.—ScA—WiA

"Teacher's pet, teacher's pet". Unknown.—ScA

"Tell her, smell her". Unknown.—OpI

"There she goes, there she goes". Unknown.—ScA—WiA

"This sidewalk is cracked". Unknown.—CoM

"Tit for tat". Unknown.—OpI—WiA

"Tommy Johnson is no good". Unknown.—OpI

"Too bad". Unknown.—ScA

"Trim, tran". Unknown.—OpI

"Twinkle, twinkle, little star, what you say". Unknown.—CoM—ScA

"Two's company". Unknown.—WiA

"Up the ladder". Unknown.—WiA

"Want a penny". Unknown.—WiA

"What, what". Unknown.—OpI

When you are there at all, that is. J. Ciardi.—CiH

"You call me names". Unknown.—ScA

"You call me this". Unknown.—CoM

"You limb of a spider". Unknown.—OpI

"You're a poet". Unknown.—WiA

Integration of the armed services of the United States. Harry S. Truman.—SuC

Intelligence

Dumb dog. J. Ridland.—LiDp

Monkeys. K. Koettner-Benigni.—NyT

Interesting facts about monsters. Florence Parry Heide.—HeG

Interlude. Myra Cohn Livingston.—LiT

International ski flying championship, Obersdorf. Elisavietta Ritchie.—KnAs

Interview with a winner. Donald Finkel.—KnAs

"**Intery,** mintery, cutery, corn". Unknown.—CoM

"Hinty, minty, cuty, corn".—SuI

"**Intie,** mintie, tootsie, lala". Unknown.—ScA

"**Into** the endless dark". See City lights

"**Into** the river". See Fishing festival

"An **intrepid** explorer named Bliss". See An explorer named Bliss

"An **invalid** since time began". See Life of the cricket

Inventions. See Inventors and inventions

Inventors and inventions

The deacon's masterpiece, or, the wonderful one-hoss shay. O. W. Holmes.—ElW

Family genius. X. J. Kennedy.—KeGh

"Gene, Gene, made a machine". Unknown.—ScA

An historic moment. W. J. Harris.—HoGo

Mechanical menagerie. X. J. Kennedy.—PrFo

"There was an old man of the Hague". E. Lear.—LiLo

"Young Frankenstein's robot invention". B. Braley.—LiLo

Inversnaid. Gerard Manley Hopkins.—MoR

Invisible cat. X. J. Kennedy.—KeGh

Invitation ("Listen, I've a big surprise"). Myra Cohn Livingston.—KeT—LiT

Invitation ("My birthday invitation"). Myra Cohn Livingston.—LiBp

Invitations

"Boys and girls come out to play". Mother Goose.

"It rains, it pains". Unknown.—OpI
"It runs all day, but never walks". Unknown.—ScA
"It rustles, it". See Homework
"It seemed the". See Christmas night
"It seemed the plum trees". See On New Year's Day, watching it snow
"It seems I always saw the Indian woman". See Long, long ago
It seems I test people. James Berry.—BeW
"It sleeps a lot". See Brand new baby
"It squinted and said". See N is for needle
"It stays all year". Unknown.—ScA
"It sushes". See Cynthia in the snow
"It sways". See Ode to la pinata
"It takes more than a wish". See To catch a fish
"It tickles me". Unknown.—WiA
"It tumbled and it crumbled". See Sea wave
"It used to be only Sunday afternoons". From Watching football on TV. Howard Nemerov.—KnAs
"It was a cough". Unknown.—BaH
"It was a dark and stormy night, some Indians were". See Story without end
"It was a dry fall". See Storm bringer
"It was a Saturday and my mother was cooking". Jo Carson.—CaS
"It was a testimony". See Gregory's house
"It was in an empty lot". See How I learned English
"It was laughing time, and the tall giraffe". See Laughing time
"It was many and many a year ago". See Annabel Lee
"It was midnight on the ocean". Unknown.—WiA
"It was my secret place". See The secret place
Italian noodles. X. J. Kennedy.—KeGh
Itinerant. Eve Merriam.—MeCh
"It's a black plastic bin bag". See Hallowe'en
"It's a hard time situation". See If sometimes blue
"It's a long walk in the dark". See John's song
"It's a stone". See Ode to el molcajete
"It's a very odd thing". See Miss T.
"It's about the ball". See Analysis of baseball
"It's always dark". See The dark
"It's better to die in the flesh of hope". See The fat black woman's motto on her bedroom door
"It's changing here". Jo Carson.—CaS
"It's Christmas, the time when we gather to make". See The remarkable cake
"It's cold, said the cricket". See Halloween concert
"It's cool under the August". See The sky is falling
"Its echoes". See Haunted house
"It's four o'clock". See What they said
"It's funny". See My puppy
"It's gettin' to where". Jo Carson.—CaS
It's great when you get in. Eugene O'Neill.—KnAs
It's gross to kiss. Kalli Dakos.—DaI
"It's hard to lose a friend". Unknown.—PrP
"It's hard to make a j". See A jamboree for j
"It's immaterial what I become". See Kyle Quinn
It's inside my sister's lunch. Kalli Dakos.—DaI
"It's just an old alley cat". See The stray cat
"It's late and I'm tired, but I don't want to sleep". See The party's over
"It's like this, Ms. L". See Annette Harrison
"It's live and evil". See The dreadful drawkcab
"It's morning in the afternoon". See Morning
"It's neither amusing nor funny". R. H. Marks.—LiLo
"It's not me". Jo Carson.—CaS
"It's odd how". See Decorations
"It's perfectly obvious why". See How to trick a chicken

"It's quiet". See Lost
"It's raining big". See Rain of leaves
"It's raining, it's pouring". Mother Goose.—CoM—OpI—ScA—WiA
"It's raining, it's raining". Mother Goose.—WaM
It's raining ("It's raining, it's raining"). See Que llueva
"It's sad when a person gets off the bus". See Byes
"It's Saturday with the gray". See Morning on this street
"It's small". See Ode to my library
"It's so still". See Spruce woods
"It's that kind of day". See That kind of day
"It's time for the party". See To friendship
"It's time, I believe". Unknown.—OpI
"It's very nice to think of how". See A kitten's thought
"It's what I've been dreading". See Are you in there
"I've always tried to be good". See Goodness
"I've been at that job". Jo Carson.—CaS
"I've been to the zoo". See At the zoo
"I've been working on my schoolbooks". Unknown.—ScA
"I've drowned seventy ants in a pool". Ann Story.—LiLo
"I've found three people now who claim they've seen". See Ghost story
"I've got a dog as thin as a rail". Unknown.—ClI—PrP
"I have a dog as thin as a rail".—ScA
"I've got a lad and he's double double-jointed". Mother Goose.—OpI
"I've got a new jacket". See New jacket
"I've got a rocket". Unknown.—WiA
"I've got the measles, want 'em too". See Free offer
"I've just begun my math". See A day in school
"I've known rivers". See The negro speaks of rivers
I've never seen a real owl. April Halprin Wayland.—LiIf
I've never written a baseball poem. Elisavietta Ritchie.—KnAs
"I've no bat for your witchcraft". See Hallowe'en ad (attention witches)
"I've read lots of articles about working mothers". See Working parents
"I've stayed in the front yard all my life". See A song in the front yard
"I've thought and thought and thought in vain". Unknown.—WiA
"I've worked this place". Jo Carson.—CaS
Ivy
Ivy. J. Yolen.—YoBe
Ivy. Jane Yolen.—YoBe

J

J is for jack-in-the-box. William Jay Smith.—SmL
J.T. never will be ten. Kalli Dakos.—DaI
"J.T.'s only nine years old". See J.T. never will be ten
Jabberwocky. From Through the looking glass. Lewis Carroll.—ElW
Jabsheh, Salwa
A pearl, tr.—NyT
Jacinto, Antonio
The rhythm of the tomtom, tr. by Don Burness.—NyT
Jack. Deborah Chandra.—LiHp
Jack A. J. Patrick Lewis.—LeA

"**Jack** and Jill". Mother Goose.—EdGl—SuO—
    WaM
"**Jack** be nimble, Jack be quick". Mother Goose.—
    EdGl—SuO—WaM
"**Jack** Hall". Unknown.—PrP
"A **jack** in the box". See Jack in the box
Jack in the box. William Jay Smith.—SmL
"**Jack**, Jack". Unknown.—WiA
Jack Jingle. Unknown.—OpT
Jack-o-lantern. X. J. Kennedy.—KeK
Jack-o'-lanterns. See Pumpkins
"**Jack** Sprat could eat no fat". Mother Goose.—
    EdGl—SuO—WaM
"**Jackie** and I cross-legged". See Brown girl, blonde
    okie
Jackie Grant. Mel Glenn.—GlBc
"**Jackie** on the porch, shouting for me to come out".
    See Walking with Jackie, sitting with a dog
Jackie Robinson. Lucille Clifton.—KnAs—MoA
Jacks. Valerie Worth.—WoAl
Jackson, Reggie (about)
    Mister October, Reggie Jackson. Unknown.—
    MoA
Jacob and Joseph. Unknown.—OpT
"**Jacob** made for his son Josie". See Jacob and
    Joseph
Jacobs, A. C.
    "Days were as great as lakes", tr.—GoT
Jacobs, Leland B.
    Queenie.—DeT
    "There is a land".—HoGo
Jacobs, Lucky
    Sacrifice bunt.—KnAs
Jacobsen, Rolf
    The memory of horses, tr. by Roger Greenwald.—
    NyT
Jacque, Florence Page
    There once was a puffin.—MoS
The **jaguar**. Ted Hughes.—CaB
Jails. See Prisons and prisoners
Jaime Milagros. Mel Glenn.—GlBc
"**Jake** had such an appetite". See Hungry Jake
"**Jake**, the twin of John Lothario". Ellen Raskin.—
    PrFo
Jamaican alphabet. Louise Bennett.—LeCa
Jamaican Caribbean proverbs, complete. Unknown
    "Because parrots are chatterers people say they are
        the only ones who eat up the fruits".—BeW
    "Befoh yu marry keep two yeye opn, afta yu
        marry shet one".—BeW
    "The boaster will make out someone else is the
        liar".—BeW
    "Call a tiger Master he'll still eat you".—BeW
    "A dog's bark isn't going to frighten the moon".—
        BeW
    "The donkey says the world isn't level ground".—
        BeW
    "Don't call an alligator a long-mouth till you have
        crossed the river".—BeW
    "Don't wait until you hear the drum beat before
        you grind your axe".—BeW
    "Every family has its deformity".—BeW
    "Good boy is a fool's nickname".—BeW
    "The great fool is as proud as a dog with two
        tails".—BeW
    "He is a clever man who drives away hunger by
        just working his jaws".—BeW
    "If nightingale sings too sweetly, jealousy will kill
        its mother".—BeW
    "If you back a monkey he'll fight a tiger".—BeW
    "A little axe can cut down a big tree".—BeW

    "The man who is all honey, flies are going to eat
        him up".—BeW
    "Many an underfed cow in the pasture is mother
        of a bull".—BeW
    "The mosquito often goes to the village for syrup
        but doesn't always get it".—BeW
    "The needle makes clothes yet the needle itself is
        naked".—BeW
    "The peacock hides its leg when its tail gets
        praises".—BeW
    "The rich and the poor do not meet".—BeW
    "When you see your neighbour's beard on fire,
        take some water and wet your own".—BeW
    "You never see a cow that kicks who doesn't
        produce a calf that kicks".—BeW
Jamaican song. James Berry.—BeW
Jamal, Mahmood
    Objectivity.—AgL
Jamboree, sels. David McCord
    "A rhyme for ham, jam".—DeS
A **jamboree** for j. Eve Merriam.—MeS
James, Eric
    Forbidden sounds.—BaH
"**James** James". See Disobedience
Jammes, Francis
    A prayer to go to paradise with the donkeys, tr.
    by Richard Wilbur.—CaB
Jams and jellies
    "Gooseberry, juiceberry". E. Merriam.—LiDd—
    MoS
"**Jane** brought a baseball bat". See I brought a worm
"**Jane**, Jane". Unknown.—WiA
Janeczko, Paul B.
    Bad.—JaB
    Bingo.—JaB—JaP
    Blanket hog.—KeT
    Bonfire.—JaB
    Brickyard.—JaB
    The bridge.—JaB
    Brothers ("Raymond slowed").—JaB
    Dancers.—JaB
    Firsts.—JaB
    Glass eye Harry Coote.—JaB
    Gus.—JaB
    History.—JaB
    Hoods.—JaB
    The kiss ("The kiss started when I danced").—JaB
    Lecture.—JaB
    Mail king.—JaB
    The monument.—JaB
    Mystery ("One Friday night").—JaB
    The poet ("Before he moved in with Miss
        Perry").—JaB
    Raymond.—JaB
    Reverend Mona.—JaB
    Roscoe.—JaB
    Ruth.—JaB
    Sisters.—JaB
    Spider ("Spider always wore sunglasses").—JaB
    Stories ("Old Lester Darby").—JaB
    Sundays.—JaB
    Thieves.—JaB
    Walker.—JaB
    Winner ("Mrs. Macey worked behind").—JaB
    The word.—JaB
Janet DeStasio. Mel Glenn.—GlBc
"**Janey** Mac, me shirt is black". See The disgruntled
    husband
Janowitz, Phyllis
    There was a man.—JaP
Jansone, Inguna
    "Do what you like with my face", tr.—NyT

January
  Carols. V. Worth.—WoA
  January. J. Updike.—FrS
  January deer. M. Singer.—SiT
  Twelfth night. V. Worth.—WoA
January. John Updike.—FrS
January deer. Marilyn Singer.—SiT
"January played". See One year
Japan
  The birthday of Buddha. J. Kirkup.—FoLe
  The doll festival. J. Kirkup.—FoLe
  Doll funerals. J. Kirkup.—FoLe
  Stars at night. I. Takenaka.—NyT
Japanese language
  "Zui zui zukkorobashi". Unknown.—YoS
Japanese nursery rhymes. See Nursery rhymes—
  Japanese
Jarman, Mark
  The gift ("When I was five my father kidnapped
  me").—JaM
Jarrell, Randall
  The bat. See Bats
  Bats.—ElW
    The bat.—LaN
  The bird of night.—LiIf
    The owl.—LaN
  The chipmunk.—MoR
    The chipmunk's day.—ElW
  The chipmunk's day. See The chipmunk
  Fly by night, sels.
    "My nest is in the hollow tree".—LiIf
  "My nest is in the hollow tree". See Fly by night
  The owl. See The bird of night
  The owl's bedtime story.—LiIf
  Say goodbye to Big Daddy.—KnAs
Jasmine. Kyongjoo Hong Ryou.—NyT
"Jason Johnson left New Jersey". Jack Prelutsky.—
  PrBe
Jastrun, Tomasz
  Father and son, tr. by Daniel Bourne.—NyT
Jauss, David
  The ghost dance, August, 1976.—JaM
  Oliver Johnson comes back to bed the morning
    after the ice storm and tells his wife why.—JaM
  Setting the traps.—JaPr
"Jawara". See Big questions
"Jay said I was yellow". See Jump
"Jaybird a-sitting on a hickory limb". Unknown.—
  WiA
Jays
  "Jaybird a-sitting on a hickory limb".
    Unknown.—WiA
  "When it is snowing". S. Cedering.—JaP
Jayyusi, Lena
  The squirrel, tr.—NyT
Jayyusi, May
  Distances of longing, tr.—NyT
  The orphan, tr.—NyT
  The pen, tr.—NyT
Jayyusi, Salma Khadra
  Ants, tr.—NyT
  Between ebb and flow, tr.—NyT
  Overture, tr.—NyT
"Je suis". Unknown.— OpI
Jealousy. See also Envy
  Brand new baby. B. S. De Regniers.—DeW
  "Did Jesus have a baby sister". D. Previn.—AgL
  Disillusion. M. Burge.—AgL
  "If nightingale sings too sweetly, jealousy will kill
    its mother". From Jamaican Caribbean
    proverbs. Unknown.—BeW

An important conversation. B. S. De Regniers.—
  DeW
Mima. W. De La Mare.—DeR—MaP
"One little kid took a limo". J. Knight.—KnT
"To sabotage the Yuletide play". X. J.
  Kennedy.—KeFb
"Jean, Jean, Jean". See Cat at the cream
Jeffers, Robinson
  Salmon fishing.—KnAs
"Jellicle cats come out tonight". See The song of the
  jellicles
"Jelly in the bowl". Unknown.—WiA
Jellyfish
  "Jellyfish stew". J. Prelutsky.—PrFo
"Jellyfish stew". Jack Prelutsky.—PrFo
"Jelly's made from jellyfish". See What you don't
  know about food
"Jemima is my name". See Mima
"Jen said, baby, don't you swaller". X. J.
  Kennedy.—KeFb
Jennie Wren. Walter De La Mare.—DeR
"Jennifer Juniper, where do you walk". Jack
  Prelutsky.—PrBe
Jennings, Elizabeth
  Clothes ("My mother keeps on telling me").—AgL
  In the night.—GoT
"Jenny got so angry". Unknown.—WiA
"Jenny had hoops she could sling in the air". See
  Jenny the juvenile juggler
Jenny the juvenile juggler. Dennis Lee.—MoR
"Jenny works with one hammer". See The hammer
  song
"Jenny Wren fell sick". See Cruel Jenny Wren
Jephson Gardens. Dennis Joseph Enright.—ElW
"Jeremiah Obadiah, puff, puff, puff". Mother
  Goose.—WaM
"Jeremy hasn't a roof on his house". See Jeremy's
  house
Jeremy's house. Lois Simmie.—BoT
"Jerry Hall". Mother Goose.—ClI—ScA
Jerusalem
  Jerusalem. Y. Amichai.—NyT
Jerusalem. Yehuda Amichai, tr. by Stephen
  Mitchell.—NyT
Jesus Christ (about). See also Christianity;
  Christmas; Easter
  "Angels from the realms of glory". J.
    Montgomery.—YoHa
  Barriers. J. Berry.—BeW
  Carol of the brown king. L. Hughes.—GoA
  Counting sheep ("I am a poor shepherd"). J.
    Yolen.—YoHa
  "Did Jesus have a baby sister". D. Previn.—AgL
  The donkey's song. J. Yolen.—YoHa
  The fir tree. J. Yolen.—YoHa
  "Go tell it on the mountain". Unknown.—LoFh
  Guardian owl. N. Farber.—LiIf
  "I danced in the morning". S. Carter.—StP
  "I find thee throned in my heart". A. MacLean.—
    StP
  "I saw a stranger yestreen". Unknown.—StP
  "Jesus Christ, thou child so wise". H. Belloc.—StP
  Journey of the Magi. T. S. Eliot.—ElW
  The legend of Rosemary. J. Yolen.—YoHa
  "Mary had a baby". Unknown.—YoHa
  Nativity play plan. J. Berry.—BeW
  "Put me not into the hands". Unknown.—StP
  Watch ("The lamb baaed gently"). J. R.
    Jimenez.—LoFh
  We three camels. J. Yolen.—YoHa
  "We three kings of Orient are". J. H. Hopkins,
    Jr.—YoHa (unat.)

K

Kay, Jackie
  Mull.—AgL
Kearney Park. Gary Soto.—SoA
Keats, John
  La belle dame sans merci.—ElW
  On the grasshopper and cricket.—ElW
Keeley, Edmund
  Healing, tr.—NyT
  The meaning of simplicity, tr.—NyT
"Keep a poem in your pocket". Beatrice Schenk De
  Regniers.—HoSt—LoFh
"Keep me a crust". See Lob-lie-by-the-fire
"Keep popping in my head". See Chocolate dreams
  and chocolate schemes
"Keep us, O Lord, as the apple of your eye".
  Unknown.—StP
"Keep watch, dear Lord, with those who work".
  Saint Augustine.—StP
"Keep your whiskers crisp and clean". See The king
  of cats sends a postcard to his wife
Keeping busy is better than nothing. John Ciardi.—
  CiH—LiLo
Keeping the horses. Roy Scheele.—JaM
Keiter, Anne
  Summer mama.—JaPr
Kekchi Indians. See Indians of the Americas—
  Kekchi
Keller, Helen
  "I believe that life is given us so we may".—StP
Kellogg, Steven
  The dream ("If everyone has the same dream").—
  SaB
Ken, Thomas
  "All praise to Thee, my God, this night".—StP
Kennedy, Monique M.
  The tongue ("You stick out your tongue"), tr.—
  NyT
Kennedy, Robert
  "Let us dedicate ourselves to what the Greeks".—
  StP
Kennedy, Thomas E.
  The tongue ("You stick out your tongue"), tr.—
  NyT
Kennedy, X. J.
  "Abner from an Alpine height".—KeFb
  The abominable baseball bat.—MoA
  Advice.—KeGh
  After Easter snow.—KeK
  Agatha Ghastly makes light of Auntie.—KeGh
  Airport.—KeK
  Airport in the grass.—MoR
  At Plymouth, the first Thanksgiving, 1621.—KeK
  "At the fireworks show, rash Randall".—KeFb
  Aunt Gilda's pincushion head.—KeGh
  Backyard volcano.—KeGh
  Basketball bragging.—KeGh
  Big Saul Fein.—KeK
  Bill Bolling's avalanche.—KeGh
  Bird sighting.—KeGh
  "Blair, to make his mother screech".—KeFb
  Blow up.—LoFh
  Braves.—KeK
  A bright idea.—LiLo
  Brother's snacks.—KeGh
  The case of the crumbled cookies.—KeGh
  The cat who aspired to higher things.—LaM
  Changelings.—KeGh
  Chocolate rabbit.—KeK
  Circus dreams.—KeK
  Collecting things.—KeK
  Cotton bottomed menace.—KeK

Cricket ("The cheerful cricket, when he sings").—
  KeK
The dental history of Flossie Fly.—KeGh
Different dads.—KeK—LiPf
A different door.—LaCc
Dodos.—KeK
"Drexel on the ballroom floor".—KeFb
Earth's birthday.—KeK
Electric eel.—WhAa
"Every time it rained, mean Merl's".—KeFb
Family genius.—KeGh
First one awake.—KeK
"For his mother's mudpack, Brent".—KeFb
"For red mouthwash, rotten Ross".—KeFb
Free offer.—KeGh
"From the boat, while Uncle Sid".—KeFb
"From zoo keepers' pails Gail steals".—KeFb
"Garth, from off the garden wall".—KeFb
Generation gap.—KeK
A giraffe's laughs last.—KeGh
The girl who makes the cymbals bang.—KeK
"Glenda, in an everglade".—KeFb
"The gnomes of Nome".—KeGh
Goldfish ("Goldfish flash past, keeping busy").—
  KeK
Grandmother in winter.—LiPg
"Greg has trained a pig that grunts".—KeFb
Guinevere Ghastly sits baby.—KeGh
"The horn on our pickup truck stayed stuck".—
  KeGh
Hot milk.—KeK
House noises.—LiPm
How to live in a howdah.—KeGh
How to treat shoes.—KeGh
"I'd like a story".—HoGo
"Ignatz Pigfats".—KeGh
"In a glacier Horace Hind".—KeFb
"In art class I gasped at the easel".—KeGh
"In her lunchbox Lena packs".—KeFb
"In the antique glass shop, Knute".—KeFb
"In the dining car, mean Myrt".—KeFb
"In the pet store Roscoe Rice".—KeFb
"In the sort of paint that glows".—KeFb
Invisible cat.—KeGh
Italian noodles.—KeGh
Jack-o-lantern.—KeK
"Jen said, baby, don't you swaller".—KeFb
"Just before the highest hill".—KeFb
"The kite that braved old Orchard Beach".—KeK
Kracken.—WhDd
"Lancelot, the scurvy knave".—KeFb
Leek soup.—KeK
A lesson ("He made fun of my Pekingese").—KeK
"Lil, to cut the rug's pile lower".—KeFb
Lines for remembering about lids.—KeK
Little people's express.—KeGh
Long distance call.—KeGh
Longest lizard.—KeGh
Louleen's feelings.—KeK
"A luckless time-traveler from Lynn".—KeGh—
  LiLo
"The mailman's such a magic guy".—KeK
Maisie's lament.—KeK
"Mal, to yank his aching molar".—KeFb
March thaw.—KeK
Martin Luther King Day.—KeK
Mechanical menagerie.—PrFo
Meteor shower.—KeK
Minotaur.—WhDd
A misspent youth.—KeGh
Mole ("The mole lives wholly in a hole").—KeGh
Mom and Pop Ghastly come up for air.—KeGh

Kennedy, X. J.—*Continued*
Mote.—KeK
"Mother, mother, bless my soul".—KeFb
Mother's nerves.—ElW
Mrs. Morizawa's morning.—KeK
My marshmallows.—KeK
"My Scottish great granduncle Milt's".—KeGh
My stupid parakeet named after you.—KeK
Narwhal.—WhAa
"Never stand under an anvil".—KeGh
New Year's advice from my Cornish grandmother.—KeK
Night fog.—KeK
Nix on picnics.—KeGh
No grosser grocer.—KeGh
"Nora, playing with Kit Kitten".—KeFb
"Now just who, muses Uncle Bill Biddle".—KeGh—LiLo
Obnoxious Nelly.—KeK
"Ocean bathing, Abner Abb".—KeFb
"Oh, how low can you go, Gosnold Goop".—KeGh
"On a day when the ocean was sharky".—KeGh—LiLo
"On a trip through Yellowstone".—KeFb
"On his laboratory table".—KeFb
"On report card day Spike Sparks".—KeFb
"On the dam, Neil spied a wheel".—KeFb
Owl ("The diet of the owl is not").—Lilf
Pacifier.—KeK
"Papa, tumbling down the sky".—KeFb
Paperclips.—KeK
Poet ("Listen, I'm talking in stumbles and bumps").—KeK
Polar dreams.—KeK
Popping popcorn.—KeK
A prickly phone call.—KeGh
Remembering ice.—KeK
Robert Robot.—KeGh
Roller coasters.—KeK
Romping in the rain.—KeK
"Round the 4H baked goods sale".—KeFb
"Said Gus Goop, that spaghetti was great".—KeGh—LiLo
Sea horse and sawhorse.—PrFo
Setting the Thanksgiving table.—KeK
Sheepshape.—KeGh
"Sheila, into Dad's right shoe".—KeFb
"Sheldon the selfish shellfish".—KeGh
"Sheldon with a welding torch".—KeFb
"Sister has a blister".—KeGh
Skunk cabbage slaw.—KeGh
Small town fireworks.—KeK
"Sneaky Ebenezer Snyder".—KeFb
"Snicketty, snacketty sneeze".—CoAz
"Snowflake souffle".—PrFo
A social mixer.—PrFo
Song for a valentine.—KeK
Special flavor.—KeGh
Stealing eggs.—PrFo
"Stealthy Steffan stuck a dead".—KeFb
Sticky situation.—LiLo
Straight scoop about scallions.—KeGh
A stupendous pincushion.—KeGh
Summer cooler.—KeK
Super strategem.—KeGh
The tables turned.—KeK
Taking down the space-trolley.—KeK
A tale of two cities.—KeGh
Telephone talk.—KeK
"Tell me, why so pale and wan".—KeFb
Ten little likenesses.—KeK

Things on a microscope slide.—KeGh
To a forgetful wishing well.—DeT
To a snowflake.—KeK
To a tuna.—KeK
"To sabotage the Yuletide play".—KeFb
"To the bottom of his drink".—KeFb
"To the bowl of champagne punch".—KeFb
Trimmed down tales.—KeGh
Trouble with baby.—KeGh
Two week car trip.—KeK
"The unicorn I tried to paint".—KeK
"An unusual man from Bound Brook".—KeGh
"The vacumn cleaner's swallowed Will".—KeGh
Valuables.—KeK
Walking Big Bo.—KeK—LiDp
Weems Ghastly's goodies.—KeGh
What I used to wonder.—KeK
What we might be, what we are.—JaP—KeGh
"Where the sun shone white hot, Cass".—KeFb
"While, unwatched, the soup pot boils".—KeFb
Whistler's father.—KeGh
"Who to trade stamps with".—KeK
Whose boo is whose.—PrFo
Why dinosaurs disappeared.—KeGh
Wicked witch's kitchen.—BaH—LiHp
Wicked witch's travels.—KeGh
Wildlife refuge.—KeGh
Wishing for winter in summer.—KeK
"With her one string ukelele".—KeFb
"With wild mushrooms Madge had found".—KeFb
Word of warning.—KeGh
Kentucky
"The sun shines bright in the old Kentucky home". From My old Kentucky home. S. C. Foster.—SuC
Kenward, Jean
Cheung Chau festival.—FoLe
Fishing festival.—FoLe
The Fourth of July ("On the Fourth of July, yes").—FoLe
Harvest moon ("She comes in silence").—FoLe
Mardi Gras.—FoLe
May day ("Twirl your ribbons").—FoLe
Mela.—FoLe
New year ("This night").—FoLe
Kenyon, Jane
November calf.—ElW
Kept home. James Berry.—BeW
Keremes, Constance Andrea
Bed mate.—HoS
"A **kernel** of corn". See Fields of corn
Kessler, Jascha
Believe it or not, tr.—NyT
"**Kettle's** for the kitchen". See A
Kevorkian, Karen
Softball dreams.—KnAs
Keyes, Robert Lord
The Yankees.—MoA
Keys
"I will give you the key". A. Lobel.—MoS
Keziah. Gwendolyn Brooks.—LiDd
Khadun, Pramila
The sky is vast.—NyT
Kick a little stone. Dorothy Aldis.—KeT
Kick and live. G. W. Porter.—SlM
Kick line. Jane Yolen.—YoDd
Kicking up. Jane Yolen.—YoBi
The **kid**. Kevin Bezner.—KnAs
Kidnap poem. Nikki Giovanni.—AgL—ElW

Kieran, John
"There's this that I like about hockey, my lad".—KnAs

Kikaku
"Butting, tumbling cat".—CaR
Nightingale, tr. by Tze-si Huang.—DeI

"**Kill** a robin or a wren". Unknown.—CaB

Killing chickens. Bruce Weigl.—JaPr

"**Kindergarten** baby". Unknown.—CoM

Kindness. See also Animals—Care; Sympathy
"Don't shoo the morning flies away". H. Yu.—GoT
"Fill your children with kindness". Unknown.—StP
"Give us grateful hearts, our Father". Unknown.—StP
Goodness. B. Andersen.—NyT
Gracious goodness. M. Piercy.—ElW
Grandmothers. D. McCord.—LiPg
Grape pickers. A. Bryan.—BrS
"Hurt no living thing". C. G. Rossetti.—DeS—StP—WhAa
"In my Missouri". M. Angelou.—AnI
Kumar Ragnath. M. Glenn.—GlBc
Mary's lamb. S. J. Hale.—SuI
"Mary had a little lamb".—EdGl (unat.)—SuO (unat.)—WaM (unat.)
"Oh, don't strike the fly". Issa.—CaR
"The runaway slave came to my house and stopt outside". From Song of myself. W. Whitman.—HoVo
The sun witness. N. Choudhurry.—AgL
Welcome here. Unknown.—GoA

King, Martin Luther (about)
The funeral of Martin Luther King, Jr. N. Giovanni.—SuC
Martin Luther King Day. X. J. Kennedy.—KeK
Martin Luther King, Jr. U. E. Perkins.—SlM

"**King** and Queen of the pelicans we". See The pelican chorus

"**King** Canute". See Kings

King David. Walter De La Mare.—DeR—MaP

"**King** David was a sorrowful man". See King David

King Henry V, sels. William Shakespeare
"I will not change my horse with any that treads".—WhAa

"The **king** in slumber when he lies down". See Part XVI: The king in slumber when he lies down

King Kong bat. William Jay Smith.—SmL

"**King** Minos had a minotaur". See Minotaur

The **king** of cats sends a postcard to his wife. Nancy Willard.—LaCc

The **king** of hearts. William Jay Smith.—SmL

The **King** of Spain. William Jay Smith.—SmL

King of the band. Amryl Johnson.—FoLe

The **King** of Yvetot. William Makepeace Thackeray.—ElW

"The **King** sent for his wise men all". See W

"The **kingfisher**". See The catch

Kingfisher. Eleanor Farjeon.—MoR

"The **kingfisher**". Unknown, tr. by Tze-si Huang.—DeI

Kings. See Rulers

Kings. Walter De La Mare.—DeR

Kings and queens. Walter De La Mare.—DeR—MaP

Kinky hair blues. Una Marson.—LeCa

A **kinsman.** Jim Wayne Miller.—JaM

Kiph. Walter De La Mare.—DeR

Kipling, Rudyard
Commissariat camels.—WhAa

If ("If you can keep your head when all about you").—ElW

Seal lullaby. See Seal mother's song

Seal mother's song.—CoAz
Seal lullaby.—WhAs

"There once was a boy of Quebec".—LiLo

The tortoise and the hedgehog.—WhAa

Kirkup, James
Baby's drinking song.—MoS
The birthday of Buddha.—FoLe
Carnival in Rio.—FoLe
The doll festival.—FoLe
Doll funerals.—FoLe
Korean butterfly dance.—FoLe
Summer full moon.—LaN

The **kiss** ("Come into the hall with me, George"). George Bogin.—JaM

The **kiss** ("The kiss started when I danced"). Paul B. Janeczko.—JaB

A **kiss** is round. Blossom Budney.—MoS

"The **kiss** started when I danced". See The kiss

"**Kisses** upon your breast, like water from a jug". See Vorobyev Hills

Kissing
"Beneath a shady tree they sat". Unknown.—ScA
Bugs. K. Kuskin.—LiDd—MoS
Cat kisses. B. Katz.—Det
"Cinderella, dressed in yellow". Unknown.—WiA
The cure. Unknown.—OpT
"Down by the river where the green grass grows". Unknown.—ScA
Fishing. L. Dangel.—JaPr
"Georgie Porgie, pudding and pie". Mother Goose.—SuO—WaM
Howie Kell suspends all lust to contemplate the universe. R. Torreson.—JaPr
"I saw Esau kissing Kate". Mother Goose.—OpI
"I wouldn't be you". Unknown.—OpI
It's gross to kiss. K. Dakos.—DaI
"I've got a lad and he's double double-jointed". Mother Goose.—OpI
"Karen and Richie sitting in a tree". Unknown.—CoM
The kiss ("Come into the hall with me, George"). G. Bogin.—JaM
The kiss ("The kiss started when I danced"). P. B. Janeczko.—JaB
A kiss is round. B. Budney.—MoS
Mistletoe. W. De La Mare.—DeR—MaP
The princess and the frog. S. C. Field.—BaH
"Rowley Powley, pudding and pie". Unknown.—OpT
"Sam and Joan sitting in a tree". Unknown.—ScA
"Sing jigmijole, the pudding bowl". Mother Goose.—WaM
"Some kiss behind a lily". Unknown.—ScA
"Two on a hammock". Unknown.—ScA
Under the mistletoe. C. Cullen.—SlM
"Wash the dishes, wipe the dishes". Mother Goose.—WaM
"We're all dry with drinking on't". Mother Goose.—WaM
"Wine and cakes for gentlemen". Mother Goose.—WaM

Kitchen table. Myra Cohn Livingston.—LiR

Kitchens
The cucumber. N. Hikmet.—NyT
The cupboard. W. De La Mare.—DeR—MaP
Fingerprint. H. Thurston.—BoT
"Give me water". M. C. Livingston.—LiMh
Grandmother in winter. X. J. Kennedy.—LiPg
Hot milk. X. J. Kennedy.—KeK

Koalas
Paula Koala. J. P. Lewis.—LeT
Koertge, Ronald
To impress the girl next door.—JaPr
Koettner-Benigni, Klara
Monkeys, tr. by Herbert Kuhner.—NyT
"A tree".—NyT
Komachi, Ono No
"Although there is".—GoT
"The cicadas sing".—GoT
"Night deepens".—GoT
Konuk, Mutlu
The cucumber, tr.—NyT
Kooser, Ted
Genuine poem, found on a blackboard in a
bowling alley in Story City, Iowa.—KnAs
Korea
Korean butterfly dance. J. Kirkup.—FoLe
Korean butterfly dance. James Kirkup.—FoLe
Koson
"Leaping flying fish".—CaR
Kracken. X. J. Kennedy.—WhDd
Kratz, E. U.
Family portrait, tr.—NyT
Krauss, Ruth
Beginning on paper.—DeS
Duet.—MoR
"Snow melting".—DeS
Song ("When your boyfriend writes you a
letter").—MoR
Kreymborg, Arthur
Life.—CoAz
Krishnasami, Christine M.
"Beside a stone three".—NyT
Kristensen, Tom
Grass ("The grass is strangely tall to me"), tr. by
Paul Borum.—NyT
Kristin Leibowitz. Mel Glenn.—GlBc
Kroll, Ernest
The California Zephyr.—MoR
Kroll, Steven
"When my friends all moved away".—JaP
Krolow, Karl
The open shutter, tr. by Kevin Perryman.—NyT
Kuan Tao Sheng
Married love, tr. by Kenneth Rexroth and Ling
Chung.—GoU
Kudzu. Eve Merriam.—MeCh
Kuhner, Herbert
Monkeys, tr.—NyT
"A tree", tr.—NyT
"Kum by yah, my Lord". Unknown.—StP
Kumar Ragnath. Mel Glenn.—GlBc
Kumin, Maxine
400 meter freestyle.—KnAs
The horses ("It has turned to snow in the
night").—JaP
Plans.—KeT
Remembering you.—KnAs
Sneeze ("There's a sort of a").—MoS
Watering trough.—JaP
Kumin, Maxine W.
Camel ("The camel's a mammal").—HoT
Kusatao
The cat ("Flourishing his head around"), tr. by
Tze-si Huang.—DeI
Kuskin, Karla
"Being lost".—HoGo
"A bug sat in a silver flower".—PrFo
Bugs.—LiDd—MoS
Catherine.—HoS
"Days that the wind takes over".—BaW

Dragon ("Let me tell you about me").—WhDd
Hughbert and the glue.—PrFo
"I have a friend who keeps on standing on her
hands".—JaP
I have a lion.—DeS
"I woke up this morning".—KeT
If ("If you").—LaCc
If I were a.—DeS
"I'm up here".—MoS
Knitted things, sels.
"There was a witch who knitted things".—
DeS
Me ("My nose is blue").—PrFo
"Moon".—LiDd
Pictures of cats.—LaCc
The porcupine ("A porcupine looks somewhat
silly").—LoFh—WhAa
The question ("People always say to me").—LiDd
Rosalie the cat.—LaCc
The rose on my cake.—KeT
Rules.—PrFo
Sitting in the sand.—MoS
Snow ("We'll play in the snow").—HoS
"Spring again".—HoS
That cat.—LaCc
"There was a mouse".—LaM
"There was a witch who knitted things". See
Knitted things
"This cat".—LaCc
"Thoughts that were put into words".—JaP
"Tree birds".—BaW
"When everything has drawn to a close".—PlW
Where would you be.—LaN
The witches' ride.—KeT
"Write about a radish".—JaP
Kwang Chin Ho. Mel Glenn.—GlBc
Kwang-kyu, Kim
The birth of a stone, tr. by Brother Anthony.—
NyT
The land of mists, tr. by Brother Anthony.—NyT
Kwanzaa
Kwanzaa is. C. McClester.—SlM
Kwanzaa is. Cedric McClester.—SlM
"Kwanzaa is a holiday". See Kwanzaa is
Kwelismith
How can I lose hope. See Sing a softblack poem
Sing a softblack poem, sels.
How can I lose hope.—SuC
Kyle Quinn. Mel Glenn.—GlBc
Kyorai
"Galloping pony".—CaR—WhAa
Kyoshi
"Above the chorus".—CaR
"On the dewy trunk".—CaR
Snake eyes, tr. by Tze-si Huang.—DeI
Kyotai
Monkey ("Out of a tree"), tr. by Tze-si Huang.—
DeI

L

L is for laundry. William Jay Smith.—SmL
"L(a". Edward Estlin Cummings.—MoR
"La-la-llamas rate as mammals". See In praise of
llamas
Labels. Arnold Adoff.—AdCh
LaBombard, Joan
Dreamers and flyers.—JaM
Labor. See Work

Labor day
Today is Labor Day. J. Foster.—FoLe
Laborers. See Work
The **labourer.** Toolsy Daby.—NyT
"The **labourer** is back from the field". See The labourer
Lacey Paget. Mel Glenn.—GlBc
Ladders
Shakes and ladders. M. Fatchen.—FaCm
"**Ladies** and gentlemen". Unknown.—ScA—WiA
"**Ladies** and gentlemen and children, too". See Boogie chant and dance
"**Ladies** and jelly spoons". Unknown.—WiA
"**Lady** bird, lady bird, turn around". Unknown.—WiA
Lady-birds. See Beetles
Lady-bugs. See Beetles
"**Lady** Hester Stanhope". William Jay Smith.—SmL
"A **lady** in a boat". Unknown.—WiA
A **lady** in Madrid. N. M. Bodecker.—LiLo
"**Lady** Jane, O Lady Jane". See The gage
The **Lady** of Shalott. Alfred Tennyson.—ElW
"A **lady** was chasing her boy round the room". Unknown.—WiA
"A **lady** who lived in Madrid". See A lady in Madrid
"A **lady** who lived in Mont.". Unknown.—LiLo
"A **lady** who lived in Uganda". See The panda
"A **lady** who lives there close to me". Jo Carson.—CaS
"A **lady** whose name was Miss Hartley". William Jay Smith.—SmL
Ladybird. Suju, tr. by Tze-si Huang.—DeI
"The **ladybird** flies off". See Ladybird
"**Ladybird,** ladybird". See "Ladybug, ladybug, fly away home"
Ladybirds. See Beetles
"**Ladybug**". Myra Cohn Livingston.—LiR
"**Ladybug,** ladybug, fly away home". Mother Goose.—ScA—WiA
"**Ladybird,** ladybird".—WaM
To the ladybird ("Ladybird, ladybird").—OpI
Ladybugs. See Beetles
Laing, Allan
"For water-ices, cheap but good".—StP
Lakes and ponds
Bullhead in summer. M. Singer.—SiT
Calligraphy. J. Yolen.—YoBi
Daddy fell into the pond. A. Noyes.—LiPf
"**Days** were as great as lakes". D. Vogel.—GoT
Dragonflyer. J. P. Lewis.—LeA
Ice fishing. D. Pendleton.—KnAs
"Jake, the twin of John Lothario". E. Raskin.—PrFo
Jump. J. Carson.—JaPr
Lost ("Desolate and lone"). C. Sandburg.—LaN
The night-swans. W. De La Mare.—DeR
"Now the pond is still". Aohozuki.—CaR
"Red bug, yellow bug, little blue". J. Prelutsky.—PrBe
The stranger ("In the nook of a wood where a pool freshed with dew"). W. De La Mare.—DeR
Strictly for the birds. M. Fatchen.—FaCm
Turtle in July. M. Singer.—SiT
Water striders. P. Fleischman.—FlJ
Lal, P.
The ship's whistle, tr.—NyT
The **lamb.** Theodore Roethke.—LiDd
"The **lamb** baaed gently". See Watch
"A **lamb** has a lambkin". See All asleep
"The **lamb** just says, I am". See The lamb

Lambert, James H.
The tale of a dog.—CoAz
Lamblin, Barbara
Medals and money, a re-evaluation.—KnAs
"**Lambs** that learn to walk in snow". See First sight
Lamento. Tomas Transtromer, tr. by May Swenson and Leif Sjoberg.—NyT
Laments. See also Death
All my secrets. M. Mack.—BoT
Annabel Lee. E. A. Poe.—ElW
Araby. W. De La Mare.—DeR
The ballad of Jimi. C. Knight.—SuC
Booman. Unknown.—OpT
The cowboy's lament. Unknown.—ElW
"Did you ever have a dog". B. S. De Regniers.—MoS
"Down-adown-derry". W. De La Mare.—DeR
The dragon's lament. T. Harvey.—FoLe
Elegy for the girl who died in the dump at Ford's Gulch. J. Johnson.—JaPr
"Estaba la paraja pinta". Unknown.—DeA
The lovely bird ("Cu cu ru, sang the lovely bird").—DeA
Euphemistic. E. Merriam.—MeCh
Exercise in preparation for a pindaric ode to Carl Hubbell. D. Schwartz.—KnAs
Fireworks ("The Fourth of July's"). M. C. Livingston.—LiR
Five of us. W. De La Mare.—DeR
The flower-fed buffaloes. V. Lindsay.—CaB
For Mugs. M. C. Livingston.—LiDp
"Garth, from off the garden wall". X. J. Kennedy.—KeFb
The great one. T. Clark.—MoA
The harlot's house. O. Wilde.—ElW
J.T. never will be ten. K. Dakos.—DaI
"Make me a grave where'er you will". From Bury me in a free land. F. E. W. Harper.—SuC
"No labor-saving machine". W. Whitman.—HoVo
"Nobody loves me". Unknown.—OpI—ScA
Oh, oh, should they take away my stove, my inexhaustible ode to joy. M. Bialoszewski.—NyT
The phantom ("Wilt thou never come again"). W. De La Mare.—DeR
Poem ("I loved my friend"). L. Hughes.—DeS—DeT—SlM
Sleep, grandmother. M. Van Doren.—SuI
The truants. W. De La Mare.—DeR—MaP
The watch ("I wakened on my hot, hard bed"). F. Cornford.—MoR
Weights, in memory of my mother, Miriam Murray nee Arnall. L. Murray.—NyT
Western wind. Unknown.—ElW
"When lilacs last in the dooryard bloom'd". W. Whitman.—HoVo
"Where have you gone". M. Evans.—SuC
"**Lamp** is off". See Night light
The **lamplighter.** Walter De La Mare.—DeR
Lamport, Felicia
Clobber the lobber.—MoR
Preparedness.—KnAs
"**Lancelot,** the scurvy knave". X. J. Kennedy.—KeFb
The **land** of counterpane. Robert Louis Stevenson.—DeT—KeT
The **land** of ho-ho-hum. William Jay Smith.—SmL
The **land** of mists. Kim Kwang-kyu, tr. by Brother Anthony.—NyT
The **Land** of Nod. Robert Louis Stevenson.—ElW
"The **land** returns from winter". See St. David's Day
"The **land** was white". Unknown.—OpI

Landau, Zishe
This evening, tr. by Irving Feldman.—GoT
Landesman, Fran
Don't do it my way.—AgL
Landesman, Miles Davis
"Heaven's in the basement".—AgL
Lane, John
You better be ready.—BoT
"A **lane** at the end of Old Pilgrim Street". See The house
Language. See also Words; also names of languages, as Spanish language
Babel. W. De La Mare.—DeR
"Crowned crane". J. Gleason.—NyT
Date-beggin sweet word them. J. Berry.—BeW
Dina Harper. M. Glenn.—GlBc
Ego-tripping. E. Merriam.—MeCh
Euphemistic. E. Merriam.—MeCh
A fishy square dance. E. Merriam.—MeCh
The grammatical witch. J. Yolen.—YoBe
Greenland's history, or the history of the Danes on Greenland. S. Holm.—NyT
How I learned English. G. Dianikian.—JaM
It came from outer space. J. Ciardi.—CiH—LiLo
Jamaican alphabet. L. Bennett.—LeCa
Jonathan Sobel. M. Glenn.—GlBc
Kwang Chin Ho. M. Glenn.—GlBc
Monkeys. K. Koettner-Benigni.—NyT
Mr. Zoo. E. Merriam.—MeCh
Old Mary. G. Brooks.—SuC
Old mountains want to turn to sand. T. Olofsson.—NyT
Polyglot. E. Merriam.—MeCh
A warning ("I know a young girl who can speak"). M. A. Webber.—LiLo
Lanier, Sidney
"My gossip, the owl, is it thou". See Sunrise
Sunrise, sels.
"My gossip, the owl, is it thou".—LiIf
Lanky Hank Farrow. Harold Witt.—KnAs
"The **lanky** hank of a she in the inn over there". See A glass of beer
A **lantern.** Walter De La Mare.—DeR
"A **lantern** lighted me to bed". See A lantern
"**Lap** 1, swimming laps". See Greg Hoffman
"**Lapped** in the light and heat of noon". See The orchard
"The **lariat** snaps, the cowboy rolls". See The closing of the rodeo
"The **lark** is but a bumpkin fowl". See The bonny, bonny owl
"The **lark** sings in heaven". See The lark's song
Larkin, Philip
First sight.—CaB—ElW
Larks
The lark's song. Seisensui.—DeI
Rabbit and lark. J. Reeves.—MoS
The **lark's** song. Seisensui, tr. by Tze-si Huang.—DeI
Larsen, Don (about)
Don Larsen's perfect game. P. Goodman.—KnAs
Lasiocampidae. Myra Cohn Livingston.—LiNe
The **last** baseball samurai. Tom Clark.—KnAs
The **last** cry of the damp fly. Dennis Lee.—PrFo
"The **last** light fails, that shallow pool of day". See Nightfall
The **last** man killed by Indians in Kimble County, Texas. Mike Angelotti.—JaM
"**Last** month when I gave my speech". See Tammy Yarbrough
The **last** mountain lion on Maple Crest Mountain. Peter Meinke.—JaM

"**Last** night". See Go to the Bahamas
"**Last** night and the night before". See "Not last night but the night before"
"**Last** night I dreamed of an old lover". See Grandmother, rocking
"**Last** night, I taught you the planets, my son". See Mr. Neil Pressman, fine arts
"**Last** night the cold wind and the rain blew". See Sunday at the end of summer
"The **last** of October". See Fall
"**Last** year changed its seasons". See In retrospect
Late ("Three small men in a small house"). Walter De La Mare.—MaP
Late ("Your street was named for berries"). Naomi Shihab Nye.—JaP
Late afternoon. Myra Cohn Livingston.—LiT
A **late** assignment. Kalli Dakos.—DaI
Late for breakfast. Mary Dawson.—KeT
Late past bedtime. Arnold Adoff.—BaW
"The **late** wind failed, high on the hill". See The fleeting
"**Latin** is a dead tongue". Unknown.—OpI
Latin language
"Amo, amas". Unknown.—OpI
"Brutus adsum jam forte". Unknown.—OpI
"Ego sum". Unknown.—OpI
"Infir taris". Unknown.—OpI
"Is ab ile here ergo". Unknown.—OpI
"Latin is a dead tongue". Unknown.—OpI
"Sum—I am a gentleman". Unknown.—OpI
"**Laugh** before you eat". Unknown.—WiA
Laughing time. William Jay Smith.—PrFo—SmL
Laughlin, James
Martha Graham.—MoR
Laughter
Bursting. D. Aldis.—PrFo
Changing. M. Angelou.—AnI
Crocodile. W. J. Smith.—SmL
Daddy fell into the pond. A. Noyes.—LiPf
The dwarf. W. De La Mare.—DeR
The giggles. M. Gardner.—PrFo
The hyena. M. Thaler.—CoAz
"I was in the garden". Unknown.—OpI
"If you have got a funnybone". J. Prelutsky.—PrFo
"It tickles me". Unknown.—WiA
Joker. E. Merriam.—MeCh
"Laugh before you eat". Unknown.—WiA
Laughing time. W. J. Smith.—PrFo—SmL
Laughter. M. Waddington.—BoT
Methuselah. E. Merriam.—MeS
Minstrel man. L. Hughes.—SuC
Mrs. Perkins. D. A. Evans.—JaPr
Night fun. J. Viorst.—KeT
"No matter how grouchy you're feeling". A. Euwer.—LiLo
Old folks laugh. M. Angelou.—AnI
The tickle rhyme. I. Serraillier.—MoS
Laughter. Miriam Waddington.—BoT
Laundresses and laundrymen. See Laundry
Laundry
Back yard. V. Worth.—DeT—WoAl
Bewitchery. E. Merriam.—MeCh
"Blair, to make his mother screech". X. J. Kennedy.—KeFb
The disgruntled husband. Unknown.—OpT
L is for laundry. W. J. Smith.—SmL
"Look at that". L. Moore.—HoS
"My mother and your mother". Unknown.—CoM—WiA
"My mother, your mother".—ScA
Old Hogan's goat. Unknown.—CoAz

Leckius, Ingemar
Locked in, tr. by May Swenson.—NyT
Lecture. Paul B. Janeczko.—JaB
Led by the Hebrew School rabbi. Judith Baumel.—KnAs
Lee, Dennis
"Billy Batter".—KeT
The coat.—KeT
The coming of teddy bears.—KeT
Dickery Dean.—KeT
"Dimpleton the simpleton".—CoAz
The dinosaur dinner.—BoT
Garbage delight.—PrFo
I eat kids yum yum.—KeT
Jenny the juvenile juggler.—MoR
The last cry of the damp fly.—PrFo
The muddy puddle.—BoT—MoS
Rattlesnake skipping song.—BoT
"Silverly".—BoT
You too lie down.—KeT
Lee, Don L.
But he was cool or, he even stopped for green lights.—ElW
Leek soup. X. J. Kennedy.—KeGh
"**Leering** across Pearl Street". See Trouble
"**Left** foot, right foot". Mother Goose.—WaM
"**Left**, left". Unknown.—ScA
"**Left**, right, I left my wife and twenty four". See Marching chant
Leg broken. Sharon Bell Mathis.—MaR
"**Leg** over leg". Mother Goose.—CII—WaM
The **legend** of Rosemary. Jane Yolen.—YoHa
Legs
Antelope ("A girl with legs like an antelope"). K. Shiraishi.—AgL
"A centipede was happy quite". Unknown.—PrP
"Donkey walks on four legs". Unknown.—OpI
Every insect. D. Aldis.—WhAa
Granny's ninety-two-year-old legs. A. Adoff.—AdIn
I have ten legs. A. Swir.—NyT
Improper moves. J. Yolen.—YoDd
Leg broken. S. B. Mathis.—MaR
The octopus ("Tell me, o octopus, I begs"). O. Nash.—CaB—WhAa
"On a mule we find two legs behind". Unknown.—ScA
Mules ("On mules . . .").—PrFo
Philander. T. Roethke.—LiLo
Taste the air. A. Bryan.—BrS
There was a man. P. Janowitz.—JaP
Walking. A. Fisher.—FiA
"**Legs** v-ed out from the groin's nugget". See The gymnasts
Leithauser, Brad
"In old Minako Wada's house".—ElW
"A **lemon** and a pickle knocked at the door". Unknown.—WiA
Lemonade stand. Myra Cohn Livingston.—KeT
"**Lend** me an ear, said Mosquito". See Think me a fable
L'Engle, Madeleine
"Dear Lord my God".—StP
Lengths of time. Phyllis McGinley.—DeS
Leonard, William Ellery
The ass in the lion's skin, tr.—CaB
Leopards
Invisible cat. X. J. Kennedy.—KeGh
Okolo the leopard warrior. C. Price.—WhDd
"They tell of a hunter named Shephard". Unknown.—LiLo
Leptopterygius. Jack Prelutsky.—PrT

"**Leptopterygius** lived in the ocean". See Leptopterygius
Lesser, Rika
Degli Sposi.—GoU
Lessie. Eloise Greenfield.—MoS
The **lesson** ("Every time I'm called to the front"). Marin Sorescu.—AgL
A **lesson** ("He made fun of my Pekingese"). X. J. Kennedy.—KeK
A **lesson** from golf. Edgar Guest.—KnAs
"**Lester** after the Western". See Strong men, riding horses
Lester tells of Wanda and the big snow. Paul Zimmer.—JaM
"**Let** me be prodigal as sun in praising you". See Geography of music
"**Let** me call you sweetheart". Unknown.—ScA
"**Let** me celebrate you, I". See A dialogue of watching
"**Let** me get up early on this summer morning". Eugene Guillevic, tr. by Teo Savory.—GoT
Let me rap you my orbital map. James Berry.—BeW
"**Let** me tell you about me". See Dragon
"**Let** my thoughts and words please you, Lord". Joan M. Burns.—StP
"**Let** nothing disturb you". Saint Teresa of Avila.—StP
Let the biter beware. Arnold Adoff.—AdCh
"**Let** the end of all bathtubs". See Watering trough
"**Let** the heavens rejoice, and let the earth be glad". From The book of psalms. Bible/Old Testament.—StP
"**Let** the rain kiss you". See April rain song
"**Let** the words of my mouth and the". From The book of psalms. Bible/Old Testament.—StP
"**Let** this be my last word". Rabindranath Tagore.—StP
"**Let** us dedicate ourselves to what the Greeks". Robert Kennedy.—StP
"**Let** us dig down". See "Ntonkale pansi"
Let us go to the woods. Unknown.—CII
"**Let** us go to the woods, says this pig". See Let us go to the woods
"**Let** us have faith that right makes might". From The Gettysburg address. Abraham Lincoln.—StP
"**Let** us in peace eat the food". Unknown.—StP
"**Let** us praise and thank God for all great and". Unknown.—StP
Let X equal half. J. F. Wilson.—LiLo
Let's be merry. Christina Georgina Rossetti.—KeT
Let's dress up. Mary Ann Hoberman.—KeT
"**Let's** dress up in grown-up clothes". See Let's dress up
"**Let's** fold perhaps". See Origami for two
Let's go, Mets. Lillian Morrison.—KnAs
"**Let's** go rolling, rolling". See Getting dirty
"**Let's** marry, said the cherry". N. M. Bodecker.—LiDd
Letter. Myra Cohn Livingston.—LiT
Letter from a witch named Flo. Jane Yolen.—YoBe
Letter from my son. Shihab Sarkar.—NyT
"**Letter** is signed—your one baby-person". See Scribbled notes picked up by owners, and rewritten because of bad grammar, bad spelling, bad writing
Letter to bee. See "Bee, I'm expecting you"
Letters and letter writing
"Dear Santa Claus". J. Prelutsky.—LoFh
Distances of longing. F. Abu Khalid.—NyT
A grandfather's last letter. N. Dubie.—JaM

Li Po
  Firefly, sels.
    "I think".—DeS
  "I think". See Firefly
"Liar, liar, lick spit". Unknown.—OpI
"Liar, liar, pants on fire". Unknown.—CoM—ScA
Liatsos, Sandra
  Night ("Night is a blanket").—HoSt
  Night music.—HoSt
  Sea wave.—HoS
  Wild geese.—HoS
Liberty. Ron Ikan.—JaPr
Libraries and librarians
  Andy Fierstein. M. Glenn.—GlBc
  Janet DeStasio. M. Glenn.—GlBc
  Kumar Ragnath. M. Glenn.—GlBc
  Library. V. Worth.—WoAl
  Mrs. Krikorian. S. Olds.—JaPr
  Ms. Yvonne Harmon, librarian. M. Glenn.—GlBc
  Ode to my library. G. Soto.—SoNe
  The poet ("Before he moved in with Miss Perry").
    P. B. Janeczko.—JaB
  Shut not your doors. W. Whitman.—HoVo
  Surprise ("The biggest"). B. McLoughland.—
    HoGo
  That girl. G. Soto.—SoA
Library. Valerie Worth.—WoAl
Licorice. John Paul Duggan.—BoT
"The lid broke, and suddenly the child". See Skater
  in blue
"Lie on your front in the summer sand". See July
Life. See also Modern life
  "Afoot and light-hearted I take to the open road".
    From Song of the open road. W. Whitman.—
    HoVo
  "All this time and at all times wait the words of
    true poems". From Song of myself. W.
    Whitman.—HoVo
  Almost a madrigal. S. Quasimodo.—GoT
  And my heart soars. Chief D. George.—BoT—
    LoFh
  The artist. A. Bryan.—BrS
  Bertha Robbins. M. Glenn.—GlBc
  Birches. R. Frost.—SuI
  Black dog, red dog. S. Dobyns.—JaPr
  A brief note to the bag lady, ma sister. Y.
    Eradam.—NyT
  The catch ("Happy to have these fish"). R.
    Carver.—KnAs
  Crossing the park. H. Moss.—SuI
  Divine delight. W. De La Mare.—DeR
  Do good. A. Bryan.—BrS
  "Don't talk to me about no options, I'm poor". J.
    Carson.—CaS
  Dreams. L. Hughes.—LoFh—SlM
  "Each day the first day". D. Hammarskjold.—StP
  Earth folk. W. De La Mare.—DeR—MaP
  Eating bread. G. Soto.—SoA
  Ex-basketball player. J. Updike.—KnAs
  Excelsior. W. Whitman.—HoVo
  "Fightin' was natural". M. Angelou.—AnI
  From the autograph album. Unknown.—MoA
  Gaze now. W. De La Mare.—DeR
  Haunted ("The rabbit in his burrow keeps"). W.
    De La Mare.—DeR
  "The heart of man has four chambers, and each
    is filled with". N. Corwin.—GoT
  Here today. W. De La Mare.—DeR
  The hill. E. Merriam.—MeS
  Honeybees. P. Fleischman.—FlJ
  Hurry. E. Merriam.—MeS

"I am the poet of the body and I am the poet of
  the soul". From Song of myself. W.
  Whitman.—HoVo
"I believe that life is given us so we may". H.
  Keller.—StP
"I celebrate myself, and sing myself". From Song
  of myself. W. Whitman.—HoVo
"I have heard what the talkers were talking, the
  talk of the". From Song of myself. W.
  Whitman.—HoVo
Ilan' life. S. J. Wallace.—LeCa
In evening air. T. Roethke.—GoT
In this deep darkness. N. Zach.—GoT
Innocency. W. De La Mare.—DeR
Insignificant. M. Angelou.—AnI
Is love. M. Angelou.—AnI
"It is no dream of mine". H. D. Thoreau.—SuI
Lamento. T. Transtromer.—NyT
Life doesn't frighten me. M. Angelou.—AgL
The life of a man is a circle. Black Elk.—SnD
A lifetime in third grade. K. Dakos.—DaI
A little girl's poem. G. Brooks.—JaP
The little shop (for a picture). W. De La Mare.—
  DeR
"Lord most giving and resourceful". Unknown.—
  StP
Love song to a stranger. J. Baez.—GoU
Lucia. L. Casalinuovo.—NyT
A lullaby ("Sleep, child, lie quiet, let be"). J.
  Agee.—GoT
"May the road rise to meet you". Unknown.—StP
Me ("As long as I live"). W. De La Mare.—DeR
Mother to son. L. Hughes.—DeT—SlM—SuC
Mrs. Earth. W. De La Mare.—DeR—MaP
Music. W. De La Mare.—DeR
"My life closed twice before its close". E.
  Dickinson.—SuI
My life story. L. Nguyen.—NyT
My 71st year. W. Whitman.—HoVo
Nocturne ("A long arm embossed with gold slides
  from the tree tops"). L.-P. Fargue.—GoT
O taste and see. D. Levertov.—ElW
Ol' man river. From Show Boat. O.
  Hammerstein.—SuC
Old Mary. G. Brooks.—SuC
On journeys through the states. W. Whitman.—
  HoVo
"Once I got a postcard from the Fiji Islands". J.
  Kaplinski.—NyT
One more time. N. Willard.—SaB
"One thought ever at the fore". W. Whitman.—
  HoVo
Or. A. Darwish.—NyT
Part XX: This brief day now over. From A child's
  day. W. De La Mare.—DeR
Patricia Lampert. M. Glenn.—GlBc
Please to remember ("Here am I"). W. De La
  Mare.—DeR
Poppies in October. S. Plath.—ElW
Propositions. N. Parra.—AgL
The quiet enemy. W. De La Mare.—DeR
Rhapsody. W. S. Braithwaite.—SlM
Rocks ("They say, no"). V. Worth.—WoAl
Sam's three wishes or life's little whirligig. W. De
  La Mare.—DeR
Say nay. E. Merriam.—MeS
Scraping the world away. C. H. Webster.—AgL
The silly song ("Hey ding a ding"). M. Mahy.—
  MaN
"Since feeling is first". E. E. Cummings.—ElW
Small wants. B. Padhi.—NyT
So I'm proud. J. Little.—LiHe

Life.—*Continued*
  Song of enchantment. W. De La Mare.—DeR—
    MaP
  The song of the mad prince. W. De La Mare.—
    DeR—ElW—MaP
  Southern road. S. A. Brown.—SuC
  "Starting from fish-shape Paumanok where I was
    born". From Starting from Paumanok. W.
    Whitman.—HoVo
  The story of your life. B. Bennett.—MoR
  Teaching numbers. G. Soto.—SoA
  The tennis. E. B. White.—KnAs
  "Thanks for today, God, for all of it". H. F.
    Couch, and S. S. Barefield.—StP
  Then as now. W. De La Mare.—DeR
  There are days. B. S. De Regniers.—DeW
  "Ticky ticky tuck". M. Smith.—AgL
  To daffodils. R. Herrick.—ElW
  "To life". Unknown.—StP
  Touching. From Songs for Nandu Bhende. N.
    Ezekiel.—AgL
  "A train is passing". P. Borum.—NyT
  "Victory, union, faith, identity, time". From
    Starting from Paumanok. W. Whitman.—HoVo
  We wear the mask. P. L. Dunbar.—SuC
  What are heavy. C. G. Rossetti.—ElW
  When I read the book. W. Whitman.—HoVo
  Wordless day. C. Shiang-hua.—NyT
  The words of the true poems. W. Whitman.—SuI
  World. A. R. Ammons.—ElW
  Yesterday. J. Little.—LiHe
Life—Conduct of life. See Conduct of life
Life—Life after death. See Immortality
Life. Arthur Kreymborg.—CoAz
Life doesn't frighten me. Maya Angelou.—AgL
Life in the forest, or, bad news, good news, bad
  news. Arnold Adoff.—AdCh
"Life is for me and is shining". See A little girl's
  poem
"Life is seldom if ever dull". See Gull
The life of a man is a circle. Black Elk.—SnD
"The life of a man is a circle from childhood". See
  The life of a man is a circle
Life of the cricket. Jorge Carrera Andrade, tr. by
  John Malcolm Brinnin.—NyT
The lifeguard. James Dickey.—KnAs
A lifetime in third grade. Kalli Dakos.—DaI
"Lift me up". Myra Cohn Livingston.—LiMh
"Lift the nozzle". Unknown.—WiA
Light
  Afterglow. J. L. Borges.—GoT
  Bed in summer. R. L. Stevenson.—DeT
  The coat. D. Lee.—KeT
  Evening dawn. H. Scott.—JaPr
  The evening light along the sound. S. Santos.—
    GoT
  In the discreet splendor. A. L. Strauss.—GoT
  The lamplighter. W. De La Mare.—DeR
  Lucia. L. Casalinuovo.—NyT
  Moon's ending. S. Teasdale.—GoT
  The moth's serenade. P. Fleischman.—FlJ
  Old deep sing song. C. Sandburg.—MoR
  The open shutter. K. Krolow.—NyT
  The prayer of the glow-worm. C. B. De
    Gasztold.—DeP
  Prism in the window. From Four poems for Roy
    G Biv. B. J. Esbensen.—EsW
  "Science". G. Nelson.—SlM
  "There's a certain slant of light". E. Dickinson.—
    GoT—SuI
  This I know. A. Corkett.—BoT

"Light a candle, then one more". See Hanukkah
  candles
"Light as a feather". Unknown.—ScA
"Light comes back again and I". See Free time
Light fabric. James Berry.—BeW
The light house keeper's white mouse. John
  Ciardi.—LaM—MoS
"Light, light". See Fireflies
"The light of dawn rose on my dreams". See The
  child in the story awakes
"The light of day". See This I know
Light rain, a downpour, and pigeons feasting on
  crumbs from a picnic in the park. Eve
  Merriam.—MeP
Light string. Valerie Worth.—WoA
Light the festival candles. Aileen Fisher.—FoLe
"Light the first of eight tonight". See Light the
  festival candles
"Light the lamp now". See Dipa, the lamp
"Lighted lanterns". See The doll festival
Lighthouse. J. Patrick Lewis.—LeE
Lighthouses
  "I'd like to be a lighthouse". R. Field.—LiDd
  The light house keeper's white mouse. J. Ciardi.—
    LaM—MoS
  Lighthouse. J. P. Lewis.—LeE
  Night fog. X. J. Kennedy.—KeK
"Lightless, unholy, eldritch thing". See The bat
Lightning. See Thunder and lightning
The lightning. May Swenson.—SuI
Lightning bugs. See Fireflies
"The lightning waked me, it slid under". See The
  lightning
Lights and lighting. See also Candles; Lighthouses
  Christmas lights. V. Worth.—WoAl
  City lights. R. Field.—DeT
  The dark ("There are six little houses up on the
    hill"). E. M. Roberts.—DeT
  "Flashing neon night". J. W. Hackett.—LaN
  A lantern. W. De La Mare.—DeR
  Light string. V. Worth.—WoA
  Night light. M. C. Livingston.—LiR
  No need to light a night light. Unknown.—HoS
  Queensboro Bridge. M. C. Livingston.—LiNe
"Lights are". See Queensboro Bridge
"The lights are all lit". See Dinosaur waltz
Lights in the dark. Eve Merriam.—MeP
Like a fire eating dragon. John Ciardi.—CiH
"Like a map blanketing a bed". See Patches of sky
"Like a nest". See Asparagus
"Like divers, we ourselves must make the jump".
  See The springboard
"Like falling rain". See The cry guy
"Like magic". Joanne Ryder.—JaP
"Like roundness of the rotating globe". See Shapes
  and actions
"Like the tides' flood". Unknown, tr. by Kenneth
  Rexroth.—GoU
"Like your books". Unknown.—WiA
Likes and dislikes
  Aelourophile. E. Merriam.—MeCh
  Aelourophobe. E. Merriam.—MeCh
  Andrea Pulovsky. M. Glenn.—GlBc
  Anteater ("The anteater makes a meal of ants").
    W. J. Smith.—PrFo—SmL
  "Birds of a feather flock together". Mother
    Goose.—WaM
    Birds of a feather.—ClI
  Bonny sailor boy. Unknown.—OpT
  Brother. M. A. Hoberman.—DeS—DeT—MoS—
    PrFo
  Bugs. K. Kuskin.—LiDd—MoS

Likes and dislikes—*Continued*

Cat ("I prefer"). M. Singer.—SiT

The cat who aspired to higher things. X. J. Kennedy.—LaM

Cats and dogs. N. M. Bodecker.—KeT—LaM—MoS

Companion. D. Manjush.—NyT

December ("I like days"). A. Fisher.—FiA—GoA

"Different people have different 'pinions". Unknown.—OpI

Do you know anyone like him. J. Ciardi.—CiH

"Eat it, it's good for you". M. A. Hoberman.—HoFa

Envying the children of San Francisco. G. Soto.—SoA

Giraffes ("Giraffes, I like them"). M. A. Hoberman.—WhAa

"Hector Protector was dressed all in green". Mother Goose.—SuO

Ho hum. J. Ciardi.—CiH

Hug o' war. S. Silverstein.—MoS

I can't abear. W. De La Mare.—DeR—MaP

"I do not like thee, Doctor Fell". Mother Goose.—OpI—SuO—WaM

"I like coffee, I like tea". Unknown.—WiA

"I like it when it's mizzly". A. Fisher.—MoS

"I love my wife and I love my baby". Unknown.—WiA

I love you it's true. C. Stewart.—AgL

The ice cream fountain mountain. E. Merriam.—MeP

"I'd like a story". X. J. Kennedy.—HoGo

"If you and your folks like me and my folks". Unknown.—WiA

"I'm in another dimension". K. Dakos.—DaI

"Jack Sprat could eat no fat". Mother Goose.—EdGl—SuO—WaM

The king of hearts. W. J. Smith.—SmL

The King of Spain. W. J. Smith.—SmL

Knoxville, Tennessee. N. Giovanni.—DeS—SlM

"Lay the cloth, knife and fork". Unknown.—OpI

"Like your books". Unknown.—WiA

Mail king. P. B. Janeczko.—JaB

Meg's egg. M. A. Hoberman.—MoS

Mice ("I think mice"). R. Fyleman.—DeS—LaM

"The mosquito often goes to the village for syrup but doesn't always get it". From Jamaican Caribbean proverbs. Unknown.—BeW

"Mother doesn't want a dog". J. Viorst.—WhAa

My favorite word. J. L. Hymes, and L. Hymes.—DeS

"My little old man and I fell out". Mother Goose.—WaM

Neck please. E. Glen.—LiPg

Night creature. L. Moore.—DeS

"Often we are foolish". Unknown.—ScA

One, two, three, four m-o-t-h-e-r. F. Holman.—LiPm

Oodles of noodles. J. L. Hymes, and L. Hymes.—PrFo

Our kitten. Unknown.—ClI

Part X: This little morsel of morsels here. From A child's day. W. De La Mare.—DeR

"Pease porridge hot, pease porridge cold". Mother Goose.—SuO—WaM

"The reason I like chocolate". N. Giovanni.—LoFh

Said the monster. L. Moore.—LiLo

Shoes. V. Worth.—WoAl

"Snow in the east". E. Merriam.—MeY—MoS

So long as there's weather. T. Kitt.—DeS

The song of the mischievous dog. D. Thomas.—DeT

"Spaghetti, spaghetti". J. Prelutsky.—MoS

Spinach. F. P. Heide.—HeG

Super strategem. X. J. Kennedy.—KeGh

"There was a young lady named Perkins". Unknown.—LiLo

Tinkering. D. Dawber.—BoT

Toni Vingelli. M. Glenn.—GlBc

"Violet picks bluebells". E. Merriam.—MeY

A vote for vanilla. E. Merriam.—MeS

What I like. M. Mahy.—MaN

Wishing for winter in summer. X. J. Kennedy.—KeK

Yawn. S. O. Huigan.—BoT

"Lil, to cut the rug's pile lower". X. J. Kennedy.—KeFb

Lilies

Song of the water lilies. E. Greenfield.—GrU

Liliuokalani, queen of Hawaii

Queen's prayer.—StP

"Limbo". See Caliban limbo

Limericks

"An abhorrent young person named Plunkett". W. J. Smith.—SmL

About learning things the hard way. J. Ciardi.—CiH

Alice. W. J. Smith.—SmL

All right, do it your way. J. Ciardi.—CiH

And they met in the middle. J. Ciardi.—CiH

April fool. J. Ciardi.—CiH—LiLo

Arthur. O. Nash.—LiLo

"As a beauty I'm not a great star". A. Euwer.—LiLo

"A barber who lived in Batavia". Unknown.—LiLo

Be kind to dumb animals. J. Ciardi.—CiH—LiLo

Be warned. M. Fatchen.—FaCm

"A beautiful lady named Psyche". Unknown.—LiLo

Beware ("When a cub, unaware being bare"). From Animalimericks. E. Merriam.—MeS

"A bicycle rider named Crockett". W. J. Smith.—SmL

"A Boston boy went out to Yuma". Unknown.—LiLo

"A bridge engineer, Mister Crumpett". Unknown.—LiLo

A bright idea. X. J. Kennedy.—LiLo

"A captain, retired from the Navy". W. J. Smith.—SmL

"A careless zookeeper named Blake". Unknown.—LiLo

"A certain young fellow, named Bobbie". Unknown.—LiLo

"A certain young man of great gumption". Unknown.—LiLo

The chow hound. J. Ciardi.—CiH

"A clever gorilla named Gus". J. Prelutsky.—PrP

"A collegiate damsel named Breeze". Unknown.—LiLo

"A contentious old person named Reagan". W. J. Smith.—SmL

"Cried a man on the Salisbury Plain". M. C. Livingston.—LiLo

"Cries a sheep to a ship on the Amazon". J. P. Lewis.—LiLo

A crusty mechanic. N. M. Bodecker.—LiLo

"A daring young lady of Guam". Unknown.—LiLo

"A decrepit old gasman, named Peter". Unknown.—LiLo

Limericks—*Continued*

"A rather polite man of Hawarden". Unknown.—LiLo

Rest in peace. J. Ciardi.—CiH

"Said a foolish young lady of Wales". L. Reed.—LiLo

"Said a lady beyond Pompton Lakes". M. Bishop.—LiLo

"Said a restless young person of Yew". M. C. Livingston.—LiLo

"Said an ogre from old Saratoga". C. Aiken.—LiLo

"Said Gus Goop, that spaghetti was great". X. J. Kennedy.—KeGh—LiLo

"Said Mrs. Isosceles Tri". C. B. Burgess.—LiLo

"Said old peeping Tom of Fort Lee". M. Bishop.—LiLo

"Said Rev. Rectangular Square". C. B. Burgess.—LiLo

"Said the condor, in tones of despair". O. Herford.—LiLo

"Said the crab, 'tis not beauty or birth". O. Herford.—LiLo

Said the monster. L. Moore.—LiLo

"A scientist living at Staines". R. Hewison.—LiLo

"A sea serpent saw a big tanker". Unknown.—LiLo—PrP

Serves him right. J. Ciardi.—CiH

"A silly young fellow named Ben". J. Prelutsky.—LiLo—PrP

"A skeleton once in Khartoum". Unknown.—LiLo

"A small boy, while learning to swim". E. Gordon.—LiLo

"A small mouse in Middleton Stoney". M. C. Livingston.—LiLo

Some rabbits. Unknown.—ClI

Sometimes even parents win. J. Ciardi.—CiH—LiLo

Speedy Sam. J. Ciardi.—CiH

Sticky situation. X. J. Kennedy.—LiLo

Stop squirming. J. Ciardi.—CiH

Summer cooler. X. J. Kennedy.—KeK

Tennis clinic. L. Morrison.—LiLo

That fish was just too fussy. J. Ciardi.—CiH

"There is a young reindeer named Donder". J. P. Lewis.—LiLo

"There once was a barber of Kew". C. Monkhouse.—LiLo

"There once was a big rattlesnake". Unknown.—LiLo

"There once was a boy of Bagdad". Unknown.—LiLo

"There once was a boy of Quebec". R. Kipling.—LiLo

"There once was a centipede neat". Unknown.—LiLo

"There once was a dancing black bear". J. P. Lewis.—LiLo

"There once was a girl of New York". C. Monkhouse.—LiLo

"There once was a man in the moon". D. McCord.—LiLo

"There once was a man who said, how". Unknown.—LiLo

"There once was a man who said, why". Unknown.—LiLo

"There once was a person of Benin". C. Monkhouse.—LiLo

"There once was a plesiosaurus". Unknown.—LiLo

"There once was a scarecrow named Joel". D. McCord.—LiLo

"There once was an old kangaroo". Unknown.—LiLo

"There once were two cats of Kilkenny". Unknown.—LiLo

    The cats of Kilkenny ("There were once . . .").—ElW—LaCc

There seems to be a problem. J. Ciardi.—CiH

"There was a faith-healer of Deal". Unknown.—LiLo

"There was a fat lady from Eye". Unknown.—LiLo

"There was a sad pig with a tail". A. Lobel.—LiLo

"There was a small maiden named Maggie". Unknown.—LiLo—PrP

    There was a young maiden (". . . called Maggie").—ClI

"There was a small pig who wept tears". A. Lobel.—HoS

"There was a young angler of Worthing". Unknown.—LiLo

"There was a young bard of Japan". Unknown.—LiLo

"There was a young damsel of Lynn". Unknown.—LiLo

"There was a young farmer of Leeds". Unknown.—LiLo—SuO

    A young farmer of Leeds.—DeS

"There was a young fellow called Hugh". M. Fatchen.—LiLo

"There was a young fellow named Hall". Unknown.—LiLo

"There was a young fellow named Shear". J. Ciardi.—LiLo

"There was a young fellow named Weir". Unknown.—LiLo

"There was a young girl named O'Neill". Unknown.—LiLo

"There was a young girl of Asturias". Unknown.—LiLo

"There was a young lady from Woosester". Unknown.—LiLo

"There was a young lady named Bright". Unknown.—LiLo

"There was a young lady named Flo". Unknown.—LiLo

"There was a young lady named Groat". W. J. Smith.—SmL

"There was a young lady named Hannah". Unknown.—LiLo

"There was a young lady named Perkins". Unknown.—LiLo

"There was a young lady named Rose". W. J. Smith.—LiLo—SmL

"There was a young lady named Ruth". Unknown.—LiLo

"There was a young lady of Bute". E. Lear.—ClI—LiLo

"There was a young lady of Crete". Unknown.—LiLo—PrP

    A young lady of Crete.—PrFo

"There was a young lady of Ealing". Unknown.—LiLo

"There was a young lady of Firle". E. Lear.—LiLo

"There was a young lady of Kent". Unknown.—LiLo

"There was a young lady of Lynn". Unknown.—LiLo

"There was a young lady of Niger". Unknown.—KeT—PrP

Limericks—*Continued*

"There was once a young woman of Oporta". L. Carroll.—LiLo

"There were three little birds in a wood". Unknown.—LiLo

"There's a girl out in Ann Arbor, Mich.". Unknown.—LiLo

"There's a tiresome young man from Bay Shore". M. Bishop.—LiLo

They had a point to make. J. Ciardi.—CiH

"They tell of a hunter named Shephard". Unknown.—LiLo

The thingamajig. J. Ciardi.—CiH

The thinker. J. Ciardi.—CiH—LiLo

"This season our tunnips was red". D. McCord.—LiLo

"A thrifty young fellow of Shoreham". Unknown.—LiLo

"'Tis a favorite project of mine". H. L. Carter.—LiLo

"A tutor who tooted the flute". Unknown.—LiLo

"Two revolting young persons named Gruen". W. J. Smith.—SmL

The unfortunate giraffe. O. Herford.—LiLo

"An unpopular youth of Cologne". Unknown.—LiLo

"An unusual man from Bound Brook". X. J. Kennedy.—KeGh

Variety. From Animalimericks. E. Merriam.—MeS

"Wailed a ghost in a graveyard at Kew". M. C. Livingston.—LiHp—LiLo

A warning ("I know a young girl who can speak"). M. A. Webber.—LiLo

"When a jolly young fisher named Fisher". Unknown.—LiLo—PrP

When you are there at all, that is. J. Ciardi.—CiH

Willis C. Sick. J. Ciardi.—CiH

Win some, lose some. J. Ciardi.—CiH

"A woman named Mrs. S. Claus". J. P. Lewis.—LiLo

The yak ("There was a most odious yak"). T. Roethke.—LiLo

"Young Frankenstein's robot invention". B. Braley.—LiLo

A young lady from Glitch. T. Kitt.—DeS

"A young man from old Terre Haute". W. J. Smith.—SmL

"Young radical Byron McNally". W. J. Smith.—SmL

Lincoln, Abraham

The Gettysburg address, sels.

"Let us have faith that right makes might".—StP

"Let us have faith that right makes might". See The Gettysburg address

Lincoln, Abraham (about)

Abraham Lincoln. S. V. Benet, and R. C. Benet.—LoFh

"Lincoln". M. C. Livingston.—LiR

To meet Mr. Lincoln. E. Merriam.—DeS

"When lilacs last in the dooryard bloom'd". W. Whitman.—HoVo

"Lincoln". Myra Cohn Livingston.—LiR

"Lincoln, Lincoln, I been thinkin'". Unknown.—CoM

"Lincoln was a long man". See Abraham Lincoln

Linden, Eddie

A drunken egotist.—AgL

Lindon, J. A.

Ruthless rhyme.—PrFo

Lindsay, Vachel

The flower-fed buffaloes.—CaB

The little turtle.—DeS—LiDd

"The moon's the north wind's cooky". See What the little girl said

The mysterious cat.—DeS—LaCc

What grandpa mouse said.—LiIf

What the little girl said.—DeT

"The moon's the north wind's cooky".—LiDd

Lindsey, Jim

"The Indians", tr.—NyT

Lindstrom, Naomi

Autumn and the sea, tr.—NyT

"A **line** in long array where they wind betwixt green islands". See Cavalry crossing a ford

Lineage. Margaret Walker.—LiPg

"**Lined** up on a station platform". See On destiny

Lines for remembering about lids. X. J. Kennedy.—KeK

"The **lines** in old people's hands". See The memory of horses

Lines to a nasturtium (a lover muses). Ann Spencer.—SuC

Link rhymes. See Build-on rhymes

"The **links** are chance, the chain is fate". See Mathematics of love

Linssen, Linda

Boy, fifteen, killed by hummingbird.—JaPr

Lion ("The beast that is most fully dressed"). William Jay Smith.—SmL

The **lion** ("He's smarter than the tabby"). J. Patrick Lewis.—LeT

The **lion** ("The lion, the lion, he dwells in the waste"). Hilaire Belloc.—ClI

The **lion** ("Oh, weep for Mr. and Mrs. Bryan"). Ogden Nash.—KeT

"The **lion** and the unicorn". Mother Goose.—EdGl

Lion dance. Trevor Millum.—FoLe

"The **lion**, the lion, he dwells in the waste". See The lion

"The **lion** walks on padded paws". See Leap and dance

Lions

"A handsome young noble of Spain". Unknown.—LiLo

Lion ("The beast that is most fully dressed"). W. J. Smith.—SmL

The lion ("He's smarter than the tabby"). J. P. Lewis.—LeT

The lion ("The lion, the lion, he dwells in the waste"). H. Belloc.—ClI

The lion ("Oh, weep for Mr. and Mrs. Bryan"). O. Nash.—KeT

"The lion and the unicorn". Mother Goose.—EdGl

Lion dance. T. Millum.—FoLe

Lions. V. Worth.—WoAl

Supper for a lion. D. Aldis.—CoAz—HoT

"There was a young fellow called Hugh". M. Fatchen.—LiLo

Lions. Valerie Worth.—WoAl

Lipscomb, Gene (about)

Say goodbye to Big Daddy. R. Jarrell.—KnAs

Listen. Walter De La Mare.—DeR

"**Listen**". Lilian Moore.—SuI

"**Listen**, I who love thee well". See The flower

"**Listen**, I'm talking in stumbles and bumps". See Poet

"**Listen**, I've a big surprise". See Invitation

Listen, Lord—a prayer. James Weldon Johnson.—SuC

"**Listen,** my children, and you shall hear". See Paul Revere's ride

"**Listen,** my children, and you shall hear of the midnight ride of Mary dear". Unknown.—WiA

"**Listen** my dear". See The flower's perfume

"**Listen,** there's a sound". See All Hallows' Eve

"**Listen** to the coal". See In memoriam John Coltrane

"**Listen** to the reading". See Mela

Listening to baseball in the car. Gail Mazur.—KnAs

"**Listening** winds". See Love letter

Lister, Daphne
Under the stairs.—BaH

Listn big brodda dread, na. James Berry.—BeW

"**Listn** the male chauvinist is mi dad". See Girls can we educate us dads

Litter. See Garbage

"A **litter** of little black foxes, and later". See Foxes

Little, Jean
About angels and age.—LiHe
About God.—LiHe
About notebooks.—LiHe
About old people.—LiHe
About poems, sort of.—LiHe
After English class.—LiHe
Afternoon in March.—LiHe
Alone ("I am alone, and lonely").—LiHe
Cartwheels.—LiHe
Clothes ("I like new clothes").—LiHe
Condensed version.—LiHe
Engaged.—LiHe
Every so often.—LiHe
Extinguished.—LiHe
Growing pains.—LiHe
He was so little.—LiHe
Hey world, here I am.—LiHe
I told you so.—LiHe
Louisa, Louisa.—LiHe
Louisa's liberation.—LiHe
Mosquitoes.—LiHe
Mother has a talk with me.—LiHe
My own day.—LiHe—LoFh
Not enough Emilys.—LiHe
Oranges ("I peel oranges neatly").—LiHe
Parsnips.—LiHe
Pearls.—LiHe
Smart remark.—BoT—LiHe
So I'm proud.—LiHe
Surprise ("I feel like the ground in winter").—LiHe
Susannah and the daisies.—LiHe
Today.—LiHe
Wars.—LiHe
"When someone I love is hurt".—LiHe
Working parents.—LiHe
Yesterday.—LiHe

Little, Lessie Jones
My yellow straw hat.—KeT

Little. Dorothy Aldis.—DeT

"A **little** after twilight". See The stranger

"**Little** Arabella Miller". Unknown.—PrP

"A **little** axe can cut down a big tree". From Jamaican Caribbean proverbs. Unknown.—BeW

"A **little** ball, a banana, a pear". See "Xiao pi qiu, xiang jiao li"

The **little** bird ("My dear Daddie bought a mansion"). Walter De La Mare.—DeR—MaP

A **little** bird ("What do you have for breakfast"). Aileen Fisher.—FiA

"**Little** birds bathe". See Part III: Little birds bathe

"**Little** birds sing with their beaks". See Singing

"**Little** Bo-Peep has lost her sheep". Mother Goose.—EdGl—SuO—WaM

"The **little** boat at anchor". See Fourth of July night

"**Little** Boy Blue, come blow your horn". Mother Goose.—EdGl—SuO—WaM

Little boy blues. Eloise Greenfield.—GrN

"**Little** brown house mouse, laugh and leap". See The house mouse

Little bush. Elizabeth Madox Roberts.—LiDd See Little bush

"**Little** cats walk with their tails up". See Confidence

"**Little** Clotilda". Unknown.—ClI

The **little** creature. Walter De La Mare.—DeR

"**Little** dabs of powder". Unknown.—ScA

"**Little** Dick was so quick". Unknown.—WiA

Little Dimity. William Jay Smith.—SmL

Little donkey close your eyes. Margaret Wise Brown.—DeT

"**Little** donkey on the hill". See Little donkey close your eyes

The **little** duck. Joso, tr. by Tze-si Huang.—DeI

"The **little** duck looks very wise". See The little duck

"The **little** fawn". See In the forest

Little fish. Basho, tr. by Tze-si Huang.—DeI

Little fly. Unknown.—ClI

"**Little** fly upon the wall". See Little fly

"**Little** frog among". Gaki, tr. by Sylvia Cassedy and Kunihiro Suetake. Haiku.—DeT

"The **little** girl". See What the little girl did

The **little** girl and the turkey. Dorothy Aldis.—DeT

"The **little** girl said". See The little girl and the turkey

A **little** girl's poem. Gwendolyn Brooks.—JaP

"**Little** gray cuckoos". See Busy

The **little** green orchard. Walter De La Mare.—DeR—MaP

"A **little** health, a little wealth". See Two precepts

"**Little** Jack Horner". See Teasing

"**Little** Jack Horner". Mother Goose.—EdGl—SuO—WaM

"**Little** Jack Sprat". Mother Goose.—ClI

"**Little** Johnny fished all day". Unknown.—PrP

"**Little** Johnny Morgan". Mother Goose.—ClI

The **little** jumping girls. See "Jump, jump, jump"

"The **little** kitten's face". See Dawn

"**Little** lamb, who made thee". William Blake.—StP

"A **little** light is going by". See Firefly

"**Little** man in coal pit goes". See Dressing a baby

"A **little** man of Teheran". Unknown.—WiA

"**Little** Ming, Little Ming". See "Xiao Ming, Xiao Ming"

"**Little** Miss Donnet". Mother Goose.—WaM

"**Little** Miss Lily, you're dreadfully silly". Mother Goose.—WaM

"**Little** Miss Muffet". Mother Goose.—EdGl—SuO—WaM

"**Little** Miss Muffet sat on a tuffet". Unknown.—ScA

"**Little** Miss Pinky all dressed in blue". Unknown.—ScA

"**Little** Miss Singer brushes her dress". From Riddle poems. James Berry.—BeW

"**Little** Miss Tuckett". Mother Goose.—ClI

Little monkey. Donald J. Bissett.—HoT

"**Little** monkey, soft and furry". See Little monkey

Little moppet. See "I had a little moppet"

"The **little** mouse". See First snowfall

"**Little** mouse, with narrow feet". See When it's snowing

"**Little** Nancy Etticoat". Mother Goose.—WaM

"The **little** nightingale". See Nightingale
The **little** old cupid. Walter De La Mare.—DeR—MaP
"A **little** old man of Derby". Mother Goose.—WaM
"**Little** Orphan Annie". Unknown.—WiA
"**Little** ostriches". From Ostrich. Alan Brownjohn.—HoT
Little people's express. X. J. Kennedy.—KeGh
"**Little** Poll Parrot". Mother Goose.—CII—WaM
"**Little** Pollie Pillikins". See A—Apple pie
"**Little** Polly Flinders". Mother Goose.—SuO—WaM
"**Little** pools". From Riddle poems. James Berry.—BeW
"**Little** Popsie-Wopsie". From Dinner table rhymes. Unknown.—OpT
"The **little** red hen does not write with a pen". See Hen
"**Little** robin redbreast". Mother Goose.—WaM
The **little** salamander. Walter De La Mare.—DeR
"**Little** Sally Water". Unknown.—WiA
"**Little** seed inside a prune". Unknown.—ScA
The **little** shop (for a picture). Walter De La Mare.—DeR
The **little** sister store. Mary Ann Hoberman.—HoFa
Little snail. Hilda Conkling.—DeS
"**Little** snail". See Snail
Little song. Langston Hughes.—KeT
"**Little** soul sister". Useni Eugene Perkins.—SlM
"A **little** sound". See Many a mickle
Little talk. Aileen Fisher.—FiA
Little things, importance of
  Big little boy. E. Merriam.—DeS
  "A child said, what is the grass, fetching it". W. Whitman.—StP
  "Dear Father". M. W. Brown.—PlW
  "Dear Father, hear and bless". Unknown.—StP
  "Don't worry if your job is small". Unknown.—PrP—ScA
  "Flower in the crannied wall". A. Tennyson.—StP
  The fly. W. De La Mare.—DeR
  "God grows weary of great kingdoms". R. Tagore.—StP
  "Hurt no living thing". C. G. Rossetti.—DeS—StP—WhAa
  In judgment of the leaf. K. Patchen.—GoU
  Insignificant. M. Angelou.—AnI
  "A little axe can cut down a big tree". From Jamaican Caribbean proverbs. Unknown.—BeW
  Little talk. A. Fisher.—FiA
  Magnifying glass ("Small grains"). V. Worth.—WoAl
  The magnifying glass ("With this round glass"). W. De La Mare.—DeR
  Mote. X. J. Kennedy.—KeK
  The tarantula. R. Whittemore.—ElW
  "To see a world in a grain of sand". From Auguries of innocence. W. Blake.—StP
  "When I walk through thy woods". M. Hakotun.—StP
"**Little** Tim Sprat". Unknown.—CII
"**Little** toad little toad mind yourself". See Jamaican song
"**Little** Tom Tucker". See "Little Tommy Tucker"
"**Little** Tommy Tadpole began to weep and wail". See Growing up
"**Little** Tommy Tittlemouse". Mother Goose.—WaM
"**Little** Tommy Tucker". Mother Goose.—SuO—WaM
  "Little Tom Tucker".—EdGl

"**Little** tree". Edward Estlin Cummings.—ElW—GoA
Little trotty wagtail. John Clare.—ElW
"**Little** trotty wagtail, he went in the rain". See Little trotty wagtail
The **little** turtle. Vachel Lindsay.—DeS—LiDd
Liu Yii Hsi
  To the tune "Glittering sword hits", tr. by Kenneth Rexroth.—GoU
"**Lives** of football men remind us". See Dedicated to F.W.
Livesay, Dorothy
  And even now.—BoT
"**Living** here". Unknown, tr. by William Stanley Merwin and J. Moussaieff Masson.—GoU
Livingston, Myra Cohn
  The amphisbaena.—WhDd
  Apple tree.—LiR
  "At the beach (1)". See Beach birthdays
  "At the beach (2)". See Beach birthdays
  At the zoo.—HoT
  Basket.—LiPg
  Beach birthdays, complete.
    "At the beach (1)".—LiBp
    "At the beach (2)".—LiBp
  Beech, to owl.—LiIf
  A beginning.—LiT
  "Below your nose".—LiMh
  Bicycle birthday.—LiBp
  The biggest questions.—LiNe
  Birds know.—LiT
  Birthday cake ("Chocolate or butter").—LiBp
  Birthday clown.—LiBp
  Birthday night.—LiBp
  Birthday secrets, complete.
    "When Joan had a birthday".—LiBp
    "When my dog had a birthday".—LiBp
  Birthday wish.—LiBp
  Black river.—LiNe
  "Blow us up".—LiMh
  "Blue legs".—LiMh
  "Bounce me".—LiMh
  Calgary.—LiNe
  Candle.—LiNe
  Christmas tree ("Covered in silver").—LiR
  Circles ("I am speaking of circles").—JaP—LiT
  Circus clown.—LiNe
  "Closed, I am a mystery".—LiMh
  Closet.—LiNe
  Coyotes ("You never see them").—LiR
  Crickets ("They tell").—LiNe
  "Cried a man on the Salisbury Plain".—LiLo
  Crystal's waltz.—LiR
  Daddy.—LiPf
  The dark ("It's always dark").—KeT
  The difference.—LiNe
  Dinosaur birthday.—LiBp
  "A discerning young lamb of Long Sutton".—LiLo
  Doll.—KeT
  The dream ("My arms").—LiNe
  "Dressed in".—LiMh
  Driving.—MoR
  Eight.—LiBp
  Envoi, Washington Square Park.—LiR
  Excuse.—LiT
  Family.—LiT
  Father ("I look for you on every street").—LiT
  February 14.—LiT
  Finding a way.—LiT
  Fireworks ("The Fourth of July's").—LiR
  First flight.—LiNe

Livingston, Myra Cohn—*Continued*
Five ("Is old enough").—LiBp
Flying west.—LiNe
Fog ("Fog sneaks in").—LiR
For a bird.—DeS
For Mugs.—LiDp
Four.—LiBp
"Four legs".—LiMh
Fourth of July ("Hurrah for the Fourth of July").—LiLo
Friendship ("Sometimes it's only Betty and Sue").—LiR
Funny glasses.—LiBp
The game ("Plastic soldiers march on the floor").—SaB
    The game ("Plastic soldiers on the floor").—LiNe
The game ("Plastic soldiers on the floor"). See The game ("Plastic soldiers march on the floor")
"Ganesha, Ganesh".—WhDd
Garage apartment.—LiT
"Give me a book".—HoGo
"Give me books, give me wings".—LiNe
"Give me water".—LiMh
Grand Canyon east, from the air.—LiR
"Gray and blue".—LiMh
The hayride.—LiBp
"He stands".—LiMh
Help ("Would it help").—LiT
"Here's a riddle".—LiMh
"Higgledy-Piggledy keeps his room tidy".—PrFo
His girlfriend.—LiT
Home ("Yelling, shouting, arguing").—LiT
I never told.—LiNe
"I polka dot the window".—LiMh
I would have come.—LiNe
"I'm sticky".—LiMh
"In bright yellow coats".—LiMh
In the middle.—LiT
"In the morning".—LiMh
"In this jungle".—HoT
Interlude.—LiT
Invitation ("Listen, I've a big surprise").—KeT—LiT
Invitation ("My birthday invitation").—LiBp
Irene.—LiR
Jim Whitehead.—LiR
June, mourning doves.—LiT
Just once.—LiNe
Kansas visit.—LiNe
Kitchen table.—LiR
"Ladybug".—LiR
Lasiocampidae.—LiNe
Late afternoon.—LiT
Leaf boats.—LiR
Lemonade stand.—KeT
Letter.—LiT
"Lift me up".—LiMh
"Lincoln".—LiR
Long ago days.—LiT
Long Beach, February.—LiR
Lost dog.—LiT
Love ("Wish they'd kiss each other").—LiT
Macaw.—LiNe
March night.—LiNe
Match.—LiT
Michael's birthday.—LiBp
Moon, two views.—LiNe
Morning at Malibu.—LiNe
Mother.—LiT
Mount St. Helens.—LiT

"Mr. Pettengill".—LiR
"My head is red".—LiMh
"My party dress". See Party dress, party shirt
"My party shirt". See Party dress, party shirt
The necklace.—LiR
New Dad.—LiT
Niagara, Canadian Horseshoe Falls.—LiNe
The night. See "The night creeps in"
"The night creeps in".—LiDd
    The night.—KeT
Night flight over Kansas.—LiNe
Night light.—LiR
Night of thunder.—LiNe
"No neck".—LiMh
Notes on a bee.—LiNe
November acorn.—LiR
"Now, a picture".—LiMh
O say.—LiR
Old spider web.—LiNe
Olive Street.—LiT
"Once they roamed".—LiMh
"One click".—LiMh
Others.—LiT
Our Christmas tree.—LiNe
Owl of night.—LiR
Party dress, party shirt, complete.
    "My party dress".—LiBp
    "My party shirt".—LiBp
Party favors.—LiBp
Party prizes.—LiBp
Party table.—LiBp
Piano recital.—LiR
Pigeons and popcorn.—LiR
"Pinning the tail on the donkey".—LiBp
Poison ivy.—LiR
Possibility.—LiR
Presents ("My friends all gave me presents").—LiBp
Puzzle.—LiR
Queensboro Bridge.—LiNe
Rain ("Summer rain").—DeS
Rain, a haiku sequence.—LiR
Readcrest drive.—LiR
Reading, fall.—LiR
Reading, spring.—LiR
Reading, summer.—LiR
Reading, winter.—LiR
Relationship.—LiT
Remembering.—LiR
Rocky Mountains, Colorado.—LiNe
S, silent shark.—LiNe
"Said a restless young person of Yew".—LiLo
School play.—LiR
"Sea shell".—LiT
Seaweed.—HoS—MoS
Secret ("The secret I told you").—LiR
The secret ("We don't mention where he went").—LiT
Secret door.—DeT
September garden.—LiNe
Seven.—LiBp
74th street.—JaP
Shortcut.—LiNe
Six.—LiBp
6:15 A.M.—LiNe
Sky tales of the Assiniboin Indians.—LiR
"A small mouse in Middleton Stoney".—LiLo
Snails.—LiR
Something strange.—LiNe
Song of peace.—LiNe
Song of the Osage woman.—LiR
Spider web.—LiT

Livingston, Myra Cohn—*Continued*
Sprinker Ice Arena.—LiR
"Squeeze me and hug me".—LiMh
Stars ("I will imagine").—LiR
Statue of Liberty.—LiNe
Statues.—LiNe
Street song.—MoS
"Stretch my ribs out wide and high".—LiMh
Summer daisies.—LiNe
10 P.M.—LiNe
Texas norther.—BaW
"There was a place".—LiT
"There was once a young fellow of Wall".—LiLo
"This book is mine".—LiNe
Tray.—LiBp
Turtle ("We found him down at Turtle Creek").—LiR
Understanding.—LiDd
Valentine hearts.—LiR
The vet.—LiR
"Wailed a ghost in a graveyard at Kew".—LiHp—LiLo
"We could be friends".—JaP
"When I sputter and rumble and pop".—LiMh
"When Joan had a birthday". See Birthday secrets
"When my dog had a birthday". See Birthday secrets
"With silver spears".—LiMh
"With yellow feathers".—LiMh
Working with mother.—KeT—LiPm—LiR
Worlds I know.—DeT
"You never see me".—LiMh
Lizard ("The beginning of a lizard"). Bundgard Povlsen, tr. by Paul Borum.—NyT
"**Lizard**". See Don't come out
Lizard ("A lean lizard). Grace Nichols.—NiCo
The **lizard** ("The lizard is a timid thing"). John Gardner.—WhAa
Lizard ("A lizard ran out on a rock and looked up, listening"). David Herbert Lawrence.—CaB
"The **lizard** is a timid thing". See The lizard
"**Lizard** outfielders". See Desert baseball
"A **lizard** ran out on a rock and looked up, listening". See Lizard
A **lizard** wriggled. Unknown.—ClI
"A **lizard** wriggled on his belly". See A lizard wriggled
Lizards
Blizzard birds. J. P. Lewis.—LeA
The chameleon. J. Gardner.—CoAz
Desert baseball. J. P. Lewis.—LeT
Don't come out. Raizan.—DeI
Is this yours. M. Fatchen.—FaCm
Lizard ("The beginning of a lizard"). B. Povlsen.—NyT
Lizard ("A lean lizard). G. Nichols.—NiCo
The lizard ("The lizard is a timid thing"). J. Gardner.—WhAa
Lizard ("A lizard ran out on a rock and looked up, listening"). D. H. Lawrence.—CaB
A lizard wriggled. Unknown.—ClI
Longest lizard. X. J. Kennedy.—KeGh
Two from the zoo. E. Merriam.—MeS
Variety. From Animalimericks. E. Merriam.—MeS
Llamas
A is for alpaca. W. J. Smith.—SmL
In praise of llamas. A. Guiterman.—CoAz
Llude sig kachoo. Eve Merriam.—MeCh
Lo, the winter is past. From The song of Solomon. Bible/Old Testament.—DeS
"**Load** of hay, load of hay". Unknown.—WiA

Lob-lie-by-the-fire. Walter De La Mare.—DeR
"**La loba**, la loba". Unknown.—DeA
The she-wolf ("Oh mama wolf, oh mama wolf").—DeA
Lobel, Arnold
Books to the ceiling.—HoGo
"Friendly Fredrick Fuddlestone".—PrFo
"I will give you the key".—MoS
"If you were a pot".—LiDd
"It rains and it pours".—LiDd
"Loose and limber".—PrFo
"Sing a song of succotash".—LiDd
"There was a man dressed all in cheese".—PrFo
"There was a sad pig with a tail".—LiLo
"There was a small pig who wept tears".—HoS
"There was a young pig from Chanute".—LiLo
"There was a young pig who, in bed".—LiLo
The **lobster** quadrille. From Alice's adventures in wonderland. Lewis Carroll.—MoR
Lobsters
The lobster quadrille. From Alice's adventures in wonderland. L. Carroll.—MoR
Locations and times. Walt Whitman.—HoVo
"**Locations** and times, what is it in me that meets them all". See Locations and times
"**Lock** the dairy door, lock the dairy door". Mother Goose.—WaM
"**Lock** yourself in the kitchen". See Chocolate dreams, five
Locked in. Ingemar Leckius, tr. by May Swenson.—NyT
Locusts
The cicada. Basho.—DeI
Cicadas. P. Fleischman.—FlJ
"On the dewy trunk". Kyoshi.—CaR
Logs. Walter De La Mare.—DeR
Lombardi, Vince (about)
For the death of Vince Lombardi. J. Dickey.—KnAs
London, Sara
Rare rhythms.—JaM
London, England
London. M. Angelou.—AnI
The London owl. E. Farjeon.—LiIf
The lord mayor's parade. S. Cook.—FoLe
Up and down. W. De La Mare.—DeR—MaP
London. Maya Angelou.—AnI
London fisherman. Unknown.—OpT
The **London** owl. Eleanor Farjeon.—LiIf
Lone. Walter De La Mare.—DeR
"**Lone** and alone she lies". See Poor Miss
Loneliness
"Ain't no hell on earth". J. Carson.—CaS
All my secrets. M. Mack.—BoT
Alone ("Alone in a house with no one to talk to"). S. Hudson.—BaH
Alone ("I am alone, and lonely"). J. Little.—LiHe
"The Bay of Tsunu". H. Kakinomoto.—GoU
Behind bars. F. Tuqan.—NyT
Boy at the window. R. Wilbur.—ElW
"Celia sat beside the seaside". Unknown.—PrP
Christmas wish. T. Johnston.—LiPf
"The cicadas sing". O. N. Komachi.—GoT
Daddy's gone. D. Chandra.—LiPf
Family portrait. E. Budianta.—NyT
Father ("I look for you on every street"). M. C. Livingston.—LiT
Footpath. S. Ngatho.—NyT
For Mugs. M. C. Livingston.—LiDp
Generations. S. Cornish.—JaPr
"Ghosty ghosty all alone". E. Merriam.—MeY
His running, my running. R. Francis.—KnAs

"The **loss** of love and youth". See Loss of love
Lost ("Desolate and lone"). Carl Sandburg.—LaN
Lost ("It's quiet"). R. H. Marks.—LiDp
Lost and found
  "Alas, alas, for Miss Mackay". Mother Goose.—
    WaM
  Among iron fragments. T. Ruebner.—GoU
  Anyone seen my. M. Fatchen.—PrFo
  The babes in the wood. Unknown.—ElW
  The bagel. D. Ignatow.—BaW
  The ball poem. J. Berryman.—KnAs
  The bandog. W. De La Mare.—DeR—MaP
  "Being lost". K. Kuskin.—HoGo
  A child's dream. F. Cornford.—ElW
  "Cock-a-doodle-doo". Mother Goose.—SuO—
    WaM
  "Days that the wind takes over". K. Kuskin.—
    BaW
  "Did you see my wife". Mother Goose.—WaM
  "Finders keepers". Unknown.—CoM—WiA
  Hideout. A. Fisher.—DeT
  "How dry I am, how wet I'll be". Unknown.—
    CoM
  "I had a little moppet". Mother Goose.—WaM
    Little moppet.—OpT
  I have a lion. K. Kuskin.—DeS
  "I wrote a letter to my love". Mother Goose.—
    WaM
  "If this book should chance to roam".
    Unknown.—OpI—WiA
  "Is your head on nice and tight". K. Dakos.—DaI
  Kiph. W. De La Mare.—DeR
  "Left foot, right foot". Mother Goose.—WaM
  "Little Bo-Peep has lost her sheep". Mother
    Goose.—EdGl—SuO—WaM
  Lost ("It's quiet"). R. H. Marks.—LiDp
  The lost cat. E. V. Rieu.—LaCc
  Lost dog. M. C. Livingston.—LiT
  The lost shoe. W. De La Mare.—DeR—MaP
  "Lucy Locket lost her pocket". Mother Goose.—
    WaM
  Lulu, lulu, I've a lilo. C. Pomerantz.—DeS—LiIf
  "Mary lost her coat". Unknown.—WiA
  Missing. A. A. Milne.—LaM
  "On Saturday night I lost my wife". Mother
    Goose.—WaM
  "One foggy autumn in Baltimore". J. Prelutsky.—
    PrBe
  Padiddle. J. P. Lewis.—LeT
  Rescue ("Bony cat"). V. Schonborg.—LaCc
  Rescue mission. A. Adoff.—AdCh
  She was hungry and cold. A. Adoff.—AdIn
  The three little kittens. E. L. Follen.—HoS
    "Three little kittens, they lost their
      mittens".—SuO (unat.)
    "Three little kittens lost their mittens".—
      EdGl (unat.)—WaM (unat.)
  Whatnot. E. Merriam.—MeS
  When I was lost. D. Aldis.—MoS
The **lost** cat. Emile Victor Rieu.—LaCc
Lost dog. Myra Cohn Livingston.—LiT
The **lost** shoe. Walter De La Mare.—DeR—MaP
Lottemoos
  "If you think".—AgL
"**Loud** roared the flames". See The fire
"**Louie** Malone yelled, reach for the sky". See Reach
  for the sky
Louisa Jones sings a praise to Caesar. Emanuel Di
  Pasquale.—LiDp
Louisa, Louisa. Jean Little.—LiHe
Louisa's liberation. Jean Little.—LiHe
Louleen's feelings. X. J. Kennedy.—KeK

Love
  Age four and my father. J. Cunningham.—LiPf
  All kinds of grands. L. Clifton.—LiPg
  "Amo, amas". Unknown.—OpI
  Among iron fragments. T. Ruebner.—GoU
  "Anna and Frankie went for a ride". Unknown.—
    ScA
  Annabel Lee. E. A. Poe.—ElW
  Annette Harrison. M. Glenn.—GlBc
  Answer to a child's question. S. T. Coleridge.—
    CaB—ElW
  Antelope ("A girl with legs like an antelope"). K.
    Shiraishi.—AgL
  The apple. J. Halevi.—GoU
  The apple charm. W. De La Mare.—DeR
  April rain song. L. Hughes.—DeS—ElW—HoS—
    LiDd—SlM—SuI
  "As I was going up Pippen Hill". Mother
    Goose.—OpT—WaM
  "As sure as a vine grows round a rafter".
    Unknown.—ScA
  "As sure as a vine grows round a stump".
    Unknown.—ScA
  "As we are so wonderfully done with each other".
    K. Patchen.—GoU
  At sunset. J. von Eichendorff.—GoT
  August 8. N. Jordan.—SlM
  Autumn garden. D. Campana.—GoT
  "Away down east, away down west". Unknown.—
    KeT
    Susianna.—OpT
  "The Bay of Tsunu". H. Kakinomoto.—GoU
  The bead mat. W. De La Mare.—DeR
  "A beautiful lady named Psyche". Unknown.—
    LiLo
  "Being to timelessness as it's to time". E. E.
    Cummings.—GoU
  "Believe me, if all those endearing young charms".
    T. Moore.—ElW
  La belle dame sans merci. J. Keats.—ElW
  Birches. R. Frost.—SuI
  A birthday. C. G. Rossetti.—ElW
  Black-eyed Susie. Unknown.—SuC
  "Bobby Shaftoe's gone to sea". Mother Goose.—
    SuO
  Bonny sailor boy. Unknown.—OpT
  Book lice. P. Fleischman.—FlJ
  Bright house. S. Fukao.—GoU
  Buick. K. Shapiro.—MoR
  C. C. Johnson. M. Glenn.—GlBc
  Caring for animals. J. Silkin.—NyT
  Carousel. J. Cunningham.—JaP
  The changeling. W. De La Mare.—DeR—MaP
  Changing. M. Angelou.—AnI
  Cheerleader. J. W. Miller.—JaPr
  "Coils the robot". F. H. Pinto.—NyT
  The comb. W. De La Mare.—DeR
  The coquette. W. De La Mare.—DeR
  Crown. D. K. Hru.—SlM
  Cruel Jenny Wren. Unknown.—ElW
  Cuernavaca. A. Pettersson.—NyT
  "Curly locks, curly locks". Mother Goose.—EdGl
  Daddy. M. C. Livingston.—LiPf
  Dear delight. W. De La Mare.—DeR
  Degli Sposi. R. Lesser.—GoU
  A dialogue of watching. K. Rexroth.—GoU
  "Did you ever have a dog". B. S. De Regniers.—
    MoS
  The digger wasp. P. Fleischman.—FlJ
  Dinosaur waltz. J. Yolen.—YoDd
  Distances of longing. F. Abu Khalid.—NyT
  "Do you carrot all for me". Unknown.—WiA

Love—*Continued*

Love ("I love you, I like you"). W. J. Smith.—SmL

Love ("Too close"). C. S. Muth.—MoR

Love ("Wish they'd kiss each other"). M. C. Livingston.—LiT

Love don't mean. E. Greenfield.—SIM

Love, it is time. K. Shapiro.—GoU

Love letter. M. Angelou.—AnI

Love letters, unmailed. E. Merriam.—MeS

"Love many, trust few". Unknown.—ScA

The love nest. L. Dangel.—JaPr

"Love rejected". L. Clifton.—SuC

Love song to a stranger. J. Baez.—GoU

Love story (for Deirdre). A. Henri.—GoU

"Loving you less than life, a little less". E. S. V. Millay.—ElW

Madonna of the evening flowers. A. Lowell.—GoU

Maisie's lament. X. J. Kennedy.—KeK

Mamaw and Frank. W. Burt.—JaPr

Many and more. M. Angelou.—AnI

"Margaret wrote a letter". Unknown.—OpT

Married love. Kuan Tao Sheng.—GoU

Marrow of my bone. M. Evans.—SuC

Marthe away (she is away). K. Rexroth.—GoU

"Mary's mad". Unknown.—WiA

Match. M. C. Livingston.—LiT

Mathematics of love. M. Hamburger.—GoU

May. C. G. Rossetti.—ElW

The meaning of simplicity. Y. Ritsos.—NyT

The mermaid. W. B. Yeats.—AgL

"Miss Buss and Miss Beale". Unknown.—OpI

Miss Cherry. W. De La Mare.—DeR

Morning on this street. G. Soto.—SoA

"Moving right along". A. Oyewole.—SIM

Mrs. Praying Mantis. J. P. Lewis.—LeA

Ms. Charlotte Kendall, biology. M. Glenn.—GlBc

Muted. P. Verlaine.—GoU

"My boyfriend's name is Jello". Unknown.—CoM—WiA

My city. J. W. Johnson.—SuC

My dog ("Here's what we think of, Gov and I"). F. Holman.—LiDp

My father's fortune. H. Scott.—JaPr

"My heart is not a plaything". Unknown.—ScA

"My love for you will never fail". Unknown.—WiA

My mother really knew. W. T. Lum.—JaM

"Naranja dulce". Unknown.—DeA

"Orange so sweet".—DeA

News for the cafeteria. S. Fisher.—JaPr

Nicoletta. W. De La Mare.—DeR

"Night deepens". O. N. Komachi.—GoT

The night piece, to Julia. R. Herrick.—ElW

No, love is not dead. R. Desnos.—GoU

"Nobody loves me". Unknown.—OpI—ScA

Nocturne ("If the deep wood is haunted, it is I"). R. Hillyer.—GoU

"Not speaking of the way". A. Yosano.—GoU

Nothing much. M. Angelou.—AnI

Now blue October. R. Nathan.—GoU

The nymph's reply to the shepherd. Sir W. Raleigh.—ElW

Ode to weddings. G. Soto.—SoNe

"O Lord, grant us to love Thee, grant that we may love". Mohammed.—StP

O mistress mine. From Twelfth night. W. Shakespeare.—ElW

On a night of the full moon. A. Lorde.—GoU

On being introduced to you. E. Merriam.—MeS

On New Year's Day, watching it snow. I. Shikibu.—GoT

On this winter after noon. A. Adoff.—AdCh

"One I love, two I love". Mother Goose.—WaM—WiA

1246. J.-U.-D. Rumi.—GoU

An open arc. S. Quasimodo.—GoT

Oranges ("The first time I walked"). G. Soto.—JaM—SoA

"Out of the cradle endlessly rocking". W. Whitman.—HoVo

The outlandish knight. Unknown.—ElW

Overture. Z. Dixon.—NyT

The owl and the pussy-cat. E. Lear.—ElW—LiDd—LoFh

The owl's bedtime story. R. Jarrell.—LiIf

Paper of pins. Unknown.—KeT

The passionate shepherd to his love. C. Marlowe.—ElW

The pelican chorus. E. Lear.—CaB—WhAa

Pet rock. C. Rylant.—JaP

The phantom ("Wilt thou never come again"). W. De La Mare.—DeR

Picnic to the earth. S. Tanikawa.—NyT

"Pigs like mud". Unknown.—WiA

Pippin in the evening. N. M. Bodecker.—LiPm

The playhouse. K. Daniels.—JaPr

Poem ("I loved my friend"). L. Hughes.—DeS—DeT—SIM

Poem II. From Twenty-one love poems. A. Rich.—GoU

Poem III. From Twenty-one love poems. A. Rich.—GoU

The poet ("Before he moved in with Miss Perry"). P. B. Janeczko.—JaB

Portrait, my wife. J. Holmes.—GoU

Preposterous. J. Hall.—JaPr

"Pretty brown baby". K. Fufuka.—SIM

"Pussycat, pussycat, wilt thou be mine". Mother Goose.—WaM

"Put out my eyes, and I can see you still". R. M. Rilke.—GoU

Ratio. L. Morrison.—GoU

"Read up and down". Unknown.—ScA—WiA

Recuerdo. E. S. V. Millay.—ElW

"Roses are red, violets are blue, sugar is sweet". Unknown.—WiA

"Roses red, violets blue, sugar is sweet, but not like you". Unknown.—ScA

Sallie. W. De La Mare.—DeR

"Sally, Sally Waters, sprinkle in the pan". Mother Goose.—WaM

"Sam and Joan sitting in a tree". Unknown.—ScA

Sappho to Eranna. R. M. Rilke.—GoU

Scribbled notes picked up by owners, and rewritten because of bad grammar, bad spelling, bad writing. J. Berry.—BeW

The secret ("Open your eyes, now, look, and see"). W. De La Mare.—DeR

A secret kept. J. Al-Harizi.—GoU

Secrets ("I doubt that you remember her, except"). R. Pack.—JaM

Seeing Granny. J. Berry.—BeW

Sending spring love to Tzu-An. H.-C. Yu.—GoU

Seven women's blessed assurance. M. Angelou.—AnI

"Should I worship Him from fear of hell". R. Al'Adawiyah.—StP

Silent noon. D. G. Rossetti.—GoU

"Since feeling is first". E. E. Cummings.—ElW

Sisters. P. B. Janeczko.—JaB

VI. P. Verlaine.—GoT

Love, it is time. Karl Shapiro.—GoU
"Love, it is time I memorized your phone". See Love, it is time
Love letter. Maya Angelou.—AnI
Love letters, unmailed. Eve Merriam.—MeS
"Love many, trust few". Unknown.—ScA
The love nest. Leo Dangel.—JaPr
"Love rejected". Lucille Clifton.—SuC
Love song to a stranger. Joan Baez.—GoU
Love songs from an ancient book, sels. Leah Goldberg, tr. by Robert Friend
"I have not seen you, even in dream".—GoT
Love story (for Deirdre). Adrian Henri.—GoU
"Loveliest of trees, the cherry now". Alfred Edward Housman.—ElW
Lovelocks. Walter De La Mare.—DeR
The lovely bird ("Cu cu ru, sang the lovely bird"). See "Estaba la paraja pinta"
"Lovely face, majestic face, face of". Unknown.—StP
Lovely mosquito. Doug MacLeod.—PrFo
"Lovely mosquito, attacking my arm". See Lovely mosquito
Love's labour's lost, sels. William Shakespeare
"When icicles hang by the wall".—LiIf Winter.—ElW
"Lovesick girls, old men in foul underwear". See The Strand Theatre
"Loving you less than life, a little less". Edna St. Vincent Millay.—ElW
Low, Alice
"School is all over".—LoFh
Some things about grandpas.—LoFh
"Low on his fours the lion". See Unstooping
Lowell, Amy
Madonna of the evening flowers.—GoU
Sea shell.—ElW—LoFh
A sprig of rosemary.—GoU
Lowell, James Russell
"And what is so rare as a day in June". See The vision of Sir Launfal
On freedom.—SuI
The vision of Sir Launfal, sels.
"And what is so rare as a day in June".—SuI
Lowell, Robert
For the Union dead, sels.
"Two months after marching through Boston".—SuC
"Two months after marching through Boston". See For the Union dead
Lowery, Mike
Sister ("You said red hair made you").—JaPr
Luanne Sheridan. Mel Glenn.—GlBc
Lucia. Lucia Casalinuovo.—NyT
Lucie-Smith, Edward
The hymn tunes.—LeCa
The tiger ("A tiger going for a stroll").—CoAz
Luck
Finding a lucky number. G. Soto.—JaM—SoA
Friday the thirteenth. A. Adoff.—AdCh
Hapless. W. De La Mare.—DeR—MaP
"I was born three months before I's due". J. Carson.—CaS
Mathematics of love. M. Hamburger.—GoU
Mischief City. T. Jones-Wynne.—BoT
"Never stand under an anvil". X. J. Kennedy.—KeGh
"See a pin and pick it up". Mother Goose.—ScA—WaM—WiA
Serendipity. E. Merriam.—MeCh
"Specks on the fingers". Unknown.—WiA
"Step on a knife". Unknown.—ScA

"Step on a spoon". Unknown.—ScA
"A luckless time-traveler from Lynn". X. J. Kennedy.—KeGh—LiLo
Lucky little birds. Eloise Greenfield.—GrU
"Lucy Locket lost her pocket". Mother Goose.—WaM
Lukeman, Mark
Playing stickball with Robbie Shea.—MoA
Lullabies
All asleep. C. Pomerantz.—PlW
Bedtime mumble. N. M. Bodecker.—PlW
"Bye, baby bunting". Mother Goose.—SuO—WaM
"Catch him, crow". Mother Goose.—WaM
A Christmas lullaby. M. Hillert.—PlW
"Coo, ah, coo". Unknown.—SnD
Good night ("Father puts the paper down"). A. Fisher.—PlW
Grandpa bear's lullaby. J. Yolen.—DeS—HoS—MoS
"Hush a bye, baby, on the tree top". Mother Goose.—EdGl
"Hush, little baby, don't say a word". Mother Goose.—SuO
Hush, little baby.—KeT
"Hush, my dear, lie still and slumber". I. Watts.—StP
"Hush thee my baby". Mother Goose.—WaM
"Hushabye baby, they're gone to milk". Mother Goose.—WaM
Little donkey close your eyes. M. W. Brown.—DeT
Lullaby ("Cat's in the alley"). J. R. Plotz.—PlW
Lullaby ("The long canoe"). R. Hillyer.—SuI
Lullaby ("Near and far, near and far"). M. Hillert.—HoSt
A lullaby ("Sleep, child, lie quiet, let be"). J. Agee.—GoT
Lullaby ("Sleep, sleep, thou lovely one"). W. De La Mare.—DeR
Lullaby for a black mother. L. Hughes.—SlM
Lullaby for a rainy night. B. J. Esbensen.—EsW
Lullaby for Suzanne. M. Stillman.—KeT
"Lullaby, oh lullaby". C. G. Rossetti.—PlW
Lully. W. De La Mare.—DeR
Mama's song. D. Chandra.—LiPm
Manhattan lullaby ("Lulled by rumble, babble, beep"). N. Farber.—KeT
Manhattan lullaby ("Now lighted windows climb the dark"). R. Field.—KeT
The mouse's lullaby. P. Cox.—KeT
Mrs. Burns' lullaby. Unknown.—OpT
New baby poem (II). E. Greenfield.—GrN
Night song. E. Merriam.—LaN
"On a still calm night when the bugs begin to bite". Unknown.—OpI
Part XX: This brief day now over. From A child's day. W. De La Mare.—DeR
"Pimpolla de canela". Unknown.—DeA
"Cinnamon shoot".—DeA
"Puva, puva, puva". Unknown.—SnD
"Rock-a-bye, baby, on the treetop". Mother Goose.—SuO—WaM
"Rockabye, baby, your cradle is hard". Unknown.—WiA
Seal mother's song. R. Kipling.—CoAz
Seal lullaby.—WhAs
"Silent night". J. Mohr.—StP (unat.)
"Sleep, sleep, sleep". Unknown.—PlW
Sweet and low. A. Tennyson.—PlW
Things ("Trains are for going"). W. J. Smith.—SmL

M

Machinery.—*Continued*
   Tinkering. D. Dawber.—BoT
   The toaster. W. J. Smith.—SmL
   Tractor. V. Worth.—WoAl
   "The vacumn cleaner's swallowed Will". X. J.
      Kennedy.—KeGh
MacInnis, Joseph
   Barracuda ("Silver").—MoR
MacIntyre, C. F.
   Dusk ("The moon is red in the foggy sky"), tr.—
      GoT
   Muted, tr.—GoU
   VI, tr.—GoT
Mack, Marguerite
   All my secrets.—BoT
McKay, Claude
   The white city.—SuC
Mackay, John Henry
   Tomorrow ("And tomorrow the sun will shine
      again").—GoT
MacKinnon, Brian
   Why because.—BoT
McLaren, Floris Clark
   Field in the wind.—BoT
MacLean, Alistair
   "I find thee throned in my heart".—StP
   "I have a secret joy in Thee, my God".—StP
   "There is a mother's heart in the heart".—StP
MacLeish, Archibald
   Yacht for sale.—KnAs
Macleod, Doug
   Anaconda.—CoAz
   Lovely mosquito.—PrFo
   Screaming.—PrFo
   Steam roller Sam.—PrFo
McLeod, Fiona
   "Deep peace of the running wave to you".—StP
MacLoughland, Beverly
   Chihuahua.—LiDp
   Secret ("Mrs. Kangaroo").—HoS
   Surprise ("The biggest").—HoGo
McMillan, Bruce
   "Bear chair".—McP
   "Blue shoe".—McP
   "Brown crown".—McP
   "Cub tub".—McP
   "Duck truck".—McP
   "Fat bat".—McP
   "Feet seat".—McP
   "Fun run".—McP
   "Goat boat".—McP
   "Grass glass".—McP
   "Green bean".—McP
   "Shirt dirt".—McP
   "Toe bow".—McP
   "Toy boy".—McP
McMillan, Ian. See Wiley, Martyn, and McMillan,
   Ian
McNaughton, Colin
   "I thought I'd take my rat to school".—PrFo
   "Monday's child is red and spotty".—PrFo
   "The water's deep".—PrFo
MacNeacail, Aonghas
   "I kept on past".—AgL
McNeil, Florence
   Everything in its place.—BoT
McReynolds, Doug
   Waiting at the St. Louis Zoo.—HoT
The **mad** nun. Dana Giola.—JaPr
"The **mad** queen in red". See Q is for queen
Maddern, Marian
   Wind's foam, tr.—NyT

"**Made** you look". Unknown.—CoM
"**Made** you stare". Unknown.—CoM
"**Mademoiselle**". Unknown.—OpI
Madgett, Naomi
   Alabama centennial.—SuC
The **madhouse**. Jared Carter.—JaM
Madonna of the evening flowers. Amy Lowell.—
   GoU
Magee, John Gillespie
   High flight. See "Oh, I have slipped the surly
      bonds of earth"
   "Oh, I have slipped the surly bonds of earth".—
      StP
      High flight.—SuI
Magee, Wes
   Questions on Christmas eve.—FoLe
   School dinner menu for 1st of April.—FoLe
"**Maggie** and Millie . . .". See "Maggie and Milly
   and Molly and May"
"**Maggie** and Milly and Molly and May". Edward
   Estlin Cummings.—SuI
   "Maggie and Millie . . .".—ElW
"**Maggie** Meek, the tail of a leek". Unknown.—WiA
"**Maghrib** is the name of the dusk". See Idh
   Mubarak
Magi
   Camels of the Kings. L. Norris.—CaB
   Carol of the brown king. L. Hughes.—GoA
   Guardian owl. N. Farber.—LiIf
   Journey of the Magi. T. S. Eliot.—ElW
   Twelfth night. V. Worth.—WoA
   We three camels. J. Yolen.—YoHa
   "We three kings of Orient are". J. H. Hopkins,
      Jr.—YoHa (unat.)
   Wise men. V. Worth.—WoA
Magic. See also Charms; Enchantment
   Caw. W. De La Mare.—DeR
   Forbidden sounds. E. James.—BaH
   "Harriet, by magic force". E. Merriam.—MeY
   Haunted ("From out the wood I watched them
      shine"). W. De La Mare.—DeR
   If the owl calls again. J. Haines.—LiIf
   Itinerant. E. Merriam.—MeCh
   Ka 'Ba. I. A. Baraka.—SuC
   The Lady of Shalott. A. Tennyson.—ElW
   Life doesn't frighten me. M. Angelou.—AgL
   The mad nun. D. Giola.—JaPr
   Magic. D. Ravikovitch.—NyT
   The magic house. J. Yolen.—LiHp—YoBe
   Magic wands. J. Yolen.—PrBe
   Magic words. Unknown.—SuI
   The old house. W. De La Mare.—DeR—MaP
   On a night of snow. E. Coatsworth.—LaCc
   "Once upon a time, she said". J. Yolen.—YoFf
   The pedlar. W. De La Mare.—DeR
   The pied piper of Hamelin, complete. R.
      Browning.—ElW
   The pumpkin ("You may not believe it, for hardly
      could I"). R. Graves.—DeS
   Queen Djenira. W. De La Mare.—DeR
   Rainbow making, magic. From Four poems for
      Roy G Biv. B. J. Esbensen.—EsW
   Song of enchantment. W. De La Mare.—DeR—
      MaP
   The song of wandering Aengus. W. B. Yeats.—
      ElW—GoU
   Sorcery. W. De La Mare.—DeR
   Suppose ("Suppose, and suppose that a wild little
      horse of magic"). W. De La Mare.—DeR
   "There is a land". L. B. Jacobs.—HoGo
   The three beggars. W. De La Mare.—DeR
   The truants. W. De La Mare.—DeR—MaP

Make-believe—*Continued*

The ship of Rio. W. De La Mare.—DeR—ElW—MaP

Somewhere. W. De La Mare.—DeR

The song of Mr. Toad. From The wind in the willows. K. Grahame.—CoAz

Sunflakes. F. Asch.—DeS—MoS

Suppose ("Suppose, and suppose that a wild little horse of magic"). W. De La Mare.—DeR

Tartary. W. De La Mare.—DeR

"Teeter-totter, bread and water". Unknown.—WiA

The tin bird. R. C. Sunico.—NyT

Transformations. T. Rozewicz.—NyT

Tree ("If only I could stand"). F. Asch.—MoS

The unicorn ("Oh this is the animal that never was"). R. M. Rilke.—WhDd

Unicorn ("The unicorn with the long white horn"). W. J. Smith.—SmL

What I used to wonder. X. J. Kennedy.—KeK

"What if". B. S. De Regniers.—DeW

What teacher said. J. P. Lewis.—LeT

What we might be, what we are. X. J. Kennedy.—JaP—KeGh

"Who knows if the moon's". E. E. Cummings.—DeS

Wouldn't it be funny. P. O'Harris.—CoAz

"You be saucer". E. Merriam.—MeY

Make believe. Harry Behn.—HoSt

"Make me a grave where'er you will". From Bury me in a free land. Frances E. W. Harper.—SuC

Makin jump shots. Michael S. Harper.—KnAs

The making of dragons. Jane Yolen.—YoFf

Makley, Mike

The new kid.—MoA

"Mal, to yank his aching molar". X. J. Kennedy.—KeFb

Mallory Wade. Mel Glenn.—GlBc

"Malvales, the mallow order, a small order". See Chips, two

"Mama". See Cancion tonta

"Mama hums a sea-song with her eyes". See Mama's song

"Mama, Mama, have you heard". Unknown.—ScA

Mama's bouquets. Ashley Bryan.—BrS

"Mama's cooking pots of couscous". See By the shores of Pago Pago

Mama's song. Deborah Chandra.—LiPm

Mamaw and Frank. William Burt.—JaPr

Mamchur, Carolyn

Together.—BoT

Mamma settles the dropout problem. Betty Gates.—SuC

Man. See Human race

Man and owl. Joan Aiken.—LiIf

"Man and woman, they enter the sea". See The bathers

Man bigot. Maya Angelou.—AnI

"A man comes in, his suit is crumpled". Sergei Timofeyev, tr. by Irina Osadchaya and Lyn Hejinian.—NyT

"The man from the land of Fandango". Margaret Mahy.—MaN

"A man I'd call tremendous, that's". See Big Saul Fein

A man in a tree. N. M. Bodecker.—LiLo

The man in red. Eloise Greenfield.—GrU

"The man in the hat (whom you see in the picture)". See The accompaniment

"The man in the moon". Mother Goose.—EdGl—WaM

"The man in the moon as he sails the sky". Unknown.—PrP

"The man is not cute". See Photograph of Managua

"A man named Philander S. Goo". See Philander

A man never cries. Jose Craveirinha, tr. by Don Burness.—NyT

A man of Pennang. N. M. Bodecker.—LiLo

"A man on third, two batters out". See Two runs will win the game

"A man runs across the ceiling". See In the dark

"The man said". See An historic moment

"A man went hunting at Ryegate". Mother Goose.—WaM

"The man who is a bigot". See Man bigot

"The man who is all honey, flies are going to eat him up". From Jamaican Caribbean proverbs. Unknown.—BeW

"A man who was fond of his skunk". David McCord.—LiLo

"Man, yu should av come". See Friday work

"Mandarin ducks". See Weasel

Mandela, Zinzi

If my right hand.—AgL

Mandela, Winnie (about)

How can I lose hope. From Sing a softblack poem. Kwelismith.—SuC

Mandelbaum, Allen

Almost a madrigal, tr.—GoT

Mandelstam, Osip

"Take from my palms, to soothe your heart".—GoU

Mandlsohn, Sol

Basso profundo.—BoT

Edward Jones.—PrFo

Nicholas tickle us.—BoT

Manger, Itzik

Evening, tr. by Miriam Waddington.—GoT

Mango. Grace Nichols.—NiCo

Manhattan lullaby ("Lulled by rumble, babble, beep"). Norma Farber.—KeT

Manhattan lullaby ("Now lighted windows climb the dark"). Rachel Field.—KeT

Manjush, Dasgupta

Companion.—NyT

Mannahatta. Walt Whitman.—HoVo

Manners

"Better to urp a burp". Unknown.—ScA

"Billy, Billy, strong and able". Unknown.—WiA

Budging line ups. K. Dakos.—DaI

"Cease your chatter". Unknown.—OpI

Company manners. E. Merriam.—MeS

A crusty mechanic. N. M. Bodecker.—LiLo

"Dave Dirt came to dinner". K. Wright.—PrFo

"I eat my peas with honey". Unknown.—ScA—WiA

If we had lunch at the White House. K. Dakos.—DaI

In public, I pick a piece or two from the plate. A. Adoff.—AdCh

Learning. J. Viorst.—PrFo

Lecture. P. B. Janeczko.—JaB

Leek soup. X. J. Kennedy.—KeGh

Lucky little birds. E. Greenfield.—GrU

"Manners in the dining room". Mother Goose.—WaM

Mosquito ("I was climbing up the sliding board"). J. P. Lewis.—JaP—LeT

The music master. J. Ciardi.—CiH

"Never take a pig to lunch". S. A. Schmeltz.—PrFo

"On top of spaghetti". Unknown.—ScA

Parsnips. J. Little.—LiHe

Manners—*Continued*
  Politeness. A. A. Milne.—DeS
  "A rather polite man of Hawarden". Unknown.—LiLo
  "Ravioli, ravioli". Unknown.—ScA
  Reason. J. Miles.—ElW
  System. R. L. Stevenson.—ElW
  Tea party. H. Behn.—LiDd
  Thank you letter. R. Klein.—FoLe
  "There was a young man so benighted". Unknown.—LiLo
  The tiger ("A tiger going for a stroll"). E. Lucie-Smith.—CoAz
  "To sup like a pup". D. Baruch.—MoS
  We must be polite. C. Sandburg.—DeS
  The woman and her pig. Unknown.—OpT
  "Yes sir, no sir". Unknown.—WiA
"**Manners** in the dining room". Mother Goose.—WaM
The **manoeuvre**. William Carlos Williams.—CaB
The **manticore**. Jeanne Steig.—WhDd
Mantis. Valerie Worth.—Woal
Many a mickle. Walter De La Mare.—DeR—MaP
"**Many** an underfed cow in the pasture is mother of a bull". From Jamaican Caribbean proverbs. Unknown.—BeW
Many and more. Maya Angelou.—AnI
"**Many** eyes". Unknown.—ScA
Maori
  Waitangi Day. D. Bateson.—FoLe
Maps
  Clouds ("Don't trust the wind"). B. J. Esbensen.—EsW
  Dennis Finch. M. Glenn.—GlBc
  The orphan. M. Al-Maghut.—NyT
  Thrum drew a small map. S. Musgrave.—BoT
Marbles
  Marbles. V. Worth.—WoAl
Marbles. Valerie Worth.—WoAl
"**Marbles** picked up". See Marbles
March
  Early March. Z. Rogow.—GoT
  Grandpa in March. A. Adoff.—MoS
  March night. M. C. Livingston.—LiNe
  March thaw. X. J. Kennedy.—KeK
  Paper dragons. S. A. Schmeltz.—BaW
March bear. Marilyn Singer.—SiT
March hares. Walter De La Mare.—DeR
March night. Myra Cohn Livingston.—LiNe
March thaw. X. J. Kennedy.—KeK
Marching. See Parades
Marching chant. Unknown.—WiA
Marching song. From The three royal monkeys. Walter De La Mare.—DeR
Mardi Gras
  Carnival in Rio. J. Kirkup.—FoLe
  Mardi Gras. J. Kenward.—FoLe
  Shrove Tuesday. A. Bonner.—FoLe
  "Victor wore a velvet cape". J. Prelutsky.—PrBe
Mardi Gras. Jean Kenward.—FoLe
"**Margaret**, Margaret, has big eyes". Unknown.—WiA
"**Margaret** wrote a letter". Unknown.—OpT
Margolis, Gary
  First green heron.—KnAs
Margolis, Richard
  I like it when.—LiPf
Marguerite. Unknown.—PrFo
"**Marguerite**, go wash your feet". See Marguerite
"**Maribelle** was dark as cloves". See Sweet talk
Marie Lucille. Gwendolyn Brooks.—KeT
Market women. Daisy Myrie.—LeCa

Markets and marketing. See also Grocery stores; Shops and shopkeepers
  Banana and mackerel. J. Berry.—BeW
  Banana talk. J. Berry.—BeW
  "Donkey, donkey, do not bray". Mother Goose.—WaM
  Esmeralda (for a picture). W. De La Mare.—DeR
  "Hie to the market, Jenny come trot". Mother Goose.—WaM
    A wasted journey.—OpT
  I have been to market. Unknown.—ClI
  Market women. D. Myrie.—LeCa
  Riding to market. Mother Goose.—OpT
  Sunny market song. J. Berry.—BeW
  Supermarket, supermarket (a jump rope rhyme). E. Merriam.—MeS
  "This little pig went to market". Unknown.—WiA
  "This little pig went to market". Mother Goose.—EdGl—SuO—WaM
    "This little piggy".—SuI
  "To market, to market". Mother Goose.—WaM
  Tradition. E. Greenfield.—GrU
  "Trit trot to market to buy a penny doll". Mother Goose.—WaM
  The woman and her pig. Unknown.—OpT
Markham, Edward Archibald
  Another dad.—AgL
Markham, Edwin
  "Teach me, Father, how to be".—StP
Marks, R. H.
  Apple bobbing.—LiHp
  "A fellow named Percival Stein".—LiLo
  From her office.—LiPg
  "It's neither amusing nor funny".—LiLo
  Lost ("It's quiet").—LiDp
  New mother.—LiPm
Marks, S. J.
  I hid you, tr.—GoU
Marley, Bob
  Sun is shining.—AgL
Marlowe, Christopher
  The passionate shepherd to his love.—ElW
Marquis, Don
  The tomcat.—LaCc
Marriage. See also Married life; Weddings
  Arroz con leche. Unknown.—DeA
    Rice and milk ("I'm rice and milk, I'd like to be wed").—DeA
  "Charlie Chuck". Unknown.—WiA
  The courtship. G. E. Lyone.—JaM
  "Forty years we courted". J. Carson.—CaS
  "El hijo del conde". Unknown.—DeA
    The count's son ("The son of the count").—DeA
  "I should worry, I should care". Unknown.—WiA
    "Me no worry, me no care".—CoM
  "Karen and Richie sitting in a tree". Unknown.—CoM
  Paper of pins. Unknown.—KeT
  A rash stipulation. Unknown.—OpT
  "Where will we get married". Unknown.—WiA
  "Whom shall I marry". Unknown.—WiA
Married life
  Beauty and the beast, an anniversary. J. Yolen.—YoFf
  "Befoh yu marry keep two yeye opn, afta yu marry shet one". From Jamaican Caribbean proverbs. Unknown.—BeW
  "Charley Barley, butter and eggs". Mother Goose.—WaM
  Daddy's gone. D. Chandra.—LiPf
  Degli Sposi. R. Lesser.—GoU

Married life—*Continued*
A dialogue of watching. K. Rexroth.—GoU
"Did you see my wife". Mother Goose.—WaM
The disgruntled husband. Unknown.—OpT
"Eaper Weaper, chimney sweeper". Unknown.—
OpI
"Either of them young 'uns married". J. Carson.—
CaS
Engaged. J. Little.—LiHe
Flame and water. J. Berry.—AgL
"Good night, sweet repose, half the bed".
Unknown.—OpI—WaM
"Have you ever, ever, ever". Unknown.—CoM
"Help, murder, police". Unknown.—CoM
Ho hum. J. Ciardi.—CiH
"I cannot remember all the times he hit me". J.
Carson.—CaS
"I had a beautiful wife". J. Carson.—CaS
"I had a little husband". Mother Goose.—WaM
"I threw my mother-in-law out". J. Carson.—CaS
"In a cottage in Fife". Mother Goose.—SuO
"Jack Sprat could eat no fat". Mother Goose.—
EdGl—SuO—WaM
"John, come sell thy fiddle". Mother Goose.—
WaM
"Julius Caesar, the Roman geezer". Unknown.—
OpI
Married love. Kuan Tao Sheng.—GoU
Meeting my best friend from the eighth grade. G.
Gildner.—KnAs
Morning on this street. G. Soto.—SoA
"My daughter got divorced". J. Carson.—CaS
"My little old man and I fell out". Mother
Goose.—WaM
"Needles and pins, needles and pins".
Unknown.—WiA
New mother. R. H. Marks.—LiPm
"On Saturday night I lost my wife". Mother
Goose.—WaM
"Peter, Peter, pumpkin eater". Mother Goose.—
EdGl—SuO—WaM
The photograph. B. Drake.—KnAs
Poem III. From Twenty-one love poems. A.
Rich.—GoU
Portrait, my wife. J. Holmes.—GoU
Relationship. M. C. Livingston.—LiT
The spaghetti nut. J. Prelutsky.—DeS
This evening. Z. Landau.—GoT
"Thomas a Didymus, hard of belief".
Unknown.—OpI
Tombmates. J. Yolen.—YoBe
TV. E. Merriam.—MeS
"When I married, I caught up". J. Holmes.—SuI
"When you are courting". Unknown.—WiA
"When you get married and live on a hill".
Unknown.—WiA
"When you get married and your husband gets
cross". Unknown.—WiA
"When you get married and your wife has twins".
Unknown.—WiA
Winner ("Mrs. Macey worked behind"). P. B.
Janeczko.—JaB
"A woman named Mrs. S. Claus". J. P. Lewis.—
LiLo
The wraggle taggle gypsies. Unknown.—ElW
"You know". J. Carson.—CaS
Married love. Kuan Tao Sheng, tr. by Kenneth
Rexroth and Ling Chung.—GoU
Marrow of my bone. Mari Evans.—SuC
Marson, Una
Kinky hair blues.—LeCa
Martha Graham. James Laughlin.—MoR

Martha Nelson speaks. George Bogin.—JaM
Marthe away (she is away). Kenneth Rexroth.—
GoU
"A Martian named Harrison Harris". Al Graham.—
LiLo
Martin, D. Roger
Hammerin' Hank.—MoA
Martin Luther King Day. X. J. Kennedy.—KeK
Martin Luther King, Jr. Useni Eugene Perkins.—
SlM
Martine Provencal. Mel Glenn.—GlBc
Marty, Sid
Too hot to sleep.—BoT
"Marvel at the". See Octopus
Marvell, Andrew
"Casting the body's vest aside". See The garden
The garden, sels.
"Casting the body's vest aside".—StP
"Marvelous Monday". See The cheerful child's week
Marvin Pickett. Mel Glenn.—KnAs
Mary, Queen of Scots (about)
The crossing of Mary of Scotland. W. J. Smith.—
SmL
Mary, Virgin (about)
"Put me not into the hands". Unknown.—StP
Mary. Walter De La Mare.—DeR
"Mary ate some marmalade". Unknown.—ScA
"Mary had a baby". Unknown.—YoHa
"Mary had a little bear". Unknown.—PrP
"Mary had a little lamb". See Mary's lamb See
Mary's lamb
"Mary had a little lamb, a little pork, a little ham".
Unknown.—ScA
"Mary had a little lamb, a lobster, and some
prunes". Unknown.—PrP
"Mary had a little lamb, its coat was black as tar".
Unknown.—WiA
"Mary had a little lamb, its coat was white as
cotton". Unknown.—WiA
"Mary had a little lamb, its fleece was white as
snow". Unknown.—WiA
"Mary had a little lamb, she set it on the shelf".
Unknown.—WiA
"Mary had a little lamb, you've heard this tale
before". Unknown.—PrFo
"Mary had a stick of gum". Unknown.—ScA
"Mary had a swarm of bees". Unknown.—ScA
"Mary lost her coat". Unknown.—WiA
"Mary, Mary, don't say no". Unknown.—WiA
"Mary, Mary, Mary". See Mary
"Mary, Mary, Queen of Scots". See The crossing of
Mary of Scotland
"Mary, Mary, quite contrary". Mother Goose.—
EdGl—SuO
"Mistress Mary".—WaM
"Mary Pary Pinder". Unknown.—OpI
"Mary went down to Grandpa's farm". Unknown.—
ClI—WiA
Mary's lamb. Sarah Josepha Hale.—SuI
"Mary had a little lamb".—EdGl (unat.)—SuO
(unat.)—WaM (unat.)
"Mary's mad". Unknown.—WiA
Masahito
Doves, tr. by Tze-si Huang.—DeI
The mask. Dakari Kamau Hru.—SlM
Masks
M is for mask. W. J. Smith.—SmL
The mask. D. K. Hru.—SlM
We wear the mask. P. L. Dunbar.—SuC
Mason, Walt
Football ("The game was ended, and the noise at
last had died away, and").—KnAs

Masson, J. Moussaieff
  "Her eyes in sleep", tr.—GoU
  "Living here", tr.—GoU
Master Rabbit. Walter De La Mare.—DeR
Masters, Edgar Lee
  Elsa Wertman.—ElW
  Hamilton Greene.—ElW
Match. Myra Cohn Livingston.—LiT
Math is brewing and I'm in trouble. Kalli Dakos.—DaI
Mathematical metric conversion version. Arnold Adoff.—AdCh
"A **mathematician** named Bath". See Let X equal half
"A **mathematician** named Lynch". Unknown.—LiLo
Mathematics
  "Arithmetic is where numbers fly". From Arithmetic. C. Sandburg.—DeS
  Brent Sorensen. M. Glenn.—GlBc
  "I went downtown". Unknown.—KeT—OpI—ScA—WiA
  "Julius Caesar said with a smile". Unknown.—OpI
  Let X equal half. J. F. Wilson.—LiLo
  Math is brewing and I'm in trouble. K. Dakos.—DaI
  Mathematical metric conversion version. A. Adoff.—AdCh
  "A mathematician named Lynch". Unknown.—LiLo
  Mathematics of love. M. Hamburger.—GoU
  Maths. D. Kalha.—AgL
  Mr. Henry Axhelm, math. M. Glenn.—GlBc
  "Multiplication is vexation". Unknown.—OpI
  The old math, one. A. Adoff.—AdCh
  The old math, two. A. Adoff.—AdCh
  Philander. T. Roethke.—LiLo
  "Said Mrs. Isosceles Tri". C. B. Burgess.—LiLo
  "Said Rev. Rectangular Square". C. B. Burgess.—LiLo
  "There was an old fellow of Trinity". Unknown.—LiLo
  "There was an old man who said, do". Unknown.—LiLo
  "There was an old man who said, Gee". Unknown.—LiLo
  They don't do math in Texas. K. Dakos.—DaI
  "'Tis a favorite project of mine". H. L. Carter.—LiLo
  A wise triangle. V. Popa.—AgL
Mathematics of love. Michael Hamburger.—GoU
Mathis, Sharon Bell
  Championship.—MaR
  Cheerleaders.—MaR
  Coach.—MaR
  Cousins.—MaR
  Ebonee.—MaR
  Football ("You twist").—MaR
  Leg broken.—MaR
  Monster man.—MaR
  Playoff pizza.—MaR
  Quarterback.—MaR
  Red dog blue fly.—MaR
  Touchdown.—MaR
  Trophy.—MaR
  Victory banquet.—MaR
Maths. Deepak Kalha.—AgL
Matinees. Katherine Soniat.—JaPr
"A **matron** well known in Montclair". William Jay Smith.—LiLo—SmL
"**Matthew,** Mark, Luke and John, hold the horse". Unknown.—OpI

"**Matthew,** Mark, Luke, and John, I'm off my horse". Unknown.—WiA
"**Matthew,** Mark, Luke, and John, stole a pig". Unknown.—WiA
Maud. Mary Swander.—JaM
Maxims. See Proverbs
May
  "April showers". Unknown.—WiA
  Fol dol do. W. De La Mare.—DeR
  Little song. L. Hughes.—KeT
  May. C. G. Rossetti.—ElW
  May day ("Oak and ivy, sycamore, ash, what shall we leave by the cottage door"). J. Nicholls.—FoLe
  May day ("Twirl your ribbons"). J. Kenward.—FoLe
  Mayflies. P. Fleischman.—FlJ
  Myrtle warblers. M. Singer.—SiT
  On May Day. A. Adoff.—AdIn
  The rural dance about the Maypole. Unknown.—MoR
May. Christina Georgina Rossetti.—ElW
"**May** all who share". Robert Herrick.—StP
May-as-well. William Jay Smith.—SmL
May day ("Oak and ivy, sycamore, ash, what shall we leave by the cottage door"). Judith Nicholls.—FoLe
May day ("Twirl your ribbons"). Jean Kenward.—FoLe
"**May** He Who is the Father in Heaven of the". Swami Akhilananda.—StP
"**May** I follow a life of compassion in pity for". Albert Schweitzer.—StP
"**May** the road rise to meet you". Unknown.—StP
"**May** we, O God, keep ourselves modest". Epictetus.—StP
"**May** your life be bright and sunny". Unknown.—WiA
Maybe. Florence Parry Heide.—HeG
"**Maybe**". See Presents
"**Maybe** it's so". See Snail's pace
"**Maybe** there's a monster". See Maybe
Mayflies. Paul Fleischman.—FlJ
Mays, Willie (about)
  Right where he left off. C. Weeden.—KnAs
Mazhar, Farhad
  On my birthday, tr. by Kabir Chowdhury and Naomi Shihab Nye.—NyT
Mazur, Gail
  Listening to baseball in the car.—KnAs
McGlynn, John H.
  Dew, tr.—NyT
Me ("As long as I live"). Walter De La Mare.—DeR
Me ("I am me"). Accabre Huntley.—AgL
Me ("My nose is blue"). Karla Kuskin.—PrFo
"**Me** and my best friend". See The ballad of Jimi
Me and my work. Maya Angelou.—AnI
"**Me** go a Granny Yard. James Berry.—BeW
"**Me** han traido una caracola". See Caracola
Me I am. Unknown.—LoFh
"**Me** me me". See Myrtle warblers
"**Me,** myself, and I". Unknown.—PrP—WiA
"**Me** no know". Unknown.—WiA
"**Me** no worry, me no care". See "I should worry, I should care"
"**Me** oh my, said the tiny, shiny ant". See Big little boy
"**Me** riddle me riddle me ree". See Riddle
The **meadow-bout** fields. Unknown.—OpT
The **meadow** mouse. Theodore Roethke.—LaM
"A **meadowlark** came back one day". See Spring song

Merriam, Eve—*Continued*
The egotistical orchestra.—MeCh
End of winter.—MoA
Eraser.—MeS
Euphemistic.—MeCh
Evergreen.—MeS
The fable of the golden pear.—MeS
Fast food.—MeS
Fiddle faddle.—MeS
Fireworks 2.—MeS
"Fish, fish, make a wish".—MeY
A fishy square dance.—MeCh
A fishy story.—MeS
"Five little monsters".—HoS
The flying pen.—MeS
From the Japanese.—MeS
Gab.—MeCh
Gazinta.—MeCh
Geography.—MeS
"Ghosty ghosty all alone".—MeY
Gift wrapping.—MeS
"Gooseberry, juiceberry".—LiDd—MoS
Grandmother, rocking.—MeS
Green with envy.—MeCh
Grump.—MeS
"Guess what I've got inside my fist".—MeY
"Harriet, by magic force".—MeY
"Hello, hello, who's calling, please".—MeY
The hiker.—MeCh
The hill.—MeS
"Hop on one foot".—MeY
"Hunter on the horse, fox on the run".—MeY
Hurry.—MeS
"I found a little stone".—MeY
"I know a boy".—MeY
"I turn out the light".—MeY
The ice cream fountain mountain.—MeP
Ice-creepers.—MeS
"I'm sorry says the machine".—MeCh
"In the woods".—MeY
Itinerant.—MeCh
A jamboree for j.—MeS
Joker.—MeCh
"Jump, jump".—MeY
Junk.—MeP
"Knobby green pickle".—MeY
Kudzu.—MeCh
Leak.—MeS
Light rain, a downpour, and pigeons feasting on
    crumbs from a picnic in the park.—MeP
Lights in the dark.—MeP
Llude sig kachoo.—MeCh
Love letters, unmailed.—MeS
"Lunch box, lunch box".—MeY
Mean song ("Snickles and podes").—MeS
Menu.—MeP
Methuselah.—MeS
Misnomer.—MeCh—PrFo
Molly's glasses.—MeP
A moose on the loose.—MeS
Mr. Zoo.—MeCh
My family tree.—MeP
"A nanny for a goat".—MeY
A new song for Old Smoky.—MeP
Night song.—LaN
The nose knows.—MeP
Notions.—MeCh
A number of words.—MeCh
An odd one. See Animalimericks
On being introduced to you.—MeS
On our way.—DeS
1, 2, 3.—MeP

Onomatopoeia.—MoR
The Optileast and the Pessimost.—MeS
Out of the city.—MeS
Parentheses.—MeCh
Parking lot full.—MeCh
Pigeons ("Other birds soar in the clouds").—MeS
"Pins and needles".—MeY
Places to hide a secret message.—DeT
The poem as a door.—MeS
A poem for a pickle.—MeP
Points of the compass.—MeS
Polyglot.—MeCh
Portmanteaux.—MeCh
Postcards.—MeCh
Prose and poetry.—MeS
"Queen Regina".—MeP
Quibble.—MeS
Rainbow writing.—MeS
A rainy day.—MeP
Reply to the question, how can you become a
    poet.—MeS
Resolution.—MeCh
A rhyme is a jump rope.—MeS
Riddle go round.—MeP
Rigmarole.—MeCh
Rodomontade in the menagerie.—MeCh
Rover.—MeP
Ruby-throated hummingbird.—MeS
Rummage.—MeS
The sappy heasons.—MeCh
Say nay.—MeS
Schenectady.—MeS
Secret hand.—MeS
Serendipity.—MeCh
The serpent's hiss.—MeCh
"Sheep, sheep, sleeps in a fold".—MeY
Silence.—MeS
"Sister Ann".—MeP
Skip rope rhyme.—MeP
Skywriting I.—MeS
Skywriting III.—MeS
"Snow in the east".—MeY—MoS
So long, see you later.—MeS
Solitude ("Solitude is a mood to share").—MeS
Someday.—MeS
Souvenir.—MeS
Specs.—MeP
Spring fever.—MeS
Starry night I.—MeS
Starry night II.—MeS
The stray cat.—LaCc—MeS
The stuck horn.—MeS
Summer rain.—MeS
Summer solstice.—MeS
Supermarket, supermarket (a jump rope
    rhyme).—MeS
"Swing me, swing me, swing me round".—MeY
"Tabby on the prowl".—MeY
Talking to the sun.—MeS
Team words.—MeCh
"Ten little apples on ten apple trees".—MeY
Three strangenesses of every day.—MeS
To meet Mr. Lincoln.—DeS
A token of unspoken.—MeCh
Traveling.—MeS
Tube time.—KeT—MeS
TV.—MeS
Two from the zoo.—MeS
Twogether.—MeCh
The ultimate product.—MeCh
Ululation.—MeS
Un-negative.—MeCh

Mice—*Continued*
The mouse ("A mouse is"). Buson.—DeI
A mouse and her house. A. Fisher.—FiH
The mouse ate the bait. M. Luton.—CoAz
Mouse dinner. A. Fisher.—KeT
"A mouse in her room woke Miss Dowd".
Unknown.—LiLo
A mouse in her room.—ClI—KeT—PrFo
The mouse in the wainscot. I. Serraillier.—LaM
Mouse under the house, mouse in the house. A.
Adoff.—AdIn
"The mouse whose name is time". R. Francis.—
KeT
The mouse's lullaby. P. Cox.—KeT
Mouseways. A. Fisher.—FiH
The old wife and the ghost. J. Reeves.—DeS
Owl ("The diet of the owl is not"). X. J.
Kennedy.—LiIf
Owl ("The owl"). V. Worth.—LiIf
Pockets. A. Fisher.—FiH
Portrait. A. Fisher.—FiH
The prayer of the mouse. C. B. De Gasztold.—
LaM
The prince. W. De La Mare.—DeR
The quiet mouse. Unknown.—CoE
"Round the 4H baked goods sale". X. J.
Kennedy.—KeFb
Six little mice. Mother Goose.—LaM
"A small mouse in Middleton Stoney". M. C.
Livingston.—LiLo
"Snicketty, snacketty sneeze". X. J. Kennedy.—
CoAz
Snow stitches. A. Fisher.—FiH
"Stealthy Steffan stuck a dead". X. J. Kennedy.—
KeFb
Surprise ("I wonder"). A. Fisher.—FiH
Sweet Suffolk owl. Unknown.—CaB—LiIf
"There was a mouse". K. Kuskin.—LaM
"There was a wee bit moosikie". Unknown.—ClI
"Three blind mice". Mother Goose.—EdGl—
WaM
Timid as a mouse. A. Fisher.—FiH
Under the snow. A. Fisher.—FiH
Wanted. R. Fyleman.—LaM
What grandpa mouse said. V. Lindsay.—LiIf
"When I found a mouse in my stew".
Unknown.—ScA
When it's snowing. A. Fisher.—FiH
Winter nests. A. Fisher.—FiH
Wouldn't it be queer. A. Fisher.—FiH
Mice ("I think mice"). Rose Fyleman.—DeS—LaM
Mice ("Mice find places"). Valerie Worth.—WoAl
Mice ("Mice in their nest"). Basho, tr. by Tze-si
Huang.—DeI
"Mice". Valerie Worth.—LaM
"Mice find places". See Mice
"Mice in their nest". See Mice
Michael, Carol
Big black dog.—CoAz
"Michael met a monster". See The silent type
Michael's birthday. Myra Cohn Livingston.—LiBp
"Mickey Mouse, he had a house". Unknown.—CoM
Microscopes
Things on a microscope slide. X. J. Kennedy.—
KeGh
"Mid autumn late autumn". See His running, my
running
"The midday sky". See The night owl
The midnight snack. James Merrill.—ElW
The midnight tennis match. Thomas Lux.—KnAs
A midsummer night's dream, sels. William
Shakespeare

"If we shadows have offended".—WhDd
"Midwives and winding sheets". See Is love
The mighty eye. Kalli Dakos.—DaI
Migration. See Birds—Migration; Immigration and
emigration
Mike and Major. Cynthia Rylant.—JaP
"Mike's sister said he". See Mike and Major
Milehigh Jeff the giant hare. Nanette Mellage.—SlM
Miles, Josephine
Reason.—ElW
Milk and milking
Chocolate dreams, four. A. Adoff.—AdCh
"Dimpleton the simpleton". D. Lee.—CoAz
Grandmother in winter. X. J. Kennedy.—LiPg
Hot milk. X. J. Kennedy.—KeK
"I went to Wisconsin". J. Prelutsky.—PrBe
A kitten's thought. O. Herford.—ElW
The milker. M. Fatchen.—FaCm
"My mother bought a donkey, she thought it was
a cow". Unknown.—WiA
"Two-legs sat on three-legs by four-legs".
Unknown.—WiA
"A milk-white bird". Unknown.—WiA
"Milk white moon, put the cows to sleep". Carl
Sandburg.—SuI
The milker. Max Fatchen.—FaCm
Milky Way
"The man in the moon as he sails the sky".
Unknown.—PrP
The Milky Way. B. J. Esbensen.—LaN
"The Milky Way is a sail". Unknown.—LaN
"The Milky Way is the wild duck's way".
Unknown.—LaN
The Milky Way. Barbara Juster Esbensen.—LaN
"The Milky Way is a sail". Unknown.—LaN
"The Milky Way is the wild duck's way".
Unknown.—LaN
Millay, Edna St. Vincent
Afternoon on a hill.—FrS—SuI
From a very little sphinx.—DeS
God's world.—StP
"Loving you less than life, a little less".—ElW
The pear tree.—ElW
Recuerdo.—ElW
Miller, Jim Wayne
Cheerleader.—JaPr
A kinsman.—JaM
Why Rosalie did it.—JaM
Miller, Mary Britton
Cat ("The black cat yawns").—KeT
Here she is.—HoT
Houses.—DeS
The miller and his son. Walter De La Mare.—DeR
Millers and mills
"Blow, wind, blow, and go, mill, go". Mother
Goose.—WaM
Five eyes. W. De La Mare.—DeR—MaP
"Margaret wrote a letter". Unknown.—OpT
The miller and his son. W. De La Mare.—DeR
"Millery millery dustipole". Mother Goose.—
WaM
To the puss moth.—OpI
White ("Once a miller, and he would say"). W.
De La Mare.—DeR
"Millery millery dustipole". Mother Goose.—WaM
To the puss moth.—OpI
Milligan, Spike
Eels.—PrFo
Pygmy elephant.—CoAz
Questions, quistions and quoshtions.—PrFo
Millman, Lawrence
"Greedy snowslide", tr.—NyT

Mills. See Millers and mills
Millum, Trevor
  Lion dance.—FoLe
  Nyepi, the day of yellow rice.—FoLe
Milne, Alan Alexander
  "A bear, however hard he tries". See Teddy bear
  The christening ("What shall I call").—LaM
  Disobedience.—KeT
  The end.—LoFh
  Furry bear.—DeS
  Missing.—LaM
  "The more it snows".—DeS
  Politeness.—DeS
  Solitude ("I have a house where I go").—LiDd
  Teddy bear, sels.
    "A bear, however hard he tries".—DeT
  The three foxes.—DeT
  Wind on the hill.—BaW
Milner, Ian
  A boy's head, tr.—NyT
Milner-Gulland, Robin
  Waiting, tr.—GoU
Milosz, Czeslaw
  Happy as a dog's tail, tr.—NyT
  I have ten legs, tr.—NyT
  Love ("I believed"), tr.—NyT
  Transformations, tr.—NyT
Mima. Walter De La Mare.—DeR—MaP
Mime. John Updike.—MoR
Mind. See also Wisdom
  "The brain is wider than the sky". E. Dickinson.—ElW
  Divine delight. W. De La Mare.—DeR
  "O mind, move in the Supreme Being". S. Brahmendra.—StP
  Resolution. E. Merriam.—MeCh
  Rummage. E. Merriam.—MeS
"Mind your own business". Unknown.—ScA
Mindoro. Ramon C. Sunico.—NyT
Mine. Lilian Moore.—MoS
"Mine are the kind that don't brown, they scorch". See My marshmallows
Mine eyes have seen the glory. From Battle hymn of the republic. Julia Ward Howe.—SuC
"Mine eyes have seen the glory of the closing of the school". Unknown.—ScA
"Mine eyes have seen the glory of the coming of the Lord". See Mine eyes have seen the glory
Miners. See Mines and mining
Mines and mining
  The pit ponies. L. Norris.—NyT
Minor, James
  "Giddy up gid".—MoR
Minotaur. X. J. Kennedy.—WhDd
Minstrel man. Langston Hughes.—SuC
"The minute I heard my first love story". See 1246
Miracles
  When angels came to Zimmer. P. Zimmer.—JaM
The mirror. William Jay Smith.—SmL
"Mirrored in the window pane". See Ivy
Mirrorment. Archie Randolph Ammons.—DeS
Mirrors. See also Reflections (mirrored)
  "One day I asked the mirror facing me". T. S. Seloti.—NyT
Mischief
  Anansi the spider. G. McDermott.—WhDd
  Apology. L. Emanuel.—JaPr
  Bad. P. B. Janeczko.—JaB
  Confession to Mrs. Robert L. Snow. G. Soto.—JaPr
  Dame Hickory. W. De La Mare.—DeR
  "Ding dong bell". Mother Goose.—SuO—WaM

"Five little monkeys". Unknown.—CoE
"For his mother's mudpack, Brent". X. J. Kennedy.—KeFb
"For red mouthwash, rotten Ross". X. J. Kennedy.—KeFb
Ginger. Unknown.—OpT
"A girl, who weighed many an oz.". Unknown.—LiLo
Halloween, the hydrant dare. G. Roberts.—JaPr
"I'm Chiquita Banana, and I'm here to say". Unknown.—CoM
"In the dining car, mean Myrt". X. J. Kennedy.—KeFb
"I've drowned seventy ants in a pool". A. Story.—LiLo
Mischief City. T. Jones-Wynne.—BoT
The mocking fairy. W. De La Mare.—DeR—MaP
"Nellie Bligh caught a fly". Unknown.—OpI
Ode to pomegranates. G. Soto.—SoNe
"On the dam, Neil spied a wheel". X. J. Kennedy.—KeFb
Part XIV: Now, dear me. From A child's day. W. De La Mare.—DeR
Part XV: Now, my dear, for gracious sake. From A child's day. W. De La Mare.—DeR
Poor substitute. K. Dakos.—DaI
"Round the 4H baked goods sale". X. J. Kennedy.—KeFb
"Sheila, into Dad's right shoe". X. J. Kennedy.—KeFb
"Sheldon with a welding torch". X. J. Kennedy.—KeFb
"Sneaky Ebenezer Snyder". X. J. Kennedy.—KeFb
"Stealthy Steffan stuck a dead". X. J. Kennedy.—KeFb
Sugar-n-spice, etc. R. Quillen.—JaPr
The time we cherry-bombed the toilet at the River Oaks. C. H. Webb.—JaPr
"To sabotage the Yuletide play". X. J. Kennedy.—KeFb
"To the bottom of his drink". X. J. Kennedy.—KeFb
"To the bowl of champagne punch". X. J. Kennedy.—KeFb
"Tom tied a kettle to the tail of a cat". Unknown.—OpI
"Where the sun shone white hot, Cass". X. J. Kennedy.—KeFb
Mischief City. Tim Jones-Wynne.—BoT
"Misericordia". Walter De La Mare.—DeR
Misnomer. Eve Merriam.—MeCh—PrFo
"Miss Beemis never married". See Dancers
"Miss Buss and Miss Beale". Unknown.—OpI
Miss Cherry. Walter De La Mare.—DeR
"Miss Lucy had a baby". Unknown.—CoM—ScA
"Miss Mary Mack, Mack, Mack". Unknown.—CoM
Miss McGillicuddy. Mary Ann Hoberman.—HoFa
"Miss, miss, little miss, miss". Unknown.—WiA
"Miss Mocking Bird". See Mocking bird
"Miss Parsons, surely you jest". See Garrett Chandler
Miss T. Walter De La Mare.—DeR—MaP
Missel thrush. Walter De La Mare.—DeR
Missing. Alan Alexander Milne.—LaM
"Mississauga rattlesnakes". See Rattlesnake skipping song
Mississippi. See "M, I, crooked letter, crooked letter, I"
Mississippi River
  "M, I, crooked letter, crooked letter, I". Unknown.—WiA

Mississippi River—*Continued*
    Mississippi.—CoM
"**Mississippi** said to Missouri". Unknown.—WiA
A **misspent** youth. X. J. Kennedy.—KeGh
Mist. See Fog
"**Mister** Beedle Baddlebug". See Tea party
Mister October, Reggie Jackson. Unknown.—MoA
"**Mister** Sometimish, Mister Sometimish". See
    Moody Mister Sometimish
Mistletoe
    Mistletoe. W. De La Mare.—DeR—MaP
    Under the mistletoe. C. Cullen.—SlM
    Winter ("Green mistletoe"). W. De La Mare.—
        DeR
Mistletoe. Walter De La Mare.—DeR—MaP
"**Mistress** Mary". See "Mary, Mary, quite contrary"
Mistress Mary. William Jay Smith.—SmL
"**Mistress** Mary, quite contrary". See Mistress Mary
Misune
    The wild goose, tr. by Tze-si Huang.—DeI
Mitchell, Adrian
    Bebe Belinda and Carl Colombus.—AgL
    A warning ("If you keep two angels in a cage").—
        AgL
Mitchell, Karen L.
    Black patent leather shoes.—JaPr
Mitchell, Lucy Sprague
    "The house of the mouse".—CoAz—LaM
Mitchell, Stephen
    Jerusalem, tr.—NyT
Mitchell, Arthur (about)
    Arthur Mitchell. M. Moore.—MoR
Mittens
    The three little kittens. E. L. Follen.—HoS
        "Three little kittens, they lost their
            mittens".—SuO (unat.)
        "Three little kittens lost their mittens".—
            EdGl (unat.)—WaM (unat.)
"**Mix** a pancake". Christina Georgina Rossetti.—
    LiDd
"A **mixture** a mingle". See Team words
Miyoshi
    "In storm-tossed grassland".—CaR
Miyoshi, Tatsuji
    Great Aso, tr. by Edith Marcombe Shiffert and
        Yuki Sawa.—NyT
Mizumura, Kazue
    "Again and again".—BaW
    "If I were a snail".—MoS
Mocking bird. Nanette Mellage.—SlM
The **mocking** fairy. Walter De La Mare.—DeR—
    MaP
Mockingbirds
    "In a Mississippi valley". J. Prelutsky.—PrBe
    Mocking bird. N. Mellage.—SlM
Modeling. See Sculpture and statues
Modern life
    Baseball canto. L. Ferlinghetti.—KnAs
    The biggest questions. M. C. Livingston.—LiNe
    Black kid in a new place. J. Berry.—BeW
    Break dance. G. Nichols.—AgL
    Brownout. T. Perez.—NyT
    But why not. M. Fatchen.—FaCm
    Checking out me history. J. Agard.—AgL
    The closing of the rodeo. W. J. Smith.—KnAs
    Clothes ("My mother keeps on telling me"). E.
        Jennings.—AgL
    "Come up an' see yer grannie". From Grannies
        and grandpas. Unknown.—OpT
    A commercial for spring. E. Merriam.—MeP
    Crowd. E. Merriam.—MeCh
    A day in school. K. Dakos.—DaI

A different image. D. Randall.—SuC
The disaster. B. Bennett.—MoR
Disco date, 1980. J. Berry.—BeW
Dodos. X. J. Kennedy.—KeK
Dream voyage to the center of the subway. E.
    Merriam.—MeS
A drunken egotist. E. Linden.—AgL
Economics. R. Wrigley.—JaPr
Enemies. C. Zolotow.—SaB
Excuse. M. C. Livingston.—LiT
Fast food. E. Merriam.—MeS
The finish. D. Hoffman.—KnAs
For my people. M. Walker.—SuC
"For peace sake". C. McClester.—SlM
From her office. R. H. Marks.—LiPg
The funeral of Martin Luther King, Jr. N.
    Giovanni.—SuC
Garage apartment. M. C. Livingston.—LiT
Girls can we educate we dads. J. Berry.—BeW
Glory falls. M. Angelou.—AnI
Hallowe'en indignation meeting. M. Fishback.—
    DeT
A hardware store as proof of the existence of
    God. N. Willard.—JaP
Health fanatic. J. C. Clarke.—AgL
How things work. G. Soto.—SoA
I believe in the theory that says we were visited
    long ago. A. Adoff.—AdCh
"I don't talk to pop stars". A. Stockbroker.—AgL
"I want to know when you get to be from a
    place". J. Carson.—CaS
"If you think". Lottemoos.—AgL
"I'm sorry says the machine". E. Merriam.—
    MeCh
"The Indians". R. Sosa.—NyT
Invitation ("Listen, I've a big surprise"). M. C.
    Livingston.—KeT—LiT
Ka 'Ba. I. A. Baraka.—SuC
London. M. Angelou.—AnI
Mamma settles the dropout problem. B. Gates.—
    SuC
A man in a tree. N. M. Bodecker.—LiLo
Me and my work. M. Angelou.—AnI
Medals and money, a re-evaluation. B.
    Lamblin.—KnAs
Meeting my best friend from the eighth grade. G.
    Gildner.—KnAs
Mothering Sunday. S. Cook.—FoLe
The mouse ("I heard a mouse"). E. Coatsworth.—
    LaM
Mum Dad and me. J. Berry.—BeW
My Jose. M. Robinson.—LiPf
My share. S. Bolat.—NyT
New mother. R. H. Marks.—LiPm
The new negro. J. E. McCall.—SuC
A new song for Old Smoky. E. Merriam.—MeP
"Oh my good Lord, I am not a young man
    anymore". J. Carson.—CaS
O say. M. C. Livingston.—LiR
O taste and see. D. Levertov.—ElW
"Old Uncle Luke, he thinks he's cute". From
    Grannies and grandpas. Unknown.—OpT
The origin of baseball. K. Patchen.—KnAs
Palm Sunday. B. Wade.—FoLe
"Priam on one side sending forth eleven". From
    Watching football on TV. H. Nemerov.—KnAs
Progress. G. E. Lyon.—JaM
A protest poem for Rosa Parks. A. Oyewole.—
    SlM
The purpose of poetry. J. Carter.—JaM
Question and answer. L. Hughes.—SuC

Monsters—*Continued*
Interesting facts about monsters. F. P. Heide.—HeG
Jabberwocky. From Through the looking glass. L. Carroll.—ElW
Kracken. X. J. Kennedy.—WhDd
Leviathan. From Book of Job. Bible/Old Testament.—WhDd
The manticore. J. Steig.—WhDd
Maybe. F. P. Heide.—HeG
Milehigh Jeff the giant hare. N. Mellage.—SlM
Minotaur. X. J. Kennedy.—WhDd
"The monster in my closet". F. P. Heide.—HeG
Monster mothers. F. P. Heide.—HeG
The ogglewop. C. West.—PrFo
The ogre. W. De La Mare.—DeR
The ombley-gombley. P. Wesley-Smith.—PrFo
"On his laboratory table". X. J. Kennedy.—KeFb
"The panteater". W. Cole.—JaP
Roc. R. Burton.—WhDd
"Said an ogre from old Saratoga". C. Aiken.—LiLo
Said the monster. L. Moore.—LiLo
"A sea serpent saw a big tanker". Unknown.—LiLo—PrP
The sign. F. P. Heide.—HeG
The silent type. F. P. Heide.—HeG
Sir John Mandeville's report on the griffin. J. Yolen.—LiDd
The snoffle. F. P. Heide.—HeG
"Something is there". L. Moore.—BaH
Sounds of winter. J. P. Lewis.—LeE
The truth about the abominable footprint. M. Baldwin.—PrFo
Under the stairs. D. Lister.—BaH
"The underwater wibbles". J. Prelutsky.—JaP
Windigo spirit. K. Stange.—BoT
The worst thing and the best thing. F. P. Heide.—HeG
The yeti. J. Gardner.—WhDd
"**Monsters** are an awful pain". See The sign
"**Monsters** are scary". See Interesting facts about monsters
"**Montague** Michael". Unknown.—LaCc
Monte Rio, California. Zack Rogow.—GoT
Montgomery, James
"Angels from the realms of glory".—YoHa
Months. See also names of months, as January
One year. N. M. Bodecker.—KeT
"Thirty days hath September". Mother Goose.—WaM
The **monument**. Paul B. Janeczko.—JaB
Monuments. See also Graves; Sculpture and statues
Concord hymn. R. W. Emerson.—ElW
The monument. P. B. Janeczko.—JaB
Ozymandias. P. B. Shelley.—ElW
"Two months after marching through Boston". From For the Union dead. R. Lowell.—SuC
Washington monument by night. C. Sandburg.—SuI
Moods
Dust of snow. R. Frost.—ElW
Grump. E. Merriam.—MeS
Moody Mister Sometimish. G. Nichols.—NiCo
The Optileast and the Pessimost. E. Merriam.—MeS
Solitude ("Solitude is a mood to share"). E. Merriam.—MeS
There are days. B. S. De Regniers.—DeW
Variety. From Animalimericks. E. Merriam.—MeS
"**Moods** and tenses". Unknown.—OpI

Moody Mister Sometimish. Grace Nichols.—NiCo
"**Mookie** and Hubie and Strawberry". See Let's go, Mets
"**Mookie** James". See Fantasti-cat
Moon
"Again and again". K. Mizumura.—BaW
"Although the wind". I. Shikibu.—GoT
Bird watcher. J. Yolen.—YoBi
Broken mirror. Zuiryu.—DeI
The cat ("Flourishing his head around"). Kusatao.—DeI
Cat at night. A. Stoutenburg.—LaCc
Cat in moonlight. D. Gibson.—DeT—LaCc
Comma in the sky. A. Fisher.—FiA
December ("Round slice of moon, December night"). F. Newman.—BoT
Dipa, the lamp. A. Bonner.—FoLe
Dusk ("The moon is red in the foggy sky"). P. Verlaine.—GoT
The early morning. H. Belloc.—KeT
Eeka, neeka. W. De La Mare.—DeR
Foxes ("A litter of little black foxes, and later"). M. A. Hoberman.—DeS
From the Japanese. E. Merriam.—MeS
Full moon ("Night on the verandah"). A. Bryan.—BrS
Full moon ("One night as Dick lay fast asleep"). W. De La Mare.—DeR—MaP
Half moon. F. Garcia Lorca.—LaN
The harvest moon ("The flame red moon, the harvest moon"). T. Hughes.—LaN
Harvest moon ("She comes in silence"). J. Kenward.—FoLe
"Hey diddle diddle, the cat and the fiddle". Mother Goose.—EdGl—SuO—WaM
Horse by moonlight. A. Blanco.—NyT
"A hungry owl hoots". Joso.—LiIf
Hymn to Cynthia. B. Jonson.—ElW
"I see the moon". Unknown.—StP
"I see the moon, the moon sees me". Unknown.—WiA
"I was born in Jacinto Vera". L. Falco.—NyT
Idh Mubarak. B. Doherty.—FoLe
In the discreet splendor. A. L. Strauss.—GoT
It is late. A. Adoff.—AdIn
"Knobby green pickle". E. Merriam.—MeY
Long Beach, February. M. C. Livingston.—LiR
"The man in the moon". Mother Goose.—EdGl—WaM
"The man in the moon as he sails the sky". Unknown.—PrP
"Milk white moon, put the cows to sleep". C. Sandburg.—SuI
"Moon". K. Kuskin.—LiDd
Moon ("I have a white cat whose name is moon"). W. J. Smith.—SmL
The moon ("The moon has a face like the clock in the hall"). R. L. Stevenson.—KeT
"The moon is a white cat". Unknown.—LaN
The moon rises slowly over the ocean. X. De-min.—NyT
Moon, two views. M. C. Livingston.—LiNe
Moon's ending. S. Teasdale.—GoT
Moonstruck. A. Fisher.—HoS—HoSt
My dress is old. Unknown.—SnD
Night ("Night is a purple pumpkin"). P. Hubbell.—LaN
Night flight over Kansas. M. C. Livingston.—LiNe
Night of the full moon. D. Batson.—FoLe
Night of thunder. M. C. Livingston.—LiNe
"Nila nila odi va". Unknown.—YoS

Moon—*Continued*

"Moon, moon, come to me".—YoS
Now day is breaking. S. Quasimodo.—GoT
"Oh, there's not much sense". Unknown.—WiA
Old man moon. A. Fisher.—DeT—FiA
On a night of the full moon. A. Lorde.—GoU
The owl on the aerial. C. Short.—LiIf
A path to the moon. B. P. Nichol.—BoT
"Ramadan". S. Cook.—FoLe
Ramadan. S. Cook.—FoLe
River moons. C. Sandburg.—LaN
Rocks ("They say, no"). V. Worth.—WoAl
Rosh Hashanah eve. H. Philip.—LoFh
"Said the wind to the moon, I will blow you out".
    From The wind and the moon. G.
    MacDonald.—DeT—LiDd
Same and different. Unknown.—DeI
The shadow ("When the last of gloaming's gone").
    W. De La Mare.—DeR
Silver. W. De La Mare.—DeR—LaN—MaP
"Silverly". D. Lee.—BoT
Sky tales of the Assiniboin Indians. M. C.
    Livingston.—LiR
"Slip past the window". From Nightdances. J.
    Skofield.—LaN
Song ("Sing to the sun"). A. Bryan.—BrS
Song of creation. Unknown.—GoT
"Song of the moon". N. Farber.—HoSt
Spell of the moon. L. Norris.—LiIf
Summer full moon. J. Kirkup.—LaN
Summer night, canoeing. B. J. Esbensen.—EsW
That cat. K. Kuskin.—LaCc
"There once was a man in the moon". D.
    McCord.—LiLo
"There was a young man of St. Kitts".
    Unknown.—LiLo
The thief. D. Chandra.—LiIf
"Watching the moon". I. Shikibu.—GoT
"The way I must enter". I. Shikibu.—GoT
"What follows king walking, yet stays". From
    Riddle poems. J. Berry.—BeW
What grandpa mouse said. V. Lindsay.—LiIf
What the little girl said. V. Lindsay.—DeT
    "The moon's the north wind's cooky".—LiDd
"Who knows if the moon's". E. E. Cummings.—
    DeS
Will ever. W. De La Mare.—DeR—MaP
The wind and the moon, complete. G.
    MacDonald.—BaW
Winter moon. L. Hughes.—DeS—LaN
"The wolf". J. P. Lewis.—LeA
Yellow man, purple man. E. Dickinson.—KeT

Moon ("I have a white cat whose name is moon").
    William Jay Smith.—SmL
The moon ("The moon has a face like the clock in
    the hall"). Robert Louis Stevenson.—KeT
"Moon". Karla Kuskin.—LiDd
"The moon dazzles the meadow". See The thief
"The moon goes over the water". See Half moon
"The moon has a face like the clock in the hall". See
    The moon
"The moon is a white cat". Unknown.—LaN
"The moon is one". See Teaching numbers
"The moon is red in the foggy sky". See Dusk
"The moon is very, very old". See Old man moon
"Moon, moon, come to me". See "Nila nila odi va"
"The moon on the one hand, the dawn on the
    other". See The early morning
The moon rises slowly over the ocean. Xu De-min,
    tr. by Edward Morin and Dennis Ding.—NyT
"The moon shines bright". Mother Goose.—WaM

"The moon shines bright and the stars give a light".
    Unknown.—OpI
"The moon that once was full, ripe and golden". See
    Ramadan
Moon, two views. Myra Cohn Livingston.—LiNe
"Moon, worn thin to the width of a quill". See
    Moon's ending
"The moon's a holy owl queen". See What grandpa
    mouse said
Moon's ending. Sara Teasdale.—GoT
"The moon's the north wind's cooky". See What the
    little girl said See What the little girl said
Moonstruck. Aileen Fisher.—HoS—HoSt
Moore, Clement Clarke
    A visit from St. Nicholas.—ElW—HoS
Moore, John Travers
    Jet.—MoR
Moore, John Travers, and Moore, Margaret
    A.—DeS
Moore, Lilian
    The chestnuts are falling.—MoR
    "Do ghouls".—PrFo
    Dragon smoke.—DeS—DeT
    Fog ("Oh this is").—BaH
    Ground hog day.—DeT
    Hey, bug.—MoS
    I'm skeleton.—BaH
    In the fog.—KeT
    "Listen".—SuI
    "Look at that".—HoS
    Mine.—MoS
    Move over.—LiDd
    Night creature.—DeS
    No one.—KeT
    Partners ("This is the wind's doing").—BaW
    Said the monster.—LiLo
    "Something is there".—BaH
    "Sometimes".—KeT
    To a red kite.—DeS
    True.—LaCc
    "Until I saw the sea".—BaW—DeS
    Waking.—MoS
    "We three".—LiHp
    Wet.—MoR
    While you were chasing a hat.—BaW
    Who.—LiDd
    Whooo.—LiIf
    Wind song.—DeS
    Witch goes shopping.—LoFh—PrFo
    Yellow weed.—LiDd
Moore, Margaret. See Moore, John Travers, and
    Moore, Margaret
Moore, Marianne
    Arthur Mitchell.—MoR
    Baseball and writing.—MoA
    Poetry ("I too, dislike it, there are things that are
    important").—SuI
Moore, Rosalie
    Catalogue, sels.
        Cats sleep fat.—LaCc
    Cats sleep fat. See Catalogue
Moore, Thomas
    "Believe me, if all those endearing young
    charms".—ElW
Moore, William H.
    Some winter pieces.—BoT
Moose
    Chocolate moose. W. J. Smith.—SmL
    A moose on the loose. E. Merriam.—MeS
A moose on the loose. Eve Merriam.—MeS
Moran, Arnaldo D. Larrosa
    The new suit, tr.—NyT

More, Saint Thomas
"These things, good Lord, that we pray for".—StP
"The **more** it snows". Alan Alexander Milne.—DeS

"**More** than two hundred". See Chips, one

Morfin, Guadulupe
Paper doll, tr. by Raul Aceves and Cristina Carrasco and Jane Taylor.—NyT

Morgan, Robert
Elevation.—JaM
Mountain bride.—JaM
Muscling rocks.—JaPr
Shaking.—JaPr

Morin, Edward
Far and close, tr.—NyT
The moon rises slowly over the ocean, tr.—NyT

Morning. See also Wake-up poems
Ants. Y. Al-Sa'igh.—NyT
An appointment. C. Shiang-hua.—NyT
"Are you ready when the Lord shall come". Unknown.—StP
At sunrise. M. Fatchen.—FaCm
The blackbird. H. Wolfe.—DeT
The border bird. W. De La Mare.—DeR
Brickyard. P. B. Janeczko.—JaB
The child in the story awakes. W. De La Mare.—DeR
Chocolate dreams, six thirty. A. Adoff.—AdCh
"Come morning". H. Yu.—GoT
Daybreak in Alabama. L. Hughes.—SuC
"Dear Lord my God". M. L'Engle.—StP
Dew. L. Suryadi.—NyT
"A diller, a dollar". Mother Goose.—SuO—WaM
"Donkey, donkey, old and gray". Mother Goose.—WaM
Dream boogie. L. Hughes.—MoR
The early morning. H. Belloc.—KeT
8 A.M. shadows. P. Hubbell.—DeS
"Eternal God". M. Takenaka.—StP
"Every morning". G. Swede.—BoT
First one awake. X. J. Kennedy.—KeK
Five ("Is old enough"). M. C. Livingston.—LiBp
"For I will consider my cat Jeoffry". From Jubilate agno. C. Smart.—StP
Good morning. M. Sipe.—DeS
Good morrow. T. Heywood.—ElW
The happy sheep. W. Thorley.—CoAz
"He that would thrive". Mother Goose.—WaM
"Here we go round the mulberry bush". Mother Goose.—EdGl—SuO—WaM
"I arise today". Saint Patrick.—StP
"I wake up". M. Rosen.—AgL
"I woke up this morning". K. Kuskin.—KeT
"In the early morning". E. Di Pasquale.—LiPg
"It is God, the creator, the gracious one". Unknown.—StP
"Let me get up early on this summer morning". E. Guillevic.—GoT
Morning at Malibu. M. C. Livingston.—LiNe
Morning athletes. M. Piercy.—KnAs
"Morning has broken". E. Farjeon.—StP
Morning horses. Basho.—DeI
Mrs. Morizawa's morning. X. J. Kennedy.—KeK
My own day. J. Little.—LiHe—LoFh
Neighborhood street. E. Greenfield.—GrN
No jewel. W. De La Mare.—DeR
Ode to Senor Leal's goat. G. Soto.—SoNe
"O God, creator of light, at the rising". Unknown.—StP
"O Lord, help me to greet the coming day in peace". Unknown.—StP
"O Lord, Thou knowest how". J. Astley.—StP

"One misty, moisty morning". Mother Goose.—MoS—SuO—WaM
The owl ("The owl hooted and told of"). Unknown.—LaN
Papa is a bear. J. P. Lewis.—LiPf
Part II: Softly, drowsily. From A child's day. W. De La Mare.—DeR
Part III: Little birds bathe. From A child's day. W. De La Mare.—DeR
Part IV: The queen of Arabia, Uanjinee. From A child's day. W. De La Mare.—DeR
Part V: England over. From A child's day. W. De La Mare.—DeR
Polyglot. E. Merriam.—MeCh
The prayer of the cock. C. B. De Gasztold.—DeP
Precious. M. Fatchen.—FaCm
Prism in the window. From Four poems for Roy G Biv. B. J. Esbensen.—EsW
The shepherd. W. De La Mare.—DeR
6:15 A.M. M. C. Livingston.—LiNe
"A slash of blue, a sweep of gray". E. Dickinson.—GoT
The song of the old mother. W. B. Yeats.—ElW
Souvenir of the ancient world. C. Drummond de Andrade.—NyT
Sparrow dreaming. B. J. Esbensen.—EsW
Spring is. B. Katz.—MoS
The sun on Easter day. N. Farber.—LoFh
Sunrise. B. J. Esbensen.—EsW
"There was an old man by Salt Lake". W. J. Smith.—SmL
"This morning, God". Unknown.—StP
"This morning I will not". H. Kakinomoto.—GoU
"Thou art the sky and thou art the nest as well". R. Tagore.—StP
Time to rise. R. L. Stevenson.—DeT—PlW
To the ancestors. Unknown.—NyT
Unseen till now. Buson.—DeI
"Wake up, Jacob". Unknown.—WiA
Waking. L. Moore.—MoS
"The way to start a day is this". From The way to start the day. B. Baylor.—DeT
What they said. Unknown.—DeS
The windhover. G. M. Hopkins.—CaB
"The year's at the spring". From Pippa passes. R. Browning.—ElW—StP
"You wake me up, Father". Unknown.—StP
Zebra ("White sun"). J. Thurman.—HoT

Morning. Bobbi Katz.—PrFo
Morning at Malibu. Myra Cohn Livingston.—LiNe
Morning athletes. Marge Piercy.—KnAs
"**Morning** comes and I awake". See The stable hymn
"**Morning** has broken". Eleanor Farjeon.—StP
Morning horses. Basho, tr. by Tze-si Huang.—DeI
"**Morning** I run with the sea". See By the sea
Morning on this street. Gary Soto.—SoA
"**Morning** sun". See A drunken egotist
The **morning** wind from the west. Arnold Adoff.—AdIn
"The **morns** are meeker than they were". Emily Dickinson.—SuI
Autumn.—DeT

Morrison, Lillian
Burning bright.—JaP
Donnybrook at Riverfront Stadium.—MoA
Great grandma.—LiPg
Let's go, Mets.—KnAs
Nine triads.—KnAs
Ratio.—GoU
Sailing, sailing.—KnAs

Mother Goose—*Continued*

A farmer went trotting.—ClI
"Fiddle-de-dee, fiddle-de-dee".—WaM
"The fiddler and his wife".—WaM
"First in a carriage".—WaM
First star. See "Star light, star bright"
"Flying-man, flying-man".—SuO
"Four and twenty tailors".—ClI
"Friday night's dream".—WaM
"Gee up, Neddy, to the fair".—WaM
"Georgie Porgie, pudding and pie".—SuO—WaM
"The giant Jim, great giant grim".—WaM
"Girls and boys, come out to play". See Come out to play
"Go to bed late".—WaM
"Go to bed, Tom".—WaM
"God be here, God be there".—WaM
"Good morrow to you, Valentine".—WaM
"Goosey goosey gander".—EdGl—SuO—WaM
"Great A, little a".—WaM
"Green cheese, yellow laces".—WaM
"Gregory Griggs, Gregory Griggs".—SuO
"Hannah Bantry in the pantry".—WaM
"Hark, hark, the dogs do bark".—WaM
"Hay is for horses".—WaM
"He that would thrive".—WaM
"Hector Protector was dressed all in green".—SuO
"Here am I".—WaM
"Here we go round the mulberry bush".—EdGl—SuO—WaM
"Here's Sulky Sue".—WaM
"Here's to thee, old apple tree".—WaM
"Hey diddle diddle, the cat and the fiddle".—EdGl—SuO—WaM
Hey diddle doubt.—ClI
"Hey ho, nobody home".—WaM
"Hiccup, hiccup, go away".—WaM
"Hickety pickety, my black hen".—SuO—WaM
"Hickory dickory dock".—EdGl—SuO—WaM
"Hie to the market, Jenny come trot".—WaM
    A wasted journey.—OpT
"Higher than a house".—WaM
"Hippity hop to the barber shop".—CoM—WaM—WiA
Hoddley, poddley.—ClI
The house that Jack built. See "This is the house that Jack built"
"Humpty Dumpty sat on a wall".—EdGl—SuO—WaM
"Hush a bye, baby, on the tree top".—EdGl
Hush, little baby. See "Hush, little baby, don't say a word"
"Hush, little baby, don't say a word".—SuO
    Hush, little baby.—KeT
"Hush thee my baby".—WaM
"Hushabye baby, they're gone to milk".—WaM
"I do not like thee, Doctor Fell".—OpI—SuO—WaM
"I had a dog whose name was Buff".—WaM
I had a little cow.—ClI
I had a little dog.—ClI
"I had a little hen".—ClI
"I had a little husband".—WaM
"I had a little moppet".—WaM
    Little moppet.—OpT
"I had a little nut tree".—EdGl—SuO
"I had two pigeons bright and gay".—WaM
"I know something I won't tell".—WaM—WiA
    Three little monkeys.—PrFo
"I love little pussy".—WaM
"I saw a ship a-sailing".—SuO
"I saw Esau kissing Kate".—OpI

"I saw three ships come sailing by".—WaM
"I wrote a letter to my love".—WaM
"Ickle, ockle, blue bockle".—WaM
"If I had a donkey that wouldn't go".—WaM
"If I'd as much money as I could spend".—WaM
"If Peter Piper picked a peck of pickled peppers". See "Peter Piper picked a peck of pickled peppers"
"If wishes were horses".—WaM
"If you are not handsome at twenty".—WaM
"I'll tell my own daddy, when he comes home".—WaM
"I'm the king of the castle".—WaM
"In a cottage in Fife".—SuO
"In an oak there liv'd an owl".—LiIf
"In the greenhouse lives a wren".—WaM
"It's raining, it's pouring".—CoM—OpI—ScA—WiA
"It's raining, it's raining".—WaM
"I've got a lad and he's double double-jointed".—OpI
"Jack and Jill".—EdGl—SuO—WaM
"Jack be nimble, Jack be quick".—EdGl—SuO—WaM
"Jack Sprat could eat no fat".—EdGl—SuO—WaM
"Jeremiah Obadiah, puff, puff, puff".—WaM
"Jerry Hall".—ClI—ScA
"John, come sell thy fiddle".—WaM
"Ladybird, ladybird". See "Ladybug, ladybug, fly away home"
"Ladybug, ladybug, fly away home".—ScA—WiA
    "Ladybird, ladybird".—WaM
    To the ladybird ("Ladybird, ladybird").—OpI
"Left foot, right foot".—WaM
"Leg over leg".—ClI—WaM
"The lion and the unicorn".—EdGl
"Little Bo-Peep has lost her sheep".—EdGl—SuO—WaM
"Little Boy Blue, come blow your horn".—EdGl—SuO—WaM
"Little Jack Horner".—EdGl—SuO—WaM
"Little Jack Sprat".—ClI
"Little Johnny Morgan".—ClI
"Little Miss Donnet".—WaM
"Little Miss Lily, you're dreadfully silly".—WaM
"Little Miss Muffet".—EdGl—SuO—WaM
"Little Miss Tuckett".—ClI
Little moppet. See "I had a little moppet"
"Little Nancy Etticoat".—WaM
"A little old man of Derby".—WaM
"Little Poll Parrot".—ClI—WaM
"Little Polly Flinders".—SuO—WaM
"Little robin redbreast".—WaM
"Little Tom Tucker". See "Little Tommy Tucker"
"Little Tommy Tittlemouse".—WaM
"Little Tommy Tucker".—SuO—WaM
    "Little Tom Tucker".—EdGl
"Lock the dairy door, lock the dairy door".—WaM
"Lucy Locket lost her pocket".—WaM
"The man in the moon".—EdGl—WaM
"A man went hunting at Ryegate".—WaM
"Manners in the dining room".—WaM
"Mary, Mary, quite contrary".—EdGl—SuO
    "Mistress Mary".—WaM
The messenger. See "Bless you, bless you, burnie-bee"
"Millery millery dustipole".—WaM
    To the puss moth.—OpI
"Mistress Mary". See "Mary, Mary, quite contrary"

Mother Goose—*Continued*
   "To market, to market".—WaM
   "To sleep easy all night".—WaM
   To the ladybird ("Ladybird, ladybird"). See "Ladybug, ladybug, fly away home"
   To the puss moth. See "Millery millery dustipole"
   "Tom, Tom, the piper's son, he learned to play when he was young".—EdGl
   "Tom, Tom, the piper's son, stole a pig and away he run".—SuO—WaM
   "Trit trot to market to buy a penny doll".—WaM
   "Two little dogs".—CII—WaM
   "Up the wooden hill to Bedfordshire".—WaM
      Pickaback up to bed (". . . to Blanket Fair").—OpT
   "Wash the dishes, wipe the dishes".—WaM
   A wasted journey. See "Hie to the market, Jenny come trot"
   Wee Willie Winkie. See "Wee Willie Winkie runs through the town"
   "Wee Willie Winkie runs through the town".—EdGl—SuO—WaM
      Wee Willie Winkie.—HoS
   "We're all dry with drinking on't".—WaM
   "We're all jolly boys".—WaM
   "We've ploughed our land".—WaM
   "When land is gone and money spent".—WaM
   "When the clouds".—WaM
   "Who are you, a dirty old man".—OpI—WaM
   "Who comes here".—WaM
   Whose little pigs.—CII
   "Willful waste brings woeful want".—WaM
   "Wine and cakes for gentlemen".—WaM
   "A wise old owl lived in an oak".—LiIf
      A wise old owl (". . . sat in an oak").—CII
   A wise old owl (". . . sat in an oak"). See "A wise old owl lived in an oak"
   "Yankee Doodle came to town".—SuO
   "Young Roger came tapping at Dolly's window".—WaM
"**Mother** got mad at me tonight and bawled me out". See Growing pains
Mother has a talk with me. Jean Little.—LiHe
"The **mother** hen". See Mother hen
Mother hen. Seibi, tr. by Tze-si Huang.—DeI
"A **mother** horse". See Mother horse
Mother horse. Issa, tr. by Tze-si Huang.—DeI
   A mother.—DeS
"A **mother** in old Alabama". William Jay Smith.—SmL
"**Mother** looms up on the prairie out there". See Believe it or not
"**Mother** made a seedy cake". Unknown.—OpI
"**Mother**, may I take a swim". Unknown.—WiA
"**Mother**, mother, bless my soul". X. J. Kennedy.—KeFb
"**Mother**, Mother, I am ill". Unknown.—OpI
"**Mother**, mother, mother, pin a rose on me". Unknown.—WiA
"**Mother** says I'm not to go". See Big black dog
"**Mother** shake the cherry tree". See Let's be merry
Mother to son. Langston Hughes.—DeT—SlM—SuC
"**Mother**, we are cold". Unknown.—SnD
Motherhood. See Mothers and motherhood
Motherhood. May Swenson.—ElW
Mothering Sunday. Stanley Cook.—FoLe
Mothers and motherhood
   About poems, sort of. J. Little.—LiHe
   Africa. A. Oyewole.—SlM
   An appointment. C. Shiang-hua.—NyT
   Atong. B. S. Santos.—NyT

Atong and his goodbye. B. S. Santos.—NyT
"Aw, lemme tell you". J. Carson.—CaS
Bats. R. Jarrell.—ElW
   The bat.—LaN
Behind bars. F. Tuqan.—NyT
Believe it or not. N. Kantchev.—NyT
Bingo. P. B. Janeczko.—JaB—JaP
Clothes ("My mother keeps on telling me"). E. Jennings.—AgL
The comb. W. De La Mare.—DeR
Come up from the fields father. W. Whitman.—HoVo
"The day I married, my mother". J. Carson.—CaS
The digger wasp. P. Fleischman.—FlJ
Disobedience. A. A. Milne.—KeT
Elsa Wertman. E. L. Masters.—ElW
Esmeralda (for a picture). W. De La Mare.—DeR
Family. M. C. Livingston.—LiT
Footpath. S. Ngatho.—NyT
"Forty years we courted". J. Carson.—CaS
The four corners of the universe. Unknown.—SnD
A friendly mouse. H. Behn.—LaM
"Go, my son, and shut the shutter". Unknown.—PrP
"Granny, Granny, please comb my hair". G. Nichols.—NiCo
Growing pains. J. Little.—LiHe
Hamilton Greene. E. L. Masters.—ElW
Help ("Would it help"). M. C. Livingston.—LiT
His girlfriend. M. C. Livingston.—LiT
House noises. X. J. Kennedy.—LiPm
I hear my mother's. R. Whitman.—LiPm
I love. B. Zephaniah.—AgL
I once dressed up. R. Fisher.—BaH
"I one my mother". Unknown.—OpI
"I see a star". A. Lopez.—LiPm
I told you so. J. Little.—LiHe
"If nightingale sings too sweetly, jealousy will kill its mother". From Jamaican Caribbean proverbs. Unknown.—BeW
If our dogs outlived us. D. Hines.—JaM
"I'll tell my own daddy, when he comes home". Mother Goose.—WaM
Industrial childhood. S. Stevenson.—NyT
Interlude. M. C. Livingston.—LiT
Invitation ("Listen, I've a big surprise"). M. C. Livingston.—KeT—LiT
"It was a Saturday and my mother was cooking". J. Carson.—CaS
Jasmine. K. Hong Ryou.—NyT
Late ("Your street was named for berries"). N. S. Nye.—JaP
Leg broken. S. B. Mathis.—MaR
"La loba, la loba". Unknown.—DeA
   The she-wolf ("Oh mama wolf, oh mama wolf").—DeA
Mama's bouquets. A. Bryan.—BrS
Mama's song. D. Chandra.—LiPm
Mamma settles the dropout problem. B. Gates.—SuC
Match. M. C. Livingston.—LiT
Mom is wow. J. Fields.—LiPm
Monster mothers. F. P. Heide.—HeG
Mosquitoes. J. Little.—LiHe
Mother. M. C. Livingston.—LiT
Mother and babe. W. Whitman.—HoVo
The mother bird. W. De La Mare.—DeR
"Mother doesn't want a dog". J. Viorst.—WhAa
Mother has a talk with me. J. Little.—LiHe
Mother horse. Issa.—DeI
   A mother.—DeS

Mountains—*Continued*
"My brother Estes". J. Carson.—CaS
The noise in the mountains. J. P. Lewis.—LeA
Old mountains want to turn to sand. T.
   Olofsson.—NyT
The prayer of the goat. C. B. De Gasztold.—DeP
Readcrest drive. M. C. Livingston.—LiR
Rocky Mountains, Colorado. M. C. Livingston.—
   LiNe
Song without end. Unknown.—WiA
"The **mournful** dodo lay in bed". See The dodo
The **mouse** ("I heard a mouse"). Elizabeth
   Coatsworth.—LaM
The **mouse** ("A mouse is"). Buson, tr. by Tze-si
   Huang.—DeI
A **mouse** and her house. Aileen Fisher.—FiH
The **mouse** ate the bait. Mildred Luton.—CoAz
"The **mouse** ate the bait off". See The mouse ate the
   bait
Mouse dinner. Aileen Fisher.—KeT
"A **mouse** doesn't dine". See Mouse dinner
"A **mouse** goes out". See In the dark of night
"A **mouse** has a house". See A mouse and her house
A **mouse** in her room. See "A mouse in her room
   woke Miss Dowd"
"A **mouse** in her room woke Miss Dowd".
   Unknown.—LiLo
A **mouse** in her room.—ClI—KeT—PrFo
The **mouse** in the wainscot. Ian Serraillier.—LaM
"A **mouse** is". See The mouse
The **mouse**, the frog, and the little red hen.
   Unknown.—HoS
Mouse under the house, mouse in the house. Arnold
   Adoff.—AdIn
"The **mouse** whose name is time". Robert Francis.—
   KeT
The **mouse's** lullaby. Palmer Cox.—KeT
Mouseways. Aileen Fisher.—FiH
Mouths
"Below your nose". M. C. Livingston.—LiMh
Big mouth. M. Fatchen.—FaCm
"Open your mouth and close your eyes".
   Unknown.—ScA
   "Open your mouth and shut your eyes".—
      WiA
The sad story of a little boy that cried.
   Unknown.—PrFo
Move over. Lilian Moore.—LiDd
Movies
Autobiographical note. V. Scannell.—JaPr
Liberty. R. Ikan.—JaPr
Matinees. K. Soniat.—JaPr
The Strand Theatre. T. Cader.—JaPr
Strong men, riding horses. G. Brooks.—SuC
The time we cherry-bombed the toilet at the
   River Oaks. C. H. Webb.—JaPr
Moving
Black kid in a new place. J. Berry.—BeW
The 1st. L. Clifton.—ElW
"Law, you know who's living". J. Carson.—CaS
Martine Provencal. M. Glenn.—GlBc
Moving. F. Steele.—JaM
The new little boy. H. Behn.—KeT
Olive Street. M. C. Livingston.—LiT
The paragon. B. Katz.—JaP
Puzzle. M. C. Livingston.—LiR
The rain falling on west train tracks, Ohio. A.
   Adoff.—AdCh
Since Hanna moved away. J. Viorst.—LoFh
Tammy Yarbrough. M. Glenn.—GlBc
There's an orange tree out there. A. Q. Urias.—
   NyT

Wanting to move. V. Mukhopadhyay.—NyT
"When my friends all moved away". S. Kroll.—
   JaP
"You know Lou Beal". J. Carson.—CaS
Moving. Frank Steele.—JaM
"**Moving** right along". Abiodun Oyewole.—SlM
Mowing. See also Harvests and harvesting
The bottoms of my sneakers are green. A. Adoff.—
   AdIn
"Lil, to cut the rug's pile lower". X. J. Kennedy.—
   KeFb
Moyne, John
558, tr.—GoU
91, tr.—GoT
1246, tr.—GoU
"There's a strange frenzy in my head", tr.—GoU
2195 In the arc of your mallet, tr.—GoU
2674 After being in love, the next responsibility,
   tr.—GoU
Mr. Alacadacca's. Walter De La Mare.—MaP See
   Mr. Alacadacca's
"**Mr.** and Mrs. Rainbow Trout". See Mr. and Mrs.
   T.
Mr. and Mrs. T. J. Patrick Lewis.—LeT
Mr. and Mrs. Turtle. J. Patrick Lewis.—LeA
"**Mr.** Axelham's cool". See Jaime Milagros
Mr. Bickerstaff. Unknown.—OpT
Mr. Desmond Klinger, music. Mel Glenn.—GlBc
Mr. Eugene Worthington, physical education. Mel
   Glenn.—GlBc
"**Mr.** Finney had a turnip". See Mr. Finney's turnip
Mr. Finney's turnip. Unknown.—HoS
"**Mr.** G., my instructor, with wild eyes". See
   Ophelia
Mr. Glump. Florence Parry Heide.—HeG
Mr. Henry Axhelm, math. Mel Glenn.—GlBc
Mr. John Fletcher, chemistry. Mel Glenn.—GlBc
Mr. Joshua Cantor. Mel Glenn.—GlBc
Mr. Neil Pressman, fine arts. Mel Glenn.—GlBc
"**Mr.** Pettengill". Myra Cohn Livingston.—LiR
Mr. Punch (for a picture). Walter De La Mare.—
   DeR
Mr. Robert Winograd, English. Mel Glenn.—GlBc
"**Mr.** Sage is very fond of saying". See Elliot West
"**Mr.** Sage tells very bad jokes". See Evan King
Mr. Slatter. N. M. Bodecker.—KeT
Mr. Smith. William Jay Smith.—SmL
Mr. Ted Sage, accounting. Mel Glenn.—GlBc
"**Mr.** Willowby's Christmas tree". Robert Barry.—
   GoA
Mr. Zoo. Eve Merriam.—MeCh
Mrs. A. Hulas. Jane Yolen.—YoDd
Mrs. Burns' lullaby. Unknown.—OpT
Mrs. Caribou. William Jay Smith.—SmL
"**Mrs.** Carlucci's cat". See Roscoe
Mrs. Earth. Walter De La Mare.—DeR—MaP
"**Mrs.** Earth makes silver black". See Mrs. Earth
"**Mrs.** Kangaroo". See Secret
Mrs. Krikorian. Sharon Olds.—JaPr
"**Mrs.** Macey worked behind". See Winner
Mrs. MacQueen. Walter De La Mare.—DeR—MaP
"**Mrs.** Mantis catches bugs". See Mrs. Praying
   Mantis
"**Mrs.** Morizawa". See Mrs. Morizawa's morning
Mrs. Morizawa's morning. X. J. Kennedy.—KeK
"**Mrs.** Peck Pigeon". Eleanor Farjeon.—DeS
Mrs. Perkins. David Allan Evans.—JaPr
"**Mrs.** Perkins wherever you are". See Mrs. Perkins
Mrs. Praying Mantis. J. Patrick Lewis.—LeA
"**Mrs.** Red she went to bed with a turban on her
   head". See Paintbox people
Mrs. Sparrow. Unknown.—OpT

"Mrs. Sue, Mrs. Sue". Unknown.—ScA
Ms. Charlotte Kendall, biology. Mel Glenn.—GlBc
Ms. Emily Parsons, history. Mel Glenn.—GlBc
"Ms. Gladstone is real nice". See Diana Marvin
"Ms. Gladstone, please tell me what to do". See C. C. Johnson
Ms. Joan Gladstone, special education. Mel Glenn.—GlBc
"Ms. L., I'm in love, but I can't tell anyone". See Victor Jeffreys
Ms. Marilyn Lindowsky, counselor. Mel Glenn.—GlBc
Ms. Nadine Sierra, French. Mel Glenn.—GlBc
Ms. Phyllis Shaw, speech. Mel Glenn.—GlBc
"Ms. Shaw". See Mercedes Lugo
Ms. Yvonne Harmon, librarian. Mel Glenn.—GlBc
"A much of motors". See Parking lot full
Mud
    Common mudlatch. W. J. Smith.—SmL
    "Lancelot, the scurvy knave". X. J. Kennedy.—KeFb
    The muddy puddle. D. Lee.—BoT—MoS
"The mud snail". Gomei, tr. by Tze-si Huang.—DeI
The muddy puddle. Dennis Lee.—BoT—MoS
Mueller, Marnie
    Strategy for a marathon.—KnAs
"Muffle the wind". See Orders
Mukhopadhyay, Vijaya
    At the ferry.—NyT
    Wanting to move.—NyT
Mules
    "On a mule we find two legs behind". Unknown.—ScA
        Mules ("On mules . . .").—PrFo
    "This little mule, he kicked so high". Unknown.—ScA
Mules ("On mules . . ."). See "On a mule we find two legs behind"
Mull. Jackie Kay.—AgL
"Multiplication is vexation". Unknown.—OpI
Mum Dad and me. James Berry.—BeW
Mumford, Erika
    The white rose, Sophie Scholl, 1921-1943.—JaM
Mummy slept late and daddy fixed breakfast. John Ciardi.—LiPf—PrFo
Munching peaches. Lee Bennett Hopkins.—HoS
"Munching peaches in the summer". See Munching peaches
Murder
    Bonny George Campbell. Unknown.—ElW
    Ghost story. R. Pack.—JaM
    The last man killed by Indians in Kimble County, Texas. M. Angelotti.—JaM
    The outlandish knight. Unknown.—ElW
    Summer killer. T. A. Broughton.—JaM
    The twa brothers. Unknown.—ElW
Murphy, Joseph Colin
    The skydivers.—KnAs
Murray, Les
    Weights, in memory of my mother, Miriam Murray nee Arnall.—NyT
Muscling rocks. Robert Morgan.—JaPr
Museums
    After a visit to the natural history museum. L. E. Richards.—SuI
    Dinosaur birthday. M. C. Livingston.—LiBp
Musgrave, Susan
    Thrum drew a small map.—BoT
Mushroom. Valerie Worth.—WoAl
"The mushroom pushes". See Mushroom
The mushroom river. Xue Di, tr. by Ping Wang and Gale Nelson.—NyT

Mushrooms
    Dance of the mushrooms. J. P. Lewis.—LeE
    Mushroom. V. Worth.—WoAl
    The mushroom river. X. Di.—NyT
    "With wild mushrooms Madge had found". X. J. Kennedy.—KeFb
"Mushrooms tipping their caps". See Dance of the mushrooms
Music. Walter De La Mare.—DeR
Music and musicians. See also Orchestras; Singing; also names of musical instruments, as Pianos; also names of muscians as Mozart, Wolfgang Amadeus
    Banjo tune. W. J. Smith.—SmL
    The bells, complete. E. A. Poe.—MoR
    Claud St. Jules. M. Glenn.—GlBc
    "A contentious old person named Reagan". W. J. Smith.—SmL
    Daybreak in Alabama. L. Hughes.—SuC
    "Disco dino dancing". J. Yolen.—YoDd
    Duet. R. Krauss.—MoR
    "A farmer in Knox, Ind.". Unknown.—LiLo
    The girl who makes the cymbals bang. X. J. Kennedy.—KeK
    Halloween concert ("It's cold, said the cricket"). A. Fisher.—FiA
    Heaven. G. Soto.—SoA
    "Heaven's in the basement". M. D. Landesman.—AgL
    "I don't talk to pop stars". A. Stockbroker.—AgL
    In memoriam John Coltrane. M. Stillman.—MoR
    Jackie Grant. M. Glenn.—GlBc
    John Coltrane ditty. D. K. Hru.—SlM
    "Johnny squeezed a concertina". J. Prelutsky.—PrBe
    Klassical dub. L. K. Johnson.—AgL
    Minstrel man. L. Hughes.—SuC
    Mr. Desmond Klinger, music. M. Glenn.—GlBc
    Music. W. De La Mare.—DeR
    Music lessons. J. Volmer.—JaPr
    My dad. A. Bryan.—BrS
    Ode to el guitarron. G. Soto.—SoNe
    Old Satchmo's gravelly voice. M. B. Tolson.—SuC
    Pan. E. B. Browning.—WhDd
    Piano. K. Shapiro.—MoR
    Piano recital. M. C. Livingston.—LiR
    Progress. G. E. Lyon.—JaM
    Recital. J. Updike.—MoR
    Rock 'n' roll band. S. Silverstein.—SuI
    Song birds. J. Yolen.—YoBi
    The song of shadows. W. De La Mare.—DeR—MaP
    Sonsito. V. H. Cruz.—MoR
    A supermarket in Guadalajara, Mexico. D. Levertov.—MoR
    "There was a young lady of Bute". E. Lear.—ClI—LiLo
    "There was a young lady of Rio". Unknown.—LiLo
    "There was a young lady of Tyre". E. Lear.—LiLo
    "There was a young lady whose chin". E. Lear.—LiLo
    "There was a young pig from Chanute". A. Lobel.—LiLo
    "There's music in a hammer". Unknown.—PrP—WiA
    "Tom, Tom, the piper's son, he learned to play when he was young". Mother Goose.—EdGl
    "A tutor who tooted the flute". Unknown.—LiLo
    When Mom plays just for me. A. H. Wayland.—LiPm

Music and musicians.—*Continued*
   A whirring. D. Aldan.—MoR
   "With her one string ukelele". X. J. Kennedy.—
      KeFb
Music lessons. Judith Volmer.—JaPr
The **music** master. John Ciardi.—CiH
Musicians. See Music and musicians
Muslim religion. See Islam
Must and May. Walter De La Mare.—MaP
"**Must** and May they were two half brothers". See
   Must and May
Mutabaruka
   You and yourself.—AgL
Muted. Paul Verlaine, tr. by C. F. MacIntyre.—GoU
Muth, Carol Sue
   Love ("Too close").—MoR
"**Muttered** centipede Slither McGrew". See Sticky
   situation
"**My** arms". See The dream
My baby brother. Mary Ann Hoberman.—HoFa
"**My** baby brother's beautiful". See My baby brother
"**My** best friend is Jimmy". See Christmas eve
   rhyme
My big brothers. Mary Ann Hoberman.—HoFa
"**My** birthday". See Eight
"**My** birthday invitation". See Invitation
My body. William Jay Smith.—SmL
"**My** boyfriend's name is Jello". Unknown.—CoM—
   WiA
My brother. Dorothy Aldis.—DeT
My brother Aaron runs outside to tell us there is a
   severe thunderstorm warning. Arnold Adoff.—
   AdIn
"**My** brother and I cut a tunnel". See Smoke
My brother Bert. Ted Hughes.—ElW
"**My** brother Estes". Jo Carson.—CaS
"**My** brother is inside the sheet". See My brother
"**My** brother kept". See Wheels
"**My** brother's always". See Brother's snacks
My cat ("My cat is asleep, white paws"). Barbara
   Juster Esbensen.—EsW
My cat ("My cat rubs my leg"). Aileen Fisher.—FiA
"**My** cat is asleep, white paws". See My cat
My cat, Mrs. Lick-a-chin. John Ciardi.—DeS—LaCc
"**My** cat rubs my leg". See My cat
"**My** children learn". See If our dogs outlived us
My city. James Weldon Johnson.—SuC
"**My** cousin Melda". Grace Nichols.—NiCo
My dad. Ashley Bryan.—BrS
My dad said. Martyn Wiley and Ian McMillan.—
   FoLe
"**My** daddy has paid the rent". See Good times
"**My** daddy is a cool dude. Karama Fufuka.—SlM
"**My** daddy rides me piggy-back". See Piggy-back
My dame. Unknown.—ClI
"**My** dame hath a lame tame crane". See My dame
"**My** daughter got divorced". Jo Carson.—CaS
"**My** daughter runs outside to busy". See Evening
   walk
"**My** dear Daddie bought a mansion". See The little
   bird
"**My** dear, do you know". See The babes in the
   wood
"**My** dentist works in a hard hat". See Why I always
   brush
My dog ("Here's what we think of, Gov and I").
   Felice Holman.—LiDp
My dog ("His nose is short and scrubby").
   Marchette Chute.—SuI
My dog ("My dog is such a gentle soul"). Max
   Fatchen.—PrFo
"**My** dog is such a gentle soul". See My dog

"**My** dolls came alive in it". See The playhouse
My dress is old. Unknown.—SnD
"**My** dress is old, but at night the moon is". See My
   dress is old
"**My** ethics were". See Basketball, a retrospective
"**My** family came from China five years ago". See
   Kwang Chin Ho
"**My** family is having dinner with the Blairs". See
   Louisa, Louisa
My family tree. Eve Merriam.—MeP
My father. Mary Ann Hoberman.—HoFa
"**My** father and his muscles". See My father toured
   the south
"**My** father died a month ago". Mother Goose.—
   WaM
"**My** father doesn't live with us". See My father
"**My** father found it after the war". See The house
   on Buder Street
"**My** father has plotted out my future". See Dennis
   Finch
"**My** father is a butcher". See "My father owns the
   butcher shop"
"**My** father left me, as he was able". Unknown.—
   ScA
"**My** father limps on the leg that healed short". See
   Hook
"**My** father owns the butcher shop". Unknown.—
   PrP—WiA
   "**My** father is a butcher".—ScA
"**My** father still calls me his little girl". See Charlene
   Cottier
"**My** father thinks the telephone". See You rang
My father toured the south. Jeanette Nichols.—
   KnAs
"**My** father was a tough cookie". See My mother
   really knew
My father's fortune. Herbert Scott.—JaPr
My father's leaving. Ira Sadoff.—JaPr
"**My** father's mother". See Seashell
My father's words. Claudia Lewis.—LiPf
My favorite word. James L. Hymes and Lucia
   Hymes.—DeS
"**My** fingers like to say hello". Lois Walfrid
   Johnson.—StP
"**My** finger's wet". Unknown.—OpI
"**My** first solo trial flight, you see". From What we
   said sitting making fantasies. James Berry.—
   BeW
My friend. Emily Hearn.—BoT
"**My** friend is". See My friend
"**My** friend Mark, he's one special boy". See Braves
"**My** friends all gave me presents". See Presents
"**My** friend's father, I love this story". See Enos
   Slaughter
"**My** friends just left me". See Loneliness
"**My** girl friend is a lulu". Unknown.—WiA
"**My** goodness, my goodness". See Christmas
"**My** gossip, the owl, is it thou". From Sunrise.
   Sidney Lanier.—LiIf
"**My** grandfather told stories in three languages". See
   Jonathan Sobel
"**My** grandma's face is rosy red". See Grandmas and
   grandpas
"**My** grandmother at her farm table". See Apple
   scoop
"**My** grandmother, I've discovered". See The smile
"**My** grandmother, my Baboo". See Neck please
"**My** grandmother pins a flower in her hair". See In
   the mirror
"**My** grandmother sold flowers in the marketplace".
   See Martine Provencal
"**My** grandmother's". See Door

My share. Salih Bolat, tr. by Yusuf Eradam.—NyT
"My shoes are new and squeaky shoes".
  Unknown.—PrP
"My sista is younga than me". See Listn big brodda
  dread, na
My sister. Margaret Mahy.—LiLo—MaN
"My sister Stephanie's in love". See Weird
"My sister's remarkably light". See My sister
"My skin sun-mixed like basic earth". See It seems
  I test people
"My son in California tells me I should retire". See
  Mr. Joshua Cantor
"My sons, said a Glurk slurping soup". See The
  music master
"My special education children whirl around me".
  See Ms. Joan Gladstone, special education
"My stick fingers click with a snicker". See Player
  piano
My stupid parakeet named after you. X. J.
  Kennedy.—KeK
"My toboggan and I carve winter". Jane Wadley.—
  BoT
My turtle. Unknown.—CoE
"My TV came down with a chill". Willard R.
  Espy.—KeT
My uncle. Mary Ann Hoberman.—HoFa
"My Uncle Ben, who's been". See Kiph
"My Uncle Demented, he's invented". See Family
  genius
"My uncle has a twinkle". See My uncle
"My Uncle Ike's an engineer". See Mechanical
  menagerie
My yellow straw hat. Lessie Jones Little.—KeT
"My youth is". See Yacht for sale
"My zoo is open to all". William Cole.—CoAz
Myrie, Daisy
  Market women.—LeCa
Myrtle warblers. Marilyn Singer.—SiT
The mysterious cat. Vachel Lindsay.—DeS—LaCc
Mystery ("One Friday night"). Paul B. Janeczko.—
  JaB
The mystery ("There was a young fellow named
  Chet"). John Ciardi.—CiH
"A mythic beast, the manticore". See The manticore
Myths
  Anansi the spider. G. McDermott.—WhDd
  Atlas. J. Yolen.—YoFf
  The centaurs. J. Stephens.—WhDd
  Cerberus. N. B. Taylor.—WhDd
  Chimera. P. S. Schott.—WhDd
  The griffin. A. Sundgaard.—WhDd
  The hippocamp. A. Sundgaard.—WhDd
  Minotaur. X. J. Kennedy.—WhDd
  Pan. E. B. Browning.—WhDd
  Pegasus. E. Farjeon.—WhDd
  The phoenix. P. Fleischman.—WhDd
  Sphinx. D. Chandra.—WhDd
  What teacher said. J. P. Lewis.—LeT

N

N is for needle. William Jay Smith.—SmL
"Na zlatom cryeltse sidelly". Unknown.—YoS
"On a golden step sat".—YoS
Names. See also Christenings
  Alphabet ball. Unknown.—WiA
    "A, my name is Alice".—CoM
  Andy Battle's song. From The three royal
    monkeys. W. De La Mare.—DeR
  "Anna banana". Unknown.—WiA

"As I was going over London Bridge".
  Unknown.—OpI
Beginning on paper. R. Krauss.—DeS
"Bill, Bill, can't sit still". Unknown.—WiA
"Billy, Billy, strong and able". Unknown.—WiA
"Burt, Burt, lost his shirt". Unknown.—WiA
Canadian Indian place names. M. Zola.—BoT
The christening ("What shall I call"). A. A.
  Milne.—LaM
"Ed, Ed, big head". Unknown.—WiA
"Edmund Clerihew Bentley". W. J. Smith.—SmL
"Frank, Frank". Unknown.—WiA
The gnat and the gnu. O. Herford.—LiLo
"Here's your fortune, here's your fame".
  Unknown.—CoM
How to tell the wild animals. C. Wells.—CoAz
"I am the youngest, so they call". A. Adoff.—
  AdIn
"I get high on butterflies". J. Roseblatt.—BoT
"I'm nobody, who are you". E. Dickinson.—ElW
"I've thought and thought and thought in vain".
  Unknown.—WiA
"Jack, Jack". Unknown.—WiA
"Jane, Jane". Unknown.—WiA
"Joe Blow". Unknown.—WiA
"Johnny-bum-bonny". Unknown.—WiA
"Katalena Magdalena Hoopensteiner Walla Walla
  Hogan". Unknown.—ScA
Little song. L. Hughes.—KeT
Lulu, lulu, I've a lilo. C. Pomerantz.—DeS—LiIf
Mannahatta. W. Whitman.—HoVo
"Margaret, Margaret, has big eyes". Unknown.—
  WiA
"Mary, Mary, don't say no". Unknown.—WiA
Mima. W. De La Mare.—DeR—MaP
Mr. Alacadacca's. W. De La Mare.—MaP
My Jose. M. Robinson.—LiPf
My name is. P. Clarke.—DeS
"My name is Yon Yonson". Unknown.—ScA
Names don't always suit. N. Prasad.—BoT
Names for the fingers. Unknown.—OpT
Names for the toes. Unknown.—OpT
"On the hill there is a mill". Unknown.—WiA
"One, two, three, a-lary, my first name is Mary".
  Unknown.—ScA—WiA
"One, two, three, Johnny". Unknown.—WiA
"Rich, Rich". Unknown.—WiA
"Robert, Bedobert, Hadobert, Gofobert".
  Unknown.—ScA
"Rose, Rose". Unknown.—WiA
"Sally bum-bally". Unknown.—WiA
Schenectady. E. Merriam.—MeS
"Sha-ame, sha-ame". Unknown.—CoM—WiA
  "Shame, shame".—ScA
The song of Snohomish. W. S. Wallace.—KnAs
"Sticks and stones". Unknown.—CoM—OpI—
  ScA—WiA
The stray cat. E. Merriam.—LaCc—MeS
A tale of two cities. X. J. Kennedy.—KeGh
"That's my name". Unknown.—CoM
Their names. G. Hyland.—JaPr
"There once was a plesiosaurus". Unknown.—
  LiLo
"There was a man". Unknown.—ClI
Too many Daves. Dr. Seuss.—ElW
Wamby or the nostalgic record book. M.
  Bracker.—MoA
Welcome, Florence. J. Steinbergh.—LiPg
Were you ever fat like me. K. Dakos.—DaI
What am I after all. W. Whitman.—HoVo
"What's your name". Unknown.—OpI
"William Penn". W. J. Smith.—SmL

Neighbors—*Continued*
"Peace between neighbors". Unknown.—StP
"She come to see your mother". J. Carson.—CaS
Stickball. C. Sullivan.—MoA
The sugar lady. F. Asch.—DeT
Summertime and the living. R. Hayden.—SuC
There was a man. P. Janowitz.—JaP
Welcome here. Unknown.—GoA
"You know Lou Beal". J. Carson.—CaS
"You know the other day we went over at George's get some eggs". J. Carson.—CaS
"You, neighbor God, if in the long night". R. M. Rilke.—StP
Neighbors. Mary Ann Hoberman.—LoFh
"Nellie Bligh caught a fly". Unknown.—OpI
Nelms, Sheryl L.
Anne Frank.—JaPr
Outhouse blues.—JaM
Nelson, Gale
The mushroom river, tr.—NyT
Nelson, Gordon
"Science".—SlM
Nemerov, Howard
"Each year brings rookies and makes veterans". See Watching football on TV
"It used to be only Sunday afternoons". See Watching football on TV
"Passing and catching overcome the world". See Watching football on TV
"Priam on one side sending forth eleven". See Watching football on TV
Sandpipers.—ElW
Sunday at the end of summer.—SuI
"To all this there are rules, the players must". See Watching football on TV
"Totemic scarabs, exoskeletal". See Watching football on TV
Watching football on TV, complete.
    "Each year brings rookies and makes veterans".—KnAs
    "It used to be only Sunday afternoons".—KnAs
    "Passing and catching overcome the world".—KnAs
    "Priam on one side sending forth eleven".—KnAs
    "To all this there are rules, the players must".—KnAs
    "Totemic scarabs, exoskeletal".—KnAs
    "We watch all afternoon, we are enthralled".—KnAs
"We watch all afternoon, we are enthralled". See Watching football on TV
Nerissa. Eloise Greenfield.—GrN
Neruda, Pablo
"What is it that upsets the volcanoes".—NyT
"A nervous young worm once got twisted". See Stop squirming
Nestlings. Jane Yolen.—YoBi
Never. Walter De La Mare.—DeR
"Never a fisherman need there be". From Fishermen's songs. Unknown.—OpT
"Never afraid of those huge creatures". See Horseback
Never be as fast as I have been, the jockey Tony DeSpirito dead at thirty-nine. Robert Hahn.—KnAs
"Never believe I leave you". See Hiding our love
"Never mind what you think". See Killing chickens
"Never put mustard on your auk". See Word of warning

"Never seems to stop until it turns to snow". See The rain falling on west train tracks, Ohio
"Never stand under an anvil". X. J. Kennedy.—KeGh
"Never take a pig to lunch". Susan Alton Schmeltz.—PrFo
"Never talk down to a glowworm". See Glowworm
"Never wondering". See Amoeba
New baby poem (I). Eloise Greenfield.—GrN
New baby poem (II). Eloise Greenfield.—GrN
"New cakes of soap". See Soap
New Dad. Myra Cohn Livingston.—LiT
A new dress. Ruth Dallas.—NyT
New England
Mending wall. R. Frost.—SuI
My lost youth. H. W. Longfellow.—SuI
Winter pause, Mt. Liberty, N.H. M. Robbins.—MoR
The new house. Maya Angelou.—AnI
New jacket. Mary Ann Hoberman.—HoFa
The new kid. Mike Makley.—MoA
The new lady barber at Ralph's Barber Shop. Leo Dangel.—JaM
The new little boy. Harry Behn.—KeT
"A new little boy moved in next door". See The new little boy
New mother. R. H. Marks.—LiPm
The new negro. James Edward McCall.—SuC
"A new pail". See Pail
A new song for Old Smoky. Eve Merriam.—MeP
The new suit. Nidia Sanabria de Romero, tr. by Arnaldo D. Larrosa Moran and Naomi Shihab Nye.—NyT
New Year. See also Rosh Hashanah
At the New Year. K. Patchen.—GoT
Beginning a new year means. R. Whitman.—LoFh
Chinese New Year. Unknown.—LoFh
Dragon dance. M. Fatchen.—FoLe
First foot. I. Serraillier.—FoLe
"God be here, God be there". Mother Goose.—WaM
"I saw three ships come sailing by". Mother Goose.—WaM
Lion dance. T. Millum.—FoLe
My New Year's resolution. R. Fisher.—FoLe
A New Year ("Here's a clean year"). M. C. Davies.—FrS
New year ("This night"). J. Kenward.—FoLe
New Year's advice from my Cornish grandmother. X. J. Kennedy.—KeK
New Year's day. V. Worth.—WoA
New Year's eve. V. Worth.—WoA
Oh calendar. J. P. Lewis.—LoFh
On New Year's Day, watching it snow. I. Shikibu.—GoT
Rosh Hashanah eve. H. Philip.—LoFh
"Traigo un ramillete". Unknown.—LoFh
    Bouquet of roses ("A bouquet of roses").—LoFh
A New Year ("Here's a clean year"). Mary Carolyn Davies.—FrS
New year ("This night"). Jean Kenward.—FoLe
New Year's advice from my Cornish grandmother. X. J. Kennedy.—KeK
New Year's day. Valerie Worth.—WoA
New Year's eve. Valerie Worth.—WoA
New York City
"Boita and Goitie sat on de coib". Unknown.—WiA
Brooklyn Bridge, a jump-rope rhyme. W. J. Smith.—SmL
Harlem night song. L. Hughes.—LaN

Nims, Bonnie
On a cold autumn day.—KeT
Nine charms against the hunter. David Wagoner.—KnAs
"**Nine** feat fiddlers had good Queen Bess". See The fiddlers
"**Nine** miles high". See Windlady
"**Nine** swallows sat on a telephone wire". See The swallows
Nine triads. Lillian Morrison.—KnAs
"**1964** and I'm parked". See White
91. Jalal-Ud-Din Rumi, tr. by John Moyne and Coleman Barks.—GoT
"A **nip** for new". Unknown.—OpI
Nix on picnics. X. J. Kennedy.—KeGh
"**No** anchovies". See Witch pizza
"**No** balls are batted". See A rainy day
No bed. Walter De La Mare.—DeR
"**No** bed, no bed, we shouted". See No bed
"**No** breath of wind". See Snow
"**No** cannon-crackers were ever more loud". See Small town fireworks
"**No** crunch of boots". See Winter pause, Mt. Liberty, N.H.
"**No** drums". See Village voices
"**No** eggs put behind the garage to rot". See Halloween, the hydrant dare
"**No** groat for a supper". See Groat nor tester
No grosser grocer. X. J. Kennedy.—KeGh
No jewel. Walter De La Mare.—DeR
"**No** jewel from the rock". See No jewel
"**No** labor-saving machine". Walt Whitman.—HoVo
No, love is not dead. Robert Desnos, tr. by Bill Zavatsky.—GoU
"**No**, love is not dead in this heart and these eyes and". See No, love is not dead
"**No** marvel, Sweet, you clap your wings". See The bird set free
"**No** matter how grouchy you're feeling". Anthony Euwer.—LiLo
No more auction block. Unknown.—SuC
"**No** more auction block for me". See No more auction block
"**No** more pencils, no more books". Unknown.—CoM—ScA
"**No** motion and". See Newborn neurological exam
"**No** neck". Myra Cohn Livingston.—LiMh
"**No** need even". See Library
No need to light a night light. Unknown.—HoS
No one. Lilian Moore.—KeT
"**No** one asked Bruno". See Wallflower
"**No** one can tell me". See Wind on the hill
No one heard him call. Dorothy Aldis.—KeT
"**No** one knows the exact moment". See Waiting for the first drop
No question. Leo Dangel.—JaPr
"**No** sooner had I drunk". See Oliver Johnson comes back to bed the morning after the ice storm and tells his wife why
Noah
Noah's prayer. C. B. De Gasztold.—DeP
"Oh, the Lord looked down from his window in the sky". Unknown.—StP
Old Noah's ark. Unknown.—DeT—HoS—SuI
The prayer of the dove. C. B. De Gasztold.—DeP
Noah's prayer. Carmen Bernos De Gasztold, tr. by Rumer Godden.—DeP
"**Nobody** knew where Gregory hid". See I never told
Nobody knows. Walter De La Mare.—DeR—MaP
"**Nobody** loves me". Unknown.—OpI—ScA
"**Nobody**, nobody told me". See Under the rose (the song of the wanderer)

"**Nobody** planted roses, he recalls". See Summertime and the living
"**Nobody** teaches". See Knowing
Nocturne ("If the deep wood is haunted, it is I"). Robert Hillyer.—GoU
Nocturne ("A long arm embossed with gold slides from the tree tops"). Leon-Paul Fargue, tr. by Kenneth Rexroth.—GoT
Nocturne of the wharves. Arna Bontemps.—SuC
Nod's song. From The three royal monkeys. Walter De La Mare.—DeR
Noise. See Sounds
The **noise** in the mountains. J. Patrick Lewis.—LeA
Nolan Ryan. Gene Fehler.—MoA
Nonsense. See also Limericks; Mother Goose; also entries under Carroll, Lewis and Lear, Edward
"A. B. C. D. Gol'fish". Unknown.—CII
"A was once an apple pie". E. Lear.—HoS
Advice. X. J. Kennedy.—KeGh
After a visit to the natural history museum. L. E. Richards.—SuI
Alas, alack. W. De La Mare.—DeR—MaP
"Anna Banana went out in the rain". J. Prelutsky.—PrBe
The antimacassar and the ottoman. W. J. Smith.—SmL
"Apples and oranges, four for a penny". Unknown.—OpI
Arymouse, arymouse. Unknown.—CII
As I looked out. Unknown.—CII
"As I was going out one day". Unknown.—ScA
"As I went out".—PrP
"As I went over the water". Mother Goose.—CII
"As I went to Bonner". Mother Goose.—CII
"As wet as a fish, as dry as a bone". Unknown.—ScA
"Away down east, away down west". Unknown.—KeT
Susianna.—OpT
Backyard volcano. X. J. Kennedy.—KeGh
Ballad of black and white. W. J. Smith.—SmL
"Bananas and cream". D. McCord.—DeT—LiDd
Banjo tune. W. J. Smith.—SmL
"A barefoot boy with shoes on". Unknown.—ScA
Basso profundo. S. Mandlsohn.—BoT
"Be kind to your web-footed friends". Unknown.—ScA
Bedtime mumble. N. M. Bodecker.—PlW
"A big bare bear". R. Heidbreder.—PrFo
Big Gumbo. W. J. Smith.—SmL
Bill Bolling's avalanche. X. J. Kennedy.—KeGh
"Billy Batter". D. Lee.—KeT
Bird sighting. X. J. Kennedy.—KeGh
"Birdie, birdie, in the sky". Unknown.—CoM—ScA
"Boom, boom, ain't it great to be crazy". Unknown.—ScA
"The boy stood on the burning deck". Unknown.—PrFo—WiA
Brother's snacks. X. J. Kennedy.—KeGh
"A bug and a flea". Unknown.—CII—OpI
"Calico ban". From Calico pie. E. Lear.—LaM
Calico pie, complete. E. Lear.—CII—LiDd
Canapes a la poste. W. J. Smith.—SmL
"Captain Flea and Sailor Snail". J. Prelutsky.—PrBe
"Celia sat beside the seaside". Unknown.—PrP
"Charley Barley, butter and eggs". Mother Goose.—WaM
Chit chat. W. J. Smith.—SmL
"Christopher Columbus, what do you think of that". Unknown.—WiA

Nonsense.—*Continued*

Mr. Slatter. N. M. Bodecker.—KeT
My old hen. Unknown.—KeT
Neet people. L. Simmie.—PrFo
"Never stand under an anvil". X. J. Kennedy.—
  KeGh
"Nicholas Narrow, tall and thin". J. Prelutsky.—
  PrBe
"Nicholas Ned". L. E. Richards.—DeS
Nix on picnics. X. J. Kennedy.—KeGh
No grosser grocer. X. J. Kennedy.—KeGh
"O was an owl who flew". E. Lear.—LiIf
Off the ground. W. De La Mare.—DeR—MaP
"Oh, dear, bread and beer". Unknown.—ScA
"Oh, how low can you go, Gosnold Goop". X. J.
  Kennedy.—KeGh
"Oh, I cannot tell the truth". Unknown.—ScA
"Oh, I had a horse, his name was Bill".
  Unknown.—ScA
"Oh, I was born one night one morn".
  Unknown.—ScA
"Oh, the cow kicked Nelly in the belly in the
  barn". Unknown.—ScA
"Oh, you may drive a horse to water".
  Unknown.—WiA
An old grey horse. Unknown.—CII
"The old hen sat on turkey eggs". Unknown.—
  WiA
Old Hogan's goat. Unknown.—CoAz
The ombley-gombley. P. Wesley-Smith.—PrFo
"On top of spaghetti". Unknown.—ScA
"Once an ant". Unknown.—WiA
"One bright morning in the middle of the night".
  Unknown.—WiA
"One bright September morning in". Unknown.—
  OpI
"One day a boy went walking". Unknown.—
  PrP—WiA
"One fine day in the middle of the night".
  Unknown.—BaH—OpI
"One misty, moisty morning". Mother Goose.—
  MoS—SuO—WaM
"One, two, three, a-lary, I spy Mistress Mary".
  Unknown.—WiA
"One, two, three, four". Mother Goose.—WaM
"Order in the court". Unknown.—ScA
The owl and the pussy-cat. E. Lear.—ElW—
  LiDd—LoFh
"P with a little o". Mother Goose.—WaM
"The panteater". W. Cole.—JaP
The pelican chorus. E. Lear.—CaB—WhAa
Pick me up. W. J. Smith.—SmL
Poor old lady. Unknown.—ElW—HoS
Postman pelican. W. J. Smith.—SmL
"Puptents and pebbles". W. J. Smith.—SmL
The purple cow. G. Burgess.—CII—KeT
"Quack, said the billy goat". C. Causley.—WhAa
The Quangle Wangle's hat. E. Lear.—CII
Rats in the garden. Mother Goose.—CII
"Red, white and green". Unknown.—ScA
The reluctant hero or barefoot in the snow. M.
  Mahy.—MaN
The remarkable cake. M. Mahy.—MaN
"Rickety pickety". J. Prelutsky.—PrBe
Rigmarole. E. Merriam.—MeCh
Robert Robot. X. J. Kennedy.—KeGh
"A robin and a robin's son". Mother Goose.—
  CII—WaM
"The robin and the wren". Unknown.—CaB—CII
"Rub a dub dub". Mother Goose.—EdGl—WaM
"Said Noble Aaron to Aaron Barron". Mother
  Goose.—WaM

"Said the monkey to the donkey". Unknown.—
  WiA
  The monkey and the donkey.—CII
"Said the monkey to the owl". Unknown.—LiIf
"Sam, Sam, dirty old man". Unknown.—CoM—
  OpI
"Sam, Sam, the butcher man". Unknown.—
  KeT—WiA
"The oausage is a cunning bird". Unknown.—PrP
Seafarer. Unknown.—OpT
"See, see, what shall I see". Mother Goose.—
  WaM
Sensible questions. M. Mahy.—MaN
"Sheldon the selfish shellfish". X. J. Kennedy.—
  KeGh
The ship in the dock. M. Rosen.—PrFo
The silly song ("Hey ding a ding"). M. Mahy.—
  MaN
"Sing me a song of teapots and trumpets". N. M.
  Bodecker.—PrFo
"Sing, sing, what shall I sing". Mother Goose.—
  CII—WaM
"Sir Samuel Squinn". F. P. Heide.—HeG
Slant-eyed peeker. W. J. Smith.—SmL
The song of the mad prince. W. De La Mare.—
  DeR—ElW—MaP
The sow came in. Unknown.—CII
Spilt milk, whodunit. W. J. Smith.—SmL
The star-crossed lovers. M. Mahy.—MaN
Steam roller Sam. D. MacLeod.—PrFo
A stupendous pincushion. X. J. Kennedy.—KeGh
T is for tub. W. J. Smith.—SmL
The table and the chair. E. Lear.—LiDd
The tarragon vinegar song. M. Mahy.—MaN
Teasing. Unknown.—CII
Television toucan. W. J. Smith.—SmL
That fish was just too fussy. J. Ciardi.—CiH
"There was a crooked man". Mother Goose.—
  DeS—EdGl—SuO—WaM
"There was a fellow". Unknown.—ScA
"There was a wee bit moosikie". Unknown.—CII
"There was an old man of Dumbree". E. Lear.—
  CII—LiIf
"There was an old man on the border". E. Lear.—
  CII
"There was an old man with a beard". E. Lear.—
  CII—KeT—LiIf—LiLo
There was an old woman ("There was an old
  woman sat spinning"). Mother Goose.—CII
There were two birds. Mother Goose.—CII
The thingamajig. J. Ciardi.—CiH
Think me a fable. J. P. Lewis.—LeT
"Three blind mice". Mother Goose.—EdGl—
  WaM
"Three, six, nine". Unknown.—CoM
"Three young rats with black felt hats". Mother
  Goose.—PrP—SuO
  Three young rats.—CII
"Tiddle liddle lightum". Mother Goose.—WaM
"Tippity toppity, upside down Roy". J.
  Prelutsky.—PrBe
The toaster. W. J. Smith.—SmL
The typewriter bird. W. J. Smith.—SmL
"The underwater wibbles". J. Prelutsky.—JaP
Unexpected summer soup. M. Mahy.—MaN
"An unusual man from Bound Brook". X. J.
  Kennedy.—KeGh
Upside-down bird. W. J. Smith.—SmL
"Uptown, downtown". C. Watson.—LiDd
Walking-stick bird. W. J. Smith.—SmL
The walrus and the carpenter. From Through the
  looking-glass. L. Carroll.—DeT—ElW—HoS

Now all the roads. Walter De La Mare.—DeR
"Now all the roads to London Town". See Now all the roads
"Now, are you a marsupial". See Are you a marsupial
"Now as the train bears west". See Night journey
Now blue October. Robert Nathan.—GoU
"Now blue October, smoky in the sun". See Now blue October
"Now Christmas is come". Washington Irving.—GoA
Now day is breaking. Salvatore Quasimodo, tr. by Jack Bevan.—GoT
"Now, dear me". See Part XIV: Now, dear me
"Now fie, o fie, how sly a face". See Part XI: Now fie, o fie, how sly a face
"Now, George is sick". Jo Carson.—CaS
"Now I lay me down to sleep". See Prayer
"Now I lay me down to sleep, a bag of peanuts at my feet". Unknown.—ScA—WiA
"Now, I'm not the one". See Garbage delight
"Now in the streets there is violence". See Electric Avenue
"Now, Jinnie, my dear, to the dwarf be off". See The dwarf
"Now just who, muses Uncle Bill Biddle". X. J. Kennedy.—KeGh—LiLo
Now lift me close. Walt Whitman.—HoVo
"Now lift me close to your face while I whisper". See Now lift me close
"Now lighted windows climb the dark". See Manhattan lullaby
"Now, my dear, for gracious sake". See Part XV: Now, my dear, for gracious sake
Now silent falls. Walter De La Mare.—DeR
"Now silent falls the clacking mill". See Now silent falls
"Now that she has knit-and-purled". See Spider
"Now the blue whale tells me". See Blue whale knowledge
"Now the luster". See New Year's day
"Now the pond is still". Aohozuki, tr. by Sylvia Cassedy and Kunihiro Suetake.—CaR
"Now they're ready, now they're waiting". See Football
"Now, through the dusk". See Part XVII: Now through the dusk
"Now we gathered for the match". See The volleyball match
"Now why did Mother go and teach". See Trouble with baby
"Now, wouldn't it be funny". See Wouldn't it be funny
Nowel. Walter De La Mare.—DeR
Nowlan, Alden
Long, long ago.—BoT
Noyes, Alfred
Daddy fell into the pond.—LiPf
"Ntonkale pansi". Unknown.—YoS
"Let us dig down".—YoS
The nude swim. Anne Sexton.—KnAs
A number of words. Eve Merriam.—MeCh
"Number one, touch your tongue". Unknown.—CoM
Numbers
Finding a lucky number. G. Soto.—JaM—SoA
Math is brewing and I'm in trouble. K. Dakos.—DaI
Numbers. E. M. Roberts.—LiDd
Teaching numbers. G. Soto.—SoA
Numbers. Elizabeth Madox Roberts.—LiDd
Numbers game. Richard Armour.—MoA

"Numbers single". See Math is brewing and I'm in trouble
Nuns
The mad nun. D. Giola.—JaPr
A nun's prayer. M. Ross.—StP
A nun's prayer. Maggie Ross.—StP
Nursery play
"A la vibora, vibora". Unknown.—YoS
"To the sea snake we will play".—YoS
Apples ("Way up high in the apple tree"). Unknown.—CoE
Balloons. Unknown.—CoE
Birthday cake ("Ten candles on a birthday cake"). Unknown.—CoE
Bluebirds. Unknown.—CoE
"Bo elai parpar nechmad". Unknown.—YoS
"Come to me, nice butterfly".—YoS
"Brow-brinker". Unknown.—WiA
Chook-chook-chook. Unknown.—CoE
Dressing a baby. Unknown.—OpT
"The eentsy, weentsy spider". Unknown.—CoE
"The elephant goes like this and that". Unknown.—PrP
The elephant.—CoE
Face play. Unknown.—OpT
Head.—WiA
A farmer went trotting. Mother Goose.—ClI
"Five little kittens". Unknown.—CoE
"Five little monkeys". Unknown.—CoE
Grandma's spectacles. Unknown.—CoE
The grasshopper ("There was a little grasshopper"). Unknown.—CoE
Great big ball. Unknown.—CoE
"Gyro gyrovoli". Unknown.—YoS
"Around the round path".—YoS
The hammer song. Unknown.—CoE
"Here are mother's knives and forks". Unknown.—CoE
"Here is daddy's hayrake". Unknown.—WiA
"Here is the beehive, where are the bees". Unknown.—WiA
The beehive.—CoE
"Here is the church". Unknown.—CoE
"Here we go round the mulberry bush". Mother Goose.—EdGl—SuO—WaM
"Here's a cup". Unknown.—CoE
"If you're happy and you know it". Unknown.—CoE
"I'm a little teapot". Unknown.—CoE
"I'm a little teapot stout".—ScA
Jack Jingle. Unknown.—OpT
"Kai veesamma kai veesu". Unknown.—YoS
"Wave your hand, wave your hand".—YoS
Knee ride. Unknown.—OpT
Knees. Unknown.—WiA
"Leg over leg". Mother Goose.—ClI—WaM
Let us go to the woods. Unknown.—ClI
My hat. Unknown.—CoE
My turtle. Unknown.—CoE
Names for the fingers. Unknown.—OpT
Names for the toes. Unknown.—OpT
"Nila nila odi va". Unknown.—YoS
"Moon, moon, come to me".—YoS
On my head. Unknown.—CoE
"One little beaver worked hard as can be". J. Knight.—KnT
"One little bunny grew carrots". J. Knight.—KnT
"One little grizzly grew grumpy". J. Knight.—KnT
"One little hippo brought a blanket". J. Knight.—KnT
"One little kid took a limo". J. Knight.—KnT

Nursery rhymes—Spanish—*Continued*
"Que linda manito". Unknown.—DeA
    A pretty little hand ("How pretty, how
      little").—DeA
Que llueva. Unknown.—DeA
    It's raining ("It's raining, it's raining").—DeA
Nursery rhymes—Tamil
"Kai veesamma kai veesu". Unknown.—YoS
    "Wave your hand, wave your hand".—YoS
"Nila nila odi va". Unknown.—YoS
    "Moon, moon, come to me".—YoS
Nursery rhymes—Yiddish
"Alef beys giml dolid". Unknown.—YoS
    "A B C D".—YoS
Nursery rhymes—Zambian
"Icipyolopyolo ca bana ba nkanga apo".
    Unknown.—YoS
    "The guinea-fowl chick says it is there".—
      YoS
"Ntonkale pansi". Unknown.—YoS
    "Let us dig down".—YoS
Nuts and nutting. See also Acorns; Peanuts
Daddy carries his empty basket on his head. A.
    Adoff.—AdIn
"I had a little nut tree". Mother Goose.—EdGl—
    SuO
"Nuts to you and nuts to me". M. A.
    Hoberman.—PrFo
The squirrel. S. Barakat.—NyT
"Nuts to you and nuts to me". Mary Ann
    Hoberman.—PrFo
Nye, Naomi Shihab
An appointment, tr.—NyT
Between ebb and flow, tr.—NyT
Famous.—JaP
Late ("Your street was named for berries").—JaP
The new suit, tr.—NyT
On my birthday, tr.—NyT
The orphan, tr.—NyT
Pitcher, tr.—NyT
The rider.—JaP
A sailor's memoirs, tr.—NyT
The squirrel, tr.—NyT
Under this sky, tr.—NyT
Valentine for Ernest Mann.—JaP
Wordless day, tr.—NyT
Nyepi, the day of yellow rice. Trevor Millum.—
    FoLe
The **nymph's** reply to the shepherd. Sir Walter
    Raleigh.—ElW

O

The **O.** M. O. R. E. Walter De La Mare.—DeR
O is for owl. William Jay Smith.—LiIf—SmL
"**O** kou aloha no". See Queen's prayer
"**O** was an owl who flew". Edward Lear.—LiIf
"**O** was once a little owl". Edward Lear.—LiIf
"**Oak** and ivy, sycamore, ash, what shall we leave
    by the cottage door". See May day
Oak apple day. Raymond Wilson.—FoLe
Oak trees
"Don't worry if your job is small". Unknown.—
    PrP—ScA
Oak apple day. R. Wilson.—FoLe
Objectivity. Mahmood Jamal.—AgL
Obnoxious Nelly. X. J. Kennedy.—KeK
"An **obnoxious** old person named Hackett". William
    Jay Smith.—LiLo—SmL

Occupations. See also names of occupations, as
    Fishers and fishing
Bonny sailor boy. Unknown.—OpT
Louisa's liberation. J. Little.—LiHe
Mom and Pop Ghastly come up for air. X. J.
    Kennedy.—KeGh
"Rich man, poor man, beggar man, thief".
    Unknown.—CoM
Ocean. See also Shore
"And God created great whales, and every living
    creature that moveth". From Book of Genesis.
    Bible/Old Testament.—WhAa
At the sea side. R. L. Stevenson.—KeT—LiDd
Away we go. W. De La Mare.—DeR
Basso profundo. S. Mandlsohn.—BoT
"Behold the wonders of the mighty deep".
    Unknown.—PrP
By the sea. E. Merriam.—MeS
Dawn ("I kindle my light over the whole
    Atlantic"). E. Sodergran.—NyT
Debt. S. Akin.—NyT
Echoes. W. De La Mare.—DeR
Haiti, skin diving. J. Shore.—KnAS
I love the sea. A. M. Cruikshank.—SlM
I swim an ocean in my sleep. N. Farber.—HoSt
Kracken. X. J. Kennedy.—WhDd
"Maggie and Milly and Molly and May". E. E.
    Cummings.—SuI
    "Maggie and Millie . . .".—ElW
The main deep. J. Stephens.—MoR
Mermaid—undersea. M. Chute.—WhDd
Mermaids ("Leagues, leagues over"). W. De La
    Mare.—DeR
The mermaids ("Sand, sand, hills of sand"). W.
    De La Mare.—DeR
Mine. L. Moore.—MoS
Ocean. J. P. Lewis.—LeE
Ocean diners. J. P. Lewis.—LeT
Old deep sing song. C. Sandburg.—MoR
Old Man Ocean. R. Hoban.—KeT—LiDd
"On a day when the ocean was sharky". X. J.
    Kennedy.—KeGh—LiLo
"Out of the cradle endlessly rocking". W.
    Whitman.—HoVo
"Protect me, O Lord". Unknown.—StP
Psalm 104. From The book of psalms. Bible/Old
    Testament.—StP
Sailing, sailing. L. Morrison.—KnAs
"A sailor went to sea, sea, sea". Unknown.—CoM
    "A sailor went to sea".—WiA
Sails, gulls, sky, sea. F. Holman.—BaW
Sand dollar. B. J. Esbensen.—EsW
Sea cliff. A. Smith.—BoT
Sea shell. A. Lowell.—ElW—LoFh
Sea timeless song. G. Nichols.—NiCo
Sea turtle. Unknown.—WhAa
Sunk Lyonesse. W. De La Mare.—DeR
The surfer. J. Wright.—MoR
There's a hole in the middle of the sea.
    Unknown.—WiA
"Think of the ocean". S. Swayne.—BoT
Tide talk. M. Fatchen.—FaCm
"Until I saw the sea". L. Moore.—BaW—DeS
"The water's deep". C. McNaughton.—PrFo
The whale ("What could hold me"). C. B. De
    Gasztold.—StP
Wild are the waves. W. De La Mare.—DeR
"The wind has such a rainy sound". C. G.
    Rossetti.—KeT
World. A. R. Ammons.—ElW

Ocean.—*Continued*
"You sea, I resign myself to you also, I guess what you". From Song of myself. W. Whitman.—HoVo
Ocean. J. Patrick Lewis.—LeE
"Ocean bathing, Abner Abb". X. J. Kennedy.—KeFb
Ocean diners. J. Patrick Lewis.—LeT
Ocelots
An odd one. From Animalimericks. E. Merriam.—LiLo—MeS
Tom Tigercat. J. P. Lewis.—LeA
"Ocka, bocka, soda crocka". Unknown.—CoM
October
Canada goose. M. Singer.—SiT
Fall. A. Fisher.—FiA
Mister October, Reggie Jackson. Unknown.—MoA
Now blue October. R. Nathan.—GoU
October ("A cold day, though only October"). G. Soto.—SoA
October ("The high fly ball"). H. J. Dawson.—MoA
October afternoons we walk around the house. A. Adoff.—AdIn
October nights. H. Cooper.—BoT
October Saturday. B. Katz.—JaP
Poppies in October. S. Plath.—ElW
October ("A cold day, though only October"). Gary Soto.—SoA
October ("The high fly ball"). Hester Jewell Dawson.—MoA
October afternoons we walk around the house. Arnold Adoff.—AdIn
"October means it's Halloween". See October nights
October nights. Harriet Cooper.—BoT
October Saturday. Bobbi Katz.—JaP
Octopus ("Marvel at the"). Valerie Worth.—WoAl
The **octopus** ("Tell me, o octopus, I begs"). Ogden Nash.—CaB—WhAa
Octopuses
Octopus ("Marvel at the"). V. Worth.—WoAl
The octopus ("Tell me, o octopus, I begs"). O. Nash.—CaB—WhAa
O'Daly, William
"What is it that upsets the volcanoes", tr.—NyT
An **odd** one. From Animalimericks. Eve Merriam.—LiLo—MeS
Ode to a day in the country. Gary Soto.—SoNe
Ode to a sneeze. George Wallace.—PrFo
Ode to el guitarron. Gary Soto.—SoNe
Ode to el molcajete. Gary Soto.—SoNe
Ode to fireworks. Gary Soto.—SoNe
Ode to La Llorona. Gary Soto.—SoNe
Ode to la pinata. Gary Soto.—SoNe
Ode to La Tortilla. Gary Soto.—SoNe
Ode to los chicharrones. Gary Soto.—SoNe
Ode to Los Raspados. Gary Soto.—SoNe
Ode to mi gato. Gary Soto.—SoNe
Ode to mi parque. Gary Soto.—SoNe
Ode to mi perrito. Gary Soto.—SoNe
Ode to my library. Gary Soto.—SoNe
Ode to Pablo's tennis shoes. Gary Soto.—SoNe
Ode to pomegranates. Gary Soto.—SoNe
Ode to Senor Leal's goat. Gary Soto.—SoNe
Ode to the Mayor. Gary Soto.—SoNe
Ode to the sprinkler. Gary Soto.—SoNe
Ode to weddings. Gary Soto.—SoNe
Ode to weight lifting. Gary Soto.—SoNe
Odors
April fool. J. Ciardi.—CiH—LiLo
Chocolate dreams, six thirty. A. Adoff.—AdCh

Lions. V. Worth.—WoAl
The nose knows. E. Merriam.—MeP
"One little skunk smelled of violets". J. Knight.—KnT
Skunk ("Skunk's footfall plods padded"). T. Hughes.—CoAz
Skunk ("Sometimes, around"). V. Worth.—WoAl
"Stealthy Steffan stuck a dead". X. J. Kennedy.—KeFb
Summer rain. E. Merriam.—MeS
"There was a man dressed all in cheese". A. Lobel.—PrFo
"Of all the birds I know, few can". See The toucan
"Of all the birds that ever I see". Unknown.—LiIf
"Of all the facts about mammals". See The elephant
"Of all the party games". See Tray
"Of all the saws I ever saw saw, I never saw a saw saw". Unknown.—WiA
"Of all the trees in England". See Trees
"Of living creatures most I prize". See Butterfly
"Of my family that, supermarket mice ate holes". See I could never convince any of the other members
Of necessity, Weeb jokes about his height. Charles Harper Webb.—JaPr
"Of obedience, faith, adhesiveness". See Thought
"Of the three wise men". See Carol of the brown king
"Of us". See Degli Sposi
Of wings. Prince Redcloud.—HoT
"Of your 'nevolent nature". See The fairy-pedlar's song
"Off". See Skate
"Off a pane the". Edward Estlin Cummings.—MoR
Off the ground. Walter De La Mare.—DeR—MaP
"Offense". See Coach
"Often I think of the beautiful town". See My lost youth
"Often I've heard the wind sigh". See Nobody knows
"Often we are foolish". Unknown.—ScA
The **ogglewop.** Colin West.—PrFo
"The ogglewop is tall and wide". See The ogglewop
O'Grady, Alison
"Great and merciful God".—StP
The **ogre.** Walter De La Mare.—DeR
"Oh, away down South where I was born". See Roll the cotton down
Oh calendar. J. Patrick Lewis.—LoFh
"Oh, Christmas time is coming again". See Emily Jane
"O Christmas tree". Unknown.—YoHa
"Oh crash". See The Fourth
"Oh, dear, bread and beer". Unknown.—ScA
O dear me. Walter De La Mare.—DeR
"Oh dear me". Unknown.—OpI
"Oh dear mother, what a rose I be". From Two dancing songs. Unknown.—OpT
"Oh did you hear". Shel Silverstein.—DeS
"Oh, do not tease the bluffalo". See The bluffalo
"Oh, do you remember, my darling". See The star-crossed lovers
"Oh, don't strike the fly". Issa, tr. by Sylvia Cassedy and Kunihiro Suetake.—CaR
"Oh, fabulous horse that's half a fish". See The hippocamp
"Oh farmer, poor farmer, you're surely". Jack Prelutsky.—PrBe
"O for a moon to light me home". See Song
"Oh ghost that follows me". From Warrior nation trilogy. Lance Henson.—SuI

"O give thanks unto the Lord". From The book of psalms. Bible/Old Testament.—StP
"O God, creator of light, at the rising". Unknown.—StP
"O God, help us not to despise or oppose". William Penn.—StP
"O God, make speed to save us". Unknown.—StP
"O God, make us able". Unknown.—StP
"O God of light, God of might". David Adam.—StP
"O God of peace, who has taught us that". Unknown.—StP
"O God, teach us to know that failure is as much". William Edward Burghardt Du Bois.—StP
"O God that bringest all things to pass". Pindar.—StP
"O God, who hast made all things beautiful". Unknown.—StP
"Oh God, who made me". See The prayer of the donkey
"O God, you have let us pass the day in peace". Unknown.—StP
"O Great Spirit, whose voice I hear in the wind". Unknown.—StP
Oh, hark. Eleanor Farjeon.—LiIf
"Oh, hark, my darling, hark". See Oh, hark
"Oh, he knew all about etymology". See A learned man
"Oh, he likes us, he's our friend". See Donkey
"O heavenly Father, protect and bless". Albert Schweitzer.—StP
"Oh, hello, Mrs. Jerome". See An important conversation
"Oh, here's to the city of Frankfurt". See A tale of two cities
"O high and glorious God". Saint Francis of Assisi.—StP
"Oh, how low can you go, Gosnold Goop". X. J. Kennedy.—KeGh
"Oh, hush thee, my baby, the night is behind us". See Seal mother's song
"Oh, I am haunted at my play". See The haunted child
"Oh, I cannot tell the truth". Unknown.—ScA
"Oh, I had a horse, his name was Bill". Unknown.—ScA
"O I have been to the meadow-bout fields". See The meadow-bout fields
"O, I have been walking". See Street song
"Oh, I have slipped the surly bonds of earth". John Gillespie Magee.—StP
High flight.—SuI
"Oh, I was born one night one morn". Unknown.—ScA
"Oh, I went down to Framingham". See Spooks
"Oh, I'm the model of a major modern witch". See Song of the modern witch
"O it's neat reading out in the snow". See Reading, winter
"O leaping crickets". See Joyful crickets
"Oh, lend me an ear and I'll happily tell". See Steam roller Sam
"Oh, little devil". Unknown.—CoM
"Oh, little playmate". Unknown.—CoM
"O little soldier with the golden helmet". See Dandelion
"O look". See Morning horses
"O look ow markit full". See Banana and mackerel
"O Lord, grant us to love Thee, grant that we may love". Mohammed.—StP
"O Lord, help me to greet the coming day in peace". Unknown.—StP

"O Lord, my day's work is over, bless all". Unknown.—StP
"O Lord my god, how excellent is your greatness". See Psalm 104
"O Lord, support us all the day long, until". Unknown.—StP
"O Lord, that lends me life". William Shakespeare.—StP
"O Lord, the meal is steaming before us". Unknown.—StP
"O Lord, Thou knowest how". Jacob Astley.—StP
"O Lord, we come this morning". See Listen, Lord—a prayer
"Oh, Mary Murple, Murple, Murple". Unknown.—ScA
"O mind, move in the Supreme Being". Sadasiva Brahmendra.—StP
"O miss, I'll give you a paper of pins". See Paper of pins
O mistress mine. From Twelfth night. William Shakespeare.—ElW
"O mistress mine, where are you roaming". See O mistress mine
"O Mrs. Mosquito, quit biting me, please". See Mosquito
"Oh my good Lord, I am not a young man anymore". Jo Carson.—CaS
"Oh my goodness, oh my dear". Clyde Watson.—LiDd
"Oh my, I want a piece of pie". Unknown.—ScA
"Ooo-ah, wanna piece of pie".—CoM
"Oh my pretty cock, oh my handsome cock". Mother Goose.—WaM
Chanticleer.—OpT
"Oh, my pretty Nicoletta". See Nicoletta
"O my soul's healer, keep me at evening". Unknown.—StP
"Oh, Norman Norton's nostrils". See Norman Norton's nostrils
Oh, oh, should they take away my stove, my inexhaustible ode to joy. Miron Bialoszewski, tr. by Andrzej Busza and Bogdan Czaykowski.—NyT
"O our mother the earth, O our father the sky". Unknown.—StP
"Oh, please will you hold baby". See Do it yourself
"Oh, policeman, policeman". Unknown.—ScA
"O purple finch". Edward Estlin Cummings.—ElW
"Oh, rare Harry Parry". Mother Goose.—WaM
"Oh, rock-a-by, baby mouse, rock-a-by, so". See The mouse's lullaby
"Oh, said the fir, still green with spring". See The fir tree
O say. Myra Cohn Livingston.—LiR
"Oh, say, can you see". Unknown.—ScA
"Oh say, kid". Unknown.—WiA
"Oh sing a song of good luck pies". See Twelve pies
"O spare us". See Clobber the lobber
"O tan-faced prairie-boy". Walt Whitman.—HoVo
O taste and see. Denise Levertov.—ElW
"Oh that I were". Mother Goose.—WaM
"Oh, the bullfrog tried to court the alligator". Unknown.—WiA
"Oh, the cow kicked Nelly in the belly in the barn". Unknown.—ScA
"Oh the dream, the dream". See The orphan
"Oh, the funniest thing I've ever seen". Unknown.—WiA
"Oh the gray cat piddled in the white cat's eye". Unknown.—OpI
"Oh, the Lord is good to me". John Chapman.—StP

"**Oh,** the Lord looked down from his window in the sky". Unknown.—StP
"**Oh,** the wily flingamango". See The flingamango
"**Oh,** there once was a puffin". See There once was a puffin
"**Oh,** there's not much sense". Unknown.—WiA
"**Oh,** they are cold". See Ching ming
"**Oh** this is". See Fog
"**Oh** this is the animal that never was". See The unicorn
"**O** thou great chief, light a candle". Unknown.—StP
"**Oh,** tongue, give sound to joy and sing". See Dragon
"**Oh,** weep for Mr. and Mrs. Bryan". See The lion
"**Oh,** what a melee". See Donnybrook at Riverfront Stadium
"**O** what can ail thee, knight at arms". See La belle dame sans merci
"**Oh,** when the saints". Unknown.—StP
"**Oh,** why can't I sing, sighed the flying fish". See The flying fish
"**Oh** will you be my wallaby". See The kangaroo's courtship
"**O** world, I cannot hold thee close enough". See God's world
"**Oh,** you gotta get a glory". Unknown.—StP
"**Oh,** you may drive a horse to water". Unknown.—WiA
"**Oh,** you never see a feather". Unknown.—WiA
"**O** you who feed the little bird". Unknown.—StP
O'Hara, Frank
   A true account of talking to the sun at Fire Island.—ElW
O'Harris, Pixie
   Wouldn't it be funny.—CoAz
O'Hehir, Brendan
   The first shoe, tr.—NyT
Oil
   Rainbow making, a mystery. From Four poems for Roy G Biv. B. J. Esbensen.—EsW
O'John, Calvin
   "Dancing teepees".—SnD
"Okay with me". See Relationship
Okolo the leopard warrior. Christine Price.—WhDd
Ol' man river. From Show Boat. Oscar Hammerstein.—SuC
"**Ol'** man river, dat ol' man river". See Ol' man river
Old age. See also Childhood recollections; Youth and age
   About old people. J. Little.—LiHe
   The emeritus. L. Nathan.—JaM
   Father William. From Alice's adventures in wonderland. L. Carroll.—LiPf
      You are old, Father William.—ElW
   Grandmother, rocking. E. Merriam.—MeS
   Granny's ninety-two-year-old legs. A. Adoff.—AdIn
   Great grandma. L. Morrison.—LiPg
   Haunted ("The rabbit in his burrow keeps"). W. De La Mare.—DeR
   Her hands. A. W. Paul.—LiPg
   "Here lies". Unknown.—BaH
   "How's mama". J. Carson.—CaS
   Ice-creepers. E. Merriam.—MeS
   In these dissenting times. A. Walker.—ElW
   Learning to read. From Sketches of southern life. F. E. W. Harper.—SuC
   Loss of love. M. Angelou.—AnI
   Marching song. From The three royal monkeys. W. De La Mare.—DeR
   Martha Nelson speaks. G. Bogin.—JaM

Maud. M. Swander.—JaM
Memories. W. Whitman.—HoVo
The memory of horses. R. Jacobsen.—NyT
Methuselah. E. Merriam.—MeS
Mr. Joshua Cantor. M. Glenn.—GlBc
Mrs. Morizawa's morning. X. J. Kennedy.—KeK
Ms. Emily Parsons, history. M. Glenn.—GlBc
My 71st year. W. Whitman.—HoVo
Old folks laugh. M. Angelou.—AnI
Old man moon. A. Fisher.—DeT—FiA
Old man's weary thoughts. G. Nichols.—NiCo
The old sailor. W. De La Mare.—DeR
The old soldier. W. De La Mare.—DeR—MaP
On a cat ageing. A. Gray.—CaB
Part IX: There was an old woman who lived in the Fens. From A child's day. W. De La Mare.—DeR
Please to remember ("Here am I"). W. De La Mare.—DeR
The purpose of poetry. J. Carter.—JaM
Queries to my seventieth year. W. Whitman.—HoVo
Rare rhythms. S. London.—JaM
"Sam, Sam, dirty old man". Unknown.—CoM—OpI
"She come to see your mother". J. Carson.—CaS
Sleep, grandmother. M. Van Doren.—SuI
Song of enchantment. W. De La Mare.—DeR—MaP
The song of Finis. W. De La Mare.—DeR—MaP
Stories ("Circling by the fire"). J. P. Lewis.—LeT—LiDp
"To get the final lilt of songs". W. Whitman.—HoVo
To old age. W. Whitman.—HoVo
"Twenty-one years". J. Carson.—CaS
The **old** Astro rotation. Unknown.—MoA
"**Old** Ben Bailey". See Done for
"An **old** billy goat". See G is for goat
"The **old** buccaneer". See P is for pirate
"An **old** couple living in Gloucester". Unknown.—LiLo
"**Old** Dan Tucker went to town". Unknown.—WiA
Old deep sing song. Carl Sandburg.—MoR
"**Old** Dr. Cox's". See Foxes
"The **old** fence". See Fence
Old folks laugh. Maya Angelou.—AnI
An **old** grey horse. Unknown.—CII
"An **old** grey horse stood on the wall". See An old grey horse
"The **old** hen sat on turkey eggs". Unknown.—WiA
Old Hogan's goat. Unknown.—CoAz
"**Old** Hogan's goat was feeling fine". See Old Hogan's goat
Old hound. Valerie Worth.—LiDp
The **old** house. Walter De La Mare.—DeR—MaP
An **old** Jamaican woman thinks about the hereafter. A. L. Hendricks.—LeCa
Old Joe Jones. Laura E. Richards.—KeT
"**Old** Joe Jones and his old dog Bones". See Old Joe Jones
"**Old** Jumpety Bumpety Hop and Go One". Unknown.—CII
The **old** king. Walter De La Mare.—DeR
"**Old** King Caraway". See Cake and sack
"**Old** King Cole was a merry old soul". Mother Goose.—EdGl—SuO—WaM
"**Old** lady Fry". Unknown.—WiA
"**Old** Lester Darby". See Stories
Old Mag. Joyce Hollingsworth-Barkley.—JaPr
Old man and the cow. Edward Lear.—DeS
   There was an old man who said.—CII

"Old man Daisy". Unknown.—WiA

"An old man from Okefenokee". William Jay Smith.—LiLo—SmL

An old man from Peru. See "There was an old man from Peru"

Old man moon. Aileen Fisher.—DeT—FiA

"Old man Moses, sick in bed". Unknown.—ScA

Old Man Ocean. Russell Hoban.—KeT—LiDd

"Old Man Ocean, how do you pound". See Old Man Ocean

Old man of Peru. See "There was an old man from Peru"

The old man of the wood. Jane Yolen.—YoBe

Old man platypus. Andrew Barton Paterson.—CoAz

The old man's comforts and how he gained them. Robert Southey.—ElW

Old man's weary thoughts. Grace Nichols.—NiCo

Old Mary. Gwendolyn Brooks.—SuC

The old math, one. Arnold Adoff.—AdCh

The old math, two. Arnold Adoff.—AdCh

"Old Mog comes in and sits on the newspaper". See Cat

"Old Mother Hubbard". Mother Goose.—EdGl—SuO—WaM

"Old Mother Ink". Unknown.—CoM

"Old Mother Shuttle". Mother Goose.—WaM

Old mountains want to turn to sand. Tommy Olofsson, tr. by Jean Pearson.—NyT

"Old Mrs. Caribou lives by a lake". See Mrs. Caribou

"Old Noah once he built an ark". See Old Noah's ark

Old Noah's ark. Unknown.—DeT—HoS—SuI

Old Obadiah. Unknown.—WiA

"Old Obadiah jumped in the fire". See Old Obadiah

"The old October ogres come". See Sounds of winter

An old person of Ware. Edward Lear.—MoS

Old photograph album, grandfather. Barbara Juster Esbensen.—EsW

"The old pig said to the little pigs". See The pigs and the charcoal-burner

The old sailor. Walter De La Mare.—DeR

Old Satchmo's gravelly voice. Melvin B. Tolson.—SuC

"Old Satchmo's gravelly voice and tapping foot". See Old Satchmo's gravelly voice

"An old scold sold a cold coal shovel". Unknown.—WiA

Old Shellover. See "Come, said old Shellover"

Old Shevchenko. Peter Oresick.—JaPr

"Old Simon swims". See Sleeping Simon

The old soldier. Walter De La Mare.—DeR—MaP

Old spider web. Myra Cohn Livingston.—LiNe

The old stone house. Walter De La Mare.—DeR—MaP

The old tailor. Walter De La Mare.—DeR

"Old Tillie Turveycombe". See Tillie

Old tom. Jane Yolen.—YoBi

"Old Tom". See Tom

"Old Uncle Luke, he thinks he's cute". From Grannies and grandpas. Unknown.—OpT

The old wife and the ghost. James Reeves.—DeS

Olds, Sharon
  Mrs. Krikorian.—JaPr

"Ole Abe (God bless 'is ole soul)". See Negro soldier's civil war chant

Olive Street. Myra Cohn Livingston.—LiT

Oliver, Mary
  How I went truant from school to visit a river.—JaPr

Oliver Johnson comes back to bed the morning after the ice storm and tells his wife why. David Jauss.—JaM

"Oliver Twist can't do this". Unknown.—ScA

Olofsson, Tommy
  Old mountains want to turn to sand, tr. by Jean Pearson.—NyT
  The shadow inside me, tr. by Jean Pearson.—NyT

Omaha Indians. See Indians of the Americas—Omaha

The ombley-gombley. Peter Wesley-Smith.—PrFo

Omens. See also Prophecies; Superstitions
  "Crow on the fence". Unknown.—CaB
  "Drop a dishrag". Unknown.—WiA
  Granny's ninety-two-year-old legs. A. Adoff.—AdIn
  "If you stub your toe". Unknown.—WiA
  "If you touch blue". Unknown.—WiA
  In the Lebanese mountains. N. Tueni.—NyT
  "Sneeze on Monday, sneeze for danger". Unknown.—WiA
  "Step in a ditch". Unknown.—CoM—WiA
  "Step in the dirt". Unknown.—WiA
  "Step on a crack". Unknown.—CoM—WiA
  "Turn to the right". Unknown.—WiA

"An ominous bird sang from its branch". See Beware

"On 41, outside Stratford". See Hitchhiking with a friend and a book that explains the Pacific Ocean

"On a broad brimmed hat". See Chit chat

On a cat ageing. Alexander Gray.—CaB

On a cold autumn day. Bonnie Nims.—KeT

"On a dark night". See Objectivity

"On a day in summer". Aileen Fisher.—HoGo

"On a day when the ocean was sharky". X. J. Kennedy.—KeGh—LiLo

"On a flat road runs the well trained runner". See The runner

"On a golden step sat". See "Na zlatom cryeltse sidelly"

"On a lonely beach the old wreck lies". See Children lost

"On a mule we find two legs behind". Unknown.—ScA

Mules ("On mules . . .").—PrFo

On a night of snow. Elizabeth Coatsworth.—LaCc

On a night of the full moon. Audre Lorde.—GoU

"On a roof in the Old City". See Jerusalem

"On a still calm night when the bugs begin to bite". Unknown.—OpI

"On a trip through Yellowstone". X. J. Kennedy.—KeFb

On being brought from Africa to America. Phillis Wheatley.—SuC

On being introduced to you. Eve Merriam.—MeS

"On Christmas Eve I turned the spit". Mother Goose.—WaM

"On days when I am sick in bed". See Sick days

On destiny. Shuntaro Tanikawa, tr. by Harold Wright.—NyT

"On either side the river lie". See The Lady of Shalott

"On Fourth of July". See Ode to fireworks

On freedom. James Russell Lowell.—SuI

"On Friday night I go backwards to bed". Mother Goose.—WaM

"On his laboratory table". X. J. Kennedy.—KeFb

On journeys through the states. Walt Whitman.—HoVo

"On journeys through the states we start". See On journeys through the states

On Limestone Street. Arnold Adoff.—AdIn

"**One** day a boy went walking". Unknown.—PrP—WiA

"**One** day, a fine day, a high flying sky day". See The cat heard the cat-bird

"**One** day a funny kind of man". See A funny man

"**One** day, beside a cactus patch". See Porcu-pain

"**One** day his captain told him". See The best in the land

"**One** day I asked my teacher". See Were you ever fat like me

"**One** day I asked the mirror facing me". Tialuga Sunia Seloti.—NyT

"**One** day I saw a downy duck". See Good morning

"**One** day I watched Ted Williams". See The kid

"**One** day, in this coldest winter, but in our". See Mouse under the house, mouse in the house

"**One** day snow leopard caught a cough". See Invisible cat

"**One-ery,** ore-ery, ickery Ann". Unknown.—SuI

"**One** ewe". See Shepherd's night count

"**One** fine day in the middle of the night". Unknown.—BaH—OpI

"**One** foggy autumn in Baltimore". Jack Prelutsky.—PrBe

"**One** foot on, one foot pushing, Esme starting". See Esme on her brother's bicycle

"**One** for anger". Unknown.—ScA

One for one. Jim Heynen.—JaPr

"**One** for the cutworm". Unknown.—WiA

"**One** for the money". Mother Goose.—ScA—WaM

"**One** for the pigeon". Mother Goose.—WaM

"**One** Friday night". See Mystery

"**One:** I do not like the way". See One, two, three, four m-o-t-h-e-r

"**One,** I don't remember". See Seven

"**One** I love, two I love". Mother Goose.—WaM—WiA

"**One** last blue patch of". See Rain, a haiku sequence

"**One** last lost". See Rescue mission

"**One** little beaver worked hard as can be". Joan Knight.—KnT

"**One** little bunny grew carrots". Joan Knight.—KnT

"**One** little grizzly grew grumpy". Joan Knight.—KnT

"**One** little hippo brought a blanket". Joan Knight.—KnT

"**One** little kid took a limo". Joan Knight.—KnT

"**One** little lamb put on records". Joan Knight.—KnT

"**One** little monkey laughed loudly". Joan Knight.—KnT

"**One** little owl played violin". Joan Knight.—KnT

"**One** little panda read music". Joan Knight.—KnT

"**One** little piggy wore leggings". Joan Knight.—KnT

"**One** little possum ate a parsnip". Joan Knight.—KnT

"**One** little skunk smelled of violets". Joan Knight.—KnT

"**One** little tiger had a tantrum". Joan Knight.—KnT

"**One** misty, moisty morning". Mother Goose.—MoS—SuO—WaM

"**One** moment take thy rest". See Alas

One more time. Nancy Willard.—SaB

"**One** morning a great gaggle slid". See When angels came to Zimmer

"**One** must have a mind of winter". See The snow man

One night. Arnold Adoff.—AdIn

"**One** night". See The visitor

"**One** night as Dick lay fast asleep". See Full moon

"**One** night two hunters, drunk, came in the tent". See At the piano

One o'clock. Katharine Pyle.—LaCc

"**One** of the clock, and silence deep". See One o'clock

"**One** of the nicest beds I know". See Autumn leaves

"**One** potato, two potato". Unknown.—CoM—SuI—WiA

"**One** runner's safe, one runner's out". See Numbers game

"**One** sack". See Monster man

"**One** summer night a little raccoon". See Raccoon

"**One** swoops in on a glider wing". See Blue herons

"**One** thing about me". See Seven women's blessed assurance

"**One** thing I really, really hate". See Spinach

"**One** thought ever at the fore". Walt Whitman.—HoVo

1246. Jalal-Ud-Din Rumi, tr. by John Moyne and Coleman Barks.—GoU

One time. William Stafford.—JaP

"**One** Tuesday night the long-haired yak". See Flight of the long-haired yak

"**One,** two, buckle my shoe". Mother Goose.—SuO

"**One,** two, grow tall". See "Meg, yergoo, yergunnas"

"**1, 2,** I love you". See Counting

"**1, 2,** my daddy, who". See Counting sheep

"**One,** two, police". See "Eins, zwei, polizei"

"**One,** two, sky blue". Unknown.—CoM

"**1, 2,** 30, 48 passengers to far vistas, lost in a trail of vapor". See Jet

"**One,** two, three". See Away we go

1, 2, 3. Eve Merriam.—MeP

"**One,** two, three, a-lary, I spy Mistress Mary". Unknown.—WiA

"**One,** two, three, a-lary, I spy Mrs. Sairy". Unknown.—CoM

"**One,** two, three, a-lary, my first name is Mary". Unknown.—ScA—WiA

"**One,** two, three a-nation". Unknown.—CoM—YoS

"**One,** two, three, a-nation, doctor, doctor". Unknown.—WiA

"**One,** two, three, four". See First foot

"**One,** two, three, four". Mother Goose.—WaM

"**One,** two, three, four, Charlie Chaplin". Unknown.—CoM

"**1, 2, 3, 4, 5**". See "Raz, dva, tree, chiteery, pyat"

"**One,** two, three, four, five, I caught a fish alive". Unknown.—WiA

"**1, 2, 3, 4, 5, 6, 7**". Unknown.—ScA

"**One,** two, three, four, five, six, seven, all good children go to heaven". Unknown.—OpI

"**One,** two, three, four, I spy Eleanor". Unknown.—WiA

One, two, three, four m-o-t-h-e-r. Felice Holman.—LiPm

"**One,** two, three, Johnny". Unknown.—WiA

"**1, 2, 3,** look out for me". Unknown.—ScA

"**One,** two, three, mother caught a flea". Unknown.—CoM

"**One** two three, one two three". See Kick line

"**One,** two, three, one, two, three". Unknown.—CoM

"**One,** two, three, the bumblebee". Unknown.—CoM

"**One,** two, tie your shoe". Unknown.—WiA

"**One** winter day". See Snowflake

"**One** without looks in tonight". See The fallow deer at the lonely house

One year. N. M. Bodecker.—KeT

"**One** year we had a picnic". See Six

O'Neill, Eugene
  It's great when you get in.—KnAs

O'Neill, Mary
    North wind ("Is your father").—BaW
"Onery, twoery". Mother Goose.—OpI
Onions
    Straight scoop about scallions. X. J. Kennedy.—
        KeGh
"Only a litter". See Kaleidoscope
An only child. Mary Ann Hoberman.—HoFa
"An only child's the only one". See An only child
"Only fools pursue". See Heron
"Only know I loved you". See Daddy
"Only light and shadow". See Night on
    neighborhood street
"Only my dad was brave enough". See Snowstorm
"Only one of me". See One
"Only the best and the finest ingredients". See The
    tarragon vinegar song
Onomatopoeia. Eve Merriam.—MoR
Oodles of noodles. James L. Hymes and Lucia
    Hymes.—PrFo
"Ooo-ah, wanna piece of pie". See "Oh my, I want
    a piece of pie"
An open arc. Salvatore Quasimodo, tr. by Jack
    Bevan.—GoT
The open door. Elizabeth Coatsworth.—KeT—LaCc
Open house. Aileen Fisher.—FiA
Open hydrant. Marci Ridlon.—DeT
"Open, shut them". Unknown.—CoE
The open shutter. Karl Krolow, tr. by Kevin
    Perryman.—NyT
"Open the closet". See Coat hangers
"Open the scrapbook and look at the past". See
    Dress code, a sedimental journey
"Open thou our lips, O Lord, and purify". Christina
    Georgina Rossetti.—StP
"Open your eyes, now, look, and see". See The
    secret
"Open your mouth and close your eyes".
    Unknown.—ScA
    "Open your mouth and shut your eyes".—WiA
"Open your mouth and shut your eyes". See "Open
    your mouth and close your eyes"
"An opera star named Maria". Unknown.—LiLo
Ophelia. Brenda Hillman.—JaM
Opossum. William Jay Smith.—SmL
Opossums
    "One little possum ate a parsnip". J. Knight.—
        KnT
    Opossum. W. J. Smith.—SmL
    "Possum pie is made of rye". Unknown.—WiA
    "Raccoon up a persimmon tree". Unknown.—
        WiA
Oppenheimer, Joel
    For Hoyt Wilhelm.—KnAs
The opposite of two. Richard Wilbur.—LoFh
Opposites
    "Detestable crow". Basho.—CaR
    The opposite of two. R. Wilbur.—LoFh
    Rabbit and lark. J. Reeves.—MoS
"The Optileast". See The Optileast and the
    Pessimost
The Optileast and the Pessimost. Eve Merriam.—
    MeS
Optimism. See Happiness; Laughter; Points of view
The optimist. Unknown.—PrFo
"The optimist fell ten stories". See The optimist
Or. Ali Darwish.—NyT
"Or one of the original Klingon kids". See I don't
    mean to say I am Martian, Morkian
"Orange so sweet". See "Naranja dulce"
Oranges
    "Dingty diddlety". Mother Goose.—WaM

"Naranja dulce". Unknown.—DeA
    "Orange so sweet".—DeA
Oranges ("The first time I walked"). G. Soto.—
    JaM—SoA
Oranges ("I peel oranges neatly"). J. Little.—LiHe
There's an orange tree out there. A. Q. Urias.—
    NyT
Oranges ("The first time I walked"). Gary Soto.—
    JaM—SoA
Oranges ("I peel oranges neatly"). Jean Little.—
    LiHe
"Oranges the tree hung around itself". See Light
    fabric
The orchard. Walter De La Mare.—DeR
Orchards
    Blackbirds. W. De La Mare.—DeR
    The little green orchard. W. De La Mare.—
        DeR—MaP
    The orchard. W. De La Mare.—DeR
Orchestras. See also Music and musicians
    Dinosaur hard rock band. J. Yolen.—YoDd
    The egotistical orchestra. E. Merriam.—MeCh
    Here comes the band. W. Cole.—DeS
    Starry night I. E. Merriam.—MeS
    "Ten tom toms". Unknown.—MoR
"Order in the court". Unknown.—ScA
"Order in the gallery". Unknown.—OpI
Orders. A. M. Klein.—BoT
Oresick, Peter
    Old Shevchenko.—JaPr
Origami for two. Pieter Dominick.—MoR
The origin of baseball. Kenneth Patchen.—KnAs
"Ormsby Slatter". See Mr. Slatter
Ornaments. Valerie Worth.—WoA
The orphan. Muhammad Al-Maghut, tr. by May
    Jayyusi and Naomi Shihab Nye.—NyT
Orphanage boy. Robert Penn Warren.—JaPr
Orphans
    Luanne Sheridan. M. Glenn.—GlBc
    The orphan. M. Al-Maghut.—NyT
    Orphanage boy. R. P. Warren.—JaPr
Orr, Bobby (about)
    High stick. B. Collins.—KnAs
Osadchaya, Irina
    "A man comes in, his suit is crumpled", tr.—NyT
Osage Indians. See Indians of the Americas—Osage
Ospreys. See Hawks
Ostrich, sels. Alan Brownjohn
    "Little ostriches".—HoT
Ostriches
    Grandmother Ostrich. W. J. Smith.—SmL
    "Little ostriches". From Ostrich. A. Brownjohn.—
        HoT
"Other birds soar in the clouds". See Pigeons
"The other day I saw a witch". See The grammatical
    witch
Others. Myra Cohn Livingston.—LiT
Otomo, Yakamochi
    "We were together".—GoU
Ouch. Max Fatchen.—FaCm
"Our baby's one". See Four
"Our balloon man has balloons". See The balloon
    man
"Our baseball team never did very much". See The
    new kid
Our canary. Lois Simmie.—PrFo
"Our canary is dusty and cold and mad". See Our
    canary
Our cat. Marchette Chute.—LaCc
"Our cat she crossed the road". Unknown.—WiA
"Our cat turns up her nose at mice". See The cat
    who aspired to higher things

"**Our** cherry tree". See Blow up
Our Christmas tree. Myra Cohn Livingston.—LiNe
"**Our** clothes are still wet from wading". See The huts at Esquimaux
"**Our** family comes from 'round the world". Mary Ann Hoberman.—HoFa
"**Our** father, hear us, and our grandfather, I mention also". Unknown.—StP
"**Our** Father in heaven". From The gospel according to Matthew. Bible/New Testament.—StP
"**Our** Father in heaven". Dick Williams.—StP
Our grandmothers. Maya Angelou.—AnI
"**Our** great fathers talked together, here they arose and". See They stooped over and came out
"**Our** history teacher says, be proud you're Canadians". See So I'm proud
"**Our** holiday activities". See At the beach
Our kitten. Unknown.—ClI
"**Our** kitten, the one we call Louie". See Our kitten
"**Our** only little girl". See My father's words
"**Our** Pacific islands are yours, O Lord". Bernard Narokobi.—StP
"**Our** puppy". See Kitchen table
"**Our** share of night to bear". Emily Dickinson.—GoT
Our tree. Marchette Chute.—DeS
"**Our** water hole should suit quite well". See Strictly for the birds
Our yak. Unknown.—ClI
The **ousel** cock. Ralph Hodgson.—ElW
Out fishing. Barbara Howes.—KnAs
Out for spring. Arnold Adoff.—AdIn
"**Out** goes the rat". Unknown.—SuI—WiA
"**Out** of a tree". See Monkey
"**Out** of green space". See Dandelion
"**Out** of my flesh that hungers". See On a night of the full moon
"**Out** of my window late at night I gape". See In the night
Out of the city. Eve Merriam.—MeS
"**Out** of the cradle endlessly rocking". Walt Whitman.—HoVo
"**Out** of the dark". See The open door
"**Out** of the east a hurricane". See Captain Lean
"**Out** there where Barnum Road hooks left". See The last mountain lion on Maple Crest Mountain
Outdoor life. See Camping and hiking; Country life; Gypsies; Nature; Sports
Outer space. See Space and space travel
Outfielder. Stephen Dunn.—MoA
Outhouse blues. Sheryl L. Nelms.—JaM
The **outlandish** knight. Unknown.—ElW
"An **outlandish** knight came from the north". See The outlandish knight
Outlaws. See Crime and criminals
"The **outlook** wasn't brilliant for the Mudville nine that day". See Casey at the bat
"The **outlook** wasn't brilliant for the Mudvillettes, it seems". See Casey's daughter at the bat
Over and under. William Jay Smith.—SmL
"**Over** every elm, the". See You too lie down
"**Over** on the hill there's a big red bull". Unknown.—WiA
"**Over** the bay". Unknown.—WiA
Over the downs. Walter De La Mare.—DeR
Over the field. May Swenson.—MoR
"**Over** the hill with a horrible growl, running". See The tables turned
"**Over** the hills". See The witches' ride
"**Over** the mirror". See Swan
"**Over** the ocean". Unknown.—WiA

"**Over** the river and through the wood". See Thanksgiving day, complete
"**Over** the river and through the wood". From Thanksgiving day. Lydia Maria Child.—HoS
"**Over** the sea". Unknown.—WiA
Overboard. May Swenson.—MoR
Overdog. Tony Johnston.—DeT
"**Overdog** Johnson is a guy". See Overdog
Overham, John
"Blessed are they that have eyes to see".—StP
Overture. Zuhur Dixon, tr. by Patricia Alanah Byrne and Salma Khadra Jayyusi.—NyT
The **owl**. See The bird of night
Owl ("The diet of the owl is not"). X. J. Kennedy.—LiIf
The **owl** ("Downhill I came, hungry, and yet not starved"). Edward Thomas.—ElW—LiIf
The **owl** ("In broad daylight"). John Gardner.—LiIf
The **owl** ("Once I was a monarch's daughter"). Unknown.—OpT
The **owl** ("The owl hooted and told of"). Unknown.—LaN
"**Owl**". See Owl of night
The **owl** ("The owl that lives in the old oak tree"). William Jay Smith.—LiIf—SmL
"The **owl**". See Owl
"**Owl**". See Prayer
The **owl**. See Song, the owl
The **owl** ("To whit, to whoo"). Conrad Aiken.—LiIf
The **owl** ("Your eyes, a searching yellow light"). Deborah Chandra.—LiIf
The **owl** and the pussy-cat. Edward Lear.—ElW—LiDd—LoFh
"The **owl** and the pussy-cat went to sea". See The owl and the pussy-cat
"**Owl** floats through the midnight wood". See Spell of the moon
"The **owl** hooted". Unknown.—LiIf
"The **owl** hooted and told of". See The owl
"The **owl**, it is said". See O is for owl
"The **owl** looked out of the ivy bush". Charles Causley.—LiIf
Owl of night. Myra Cohn Livingston.—LiR
The **owl** on the aerial. Clarice Short.—LiIf
"**Owl**, owl". See Lulu, lulu, I've a lilo
The **owl** takes off at Upper Black Eddy, Pa. Emanuel Di Pasquale.—LiIf
"The **owl** that lives in the old oak tree". See The owl
Owl ("The owl"). Valerie Worth.—LiIf
Owls
Aesthetic curiosity. A. M. Klein.—BoT
All eyes. J. P. Lewis.—LeA—LiIf
Barn owl. M. Singer.—SiT
Beech, to owl. M. C. Livingston.—LiIf
Beware ("Did I dream the owl or was it really there"). M. Robinson.—LiIf
The bird of night. R. Jarrell.—LiIf
    The owl.—LaN
The bonny, bonny owl. Sir W. Scott.—LiIf
"Brown owls come here in the blue evening". Unknown.—LiIf
The canal bank. J. Stephens.—LiIf
Careful, mouse. A. Fisher.—FiH
The dark ("There are six little houses up on the hill"). E. M. Roberts.—LaN
"Five little owls in the old elm tree". Unknown.—WhAa
Ghosts ("A cold and starry darkness moans"). H. Behn.—BaH—LiIf
"God save the owls". From Alabama. J. Fields.—LiIf

P

Parrots

"Because parrots are chatterers people say they are the only ones who eat up the fruits". From Jamaican Caribbean proverbs. Unknown.—BeW

I'm a parrot. G. Nichols.—NiCo

"Little Poll Parrot". Mother Goose.—ClI—WaM

Macaw. M. C. Livingston.—LiNe

My stupid parakeet named after you. X. J. Kennedy.—KeK

Parakeets ("Parakeets wheel"). G. Nichols.—NiCo

The parakeets ("They talk all day"). A. Blanco.—NyT

Parrot (from Trinidad). W. J. Smith.—SmL

Parrot (from Zambezi). W. J. Smith.—SmL

Why there are no cats in the forest. S. Dumdum.—NyT

Parsnips. Jean Little.—LiHe

Part I: I sang a song to Rosamund Rose. From A child's day. Walter De La Mare.—DeR

Part II: Softly, drowsily. From A child's day. Walter De La Mare.—DeR

Part III: Little birds bathe. From A child's day. Walter De La Mare.—DeR

Part IV: The queen of Arabia, Uanjinee. From A child's day. Walter De La Mare.—DeR

Part V: England over. From A child's day. Walter De La Mare.—DeR

Part VI: Thousands of years ago. From A child's day. Walter De La Mare.—DeR

Part VII: When safe in to the fields Ann got. From A child's day. Walter De La Mare.—DeR

Part VIII: When she was in her garden. From A child's day. Walter De La Mare.—DeR

Part IX: There was an old woman who lived in the Fens. From A child's day. Walter De La Mare.—DeR

Part X: This little morsel of morsels here. From A child's day. Walter De La Mare.—DeR

Part XI: Now fie, o fie, how sly a face. From A child's day. Walter De La Mare.—DeR

Part XII: Ann, upon the stroke of three. From A child's day. Walter De La Mare.—DeR

Part XIII: As soon as ever twilight comes. From A child's day. Walter De La Mare.—DeR

Part XIV: Now, dear me. From A child's day. Walter De La Mare.—DeR

Part XV: Now, my dear, for gracious sake. From A child's day. Walter De La Mare.—DeR

Part XVI: The king in slumber when he lies down. From A child's day. Walter De La Mare.—DeR

Part XVII: Now through the dusk. From A child's day. Walter De La Mare.—DeR

Part XVIII: He squats by the fire. From A child's day. Walter De La Mare.—DeR

Part XIX: Sadly, o, sadly, the sweet bells of Baddeley. From A child's day. Walter De La Mare.—DeR

Part XX: This brief day now over. From A child's day. Walter De La Mare.—DeR

Parties

And after. J. Yolen.—YoDd

The barkday party. J. Berry.—BeW

Birthday clown. M. C. Livingston.—LiBp

The blackbirds' party. A. Bryan.—BrS

Celebration. A. Lopez.—DeT

Chocolate moose. W. J. Smith.—SmL

Deck the halls. Unknown.—YoHa

Dinosaur dances. J. Yolen.—YoDd

"Every party needs a pooper". Unknown.—CoM

Funny glasses. M. C. Livingston.—LiBp

The hayride. M. C. Livingston.—LiBp

Invitation ("My birthday invitation"). M. C. Livingston.—LiBp

Leaps of feeling. J. Berry.—BeW

"Left foot, right foot". Mother Goose.—WaM

The little bird ("My dear Daddie bought a mansion"). W. De La Mare.—DeR—MaP

"Little Clotilda". Unknown.—ClI

Michael's birthday. M. C. Livingston.—LiBp

"My party dress". From Party dress, party shirt. M. C. Livingston.—LiBp

"My party shirt". From Party dress, party shirt. M. C. Livingston.—LiBp

The new suit. N. Sanabria de Romero.—NyT

New Year's eve. V. Worth.—WoA

"Now Christmas is come". W. Irving.—GoA

Ode to la pinata. G. Soto.—SoNe

Party favors. M. C. Livingston.—LiBp

Party prizes. M. C. Livingston.—LiBp

Party table. M. C. Livingston.—LiBp

The party's over. R. Edwards.—FoLe

"Pinning the tail on the donkey". M. C. Livingston.—LiBp

Presents ("My friends all gave me presents"). M. C. Livingston.—LiBp

The rose on my cake. K. Kuskin.—KeT

Sephina. W. De La Mare.—DeR

Shrove Tuesday. A. Bonner.—FoLe

Six. M. C. Livingston.—LiBp

Tea party. H. Behn.—LiDd

"There was a young man of Bengal". Unknown.—LiLo—PrP

  There was a young man.—ClI

"There was a young man so benighted". Unknown.—LiLo

"There was a young person called Smarty". Unknown.—LiLo

"There was an old man from the coast". W. J. Smith.—SmL

To friendship. E. Greenfield.—GrU

"To the bowl of champagne punch". X. J. Kennedy.—KeFb

Tray. M. C. Livingston.—LiBp

Victory banquet. S. B. Mathis.—MaR

"We're all dry with drinking on't". Mother Goose.—WaM

"When Joan had a birthday". From Birthday secrets. M. C. Livingston.—LiBp

Whodunnit. E. Merriam.—MeCh

Parting

The apple. J. Halevi.—GoU

Atong. B. S. Santos.—NyT

Atong and his goodbye. B. S. Santos.—NyT

"The Bay of Tsunu". H. Kakinomoto.—GoU

Byes. M. Redoles.—AgL

Coming home on my own. J. Berry.—BeW

Daddy's gone. D. Chandra.—LiPf

Distances of longing. F. Abu Khalid.—NyT

Early love. H. Scott.—JaM

"Good-bye my fancy". W. Whitman.—HoVo

Hiding our love. C. Kizer.—GoU

"I have not seen you, even in dream". From Love songs from an ancient book. L. Goldberg.—GoT

Leaving. A. Bryan.—BrS

"My life closed twice before its close". E. Dickinson.—SuI

"Naranja dulce". Unknown.—DeA

  "Orange so sweet".—DeA

Now lift me close. W. Whitman.—HoVo

Part XX: This brief day now over. From A child's day. W. De La Mare.—DeR

Peacocks—*Continued*
"The peacock hides its leg when its tail gets praises". From Jamaican Caribbean proverbs. Unknown.—BeW
"When a peacock loudly calls". Unknown.—WhAa
Peak and Puke. Walter De La Mare.—DeR—MaP
"A **peanut** sat on a railroad track". Unknown.—KeT—PrP
"A peanut sat on the railroad track".—WiA
The peanut song ("Oh, a peanut sat . . .").—CoE
"A **peanut** sat on the railroad track". See "A peanut sat on a railroad track"
The **peanut** song ("Oh, a peanut sat . . ."). See "A peanut sat on a railroad track"
Peanuts
"Now I lay me down to sleep, a bag of peanuts at my feet". Unknown.—ScA—WiA
"A peanut sat on a railroad track". Unknown.—KeT—PrP
"A peanut sat on the railroad track".—WiA
The peanut song ("Oh, a peanut sat . . .").—CoE
Pigeons and peanuts for sale. N. Mellage.—SlM
The **pear** tree. Edna St. Vincent Millay.—ElW
A **pearl**. Fawziyya Abu Khalid, tr. by Salwa Jabsheh and John Heath-Stubbs.—NyT
"**Pearl** Avenue runs past the high school lot". See Ex-basketball player
Pearlman, Bill
The volleyball match.—KnAs
Pearls
A pearl. F. Abu Khalid.—NyT
Pearls. J. Little.—LiHe
Pearls. Jean Little.—LiHe
Pears and pear trees
The fable of the golden pear. E. Merriam.—MeS
The pear tree. E. S. V. Millay.—ElW
Pearson, Jean
Old mountains want to turn to sand, tr.—NyT
The shadow inside me, tr.—NyT
"**Pease** porridge hot, pease porridge cold". Mother Goose.—SuO—WaM
"**Pease-porridge** hot, pease-porridge cold". Unknown.—OpI
"**Pease** porridge hot, pease porridge cold". Unknown.—ScA
Peavy, Linda
The telling tree.—JaPr
Pebbles. Valerie Worth.—WoAl
"**Pebbles** belong to no one". See Pebbles
"**Peck**, peck, peck". See Baby chick
Peddlers and vendors
All hot (the chestnut man). W. De La Mare.—DeR
"Apples and oranges, four for a penny". Unknown.—OpI
The balloon man. D. Aldis.—DeT
"Beneath a blue umbrella". J. Prelutsky.—PrBe
Bread and cherries. W. De La Mare.—DeR—MaP
"Chick, chick, chatterman". Unknown.—WiA
Cockles and mussels. Unknown.—ElW
Drinking water coconut. G. Nichols.—NiCo
The fairy-pedlar's song. From Crossings. W. De La Mare.—DeR
How to sell things. G. Soto.—SoA
"Idaho Rose, dressed in polka dot clothes". J. Prelutsky.—PrBe
"If I'd as much money as I could spend". Mother Goose.—WaM
"In just-spring". E. E. Cummings.—ElW
Jim Whitehead. M. C. Livingston.—LiR

Lemonade stand. M. C. Livingston.—KeT
Market women. D. Myrie.—LeCa
Martine Provencal. M. Glenn.—GlBc
"Una mexicana". Unknown.—YoS
Old Joe Jones. L. E. Richards.—KeT
The pedlar. W. De La Mare.—DeR
Pigeons and peanuts for sale. N. Mellage.—SlM
"Scrub weel yer fresh fish". From Fishermen's songs. Unknown.—OpT
The seller. E. Greenfield.—GrN
"Simple Simon met a pieman". Mother Goose.—EdGl—SuO—WaM
"Smiling girls, rosy boys". Mother Goose.—WaM
Pedlar's song .—OpT
The song of the banana man. E. Jones.—LeCa
"Still it was nice". L. Clifton.—ElW
Times Square shoeshine competition. M. Angelou.—MoR
Tinker man. Unknown.—MoR
The used carpet salesman. J. Yolen.—YoBe
Pederson, Cynthia S.
Pogoing.—MoR
The **pedlar**. Walter De La Mare.—DeR
Pedlar's song . See "Smiling girls, rosy boys"
Pegasus. Eleanor Farjeon.—WhDd
The **pelican** chorus. Edward Lear.—CaB—WhAa
Pelicanaries. J. Patrick Lewis.—LeA
"**Pelicanaries** are homely birds". See Pelicanaries
Pelicans
The beak of the pelican. J. P. Lewis.—LeA
The pelican chorus. E. Lear.—CaB—WhAa
The **pen**. Muhammad Al-Ghuzzi, tr. by May Jayyusi and John Heath-Stubbs.—NyT
Pencils. Barbara Juster Esbensen.—EsW
Pencils and pens
Eraser. E. Merriam.—MeS
The flying pen. E. Merriam.—MeS
"If you find a little feather". B. S. De Regniers.—HoT—MoS
"My head doth ache". Unknown.—OpI
The pen. M. Al-Ghuzzi.—NyT
Pencils. B. J. Esbensen.—EsW
"September is". B. Katz.—MoS
Ways of composing. E. Merriam.—MeS
Pendleton, Denise
Ice fishing.—KnAs
Penguin ("I think it must be very nice"). William Jay Smith.—SmL
The **penguin** ("The penguin isn't meat, fish or bird"). Ricardo Yanez, tr. by Raul Aceves and Arturo Suarez and Jane Taylor.—NyT
"The **penguin** isn't meat, fish or bird". See The penguin
Penguins
Enigma sartorial. L. W. Rhu.—WhAa
Penguin ("I think it must be very nice"). W. J. Smith.—SmL
The penguin ("The penguin isn't meat, fish or bird"). R. Yanez.—NyT
Penguins. J. P. Lewis.—LeA
Penguins. J. Patrick Lewis.—LeA
Penn, William
"O God, help us not to despise or oppose".—StP
The **penny** owing. Walter De La Mare.—DeR
Pens. See Pencils and pens
People. See also Crowds; Human race
People—**portraits**. See also Boys and boyhood; Girls and girlhood
About old people. J. Little.—LiHe
Airport. X. J. Kennedy.—KeK
Anyone seen my. M. Fatchen.—PrFo
The ass in the lion's skin. Aesop.—CaB

People—portraits—women—*Continued*

A glass of beer. J. Stephens.—ElW
Granny ("Granny had a way with fruit trees"). A. Bryan.—BrS
Gus. P. B. Janeczko.—JaB
"Her eyes in sleep". Unknown.—GoU
How can I lose hope. From Sing a softblack poem. Kwelismith.—SuC
"I am created in the image of God". E. Tapia.—StP
"I cannot remember all the times he hit me". J. Carson.—CaS
"I want to tell". J. Carson.—CaS
In the mirror. M. Robinson.—LiPg
Joan Benoit. R. Ferrarelli.—KnAs
Learning to read. From Sketches of southern life. F. E. W. Harper.—SuC
Long, long ago. A. Nowlan.—BoT
Lovelocks. W. De La Mare.—DeR
Lucia. L. Casalinuovo.—NyT
Mamaw and Frank. W. Burt.—JaPr
Market women. D. Myrie.—LeCa
Maud. M. Swander.—JaM
Morning athletes. M. Piercy.—KnAs
Mrs. Krikorian. S. Olds.—JaPr
Mrs. MacQueen. W. De La Mare.—DeR—MaP
Mrs. Morizawa's morning. X. J. Kennedy.—KeK
The new lady barber at Ralph's Barber Shop. L. Dangel.—JaM
Night garden with ladies. D. Stein.—GoT
Ode to La Llorona. G. Soto.—SoNe
Old Mag. J. Hollingsworth-Barkley.—JaPr
"On the mountain is a woman". Unknown.—ScA
One for one. J. Heynen.—JaPr
Our grandmothers. M. Angelou.—AnI
Part IX: There was an old woman who lived in the Fens. From A child's day. W. De La Mare.—DeR
Patches of sky. D. Greger.—SuI
The poet ("Before he moved in with Miss Perry"). P. B. Janeczko.—JaB
Poor Miss ("Lone and alone she lies"). W. De La Mare.—DeR—MaP
Portrait, my wife. J. Holmes.—GoU
Pumping iron. D. Ackerman.—KnAs
Reverend Mona. P. B. Janeczko.—JaB
"Ride a cockhorse to Banbury Cross". Mother Goose.—SuO—WaM
Sam's world. S. Cornish.—LiPm
Secrets ("She slits empty feed sacks"). L. Schandelmeier.—JaPr
Seven women's blessed assurance. M. Angelou.—AnI
Sister ("You said red hair made you"). M. Lowery.—JaPr
Softball dreams. K. Kevorkian.—KnAs
Sonja Henie Sonnet. E. Field.—KnAs
A story about Afiya. J. Berry.—BeW
The sugar lady. F. Asch.—DeT
"There was a young lady named Groat". W. J. Smith.—SmL
"There was an old lady named Brown". W. J. Smith.—SmL
"There was an old lady named Hart". W. J. Smith.—LiLo—SmL
"There was an old woman lived under a hill". Mother Goose.—WaM
To those of my sisters who kept their naturals. G. Brooks.—SuC
"Violet picks bluebells". E. Merriam.—MeY
Whiskers meets Polly. M. Stillman.—KeT
A widow's weeds. W. De La Mare.—DeR—MaP

Winner ("Mrs. Macey worked behind"). P. B. Janeczko.—JaB
"A woman named Mrs. S. Claus". J. P. Lewis.—LiLo
Women are different. M. Prescod.—AgL
Women's tug of war at Lough Arrow. T. Gallagher.—KnAs

People—size

Basketball. N. Giovanni.—DeT
Big and little. W. J. Smith.—SmL
Big Gumbo. W. J. Smith.—SmL
Big little boy. E. Merriam.—DeS
Big Saul Fein. X. J. Kennedy.—KeK
Billy Ray Smith. O. Nash.—KnAs
Elevation. R. Morgan.—JaM
"Fat and Skinny had a race". Unknown.—WiA
The fat black woman's motto on her bedroom door. G. Nichols.—AgL
"Fat, fat, the water rat". Unknown.—ScA
A fat poem. G. Nichols.—AgL
"Fatty, fatty, boom a latty". Unknown.—PrP
He was so little. J. Little.—LiHe
"Here I stand all fat and chunky". Unknown.—ScA
"I had a little brother". Unknown.—PrP—WiA
"I had a little husband". Mother Goose.—WaM
"I would reduce". Unknown.—ScA
"Jack Hall". Unknown.—PrP
"Jerry Hall". Mother Goose.—ClI—ScA
"K is for plump little Kate". Unknown.—LiLo
Lanky Hank Farrow. H. Witt.—KnAs
Little. D. Aldis.—DeT
Little Dimity. W. J. Smith.—SmL
My sister. M. Mahy.—LiLo—MaN
"Nicholas Narrow, tall and thin". J. Prelutsky.—PrBe
Of necessity, Weeb jokes about his height. C. H. Webb.—JaPr
A rash stipulation. Unknown.—OpT
The reluctant hero or barefoot in the snow. M. Mahy.—MaN
Say goodbye to Big Daddy. R. Jarrell.—KnAs
"Skinny bone, skinny bone". Unknown.—ScA
"Skinny, skinny, run for your life". Unknown.—WiA
The sleeper. E. Field.—KnAs
"There once was a girl of New York". C. Monkhouse.—LiLo
"There was a fat lady from Eye". Unknown.—LiLo
"There was a maid on Scrabble Hill". Mother Goose.—SuO
"There was a young damsel of Lynn". Unknown.—LiLo
"There was a young lady named Flo". Unknown.—LiLo
"There was a young lady of Lynn". Unknown.—LiLo
"There was an old fellow named Green". Unknown.—LiLo
"There was an old maid of Berlin". E. Gordon.—LiLo
"There was an old man of the Nore". Unknown.—LiLo
"There was an old person of Dutton". E. Lear.—LiLo
"There was once a young fellow of Wall". M. C. Livingston.—LiLo
"There was once a young woman of Oporta". L. Carroll.—LiLo
Uncle Fred. M. Fatchen.—FaCm

People—size—*Continued*
  What Saundra said about being short. J. Hall.—
    JaM
  Wilt Chamberlain. R. R. Knudson.—KnAs
People. William Jay Smith.—SmL
"People always say to me". See The question
People of gleaming cities, and of the lion's and the
    leopard's brood. Sharon Bourke.—SuC
"The people of Neet have triangular feet". See Neet
    people
"People say the chameleon can take on the hue".
    See The chameleon
"People sprinting to and fro". See Airport
"The people who keep losing things". See Anyone
    seen my
"People who know tigers". See How to tell a tiger
Pepper tree. Gary Soto.—SoA
Perez, Tony
  Brownout.—NyT
  Volunteer worker.—NyT
"The perfect ice of the thin keys must break". See
    Piano
The perfect reactionary. Hughes Mearns.—PrFo
Perfection
  "And what is so rare as a day in June". From The
    vision of Sir Launfal. J. R. Lowell.—SuI
  The deacon's masterpiece, or, the wonderful one-
    hoss shay. O. W. Holmes.—ElW
  Some things don't make any sense at all. J.
    Viorst.—DeT
Perkins, Useni Eugene
  Ayo.—SlM
  Ballad of John Henry.—SlM
  Black is beautiful.—SlM
  "Hey black child".—SlM
  "Little soul sister".—SlM
  Martin Luther King, Jr.—SlM
  Nationhood.—SlM
Perry, Phyllis J.
  Halloween ("Hooting howling hissing witches").—
    BaH
Perryman, Kevin
  Improvisation.—NyT
  The open shutter, tr.—NyT
Perseverance
  Another mountain. A. Oyewole.—SlM
  Dreams. L. Hughes.—LoFh—SlM
  Kick and live. G. W. Porter.—SlM
  Mother to son. L. Hughes.—DeT—SlM—SuC
  "Moving right along". A. Oyewole.—SlM
  "Say not the struggle nought availeth". A. H.
    Clough.—ElW
  74th street. M. C. Livingston.—JaP
  Try, try again. T. H. Palmer.—SuI
  Upon the snail. J. Bunyan.—CaB
A person in Spain. N. M. Bodecker.—LiLo
A person in Stirling. N. M. Bodecker.—LiLo
The personable porcupine. Wilbur G. Howcroft.—
  CoAz
Personal beauty. See Beauty, personal
A personal experience. Oliver Herford.—LiLo
Pessimism. See Despair; Melancholy; Points of view
Pet rock. Cynthia Rylant.—JaP
The petal. Ryukyo, tr. by Tze-si Huang.—DeI
"A petal lightly dropped". See The petal
"Pete and repeat were walking down". See Endless
    riddle
Pete at the zoo. Gwendolyn Brooks.—HoT—KeT
"Peter, Peter, pumpkin eater". Mother Goose.—
  EdGl—SuO—WaM
"Peter Piper picked a peck of pickled peppers".
  Mother Goose.—EdGl—SuO

"If Peter Piper picked a peck of pickled
    peppers".—WiA
"Peter went, and nobody there". See The sea body
"Peter White will ne'er go right". Mother Goose.—
  WaM
"Peter's Pop kept a lollipop shop". Unknown.—OpI
Petrified minute. Zoltan Zelk, tr. by Barbara
    Howes.—NyT
Pets. See also Animals; also names of pets, as Cats
  Aquarium. V. Worth.—WoAl
  The bird set free. W. De La Mare.—DeR
  The black snake. P. Hubbell.—HoT
  Captive bird. Boethius.—CaB
  The christening ("What shall I call"). A. A.
    Milne.—LaM
  David's mouse. P. Hubbell.—LaM
  George's pet. M. Mahy.—MaN
  Goldfish ("I have four fish with poppy eyes"). A.
    Fisher.—MoS
  Hot dog. S. Silverstein.—PrFo
  Houseboat mouse. C. Sullivan.—SuI
  "I dribbled catsup on my pet". J. Prelutsky.—PrP
  I had a cat. Unknown.—ClI
  I have a lion. K. Kuskin.—DeS
  "I made my dog a valentine". J. Prelutsky.—LoFh
  "I thought I'd take my rat to school". C.
    McNaughton.—PrFo
  "In the pet store Roscoe Rice". X. J. Kennedy.—
    KeFb
  A kitten ("A kitten, a black one"). A. Fisher.—
    LaCc
  The light house keeper's white mouse. J. Ciardi.—
    LaM—MoS
  "Little Tim Sprat". Unknown.—ClI
  Man and owl. J. Aiken.—LiIf
  "Mary had a little bear". Unknown.—PrP
  Mary's lamb. S. J. Hale.—SuI
    "Mary had a little lamb".—EdGl (unat.)—
      SuO (unat.)—WaM (unat.)
  The meadow mouse. T. Roethke.—LaM
  Missing. A. A. Milne.—LaM
  "Mother doesn't want a dog". J. Viorst.—WhAa
  My brother Bert. T. Hughes.—ElW
  My stupid parakeet named after you. X. J.
    Kennedy.—KeK
  "Old Mother Hubbard". Mother Goose.—EdGl—
    SuO—WaM
  The personable porcupine. W. G. Howcroft.—
    CoAz
  Pet rock. C. Rylant.—JaP
  Pets. D. Pettiward.—CoAz
  Scribbled notes picked up by owners, and
    rewritten because of bad grammar, bad spelling,
    bad writing. J. Berry.—BeW
  "There was a man, now please take note".
    Unknown.—PrP
  Tiny Tony and his pony. C. West.—PrFo
  Turtle ("We found him down at Turtle Creek").
    M. C. Livingston.—LiR
  "What if". B. S. De Regniers.—DeW
Pets. Daniel Pettiward.—CoAz
"Pets are the hobby of my brother Bert". See My
    brother Bert
Pettersson, Aline
  Cuernavaca, tr. by Judith Infante.—NyT
Pettit, Michael
  Celestial.—JaM
  Driving lesson.—JaM
The pettitoes. Unknown.—ClI
"The pettitoes are little feet". See The pettitoes
Pettiward, Daniel
  Pets.—CoAz

"Petulance is purple". See Spectrum
"Petulant priests, greedy". See Savior
The **phantom** ("Upstairs in the large closet, child"). Walter De La Mare.—DeR
The **phantom** ("Wilt thou never come again"). Walter De La Mare.—DeR
Phantoms. See Ghosts
The **pheasant.** Buson, tr. by Tze-si Huang.—DeI
"A **pheasant** flew up". See Surprise
Philander. Theodore Roethke.—LiLo
Philip, Harry
  Rosh Hashanah eve.—LoFh
Phillips, Louis
  The elephant ("Of all the facts about mammals").—CoAz
Phoenix
  The phoenix. P. Fleischman.—WhDd
  The phoenix. Paul Fleischman.—WhDd
The **photograph.** Barbara Drake.—KnAs
Photograph of Managua. From Nicaragua libre. June Jordan.—AgL
Photographs and photography
  The finish. D. Hoffman.—KnAs
  The Hongo Store, 29 miles volcano, Hilo, Hawaii. G. K. Hongo.—JaM
  A kinsman. J. W. Miller.—JaM
  Long ago days. M. C. Livingston.—LiT
  Old photograph album, grandfather. B. J. Esbensen.—EsW
  "One click". M. C. Livingston.—LiMh
  The photograph. B. Drake.—KnAs
  Photograph of Managua. From Nicaragua libre. J. Jordan.—AgL
Physicians. See Doctors
Piano. Karl Shapiro.—MoR
Piano recital. Myra Cohn Livingston.—LiR
Pianos
  Music lessons. J. Volmer.—JaPr
  Piano. K. Shapiro.—MoR
  Piano recital. M. C. Livingston.—LiR
  Player piano. J. Updike.—MoR
  When Mom plays just for me. A. H. Wayland.—LiPm
Piche, Jorge D.
  A short story, tr.—NyT
"**Pick** a color". See Urban rainbow
Pick me up. William Jay Smith.—SmL
"**Pick** me up with a pile of blocks". See Pick me up
Pick up your room. Mary Ann Hoberman.—HoFa
"**Pick** up your room, my mother says". See Pick up your room
Pickaback up to bed (". . . to Blanket Fair"). See "Up the wooden hill to Bedfordshire"
"The **pickety** fence". David McCord.—HoS
Pickles
  "Peter Piper picked a peck of pickled peppers". Mother Goose.—EdGl—SuO
    "If Peter Piper picked a peck of pickled peppers".—WiA
The **picnic.** Dorothy Aldis.—HoS
Picnic to the earth. Shuntaro Tanikawa, tr. by Harold Wright.—NyT
Picnics
  Child in a blue linen dress. H. Sorrells.—JaM
  Grape sherbert. R. Dove.—JaM
  Little bush. E. M. Roberts.—LiDd
  Ode to mi parque. G. Soto.—SoNe
  "One little beaver worked hard as can be". J. Knight.—KnT
  "One little hippo brought a blanket". J. Knight.—KnT
  Out of the city. E. Merriam.—MeS

The picnic. D. Aldis.—HoS
Picnic to the earth. S. Tanikawa.—NyT
Supper ("I supped where bloomed the red red rose"). W. De La Mare.—DeR
The tent. W. De La Mare.—DeR
The **picture.** Walter De La Mare.—DeR—MaP
The **picture-book.** Walter De La Mare.—DeR
Pictures. See Painting and pictures; Photographs and photography
Pictures of cats. Karla Kuskin.—LaCc
Pie. Valerie Worth.—WoAl
The **pied** piper of Hamelin, complete. Robert Browning.—ElW
The **pied** piper of Hamelin, sels. Robert Browning
  "Hamelin Town's in Brunswick".—CaB
Piercy, Marge
  Gracious goodness.—ElW
  Morning athletes.—KnAs
Pies. See also Desserts; Food and eating
  A—Apple pie. W. De La Mare.—DeR
  "Baby and I". Mother Goose.—PrP—WaM
  Defiance. Unknown.—OpT
  "Lancelot, the scurvy knave". X. J. Kennedy.—KeFb
  "Little Jack Horner". Mother Goose.—EdGl—SuO—WaM
  "Me, myself, and I". Unknown.—PrP—WiA
  "Nellie Bligh caught a fly". Unknown.—OpI
  "Oh my, I want a piece of pie". Unknown.—ScA
    "Ooo-ah, wanna piece of pie".—CoM
  "P-U-N-kin". Mother Goose.—WaM
  Pie. V. Worth.—WoAl
  "Possum pie is made of rye". Unknown.—WiA
  "The Queen of Hearts". Mother Goose.—EdGl—SuO
  Rocky Mountains, Colorado. M. C. Livingston.—LiNe
  "Round about, round about". Mother Goose.—WaM
  "Simple Simon met a pieman". Mother Goose.—EdGl—SuO—WaM
  "Sing a song of sixpence". Mother Goose.—EdGl—SuO—WaM
  "St. Thomas's Day is past and gone". Mother Goose.—WaM
  "There was an old lady of Rye". Unknown.—LiLo
  Twelve pies. J. Yolen.—YoHa
Pig ("The pig is bigger"). Valerie Worth.—WoAl
Pig ("Pigs are always awfully dirty"). William Jay Smith.—SmL
"The **pig** is bigger". See Pig
A **pig** tale. James Reeves.—DeS
"The **pig** was first seen by the men at Gillis Mill". See The terrible pig
Pigeon and wren. Unknown.—CaB
"The **pigeon** shed". See Pigeons
Pigeon toed pigeons. William Jay Smith.—SmL
"**Pigeon** toed pigeons on the grass, alas". See Pigeon toed pigeons
Pigeons
  Doves. Masahito.—DeI
  "I had two pigeons bright and gay". Mother Goose.—WaM
  "I'd like to have a purple pigeon". From What we said sitting making fantasies. J. Berry.—BeW
  June, mourning doves. M. C. Livingston.—LiT
  Light rain, a downpour, and pigeons feasting on crumbs from a picnic in the park. E. Merriam.—MeP
  The miller and his son. W. De La Mare.—DeR
  "Mrs. Peck Pigeon". E. Farjeon.—DeS

Play.—*Continued*
A southern circular saying. Unknown.—WiA
"The spades go tulips together". Unknown.—CoM
Spring thaw. M. Vinz.—JaP
Stickball. C. Sullivan.—MoA
Story without end. Unknown.—WiA
Summer doings. W. Cole.—HoGo
Sunflakes. F. Asch.—DeS—MoS
The swing ("How do you like to go up in a swing"). R. L. Stevenson.—DeS—HoS—KeT—LiDd
"Swing me, swing me, swing me round". E. Merriam.—MeY
Taking down the space-trolley. X. J. Kennedy.—KeK
Things ("Went to the corner"). E. Greenfield.—SIM
"Tid, mid, misere". Unknown.—OpI
Timmy and Tawanda. G. Brooks.—SIM
To a squirrel at Kyle-na-no. W. B. Yeats.—DeS—LiDd
"Tra-la-la-boom-de-ay". Unknown.—CoM
Transformations. T. Rozewicz.—NyT
Tree house. S. Silverstein.—DeS
"Trois fois passera". Unknown.—YoS
   "Three times by she passes".—YoS
"Under the bamboo, under the tree". Unknown.—CoM
"Up the ladder and down the wall". Unknown.—OpI
Vistasp. G. Patel.—NyT
Walking with Jackie, sitting with a dog. G. Soto.—JaPr
What Johnny told me. J. Ciardi.—KeT
Whenever. M. A. Hoberman.—MoS
Where go the boats. R. L. Stevenson.—ElW—KeT
"Zui zui zukkorobashi". Unknown.—YoS
"Play moonlight". See Crab dance
"A player, name of Wambsganss". See Wamby or the nostalgic record book
Player piano. John Updike.—MoR
The **playhouse.** Kate Daniels.—JaPr
Playing dirty. Max Fatchen.—FaCm
"Playing on the harp and". See Angel tunes
Playing stickball with Robbie Shea. Mark Lukeman.—MoA
"Playing upon the hill three centaurs were". See The centaurs
Playmate ("And because"). Keith Wilson.—JaPr
The **playmate** ("Weep no more, nor grieve, nor sigh"). Walter De La Mare.—DeR
Playoff pizza. Sharon Bell Mathis.—MaR
Please. Judith Thurman.—MoS
"Please, how does one spell definite". See Inquisitiveness
"Please, Lord, send summat good to eat". From Dinner table rhymes. Unknown.—OpT
"Please Mum please". See Skateboard flyer
"Please please what is your pleasure". See Itinerant
"Please snow cloud". See Please
Please to remember ("He comes to see us every year"). Geoffrey Holloway.—FoLe
Please to remember ("Here am I"). Walter De La Mare.—DeR
"Please to remember the fifth of November". Unknown.—OpI
Plenty-Coups
We chased butterflies.—SnD
Plomer, William
Anglo-Swiss, or a day among the Alps, sels.
   "Away she flies and he follows".—MoR

"Away she flies and he follows". See Anglo-Swiss, or a day among the Alps
Plotz, John R.
Lullaby ("Cat's in the alley").—PlW
Plumly, Stanley
Karate.—KnAs
"Plump Mrs. Brown, we may suppose". See Esmeralda (for a picture)
"Plunk a plunk, plunk a plunk". See Banjo tune
Pockets. Aileen Fisher.—FiH
Pods pop and grin. James Berry.—BeW
Poe, Edgar Allan
Annabel Lee.—ElW
The bells, complete.—MoR
The bells, sels.
   "Hear the sledges with the bells".—GoA
Eldorado.—MoR
"Hear the sledges with the bells". See The bells
The raven.—SuI
Poem ("As the cat"). William Carlos Williams.—MoR
Poem ("I loved my friend"). Langston Hughes.—DeS—DeT—SIM
Poem ("If I write"). Robert Currie.—JaP
The **poem** as a door. Eve Merriam.—MeS
Poem at thirty. Sonia Sanchez.—SuC
A **poem** for a pickle. Eve Merriam.—MeP
A **poem** for Magic. Quincy Troupe.—SIM
Poem for my son. Bibhu Padhi.—NyT
Poem II. From Twenty-one love poems. Adrienne Rich.—GoU
The **poem** that got away. Felice Holman.—JaP
Poem III. From Twenty-one love poems. Adrienne Rich.—GoU
"The poem's a ball". See Verse play
"Poems can give you". Sandra Bogart.—BoT
The **poet** ("Before he moved in with Miss Perry"). Paul B. Janeczko.—JaB
Poet ("Listen, I'm talking in stumbles and bumps"). X. J. Kennedy.—KeK
The **poet** speaks. John Henrik Clarke.—SIM
Poetry ("I too, dislike it, there are things that are important"). Marianne Moore.—SuI
Poetry ("What is poetry, who knows"). Eleanor Farjeon.—ElW
Poetry lesson number one. Wanda Coleman.—JaPr
"The poetry of earth is never dead". See On the grasshopper and cricket
Poetry was like this. Al Mahmud, tr. by Kabir Chowdhury.—NyT
"Poetry was the memory of adolescence". See Poetry was like this
Poets and poetry. See also names of poets, as Shakespeare, William (about); also names of verse forms, as Limericks
About poems, sort of. J. Little.—LiHe
After English class. J. Little.—LiHe
"All this time and at all times wait the words of true poems". From Song of myself. W. Whitman.—HoVo
And then. P. Redcloud.—HoGo
"Beneath a shady tree they sat". Unknown.—ScA
Catch ("Two boys uncoached are tossing a poem together"). R. Francis.—KnAs
"Coils the robot". F. H. Pinto.—NyT
"A decrepit old gasman, named Peter". Unknown.—LiLo
Dreamers and flyers. J. LaBombard.—JaM
Fireworks 2. E. Merriam.—MeS
Flying kites. Q. Troupe.—SIM
Freedom. W. Dissanayake.—NyT
The gatherer. A. Al-Mak.—NyT

Prayers.—*Continued*

"Give to us eyes". Unknown.—StP

"Give us a pure heart". D. Hammarskjold.—StP

"Give us grateful hearts, our Father". Unknown.—StP

"Glory to thee, glory to thee, O Lord". Dadu.—StP

"Go well and safely". Unknown.—StP

"God before me, God behind me". Unknown.—StP

"God bless all those that I love". Unknown.—StP

"God bless us, every one". C. Dickens.—StP

"God is, I know that". Unknown.—StP

"God is light". Unknown.—StP

"Good Lord, help me to win if I may". Unknown.—StP

"Goosey goosey gander". Mother Goose.—EdGl—SuO—WaM

"Great and merciful God". A. O'Grady.—StP

"Great spirit". From Warrior nation trilogy. L. Henson.—SuI

"Have mercy on me, o beneficent one". Unknown.—StP

"He prayeth best, who loveth best". From The rime of the ancient mariner. S. T. Coleridge.—StP

"Hear me, four quarters of the world". Black Elk.—StP

"Heavenly Father, bless us". Unknown.—StP

"Holy, holy, holy Lord, God of power and might". Unknown.—StP

"Hoping is knowing that there is love". Unknown.—StP

"I am here, Lord". J. M. Burns.—StP

"I am small". Unknown.—StP

"I arise today". Saint Patrick.—StP

"I find thee throned in my heart". A. MacLean.—StP

"I have a secret joy in Thee, my God". A. MacLean.—StP

"I see the moon". Unknown.—StP

"In my little bed I lie". Unknown.—StP

"In the name of God". Unknown.—StP

"In Tsegihi". Unknown.—StP

"It is God, the creator, the gracious one". Unknown.—StP

"Jesus Christ, thou child so wise". H. Belloc.—StP

"Keep us, O Lord, as the apple of your eye". Unknown.—StP

"Keep watch, dear Lord, with those who work". Saint Augustine.—StP

"Kum by yah, my Lord". Unknown.—StP

"Let my thoughts and words please you, Lord". J. M. Burns.—StP

"Let the words of my mouth and the". From The book of psalms. Bible/Old Testament.—StP

"Let us dedicate ourselves to what the Greeks". R. Kennedy.—StP

"Let us in peace eat the food". Unknown.—StP

"Let us praise and thank God for all great and". Unknown.—StP

Listen, Lord—a prayer. J. W. Johnson.—SuC

"The Lord bless us, and keep us". From The book of numbers. Bible/Old Testament.—StP

"Lord, help me to find the good and praise it". Unknown.—StP

"Lord, isn't your creation wasteful". H. Camara.—StP

"Lord of the springtime, father of flower". W. E. B. Du Bois.—StP

"Lord, you made the world and everything in it, you". F. Kaan.—StP

"May all who share". R. Herrick.—StP

"May we, O God, keep ourselves modest". Epictetus.—StP

"My fingers like to say hello". L. W. Johnson.—StP

Noah's prayer. C. B. De Gasztold.—DeP

"Not because we know how to pray". Unknown.—StP

"Not my brother, not my sister". Unknown.—StP

"Now I lay me down to sleep, a bag of peanuts at my feet". Unknown.—ScA—WiA

A nun's prayer. M. Ross.—StP

"O give thanks unto the Lord". From The book of psalms. Bible/Old Testament.—StP

"O God, creator of light, at the rising". Unknown.—StP

"O God, help us not to despise or oppose". W. Penn.—StP

"O God, make speed to save us". Unknown.—StP

"O God, make us able". Unknown.—StP

"O God of light, God of might". D. Adam.—StP

"O God of peace, who has taught us that". Unknown.—StP

"O God that bringest all things to pass". Pindar.—StP

"O God, you have let us pass the day in peace". Unknown.—StP

"O heavenly Father, protect and bless". A. Schweitzer.—StP

"O high and glorious God". Saint Francis of Assisi.—StP

"O Lord, grant us to love Thee, grant that we may love". Mohammed.—StP

"O Lord, help me to greet the coming day in peace". Unknown.—StP

"O Lord, my day's work is over, bless all". Unknown.—StP

"O Lord, support us all the day long, until". Unknown.—StP

"O Lord, the meal is steaming before us". Unknown.—StP

"O Lord, Thou knowest how". J. Astley.—StP

"O my soul's healer, keep me at evening". Unknown.—StP

"O our mother the earth, O our father the sky". Unknown.—StP

"Oh, the Lord is good to me". J. Chapman.—StP

"O thou great chief, light a candle". Unknown.—StP

"Open thou our lips, O Lord, and purify". C. G. Rossetti.—StP

Or. A. Darwish.—NyT

"Our father, hear us, and our grandfather, I mention also". Unknown.—StP

"Our Father in heaven". From The gospel according to Matthew. Bible/New Testament.—StP

"Our Pacific islands are yours, O Lord". B. Narokobi.—StP

"Please, Lord, send summat good to eat". From Dinner table rhymes. Unknown.—OpT

"Praised be my Lord God for all his creatures". Saint Francis of Assisi.—StP

Prayer ("Now I lay me down to sleep"). Unknown.—HoS

The prayer of the cat. C. B. De Gasztold.—DeP

The prayer of the cock. C. B. De Gasztold.—DeP

The prayer of the dog. C. B. De Gasztold.—DeP

The prayer of the donkey. C. B. De Gasztold.—DeP

The prayer of the dove. C. B. De Gasztold.—DeP

Prelutsky, Jack—*Continued*
"Four fat goats upon a boat".—PrBe
"Four furry seals, four funny fat seals".—CoAz
Ghost.—BaH
The goblin.—KeT
Help ("Can anybody tell me, please").—PrFo
The house mouse.—LaM
I am flying.—BaW
"I do not mind you, winter wind".—BaW
"I dribbled catsup on my pet".—PrP
"I had a little secret".—PrBe
"I made my dog a valentine".—LoFh
"I met a dragon face to face".—HoGo
"I went to Wisconsin".—PrBe
"Idaho Rose, dressed in polka dot clothes".—PrBe
"If you have got a funnybone".—PrFo
Iguanodon.—PrT
"In a Mississippi valley".—PrBe
"In downtown Philadelphia".—PrBe
"Jason Johnson left New Jersey".—PrBe
"Jellyfish stew".—PrFo
"Jennifer Juniper, where do you walk".—PrBe
"Jiggity jumpity jog".—PrBe
"John Poole left Sedalia".—PrBe
"Johnny squeezed a concertina".—PrBe
Leptopterygius.—PrT
Long gone.—WhAa
"My mother says I'm sickening".—PrFo
"Nicholas Narrow, tall and thin".—PrBe
"Oh farmer, poor farmer, you're surely".—PrBe
"One foggy autumn in Baltimore".—PrBe
The pancake collector.—PrFo
"Patter pitter caterpillar".—PrBe
"Polly saw a butterfly".—PrBe
Quetzalcoatlus.—PrT
"Red bug, yellow bug, little blue".—PrBe
"Rickety pickety".—PrBe
"Robin spied a chubby worm".—PrBe
Seismosaurus.—PrT
"Seven piglets, pink and gray".—PrBe
"A silly young fellow named Ben".—LiLo—PrP
The spaghetti nut.—DeS
"Spaghetti, spaghetti".—MoS
Stegosaurus.—PrT
"Tailor had a needle".—PrBe
"There's someone I know".—DeS
"Tippity toppity, upside down Roy".—PrBe
Triceratops.—PrT
Tyrannosaurus ("Tyrannosaurus was a beast").—PrT
"An unassuming owl".—LiIf
"The underwater wibbles".—JaP
"Victor wore a velvet cape".—PrBe
"We each wore half a horse".—FoLe
We heard Wally wail.—JaP
"What happens to the colors".—PlW
The witch ("She comes by night, in fearsome flight").—DeT
Yak ("Yickity yackity, yickity yak").—WhAa
Premonitions. See Omens; Prophecies
Preparedness. Felicia Lamport.—KnAs
Preposterous. Jim Hall.—JaPr
Prescod, Marsha
Women are different.—AgL
Presents. See Gifts and giving
Presents ("Maybe"). Valerie Worth.—WoA
Presents ("My friends all gave me presents"). Myra Cohn Livingston.—LiBp
"A **pretentious** old man of the Bosporus". See A bright idea
"**Pretty** brown baby". Karama Fufuka.—SlM
"**Pretty** flowers bloomin". See Good flower blues

Pretty is. Ashley Bryan.—BrS
A **pretty** little hand ("How pretty, how little"). See "Que linda manito"
Previn, Dory
"Did Jesus have a baby sister".—AgL
"**Priam** on one side sending forth eleven". From Watching football on TV. Howard Nemerov.—KnAs
Price, Christine
Okolo the leopard warrior.—WhDd
Price, David Watkin
Saint David's Day.—FoLe
A **prickly** phone call. X. J. Kennedy.—KeGh
Pride
"Aw, lemme tell you". J. Carson.—CaS
Black is beautiful. U. E. Perkins.—SlM
Color. L. Hughes.—SlM
"Come times sometimes". J. Carson.—CaS
"Fine black kinfolk". D. K. Hru.—SlM
"First come I, my name is Jowett". Unknown.—OpI
Hamilton Greene. E. L. Masters.—ElW
"Have mercy on me, o beneficent one". Unknown.—StP
"It's not me". J. Carson.—CaS
Ka 'Ba. I. A. Baraka.—SuC
"A lady who lives there close to me". J. Carson.—CaS
Mamaw and Frank. W. Burt.—JaPr
Marvin Pickett. M. Glenn.—KnAs
Monster mothers. F. P. Heide.—HeG
My father's words. C. Lewis.—LiPf
My people. L. Hughes.—SlM
The mysterious cat. V. Lindsay.—DeS—LaCc
Ode to weight lifting. G. Soto.—SoNe
Ozymandias. P. B. Shelley.—ElW
People of gleaming cities, and of the lion's and the leopard's brood. S. Bourke.—SuC
Photograph of Managua. From Nicaragua libre. J. Jordan.—AgL
Pride. D. Ravikovitch.—NyT
So I'm proud. J. Little.—LiHe
To those of my sisters who kept their naturals. G. Brooks.—SuC
"An unassuming owl". J. Prelutsky.—LiIf
Winner ("What I remember most"). G. Fehler.—MoA
Pride. Dahlia Ravikovitch, tr. by Chana Bloch and Ariel Bloch.—NyT
Pridmore, Jane
In the dark.—BaH
The **prince.** Walter De La Mare.—DeR
Prince Rama comes to Longsight. John Cunliffe.—FoLe
Princes and princesses
Goose-wing chariot. Unknown.—OpT
"I had a little nut tree". Mother Goose.—EdGl—SuO
I met at eve. W. De La Mare.—DeR
The owl ("Once I was a monarch's daughter"). Unknown.—OpT
The prince. W. De La Mare.—DeR
The princess and the frog. S. C. Field.—BaH
The song of the mad prince. W. De La Mare.—DeR—ElW—MaP
The **princess** and the frog. Susan Cohen Field.—BaH
"A **princess** kissed a frog one day". See The princess and the frog
"**Printing** ideograms". See Calgary
Prism in the window. From Four poems for Roy G Biv. Barbara Juster Esbensen.—EsW

The **prison** cell. Mahmud Darwish, tr. by Ben Bennani.—NyT

Prisons and prisoners
  Behind bars. F. Tuqan.—NyT
  Locked in. I. Leckius.—NyT
  The prison cell. M. Darwish.—NyT
  Southern road. S. A. Brown.—SuC
  Tending the garden. E. Pankey.—JaM
  To sit in solemn silence. W. S. Gilbert.—MoR

Professions. See names of professions, as Doctors

A **professor** called Chesterton. William Schwenck Gilbert.—LiLo

Progress
  Alabama centennial. N. Madgett.—SuC
  The closing of the rodeo. W. J. Smith.—KnAs
  "The first time I sat in a restaurant". J. Carson.—CaS
  Houses. M. B. Miller.—DeS
  "It's changing here". J. Carson.—CaS
  Kansas visit. M. C. Livingston.—LiNe
  New mother. R. H. Marks.—LiPm
  The new negro. J. E. McCall.—SuC
  "Oh my good Lord, I am not a young man anymore". J. Carson.—CaS
  "One day". J. Carson.—CaS
  Progress. G. E. Lyon.—JaM
  Question and answer. L. Hughes.—SuC
  Remodeling the hermit's cabin. F. Chappell.—JaM
  "See, steamers steaming through my poems". From Starting from Paumanok. W. Whitman.—HoVo
  "You can always tell a tourist town". J. Carson.—CaS

Progress. George Ella Lyon.—JaM

Promises
  "Hangy Bangy cut my throat". Unknown.—OpI
  "My finger's wet". Unknown.—OpI
  Nocturne ("A long arm embossed with gold slides from the tree tops"). L.-P. Fargue.—GoT
  The pied piper of Hamelin, complete. R. Browning.—ElW
  "Preacher, don't send me". M. Angelou.—AnI
  Stopping by woods on a snowy evening. R. Frost.—DeS—DeT—ElW—SuI
  "Walk together children". From Walk together children. Unknown.—SuC
  The wind is from the north. R. Hillyer.—GoT
  The yes and the no, Redondo. G. Pape.—JaPr

Prophecies. See also Omens
  Gambler. E. Stuckey.—AgL
  Glass eye Harry Coote. P. B. Janeczko.—JaB
  "Mother, mother, bless my soul". X. J. Kennedy.—KeFb
  The raven. E. A. Poe.—SuI
  "Whistling girls and crowing hens". Unknown.—WiA

Propositions. Nicanor Parra.—AgL

Prose and poetry. Eve Merriam.—MeS

"**Protect** me, O Lord". Unknown.—StP

"**Protected** by thick brick walls". See International ski flying championship, Obersdorf

"**Protector** of pharaohs". See The griffin

A **protest** poem for Rosa Parks. Abiodun Oyewole.—SlM

"**Proud** on his board". See Iron man

"**Proud** woman". See Mamaw and Frank

Proverbs. See also Superstitions
  "April showers". Unknown.—WiA
  "Ask me no questions". Unknown.—WiA

"Because parrots are chatterers people say they are the only ones who eat up the fruits". From Jamaican Caribbean proverbs. Unknown.—BeW

"Befoh yu marry keep two yeye opn, afta yu marry shet one". From Jamaican Caribbean proverbs. Unknown.—BeW

"Berries red, have no dread". Unknown.—ScA

"Birds of a feather flock together". Mother Goose.—WaM
  Birds of a feather.—ClI

"The boaster will make out someone else is the liar". From Jamaican Caribbean proverbs. Unknown.—BeW

"Break master neck but nuh break master law". Unknown.—LeCa

"Call a tiger Master he'll still eat you". From Jamaican Caribbean proverbs. Unknown.—BeW

"Corn knee high". Unknown.—ScA

"A dog's bark isn't going to frighten the moon". From Jamaican Caribbean proverbs. Unknown.—BeW

"The donkey says the world isn't level ground". From Jamaican Caribbean proverbs. Unknown.—BeW

"Don't call an alligator a long-mouth till you have crossed the river". From Jamaican Caribbean proverbs. Unknown.—BeW

"Don't wait until you hear the drum beat before you grind your axe". From Jamaican Caribbean proverbs. Unknown.—BeW

"Every family has its deformity". From Jamaican Caribbean proverbs. Unknown.—BeW

"Finders keepers". Unknown.—CoM—WiA

"Good boy is a fool's nickname". From Jamaican Caribbean proverbs. Unknown.—BeW

"The great fool is as proud as a dog with two tails". From Jamaican Caribbean proverbs. Unknown.—BeW

"He is a clever man who drives away hunger by just working his jaws". From Jamaican Caribbean proverbs. Unknown.—BeW

"If a rooster crows when he goes to bed". Unknown.—WhAa—WiA

"If ifs and ans". Unknown.—OpI

"If nightingale sings too sweetly, jealousy will kill its mother". From Jamaican Caribbean proverbs. Unknown.—BeW

"If wishes were horses". Mother Goose.—WaM

"If you back a monkey he'll fight a tiger". From Jamaican Caribbean proverbs. Unknown.—BeW

"A little axe can cut down a big tree". From Jamaican Caribbean proverbs. Unknown.—BeW

"The man who is all honey, flies are going to eat him up". From Jamaican Caribbean proverbs. Unknown.—BeW

"Many an underfed cow in the pasture is mother of a bull". From Jamaican Caribbean proverbs. Unknown.—BeW

"Monkey see, monkey do". Unknown.—WiA

"The mosquito often goes to the village for syrup but doesn't always get it". From Jamaican Caribbean proverbs. Unknown.—BeW

"The needle makes clothes yet the needle itself is naked". From Jamaican Caribbean proverbs. Unknown.—BeW

"The peacock hides its leg when its tail gets praises". From Jamaican Caribbean proverbs. Unknown.—BeW

Proverbs.—*Continued*
    "Pumpkin neba bear watermelan". Unknown.—LeCa
    "Rain before seven". Unknown.—WiA
    "Rainbow at night, sailor's delight". Unknown.—WiA
    "Red sky at night". Mother Goose.—WaM
    "The rich and the poor do not meet". From Jamaican Caribbean proverbs. Unknown.—BeW
    Rodomontade in the menagerie. E. Merriam.—MeCh
    "Sickness come di gallop, but e tek e own time fo walk' way". Unknown.—LeCa
    "Sticks and stones". Unknown.—CoM—OpI—ScA—WiA
    "A sunshiny shower". Unknown.—WiA
    Two precepts. Unknown.—OpT
    "Two's company". Unknown.—WiA
    "When you see your neighbour's beard on fire, take some water and wet your own". From Jamaican Caribbean proverbs. Unknown.—BeW
    "Whistling girls and crowing hens". Unknown.—WiA
    "Willful waste brings woeful want". Mother Goose.—WaM
    "You live in de cement house, and no worry de hurricane". Unknown.—LeCa
    "You never see a cow that kicks who doesn't produce a calf that kicks". From Jamaican Caribbean proverbs. Unknown.—BeW
The **provident** puffin. Oliver Herford.—LiLo
Psalm 23. See "The Lord is my shepherd, I shall not want"
Psalm 104. From The book of psalms. Bible/Old Testament.—StP
Psalms
    "Let the heavens rejoice, and let the earth be glad". From The book of psalms. Bible/Old Testament.—StP
    "Let the words of my mouth and the". From The book of psalms. Bible/Old Testament.—StP
    "The Lord is my shepherd, I shall not want". From The book of psalms. Bible/Old Testament.—StP
        Psalm 23.—SuC
    "O give thanks unto the Lord". From The book of psalms. Bible/Old Testament.—StP
    "Where can I go then from your spirit". From The book of psalms. Bible/Old Testament.—StP
"The **public** library was saying things". See That girl
Puddles
    "Doctor Foster went to Gloucester". Mother Goose.—SuO—WaM
    "Every time it rained, mean Merl's". X. J. Kennedy.—KeFb
    Getting dirty. D. Charles.—KeT
    "A luckless time-traveler from Lynn". X. J. Kennedy.—KeGh—LiLo
    The muddy puddle. D. Lee.—BoT—MoS
    Puddles. F. Asch.—MoS
Puddles. Frank Asch.—MoS
Puffins
    The provident puffin. O. Herford.—LiLo
    There once was a puffin. F. P. Jacque.—MoS
Pull hitter. R. Gerry Fabian.—MoA
"**Pulling** chair cushions into the garage". See October afternoons we walk around the house
Pumping iron. Diane Ackerman.—KnAs

Pumpkin ("After its lid"). Valerie Worth.—BaH—WoAl
The **pumpkin** ("Ah, on Thanksgiving day, when from east and from west"). John Greenleaf Whittier.—SuI
The **pumpkin** ("You may not believe it, for hardly could I"). Robert Graves.—DeS
"**Pumpkin** neba bear watermelan". Unknown.—LeCa
Pumpkin people. John Ridland.—LiHp
"The **pumpkin** people camp inside". See Pumpkin people
"**Pumpkin**, pumpkin, pumpkin bright". N. M. Bodecker.—LiHp
Pumpkins
    Carving pumpkins with my father. L. Rosenberg.—LiPf
    Hallowe'en ("Tonight is the night"). H. Behn.—LiHp
    It is late. A. Adoff.—AdIn
    Jack. D. Chandra.—LiHp
    Jack-o-lantern. X. J. Kennedy.—KeK
    "P-U-N-kin". Mother Goose.—WaM
    "Peter, Peter, pumpkin eater". Mother Goose.—EdGl—SuO—WaM
    Pumpkin ("After its lid"). V. Worth.—BaH—WoAl
    The pumpkin ("Ah, on Thanksgiving day, when from east and from west"). J. G. Whittier.—SuI
    The pumpkin ("You may not believe it, for hardly could I"). R. Graves.—DeS
    Pumpkin people. J. Ridland.—LiHp
    "Pumpkin, pumpkin, pumpkin bright". N. M. Bodecker.—LiHp
    To pumpkins at pumpkin time. G. Tall.—BaH
    Watchdogs. J. Thomas.—LiHp
"**Punch** and Judy fought for a pie". Unknown.—PrFo
Punch, boys, punch. Unknown.—OpT
Punctuation
    Call the periods, call the commas. K. Dakos.—DaI
    "Charles the First walked and talked". Unknown.—OpI
    "Every lady in the land". Unknown.—OpI
    "I saw a peacock with a fiery tail". Unknown.—ScA
    Parentheses. E. Merriam.—MeCh
    The question mark. G. Emin.—NyT
Punishment
    Don't you remember how sick you are. K. Dakos.—DaI
    The fastest belt in town. G. Nichols.—NiCo
    Go to the Bahamas. K. Dakos.—DaI
    "Little Polly Flinders". Mother Goose.—SuO—WaM
    "Mary Pary Pinder". Unknown.—OpI
    "A nip for new". Unknown.—OpI
    Sales talk for Annie. M. Bishop.—ElW
    "Sing jigmijole, the pudding bowl". Mother Goose.—WaM
    "There was an old woman who lived in a shoe". Mother Goose.—EdGl—SuI—SuO—WaM
    The three little kittens. E. L. Follen.—HoS
        "Three little kittens, they lost their mittens".—SuO (unat.)
        "Three little kittens lost their mittens".—EdGl (unat.)—WaM (unat.)
    "Tom, Tom, the piper's son, stole a pig and away he run". Mother Goose.—SuO—WaM
    We heard Wally wail. J. Prelutsky.—JaP
Puppies. See Dogs

R

Railroads—*Continued*
  Traveling. E. Merriam.—MeS
  What the engines said (the joining of the Union
    Pacific and Central Pacific Railroads, May 10,
    1869). B. Harte.—SuI
  Window ("Night from a railroad car window"). C.
    Sandburg.—DeT

Rain
  April. L. Clifton.—LiDd
  April rain song. L. Hughes.—DeS—ElW—HoS—
    LiDd—SlM—SuI
  "April showers". Unknown.—WiA
  "Bella had a new umbrella". E. Merriam.—PrFo
  City rain. V. Schonborg.—LaN
  Conversation. Buson.—DeS
  "Cried a man on the Salisbury Plain". M. C.
    Livingston.—LiLo
  "Crow on the fence". Unknown.—CaB
  The dark and falling summer. D. Schwartz.—
    GoT—SuI
  A different door. X. J. Kennedy.—LaCc
  "Do ghouls". L. Moore.—PrFo
  "Doctor Foster went to Gloucester". Mother
    Goose.—SuO—WaM
  Esmeralda (for a picture). W. De La Mare.—DeR
  "Farewell, my younger brother". Unknown.—SnD
  Galoshes. R. Bacmeister.—DeS
  Great Aso. T. Miyoshi.—NyT
  "I am the rain". G. Nichols.—NiCo
  "I like it when it's mizzly". A. Fisher.—MoS
  "I polka dot the window". M. C. Livingston.—
    LiMh
  "If a rooster crows when he goes to bed".
    Unknown.—WhAa—WiA
  Improvisation. K. Perryman.—NyT
  "In the night". Unknown.—GoT—LaN
  "In time of silver rain". L. Hughes.—FrS
  It rained in the park today. J. Thurman.—MoS
  "It rains and it pours". A. Lobel.—LiDd
  "It rains, it pains". Unknown.—OpI
  "It's raining, it's pouring". Mother Goose.—
    CoM—OpI—ScA—WiA
  "It's raining, it's raining". Mother Goose.—WaM
  Leaf boats. M. C. Livingston.—LiR
  Light rain, a downpour, and pigeons feasting on
    crumbs from a picnic in the park. E.
    Merriam.—MeP
  "Little frog among". Gaki.—CaR
    Haiku.—DeT
  Little trotty wagtail. J. Clare.—ElW
  Lullaby for a rainy night. B. J. Esbensen.—EsW
  March night. M. C. Livingston.—LiNe
  The mouse ("A mouse is"). Buson.—DeI
  Nicely, nicely. Unknown.—SnD
  Nix on picnics. X. J. Kennedy.—KeGh
  A person in Spain. N. M. Bodecker.—LiLo
  The prayer of the little ducks. C. B. De
    Gasztold.—DeS—StP
  Que llueva. Unknown.—DeA
    It's raining ("It's raining, it's raining").—DeA
  Rain ("How does"). A. Fisher.—FiA
  Rain ("I woke in the swimming dark"). W. De La
    Mare.—DeR
  Rain ("Pitter-pat, pitter-pat"). Unknown.—CoE
  Rain ("The rain is raining all around"). R. L.
    Stevenson.—DeS—ElW—HoS
  Rain ("Summer rain"). M. C. Livingston.—DeS
  Rain, a haiku sequence. M. C. Livingston.—LiR
  "Rain before seven". Unknown.—WiA
  Rain coming. A. Bryan.—BrS
  Rain drops. S. B. Wood.—MoR
  "The rain it raineth all around". Unknown.—OpI

Rain of leaves. A. Fisher.—DeT—FiA
  Rain poem. E. Coatsworth.—DeS
  "Rain, rain, go away". Mother Goose.—DeS—
    EdGl—WiA
  "Rain, rain, go to Spain". Unknown.—ScA
  A rainy day. E. Merriam.—MeP
  Romping in the rain. X. J. Kennedy.—KeK
  Saint Swithin's Day. A. Bonner.—FoLe
  "Showery, flowery". Unknown.—ScA
  "Slippy". Unknown.—ScA
  So dry this July. A. Adoff.—AdIn
  Spring rain. J. P. Lewis.—LeE
  Summer rain. E. Merriam.—MeS
  Summer shower. D. McCord.—KeT
  Sunday at the end of summer. H. Nemerov.—SuI
  "A sunshiny shower". Unknown.—WiA
  10 P.M. M. C. Livingston.—LiNe
  "Thank God for rain". Unknown.—StP
  "There was a young man on a plain". W. J.
    Smith.—SmL
  To the rain. Unknown.—OpI
  To the thawing wind. R. Frost.—ElW
  Waiting for the first drop. R. Souster.—BoT
  Weather ("Dot a dot dot, dot a dot dot"). E.
    Merriam.—DeS—KeT
  Western wind. Unknown.—ElW
  "What did the blackbird say to the crow".
    Unknown.—ScA
  Wildlife refuge. X. J. Kennedy.—KeGh
  "The wind, the wind". Unknown.—ScA
  Windshield wiper. E. Merriam.—MeCh
Rain ("How does"). Aileen Fisher.—FiA
Rain ("I woke in the swimming dark"). Walter De
    La Mare.—DeR
"Rain". See Leaf boats
Rain ("Pitter-pat, pitter-pat"). Unknown.—CoE
Rain ("The rain is raining all around"). Robert
    Louis Stevenson.—DeS—ElW—HoS
Rain ("Summer rain"). Myra Cohn Livingston.—
    DeS
Rain, a haiku sequence. Myra Cohn Livingston.—
    LiR
"Rain before seven". Unknown.—WiA
Rain coming. Ashley Bryan.—BrS
Rain drops. Sallie Burrow Wood.—MoR
"Rain drops spot". See Rain drops
The **rain** falling on west train tracks, Ohio. Arnold
    Adoff.—AdCh
"Rain falling, what things do you grow". See River
    winding
"Rain is good". See April
"The rain is raining all around". See Rain
"The rain it raineth all around". Unknown.—OpI
Rain of leaves. Aileen Fisher.—DeT—FiA
Rain poem. Elizabeth Coatsworth.—DeS
"Rain poured down, the house". See The rescue
"Rain, rain, go away". Mother Goose.—DeS—
    EdGl—WiA
"Rain, rain, go away, come another summer's day".
    See To the rain
"Rain, rain, go to Spain". Unknown.—ScA
"The rain was full of the freshness". See The dark
    and falling summer
"The rain was like a little mouse". See Rain poem
The **rainbow**. Walter De La Mare.—DeR
"Rainbow at night, sailor's delight". Unknown.—
    WiA
Rainbow crow. Nancy Van Laan.—WhDd
Rainbow making, a mystery. From Four poems for
    Roy G Biv. Barbara Juster Esbensen.—EsW
Rainbow making, magic. From Four poems for Roy
    G Biv. Barbara Juster Esbensen.—EsW

Rainbow writing. Eve Merriam.—MeS
Rainbows
  Bubbles. C. Sandburg.—DeT
  The rainbow. W. De La Mare.—DeR
  "Rainbow at night, sailor's delight". Unknown.—
  WiA
  Rainbow making, a mystery. From Four poems
    for Roy G Biv. B. J. Esbensen.—EsW
  Rainbow making, magic. From Four poems for
    Roy G Biv. B. J. Esbensen.—EsW
  Rainbow writing. E. Merriam.—MeS
  "Red and blue and delicate green". Unknown.—
  WiA
  Riddling song. Unknown.—OpT
"Raindrops". See March night
A **rainy** day. Eve Merriam.—MeP
"Raising frogs for profit". Unknown.—PrFo
Raizan
  Don't come out, tr. by Tze-si Huang.—DeI
Raleigh, Sir Walter
  "Give me my scallop shell of quiet".—StP
  The nymph's reply to the shepherd.—ElW
Ramadan. Stanley Cook.—FoLe
"Ramadan". Stanley Cook.—FoLe
"Ran against walls". See Jackie Robinson
Randall, Dudley
  Ballad of Birmingham.—ElW
  A different image.—SuC
  George.—SuC
  The melting pot.—SuC
Ranetsu
  The snail ("The snail sticks out his horn"), tr. by
    Tze-si Huang.—DeI
Rare rhythms. Sara London.—JaM
"Rare-sweet the air in that unimagined country".
  See The unfinished dream
A **rash** stipulation. Unknown.—OpT
Raskin, Ellen
  "Jake, the twin of John Lothario".—PrFo
Rat a tat tat. Mother Goose.—ClI
"Rat a tat tat, who is that". See Rat a tat tat
"A rather polite man of Hawarden". Unknown.—
  LiLo
"Rather unexpectedly, the lights went out". See
  Brownout
Ratio. Lillian Morrison.—GoU
Rats
  Defiance. Unknown.—OpT
  "Hamelin Town's in Brunswick". From The pied
    piper of Hamelin. R. Browning.—CaB
  "He was a rat, and she was a rat". Unknown.—
    ClI
  "Jerry Hall". Mother Goose.—ClI—ScA
  "Little Tim Sprat". Unknown.—ClI
  The pied piper of Hamelin, complete. R.
    Browning.—ElW
  Rats in the garden. Mother Goose.—ClI
  There was a rat. Mother Goose.—ClI
Rats in the garden. Mother Goose.—ClI
"Rats in the garden, catch 'em Towser". See Rats in
  the garden
Rattlesnake meat. Ogden Nash.—PrFo
Rattlesnake skipping song. Dennis Lee.—BoT
"Ravana's gone". See Divali
The **raven**. Edgar Allan Poe.—SuI
Ravens
  The raven. E. A. Poe.—SuI
  Ravens. Unknown.—DeI
  The raven's tomb. W. De La Mare.—DeR
Ravens. Unknown, tr. by Tze-si Huang.—DeI
The **raven's** tomb. Walter De La Mare.—DeR

Ravikovitch, Dahlia
  Magic, tr. by Chana Bloch and Ariel Bloch.—NyT
  Pride, tr. by Chana Bloch and Ariel Bloch.—NyT
"Ravioli, ravioli". Unknown.—ScA
Raw carrots. Valerie Worth.—WoAl
"Raw carrots taste". See Raw carrots
Rawnsley, Irene
  Ching ming.—FoLe
  Holi.—FoLe
Ray, Lila
  Cat ("Again and again through the day"), tr.—
    NyT
  Day-dream, tr.—NyT
Ray, Tarapada
  My great grand uncle.—NyT
  The ship's whistle, tr. by Shyamasree Devi and P.
    Lal.—NyT
Raymond. Paul B. Janeczko.—JaB
"Raymond slowed". See Brothers
"Raz, dva, tree, chiteery, pyat". Unknown.—YoS
  "1, 2, 3, 4, 5".—YoS
"Razzle dazzle". See Whiskers meets Polly
Reach for the sky. Unknown.—ScA
"Read up and down". Unknown.—ScA—WiA
Readcrest drive. Myra Cohn Livingston.—LiR
The **reader**. Buson, tr. by Tze-si Huang.—DeI
Reading. See Books and reading
Reading, fall. Myra Cohn Livingston.—LiR
Reading in the autumn. Shen Chou.—SuI
Reading, spring. Myra Cohn Livingston.—LiR
Reading, summer. Myra Cohn Livingston.—LiR
Reading, winter. Myra Cohn Livingston.—LiR
Reaney, James
  The royal visit.—BoT
  Windlady.—BoT
Reason. Josephine Miles.—ElW
"The reason I like chocolate". Nikki Giovanni.—
  LoFh
Reavin, Sam
  Fields of corn.—MoS
"Rebecca Jane". See The porcupine
Rebus Valentine. Unknown.—LoFh
Recipe for a hippopotamus sandwich. Shel
  Silverstein.—PrFo
Recipe for Thanksgiving Day soup. Dorothy
  Farmiloe.—BoT
Recital. John Updike.—MoR
Recuerdo. Edna St. Vincent Millay.—ElW
"Red and blue and delicate green". Unknown.—
  WiA
Red and gray in city park. J. Patrick Lewis.—LeT
"Red bug, yellow bug, little blue". Jack Prelutsky.—
  PrBe
Red dog blue fly. Sharon Bell Mathis.—MaR
The **red** dragonfly. Basho, tr. by Tze-si Huang.—DeI
"Red dragonfly on". Soseki, tr. by Sylvia Cassedy
  and Kunihiro Suetake.—CaR
The **red** fox. J. Patrick Lewis.—LeE
The **red** hen. James S. Tippett.—WhAa
The **red** leaf. Page Sullivan.—SuI
"Red rocks". See Grand Canyon east, from the air
"Red sky at night". Mother Goose.—WaM
The **Red** Stockings. George Ellard.—MoA
"Red stockings, blue stockings". Mother Goose.—
  WaM
"Red, white, and blue". Unknown.—YoS
"Red, white, and blue, I don't speak to you".
  Unknown.—OpI
"Red, white and green". Unknown.—ScA
"Red white blue". See "Rood wit blauw"
Redbird, Duke
  "My moccasins have not walked".—BoT

Redcloud, Prince
And then.—HoGo
Of wings.—HoT
Redoles, Mauricio
Byes.—AgL
Reed, Langford
"Said a foolish young lady of Wales".—LiLo
Rees, Timothy
"God is love, and love enfolds us".—StP
Reeves, James
"The bogus-boo".—BaH
The four horses.—KeT
The old wife and the ghost.—DeS
A pig tale.—DeS
Rabbit and lark.—MoS
W.—DeS
The wind ("I can get through a doorway without
any key").—BaW
"Reflected". See Round mirrors
Reflections (mirrored). See also Mirrors
Broken mirror. Zuiryu.—DeI
Calligraphy. J. Yolen.—YoBi
Coffeepot face. A. Fisher.—FiA
I hear the usual thump. A. Adoff.—AdIn
Kaleidoscope. V. Worth.—WoAl
"The kingfisher". Unknown.—DeI
The mirror. W. J. Smith.—SmL
"One day I asked the mirror facing me". T. S.
Seloti.—NyT
Puddles. F. Asch.—MoS
River moons. C. Sandburg.—LaN
Round mirrors. Issa.—DeI
"Said an ogre from old Saratoga". C. Aiken.—
LiLo
The star in the pail. D. McCord.—LaN
Swan ("Over the mirror"). J. Yolen.—YoBi
Regina Kelsey. Mel Glenn.—GlBc
Reikan
Dreams of flowers, tr. by Tze-si Huang.—DeI
Reindeer
R is for reindeer. W. J. Smith.—SmL
"There is a young reindeer named Donder". J. P.
Lewis.—LiLo
Relationship. Myra Cohn Livingston.—LiT
Relatives. See also names of relatives, as Uncles
Brothers ("We're related, you and I"). L.
Hughes.—SlM
Cousins. S. B. Mathis.—MaR
"Cousins are cozy". M. A. Hoberman.—HoFa
Do it yourself. M. Fatchen.—FaCm
"Fine black kinfolk". D. K. Hru.—SlM
A funny old person. Unknown.—CII
I want you to meet. D. McCord.—DeS
A kinsman. J. W. Miller.—JaM
Knee ride. Unknown.—OpT
"My cousin Melda". G. Nichols.—NiCo
Relatives. M. A. Hoberman.—HoFa
Timmy and Tawanda. G. Brooks.—SlM
Relatives. Mary Ann Hoberman.—HoFa
Religions. See Buddhism; Christianity; Faith;
Hinduism; Islam; Judaism
The **reluctant** hero or barefoot in the snow.
Margaret Mahy.—MaN
The **remarkable** cake. Margaret Mahy.—MaN
Remember. David Ward.—FoLe
"Remember, the noise of moonlight". See In the
Lebanese mountains
"Remember us to Eagle Rock". See Eagle rock
Remembering, sels. Xue Di, tr. by Iona Cook and
Keith Waldrop
"My mouth is a horse's mouth".—NyT
"Remembering". See Irene

Remembering. Myra Cohn Livingston.—LiR
Remembering ice. X. J. Kennedy.—KeK
Remembering Oscar eel. J. Patrick Lewis.—LeA
Remembering you. Maxine Kumin.—KnAs
Remembrance Day ("Poppies, oh, miss"). Judith
Nicholls.—FoLe
Remembrance Day ("To some"). John Kitching.—
FoLe
Remodeling the hermit's cabin. Fred Chappell.—
JaM
Reply to the question, how can you become a poet.
Eve Merriam.—MeS
Reptiles. See names of reptiles, as Snakes
Requiem. Paul Fleischman.—FlJ
Requiems. See Laments
Rescue ("Bony cat"). Virginia Schonborg.—LaCc
The **rescue** ("Rain poured down, the house").
Barbara Juster Esbensen.—EsW
Rescue ("Sunday, beginning the week late"). Eric
Trethewey.—JaPr
Rescue mission. Arnold Adoff.—AdCh
Resistance, Brother
Dollar horror.—AgL
Resolution. Eve Merriam.—MeCh
Rest in peace. John Ciardi.—CiH
Restaurants
Dinosaur waltz. J. Yolen.—YoDd
"An epicure, dining at Crewe". Unknown.—LiLo
Monte Rio, California. Z. Rogow.—GoT
Playoff pizza. S. B. Mathis.—MaR
Ruth. P. B. Janeczko.—JaB
"When I found a mouse in my stew".
Unknown.—ScA
Return of the native. Imamu Amiri Baraka.—SuC
Revenge
The antelope ("When one of us hit"). D. A.
Evans.—JaPr
City nomad. J. Berry.—BeW
Economics. R. Wrigley.—JaPr
Eraser. E. Merriam.—MeS
"Every time it rained, mean Merl's". X. J.
Kennedy.—KeFb
The gage. W. De La Mare.—DeR
Grool. F. P. Heide.—HeG
"I wish I were a grapefruit". Unknown.—CoM
A lesson ("He made fun of my Pekingese"). X. J.
Kennedy.—KeK
No question. L. Dangel.—JaPr
"Tit for tat". Unknown.—OpI—WiA
Revere, Paul (about)
Paul Revere's ride. H. W. Longfellow.—ElW—SuI
Reverend Mona. Paul B. Janeczko.—JaB
Reverie. Walter De La Mare.—DeR
Revolution
Greenland's history, or the history of the Danes
on Greenland. S. Holm.—NyT
Revolution—American. See United States—
History—Revolution
Rexroth, Kenneth
"The Bay of Tsunu", tr.—GoU
"Black hair", tr.—GoU
Bright house, tr.—GoU
A dialogue of watching.—GoU
Evening comes, tr.—GoT
From the most distant time, tr.—GoT
"I wish I were close", tr.—GoU
"Like the tides' flood", tr.—GoU
Married love, tr.—GoU
Marthe away (she is away).—GoU
Nocturne ("A long arm embossed with gold slides
from the tree tops"), tr.—GoT
"Not speaking of the way", tr.—GoU

Rexroth, Kenneth—*Continued*
  Raccoon ("The raccoon wears a black mask").—CoAz
  Sending spring love to Tzu-An, tr.—GoU
  Snow on Lotus Mountain, tr.—GoT
  "This morning I will not", tr.—GoU
  To the tune "Glittering sword hits", tr.—GoU
  "We were together", tr.—GoU
Rhapsody. William Stanley Braithwaite.—SlM
Rhinoceros ("I often wonder whether"). Mary Ann Hoberman.—WhAa
Rhinoceros ("You may hang your hat on the nose of the Rhino"). William Jay Smith.—SmL
Rhinoceros stew. Mildred Luton.—PrFo
Rhinoceroses
  How the rhinoceros got his nose. J. P. Lewis.—LeA
  Just friends. M. Fatchen.—FaCm
  Rhinoceros ("I often wonder whether"). M. A. Hoberman.—WhAa
  Rhinoceros ("You may hang your hat on the nose of the Rhino"). W. J. Smith.—SmL
  Rhinoceros stew. M. Luton.—PrFo
Rhu, Lucy W.
  Enigma sartorial.—WhAa
Rhyme. Elizabeth Coatsworth.—MoS
"A rhyme for ham, jam". From Jamboree. David McCord.—DeS
Rhyme for night. Joan Aiken.—KeT
A rhyme is a jump rope. Eve Merriam.—MeS
"A rhyme is a jump rope, let's begin". See A rhyme is a jump rope
Rhymes (about)
  "My father left me, as he was able". Unknown.—ScA
  "A rhyme for ham, jam". From Jamboree. D. McCord.—DeS
  A rhyme is a jump rope. E. Merriam.—MeS
  W. J. Reeves.—DeS
  What they said. Unknown.—DeS
The rhythm of the tomtom. Antonio Jacinto, tr. by Don Burness.—NyT
"The rhythm of the tomtom does not beat in my blood". See The rhythm of the tomtom
Rice, Grantland
  Babe Didrikson.—KnAs
Rice and milk ("I'm rice and milk, I'd like to be wed"). See Arroz con leche
Rich, Adrienne
  Poem II. See Twenty-one love poems
  Poem III. See Twenty-one love poems
  The springboard.—KnAs
  Twenty-one love poems, sels.
    Poem II.—GoU
    Poem III.—GoU
"The rich and the poor do not meet". From Jamaican Caribbean proverbs. Unknown.—BeW
"Rich man, poor man, beggar man, thief". Unknown.—CoM
"Rich, Rich". Unknown.—WiA
"Richard Dick upon a stick". Mother Goose.—WaM
Richards, Laura E.
  After a visit to the natural history museum.—SuI
  A cat may look at a King.—WhAa
  Eletelephony.—DeS—SuI
  Emily Jane.—ElW
  "Nicholas Ned".—DeS
  Old Joe Jones.—KeT
Riches. See Wealth
"Rickety pickety". Jack Prelutsky.—PrBe

Ridd, Julie
  Toes.—AgL
Riddle. Grace Nichols.—NiCo
Riddle go round. Eve Merriam.—MeP
"Riddle go round and roundabout". See Riddle go round
"Riddle me no". See Fiddle faddle
Riddle me rhyme. David McCord.—LiIf
"Riddle me, riddle me, ree". See Riddle me rhyme
"Riddle me, riddle me, what is that". Unknown.—WiA
"Riddle my this, riddle my that". From Riddle poems. James Berry.—BeW
Riddle poems, complete. James Berry
  "Boy is sent for something".—BeW
  "Eyes ablaze looking up".—BeW
  "Hill is my pillow, I have my own bed".—BeW
  "Little Miss Singer brushes her dress".—BeW
  "Little pools".—BeW
  "Riddle my this, riddle my that".—BeW
  "Rooms are full, hall is full, but".—BeW
  "Waltzing for leaves".—BeW
  "What follows king walking, yet stays".—BeW
  "What is vessel of gold sent off".—BeW
  "What's hearty as a heart, round as a ring".—BeW
Riddles
  "Adam and Eve and Pinch-me". Unknown.—OpI—WiA
  "As I was going over London Bridge". Unknown.—OpI
  "As I was going to St. Ives". Unknown.—ScA
  "As I went through a field of wheat". Unknown.—WiA
  "As I went up a slippery gap". Unknown.—OpT
  "Below your nose". M. C. Livingston.—LiMh
  "Big at each end and little in the middle". Unknown.—WiA
  "Big at the bottom, little at the top". Unknown.—WiA
  "Blow us up". M. C. Livingston.—LiMh
  "Blue legs". M. C. Livingston.—LiMh
  "Bounce me". M. C. Livingston.—LiMh
  "Boy is sent for something". From Riddle poems. J. Berry.—BeW
  "Brothers and sisters have I none". Unknown.—OpI
  "Closed, I am a mystery". M. C. Livingston.—LiMh
  "Dressed in". M. C. Livingston.—LiMh
  "East, west, north, south". Unknown.—WiA
  Eeka, neeka. W. De La Mare.—DeR
  Endless riddle. Unknown.—WiA
  "Eyes ablaze looking up". From Riddle poems. J. Berry.—BeW
  "Feed it, it will grow high". Unknown.—ScA
  "The first letter in my name". Unknown.—ScA
  Fish riddle. Unknown.—CaB
  "Flies forever". Unknown.—ScA
  "Four legs". M. C. Livingston.—LiMh
  "Four stiff-standers". Unknown.—CaB—ScA
  "Give me water". M. C. Livingston.—LiMh
  "Gray and blue". M. C. Livingston.—LiMh
  "He stands". M. C. Livingston.—LiMh
  "Here's a riddle". M. C. Livingston.—LiMh
  "Higher than a house". Mother Goose.—WaM
  "Hill is my pillow, I have my own bed". From Riddle poems. J. Berry.—BeW
  "House full, yard full". Unknown.—WiA
  "I polka dot the window". M. C. Livingston.—LiMh

Riddles—*Continued*

"I saw a peacock with a fiery tail". Unknown.—ScA
"I washed my hands in water". Unknown.—WiA
"I went to the town". Unknown.—OpT
"I'm sticky". M. C. Livingston.—LiMh
"In bright yellow coats". M. C. Livingston.—LiMh
"In marble halls as white as milk". Unknown.—CaB—OpT
"In the beginning". Unknown.—ScA
"In the morning". M. C. Livingston.—LiMh
"It has a head like a cat, feet like a cat". Unknown.—WiA
"It is in the rock, but not in the stone". Unknown.—OpI
"It runs all day, but never walks". Unknown.—ScA
"It stays all year". Unknown.—ScA
"A jumper of ditches". Unknown.—OpT
"The land was white". Unknown.—OpI
"Lift me up". M. C. Livingston.—LiMh
"Light as a feather". Unknown.—ScA
"Little Miss Singer brushes her dress". From Riddle poems. J. Berry.—BeW
"Little Nancy Etticoat". Mother Goose.—WaM
"Little pools". From Riddle poems. J. Berry.—BeW
"Long, slim, slick fellow". Unknown.—WiA
"Many eyes". Unknown.—ScA
"A milk-white bird". Unknown.—WiA
"My head is red". M. C. Livingston.—LiMh
"No neck". M. C. Livingston.—LiMh
"Now, a picture". M. C. Livingston.—LiMh
"On the hill there is a mill". Unknown.—WiA
"Once they roamed". M. C. Livingston.—LiMh
"One click". M. C. Livingston.—LiMh
"Over on the hill there's a big red bull". Unknown.—WiA
"Railroad crossing, look out for cars". Unknown.—WiA
    "Railroad crossing, look out for the cars".—OpI
"Red and blue and delicate green". Unknown.—WiA
Riddle. G. Nichols.—NiCo
Riddle go round. E. Merriam.—MeP
Riddle me rhyme. D. McCord.—LiIf
"Riddle me, riddle me, what is that". Unknown.—WiA
"Riddle my this, riddle my that". From Riddle poems. J. Berry.—BeW
Riddling song. Unknown.—OpT
"Rooms are full, hall is full, but". From Riddle poems. J. Berry.—BeW
"Round and round the rugged rock the ragged rascal ran". Unknown.—ScA—WiA
"Round as a doughnut". Unknown.—WiA
"A snow white bird". Unknown.—ScA
"Squeeze me and hug me". M. C. Livingston.—LiMh
"Stretch my ribs out wide and high". M. C. Livingston.—LiMh
There was a knight. Unknown.—ElW
"Thirty-two white horses". Unknown.—WiA
"Thirty white cows standing in a stall". Unknown.—ScA
"Two-legs sat on three-legs by four-legs". Unknown.—WiA
"Upon the hill there is a yellow house". Unknown.—WiA

"Waltzing for leaves". From Riddle poems. J. Berry.—BeW
"What follows king walking, yet stays". From Riddle poems. J. Berry.—BeW
"What has". Unknown.—WiA
"What in the world". E. Merriam.—DeS
"What is it you always see". Unknown.—ScA
"What is the difference". Unknown.—ScA
"What is vessel of gold sent off". From Riddle poems. J. Berry.—BeW
"What's hearty as a heart, round as a ring". From Riddle poems. J. Berry.—BeW
"What's in the church". Unknown.—WiA
"When I sputter and rumble and pop". M. C. Livingston.—LiMh
"White bird featherless". Unknown.—OpT
"Who, who, who is it". E. Merriam.—LiIf
"Widdicote, waddicote". Unknown.—OpT
The wind ("I can get through a doorway without any key"). J. Reeves.—BaW
"With silver spears". M. C. Livingston.—LiMh
"With yellow feathers". M. C. Livingston.—LiMh
"Without a bridle or a saddle". Unknown.—OpT
"You never see me". M. C. Livingston.—LiMh
"YYUR". Unknown.—WiA

Riddling song. Unknown.—OpT
"**Ride** a cock-horse to Coventry Cross". See Riding to market
"**Ride** a cockhorse to Banbury Cross". Mother Goose.—SuO—WaM
"**Ride** a horse to Boston". Mother Goose.—WaM
"**Ride** away, ride away". Mother Goose.—ClI
The **ride-by-nights**. Walter De La Mare.—DeR—MaP
The **rider**. Naomi Shihab Nye.—JaP

Rides and riding

Donkey. E. Greenfield.—GrU
The donkey and the man. J. Berry.—BeW
"First in a carriage". Mother Goose.—WaM
The hayride. M. C. Livingston.—LiBp
How to live in a howdah. X. J. Kennedy.—KeGh
"John Poole left Sedalia". J. Prelutsky.—PrBe
Knee ride. Unknown.—OpT
"Listen, my children, and you shall hear of the midnight ride of Mary dear". Unknown.—WiA
"Little Johnny Morgan". Mother Goose.—ClI
"Mary had a little lamb, its fleece was white as snow". Unknown.—WiA
The north wind ("Once, when I was young I knew the wind"). J. Lysyk.—BoT
"Old Dan Tucker went to town". Unknown.—WiA
"Richard Dick upon a stick". Mother Goose.—WaM
"Ride away, ride away". Mother Goose.—ClI
Riding in style. Unknown.—OpT
Wheels. J. Daniels.—JaPr
Wicked witch's travels. X. J. Kennedy.—KeGh

Rides and riding—Horse

Billy could ride. J. W. Riley.—KnAs
Bonny George Campbell. Unknown.—ElW
Bronco busting, event #1. M. Swenson.—KnAs—MoR
Cavalry crossing a ford. W. Whitman.—ElW
"A certain young fellow, named Bobbie". Unknown.—LiLo
A farmer went trotting. Mother Goose.—ClI
"Giddy up gid". J. Minor.—MoR
"A gigantic beauty of a stallion, fresh and responsive to my caresses". From Song of myself. W. Whitman.—SuI
    Stallion.—KnAs

Rides and riding—Horse—*Continued*

Horseback. C. Kizer.—KnAs

The horseman ("I heard a horseman"). W. De La Mare.—DeR—MaP

The horseman ("There was a horseman rode so fast"). W. De La Mare.—DeR—MaP

The huntsmen. W. De La Mare.—DeR—MaP

"I will not change my horse with any that treads". From King Henry V. W. Shakespeare.—WhAa

"Matthew, Mark, Luke and John, hold the horse". Unknown.—OpI

"Matthew, Mark, Luke, and John, I'm off my horse". Unknown.—WiA

"My horse, fly like a bird". V. D. H. Sneve.—SnD

Never be as fast as I have been, the jockey Tony DeSpirito dead at thirty-nine. R. Hahn.—KnAs

Paul Revere's ride. H. W. Longfellow.—ElW—SuI

Polo ponies practicing. W. Stevens.—KnAs

Reverie. W. De La Mare.—DeR

"Ride a cockhorse to Banbury Cross". Mother Goose.—SuO—WaM

"Ride a horse to Boston". Mother Goose.—WaM

Riding lesson. H. Taylor.—KnAs

Riding to market. Mother Goose.—OpT

Suppose ("Suppose, and suppose that a wild little horse of magic"). W. De La Mare.—DeR

Whoa. M. Fatchen.—FaCm

Windy nights. R. L. Stevenson.—DeS—DeT—MoR

"Yankee Doodle came to town". Mother Goose.—SuO

Riding in style. Unknown.—OpT

Riding lesson. Henry Taylor.—KnAs

Riding to market. Mother Goose.—OpT

Ridland, John

Dumb dog.—LiDp

Pumpkin people.—LiHp

Ridlon, Marci

Open hydrant.—DeT

Rieu, Emile Victor

The flattered flying fish.—ElW

The lost cat.—LaCc

The paint box.—ElW

Soliloquy of a tortoise on revisiting the lettuce beds after an interval of one hour while supposed to be sleeping in a clump of blue hollyhocks.—ElW

Rifka, Fuad

Diary of a woodcutter, sels.

"Wrinkles in the lake".—NyT

"Wrinkles in the lake". See Diary of a woodcutter

Riggs, Dionis

At the beach ("The waves are erasing the footprints"), tr.—NyT

"**Right** off the". See Just once

"**Right** on the alley". See Garage apartment

Right where he left off. Craig Weeden.—KnAs

Rigmarole. Eve Merriam.—MeCh

Riley, James Whitcomb

Billy could ride.—KnAs

Rilke, Rainer Maria

"Put out my eyes, and I can see you still".—GoU

Sappho to Eranna, tr. by Edward Snow.—GoU

The unicorn ("Oh this is the animal that never was").—WhDd

"You, neighbor God, if in the long night".—StP

The **rime** of the ancient mariner, complete. Samuel Taylor Coleridge.—ElW

The **rime** of the ancient mariner, sels. Samuel Taylor Coleridge

"He prayeth best, who loveth best".—StP

"**Rin** Tin Tin swallowed a pin". Unknown.—WiA

"**Ring** a ring o' roses". See "Ring around a rosey"

"**Ring** a ring of roses". See "Ring around a rosey"

"**Ring** around a rosey". Mother Goose.—WaM

"Ring a ring o' roses".—SuO

"Ring a ring of roses".—EdGl

"The **ring** so worn, as you behold". See His mother's wedding ring

Rings. See Jewelry

Rio de Janiero, Brazil

Carnival in Rio. J. Kirkup.—FoLe

Rios, Alberto

The purpose of altar boys.—JaPr

"There was a roof over our heads".—SuI

"The **rising** moon pulls". See Summer night, canoeing

Ritchie, Elisavietta

International ski flying championship, Obersdorf.—KnAs

I've never written a baseball poem.—KnAs

Ritchings, Joan Drew

Attic dance.—MoR

Rites of passage. Dorianne Laux.—JaPr

Ritsos, Yannis

Healing, tr. by Edmund Keeley.—NyT

The meaning of simplicity, tr. by Edmund Keeley.—NyT

The **river.** Charlotte Zolotow.—FrS

"The **river** is famous to the fish". See Famous

River lovers. J. Patrick Lewis.—LeA

River moons. Carl Sandburg.—LaN

"The **river** turns". See The pike

River winding. Charlotte Zolotow.—LiDd

Rivers. See also names of rivers, as Mississippi River

Afton water. R. Burns.—ElW

Black river. M. C. Livingston.—LiNe

Bonum omen. W. De La Mare.—DeR

The brook. A. Tennyson.—ElW

Cavalry crossing a ford. W. Whitman.—ElW

Dreamland. W. De La Mare.—DeR

"From its sources which well". From The cataract of Lodore. R. Southey.—MoR

Half moon. F. Garcia Lorca.—LaN

"Hill is my pillow, I have my own bed". From Riddle poems. J. Berry.—BeW

How I went truant from school to visit a river. M. Oliver.—JaPr

Inversnaid. G. M. Hopkins.—MoR

"It runs all day, but never walks". Unknown.—ScA

"Lord, Thou mighty river, all knowing, all seeing". G. Nanak.—StP

Monte Rio, California. Z. Rogow.—GoT

Mountain brook. E. Coatsworth.—FrS

The mushroom river. X. Di.—NyT

The negro speaks of rivers. L. Hughes.—SuC

Night magic. C. Lewis.—LaN

Ol' man river. From Show Boat. O. Hammerstein.—SuC

Part VII: When safe in to the fields Ann got. From A child's day. W. De La Mare.—DeR

The pike ("The river turns"). T. Roethke.—KnAs

The river. C. Zolotow.—FrS

River lovers. J. P. Lewis.—LeA

Schoolcrafts's diary, written on the Missouri, 1830. R. Bly.—SuI

Thames. W. De La Mare.—DeR

Where go the boats. R. L. Stevenson.—ElW—KeT

Roach, Eloise

Watch ("The lamb baaed gently"), tr.—LoFh

Roads and streets
"Afoot and light-hearted I take to the open road". From Song of the open road. W. Whitman.—HoVo
Hitchhiking with a friend and a book that explains the Pacific Ocean. G. Soto.—SoA
Mouseways. A. Fisher.—FiH
Neighborhood street. E. Greenfield.—GrN
Night sounds. F. Holman.—HoSt—LaN
"One day". J. Carson.—CaS
Roadside. V. Worth.—WoAl
South ("Today's cool asphalt . . . where had the cars gone"). T. Gunn.—ElW
Telephone poles. V. Worth.—WoAl
Up and down. W. De La Mare.—DeR—MaP
"**Roads** run by". See Always wondering
Roadside. Valerie Worth.—WoAl
"**Roaming** these furry prairies". See Fleas
Robbins, Martin
Winter pause, Mt. Liberty, N.H.—MoR
"**Robert,** Bedobert, Hadobert, Gofobert". Unknown.—ScA
Robert Robot. X. J. Kennedy.—KeGh
"**Robert** Robot, go unscrew". See Robert Robot
Roberts, Elizabeth Madox
The dark ("There are six little houses up on the hill").—LaN
Father's story.—SuI
Firefly.—DeS—LiDd—StP—WhAa
The hens.—LiDd
Little bush.—LiDd
Numbers.—LiDd
The rabbit ("When they said the time to hide was mine").—ElW
The woodpecker ("The woodpecker pecked out a little round hole").—KeT
Roberts, George
Halloween, the hydrant dare.—JaPr
High school.—JaPr
The **robin** ("As little Bess was walking home"). Walter De La Mare.—DeR
Robin ("Suddenly spring wings"). J. Patrick Lewis.—LeA
"A **robin** and a robin's son". Mother Goose.—CII—WaM
"The **robin** and the wren". Unknown.—CaB—CII
"The **robin** cam' to the wren's door". See Mrs. Burns' lullaby
"**Robin** spied a chubby worm". Jack Prelutsky.—PrBe
Robins
Betsy Robin. W. J. Smith.—SmL
Cruel Jenny Wren. Unknown.—ElW
An epitaph on a robin redbreast. S. Rogers.—CaB
First robin. J. Yolen.—YoBi
"Kill a robin or a wren". Unknown.—CaB
"Little robin redbreast". Mother Goose.—WaM
Mrs. Burns' lullaby. Unknown.—OpT
Nestlings. J. Yolen.—YoBi
"The north wind doth blow". Mother Goose.—DeS—SuO—WaM
The robin ("As little Bess was walking home"). W. De La Mare.—DeR
Robin ("Suddenly spring wings"). J. P. Lewis.—LeA
"A robin and a robin's son". Mother Goose.—CII—WaM
"The robin and the wren". Unknown.—CaB—CII
"Robin spied a chubby worm". J. Prelutsky.—PrBe
Robins. V. Worth.—WoAl
Robins. Valerie Worth.—WoAl

Robinson, Edwin Arlington
The sheaves.—SuI
Robinson, Martha
Beware ("Did I dream the owl or was it really there").—LiIf
In the mirror.—LiPg
My Jose.—LiPf
Robinson, Jackie (about)
Jackie Robinson. L. Clifton.—KnAs—MoA
"**Robinson** one". Unknown.—OpI
Robots
"Coils the robot". F. H. Pinto.—NyT
Robert Robot. X. J. Kennedy.—KeGh
"Young Frankenstein's robot invention". B. Braley.—LiLo
Roc. Richard Burton.—WhDd
"**Rock-a-bye,** baby, on the treetop". Mother Goose.—SuO—WaM
Rock 'n' roll band. Shel Silverstein.—SuI
"**Rockabye,** baby, your cradle is hard". Unknown.—WiA
Rocks ("Big rocks into pebbles"). Florence Parry Heide.—DeS
Rocks ("They say, no"). Valerie Worth.—WoAl
Rocks and stones
The birth of a stone. K. Kwang-kyu.—NyT
Eagle rock. G. Hewitt.—JaPr
Flint. C. G. Rossetti.—ElW
Geode. B. J. Esbensen.—EsW
"I found a little stone". E. Merriam.—MeY
Kick a little stone. D. Aldis.—KeT
Muscling rocks. R. Morgan.—JaPr
Ode to el molcajete. G. Soto.—SoNe
Pebbles. V. Worth.—WoAl
Pride. D. Ravikovitch.—NyT
Rocks ("Big rocks into pebbles"). F. P. Heide.—DeS
Rocks ("They say, no"). V. Worth.—WoAl
Secrets ("I doubt that you remember her, except"). R. Pack.—JaM
"This is my rock". D. McCord.—KeT—LiDd
Rocky Mountains, Colorado. Myra Cohn Livingston.—LiNe
Rodeos
Bronco busting, event #1. M. Swenson.—KnAs—MoR
The closing of the rodeo. W. J. Smith.—KnAs
Rodomontade in the menagerie. Eve Merriam.—MeCh
Rodriguez, Blanca
Surprise ("A balloon, my Daddy brought for me"), tr. by Aurelio Major.—NyT
Roethke, Theodore
The bat ("By day the bat is cousin to the mouse").—CoAz—DeS—ElW
The hippo.—HoT
In evening air.—GoT
The lamb.—LiDd
The meadow mouse.—LaM
My papa's waltz.—ElW
Night journey.—MoR
Philander.—LiLo
The pike ("The river turns").—KnAs
The sloth.—ElW
The whale ("There was a most monstrous whale").—CoAz
The yak ("There was a most odious yak").—LiLo
"**Roger** came to Beaver". See Pet rock
Roger the dog. Ted Hughes.—ElW
Rogers, Samuel
An epitaph on a robin redbreast.—CaB

Rogow, Zack
 Early March.—GoT
 Monte Rio, California.—GoT
 Nantucket.—GoT
Roistering. Unknown.—OpT
Roka
 The swan ("The white swan, swimming"), tr. by
  Tze-si Huang.—DeI
Roll the cotton down. Unknown.—SuC
Roller-coasters
 "Just before the highest hill". X. J. Kennedy.—
  KeK
 Roller coasters. X. J. Kennedy.—KeK
Roller coasters. X. J. Kennedy.—KeK
"The **roller** skates that Mary had". See Thud
"**Roly** poly Hobart". See Willy nilly
Romance. See Adventure and adventurers; Knights
  and knighthood; Love
"The **Romans** built their road and path". See
  Playing dirty
Romping in the rain. X. J. Kennedy.—KeK
Ronnie Schwinck. David Allan Evans.—JaPr
"**Rood** wit blauw". Unknown.—YoS
 "Red white blue".—YoS
The **room** (for a picture). Walter De La Mare.—DeR
Rooms
 Closet. M. C. Livingston.—LiNe
 "I wish that my room had a floor". G. Burgess.—
  LiLo—PrFo
 The room (for a picture). W. De La Mare.—DeR
 Whenever. M. A. Hoberman.—MoS
"**Rooms** are full, hall is full, but". From Riddle
  poems. James Berry.—BeW
"The **rooms** in a pencil". See Pencils
"The **rooms** in her small apartment". See Great
  grandma
"The **rooster** is ridiculous". See Bragging in the
  barnyard
Roosters. Elizabeth Coatsworth.—WhAs
Rosalie the cat. Karla Kuskin.—LaCc
Roscoe. Paul B. Janeczko.—JaB
Rose, Pete (about)
 The last baseball samurai. T. Clark.—KnAs
The **rose** on my cake. Karla Kuskin.—KeT
"**Rose**, Rose". Unknown.—WiA
Roseblatt, Joe
 "I get high on butterflies".—BoT
Rosebush. Valerie Worth.—WoAl
Rosen, Michael
 "The angry hens from Never-when".—PrFo
 "I wake up".—AgL
 The ship in the dock.—PrFo
Rosenberg, Liz
 Carving pumpkins with my father.—LiPf
 My mother's face.—LiPm
 Trick or treating at age eight.—LiHp
Roses
 The bees' song. W. De La Mare.—DeR—MaP
 "My mother and I". E. Di Pasquale.—LiPm
 Rosebush. V. Worth.—WoAl
 "Traigo un ramillete". Unknown.—LoFh
  Bouquet of roses ("A bouquet of roses").—
   LoFh
"**Roses** and a tulip". Charlotte Pomerantz.—JaP
"**Roses** are red, cabbages are green". Unknown.—
  ScA
"**Roses** are red, violets are black". Unknown.—
  CoM—ScA
"**Roses** are red, violets are blue, a face like yours".
  Unknown.—ScA
"**Roses** are red, violets are blue, do you hate me".
  Unknown.—CoM

"**Roses** are red, violets are blue, grass is green".
  Unknown.—WiA
"**Roses** are red, violets are blue, if I looked like
  you". Unknown.—CoM
"**Roses** are red, violets are blue, sugar is sweet".
  Unknown.—WiA
"**Roses** are red, violets are blue, what you need".
  Unknown.—WiA
"**Roses** red, violets blue, sugar is sweet, but not like
  you". Unknown.—ScA
Rosh Hashanah
 Rosh Hashanah eve. H. Philip.—LoFh
Rosh Hashanah eve. Harry Philip.—LoFh
Ross, Jerry, and Adler, Richard
 Damn Yankees, sels.
  Heart.—KnAs
 Heart. See Damn Yankees
Ross, Maggie
 A nun's prayer.—StP
Rossetti, Christina Georgina
 A birthday.—ElW
 The caterpillar ("Brown and furry").—DeS—
  DeT—ElW
 The city mouse and the garden mouse.—LaM
 Clouds ("White sheep, white sheep").—DeS
 "Ferry me across the water".—KeT
 Flint.—ElW
 Fly away. See The swallow
 "A house of cards".—DeT
 "Hurt no living thing".—DeS—StP—WhAa
 Let's be merry.—KeT
 "Lullaby, oh lullaby".—PlW
 May.—ElW
 "Mix a pancake".—LiDd
 "Open thou our lips, O Lord, and purify".—StP
 Song ("When I am dead, my dearest").—ElW
 The swallow.—DeT
  Fly away.—FrS
 What are heavy.—ElW
 "What can I give him".—StP
 What is pink.—DeS—ElW
 "Who has seen the wind".—BaW—DeS—KeT—
  LiDd—MoS—StP
 "The wind has such a rainy sound".—KeT
Rossetti, Dante Gabriel
 Silent noon.—GoU
"**Rosy** the blossom that breaks in May". See Apple-
  fall
"**Round** about, round about". Mother Goose.—WaM
"**Round** about the rosebush". Mother Goose.—WaM
"**Round** and round the rugged rock the ragged rascal
  ran". Unknown.—ScA—WiA
"**Round** as a doughnut". Unknown.—WiA
"**Round** as a pot". See The witch's cauldron
"**Round** is the moon". See A kiss is round
Round mirrors. Issa, tr. by Tze-si Huang.—DeI
"**Round** or square". See Hats
"**Round** slice of moon, December night". See
  December
"**Round** the 4H baked goods sale". X. J. Kennedy.—
  KeFb
The **roundhouse.** Raymond Souster.—BoT
"**Roused** us last night". See West wind
Rover. Eve Merriam.—MeP
"**Rover** is a wonder dog". See Rover
"**Row**, row, row". N. M. Bodecker.—LiDd
"**Row**, row, row your boat". Unknown.—ScA
"**Rowley** Powley, pudding and pie". Unknown.—
  OpT
"**Rowsty** dowt". Mother Goose.—WaM
Rowthorn, Jeffery
 "Creating God, your fingers trace".—StP

The **royal** visit. James Reaney.—BoT
Rozewicz, Tadeusz
  Father ("My old father walks through").—AgL
  Transformations, tr. by Czeslaw Milosz.—NyT
Rozo-Moorhouse, Teresa
  "Childhood is the only lasting flower", tr.—NyT
"**Rub** a dub dub". Mother Goose.—EdGl—WaM
"**Rub** a dub dub". Unknown.—WiA
"**Rubber** bands seem very nice". See Beware of
  rubber bands
"**Rubbing** the naked white of our legs". See Zora
"**Ruby,** amethyst, emerald, diamond". See Precious
  stones
Ruby-throated hummingbird. Eve Merriam.—MeS
Rudolph is tired of the city. Gwendolyn Brooks.—
  SlM
Ruebner, Tuvia
  Among iron fragments, tr. by Robert Friend.—
  GoU
Ruffin, Paul
  Jody Walker, the first voice.—JaPr
Rugs
  "Lil, to cut the rug's pile lower". X. J. Kennedy.—
  KeFb
  The used carpet salesman. J. Yolen.—YoBe
The **ruin.** Walter De La Mare.—DeR—MaP
Rulers. See also Princes and princesses; also names
  of rulers, as Mary, Queen of Scots
  Bragging in the barnyard. J. P. Lewis.—LeA
  "Brown crown". B. McMillan.—McP
  Cake and sack. W. De La Mare.—DeR—MaP
  Camels of the Kings. L. Norris.—CaB
  A cat may look at a King. L. E. Richards.—WhAa
  "Charles the First walked and talked".
  Unknown.—OpI
  The golden stair. J. Yolen.—YoFf
  Gone ("Where's the Queen of Sheba"). W. De La
  Mare.—DeR
  "Hector Protector was dressed all in green".
  Mother Goose.—SuO
  Honeybees. P. Fleischman.—FlJ
  K is for king. W. J. Smith.—SmL
  The King of Spain. W. J. Smith.—SmL
  King of the band. A. Johnson.—FoLe
  The King of Yvetot. W. M. Thackeray.—ElW
  Kings. W. De La Mare.—DeR
  Kings and queens. W. De La Mare.—DeR—MaP
  Lion ("The beast that is most fully dressed"). W.
  J. Smith.—SmL
  "Na zlatom cryeltse sidelly". Unknown.—YoS
    "On a golden step sat".—YoS
  "Nebuchadnezzar the King of the Jews".
  Unknown.—OpI
  Oak apple day. R. Wilson.—FoLe
  The old king. W. De La Mare.—DeR
  "Old King Cole was a merry old soul". Mother
  Goose.—EdGl—SuO—WaM
  Ozymandias. P. B. Shelley.—ElW
  Part IV: The queen of Arabia, Uanjinee. From A
  child's day. W. De La Mare.—DeR
  Part XVI: The king in slumber when he lies
  down. From A child's day. W. De La Mare.—
  DeR
  The pelican chorus. E. Lear.—CaB—WhAa
  Pictures of cats. K. Kuskin.—LaCc
  Plans gone wrong. M. Mahy.—MaN
  "Pussycat, pussycat, where have you been".
  Mother Goose.—SuO—WaM
  Q is for queen. W. J. Smith.—SmL
  Queen Djenira. W. De La Mare.—DeR
  Queen Nefertiti. Unknown.—KeT

"The Queen of Hearts". Mother Goose.—EdGl—
  SuO
The Queen of the Nile. W. J. Smith.—SmL
Queen of the world (or king). B. S. De Regniers.—
  DeW
"Queen, Queen Caroline". Unknown.—KeT—OpI
"Queen Regina". E. Merriam.—MeP
Queen's prayer. Liliuokalani, queen of Hawaii.—
  StP
The royal visit. J. Reaney.—BoT
"Sing a song of sixpence". Mother Goose.—
  EdGl—SuO—WaM
The song of the mad prince. W. De La Mare.—
  DeR—ElW—MaP
Tartary. W. De La Mare.—DeR
The thief at Robin's castle. W. De La Mare.—
  DeR—MaP
Tyrannosaurus ("He strides onto the dance
  floor"). J. Yolen.—YoDd
W. J. Reeves.—DeS
We three camels. J. Yolen.—YoHa
What grandpa mouse said. V. Lindsay.—LiIf
Rules
  Disobedience. A. A. Milne.—KeT
  "My mother says I'm sickening". J. Prelutsky.—
  PrFo
  "Order in the gallery". Unknown.—OpI
  Rules. K. Kuskin.—PrFo
  "To all this there are rules, the players must".
  From Watching football on TV. H. Nemerov.—
  KnAs
Rules. Karla Kuskin.—PrFo
Rules for the elephant parade. J. Patrick Lewis.—
  LeA
"**Rumba** rumba". See Carnival in Rio
Rumi, Jalal-Ud-Din
  558, tr. by John Moyne and Coleman Barks.—
  GoU
  "Flowers every night".—StP
  91, tr. by John Moyne and Coleman Barks.—GoT
  1246, tr. by John Moyne and Coleman Barks.—
  GoU
  "There's a strange frenzy in my head".—GoU
  2195 In the arc of your mallet, tr. by John Moyne
  and Coleman Barks.—GoU
  2674 After being in love, the next responsibility,
  tr. by John Moyne and Coleman Barks.—GoU
Rummage. Eve Merriam.—MeS
"A **rumpled** sheet". See The term
"**Rumpty-iddity,** row row row". Mother Goose.—
  WaM
Runagate runagate. Robert Hayden.—SuC
The **runaway.** Robert Frost.—ElW
The **runaway** girl. Gregory Corso.—JaPr
"The **runaway** slave came to my house and stopt
  outside". From Song of myself. Walt
  Whitman.—HoVo
Runaway teen. William Stafford.—JaPr
Runaways
  Runagate runagate. R. Hayden.—SuC
  The runaway. R. Frost.—ElW
  The runaway girl. G. Corso.—JaPr
  "The runaway slave came to my house and stopt
  outside". From Song of myself. W. Whitman.—
  HoVo
  Runaway teen. W. Stafford.—JaPr
  The wraggle taggle gypsies. Unknown.—ElW
The **runner.** Walt Whitman.—KnAs
Runners and running
  Afternoon in March. J. Little.—LiHe
  Birthday on the beach. O. Nash.—KnAs
  City to surf. D. Bateson.—FoLe

Runners and running—*Continued*
 Crystal Rowe, track star. M. Glenn.—MoR
 "Dig your starting holes deep". From To James.
  F. Horne.—SuC
 The finish. D. Hoffman.—KnAs
 The four corners of the universe. Unknown.—
  SnD
 "Fun run". B. McMillan.—McP
 Health fanatic. J. C. Clarke.—AgL
 His running, my running. R. Francis.—KnAs
 Hurdler. G. Butcher.—KnAs
 I have ten legs. A. Swir.—NyT
 Interview with a winner. D. Finkel.—KnAs
 Joan Benoit. R. Ferrarelli.—KnAs
 Lessie. E. Greenfield.—MoS
 Morning athletes. M. Piercy.—KnAs
 The photograph. B. Drake.—KnAs
 Prefontaine. C. Ghigna.—KnAs
 The runner. W. Whitman.—KnAs
 Running. R. Wilbur.—KnAs
 "Sometimes running". J. Ciardi.—MoR
 Strategy for a marathon. M. Mueller.—KnAs
 To an athlete dying young. A. E. Housman.—ElW
 Touchdown. S. B. Mathis.—MaR
 We chased butterflies. Plenty-Coups.—SnD
Running. Richard Wilbur.—KnAs
"**Running** to school". Unknown.—ScA
"**Runs** falls rises stumbles on from darkness into
 darkness". See Runagate runagate
Runyon, Damon
 Babe Ruth.—KnAs
The **rural** dance about the Maypole. Unknown.—
 MoR
Russian language
 "Na zlatom cryeltse sidelly". Unknown.—YoS
  "On a golden step sat".—YoS
 "Raz, dva, tree, chiteery, pyat". Unknown.—YoS
  "1, 2, 3, 4, 5".—YoS
Russian nursery rhymes. See Nursery rhymes—
 Russian
"**Rusty** nail, went to jail". Unknown.—WiA
"The **rusty** spigot". See Onomatopoeia
Ruth, George Herman "Babe" (about)
 Along came Ruth. F. Frick.—MoA
 Babe and Lou. F. Douskey.—KnAs
 Babe Ruth. D. Runyon.—KnAs
Ruth. Paul B. Janeczko.—JaB
Ruthless rhyme. J. A. Lindon.—PrFo
Rutsala, Vern
 Skaters ("There are many tonight and the
  rink").—KnAs
Ryan, Nolan (about)
 Nolan Ryan. G. Fehler.—MoA
Ryder, Joanne
 Enchantment.—JaP
 "Like magic".—JaP
Rylant, Cynthia
 Forgotten.—JaP
 Mike and Major.—JaP
 Pet rock.—JaP
Ryukyo
 The petal, tr. by Tze-si Huang.—DeI

S

S is for springs. William Jay Smith.—SmL
S, silent shark. Myra Cohn Livingston.—LiNe
Saba, Umberto
 Woman, tr. by Thomas G. Bergin.—GoU

Sachs, Marilyn
 I was there.—SaB
The **sacred**. Stephen Dunn.—JaM
Sacrifice bunt. Lucky Jacobs.—KnAs
"The **sad** bells sound". See Strangers
The **sad** story of a little boy that cried. Unknown.—
 PrFo
"**Sadly**, o, sadly, the sweet bells of Baddeley". See
 Part XIX: Sadly, o, sadly, the sweet bells of
 Baddeley
Sadness. See also Despair; Grief; Melancholy
 "All day I hear the noise of waters". J. Joyce.—
  ElW
 Alone ("I am alone, and lonely"). J. Little.—LiHe
 Black dog, red dog. S. Dobyns.—JaPr
 The blues. L. Hughes.—KeT
 Byes. M. Redoles.—AgL
 Down by the salley gardens. W. B. Yeats.—ElW
 February 14. M. C. Livingston.—LiT
 Growing pains. J. Little.—LiHe
 Hapless. W. De La Mare.—DeR—MaP
 Household. P. Booth.—JaPr
 Infant sorrow. W. Blake.—ElW
 King David. W. De La Mare.—DeR—MaP
 Leaving. A. Bryan.—BrS
 Little boy blues. E. Greenfield.—GrN
 Minstrel man. L. Hughes.—SuC
 Poem ("I loved my friend"). L. Hughes.—DeS—
  DeT—SlM
 They told me. W. De La Mare.—DeR
 Tired Tim. W. De La Mare.—DeR—MaP
 Why ("Why do you weep, Mother, why do you
  weep"). W. De La Mare.—DeR
Sadoff, Ira
 My father's leaving.—JaPr
Safety
 The dream keeper. L. Hughes.—SlM
 "I used to work down". J. Carson.—CaS
 "I worked there as a secretary". J. Carson.—CaS
 "I've been at that job". J. Carson.—CaS
 The owl ("Downhill I came, hungry, and yet not
  starved"). E. Thomas.—ElW—LiIf
 When I tell you I'm scared. B. S. De Regniers.—
  DeW
Safety pin. Valerie Worth.—WoAl
"**Said** a foolish young lady of Wales". Langford
 Reed.—LiLo
"**Said** a lady beyond Pompton Lakes". Morris
 Bishop.—LiLo
"**Said** a restless young person of Yew". Myra Cohn
 Livingston.—LiLo
"**Said** a salty old skipper from Wales". See Iron men
 and wooden ships
"**Said** an ogre from old Saratoga". Conrad Aiken.—
 LiLo
"**Said** Arlene Francis to Granville Hicks". William
 Jay Smith.—SmL
"**Said** Dorothy Hughes to Helen Hocking". William
 Jay Smith.—SmL
"**Said** General Shoup to Adja Yunkers". William Jay
 Smith.—SmL
"**Said** Gus Goop, that spaghetti was great". X. J.
 Kennedy.—KeGh—LiLo
"**Said** Justice Douglas to Douglass Cater". William
 Jay Smith.—SmL
"**Said** Marcia Brown to Carlos Baker". William Jay
 Smith.—SmL
"**Said** Mr. Smith, I really cannot". See Bones
"**Said** Mrs. Isosceles Tri". Clinton Brooks Burgess.—
 LiLo
"**Said** Noble Aaron to Aaron Barron". Mother
 Goose.—WaM

"Said Ogden Nash to Phyllis McGinley". William Jay Smith.—SmL
"Said old peeping Tom of Fort Lee". Morris Bishop.—LiLo
"Said, pull her up a bit will you, Mac, I want to unload there". See Reason
"Said Rev. Rectangular Square". Clinton Brooks Burgess.—LiLo
"Said the circus man, oh what do you like". See The circus, or one view of it
"Said the condor, in tones of despair". Oliver Herford.—LiLo
"Said the crab, 'tis not beauty or birth". Oliver Herford.—LiLo
"Said the duck to the kangaroo". See The duck and the kangaroo
"Said the first little chicken". See The chickens
"Said the first little chicken". See Five little chickens
"Said the monkey to the donkey". Unknown.—WiA
The monkey and the donkey.—ClI
"Said the monkey to the owl". Unknown.—LiIf
Said the monster. Lilian Moore.—LiLo
"Said the monster, you all think that I". See Said the monster
"Said the Queen of the Nile". See The Queen of the Nile
"Said the shark to the flying fish over the phone". See The flattered flying fish
"Said the table to the chair". See The table and the chair
"Said the turtle to the turkey". See The turkey's wattle
"Said the wind to the moon". See The wind and the moon, complete
"Said the wind to the moon, I will blow you out". From The wind and the moon. George MacDonald.—DeT—LiDd
The sailboat race. Eloise Greenfield.—GrU
Sailing. See Boats and boating; Ships
Sailing, sailing. Lillian Morrison.—KnAs
"A sailor went to sea". See "A sailor went to sea, sea, sea"
"A sailor went to sea, sea, sea". Unknown.—CoM
"A sailor went to sea".—WiA
"Sailorman, I'll give to you". See The silver penny
Sailors. See Seafaring life
A sailor's memoirs. Muhammad Al-Fayiz, tr. by Issa Boullata and Naomi Shihab Nye.—NyT
"Sails against the wind like gulls". See Sails, gulls, sky, sea
Sails, gulls, sky, sea. Felice Holman.—BaW
Saint David's Day
  Saint David's Day. D. W. Price.—FoLe
  St. David's Day ("The land returns from winter"). S. Cook.—FoLe
Saint David's Day. David Watkin Price.—FoLe
St. David's Day ("The land returns from winter"). Stanley Cook.—FoLe
Saint George's Day
  The dragon's lament. T. Harvey.—FoLe
Saint Lucy's Night
  Crown of light festival. D. Bateson.—FoLe
Saint Patrick's Day
  Little people's express. X. J. Kennedy.—KeGh
Saint Swithin's Day
  Saint Swithin's Day. A. Bonner.—FoLe
Saint Swithin's Day. Ann Bonner.—FoLe
Saint Valentine's Day
  February 14. M. C. Livingston.—LiT
  February 14th. A. Bonner.—FoLe

"A fellow named Percival Stein". R. H. Marks.—LiLo
"Good morrow to you, Valentine". Mother Goose.—WaM
"I made my dog a valentine". J. Prelutsky.—LoFh
"Postman, postman, at the gate". Unknown.—OpI
Rebus Valentine. Unknown.—LoFh
Song for a valentine. X. J. Kennedy.—KeK
"There's someone I know". J. Prelutsky.—DeS
Valentine for Ernest Mann. N. S. Nye.—JaP
Valentine hearts. M. C. Livingston.—LiR
Valentines. A. Fisher.—FiA
Valentine's day. A. Fisher.—FiA
Saints. See also names of saints, as Luke
"Alone with none but Thee, my God". Saint Columba.—StP
"From silly devotions". Saint Teresa of Avila.—StP
"Keep watch, dear Lord, with those who work". Saint Augustine.—StP
"Oh, when the saints". Unknown.—StP
Salamanders
  The little salamander. W. De La Mare.—DeR
"The sale began, young girls were there". See The slave auction
Sales talk for Annie. Morris Bishop.—ElW
Salkey, Andrew
  A song for England.—AgL
Sallie. Walter De La Mare.—DeR
"Sally bum-bally". Unknown.—WiA
"Sally gave harmonicas". See Party favors
"Sally go round the sun". Mother Goose.—WaM
"Sally over the water". Unknown.—WiA
"Sally, Sally Waters, sprinkle in the pan". Mother Goose.—WaM
Salmon fishing. Robinson Jeffers.—KnAs
Salt and memory, a tribute to Marc Chagall. Zoltan Zelk, tr. by Barbara Howes.—NyT
Sam. Walter De La Mare.—DeR—MaP
"Sam and Joan sitting in a tree". Unknown.—ScA
"Sam, Sam, dirty old man". Unknown.—CoM—OpI
"Sam, Sam, the butcher man". Unknown.—KeT—WiA
"Sam Speer, watching the black ball". See The last man killed by Indians in Kimble County, Texas
"Sam the soup maker tried to fry ice". See All right, do it your way
Samantha. Colin West.—PrFo
Same and different. Unknown, tr. by Tze-si Huang.—DeI
"Sam's mother has". See Sam's world
Sam's three wishes or life's little whirligig. Walter De La Mare.—DeR
Sam's world. Sam Cornish.—LiPm
San Francisco
  Kearney Park. G. Soto.—SoA
Sanabria de Romero, Nidia
  The new suit, tr. by Arnaldo D. Larrosa Moran and Naomi Shihab Nye.—NyT
Sanchez, Sonia
  Haiku ("I have looked into").—SlM
  Poem at thirty.—SuC
Sand
  "At the beach (1)". From Beach birthdays. M. C. Livingston.—LiBp
  "At the beach (2)". From Beach birthdays. M. C. Livingston.—LiBp
  The chatelaine. Unknown.—OpT
  Five ("Five little children"). C. Tringress.—MoS
  Mine. L. Moore.—MoS
  Rocks ("Big rocks into pebbles"). F. P. Heide.—DeS

Sand—*Continued*
Sand house. J. P. Lewis.—LeE
Sand dollar. Barbara Juster Esbensen.—EsW
Sand house. J. Patrick Lewis.—LeE
"Sand, sand, hills of sand". See The mermaids
Sandburg, Carl
Arithmetic, sels.
"Arithmetic is where numbers fly".—DeS
"Arithmetic is where numbers fly". See Arithmetic
Bubbles.—DeT
Buffalo dusk.—CaB—DeS—ElW
The family of man, sels.
Names.—WhAa
Fog ("The fog comes").—DeT
Fourth of July night.—LaN
Hits and runs.—KnAs
Lost ("Desolate and lone").—LaN
"Milk white moon, put the cows to sleep".—SuI
Names. See The family of man
Old deep sing song.—MoR
Paper I.—DeS
Paper II.—DeS
"The place where a great city stands is not the place of stretch'd wharves, docks". See Song of the broad-axe
Potomac town in February.—LiDd
River moons.—LaN
Skyscraper.—SuI
Song of the broad-axe, sels.
"The place where a great city stands is not the place of stretch'd wharves, docks".—SuI
Stars ("The stars are too many to count").—HoSt
There are different gardens.—SuI
Washington monument by night.—SuI
We must be polite.—DeS
Window ("Night from a railroad car window").—DeT
Worms and the wind.—CaB
"Sandpaper kisses". See Cat kisses
The **sandpiper**. Celia Thaxter.—SuI
Sandpipers
The sandpiper. C. Thaxter.—SuI
Sandpipers. H. Nemerov.—ElW
"Sandpipers running along the beach". J. A. P. Spencer.—StP
Sandpipers. Howard Nemerov.—ElW
"Sandpipers running along the beach". Joseph A. P. Spencer.—StP
"The sandy cat by the farmer's chair". See Summer evening
"Sandy's in love with Timmy". See It's gross to kiss
Santa Claus
Christmas eve rhyme. C. MacCullers.—GoA
"Dear Santa Claus". J. Prelutsky.—LoFh
"Jolly old Saint Nicholas". Unknown.—YoHa
The North Pole express. J. Yolen.—YoHa
Questions on Christmas eve. W. Magee.—FoLe
Santa Claus ("Hast thou, in fancy, trodden where lie"). W. De La Mare.—DeR
Santa Claus ("Santa Claus is"). V. Worth.—WoA
Santa rides. J. Yolen.—YoHa
"There is a young reindeer named Donder". J. P. Lewis.—LiLo
A visit from St. Nicholas. C. C. Moore.—ElW—HoS
What I used to wonder. X. J. Kennedy.—KeK
"A woman named Mrs. S. Claus". J. P. Lewis.—LiLo
Santa Claus ("Hast thou, in fancy, trodden where lie"). Walter De La Mare.—DeR

Santa Claus ("Santa Claus is"). Valerie Worth.—WoA
"Santa Claus is". See Santa Claus
Santa rides. Jane Yolen.—YoHa
Santoka
The crow ("A crow"), tr. by Tze-si Huang.—DeI
Santos, Benilda S.
Atong, tr. by Ramon C. Sunico.—NyT
Atong and his goodbye, tr. by Ramon C. Sunico.—NyT
Santos, Sherod
The evening light along the sound.—GoT
Sappho
"Thank you, my dear".—GoU
Sappho to Eranna. Rainer Maria Rilke, tr. by Edward Snow.—GoU
The **sappy** heasons. Eve Merriam.—MeCh
"Saps rising, ground's warming". See Grasshoppers
"Sara Cynthia Sylvia Stout would not take the garbage out". Shel Silverstein.—ElW
Sarkar, Shihab
Letter from my son.—NyT
Sarton, May
Letters from Maine, sels.
"There was your voice, astonishment".—GoU
"There was your voice, astonishment". See Letters from Maine
"Sasparilla". Unknown.—ScA
Satan. See Devil
"The satin sea lions". See Sea lions
Sato, Hiro
Kappa.—WhDd
"Saturday evening grows". See Jasmine
Saturday fielding practice. Lillian Morrison.—LiPf
"Saturday night". See Bingo
Saucer hat lady. Eloise Greenfield.—GrU
"Saucer on his head, carapace on his back". See Kappa
"The sausage is a cunning bird". Unknown.—PrP
"Savage lion in the zoo". See Supper for a lion
Savior. Maya Angelou.—AnI
Savory, Teo
"Let me get up early on this summer morning", tr.—GoT
Sawa, Yuki
Great Aso, tr.—NyT
Stars at night, tr.—NyT
Sawdust song ("Sawdust sings, sawdust songs"). See "Aserrin, aserran"
Say goodbye to Big Daddy. Randall Jarrell.—KnAs
Say nay. Eve Merriam.—MeS
"Say not the struggle nought availeth". Arthur Hugh Clough.—ElW
Says, sels. Walt Whitman
"I say whatever tastes sweet to the most perfect person, that".—HoVo
"Says the humpbacked zebu". See Z is for zebu
"Says the prancing French poodle". See D is for dog
"A scallion has a scad of skins". See Straight scoop about scallions
Scannell, Vernon
Autobiographical note.—JaPr
Scarecrow Christmas. Pie Corbett.—FoLe
Scarecrows
"Oh farmer, poor farmer, you're surely". J. Prelutsky.—PrBe
Scarecrow Christmas. P. Corbett.—FoLe
"There once was a scarecrow named Joel". D. McCord.—LiLo
Scary things. Julie Holder.—BaH
"The scent of bramble fills the air". See The sleeping beauty

Schandelmeier, Linda
Secrets ("She slits empty feed sacks").—JaPr
Scheele, Roy
Keeping the horses.—JaM
Nothing but net.—KnAs
Schell, Jessie
Zora.—JaPr
Schenectady. Eve Merriam.—MeS
Schmeltz, Susan Alton
"Never take a pig to lunch".—PrFo
Paper dragons.—BaW
Scholl, Sophie (about)
The white rose, Sophie Scholl, 1921-1943. E. Mumford.—JaM
Schonborg, Virginia
"The air was damp". See Song of ships
City rain.—LaN
Rescue ("Bony cat").—LaCc
Song of ships, sels.
"The air was damp".—LaN
School. See also Teachers and teaching
Alley cat school. F. Asch.—LaCc
Andrea Pulovsky. M. Glenn.—GlBc
Anne Frank. S. L. Nelms.—JaPr
April fool. J. Ciardi.—CiH—LiLo
"April fool, go to school". Unknown.—WiA
Arnold Flitterman. M. Glenn.—GlBc
Bad. P. B. Janeczko.—JaB
Beginning of term. Unknown.—OpI
Belinda Enriquez. M. Glenn.—GlBc
Bonfire. P. B. Janeczko.—JaB
Brent Sorensen. M. Glenn.—GlBc
Budging line ups. K. Dakos.—DaI
"The bus weaves its way through the jungle home". M. Wayne.—LeCa
Caleb's desk is a mess. K. Dakos.—DaI
Championship. S. B. Mathis.—MaR
Checking out me history. J. Agard.—AgL
Cheerleader. J. W. Miller.—JaPr
Chocolate dreams and chocolate schemes. A. Adoff.—AdCh
Claud St. Jules. M. Glenn.—GlBc
"A collegiate damsel named Breeze". Unknown.—LiLo
Cruel boys. G. Soto.—JaM
A day in school. K. Dakos.—DaI
Diana Marvin. M. Glenn.—GlBc
"A diller, a dollar". Mother Goose.—SuO—WaM
Dina Harper. M. Glenn.—GlBc
"Don't talk to me about no options, I'm poor". J. Carson.—CaS
Don't you remember how sick you are. K. Dakos.—DaI
Drawing by Ronnie C., grade one. Lechlitner. Ruth.—GoT
The dunce. W. De La Mare.—DeR—MaP
Excuse. M. C. Livingston.—LiT
First day of school. A. Fisher.—FiA
"Fool, fool, April fool". Unknown.—OpI
Football ("Now they're ready, now they're waiting"). F. S. Fitzgerald.—KnAs
"Four more days and we are free". Unknown.—WiA
Gardner Todd. M. Glenn.—GlBc
Garrett Chandler. M. Glenn.—GlBc
Gayle Buckingham. M. Glenn.—GlBc
Getting nowhere. J. Berry.—BeW
Go to the Bahamas. K. Dakos.—DaI
"Hark, the herald angels shout". Unknown.—ScA
Hector Velasquez. M. Glenn.—GlBc
"Heigh ho, heigh ho, it's off to school we go". Unknown.—ScA

Help ("Any magazines"). M. Fatchen.—FaCm
Herby Wall. M. Glenn.—GlBc
High school. G. Roberts.—JaPr
Homework. B. J. Esbensen.—EsW
How I went truant from school to visit a river. M. Oliver.—JaPr
I brought a worm. K. Dakos.—DaI
I can't go back to school. M. P. Hearn.—JaP
I have no time to visit with King Arthur. K. Dakos.—DaI
"I love to do my homework". Unknown.—PrFo
"I thought I'd take my rat to school". C. McNaughton.—PrFo
I won the prize. K. Dakos.—DaI
Idyll. J. Updike.—KnAs
If you're not here, please raise your hand. K. Dakos.—DaI
"I'm going to die". K. Dakos.—DaI
"I'm in another dimension". K. Dakos.—DaI
In this last class before lunch, I close my eyes. A. Adoff.—AdCh
It's inside my sister's lunch. K. Dakos.—DaI
"It's time, I believe". Unknown.—OpI
"I've been working on my schoolbooks". Unknown.—ScA
Jimmy Zale. M. Glenn.—GlBc
Kumar Ragnath. M. Glenn.—GlBc
Kwang Chin Ho. M. Glenn.—GlBc
Lanky Hank Farrow. H. Witt.—KnAs
A late assignment. K. Dakos.—DaI
"Latin is a dead tongue". Unknown.—OpI
Led by the Hebrew School rabbi. J. Baumel.—KnAs
The lesson ("Every time I'm called to the front"). M. Sorescu.—AgL
A lifetime in third grade. K. Dakos.—DaI
Look out. M. Fatchen.—PrFo
Luanne Sheridan. M. Glenn.—GlBc
Lunchbox. V. Worth.—MoS
Mallory Wade. M. Glenn.—GlBc
Mamma settles the dropout problem. B. Gates.—SuC
Marvin Pickett. M. Glenn.—KnAs
"Mary had a stick of gum". Unknown.—ScA
Mary's lamb. S. J. Hale.—SuI
"Mary had a little lamb".—EdGl (unat.)—SuO (unat.)—WaM (unat.)
Math is brewing and I'm in trouble. K. Dakos.—DaI
Mercedes Lugo. M. Glenn.—GlBc
The mighty eye. K. Dakos.—DaI
"Mine eyes have seen the glory of the closing of the school". Unknown.—ScA
"Moods and tenses". Unknown.—OpI
Ms. Marilyn Lindowsky, counselor. M. Glenn.—GlBc
Ms. Nadine Sierra, French. M. Glenn.—GlBc
"Multiplication is vexation". Unknown.—OpI
"My head doth ache". Unknown.—OpI
My homework isn't done. K. Dakos.—DaI
My own day. J. Little.—LiHe—LoFh
Napoleon. M. Holub.—NyT
"Naughty little Margaret". Unknown.—ScA
"A nip for new". Unknown.—OpI
"No more pencils, no more books". Unknown.—CoM—ScA
The Notre Dame victory march. J. Shea.—KnAs
"On report card day Spike Sparks". X. J. Kennedy.—KeFb
Ophelia. B. Hillman.—JaM
"Over the bay". Unknown.—WiA
"Over the ocean". Unknown.—WiA

School.—*Continued*
"Over the sea". Unknown.—WiA
Paper doll. G. Morfin.—NyT
Patricia Lampert. M. Glenn.—GlBc
Playoff pizza. S. B. Mathis.—MaR
Poor substitute. K. Dakos.—DaI
Preposterous. J. Hall.—JaPr
Puzzle. M. C. Livingston.—LiR
"Row, row, row your boat". Unknown.—ScA
"Running to school". Unknown.—ScA
The sacred. S. Dunn.—JaM
School dinner menu for 1st of April. W. Magee.—FoLe
"School is all over". A. Low.—LoFh
School play. M. C. Livingston.—LiR
September. L. Clifton.—SlM
"September is". B. Katz.—MoS
Shakespeare's gone. K. Dakos.—DaI
She should have listened to me. K. Dakos.—DaI
"Sheldon with a welding torch". X. J. Kennedy.—KeFb
Skateboard flyer. J. Berry.—BeW
The sleeper. E. Field.—KnAs
Speech class, for Joe. J. Daniels.—JaP
"Strawberry shortcake". Unknown.—ScA
Summer goes. R. Hoban.—LoFh
Summer vacation. K. Fufuka.—SlM
T. C. Tyler. M. Glenn.—GlBc
Teach the making of summer. J. Berry.—BeW
"Teacher's pet, teacher's pet". Unknown.—ScA
That girl. G. Soto.—SoA
There's a cobra in the bathroom. K. Dakos.—DaI
They don't do math in Texas. K. Dakos.—DaI
"This time tomorrow, where shall I be". Unknown.—OpI
Three thirty. A. Adoff.—AdCh
Today. J. Little.—LiHe
"Today's the case". Unknown.—OpI
Toni Vingelli. M. Glenn.—GlBc
"Tonight, tonight, the pillow fight". Unknown.—WiA
Valerie O'Neill. M. Glenn.—GlBc
Victory banquet. S. B. Mathis.—MaR
Warren Christopher. M. Glenn.—GlBc
What I remember about the 6th grade. M. Vinz.—JaP
"When ice cream grows on spaghetti trees". Unknown.—PrFo
"When land is gone and money spent". Mother Goose.—WaM
"Where the sun shone white hot, Cass". X. J. Kennedy.—KeFb
The wind is calling me away. K. Dakos.—DaI
You can do better. K. Dakos.—DaI
You've got to learn the white man's game. M. M. Smith.—KnAs
Zimmer in grade school. P. Zimmer.—JaPr
"A school-bus driver from Deering". See A driver from Deering
School dinner menu for 1st of April. Wes Magee.—FoLe
"School is all over". Alice Low.—LoFh
School play. Myra Cohn Livingston.—LiR
Schoolcrafts's diary, written on the Missouri, 1830. Robert Bly.—SuI
"Schoolgirls are heroes". See A short note on schoolgirls
Schott, Penelope Scambly
Chimera.—WhDd
Schwartz, Delmore
The dark and falling summer.—GoT—SuI

Exercise in preparation for a pindaric ode to Carl Hubbell.—KnAs
Schwartz, Howard
Wandering chorus, tr.—GoT
Schweitzer, Albert
"May I follow a life of compassion in pity for".—StP
"O heavenly Father, protect and bless".—StP
Science
"Science". G. Nelson.—SlM
"A scientist living at Staines". R. Hewison.—LiLo
"When I heard the learn'd astronomer". W. Whitman.—HoVo
"Science". Gordon Nelson.—SlM
"A scientist living at Staines". R.J.P. Hewison.—LiLo
"Scones and pancakes roun' the table". Unknown.—StP
Scotland
First foot. I. Serraillier.—FoLe
A history of golf, sort of. T. L. Hirsch.—KnAs
"My Scottish great granduncle Milt's". X. J. Kennedy.—KeGh
Scott, Herbert
A brief reversal, 1941.—JaPr
Early love.—JaM
Evening dawn.—JaPr
My father's fortune.—JaPr
That summer.—JaPr
Scott, Sir Walter
The bonny, bonny owl.—LiIf
"Scott and I bent". See Heaven
Scraping the world away. Clive Herbert Webster.—AgL
"Scrawny, Bumper, Zip". See Their names
Screaming. Doug MacLeod.—PrFo
"A screech across the sands". See Mr. Punch (for a picture)
Scribbled notes picked up by owners, and rewritten because of bad grammar, bad spelling, bad writing. James Berry.—BeW
"Scrub weel yer fresh fish". From Fishermen's songs. Unknown.—OpT
"The scruffy reds". See Winter choosing
Sculpture and statues
"Alla en la fuente". Unknown.—DeA
The fountain ("There in the fountain").—DeA
The little old cupid. W. De La Mare.—DeR—MaP
Ozymandias. P. B. Shelley.—ElW
Sphinx. D. Chandra.—WhDd
The statue. A. Grilikhes.—MoR
Statue of Liberty. M. C. Livingston.—LiNe
Statues. M. C. Livingston.—LiNe
Sea. See Ocean
The sea body. Walter De La Mare.—MaP
Sea cliff. A.J.M. Smith.—BoT
The sea gull's eye. Russell Hoban.—JaP
Sea horse and sawhorse. X. J. Kennedy.—PrFo
"A sea horse saw a sawhorse". See Sea horse and sawhorse
"The sea laments". See Echoes
Sea life. See names of sea life, as Whales
Sea lions. Valerie Worth.—WoAl
Sea school. Barbara Howes.—LeCa
"A sea serpent saw a big tanker". Unknown.—LiLo—PrP
Sea shell. Amy Lowell.—ElW—LoFh
"Sea shell". Myra Cohn Livingston.—LiT
"Sea shell, sea shell". See Sea shell
Sea thing. Max Fatchen.—FaCm
Sea timeless song. Grace Nichols.—NiCo

Sea turtle. Unknown.—WhAa
"The sea washes England". See Babel
Sea wave. Sandra Liatsos.—HoS
Seafarer. Unknown.—OpT
Seafaring life. See also Fishers and fishing; Pirates; Ships
  Andy Battle's and Nod's song. W. De La Mare.—MaP
    Yeo ho.—DeR
  Araby. W. De La Mare.—DeR
  "Bobby Shaftoe's gone to sea". Mother Goose.—SuO
  Bonny sailor boy. Unknown.—OpT
  Captain Lean. W. De La Mare.—DeR
  Cheerily man. Unknown.—MoR
  The Englishman. W. De La Mare.—DeR
  Gone ("Bright sun, hot sun, oh, to be"). W. De La Mare.—DeR
  "I'm Popeye, the sailorman". Unknown.—CoM
  The necklace. M. C. Livingston.—LiR
  Nocturne of the wharves. A. Bontemps.—SuC
  The old sailor. W. De La Mare.—DeR
  The picture. W. De La Mare.—DeR—MaP
  "Red sky at night". Mother Goose.—WaM
  The rime of the ancient mariner, complete. S. T. Coleridge.—ElW
  "A sailor went to sea, sea, sea". Unknown.—CoM
    "A sailor went to sea".—WiA
  A sailor's memoirs. M. Al-Fayiz.—NyT
  Sea shell. A. Lowell.—ElW—LoFh
  Seafarer. Unknown.—OpT
  Thames. W. De La Mare.—DeR
"Seagull, seagull, sit on the sand". See To the seagull
Seagulls. See Gulls
Seal. William Jay Smith.—SmL
Seal at the zoo. Lee Bennett Hopkins.—HoT
Seal lullaby. See Seal mother's song
Seal mother's song. Rudyard Kipling.—CoAz
  Seal lullaby.—WhAs
"Sealed wax cells". See Honeycomb
Seals (animals)
  "Four furry seals, four funny fat seals". J. Prelutsky.—CoAz
  Sea lions. V. Worth.—WoAl
  Seal. W. J. Smith.—SmL
  Seal at the zoo. L. B. Hopkins.—HoT
  Seal mother's song. R. Kipling.—CoAz
    Seal lullaby.—WhAs
Seamen. See Seafaring life
Seashell. Valerie Worth.—WoAl
Seashells. See Shells
Seashore. See Shore
Seasons. See also names of seasons, as Autumn; also names of months, as January
  Come, gone. W. De La Mare.—DeR
  Coming and going. R. Francis.—KeT
  Country calendar. E. Merriam.—MeS
  Crow ("Jump-Johnny Peacoat"). J. P. Lewis.—LeT
  Deciduous. E. Merriam.—MeS
  Evergreen. E. Merriam.—MeS
  Fireworks 2. E. Merriam.—MeS
  Four seasons. Unknown.—DeS
  From the most distant time. L. Wu-ti.—GoT
  Garden calendar. N. M. Bodecker.—KeT
  He saved a lot of time by not working. J. Ciardi.—CiH
  "The heart of man has four chambers, and each is filled with". N. Corwin.—GoT
  In retrospect. M. Angelou.—GoU
  Now blue October. R. Nathan.—GoU

O dear me. W. De La Mare.—DeR
On journeys through the states. W. Whitman.—HoVo
On the grasshopper and cricket. J. Keats.—ElW
Our tree. M. Chute.—DeS
Points of the compass. E. Merriam.—MeS
Reply to the question, how can you become a poet. E. Merriam.—MeS
Rosebush. V. Worth.—WoAl
The sappy heasons. E. Merriam.—MeCh
Stars ("If to the heavens you lift your eyes"). W. De La Mare.—DeR
There was a sound of airy seasons passing. S. Quasimodo.—GoT
"There was a young fellow named Hall". Unknown.—LiLo
"Wrinkles in the lake". From Diary of a woodcutter. F. Rifka.—NyT
Seaweed. Myra Cohn Livingston.—HoS—MoS
"Seaweed from high tide". See Seaweed
Second song, to the same. Alfred Tennyson.—LiIf
Secret ("Mrs. Kangaroo"). Beverly McLoughland.—HoS
The secret ("Open your eyes, now, look, and see"). Walter De La Mare.—DeR
Secret ("The secret I told you"). Myra Cohn Livingston.—LiR
The secret ("We don't mention where he went"). Myra Cohn Livingston.—LiT
Secret door. Myra Cohn Livingston.—DeT
Secret hand. Eve Merriam.—MeS
"The secret I told you". See Secret
A secret kept. Judah Al-Harizi, tr. by Robert Mezey.—GoU
The secret place. Tomie De Paola.—DeT
Secrets
  Big sister. M. A. Hoberman.—HoFa
  Closet. M. C. Livingston.—LiNe
  558. J.-U.-D. Rumi.—GoU
  For forest. G. Nichols.—NiCo
  Hideout. A. Fisher.—DeT
  Hiding our love. C. Kizer.—GoU
  "I had a little secret". J. Prelutsky.—PrBe
  "I know a secret". Unknown.—WiA
  "I know something I won't tell". Mother Goose.—WaM—WiA
    Three little monkeys.—PrFo
  I never told. M. C. Livingston.—LiNe
  In autumn. B. J. Esbensen.—EsW
  Jody Walker, the first voice. P. Ruffin.—JaPr
  Keziah. G. Brooks.—LiDd
  Lulu, lulu, I've a lilo. C. Pomerantz.—DeS—LiIf
  Places to hide a secret message. E. Merriam.—DeT
  The secret ("Open your eyes, now, look, and see"). W. De La Mare.—DeR
  Secret ("The secret I told you"). M. C. Livingston.—LiR
  The secret ("We don't mention where he went"). M. C. Livingston.—LiT
  Secret door. M. C. Livingston.—DeT
  Secret hand. E. Merriam.—MeS
  A secret kept. J. Al-Harizi.—GoU
  The secret place. T. De Paola.—DeT
  Secrets ("I doubt that you remember her, except"). R. Pack.—JaM
  Secrets ("She slits empty feed sacks"). L. Schandelmeier.—JaPr
  Shortcut. M. C. Livingston.—LiNe
  The song of the secret. W. De La Mare.—DeR—MaP
  Telephone talk. X. J. Kennedy.—KeK

Selfishness
"Sheldon the selfish shellfish". X. J. Kennedy.—KeGh
The **seller**. Eloise Greenfield.—GrN
Seloti, Tialuga Sunia
"One day I asked the mirror facing me".—NyT
Sending spring love to Tzu-An. Hsiian-Chi Yu, tr. by Kenneth Rexroth and Ling Chung.—GoU
Sengupta, Bhabani
Under this sky, tr.—NyT
Sengupta, Samarendra
Day-dream, tr. by Lila Ray.—NyT
Senses. See also Odors; Sight; Sounds; Taste; Touch
Sensible questions. Margaret Mahy.—MaN
Sephina. Walter De La Mare.—DeR
September
It's great when you get in. E. O'Neill.—KnAs
September. L. Clifton.—SlM
"September is". B. Katz.—MoS
Timber rattlesnake. M. Singer.—SiT
September. Lucille Clifton.—SlM
September garden. Myra Cohn Livingston.—LiNe
"**September** is". Bobbi Katz.—MoS
Serendipity. Eve Merriam.—MeCh
"A **series** of small, on". See Insignificant
The **serpent's** hiss. Eve Merriam.—MeCh
Serraillier, Ian
First foot.—FoLe
The mouse in the wainscot.—LaM
The tickle rhyme.—MoS
The visitor ("A crumbling churchyard, the sea, and the moon").—BaH
Serves him right. John Ciardi.—CiH
"A **set** of bookends where". See Parentheses
"**Set** your watch, the weather said". See On time
Setting the Thanksgiving table. X. J. Kennedy.—KeK
Setting the traps. David Jauss.—JaPr
Seuss, Dr. (pseud. of Theodor Geisel)
If we didn't have birthdays.—LoFh
Too many Daves.—ElW
Seven. Myra Cohn Livingston.—LiBp
"**Seven** little rabbits". John Becker.—HoS
"**Seven** piglets, pink and gray". Jack Prelutsky.—PrBe
"**Seven** sweet notes". See Echo
Seven women's blessed assurance. Maya Angelou.—AnI
"**Seventeen** and countless times french-kissed". See Cheerleader
The **seventh** round. James Merrill.—KnAs
74th street. Myra Cohn Livingston.—JaP
Sewing
Basket. M. C. Livingston.—LiPg
The coat. D. Lee.—KeT
Dressmaking screamer. W. J. Smith.—SmL
N is for needle. W. J. Smith.—SmL
"Oh, the funniest thing I've ever seen". Unknown.—PrP—WiA
"Pins and needles". E. Merriam.—MeY
"Tailor had a needle". J. Prelutsky.—PrBe
"There was an old man of the Cape". R. L. Stevenson.—LiLo
"A thrifty young fellow of Shoreham". Unknown.—LiLo
Tillie. W. De La Mare.—DeR—MaP
"Work, work, work". From The song of the shirt. T. Hood.—MoR
Sex
"As we are so wonderfully done with each other". K. Patchen.—GoU
Bad. P. B. Janeczko.—JaB

"Black hair". A. Yosano.—GoU
Born that way. M. Angelou.—AnI
Boys' night out. M. Vinz.—JaPr
Elsa Wertman. E. L. Masters.—ElW
Generations. S. Cornish.—JaPr
"Her eyes in sleep". Unknown.—GoU
Known to Eve and me. M. Angelou.—AnI
Love song to a stranger. J. Baez.—GoU
Not quite Kinsey. G. Hyland.—JaPr
On a night of the full moon. A. Lorde.—GoU
Regina Kelsey. M. Glenn.—GlBc
A secret kept. J. Al-Harizi.—GoU
Song of the queen bee. E. B. White.—ElW
Summer killer. T. A. Broughton.—JaM
Trouble. J. Wright.—JaPr
A war baby looks back. J. Holden.—JaPr
Sexton, Anne
The nude swim.—KnAs
Young.—AgL—JaPr
"**Sha-ame**, sha-ame". Unknown.—CoM—WiA
"Shame, shame".—ScA
Shadow ("Silhouette"). Richard Bruce.—SuC
The **shadow** ("When the last of gloaming's gone"). Walter De La Mare.—DeR
The **shadow** inside me. Tommy Olofsson, tr. by Jean Pearson.—NyT
"A **shadow** is floating through the moonlight". See The bird of night
"**Shadow** lit with yellow eyes". Tony Johnston.—LiIf
"A **shadow** of a shadow". See The warlock's cat
Shadowboxing. James Tate.—KnAs
Shadows
Candle. M. C. Livingston.—LiNe
Cat at night. A. Stoutenburg.—LaCc
8 A.M. shadows. P. Hubbell.—DeS
Ground hog day. L. Moore.—DeT
Shadow ("Silhouette"). R. Bruce.—SuC
The shadow ("When the last of gloaming's gone"). W. De La Mare.—DeR
The shadow inside me. T. Olofsson.—NyT
Shadowboxing. J. Tate.—KnAs
Shadows. W. De La Mare.—DeR
The song of shadows. W. De La Mare.—DeR—MaP
Shadows. Walter De La Mare.—DeR
"**Shadows** on the wall". See Life doesn't frighten me
"**Shake** your brown feet, honey". See Song for a banjo dance
Shakes and ladders. Max Fatchen.—FaCm
Shakespeare, William
Cymbeline, sels.
"Fear no more the heat o' the sun".—ElW
"Fear no more the heat o' the sun". See Cymbeline
"I will not change my horse with any that treads". See King Henry V
"If we shadows have offended". See A midsummer night's dream
King Henry V, sels.
"I will not change my horse with any that treads".—WhAa
Love's labour's lost, sels.
"When icicles hang by the wall".—LiIf
Winter.—ElW
A midsummer night's dream, sels.
"If we shadows have offended".—WhDd
"O Lord, that lends me life".—StP
O mistress mine. See Twelfth night
Twelfth night, sels.
O mistress mine.—ElW
"When icicles hang by the wall". See Love's labour's lost

Shore.—*Continued*
Autumn and the sea. J. Heraud.—NyT
Away we go. W. De La Mare.—DeR
The bathers. K. Shapiro.—KnAs
"The Bay of Tsunu". H. Kakinomoto.—GoU
By the sea. E. Merriam.—MeS
Caught. G. Dubois.—KnAs
"Celia sat beside the seaside". Unknown.—PrP
The chatelaine. Unknown.—OpT
Children lost. M. Fatchen.—FaCm
City to surf. D. Bateson.—FoLe
Crab. V. Worth.—WoAl
Crab dance. G. Nichols.—NiCo
"Daisy and Lily". From Waltz. E. Sitwell.—MoR
"Down by the ocean, down by the sea".
   Unknown.—ScA
Duet. R. Krauss.—MoR
Echoes. W. De La Mare.—DeR
The evening light along the sound. S. Santos.—
   GoT
Fisherman. D. Brand.—BoT
Five ("Five little children"). C. Tringress.—MoS
"Galloping pony". Kyorai.—CaR—WhAa
Gracious goodness. M. Piercy.—ElW
Haiti, skin diving. J. Shore.—KnAS
The hungry waves. D. Aldis.—DeT
It's great when you get in. E. O'Neill.—KnAs
July. F. Newman.—BoT
"The kite that braved old Orchard Beach". X. J.
   Kennedy.—KeK
Laughter. M. Waddington.—BoT
Long Beach, February. M. C. Livingston.—LiR
"Maggie and Milly and Molly and May". E. E.
   Cummings.—SuI
      "Maggie and Millie . . .".—ElW
The main deep. J. Stephens.—MoR
The mermaids ("Sand, sand, hills of sand"). W.
   De La Mare.—DeR
Mine. L. Moore.—MoS
The moon rises slowly over the ocean. X.
   De-min.—NyT
Morning at Malibu. M. C. Livingston.—LiNe
Nantucket. Z. Rogow.—GoT
Night fog. X. J. Kennedy.—KeK
Nocturne of the wharves. A. Bontemps.—SuC
"One foggy autumn in Baltimore". J. Prelutsky.—
   PrBe
"Out of the cradle endlessly rocking". W.
   Whitman.—HoVo
The picnic. D. Aldis.—HoS
The pool in the rock. W. De La Mare.—DeR
Remembering. M. C. Livingston.—LiR
Rocks ("Big rocks into pebbles"). F. P. Heide.—
   DeS
Sails, gulls, sky, sea. F. Holman.—BaW
Sam. W. De La Mare.—DeR—MaP
Sand dollar. B. J. Esbensen.—EsW
Sand house. J. P. Lewis.—LeE
The sandpiper. C. Thaxter.—SuI
Sandpipers. H. Nemerov.—ElW
"Sandpipers running along the beach". J. A. P.
   Spencer.—StP
The sea body. W. De La Mare.—MaP
Sea cliff. A. Smith.—BoT
The sea gull's eye. R. Hoban.—JaP
Sea horse and sawhorse. X. J. Kennedy.—PrFo
Sea shell. A. Lowell.—ElW—LoFh
Seaweed. M. C. Livingston.—HoS—MoS
"She sells sea shells by the seashore".
   Unknown.—WiA
Sitting in the sand. K. Kuskin.—MoS
Song of the sea and people. J. Berry.—BeW

South ("But today I recapture the islands'"). E.
   Brathwaite.—LeCa
Souvenir. E. Merriam.—MeS
Starfish. V. Worth.—WoAl
The storm ("First there were two of us, then there
   were three of us"). W. De La Mare.—DeR
Summer doings. W. Cole.—HoGo
The surfer. J. Wright.—MoR
Surfers at Santa Cruz. P. Goodman.—KnAs
Swimming in the Pacific. R. P. Warren.—KnAs
"There's a tiresome young man from Bay Shore".
   M. Bishop.—LiLo
Tide talk. M. Fatchen.—FaCm
Tidings. M. Bevan.—CaB
Trip to the seashore. L. Simmie.—BoT
"Until I saw the sea". L. Moore.—BaW—DeS
A visit from the sea. R. L. Stevenson.—CaB
The walrus and the carpenter. From Through the
   looking-glass. L. Carroll.—DeT—ElW—HoS
"The water's deep". C. McNaughton.—PrFo
World. A. R. Ammons.—ElW
"You sea, I resign myself to you also, I guess what
   you". From Song of myself. W. Whitman.—
   HoVo
Short, Clarice
The owl on the aerial.—LiIf
A **short** long story. Julia Cunningham.—JaP
A **short** note on schoolgirls. Alison Campbell.—AgL
"**Short** ones, fat ones". See Backsides
A **short** story. David Escobar Galindo, tr. by Jorge
   D. Piche.—NyT
Shortcut. Myra Cohn Livingston.—LiNe
"**Should** I worship Him from fear of hell". Rabi'ah
   Al'Adawiyah.—StP
"**Should** you, my lord, while you pursue my song".
   From To the right honorable William, Earl of
   Dartmouth. Phillis Wheatley.—SuI
Show Boat, sels. Oscar Hammerstein
   Ol' man river.—SuC
"A **shower**, a sprinkle". See Summer rain
"**Showery**, flowery". Unknown.—ScA
"A **showy** gesture". See The cardinal
"**Shrill** rang the squeak in the empty house". See
   Lone
The **shriving.** Jared Carter.—JaM
Shrove Tuesday. Ann Bonner.—FoLe
Shub, Elizabeth
   "Sleep, sleep, sleep", tr.—PlW
Shurbanov, Alexander
   Believe it or not, tr.—NyT
Shut not your doors. Walt Whitman.—HoVo
"**Shut** not your doors to me proud libraries". See
   Shut not your doors
"**Shut** one eye then the other". See Before the game
"**Shut** the windows". See Hurricane
Shy. Mary Ann Hoberman.—HoFa
Sick days. Mary Ann Hoberman.—HoFa
The **sick-room.** R. A. Simpson.—NyT
Sickness
Bones. W. De La Mare.—PrFo
The breath of death (the cigarette). L. Sissay.—
   AgL
A brief reversal, 1941. H. Scott.—JaPr
"Caroline Pink, she fell down the sink".
   Unknown.—OpI
Cruel Jenny Wren. Unknown.—ElW
The cure. Unknown.—OpT
The dodo ("The mournful dodo lay in bed"). P.
   Wesley-Smith.—PrFo
Don't you remember how sick you are. K.
   Dakos.—DaI

Sickness—*Continued*
"Every time I get a little headache". J. Carson.—CaS
"I met my boyfriend at the candy store". Unknown.—CoM
"I went down to Johnny's house". Unknown.—WiA
"Jeremiah Obadiah, puff, puff, puff". Mother Goose.—WaM
Kept home. J. Berry.—BeW
The land of counterpane. R. L. Stevenson.—DeT—KeT
Llude sig kachoo. E. Merriam.—MeCh
"Miss Lucy had a baby". Unknown.—CoM—ScA
"Mother made a seedy cake". Unknown.—OpI
"Mother, Mother, I am ill". Unknown.—OpI
"My TV came down with a chill". W. R. Espy.—KeT
"Now, George is sick". J. Carson.—CaS
"Old man Moses, sick in bed". Unknown.—ScA
Olive Street. M. C. Livingston.—LiT
Poor Henry. W. De La Mare.—DeR—MaP
"Quick, quick". Unknown.—OpI
Sailing, sailing. L. Morrison.—KnAs
"She come to see your mother". J. Carson.—CaS
Sick days. M. A. Hoberman.—HoFa
The sick-room. R. A. Simpson.—NyT
"Sickness come di gallop, but e tek e own time fo walk' way". Unknown.—LeCa
"There was a young girl named O'Neill". Unknown.—LiLo
"There was a young lady of Spain". Unknown.—LiLo
"To the medicine man's house they have led me". Unknown.—LiIf
"Up the river". Unknown.—WiA
"**Sickness** come di gallop, but e tek e own time fo walk' way". Unknown.—LeCa
The **sidewalk** racer, or on the skateboard. Lillian Morrison.—JaP—KnAs
Sidewalks. Valerie Worth.—WoAl
"**Sidewalks** wear out". See Sidewalks
Sight
Gazebo. E. Greenfield.—GrU
The owl ("In broad daylight"). J. Gardner.—LiIf
The owl ("The owl that lives in the old oak tree"). W. J. Smith.—LiIf—SmL
Specs. E. Merriam.—MeP
What all the owls know. J. Hollander.—LiIf
The woods at night. M. Swenson.—LiIf
The **sign**. Florence Parry Heide.—HeG
"**Signals** signals hey". See Red dog blue fly
Signs
The sign. F. P. Heide.—HeG
Sikhs
Mela. J. Kenward.—FoLe
Silence
"All is silent". H. Ping-hsin.—StP
The crow ("A crow"). Santoka.—DeI
The frog ("Breaking the silence"). Basho.—DeI
I told you so. J. Little.—LiHe
The meaning of simplicity. Y. Ritsos.—NyT
Muted. P. Verlaine.—GoU
My father's fortune. H. Scott.—JaPr
Now silent falls. W. De La Mare.—DeR
The old king. W. De La Mare.—DeR
"Order in the gallery". Unknown.—OpI
Orders. A. M. Klein.—BoT
Silence. E. Merriam.—MeS
Silent noon. D. G. Rossetti.—GoU
"There was a boy, ye knew him well, ye cliffs". From The prelude. W. Wordsworth.—LiIf

"This cat". K. Kuskin.—LaCc
Tomorrow ("And tomorrow the sun will shine again"). J. H. Mackay.—GoT
Wordless day. C. Shiang-hua.—NyT
"The **silence**". See The cicada
Silence. Eve Merriam.—MeS
"**Silence** in the court". Unknown.—ScA
"**Silence** stilled the meadow". See Grasshopper
"**Silence** was my father's fortune". See My father's fortune
"**Silent** night". Joseph Mohr.—StP (unat.)
Silent noon. Dante Gabriel Rossetti.—GoU
"The **silent** shark". See S, silent shark
The **silent** type. Florence Parry Heide.—HeG
Silesius, Angelus
"Everyone to his own".—StP
"**Silhouette**". See Shadow
Silhouettes. Max Fatchen.—FaCm
Silkin, Jon
Caring for animals.—NyT
Silko, Leslie Marmon
Where mountain lion lay down with deer.—SuI
"The **silliest** fowl, the most absurd". See Gooney bird
Silly Billy. Max Fatchen.—FaCm
"**Silly** bird is Mr. Owl". See All eyes
"A **silly** old skinflint named Quince". See Rest in peace
Silly questions. Jane Yolen.—YoBe
Silly Sallie. Walter De La Mare.—DeR
"**Silly** Sallie, silly Sallie". See Silly Sallie
The **silly** song ("Hey ding a ding"). Margaret Mahy.—MaN
Silly song ("Mama"). See Cancion tonta
"A **silly** young fellow named Ben". Jack Prelutsky.—LiLo—PrP
"A **silly** young person in Stirling". See A person in Stirling
Silver (color)
Silver. W. De La Mare.—DeR—LaN—MaP
"**Silver**". See Barracuda
Silver. Walter De La Mare.—DeR—LaN—MaP
The **silver** penny. Walter De La Mare.—DeR
"A **silver** scaled dragon with jaws flaming red". See The toaster
"**Silverly**". Dennis Lee.—BoT
Silverstein, Shel
Fancy dive.—KnAs
The Fourth.—MoR
Gooloo.—PrFo
Hot dog.—PrFo
Hug o' war.—MoS
"Oh did you hear".—DeS
Recipe for a hippopotamus sandwich.—PrFo
Rock 'n' roll band.—SuI
"Sara Cynthia Sylvia Stout would not take the garbage out".—ElW
Tree house.—DeS
Simic, Charles
Before the game, tr.—NyT
Wolf-ancestry, tr.—NyT
Simmerman, Jim
Almost dancing.—JaM
Simmie, Lois
Attic fanatic.—PrFo
Jeremy's house.—BoT
Neet people.—PrFo
Our canary.—PrFo
Trip to the seashore.—BoT
"A **simple** child". See We are seven
"**Simple** Simon met a pieman". Mother Goose.—EdGl—SuO—WaM

Simpson, R. A.
    The sick-room.—NyT
"Since feeling is first". Edward Estlin Cummings.—
    ElW
Since Hanna moved away. Judith Viorst.—LoFh
"Since sown". See The harvest queen
"Since we're not young, weeks have to do time". See
    Poem III
Sing a softblack poem, sels. Kwelismith
    How can I lose hope.—SuC
"Sing a softblack poem fora". See How can I lose
    hope
"Sing a song of colors". See Song of the water lilies
"Sing a song of kittens". Elizabeth Coatsworth.—
    LaCc
"Sing a song of popcorn". From A popcorn song.
    Nancy Byrd Turner.—DeS
"Sing a song of sixpence". Mother Goose.—EdGl—
    SuO—WaM
"Sing a song of succotash". Arnold Lobel.—LiDd
"Sing aloud". See Song of peace
"Sing in the silver fog of night". See The spun gold
    fox
"Sing jigmijole, the pudding bowl". Mother
    Goose.—WaM
"Sing me a song of teapots and trumpets". N. M.
    Bodecker.—PrFo
"Sing, sing, what shall I sing". Mother Goose.—
    ClI—WaM
"Sing to the sun". See Song
Singer, Marilyn
    "April is a dog's dream".—SiT
    Barn owl.—SiT
    Beavers in November.—SiT
    Bullhead in autumn.—SiT
    Bullhead in spring.—SiT
    Bullhead in summer.—SiT
    Bullhead in winter.—SiT
    Canada goose.—SiT
    Cat ("I prefer").—SiT
    Cow ("I approve of June").—SiT
    Deer mouse ("Get get get get get").—SiT
    Dragonfly.—SiT
    January deer.—SiT
    March bear.—SiT
    Myrtle warblers.—SiT
    Timber rattlesnake.—SiT
    Turtle in July.—SiT
"A **singer**, who sang". See Basso profundo
Singers. See Singing
Singh, Gobind
    "Lord, thou art the Hindu, the Moslem, the
    Turk".—StP
Singing
    Angel tunes. J. Yolen.—YoHa
    "As I was going along, along". Mother Goose.—
    MoS
    "Aserrin, aserran". Unknown.—DeA
        Sawdust song ("Sawdust sings, sawdust
        songs").—DeA
    At the piano. A. Hudgins.—JaM
    Basso profundo. S. Mandlsohn.—BoT
    Carols. V. Worth.—WoA
    Cheerily man.—MoR
    Crickets ("We cannot say that crickets sing"). H.
    Behn.—WhAa
    Diggin sing. J. Berry.—BeW
    Dragon ("Oh, tongue, give sound to joy and
    sing"). A. McCaffrey.—WhDd
    "An extinct old ichthyosaurus". Unknown.—LiLo
    Father Wolf's midnight song. J. Yolen.—LaN

"God save the owls". From Alabama. J. Fields.—
    LiIf
Harlem night song. L. Hughes.—LaN
"Here we come a-wassailing". Unknown.—YoHa
The hymn tunes. E. Lucie-Smith.—LeCa
I hear America singing. W. Whitman.—HoVo
"In the church". E. Greenfield.—GrN
John's song. J. Aiken.—KeT
"Knock at the knocker". Unknown.—OpI
The lark's song. Seisensui.—DeI
Let me rap you my orbital map. J. Berry.—BeW
"Little Tommy Tucker". Mother Goose.—SuO—
    WaM
        "Little Tom Tucker".—EdGl
Louisa Jones sings a praise to Caesar. E. Di
    Pasquale.—LiDp
Mama's song. D. Chandra.—LiPm
Night music. S. Liatsos.—HoSt
"Oh, when the saints". Unknown.—StP
"An old man from Okefenokee". W. J. Smith.—
    LiLo—SmL
"One little owl played violin". J. Knight.—KnT
One more time. N. Willard.—SaB
"An opera star named Maria". Unknown.—LiLo
"Out of the cradle endlessly rocking". W.
    Whitman.—HoVo
"The owl looked out of the ivy bush". C.
    Causley.—LiIf
The quartette. W. De La Mare.—DeR—MaP
"Sing me a song of teapots and trumpets". N. M.
    Bodecker.—PrFo
Singing. D. Aldis.—DeT
Singing carols. J. Yolen.—YoHa
"The sodden moss sinks underfoot when we cross
    half-frozen bays and". A. Debeljak.—NyT
The solitary reaper. W. Wordsworth.—ElW
Song ("Sing to the sun"). A. Bryan.—BrS
Song of enchantment. W. De La Mare.—DeR—
    MaP
Song of peace. M. C. Livingston.—LiNe
Song of the water lilies. E. Greenfield.—GrU
The spun gold fox. P. Hubbell.—LaN
"Then let us sing merrily, merrily now". Mother
    Goose.—WaM
"There was an old person of Bray". E. Lear.—ClI
"There was an old person of Tring". Unknown.—
    LiLo
"There were three little birds in a wood".
    Unknown.—LiLo
"This old hammer". Unknown.—MoR
Singing. Dorothy Aldis.—DeT
Singing carols. Jane Yolen.—YoHa
Singing games
    "Do your ears hang low". Unknown.—ScA
    "The eentsy, weentsy spider". Unknown.—CoE
    The hammer song. Unknown.—CoE
    "Here we go round the mulberry bush". Mother
    Goose.—EdGl—SuO—WaM
    "If you're happy and you know it". Unknown.—
    CoE
    Jack Jingle. Unknown.—OpT
    On my head. Unknown.—CoE
    "Ring around a rosey". Mother Goose.—WaM
        "Ring a ring o' roses".—SuO
        "Ring a ring of roses".—EdGl
    This old man. Unknown.—CoE
Sioux Indians. See Indians of the Americas—Sioux
"Sip a little". See Baby's drinking song
Sipe, Muriel
    Good morning.—DeS
Sir John Mandeville's report on the griffin. Jane
    Yolen.—LiDd

"**Sir** Samuel Squinn". Florence Parry Heide.—HeG
"**Sir** Walter Raleigh". William Jay Smith.—SmL
Sissay, Lemn
The breath of death (the cigarette).—AgL
"**Sistas** and broddas and everybody". See Nativity
play plan
Sister ("You said red hair made you"). Mike
Lowery.—JaPr
Sister ("Younger than they"). H. R. Coursen.—JaPr
"**Sister** Ann". Eve Merriam.—MeP
"**Sister** has a blister". X. J. Kennedy.—KeGh
"**Sister** has a boyfriend". Unknown.—ScA
"**Sister** with sister, dark and fair". See Asleep
Sisters. See Brothers and sisters
Sisters. Paul B. Janeczko.—JaB
"**Sisters**". See To those of my sisters who kept their
naturals
"**Sit** down, inhale, exhale". See To the young who
want to die
"**Sit** on your thumb". Unknown.—OpI
Sitting Bull (about)
The ghost dance, August, 1976. D. Jauss.—JaM
Sitting in the sand. Karla Kuskin.—MoS
"**Sitting** in the sand and the sea comes up". See
Sitting in the sand
"**Sitting** under the mistletoe". See Mistletoe
Sitwell, Edith
"Daisy and Lily". See Waltz
Waltz, sels.
"Daisy and Lily".—MoR
Sitwell, Sacheverell
Dandelion ("These lions, each by a daisy
queen").—ElW
Six. Myra Cohn Livingston.—LiBp
VI. Paul Verlaine, tr. by C. F. MacIntyre.—GoT
Six birds. J. Patrick Lewis.—LeA
6:15 A.M. Myra Cohn Livingston.—LiNe
"**Six** little ducks". Unknown.—CoE
Six little mice. Mother Goose.—LaM
"**Six** little mice sat down to spin". See Six little
mice
"**Six** slim slick sycamore saplings". Unknown.—
WiA
"**Six** thirty, as usual, and I am so sleepy". See
Chocolate dreams, six thirty
"**Sixty** needles and sixty pins". Unknown.—WiA
Size. See also People—size
Anaconda. D. Macleod.—CoAz
Before you fix your next peanut butter sandwich,
read this. F. P. Heide.—HeG
Believe it or not. N. Kantchev.—NyT
Dog's song. R. Wallace.—KeT
The elephant ("Of all the facts about mammals").
L. Phillips.—CoAz
The house of a mouse. A. Fisher.—FiH
"The house of the mouse". L. S. Mitchell.—
CoAz—LaM
"If I were smaller than I am, small as a turtle".
From If I were smaller than I am. J.
Sweeney.—MoS
Pig ("The pig is bigger"). V. Worth.—WoAl
The prayer of the elephant. C. B. De Gasztold.—
DeP
Pygmy elephant. S. Milligan.—CoAz
Seismosaurus. J. Prelutsky.—PrT
A short story. D. E. Galindo.—NyT
"This big cat". B. S. De Regniers.—MoS
"This soul of mine within the heart is smaller".
Unknown.—StP
Walking Big Bo. X. J. Kennedy.—KeK—LiDp
"Way down south where bananas grow".
Unknown.—PrP—WiA

Way down south.—ClI
The whale ("There was a most monstrous
whale"). T. Roethke.—CoAz
The whale ("What could hold me"). C. B. De
Gasztold.—StP
Sjoberg, Leif
Dawn ("I kindle my light over the whole
Atlantic"), tr.—NyT
Lamento, tr.—NyT
Skate. Laurel Blossom.—KnAs
Skateboard flyer. James Berry.—BeW
Skateboards and skateboarding
The sidewalk racer, or on the skateboard. L.
Morrison.—JaP—KnAs
Skateboard flyer. J. Berry.—BeW
Skater in blue. Jay Parini.—KnAs
The **skaters** ("Black swallows swooping or gliding").
John Gould Fletcher.—KnAs
Skaters ("There are many tonight and the rink").
Vern Rutsala.—KnAs
Skating
High stick. B. Collins.—KnAs
Hockey. S. Blaine.—KnAs
74th street. M. C. Livingston.—JaP
Skate. L. Blossom.—KnAs
Skater in blue. J. Parini.—KnAs
The skaters ("Black swallows swooping or
gliding"). J. G. Fletcher.—KnAs
Skaters ("There are many tonight and the rink").
V. Rutsala.—KnAs
Skating in Pleasant Hill, Ohio. K. Iddings.—KnAs
Sonja Henie Sonnet. E. Field.—KnAs
Sprinker Ice Arena. M. C. Livingston.—LiR
"There was once a most charming young miss".
Unknown.—LiLo
Thud. M. Fatchen.—FaCm
To Kate, skating better than her date. D.
Daiches.—KnAs
"We're racing, racing down the walk". P.
McGinley.—DeT
Skating in Pleasant Hill, Ohio. Kathleen Iddings.—
KnAs
Skeleton. Lee Bartlett.—LiHp
"A **skeleton** once in Khartoum". Unknown.—LiLo
Skeletons
Halloween concert ("Elbows bent, tireless"). B. J.
Esbensen.—LiHp
I'm skeleton. L. Moore.—BaH
Skeleton. L. Bartlett.—LiHp
"A skeleton once in Khartoum". Unknown.—
LiLo
The visitor ("A crumbling churchyard, the sea,
and the moon"). I. Serraillier.—BaH
Sketches of southern life, sels. Frances E. W. Harper
Learning to read.—SuC
Ski song of the U.S. Army's tenth mountain
division. W. T. Levitt.—KnAs
Skiing
"Away she flies and he follows". From Anglo-
Swiss, or a day among the Alps. W. Plomer.—
MoR
International ski flying championship, Obersdorf.
E. Ritchie.—KnAs
Remembering you. M. Kumin.—KnAs
Ski song of the U.S. Army's tenth mountain
division. W. T. Levitt.—KnAs
"**Skiing** the mountain alone". See Remembering you
"**Skimming**". See The sidewalk racer, or on the
skateboard
Skin
Ankylosaurus. J. Prelutsky.—PrT

Skin—*Continued*
   "An Eskimo sleeps in his white bearskin".
      Unknown.—PrP
   "I'm a little Hindoo". Unknown.—WiA
   Rhinoceros ("I often wonder whether"). M. A.
      Hoberman.—WhAa
   "Sir Samuel Squinn". F. P. Heide.—HeG
   When ("Once there was a little boy").
      Unknown.—OpT
"Skin back your teeth, damn you". See Why are
   they happy people
"Skinny bone, skinny bone". Unknown.—ScA
"A skinny man". See Edward Jones
"Skinny, skinny, run for your life". Unknown.—
   WiA
"Skip on, big man, steady steady". See Boxer man
   in a skippin workout
Skip rope rhyme. Eve Merriam.—MeP
Skipping
   Boxer man in a skippin workout. J. Berry.—BeW
   "Hippity hop to the barber shop". Mother
      Goose.—CoM—WaM—WiA
   Rattlesnake skipping song. D. Lee.—BoT
   Skip rope rhyme. E. Merriam.—MeP
   "Up the ladder and down the wall". Unknown.—
      OpI
Skloot, Floyd
   Hook.—KnAs
"Skoe min hest". Unknown.—YoS
"Shoe my horse".—YoS
Skofield, James
   Nightdances, sels.
      "Slip past the window".—LaN
   "Slip past the window". See Nightdances
Skunk ("Skunk's footfall plods padded"). Ted
   Hughes.—CoAz
Skunk ("Sometimes, around"). Valerie Worth.—
   WoAl
Skunk cabbage slaw. X. J. Kennedy.—KeGh
"Skunk cabbage slaw has one bad flaw". See Skunk
   cabbage slaw
"Skunk doesn't smell". See The nose knows
"A skunk sat on a stump, the stump thunk the
   skunk". Unknown.—WiA
Skunks
   April fool. J. Ciardi.—CiH—LiLo
   "A man who was fond of his skunk". D.
      McCord.—LiLo
   The nose knows. E. Merriam.—MeP
   "One little skunk smelled of violets". J. Knight.—
      KnT
   Skunk ("Skunk's footfall plods padded"). T.
      Hughes.—CoAz
   Skunk ("Sometimes, around"). V. Worth.—WoAl
   "A skunk sat on a stump, the stump thunk the
      skunk". Unknown.—WiA
"Skunk's footfall plods padded". See Skunk
Sky
   April. L. Clifton.—LiDd
   Brooms. D. Aldis.—DeT
   Calgary. M. C. Livingston.—LiNe
   The dome of night. C. Lewis.—LaN
   Drawing by Ronnie C., grade one. Lechlitner.
      Ruth.—GoT
   "Far to the west". Unknown.—SnD
   Groundhog Day. M. Pomeroy.—CoAz
   Hazard's optimism. W. Meredith.—KnAs
   "Higher than a house". Mother Goose.—WaM
   "I think". From Firefly. Li Po.—DeS
   Jeremy's house. L. Simmie.—BoT
   Jet. J. T. Moore.—MoR
   The Milky Way. B. J. Esbensen.—LaN

Of wings. P. Redcloud.—HoT
   "Oh, I have slipped the surly bonds of earth". J.
      G. Magee.—StP
      High flight.—SuI
   "Red sky at night". Mother Goose.—WaM
   Sky. G. Nichols.—NiCo
   The sky is vast. P. Khadun.—NyT
   Sky tales of the Assiniboin Indians. M. C.
      Livingston.—LiR
   "A slash of blue, a sweep of gray". E.
      Dickinson.—GoT
   Song ("Don't you ever"). Unknown.—DeT
   "There's a certain slant of light". E. Dickinson.—
      GoT—SuI
   Under this sky. Z. Hyder.—NyT
   Wandering chorus. E. Blum.—GoT
   "Widdicote, waddicote". Unknown.—OpT
   The wild goose. Misune.—DeI
   Will ever. W. De La Mare.—DeR—MaP
   Wynken, Blynken, and Nod. E. Field.—ElW
Sky. Grace Nichols.—NiCo
"Sky-flowers". See Two ways to look at kites
"The sky is a blue vault". See Sky tales of the
   Assiniboin Indians
"The sky is blue, how old are you". Unknown.—
   CoM
The sky is falling. Diane Dawber.—BoT
"The sky is so blue after last night". See I meet
   sweet Sue for a walk on a cold and sunny
   afternoon
The sky is vast. Pramila Khadun.—NyT
"The sky surrounds me". See Alone on a broom
Sky tales of the Assiniboin Indians. Myra Cohn
   Livingston.—LiR
"The sky was yellow". See Halloween
The skydivers. Joseph Colin Murphy.—KnAs
Skylarks. See Larks
Skyscraper. Carl Sandburg.—SuI
Skyscrapers
   Braves. X. J. Kennedy.—KeK
   City lights. R. Field.—DeT
   Houses. M. B. Miller.—DeS
   Skyscraper. C. Sandburg.—SuI
   Skyscrapers. R. Field.—HoSt
   To a giraffe. P. Hubbell.—HoT
Skyscrapers. Rachel Field.—HoSt
Skywriting I. Eve Merriam.—MeS
Skywriting III. Eve Merriam.—MeS
Slant-eyed peeker. William Jay Smith.—SmL
"The slant-eyed peeker sits on a low bough". See
   Slant-eyed peeker
"A slash of blue, a sweep of gray". Emily
   Dickinson.—GoT
Slaughter, Enos (about)
   Enos Slaughter. J. L. Havelin.—KnAs
The slave and the iron lace. Margaret Danner.—SuC
The slave auction. Frances E. W. Harper.—SuC
Slavery
   "All hail, thou truly noble chief". From To
      Cinque. J. M. Whitfield.—SuC
   Andy Battle's and Nod's song. W. De La Mare.—
      MaP
      Yeo ho.—DeR
   Aunt Sue's stories. L. Hughes.—SlM
   The funeral of Martin Luther King, Jr. N.
      Giovanni.—SuC
   "Go down, Moses". From Go down, Moses.
      Unknown.—SuC
   Harriet Tubman. E. Greenfield.—SlM
   I have had two masters. From Narrative of the
      life of Frederick Douglass. F. Douglass.—SuC

Slavery—*Continued*

Learning to read. From Sketches of southern life. F. E. W. Harper.—SuC

"Make me a grave where'er you will". From Bury me in a free land. F. E. W. Harper.—SuC

Mean to be free. Unknown.—SuC

Negro soldier's civil war chant. Unknown.—SuC

No more auction block. Unknown.—SuC

On being brought from Africa to America. P. Wheatley.—SuC

On freedom. J. R. Lowell.—SuI

Our grandmothers. M. Angelou.—AnI

Runagate runagate. R. Hayden.—SuC

"The runaway slave came to my house and stopt outside". From Song of myself. W. Whitman.—HoVo

Seder. J. Nicholls.—FoLe

"Should you, my lord, while you pursue my song". From To the right honorable William, Earl of Dartmouth. P. Wheatley.—SuI

The slave and the iron lace. M. Danner.—SuC

The slave auction. F. E. W. Harper.—SuC

Southern mansion. A. Bontemps.—SuC

Strong men. S. A. Brown.—SuC

"The sun shines bright in the old Kentucky home". From My old Kentucky home. S. C. Foster.—SuC

"When I was young, I used to wait". From The blue-tail fly. Unknown.—SuC

Sleds and sleighs

"Hear the sledges with the bells". From The bells. E. A. Poe.—GoA

"My toboggan and I carve winter". J. Wadley.—BoT

"Over the river and through the wood". From Thanksgiving day. L. M. Child.—HoS

Thanksgiving day, complete. L. M. Child.—FoLe—SuI

Sleep. See also Bedtime; Dreams; Lullabies

Afton water. R. Burns.—ElW

Asleep. W. De La Mare.—DeR

Bullhead in winter. M. Singer.—SiT

Cats ("Cats sleep"). E. Farjeon.—ElW

A clear midnight. W. Whitman.—HoVo

Full moon ("One night as Dick lay fast asleep"). W. De La Mare.—DeR—MaP

Going into dream. E. Farjeon.—HoSt

Grandpa bear's lullaby. J. Yolen.—DeS—HoS—MoS

"He that would thrive". Mother Goose.—WaM

The house of dream. W. De La Mare.—DeR

I met at eve. W. De La Mare.—DeR

I swim an ocean in my sleep. N. Farber.—HoSt

"If once you have slept on an island". R. Field.—LoFh

John Boatman. Unknown.—OpT

Lawanda's walk. E. Greenfield.—GrN

"Little Boy Blue, come blow your horn". Mother Goose.—EdGl—SuO—WaM

A lullaby ("Sleep, child, lie quiet, let be"). J. Agee.—SuI

"Milk white moon, put the cows to sleep". C. Sandburg.—SuI

Mother cat's purr. J. Yolen.—LaCc—MoS

Night sounds. F. Holman.—HoSt—LaN

Part XVII: Now through the dusk. From A child's day. W. De La Mare.—DeR

Rhyme for night. J. Aiken.—KeT

The shadow inside me. T. Olofsson.—NyT

"Sheep, sheep, sleeps in a fold". E. Merriam.—MeY

The sleeping beauty. W. De La Mare.—DeR

Song ("O for a moon to light me home"). W. De La Mare.—DeR

Three strangenesses of every day. E. Merriam.—MeS

"Sleep, child, lie quiet, let be". See A lullaby

"Sleep coming down". See New baby poem (II)

Sleep, grandmother. Mark Van Doren.—SuI

"Sleep, grandmother, sleep". See Sleep, grandmother

"Sleep, sleep, sleep". Unknown, tr. by Elizabeth Shub.—PlW

"Sleep, sleep, thou lovely one". See Lullaby

"Sleep the half sleep". See Mother cat's purr

The sleeper. Edward Field.—KnAs

The sleeping beauty. Walter De La Mare.—DeR

Sleeping Simon. Deborah Chandra.—LiDp

Sleepyhead. Walter De La Mare.—DeR

"Sliced in half, the moon". See Moon, two views

"Sliding over stones". See The serpent's hiss

"Slim dragonfly". See Arthur Mitchell

"Slip past the window". From Nightdances. James Skofield.—LaN

"Slipping in my black patent leather shoes". See Black patent leather shoes

"Slippy". Unknown.—ScA

The sloth. Theodore Roethke.—ElW

Sloths

The sloth. T. Roethke.—ElW

"Slowly, silently, now the moon". See Silver

"Slowly, slowly he cruises". See The barracuda

Slug ("She pokes along, this coatless snail"). J. Patrick Lewis.—LeA

Slug ("The slug slides sly"). Valerie Worth.—WoAl

"The slug slides sly". See Slug

The sluggard. Isaac Watts.—ElW

"Sluggardy-guise". Unknown.—OpI

Slugs

Nothing at all. Shiki.—DeI

Slug ("She pokes along, this coatless snail"). J. P. Lewis.—LeA

Slug ("The slug slides sly"). V. Worth.—WoAl

"A small boy, while learning to swim". Elizabeth Gordon.—LiLo

A small discovery. James A. Emanuel.—DeT—LiDd

"Small grains". See Magnifying glass

"A small mouse in Middleton Stoney". Myra Cohn Livingston.—LiLo

"The small ones wanted pieces of me". See Volunteer worker

Small town fireworks. X. J. Kennedy.—KeK

Small wants. Bibhu Padhi.—NyT

"A small woolly llama". See A is for alpaca

Smart, Christopher

"For I will consider my cat Jeoffry". See Jubilate agno

Jubilate agno, sels.

"For I will consider my cat Jeoffry".—StP

Smart remark. Jean Little.—BoT—LiHe

"Smarty, smarty, smarty". Unknown.—WiA

Smells. See Odors

The smile. Joan Aiken.—LiPg

Smiley, Norene

Winter yard.—BoT

"Smiling girls, rosy boys". Mother Goose.—WaM

Pedlar's song .—OpT

Smith, A.J.M.

Sea cliff.—BoT

Smith, Dave

Blues for Benny "Kid" Paret.—KnAs

Smith, Ken

Agies's advice.—AgL

Smith, Mbembe Milton
  You've got to learn the white man's game.—KnAs
Smith, Michael
  "Ticky ticky tuck".—AgL
Smith, Naomi Royde
  The rabbit ("The rabbit has a charming face").—
    CaB
Smith, R. T.
  A victory.—JaM
Smith, Stephen L.
  An appointment, tr.—NyT
  Wordless day, tr.—NyT
Smith, Stevie
  Papa loves baby.—ElW
Smith, William Jay
  A is for alpaca.—SmL
  "An abhorrent young person named Plunkett".—
    SmL
  Alice.—SmL
  Anteater ("The anteater makes a meal of ants").—
    PrFo—SmL
  Antelope ("When he takes a bath, the
    antelope").—SmL
  The antimacassar and the ottoman.—SmL
  Apples ("Some people say that apples are red").—
    SmL
  B is for bats.—SmL
  Bad boy's swan song.—SmL
  Ballad of black and white.—SmL
  Banjo tune.—SmL
  Bay breasted barge bird.—SmL
  "Beatrix Potter".—SmL
  Betsy Robin.—SmL
  "A bicycle rider named Crockett".—SmL
  Big and little.—SmL
  Big Gumbo.—SmL
  The black widow, a cautionary tale.—SmL
  Brooklyn Bridge, a jump-rope rhyme.—SmL
  Butterfly ("Of living creatures most I prize").—
    SmL
  C is for cabbages.—SmL
  Camel ("The camel is a long legged humpbacked
    beast").—SmL
  Canapes a la poste.—SmL
  "A captain, retired from the Navy".—SmL
  Cat ("Cats are not at all like people").—LaCc—
    SmL
  Cat whiskered Catbird.—SmL
  Chit chat.—SmL
  Chocolate moose.—SmL
  The closing of the rodeo.—KnAs
  Coati-mundi.—SmL
  Collector bird.—SmL
  Common mudlatch.—SmL
  "A contentious old person named Reagan".—SmL
  Cow ("Cows are not supposed to fly").—SmL
  Crocodile.—SmL
  The crossing of Mary of Scotland.—SmL
  D is for dog.—SmL
  Dictionary.—SmL
  Dog ("Dogs are quite a bit like people").—LiDp—
    SmL
  Dollar bird.—SmL
  Dragon ("A dragon named Ernest Belflour").—
    SmL
  Dressmaking screamer.—SmL
  E is for egg.—SmL
  The Easter parade.—LoFh—SmL
  "An eccentric explorer named Hayter".—SmL
  "Edmund Clerihew Bentley".—SmL
  Elephant ("When you put me up on the elephant's
    back").—SmL

  Executive Eagle.—SmL
  F is for frog-boy.—SmL
  Faucet.—SmL
  Fish ("Look at the fish").—SmL
  Flight of the long-haired yak.—SmL
  The flight of the one-eyed bat.—SmL
  The floor and the ceiling.—SmL
  Fox and crow.—SmL
  G is for goat.—SmL
  Giraffe ("When I invite the giraffe to dine").—
    SmL
  Gondola swan.—SmL
  Gooney bird.—SmL
  Grandmother Ostrich.—SmL
  The grease monkey and the powder puff.—SmL
  Gull.—SmL
  H is for hat.—SmL
  Hackle bird.—SmL
  Hats.—SmL
  Having.—SmL
  Hen.—SmL
  Hippopotamus.—SmL
  Hoolie bird.—SmL
  Horn-rimmed hen.—SmL
  Hot and cold tin can surprise.—SmL
  I is for inkspot.—SmL
  J is for jack-in-the-box.—SmL
  Jack in the box.—SmL
  Jittery Jim.—SmL
  K is for king.—SmL
  Kangaroo.—SmL
  King Kong bat.—SmL
  The king of hearts.—SmL
  The King of Spain.—SmL
  L is for laundry.—SmL
  "Lady Hester Stanhope".—SmL
  "A lady whose name was Miss Hartley".—SmL
  The land of ho-ho-hum.—SmL
  Laughing time.—PrFo—SmL
  Lion ("The beast that is most fully dressed").—
    SmL
  Little Dimity.—SmL
  Love ("I love you, I like you").—SmL
  M is for mask.—SmL
  "A matron well known in Montclair".—LiLo—
    SmL
  May-as-well.—SmL
  The mirror.—SmL
  Mistress Mary.—SmL
  Mole ("Jiminy jiminy jukebox, wheatcakes,
    crumbs").—SmL
  Molly Mock Turtle.—SmL
  Monkey ("High on a banyan tree in a row").—
    SmL
  Moon ("I have a white cat whose name is
    moon").—SmL
  "A mother in old Alabama".—SmL
  Mr. Smith.—SmL
  Mrs. Caribou.—SmL
  My body.—SmL
  N is for needle.—SmL
  O is for owl.—Lilf—SmL
  "An obnoxious old person named Hackett".—
    LiLo—SmL
  "An old man from Okefenokee".—LiLo—SmL
  Opossum.—SmL
  Over and under.—SmL
  The owl ("The owl that lives in the old oak
    tree").—Lilf—SmL
  P is for pirate.—SmL
  The panda.—SmL
  Parrot (from Trinidad).—SmL

Smith, William Jay—*Continued*
Parrot (from Zambezi).—SmL
Penguin ("I think it must be very nice").—SmL
People.—SmL
Pick me up.—SmL
Pig ("Pigs are always awfully dirty").—SmL
Pigeon toed pigeons.—SmL
Polar bear ("The polar bear never makes his bed").—KeT—SmL
Postman pelican.—SmL
"Puptents and pebbles".—SmL
Q is for queen.—SmL
The Queen of the Nile.—SmL
"A querulous cook from Pomona".—SmL
R is for reindeer.—SmL
Raccoon ("One summer night a little raccoon").—SmL
Rhinoceros ("You may hang your hat on the nose of the Rhino").—SmL
S is for springs.—SmL
"Said Arlene Francis to Granville Hicks".—SmL
"Said Dorothy Hughes to Helen Hocking".—SmL
"Said General Shoup to Adja Yunkers".—SmL
"Said Justice Douglas to Douglass Cater".—SmL
"Said Marcia Brown to Carlos Baker".—SmL
"Said Ogden Nash to Phyllis McGinley".—SmL
Seal.—SmL
"Sir Walter Raleigh".—SmL
Slant-eyed peeker.—SmL
Spilt milk, whodunit.—SmL
Subway centipede.—SmL
Swan ("You have seen the world, you have seen the zoo").—SmL
T is for tub.—SmL
Tapir.—SmL
Television toucan.—SmL
"There was a young lady named Groat".—SmL
"There was a young lady named Rose".—LiLo—SmL
"There was a young man from Alassio".—SmL
"There was a young man on a plain".—SmL
"There was a young person named Crockett".—LiLo—SmL
"There was an old lady from Java".—SmL
"There was an old lady named Brown".—SmL
"There was an old lady named Crockett".—LiLo—SmL
"There was an old lady named Hart".—LiLo—SmL
"There was an old man by Salt Lake".—SmL
"There was an old man from Japan".—SmL
"There was an old man from Luray".—LiLo—SmL
"There was an old man from the coast".—SmL
"There was an old man of Toulon".—SmL
"There was an old person from Queens".—SmL
"There was an old person who said".—SmL
"There was an old woman from Winnipeg".—SmL
"There was an old woman named Piper".—KeT—SmL
"There was an old woman named Porter".—SmL
"There was an old woman named Ware".—SmL
Things ("Trains are for going").—SmL
Tiger ("A hunter cried out when he spotted a tiger").—SmL
The toaster.—SmL
"Two revolting young persons named Gruen".—SmL
The typewriter bird.—SmL
U is for up.—SmL

Unicorn ("The unicorn with the long white horn").—SmL
Up the hill.—LiDd—SmL
Upside-down bird.—SmL
V is for volcano.—SmL
A visit to the mayor.—SmL
W is for well.—SmL
Walking-stick bird.—SmL
Water buffalo.—SmL
Whale ("When I swam underwater I saw a blue whale").—SmL
"What difference did it make to Longfellow".—SmL
When candy was chocolate.—SmL
Why ("Why do apricots look like eggs").—SmL
"William Penn".—SmL
World champions.—KnAs
X is for x.—SmL
Y is for yarn.—SmL
Yak ("The long haired yak has long black hair").—SmL
"A young man from old Terre Haute".—SmL
"Young radical Byron McNally".—SmL
Z is for zebu.—SmL
Zebra ("Are zebras black with broad white stripes").—SmL
Zipper bird.—SmL
Smith, Billy Ray (about)
Billy Ray Smith. O. Nash.—KnAs
Smith, John (about)
"John Smith and his son, John Smith". W. Stevens.—ElW—KeT
"Smitty on the railroad, picking up sticks". Unknown.—WiA
Smoke
The breath of death (the cigarette). L. Sissay.—AgL
Dragon smoke. L. Moore.—DeS—DeT
"House full, yard full". Unknown.—WiA
The morning wind from the west. A. Adoff.—AdIn
The roundhouse. R. Souster.—BoT
Smoke. E. Pankey.—JaPr
Smoke. Eric Pankey.—JaPr
"Smooth it feels". See Driving
Snail ("Little snail"). Langston Hughes.—SlM
The **snail** ("The snail sticks out his horn"). Ranetsu, tr. by Tze-si Huang.—DeI
Snail ("Snail upon the wall"). John Drinkwater.—DeS—LiDd—WhAa
"The **snail** does the holy". Gilbert Keith Chesterton.—StP
"Snail, snail, come out of your hole". See To the snail
"The **snail** sticks out his horn". See The snail
Snail ("They have brought me a snail"). See Caracola ("Me han traido una caracola")
"Snail upon the wall". See Snail
Snails
Aquarium. V. Worth.—WoAl
Caracola ("Me han traido una caracola"). F. Garcia Lorca.—DeT
  Snail ("They have brought me a snail").—DeT
"Come, said old Shellover". W. De La Mare.—MaP
  Old Shellover.—DeR
"Did you ever ever ever". Unknown.—WiA
"Four and twenty tailors". Mother Goose.—ClI
"If I were a snail". K. Mizumura.—MoS
Little snail. H. Conkling.—DeS

"The **soap** bubble's". See Soap bubble
Soccer
    Pair of hands against football. J. Berry.—BeW
    Soccer at the Meadowlands. D. Ackerman.—KnAs
Soccer at the Meadowlands. Diane Ackerman.—KnAs
A **social** mixer. X. J. Kennedy.—PrFo
Socrates
    "It is a comely fashion to be glad".—StP
"The **sodden** moss sinks underfoot when we cross half-frozen bays and". Ales Debeljak, tr. by Christopher Merrill.—NyT
Sodergran, Edith
    Dawn ("I kindle my light over the whole Atlantic"), tr. by Daisy Aldan and Leif Sjoberg.—NyT
"**Soft** and warm, and sings". See A cat is
"**Soft** voice reading". See I hear my mother's
Softball dreams. Karen Kevorkian.—KnAs
"**Softly,** drowsily". See Part II: Softly, drowsily
Sokan
    The egrets ("That flight of egrets"), tr. by Tze-si Huang.—DeI
"A **soldier,** lately assigned a billet". See The black widow, a cautionary tale
Soldiers. See also War
    Around the campfire. A. Hudgins.—JaM
    Cavalry crossing a ford. W. Whitman.—ElW
    Come up from the fields father. W. Whitman.—HoVo
    The enlistment of free blacks as Continental soldiers. J. Thomas.—SuC
    The game ("Plastic soldiers march on the floor"). M. C. Livingston.—SaB
        The game ("Plastic soldiers on the floor").—LiNe
    Integration of the armed services of the United States. H. S. Truman.—SuC
    Marching chant. Unknown.—WiA
    Negro soldier's civil war chant. Unknown.—SuC
    The old soldier. W. De La Mare.—DeR—MaP
    The portrait of a warrior. W. De La Mare.—DeR
    Remembrance Day ("Poppies, oh, miss"). J. Nicholls.—FoLe
    Remembrance Day ("To some"). J. Kitching.—FoLe
    Ski song of the U.S. Army's tenth mountain division. W. T. Levitt.—KnAs
    The soldier's camp. Unknown.—OpT
    The song of soldiers. W. De La Mare.—DeR—MaP
    "They had supposed their formula was fixed". From The white troops had their orders but the negroes looked like men. G. Brooks.—SuC
    "Two months after marching through Boston". From For the Union dead. R. Lowell.—SuC
    When Johnny comes marching home again. Unknown.—LoFh
    "Who comes here". Mother Goose.—WaM
The **soldier's** camp. Unknown.—OpT
"**Solemn** bells in steeples sing". See Martin Luther King Day
"**Solid** soup". See School dinner menu for 1st of April
Soliloquy of a tortoise on revisiting the lettuce beds after an interval of one hour while supposed to be sleeping in a clump of blue hollyhocks. Emile Victor Rieu.—ElW
The **solitary** reaper. William Wordsworth.—ElW
Solitude. See also Loneliness; Silence
    Alone ("I am alone, and lonely"). J. Little.—LiHe
    Alone in winter. J. P. Lewis.—LeT

And suddenly it's evening. S. Quasimodo.—GoT
    At sunset. J. von Eichendorff.—GoT
    Boy alone at noon. J. Berry.—BeW
    By myself. E. Greenfield.—SlM
    Crowd. E. Merriam.—MeCh
    Daffodils. W. Wordsworth.—FrS
        "I wandered lonely as a cloud".—ElW
    The giraffes ("I think before they saw me the giraffes"). R. Fuller.—ElW
    Goodness. B. Andersen.—NyT
    Haunted ("The rabbit in his burrow keeps"). W. De La Mare.—DeR
    "Here am I". Mother Goose.—WaM
    The hill. E. Merriam.—MeS
    I am home, said the turtle. J. Ciardi.—CoAz
    The journey ("When the high road"). W. De La Mare.—DeR
    Keeping the horses. R. Scheele.—JaM
    Kept home. J. Berry.—BeW
    Keziah. G. Brooks.—LiDd
    Martha Nelson speaks. G. Bogin.—JaM
    Mother. M. C. Livingston.—LiT
    Now day is breaking. S. Quasimodo.—GoT
    An open arc. S. Quasimodo.—GoT
    Orders. A. M. Klein.—BoT
    Owls ("Wait, the great horned owls"). W. D. Snodgrass.—LiIf
    Snow on Lotus Mountain. L. C. Ch'ing.—GoT
    The solitary reaper. W. Wordsworth.—ElW
    Solitude ("I have a house where I go"). A. A. Milne.—LiDd
    Solitude ("Solitude is a mood to share"). E. Merriam.—MeS
    Solitude ("Wish, and it's thine, the changeling piped"). W. De La Mare.—DeR
    Sometimes. M. A. Hoberman.—HoFa
    Stopping by woods on a snowy evening. R. Frost.—DeS—DeT—ElW—SuI
    "This is my rock". D. McCord.—KeT—LiDd
    To sit in solemn silence. W. S. Gilbert.—MoR
    Twilight of the outward life. H. von Hofmannsthal.—GoT
    "Watching the moon". I. Shikibu.—GoT
Solitude ("I have a house where I go"). Alan Alexander Milne.—LiDd
Solitude ("Solitude is a mood to share"). Eve Merriam.—MeS
Solitude ("Wish, and it's thine, the changeling piped"). Walter De La Mare.—DeR
"**Solitude** is a mood to share". See Solitude
"**Some** at beaches". See Summer doings
"**Some** bugs pinch". See Song of the bugs
Some cook. John Ciardi.—PrFo
"**Some** dinosaurs dance lightly". See Partners
"**Some** doors". See Doors
"**Some** fat lady in a mink". See For people who can't open their hoods
"**Some** flowers close their petals". See Flowers at night
"**Some** Greek statue". See The statue
"**Some** hae meat and canna eat". Robert Burns.—StP
"**Some** hornets one day in a nest". See They had a point to make
"**Some** kiss behind a lily". Unknown.—ScA
"**Some** like cats, and some like dogs". See Cats and dogs
"**Some** nights they meet". See The meeting
"**Some** of the cats I know about". See My cat, Mrs. Lick-a-chin
"**Some** of the girls are playing jacks". See Narcissa
"**Some** of the time". See Working with mother

Some one. Walter De La Mare.—DeR—DeS—KeT—LiDd—MaP

"Some one came knocking". See Some one

"Some one is always sitting there". See The little green orchard

"Some people say that apples are red". See Apples

"Some people say that fleas are black". Unknown.—ScA

Some rabbits. Unknown.—ClI

"Some rabbits came over from Arden". See Some rabbits

Some sights sometimes seen and seldom seen. William Cole.—KeT

Some things about grandpas. Alice Low.—LoFh

Some things don't make any sense at all. Judith Viorst.—DeT

Some things go together, sels. Charlotte Zolotow
"Hats with heads".—MoS

"Some think electric eel lacks look". See Electric eel

"Some traffic jam, it takes a whole". See Two week car trip

Some winter pieces. William H. Moore.—BoT

"Some words get read". See A token of unspoken

"Some write for pleasure". Unknown.—WiA

"Some years back I worked a strip mine". See Lester tells of Wanda and the big snow

"Somebody calls somebody". See Cow's complaint

"Somebody loves you". Unknown.—ScA

"Somebody must have". See A gift horse

"Somebody said that it couldn't be done". Unknown.—PrFo

"Somebody who is growin". See A toast for everybody who is growin

Someday. Eve Merriam.—MeS

"Someday wooed a peacock". See Someday

"Somehow the hen". See Egg

"Someone had been walking in and out". See The origin of baseball

"Someone pouring light". See The open shutter

"Someone raked the gray, brushed earth of Utah". See Flying west

"Something in my head". See Quarterback

"Something is there". Lilian Moore.—BaH

Something left to say. Katherine Soniat.—JaM

Something strange. Myra Cohn Livingston.—LiNe

"Something there is that doesn't love a wall". See Mending wall

"Something told the wild geese". Rachel Field.—FrS

"Sometime this winter if you go". See Snowflakes

Sometimes. Mary Ann Hoberman.—HoFa

"Sometimes". Lilian Moore.—KeT

"Sometimes, around". See Skunk

Sometimes even parents win. John Ciardi.—CiH—LiLo

"Sometimes I like to be alone". See Sometimes

"Sometimes I'm afraid". See When I tell you I'm scared

"Sometimes in the tangled boughs". See A dream of paradise in the shadow of war

"Sometimes it's only Betty and Sue". See Friendship

"Sometimes running". John Ciardi.—MoR

"Sometimes there's a mountain". See Another mountain

"Sometimes when I don't want to go". See Shy

"Sometimes when I'm lonely". See Hope

"Sometimes when we go out for walks". See Four generations

"Sometimes you almost get a punch in". See Shadowboxing

Somewhere. Walter De La Mare.—DeR

"Somewhere I have never travelled, gladly beyond". Edward Estlin Cummings.—GoU

"Son". See Father and I in the woods

Son to mother. Maya Angelou.—AnI

Song ("Don't you ever"). Unknown.—DeT

Song ("I placed my dream in a boat"). Cecilia Meireles, tr. by Eloah F. Giacomelli.—NyT

Song ("Love is a green girl"). Michael Stillman.—KeT

Song ("O for a moon to light me home"). Walter De La Mare.—DeR

Song ("Sing to the sun"). Ashley Bryan.—BrS

Song ("When I am dead, my dearest"). Christina Georgina Rossetti.—ElW

Song ("When your boyfriend writes you a letter"). Ruth Krauss.—MoR

Song birds. Jane Yolen.—YoBi

Song for a banjo dance. Langston Hughes.—SuC

Song for a valentine. X. J. Kennedy.—KeK

A song for England. Andrew Salkey.—AgL

A song in the front yard. Gwendolyn Brooks.—ElW

Song of creation. Unknown.—GoT

Song of enchantment. Walter De La Mare.—DeR—MaP

"A song of enchantment I sang me there". See Song of enchantment

The song of Finis. Walter De La Mare.—DeR—MaP

A song of greatness. Unknown, tr. by Mary Austin.—SuI

The song of Mr. Toad. From The wind in the willows. Kenneth Grahame.—CoAz

Song of myself, sels. Walt Whitman
"All this time and at all times wait the words of true poems".—HoVo
"A gigantic beauty of a stallion, fresh and responsive to my caresses".—SuI
Stallion.—KnAs
"I am of old and young, of the foolish as much as the wise".—SuI
"I am the poet of the body and I am the poet of the soul".—HoVo
"I celebrate myself, and sing myself".—HoVo
"I have heard what the talkers were talking, the talk of the".—HoVo
"I think I could turn and live with animals, they are so placid".—HoVo
"The runaway slave came to my house and stopt outside".—HoVo
"You sea, I resign myself to you also, I guess what you".—HoVo

Song of peace. Myra Cohn Livingston.—LiNe

The song of seven. Walter De La Mare.—DeR

The song of shadows. Walter De La Mare.—DeR—MaP

Song of ships, sels. Virginia Schonborg
"The air was damp".—LaN

The song of Snohomish. William S. Wallace.—KnAs

The song of soldiers. Walter De La Mare.—DeR—MaP

The song of Solomon, sels. Bible/Old Testament
Lo, the winter is past.—DeS

Song of summer. Margaret Wise Brown.—MoS

The song of the banana man. Evan Jones.—LeCa

Song of the broad-axe, sels. Carl Sandburg
"The place where a great city stands is not the place of stretch'd wharves, docks".—SuI

Song of the bugs. Margaret Wise Brown.—MoS

The song of the jellicles. Thomas Stearns Eliot.—DeT—LaCc—SuI

The song of the mad prince. Walter De La Mare.—DeR—ElW—MaP

Sorescu, Marin
The lesson ("Every time I'm called to the front").—AgL
Sorrells, Helen
Child in a blue linen dress.—JaM
Sorrow. See Grief
"Sorry, sorry Mrs. Lorry". Nanette Mellage.—SlM
Sosa, Roberto
"The Indians".—NyT
Soseki
"Red dragonfly on".—CaR
Soseki, Muso
House of spring, tr. by William Stanley Merwin and Soiku Shigematsu.—NyT
Soto, Gary
Autumn with a daughter who's just catching on.—SoA
Black hair.—JaP—SoA
Brown girl, blonde okie.—SoA
Confession to Mrs. Robert L. Snow.—JaPr
Cruel boys.—JaM
Eating bread.—SoA
Envying the children of San Francisco.—SoA
Evening walk.—SoA
Failing in the presence of ants.—SoA
Finding a lucky number.—JaM—SoA
Heaven.—SoA
Hitchhiking with a friend and a book that explains the Pacific Ocean.—SoA
How things work.—SoA
How to sell things.—SoA
In August.—SoA
Kearney Park.—SoA
Looking around, believing.—SoA
Morning on this street.—SoA
October ("A cold day, though only October").—SoA
Ode to a day in the country.—SoNe
Ode to el guitarron.—SoNe
Ode to el molcajete.—SoNe
Ode to fireworks.—SoNe
Ode to La Llorona.—SoNe
Ode to la pinata.—SoNe
Ode to La Tortilla.—SoNe
Ode to los chicharrones.—SoNe
Ode to Los Raspados.—SoNe
Ode to mi gato.—SoNe
Ode to mi parque.—SoNe
Ode to mi perrito.—SoNe
Ode to my library.—SoNe
Ode to Pablo's tennis shoes.—SoNe
Ode to pomegranates.—SoNe
Ode to Senor Leal's goat.—SoNe
Ode to the Mayor.—SoNe
Ode to the sprinkler.—SoNe
Ode to weddings.—SoNe
Ode to weight lifting.—SoNe
Oranges ("The first time I walked").—JaM—SoA
Pepper tree.—SoA
Target practice.—JaPr
Teaching numbers.—SoA
That girl.—SoA
Walking with Jackie, sitting with a dog.—JaPr
Where we could go.—SoA
Soul. See also Death; Immortality
"Casting the body's vest aside". From The garden. A. Marvell.—StP
"I sought my soul". Unknown.—StP
The mask. D. K. Hru.—SlM
"Oh, you gotta get a glory". Unknown.—StP
"The soul that you have given me, O God". Unknown.—StP

"This soul of mine within the heart is smaller". Unknown.—StP
Who am I. K. Grosvenor.—SlM
"The **soul** that you have given me, O God". Unknown.—StP
The **sound**. Shiki, tr. by Tze-si Huang.—DeI
"The **sound** of must". See A word or two with you
"The **sound** of the bats". See The sound
"**Sound** the bell, sound the bell". Unknown.—ScA
Sounds
"Above the chorus". Kyoshi.—CaR
The accompaniment. W. De La Mare.—DeR
"The air was damp". From Song of ships. V. Schonborg.—LaN
"All day I hear the noise of waters". J. Joyce.—ElW
April rain song. L. Hughes.—DeS—ElW—HoS—LiDd—SlM—SuI
Around my room. W. J. Smith.—KeT—LiDd—SmL
Autumn and the sea. J. Heraud.—NyT
The bees' song. W. De La Mare.—DeR—MaP
Bell. V. Worth.—WoAl
The bells, complete. E. A. Poe.—MoR
"Bow-wow, says the dog". Mother Goose.—SuO
"Bubble, said the kettle". Unknown.—PrP
Cacophony. E. Merriam.—MeCh
"The cars in Caracas". J. Updike.—MoR
Cicadas. P. Fleischman.—FlJ
"Crick, crack". E. Merriam.—BaW
Crickets ("They tell"). M. C. Livingston.—LiNe
"Did you ever hear such a noise and clamor". Unknown.—WiA
Father's magic. E. Di Pasquale.—LiPf
Forbidden sounds. E. James.—BaH
The frog ("Breaking the silence"). Basho.—DeI
Galoshes. R. Bacmeister.—DeS
Grasshopper ("Silence stilled the meadow"). J. P. Lewis.—LeE
"Her eyes in sleep". Unknown.—GoU
The horn. W. De La Mare.—DeR
"The horn on our pickup truck stayed stuck". X. J. Kennedy.—KeGh
House noises. X. J. Kennedy.—LiPm
I hear my mother's. R. Whitman.—LiPm
I speak, I say, I talk. A. L. Shapiro.—DeT
"I went down to the lily pond". Unknown.—WiA
Ice-creepers. E. Merriam.—MeS
"I'd like a great satellite-looking dish". From What we said sitting making fantasies. J. Berry.—BeW
In memoriam John Coltrane. M. Stillman.—MoR
"In the antique glass shop, Knute". X. J. Kennedy.—KeFb
"In the night". Unknown.—GoT—LaN
Inside. K. Chiha.—NyT
Ivy. J. Yolen.—YoBe
A jamboree for j. E. Merriam.—MeS
Joker. E. Merriam.—MeCh
The land of mists. K. Kwang-kyu.—NyT
Leak. E. Merriam.—MeS
Life. A. Kreymborg.—CoAz
"Listen". L. Moore.—SuI
Lost ("Desolate and lone"). C. Sandburg.—LaN
Lullaby for a rainy night. B. J. Esbensen.—EsW
Manhattan lullaby ("Lulled by rumble, babble, beep"). N. Farber.—KeT
Many a mickle. W. De La Mare.—DeR—MaP
Mountain tambourine. P. Van Toorn.—NyT
"A mouse in her room woke Miss Dowd". Unknown.—LiLo
A mouse in her room.—ClI—KeT—PrFo

The **spaghetti** nut. Jack Prelutsky.—DeS
"**Spaghetti**, spaghetti". Jack Prelutsky.—MoS
"**Spahn** and Sain". Unknown.—MoA
Spanish language
    "A la vibora, vibora". Unknown.—YoS
        "To the sea snake we will play".—YoS
    "Alla en la fuente". Unknown.—DeA
        The fountain ("There in the fountain").—DeA
    Arroz con leche. Unknown.—DeA
        Rice and milk ("I'm rice and milk, I'd like to be wed").—DeA
    "Aserrin, aserran". Unknown.—DeA
        Sawdust song ("Sawdust sings, sawdust songs").—DeA
    Cancion tonta. F. Garcia Lorca.—DeT
        Silly song ("Mama").—DeT
    Caracola ("Me han traido una caracola"). F. Garcia Lorca.—DeT
        Snail ("They have brought me a snail").—DeT
    "Un elefante se balanceaba". Unknown.—DeA
        The graceful elephant ("One elephant balanced gracefully").—DeA
    "En la puerta del cielo". Unknown.—DeA
        "At heaven's gate".—DeA
    "Estaba la paraja pinta". Unknown.—DeA
        The lovely bird ("Cu cu ru, sang the lovely bird").—DeA
    "El hijo del conde". Unknown.—DeA
        The count's son ("The son of the count").—DeA
    "La loba, la loba". Unknown.—DeA
        The she-wolf ("Oh mama wolf, oh mama wolf").—DeA
    "Una mexicana". Unknown.—YoS
    "Naranja dulce". Unknown.—DeA
        "Orange so sweet".—DeA
    "Pimpolla de canela". Unknown.—DeA
        "Cinnamon shoot".—DeA
    "Que linda manito". Unknown.—DeA
        A pretty little hand ("How pretty, how little").—DeA
    Que llueva. Unknown.—DeA
        It's raining ("It's raining, it's raining").—DeA
    "Traigo un ramillete". Unknown.—LoFh
        Bouquet of roses ("A bouquet of roses").—LoFh
Spanish nursery rhymes. See Nursery rhymes—Spanish
Sparrow ("A hummingbird hums"). Kaye Starbird.—WhAa
Sparrow ("Nothing is less"). Valerie Worth.—WoAl
Sparrow ("Year we worked"). Ewondo-Beti, tr. by Judith Gleason.—NyT
Sparrow dreaming. Barbara Juster Esbensen.—EsW
Sparrows
    "All at once, the storm". Buson.—CaR
    Mrs. Sparrow. Unknown.—OpT
    Sparrow ("A hummingbird hums"). K. Starbird.—WhAa
    Sparrow ("Nothing is less"). V. Worth.—WoAl
    Sparrow dreaming. B. J. Esbensen.—EsW
"**Speak** not—whisper not". See The sunken garden
Special flavor. X. J. Kennedy.—KeGh
"**Specks** on the fingers". Unknown.—WiA
Specs. Eve Merriam.—MeP
Spectrum. Mari Evans.—SuC
Speech
    Babel. W. De La Mare.—DeR
    "Boita and Goitie sat on de coib". Unknown.—WiA
    "Bow-wow, says the dog". Mother Goose.—SuO

Hector Velasquez. M. Glenn.—GlBc
    "I with I wath a fith". Unknown.—ScA
    "Ladles and jelly spoons". Unknown.—WiA
    Ms. Phyllis Shaw, speech. M. Glenn.—GlBc
    My little boy. H. Dumas.—AgL
    "My name is Yon Yonson". Unknown.—ScA
    Speech class, for Joe. J. Daniels.—JaP
    Tammy Yarbrough. M. Glenn.—GlBc
    Ululation. E. Merriam.—MeS
Speech class, for Joe. Jim Daniels.—JaP
Speed
    The horseman ("There was a horseman rode so fast"). W. De La Mare.—DeR—MaP
    Hurry. E. Merriam.—MeS
    Nolan Ryan. G. Fehler.—MoA
    Speedy Sam. J. Ciardi.—CiH
    "There was a young lady named Bright". Unknown.—LiLo
Speedy Sam. John Ciardi.—CiH
"**Speedy** Sam, while exploring a cave". See Speedy Sam
Spelius, Carol D.
    The swimmer's chant.—MoR
Spell of the moon. Leslie Norris.—LiIf
Spell potatoes. Unknown.—WiA
    Potato.—CoM
Spell to banish a pimple. John Agard.—AgL
Spelling
    Aa couple of doubbles. E. Merriam.—MeCh
    "B, u, hippity". Unknown.—WiA
    Banananananananana. W. Cole.—PrFo
    "Can you count". Unknown.—WiA
    "Chicken in the car". Unknown.—WiA
        "A chicken in the car".—ScA
        Chicago.—CoM
    Constantinople. Unknown.—CoM
    Ego-tripping. E. Merriam.—MeCh
    Finis. Unknown.—OpI
    The gnat and the gnu. O. Herford.—LiLo
    "H, u, uckle". Unknown.—WiA
    "A knife and a fork". Unknown.—ScA—WiA
        New York ("Knife and fork").—CoM
    "M, I, crooked letter, crooked letter, I". Unknown.—WiA
        Mississippi.—CoM
    "A needle and a pin". Unknown.—WiA
    "P with a little o". Mother Goose.—WaM
    "Pease-porridge hot, pease-porridge cold". Unknown.—OpI
    Quibble. E. Merriam.—MeS
    "Railroad crossing, look out for cars". Unknown.—WiA
        "Railroad crossing, look out for the cars".—OpI
    "Snoopy, snippin'". Unknown.—WiA
    Spell potatoes. Unknown.—WiA
        Potato.—CoM
    "T, u, turkey, t, u, ti". Unknown.—WiA
    We heard Wally wail. J. Prelutsky.—JaP
Spells. Jane Yolen.—YoBe
Spencer, Ann
    Lines to a nasturtium (a lover muses).—SuC
Spencer, Joseph A. P.
    "Sandpipers running along the beach".—StP
Spencer, Theodore
    The circus, or one view of it.—MoR
Sphinx. Deborah Chandra.—WhDd
Spices
    A vote for vanilla. E. Merriam.—MeS
Spider ("Now that she has knit-and-purled"). J. Patrick Lewis.—LeT

Spider ("Spider always wore sunglasses"). Paul B. Janeczko.—JaB
"**Spider** always wore sunglasses". See Spider
The **spider** and the fly. Mary Howitt.—ElW
Spider on the floor. Unknown.—BaH
Spider web. Myra Cohn Livingston.—LiT
Spiders. See also Cobwebs
    Anansi the spider. G. McDermott.—WhDd
    The black widow, a cautionary tale. W. J. Smith.—SmL
    "The eentsy, weentsy spider". Unknown.—CoE
    "Un elefante se balanceaba". Unknown.—DeA
        The graceful elephant ("One elephant balanced gracefully").—DeA
    Hallowe'en ad (attention witches). G. Tall.—BaH
    "Little Miss Muffet". Mother Goose.—EdGl—SuO—WaM
    Old spider web. M. C. Livingston.—LiNe
    "Sneaky Ebenezer Snyder". X. J. Kennedy.—KeFb
    Spider ("Now that she has knit-and-purled"). J. P. Lewis.—LeT
    The spider and the fly. M. Howitt.—ElW
    Spider on the floor. Unknown.—BaH
    Spider web. M. C. Livingston.—LiT
    Spiders. A. Fisher.—FiA
    The tarantula. R. Whittemore.—ElW
    Teasing. Unknown.—CII
    The visitor ("One night"). S. O. Huigan.—BoT
    "You limb of a spider". Unknown.—OpI
Spiders. Aileen Fisher.—FiA
"**Spiders** are so sort-of-thing". See Spiders
Spilka, Arnold
    Boo hoo.—PrFo
Spilt milk, whodunit. William Jay Smith.—SmL
"**Spin** a coin, spin a coin". See Queen Nefertiti
Spinach. Florence Parry Heide.—HeG
"**Spined** with sparks". See Starfish
The **spinning** earth. Aileen Fisher.—FiA
Spirit. See Soul
Spirits. See Ghosts
Spite shots labels. James Berry.—BeW
The **splendor** falls. Alfred Tennyson.—ElW
"The **splendor** falls on castle walls". See The splendor falls
Spooks. Nathalia Crane.—BaH
Sports. See also Athletes and athletics; Games; also names of games, as Baseball; also names of sports, as Fishers and fishing
    Audrey Reynolds. M. Glenn.—GlBc
    The boxing match. D. Ignatow.—KnAs
    Clean. L. Newman.—KnAs
    Don't howl. J. Berry.—BeW
    Karate. S. Plumly.—KnAs
    Medals and money, a re-evaluation. B. Lamblin.—KnAs
    Nine triads. L. Morrison.—KnAs
    Ode to weight lifting. G. Soto.—SoNe
    Ouch. M. Fatchen.—FaCm
    Pole vaulter. D. A. Evans.—KnAs
    Polo ponies practicing. W. Stevens.—KnAs
    Quick ball man, for Michael Holding. J. Berry.—BeW
    The standing broad jump. R. Frost.—KnAs
    Toni Vingelli. M. Glenn.—GlBc
    Unsound condition. R. Armour.—KnAs
    The volleyball match. B. Pearlman.—KnAs
    Women's tug of war at Lough Arrow. T. Gallagher.—KnAs
    You've got to learn the white man's game. M. M. Smith.—KnAs
"A **spot** of black ink". See I is for inkspot

"The **spotted** cat hops". See Cat
"The **spotted** frog". See Frog
"**Spread** out on". See Light string
A **sprig** of rosemary. Amy Lowell.—GoU
Spring. See also March; April; May; also Seasons
    After the last hard freeze in early spring weather. A. Adoff.—AdIn
    April 1st. A. Bonner.—FoLe
    "April is a dog's dream". M. Singer.—SiT
    "Bee, I'm expecting you". E. Dickinson.—WhAa
        Letter to bee.—KeT
    "Beneath this stone, a lump of clay". Unknown.—BaH
    The black bull. Basho.—DeI
    "Blackbird, whistle". Unknown.—ScA
    Blackbirds. W. De La Mare.—DeR
    Bullhead in spring. M. Singer.—SiT
    Calligraphy. J. Yolen.—YoBi
    Ching ming. I. Rawnsley.—FoLe
    Come, gone. W. De La Mare.—DeR
    A commercial for spring. E. Merriam.—MeP
    The cucumber. N. Hikmet.—NyT
    "Daffy-down-dilly is new come to town". Mother Goose.—SuO
        "Daffy-down-dilly has just come to town".—ScA
    Early March. Z. Rogow.—GoT
    Easter. S. Cook.—FoLe
    End of winter. E. Merriam.—MoA
    First robin. J. Yolen.—YoBi
    First sight. P. Larkin.—CaB—ElW
    "Four ducks on a pond". W. Allingham.—ElW
    "Good-by my winter suit". N. M. Bodecker.—MoS
    Grandpa in March. A. Adoff.—MoS
    Grasshoppers. P. Fleischman.—FlJ
    Groundhog Day. M. Pomeroy.—CoAz
    Holi. I. Rawnsley.—FoLe
    House of spring. M. Soseki.—NyT
    "I heard a bird sing". O. Herford.—DeS
    "In just-spring". E. E. Cummings.—ElW
    "In time of silver rain". L. Hughes.—FrS
    Lo, the winter is past. From The song of Solomon. Bible/Old Testament.—DeS
    March bear. M. Singer.—SiT
    March night. M. C. Livingston.—LiNe
    My brother Aaron runs outside to tell us there is a severe thunderstorm warning. A. Adoff.—AdIn
    Not enough Emilys. J. Little.—LiHe
    On time. A. Fisher.—FiA
    Out for spring. A. Adoff.—AdIn
    Potomac town in February. C. Sandburg.—LiDd
    Reading, spring. M. C. Livingston.—LiR
    Robin ("Suddenly spring wings"). J. P. Lewis.—LeA
    Saint David's Day. D. W. Price.—FoLe
    St. David's Day ("The land returns from winter"). S. Cook.—FoLe
    Sending spring love to Tzu-An. H.-C. Yu.—GoU
    Snowman sniffles. N. M. Bodecker.—KeT
    Song of summer. M. W. Brown.—MoS
    Spring ("In spring, the old"). V. Worth.—WoA
    Spring ("To tangled grass I cling"). M. F. Fraser.—SuI
    "Spring again". K. Kuskin.—HoS
    Spring fever. E. Merriam.—MeS
    Spring is. B. Katz.—MoS
    Spring poem. C. Thibaudeau.—NyT
    Spring rain. J. P. Lewis.—LeE
    Spring song. A. Fisher.—FiA
    Spring thaw. M. Vinz.—JaP

The **swallow**. Christina Georgina Rossetti.—DeT
Fly away.—FrS
Swallows
Kicking up. J. Yolen.—YoBi
The swallow. C. G. Rossetti.—DeT
Fly away.—FrS
The swallows. E. Coatsworth.—KeT
The **swallows**. Elizabeth Coatsworth.—KeT
Swamps
"Be kind to your web-footed friends".
Unknown.—ScA
Gnats. Unknown.—DeI
Swan ("Over the mirror"). Jane Yolen.—YoBi
The **swan** ("The white swan, swimming"). Roka, tr. by Tze-si Huang.—DeI
Swan ("You have seen the world, you have seen the zoo"). William Jay Smith.—SmL
"The **swan** has a neck that is curly and long". See Necks
Swander, Mary
Maud.—JaM
Swans
Gondola swan. W. J. Smith.—SmL
The night-swans. W. De La Mare.—DeR
Silhouettes. M. Fatchen.—FaCm
Swan ("Over the mirror"). J. Yolen.—YoBi
The swan ("The white swan, swimming"). Roka.—DeI
Swan ("You have seen the world, you have seen the zoo"). W. J. Smith.—SmL
Swayne, Siobhan
"Think of the ocean".—BoT
Swede, George
"Every morning".—BoT
The fox and the hounds.—BoT
Winter walk in forest.—BoT
The yellow tulip.—BoT
Sweden
Crown of light festival. D. Bateson.—FoLe
Sweeney, Jacqueline
Cogs and gears and wheels and springs.—MoS
"First time at third".—MoA
If I were smaller than I am, sels.
"If I were smaller than I am, small as a turtle".—MoS
"If I were smaller than I am, small as a turtle". See If I were smaller than I am
"**Sweep** thy faint strings, musician". See The song of shadows
Sweet and low. Alfred Tennyson.—PlW
"**Sweet** and low, sweet and low". See Sweet and low
Sweet like a crow. Michael Ondaatje.—NyT
"**Sweet** Peridarchus was a prince". See The prince
Sweet sixteen. Eunice De Souza.—AgL
Sweet Suffolk owl. Unknown.—CaB—LiIf
"**Sweet** Suffolk owl, so trimly dight". See Sweet Suffolk owl
"**Sweet**, sweet, sweet, O Pan". See Pan
Sweet talk. Ashley Bryan.—BrS
Sweets. Valerie Worth.—WoAl
Swenson, May
Analysis of baseball.—KnAs—SuI
Bronco busting, event #1.—KnAs—MoR
Choosing craft.—KnAs
Lamento, tr.—NyT
The lightning.—SuI
Locked in, tr.—NyT
Motherhood.—ElW
Night practice.—MoR
Over the field.—MoR
Overboard.—MoR
Painting the gate.—KeT

Southbound on the freeway.—SuI
Watching the Jets lose to Buffalo at Shea.—KnAs
The woods at night.—LiIf
The **swimmer's** chant. Carol D. Spelius.—MoR
Swimming and diving
The bathers. K. Shapiro.—KnAs
"A daring young lady of Guam". Unknown.—LiLo
"The day is hot and icky and the sun sticks to my skin". E. Greenfield.—MoS
Fancy dive. S. Silverstein.—KnAs
400 meter freestyle. M. Kumin.—KnAs
Goldfish ("Goldfish flash past, keeping busy"). X. J. Kennedy.—KeK
Greg Hoffman. M. Glenn.—MoR
Haiti, skin diving. J. Shore.—KnAS
It's great when you get in. E. O'Neill.—KnAs
"Jake, the twin of John Lothario". E. Raskin.—PrFo
The lifeguard. J. Dickey.—KnAs
Medals and money, a re-evaluation. B. Lamblin.—KnAs
"Mother, may I take a swim". Unknown.—WiA
Mr. and Mrs. T. J. P. Lewis.—LeT
The mystery ("There was a young fellow named Chet"). J. Ciardi.—CiH
The nude swim. A. Sexton.—KnAs
"Ocean bathing, Abner Abb". X. J. Kennedy.—KeFb
Ode to the sprinkler. G. Soto.—SoNe
"On a day when the ocean was sharky". X. J. Kennedy.—KeGh—LiLo
Overboard. M. Swenson.—MoR
Sea school. B. Howes.—LeCa
Sleeping Simon. D. Chandra.—LiDp
"A small boy, while learning to swim". E. Gordon.—LiLo
The springboard. A. Rich.—KnAs
Swan ("Over the mirror"). J. Yolen.—YoBi
The swimmer's chant. C. D. Spelius.—MoR
Swimming in the Pacific. R. P. Warren.—KnAs
That summer. H. Scott.—JaPr
There seems to be a problem. J. Ciardi.—CiH
"There was an old woman named Porter". W. J. Smith.—SmL
"The water's deep". C. McNaughton.—PrFo
The yes and the no, Redondo. G. Pape.—JaPr
"You sea, I resign myself to you also, I guess what you". From Song of myself. W. Whitman.—HoVo
Swimming in the Pacific. Robert Penn Warren.—KnAs
The **swing** ("How do you like to go up in a swing"). Robert Louis Stevenson.—DeS—HoS—KeT—LiDd
The **swing** ("The wind blows strong and the swing rides free"). Marchette Chute.—BaW
"**Swing** dat hammer—hunh". See Southern road
"**Swing** me, swing me, swing me round". Eve Merriam.—MeY
A **swing** song. William Allingham.—KeT
"**Swing**, swing". See A swing song
"**Swing** your dino, dipsy do". See Square dance
"**Swing** your honey like swinging on a gate". See Dance calls
Swinging
At the playground. W. Stafford.—JaP—KeT
"Catch him, crow". Mother Goose.—WaM
"Hello and goodbye". M. A. Hoberman.—LiDd
"Huchdjeho niochdzi". Unknown.—YoS
"Come, ye wood rats, here to me".—YoS
"I went to my father's garden". Unknown.—OpI

Swinging—*Continued*
  The swing ("How do you like to go up in a swing"). R. L. Stevenson.—DeS—HoS—KeT—LiDd
  The swing ("The wind blows strong and the swing rides free"). M. Chute.—BaW
  "Swing me, swing me, swing me round". E. Merriam.—MeY
  A swing song. W. Allingham.—KeT
  Wouldn't you. J. Ciardi.—MoS
"Swinging pom-poms". See Cheerleaders
Swinging the river. Charles Harper Webb.—JaPr
Swir, Anna
  Happy as a dog's tail, tr. by Czeslaw Milosz and Leonard Nathan.—NyT
  I have ten legs, tr. by Czeslaw Milosz and Leonard Nathan.—NyT
Sylvie and Bruno, sels. Lewis Carroll
  There was a pig.—ClI
Sympathy. See also Friendship; Kindness
  Another dad. E. A. Markham.—AgL
  Boy at the window. R. Wilbur.—ElW
  "God is love, and love enfolds us". T. Rees.—StP
  "If you think". Lottemoos.—AgL
  Me and my work. M. Angelou.—AnI
  Napoleon. M. Holub.—NyT
  "Poor bird". W. De La Mare.—DeR
  What Tomas said in a pub. J. Stephens.—ElW
System. Robert Louis Stevenson.—ElW

T

T. C. Tyler. Mel Glenn.—GlBc
"T for time to be together". See All in a word
T is for tub. William Jay Smith.—SmL
"T, u, turkey, t, u, ti". Unknown.—WiA
"Tabby on the prowl". Eve Merriam.—MeY
"Tabby or tom". See Aelourophile
The table and the chair. Edward Lear.—LiDd
Table manners. See Manners
Tableau. Keith Wilson.—JaPr
Tables
  "Diamonds, hearts, kings and aces". M. Wayne.—LeCa
  Kitchen table. M. C. Livingston.—LiR
  "Roses and a tulip". C. Pomerantz.—JaP
  The table and the chair. E. Lear.—LiDd
The tables turned. X. J. Kennedy.—KeK
Tableware
  "Alas, alas, for Miss Mackay". Mother Goose.—WaM
  "Gilly, gilly, gilly, gilly". Unknown.—ScA
  "Here are mother's knives and forks". Unknown.—CoE
  "Here's a cup". Unknown.—CoE
  "I eat my peas with honey". Unknown.—ScA—WiA
  "I'm a little teapot". Unknown.—CoE
    "I'm a little teapot stout".—ScA
  "A knife and a fork". Unknown.—ScA—WiA
    New York ("Knife and fork").—CoM
  Pitcher. R. Ferrer de Arrellaga.—NyT
  "Step on a knife". Unknown.—ScA
  "Step on a spoon". Unknown.—ScA
  "With silver spears". M. C. Livingston.—LiMh
Tadpoles. See Frogs and toads
Tafari, Levi
  The tongue ("The tongue was the very first instrument").—AgL

Tafdrup, Pia
  The tongue ("You stick out your tongue"), tr. by Monique M. Kennedy and Thomas E. Kennedy.—NyT
Tagore, Rabindranath
  "God grows weary of great kingdoms".—StP
  "Let this be my last word".—StP
  "Thou art the sky and thou art the nest as well".—StP
"The tail of a fox will show no matter how hard he tries to hide it". Unknown.—WhAa
"Tailor had a needle". Jack Prelutsky.—PrBe
Tailors
  "Four and twenty tailors". Mother Goose.—ClI
  Itinerant. E. Merriam.—MeCh
  Jacob and Joseph. Unknown.—OpT
  The old tailor. W. De La Mare.—DeR
  Six little mice. Mother Goose.—LaM
  "Tailor had a needle". J. Prelutsky.—PrBe
  "There was a young damsel of Lynn". Unknown.—LiLo
Tails
  The christening ("What shall I call"). A. A. Milne.—LaM
  "Geat but not naudy". Unknown.—WiA
  Growing up ("Little Tommy Tadpole began to weep and wail"). C. J. Dennis.—CoAz
  Happy as a dog's tail. A. Swir.—NyT
  Is this yours. M. Fatchen.—FaCm
  "Little Bo-Peep has lost her sheep". Mother Goose.—EdGl—SuO—WaM
  "Mary had a little lamb, she set it on the shelf". Unknown.—WiA
  "Oh, you never see a feather". Unknown.—WiA
  The pheasant. Buson.—DeI
  "The raccoon's tail is ring-around". Unknown.—WiA
  Tails. R. Bennett.—DeS
  The tale of a dog. J. H. Lambert.—CoAz
  "There was a little dog and he had a little tail". Unknown.—PrP
    There was a little dog (". . . and he had a tail").—ClI
  "There was a sad pig with a tail". A. Lobel.—LiLo
  "Three blind mice". Mother Goose.—EdGl—WaM
  Wiggle waggle, wiggle waggle. Unknown.—ClI
Tails. Rowena Bennett.—DeS
Take away some but leave some. James Berry.—BeW
"Take from my palms, to soothe your heart". Osip Mandelstam, tr. by Clarence Brown and William Stanley Merwin.—GoU
"Take, if you can, a moose". See Chocolate moose
"Take it to the hoop, Magic Johnson". See A poem for Magic
"Take me, or leave me, I'm not thine". See Never
"Take me out to the ball game". Jack Norworth.—KnAs—MoA
"Take me, Virginia". See Forgive
"Take my head for the guillotine". See My homework isn't done
"Take the leaf of a tree". See Reply to the question, how can you become a poet
"Take the nastiness that turns me into disgrace". See Take away some but leave some
Takenaka, Iku
  Stars at night, tr. by Edith Marcombe Shiffert and Yuki Sawa.—NyT
Takenaka, Masao
  "Eternal God".—StP

"Taking a pen in your uncertain fingers". See The pen

Taking down the space-trolley. X. J. Kennedy.—KeK

"Taking off". See Beginning a new year means

Taking turns. Norma Farber.—KeT

The tale of a dog. James H. Lambert.—CoAz

A tale of two cities. X. J. Kennedy.—KeGh

Talking
"Because parrots are chatterers people say they are the only ones who eat up the fruits". From Jamaican Caribbean proverbs. Unknown.—BeW
Big mouth. M. Fatchen.—FaCm
Bird talk. A. Fisher.—FiA
"Bubble, said the kettle". Unknown.—PrP
"Did he say I said you said she said that". Unknown.—WiA
"Don't say it, don't say it". Unknown.—ScA
Every chance we got. C. H. Webb.—JaPr
Four generations. M. A. Hoberman.—HoFa
Glowworm. D. McCord.—MoS
"He is a clever man who drives away hunger by just working his jaws". From Jamaican Caribbean proverbs. Unknown.—BeW
"I don't talk to pop stars". A. Stockbroker.—AgL
"I have a friend who keeps on standing on her hands". K. Kuskin.—JaP
"I have heard what the talkers were talking, the talk of the". From Song of myself. W. Whitman.—HoVo
"I hear you say I say I say after every word I say I say". Unknown.—WiA
I speak, I say, I talk. A. L. Shapiro.—DeT
Jocelyn Ridley. M. Glenn.—GlBc
Little bush. E. M. Roberts.—LiDd
Little talk. A. Fisher.—FiA
The meeting. E. Greenfield.—GrN
Mercedes Lugo. M. Glenn.—GlBc
Mother has a talk with me. J. Little.—LiHe
"Mr. Pettengill". M. C. Livingston.—LiR
Ms. Phyllis Shaw, speech. M. Glenn.—GlBc
"My fingers like to say hello". L. W. Johnson.—StP
Owls talking. D. McCord.—LiIf
The parakeets ("They talk all day"). A. Blanco.—NyT
"Red, white, and blue, I don't speak to you". Unknown.—OpI
The silent type. F. P. Heide.—HeG
Speech class, for Joe. J. Daniels.—JaP
Talking to the sun. E. Merriam.—MeS
"Tattletale, tattletale". Unknown.—ScA—WiA
Teach the making of summer. J. Berry.—BeW
Telephone talk. X. J. Kennedy.—KeK
The telling tree. L. Peavy.—JaPr
"There was an old man from Luray". W. J. Smith.—LiLo—SmL
"There was an old woman named Piper". W. J. Smith.—KeT—SmL
To you. W. Whitman.—HoVo
TV. E. Merriam.—MeS
"Two deep clear eyes". W. De La Mare.—DeR
"Two little dogs". Mother Goose.—ClI—WaM
"A very wise bird with a very long beak". Unknown.—PrP
Village voices. A. Bryan.—BrS
A visit to the mayor. W. J. Smith.—SmL
"A wise old owl lived in an oak". Mother Goose.—LiIf
A wise old owl ("... sat in an oak").—ClI

Talking to the sun. Eve Merriam.—MeS

Tall, Grace
Hallowe'en ad (attention witches).—BaH
To pumpkins at pumpkin time.—BaH

Tall, Grace Cornell
Winter is a wolf.—BaW

"Tall and blue". See Sky

"Tall times". See Mount St. Helens

"Tall treasure". See Trophy

"Tallyho, tallyho". See The hunt

Tamil language
"Kai veesamma kai veesu". Unknown.—YoS
"Wave your hand, wave your hand".—YoS
"Nila nila odi va". Unknown.—YoS
"Moon, moon, come to me".—YoS

Tamil nursery rhymes. See Nursery rhymes—Tamil

Tamm, Riina
"Once I got a postcard from the Fiji Islands", tr.—NyT

Tammy Yarbrough. Mel Glenn.—GlBc

Tanikawa, Shuntaro
On destiny, tr. by Harold Wright.—NyT
Picnic to the earth, tr. by Harold Wright.—NyT

"Tantrums of flame gush". See Five haiku

Tapia, Elizabeth
"I am created in the image of God".—StP

Tapir. William Jay Smith.—SmL

Tapirs
Tapir. W. J. Smith.—SmL

Tarantella. Hilaire Belloc.—MoR

The tarantula. Reed Whittemore.—ElW

Target practice. Gary Soto.—JaPr

The tarragon vinegar song. Margaret Mahy.—MaN

Tartary. Walter De La Mare.—DeR

"Tarzan, Tarzan, in a tree". Unknown.—CoM

Taste
Poor Henry. W. De La Mare.—DeR—MaP
Rattlesnake meat. O. Nash.—PrFo
Raw carrots. V. Worth.—WoAl
Sweets. V. Worth.—WoAl
The tongue ("The tongue was the very first instrument"). L. Tafari.—AgL
A vote for vanilla. E. Merriam.—MeS

Taste the air. Ashley Bryan.—BrS

Tate, James
Shadowboxing.—KnAs

"Tattletale, tattletale". Unknown.—ScA—WiA

Taunts. See Insults

Taverns. See Inns and taverns

Taxicabs
Santa rides. J. Yolen.—YoHa
Theatre hour. O. Nash.—SuI

Taylor, Alexander
Goodness, tr.—NyT

Taylor, Henry
Riding lesson.—KnAs

Taylor, Jane
The star.—SuI
"Twinkle, twinkle, little star".—EdGl (unat.)—WaM (unat.)
"Twinkle, twinkle, little star". See The star

Taylor, Jane
Paper doll, tr.—NyT
The penguin ("The penguin isn't meat, fish or bird"), tr.—NyT

Taylor, N. B.
Cerberus.—WhDd

"Tbl". Virginia Driving Hawk Sneve.—SnD

Tea parties
"Here's a cup". Unknown.—CoE
"Polly put the kettle on". Mother Goose.—EdGl—SuO—WaM

Tea party. Harry Behn.—LiDd

Telephones—*Continued*
I would have come. M. C. Livingston.—LiNe
"I'm sorry says the machine". E. Merriam.—MeCh
Long distance call. X. J. Kennedy.—KeGh
Love, it is time. K. Shapiro.—GoU
The telephone. R. Frost.—SuI
Telephone poles. V. Worth.—WoAl
Telephone talk. X. J. Kennedy.—KeK
"There was your voice, astonishment". From Letters from Maine. M. Sarton.—GoU
"We could be friends". M. C. Livingston.—JaP
You rang. M. Fatchen.—FaCm
Televised. Maya Angelou.—AnI
"**Televised** news turns". See Televised
Television
The disaster. B. Bennett.—MoR
Enemies. C. Zolotow.—SaB
Explaining. D. B. Axelrod.—JaPr
The home-watcher. M. Bracker.—MoA
"It used to be only Sunday afternoons". From Watching football on TV. H. Nemerov.—KnAs
A man in a tree. N. M. Bodecker.—LiLo
"My TV came down with a chill". W. R. Espy.—KeT
"Now, a picture". M. C. Livingston.—LiMh
"Passing and catching overcome the world". From Watching football on TV. H. Nemerov.—KnAs
Silly questions. J. Yolen.—YoBe
Televised. M. Angelou.—AnI
Tube time. E. Merriam.—KeT—MeS
TV. E. Merriam.—MeS
"We watch all afternoon, we are enthralled". From Watching football on TV. H. Nemerov.—KnAs
"With yellow feathers". M. C. Livingston.—LiMh
"The **television** toucan". See Television toucan
Television toucan. William Jay Smith.—SmL
"**Tell** her, smell her". Unknown.—OpI
Tell me. Barbara Juster Esbensen.—EsW
"**Tell** me, o octopus, I begs". See The octopus
"**Tell** me quick before I faint". Unknown.—ScA
"**Tell** me, why so pale and wan". X. J. Kennedy.—KeFb
"**Tell** tale tit". Unknown.—OpI
The **telling** tree. Linda Peavy.—JaPr
Temple for tomorrow. From The negro artist and the racial mountain. Langston Hughes.—SuC
"**Ten** candles on a birthday cake". See Birthday cake
Ten fat peas. Unknown.—CoE
"**Ten** fat peas in a peapod pressed". See Ten fat peas
Ten in the bed. Unknown.—CoE
"**Ten** in the morning". See City to surf
"**Ten** little apples on ten apple trees". Eve Merriam.—MeY
Ten little fingers. Unknown.—CoE
Ten little firefighters. Unknown.—CoE
"**Ten** little firefighters sleeping in a row". See Ten little firefighters
Ten little likenesses. X. J. Kennedy.—KeK
10 P.M. Myra Cohn Livingston.—LiNe
"**Ten** tom toms". Unknown.—MoR
Tending the garden. Eric Pankey.—JaM
"**Tendril** green unfurls to rose". See Country calendar
Tennis
Clobber the lobber. F. Lamport.—MoR
In the spring. J. Hall.—JaM
The midnight tennis match. T. Lux.—KnAs
Preparedness. F. Lamport.—KnAs
The tennis. E. B. White.—KnAs
Tennis clinic. L. Morrison.—LiLo

Tennis in the city. F. Higgins.—KnAs
The **tennis.** Elwyn Brooks White.—KnAs
Tennis clinic. Lillian Morrison.—LiLo
Tennis in the city. Frank Higgins.—KnAs
Tennyson, Alfred
The brook.—ElW
The eagle ("He clasps the crag with crooked hands").—CaB—ElW
"Flower in the crannied wall".—StP
The Lady of Shalott.—ElW
The owl. See Song, the owl
Second song, to the same.—LiIf
Song, the owl.—LiIf
The owl.—ElW
The splendor falls.—ElW
Sweet and low.—PlW
The **tent.** Walter De La Mare.—DeR
Tents
The tent. W. De La Mare.—DeR
Teresa of Avila, Saint
"From silly devotions".—StP
"Let nothing disturb you".—StP
The **term.** William Carlos Williams.—BaW
The **terrible** pig. Unknown.—ScA
Tewa Indians. See Indians of the Americas—Tewa
Texas
They don't do math in Texas. K. Dakos.—DaI
Texas norther. Myra Cohn Livingston.—BaW
Thackeray, William Makepeace
The King of Yvetot.—ElW
Thaler, Mike
The hyena.—CoAz
Sheep.—CoAz
Thames. Walter De La Mare.—DeR
"**Thank** God for rain". Unknown.—StP
"**Thank** you". See Thanksgiving
Thank you letter. Robin Klein.—FoLe
"**Thank** you, my dear". Sappho, tr. by Mary Barnard.—GoU
Thankfulness
All in a word. A. Fisher.—FiA—HoS
"All things bright and beautiful". C. F. Alexander.—StP
At the New Year. K. Patchen.—GoT
"Baby's heart is lifted up". R. L. Gales.—StP
The bead mat. W. De La Mare.—DeR
"Bless the meat". Unknown.—OpI
Counting sheep ("I am a poor shepherd"). J. Yolen.—YoHa
"Each time we eat". Unknown.—StP
"For all that has been, thanks". D. Hammarskjold.—StP
"For cities and towns, factories and farms, flowers". Unknown.—StP
"For every cup and plateful". Unknown.—StP
"For water-ices, cheap but good". A. Laing.—StP
"Give me a good digestion, Lord". T. H. B. Webb.—StP
"Give me my scallop shell of quiet". Sir W. Raleigh.—StP
"Glory be to God for dappled things". G. M. Hopkins.—StP
"God is great". Unknown.—StP
Grace. W. De La Mare.—DeR
"Have mercy on me, o beneficent one". Unknown.—StP
I thank God I'm free at las'. Unknown.—SuC
"I thank you God for most this amazing". E. E. Cummings.—StP
A kitten's thought. O. Herford.—ElW
Kumar Ragnath. M. Glenn.—GlBc
"Let us in peace eat the food". Unknown.—StP

There are days. Beatrice Schenk De Regniers.—DeW
There are different gardens. Carl Sandburg.—SuI
"There are glad days". See There are days
"There are gold ships". Unknown.—WiA
"There are lots of queer things that discoverers do". See Christopher Columbus
"There are many and more". See Many and more
"There are many tonight and the rink". See Skaters
"There are many who say that a dog has its day". See The song of the mischievous dog
"There are no ghosts". See Trick or treating at age eight
"There are not enough Emilys in the world". See Not enough Emilys
"There are six little houses up on the hill". See The dark
"There are so many different flavors to find". See The ice cream fountain mountain
"There are some things I want to know about". Jo Carson.—CaS
"There are stars above Japan". See Stars at night
"There are times when I can't move". Roberto Juarroz, tr. by William Stanley Merwin.—NyT
"There aren't any ghosts". See Night scare
"There came a gray owl at sunset". Unknown.—LiIf
"There came a pedlar to an evening house". See The pedlar
"There came a thief one night to Robin's castle". See The thief at Robin's castle
"There came an old sailor". See The old sailor
"There came an old soldier to my door". See The old soldier
"There flows a wonderful water". See Thames
"There goes the wapiti". See The wapiti
"There I was and in it came". See The poem that got away
"There is a boy here like me who catches fish". See Mull
"There is a girl in West Shopping Mall, Missouri". See A nature story
"There is a girl on our street". Unknown.—ScA
"There is a land". Leland B. Jacobs.—HoGo
"There is a magic melting pot". See The melting pot
"There is a mother's heart in the heart". Alistair MacLean.—StP
"There is a wordless tomorrow". See Wordless day
"There is a young reindeer named Donder". J. Patrick Lewis.—LiLo
"There is always". See Leaving
"There is an amazing bird". See The tin bird
"There is an animal known as a skink". See Two from the zoo
"There is an old lady who lives down the hall". See The sugar lady
"There is more". See Mosquito
"There is no break". See August 8
"There is no frigate like a book". Emily Dickinson.—DeT—ElW
"There is no impeding". See Sailing, sailing
"There is no swimming". See Ode to the sprinkler
"There is nobody anywhere near him". See Day-dream
"There is one word". See My favorite word
"There is only one horse on all the earth". See Names
"There is this place I know". See This place
"There never was yet a boy or a man". See Tinker man
"There once was a barber of Kew". Cosmo Monkhouse.—LiLo

"There once was a bear in a tree". See Paying through the nose
"There once was a big rattlesnake". Unknown.—LiLo
"There once was a boy of Bagdad". Unknown.—LiLo
"There once was a boy of Quebec". Rudyard Kipling.—LiLo
"There once was a boy with a nose". See The elephant boy
"There once was a centipede neat". Unknown.—LiLo
"There once was a dancing black bear". J. Patrick Lewis.—LiLo
"There once was a fat little pig named Alice". See Alice
"There once was a Feeble so few". See When you are there at all, that is
"There once was a finicky ocelot". See An odd one
"There once was a girl of New York". Cosmo Monkhouse.—LiLo
"There once was a man in the moon". David McCord.—LiLo
"There once was a man who said, how". Unknown.—LiLo
"There once was a man who said, why". Unknown.—LiLo
"There once was a Martian named Zed". See It came from outer space
"There once was a person of Benin". Cosmo Monkhouse.—LiLo
"There once was a plesiosaurus". Unknown.—LiLo
"There once was a provident puffin". See The provident puffin
There once was a puffin. Florence Page Jacque.—MoS
"There once was a scarecrow named Joel". David McCord.—LiLo
"There once was a sweet little mousicle". See Is it possicle
"There once was a thingamajig". See The thingamajig
"There once was a trout on a plate". See The hopeful trout, poor fish
"There once was a witch of Willowby Wood". From The witch of Willowby Wood. Rowena Bennett.—DeS
"There once was an ape in a zoo". See Be kind to dumb animals
"There once was an old kangaroo". Unknown.—LiLo
There once was an owl. John Ciardi.—LiIf
"There once was an owl perched on a shed". See There once was an owl
"There once was an oyster whose head". See Ho hum
"There once were two backcountry geezers". See Friendship
"There once were two cats of Kilkenny". Unknown.—LiLo
The cats of Kilkenny ("There were once . . .").—ElW—LaCc
"There sate good Queen Bess, oh". Walter De La Mare.—DeR
There seems to be a problem. John Ciardi.—CiH
"There she goes, there she goes". Unknown.—ScA—WiA
"There was a bee". Mother Goose.—WaM
"There was a boy, ye knew him well, ye cliffs". From The prelude. William Wordsworth.—LiIf
"There was a brave hunter named Fred". See He was brave, but not for long

"There was a young lady named Flo". Unknown.—LiLo

"There was a young lady named Groat". William Jay Smith.—SmL

"There was a young lady named Hannah". Unknown.—LiLo

"There was a young lady named Perkins". Unknown.—LiLo

"There was a young lady named Rose". William Jay Smith.—LiLo—SmL

"There was a young lady named Ruth". Unknown.—LiLo

"There was a young lady named Sue". See Keeping busy is better than nothing

"There was a young lady of Bute". Edward Lear.—CII—LiLo

"There was a young lady of Crete". Unknown.—LiLo—PrP
   A young lady of Crete.—PrFo

"There was a young lady of Ealing". Unknown.—LiLo

"There was a young lady of Firle". Edward Lear.—LiLo

"There was a young lady of Kent". Unknown.—LiLo

"There was a young lady of Lynn". Unknown.—LiLo

"There was a young lady of Niger". Unknown.—KeT—PrP
   "There was a young woman from Niger".—LiLo

"There was a young lady of Norway". Edward Lear.—LiLo

"There was a young lady of Rio". Unknown.—LiLo

"There was a young lady of Ryde". See "There was an old woman of Ryde"

"There was a young lady of Spain". Unknown.—LiLo

"There was a young lady of Tyre". Edward Lear.—LiLo

"There was a young lady whose chin". Edward Lear.—LiLo

"There was a young lady whose nose". Edward Lear.—LiLo

"There was a young maid who said, why". Unknown.—LiLo

"There was a young maiden called Eighmy". Unknown.—LiLo

There was a young maiden (". . . called Maggie"). See "There was a small maiden named Maggie"

There was a young man. See "There was a young man of Bengal"

"There was a young man from Alassio". William Jay Smith.—SmL

"There was a young man from Port Jervis". See Tennis clinic

"There was a young man from the city". Unknown.—LiLo

"There was a young man, let me say". David McCord.—LiLo

"There was a young man of Bengal". Unknown.—LiLo—PrP
   There was a young man.—CII

"There was a young man of Devizes". Unknown.—LiLo

"There was a young man of St. Kitts". Unknown.—LiLo

"There was a young man on a plain". William Jay Smith.—SmL

"There was a young man on a ship". See Willis C. Sick

"There was a young man so benighted". Unknown.—LiLo

"There was a young person called Smarty". Unknown.—LiLo

"There was a young person named Crockett". William Jay Smith.—LiLo—SmL

"There was a young pig from Chanute". Arnold Lobel.—LiLo

"There was a young pig who, in bed". Arnold Lobel.—LiLo

"There was a young prince in Bombay". Walter Parke.—LiLo

"There was a young woman from Niger". See "There was a young lady of Niger"

"There was an old crow". Mother Goose.—WaM

"There was an old crusty mechanic". See A crusty mechanic

"There was an old fellow named Green". Unknown.—LiLo

"There was an old fellow of Trinity". Unknown.—LiLo

"There was an old lady from Java". William Jay Smith.—SmL

"There was an old lady named Brown". William Jay Smith.—SmL

"There was an old lady named Carr". Unknown.—LiLo

"There was an old lady named Crockett". William Jay Smith.—LiLo—SmL

"There was an old lady named Hart". William Jay Smith.—LiLo—SmL

"There was an old lady of Rye". Unknown.—LiLo

"There was an old looney of Rhyme". Unknown.—LiLo

"There was an old maid of Berlin". Elizabeth Gordon.—LiLo

"There was an old man by Salt Lake". William Jay Smith.—SmL

"There was an old man from Japan". William Jay Smith.—SmL

"There was an old man from Luray". William Jay Smith.—LiLo—SmL

"There was an old man from Peru". Unknown.—ScA
   An old man from Peru.—PrFo
   Old man of Peru.—DeS

"There was an old man from the coast". William Jay Smith.—SmL

"There was an old man from the Rhine". Unknown.—LiLo

"There was an old man of Blackheath". Unknown.—LiLo

"There was an old man of Calcutta". See Arthur

"There was an old man of Dumbree". Edward Lear.—CII—LiIf

"There was an old man of Khartoum". Unknown.—LiLo

"There was an old man of Tarentum". Unknown.—LiLo

"There was an old man of the Cape". Robert Louis Stevenson.—LiLo

"There was an old man of the Hague". Edward Lear.—LiLo

"There was an old man of the Isles". Edward Lear.—LiLo

"There was an old man of the Nore". Unknown.—LiLo

"There was an old man of Toulon". William Jay Smith.—SmL

"There was an old man on a hill". See Serves him right

"There was an old man on the border". Edward Lear.—CII

"There's music in a hammer". Unknown.—PrP—WiA

"There's nothing like a party, nothing". See Leaps of feeling

"There's room in the bus". See Jittery Jim

"There's someone I know". Jack Prelutsky.—DeS

"There's this that I like about hockey, my lad". John Kieran.—KnAs

"These are the saddest of possible words". See Baseball's sad lexicon

"These buildings are too close to me". See Rudolph is tired of the city

"These lions, each by a daisy queen". See Dandelion

"These things, good Lord, that we pray for". Saint Thomas More.—StP

These yet to be United States. Maya Angelou.—AnI

"They all must fall". Muhammad Ali.—KnAs

"They always". See Lunchbox

"They are busy in the moon". See Night garden with ladies

"They are flutes". See Ode to La Tortilla

"They are out all together". See One night

"They are shaped". See Ode to los chicharrones

"They are slaves who fear to speak". See On freedom

They ask why. Maya Angelou.—AnI

"They can't see their pictures". See Package of trees

"They come like the ghosts of horses, shyly". See The pit ponies

They don't do math in Texas. Kalli Dakos.—DaI

"They dragged you from homeland". See Strong men

"They dressed us up in black". See The funeral

"They forbade this place alone to us, my parents". See Elegy for the girl who died in the dump at Ford's Gulch

"They furnish shade to others". Unknown.—StP

They had a point to make. John Ciardi.—CiH

"They had supposed their formula was fixed". From The white troops had their orders but the negroes looked like men. Gwendolyn Brooks.—SuC

"They have a certain beauty, those wheeled". See Over the field

"They have come by carloads". See Surfers at Santa Cruz

"They have spent their". See Old folks laugh

"They looked for me". See Hideout

"They mocked him when he said". See A short long story

"They mowed the meadow down below". See The island

"They must be here somewhere". See Padiddle

"They open up their beaks and throats". See Ocean diners

"They said, "Wait," well, I waited". See Alabama centennial

"They say, no". See Rocks

"They say Revis found a flatrock". See Mountain bride

"They say she weeps". See Ode to La Llorona

"They shall all be here one day". See At the ferry

"They stare at you". See Owls

They stooped over and came out. Unknown.—GoT

"They strolled down the lane together". Unknown.—PrP

"They talk all day". See The parakeets

"They tell". See Crickets

"They tell of a hunter named Shephard". Unknown.—LiLo

They told me. Walter De La Mare.—DeR

"They told me Pan was dead, but I". See They told me

"They told me the water was lovely". See It's great when you get in

"They try to say what you are, spiritual or sexual". See 558

"They wait under Pablo's bed". See Ode to Pablo's tennis shoes

"They walk together". See Under the Sunday tree

"They went to sea in a sieve, they did". See The jumblies

"They went with axe and rifle, when the trail was still to blaze". See Western wagons

They were my people. Grace Nichols.—NiCo

"They were those who cut cane". See They were my people

"They're checking the ping pong ball". See Unsound condition

"They're lucky little birds". See Lucky little birds

Thibaudeau, Colleen
Spring poem.—NyT
White bracelets.—NyT

"Thick in its glass". See Poor Henry

The **thief**. Deborah Chandra.—LiIf

The **thief** at Robin's castle. Walter De La Mare.—DeR—MaP

Thieves
A—Apple pie. W. De La Mare.—DeR
Calling all cars. M. Fatchen.—FaCm
"Charley, Charley". Mother Goose.—WaM
"Dingty diddlety". Mother Goose.—WaM
"Don't steal this book, my little lad". Unknown.—ScA
"Do not steal this book, my lad".—OpI
"From zoo keepers' pails Gail steals". X. J. Kennedy.—KeFb
The honey robbers. W. De La Mare.—DeR—MaP
"It is a sin". Unknown.—WiA
"A lemon and a pickle knocked at the door". Unknown.—WiA
"Little Poll Parrot". Mother Goose.—ClI—WaM
"A maiden caught stealing a dahlia". Unknown.—LiLo
"Matthew, Mark, Luke, and John, stole a pig". Unknown.—WiA
"Millery millery dustipole". Mother Goose.—WaM
To the puss moth.—OpI
"Not last night but the night before". Unknown.—OpI—ScA
"Last night and the night before".—WiA
1, 2, 3. E. Merriam.—MeP
Peak and Puke. W. De La Mare.—DeR—MaP
"Policeman, policeman, don't catch me". Unknown.—WiA
"The Queen of Hearts". Mother Goose.—EdGl—SuO
"The rain it raineth all around". Unknown.—OpI
Reach for the sky. Unknown.—ScA
"Steal not this book for fear of shame". Unknown.—OpI
Stealing eggs. X. J. Kennedy.—PrFo
The thief at Robin's castle. W. De La Mare.—DeR—MaP
Thieves. P. B. Janeczko.—JaB
"This book is one thing". Unknown.—OpI
"Tom, Tom, the piper's son, stole a pig and away he run". Mother Goose.—SuO—WaM
The truants. W. De La Mare.—DeR—MaP
Who really. W. De La Mare.—DeR

Thieves. Paul B. Janeczko.—JaB

"Thin frozen". See Winter dusk

"The **thing** about a gull is not the soaring flight".
    See The sea gull's eye
"The **thing** about a shark is, teeth". See About the
    teeth of sharks
"The **thing** to remember when you go to bed". See
    Advice on how to sleep well Halloween night
The **thingamajig**. John Ciardi.—CiH
Things ("Trains are for going"). William Jay
    Smith.—SmL
Things ("Went to the corner"). Eloise Greenfield.—
    SIM
Things on a microscope slide. X. J. Kennedy.—
    KeGh
"The **things** to draw with compasses". See Circles
"**Think** about the way we'll meet". See A beginning
Think me a fable. J. Patrick Lewis.—LeT
"**Think** of all the people". See The world's so big
"**Think** of the muscles". See Windy tree
"**Think** of the ocean". Siobhan Swayne.—BoT
"**Think,** said the robin". See Bird talk
The **thinker**. John Ciardi.—CiH—LiLo
"**Thinking** about you". See Ratio
Thinking green. Earthworks Group.—LoFh
Thirst
    Drinking water coconut. G. Nichols.—NiCo
"**Thirty** days hath September". Mother Goose.—
    WaM
"**Thirty-two** white horses". Unknown.—WiA
"**Thirty** white cows standing in a stall". Unknown.—
    ScA
"**This** afternoon". See Three o'clock
"**This** big cat". Beatrice Schenk De Regniers.—MoS
"**This** bird was happy once in the high trees". See
    Captive bird
"**This** book is mine". Myra Cohn Livingston.—LiNe
"**This** book is one thing". Unknown.—OpI
"**This** box contains". See The old math, two
"**This** brief day now over". See Part XX: This brief
    day now over
"**This** butterfly". See The reader
"**This** cat". Karla Kuskin.—LaCc
"**This** cat, see, yellow". See Tom cat
"**This** cigarette of which I light". See The breath of
    death (the cigarette)
"**This** clock". See Clock
"**This** darksome burn, horseback brown". See
    Inversnaid
"**This** drought has cracked". See So dry this July
This evening. Zishe Landau, tr. by Irving
    Feldman.—GoT
"**This** feather-soft creature". See A goldfinch
"**This** giant white". See Lighthouse
"**This** guy is an animal, a pig, squealing sinus
    breathing". See Wrestling the beast
This house is the center. Arnold Adoff.—AdIn
This I know. Anne Corkett.—BoT
"**This** is a fervent time". See The skydivers
"**This** is a snake, perhaps you've read of it". See The
    snake
"**This** is a song". See Touching
This is just to say. William Carlos Williams.—ElW
"**This** is mint and here are three pinks". See Gift
"**This** is my bicycle birthday". See Bicycle birthday
"**This** is my rock". David McCord.—KeT—LiDd
"**This** is my turtle". See My turtle
"**This** is not a poem about Indians". See Indian trail
"**This** is the church". Unknown.—WiA
"**This** is the day the circus comes". See A circus
    garland
"**This** is the end of winter's reign". See Easter
"**This** is the house that Jack built". Mother
    Goose.—SuO

The house that Jack built.—HoS
"**This** is the man that broke the barn". See A story
    for five toes
"**This** is the month". See December
"**This** is the night of Halloween". Unknown.—OpI
"**This** is the only junkyard in this county". Jo
    Carson.—CaS
"**This** is the time of gentle rain". See 10 P.M.
"**This** is the way". See Balloons
"**This** is the Wiggledywasticus". See After a visit to
    the natural history museum
"**This** is the wind's doing". See Partners
"**This** is thy hour, O Soul, thy free flight into the
    wordless". See A clear midnight
"**This** land is nothing that I know". See Kansas visit
"**This** little morsel of morsels here". See Part X:
    This little morsel of morsels here
"**This** little mule, he kicked so high". Unknown.—
    ScA
"**This** little pig went to market". Unknown.—WiA
"**This** little pig went to market". Mother Goose.—
    EdGl—SuO—WaM
  "**This** little piggy".—SuI
"**This** little piggy". See "This little pig went to
    market"
"**This** monarch butterfly". See On May Day
"**This** morning, God". Unknown.—StP
"**This** morning I argued with a friend". See
    Listening to baseball in the car
"**This** morning, I saw Susan Rosenthal standing in
    the snow". See About angels and age
"**This** morning I will not". Hitomaro Kakinomoto,
    tr. by Kenneth Rexroth.—GoU
"**This** night". See New year
This night. Leah Goldberg, tr. by Robert Friend.—
    GoT
"**This** night and all its silence". See This night
"**This** old hammer". Unknown.—MoR
This old man. Unknown.—CoE
"**This** old man grazed thirty head of cattle". See The
    purpose of poetry
"**This** old man, he played one". See This old man
"**This** one saw a hare". See "Celui-ci a vu un lievre"
"**This** pearl". See A pearl
"**This** pig got in the barn". Unknown.—ClI
This place. Eloise Greenfield.—GrU
"**This** sad house". See Household
"**This** season our tunnips was red". David
    McCord.—LiLo
"**This** ship in the dock was at the end of its trip".
    See The ship in the dock
"**This** sidewalk is cracked". Unknown.—CoM
"**This** small". See Magnet
"**This** soul of mine within the heart is smaller".
    Unknown.—StP
"**This** stick here". See Beavers in November
"**This** time, from across the water". C. Aleph
    Kamal.—LeCa
"**This** time tomorrow, where shall I be".
    Unknown.—OpI
This tooth. Lee Bennett Hopkins.—KeT
"**This** train don't carry no gamblers, this train".
    Unknown.—StP
"**This** tree, by April wreathed in flowers". See Logs
"**Thistle** and darnel and dock grew there". See
    Nicholas Nye
Thomas, Dylan
    The song of the mischievous dog.—DeT
Thomas, Edward
    The gallows.—ElW
    The owl ("Downhill I came, hungry, and yet not
        starved").—ElW—LiIf

Thomas, Edward—*Continued*
"Will you come".—MoR
Thomas, Jim
Chore boy.—LiPm
Free time.—LiPm
Watchdogs.—LiHp
Thomas, John
The enlistment of free blacks as Continental soldiers.—SuC
Thomas, Joyce Carol
The gingerbread grandma.—LiPg
"Thomas a Didymus, hard of belief". Unknown.—OpI
Thoreau, Henry David
"It is no dream of mine".—SuI
Thorley, Wilfred
The happy sheep.—CoAz
Thorny. William Cole.—CoAz
"Those good students who only loved working". See Led by the Hebrew School rabbi
"Those presents". See Christmas morning
Those who do not study history are doomed. Arnold Adoff.—AdCh
Those winter Sundays. Robert Hayden.—ElW
"Thou art my father, who is my mother". Unknown.—StP
"Thou art the sky and thou art the nest as well". Rabindranath Tagore.—StP
"Thou dawnest beautifully in the horizon". Unknown.—StP
Thou reader. Walt Whitman.—HoVo
"Thou reader throbbest life and pride and love the same as I". See Thou reader
"Thou that hast given so much to me". George Herbert.—StP
"Though fiends". See Next day
Thought. See also Mind
A boy's head. M. Holub.—NyT
Idea. Shiki.—DeI
In the night. E. Jennings.—GoT
My dog ("Here's what we think of, Gov and I"). F. Holman.—LiDp
Rummage. E. Merriam.—MeS
Shapes and actions. J. Berry.—BeW
A short story. D. E. Galindo.—NyT
Sometimes. M. A. Hoberman.—HoFa
The telephone. R. Frost.—SuI
The waterbeetle. H. Belloc.—CaB
Thought. Walt Whitman.—HoVo
Thoughts. Eloise Greenfield.—GrU
"Thoughts that were put into words". Karla Kuskin.—JaP
"A thousand doors ago". See Young
"A thousand years ago, or maybe more". See Waitangi Day
"Thousands of years ago". See Part VI: Thousands of years ago
"Thousandz of thornz there be". See The bees' song
"A thread of red ants". See Ants
"Three and thirty birds there stood". See Melmillo
The three beggars. Walter De La Mare.—DeR
"Three blind mice". Mother Goose.—EdGl—WaM
"Three dwarfs there were which lived in an isle". See The isle of Lone
The three foxes. Alan Alexander Milne.—DeT
Three ghostesses. Unknown.—LoFh
"Three grand arcs". See Nine triads
Three gray geese ("... in a green field grazing") . See "Three gray geese in the green grass grazing"
"Three gray geese in the green grass grazing". Unknown.—WiA

Three gray geese ("... in a green field grazing") .—ClI
"Three jolly farmers". See Off the ground
"Three jolly gentlemen". See The huntsmen
"Three little ghostesses". See Three ghostesses
"Three little girls dressed all in white". Unknown.—WiA
The three little kittens. Eliza Lee Follen.—HoS
"Three little kittens, they lost their mittens".—SuO (unat.)
"Three little kittens lost their mittens".—EdGl (unat.)—WaM (unat.)
"Three little kittens lost their mittens". See The three little kittens See The three little kittens
"Three little kittens, they lost their mittens". See The three little kittens
Three little monkeys. See "I know something I won't tell"
"Three little monkeys". See Monkeys on the bed
Three o'clock. Valerie Worth.—WoA
"Three of us here on the hill". See The hill
"Three robbers trying to get rich rich rich". See 1, 2, 3
The three royal monkeys, sels. Walter De La Mare
Andy Battle's song.—DeR
Marching song.—DeR
Nod's song.—DeR
The water midden's song.—DeR
"Three, six, nine". Unknown.—CoM
"Three small men in a small house". See Late
Three strangenesses of every day. Eve Merriam.—MeS
Three thirty. Arnold Adoff.—AdCh
"Three times by she passes". See "Trois fois passera"
"Three times iron bars". See "Dreimal eiserne stangen"
"Three times it cried". See The deer on the mountain
"Three times they called". See Code blue
"Three wise men of Gotham". Mother Goose.—WaM
Three young rats. See "Three young rats with black felt hats"
"Three young rats with black felt hats". Mother Goose.—PrP—SuO
Three young rats.—ClI
Thrift
A nature story. A. Adoff.—AdCh
"Willful waste brings woeful want". Mother Goose.—WaM
"A thrifty young fellow of Shoreham". Unknown.—LiLo
"Through joy and sorrow we have". See At sunset
"Through moonlight's milk". See Cat in moonlight
"Through my house in sunny weather". See The dictionary bird
"Through the green twilight of a hedge". See The mother bird
Through the looking glass, sels. Lewis Carroll
"I passed by his garden, and marked, with one eye".—LiIf
Jabberwocky.—ElW
The walrus and the carpenter.—DeT—ElW—HoS
"Through the revolving door". See Alligator on the escalator
"Through the sunshine". See Easter's coming
"Through the teeth". Unknown.—ScA—WiA
"Thrum drew". See Thrum drew a small map
Thrum drew a small map. Susan Musgrave.—BoT
The thrush. Walter De La Mare.—DeR
Thud. Max Fatchen.—FaCm

Tongue-twisters—*Continued*
"Peter Piper picked a peck of pickled peppers".
Mother Goose.—EdGl—SuO
"If Peter Piper picked a peck of pickled
peppers".—WiA
Punch, boys, punch. Unknown.—OpT
"Round and round the rugged rock the ragged
rascal ran". Unknown.—ScA—WiA
Sea horse and sawhorse. X. J. Kennedy.—PrFo
"She sells sea shells by the seashore".
Unknown.—WiA
Sheepshape. X. J. Kennedy.—KeGh
"Six slim slick sycamore saplings". Unknown.—
WiA
"A skunk sat on a stump, the stump thunk the
skunk". Unknown.—WiA
"Theophilus, the thistle sifter, while sifting a sifter
full". Unknown.—WiA
"Three gray geese in the green grass grazing".
Unknown.—WiA
Three gray geese (". . . in a green field
grazing") .—CII
"Toy boat, toy boat, toy boat". Unknown.—WiA
"A tutor who tooted the flute". Unknown.—LiLo
Unfinished knews item. E. Merriam.—MeCh
Wamby or the nostalgic record book. M.
Bracker.—MoA
Weather ("Whether the weather be fine").
Unknown.—SuI
"When a jolly young fisher named Fisher".
Unknown.—LiLo—PrP
"The tongue was the very first instrument". See The
tongue
Tongues
Cat bath ("In the midst"). V. Worth.—LaCc—
WoAl
"Liar, liar, pants on fire". Unknown.—CoM—ScA
Ode to el molcajete. G. Soto.—SoNe
"Tell tale tit". Unknown.—OpI
"There was an old man from Luray". W. J.
Smith.—LiLo—SmL
"Thirty white cows standing in a stall".
Unknown.—ScA
The tongue ("The tongue was the very first
instrument"). L. Tafari.—AgL
The tongue ("You stick out your tongue"). P.
Tafdrup.—NyT
Toni Vingelli. Mel Glenn.—GlBc
"Tonight I lie staring into the unlit neighborhood".
See Apology
"Tonight is the night". See Hallowe'en
"Tonight their voices screeched". See Daddy's gone
"Tonight, tonight, the pillow fight". Unknown.—
WiA
"Tonio told me at catechism". See The purpose of
altar boys
"Tony eats apples". See Ode to weight lifting
"Tony said, boys are better". See Girls can, too
"Too aware of endings, I search among". See Child
in a blue linen dress
"Too bad". Unknown.—ScA
"Too close". See Love
Too hot to sleep. Sid Marty.—BoT
Too many Daves. Dr. Seuss.—ElW
"Too young to milk". See Chore boy
Tools
Compass. V. Worth.—WoAl
"East, west, north, south". Unknown.—WiA
Hose. V. Worth.—DeT—WoAl
Pail. V. Worth.—WoAl
Ways of composing. E. Merriam.—MeS
"A tooth fell out". See But then

"Toothless, she kisses". See Seeing Granny
"The top of a hill". See How to tell the top of a hill
Torei
Energy, tr. by Tze-si Huang.—DeI
Tori
The catch ("The kingfisher"), tr. by Tze-si
Huang.—DeI
Torreson, Rodney
Howie Kell suspends all lust to contemplate the
universe.—JaPr
The tortoise and the hedgehog. Rudyard Kipling.—
WhAa
Tortoises. See Turtles and tortoises
"Totemic scarabs, exoskeletal". From Watching
football on TV. Howard Nemerov.—KnAs
The toucan. Pyke Johnson.—CoAz
Toucans
Television toucan. W. J. Smith.—SmL
The toucan. P. Johnson.—CoAz
Touch
Love letters, unmailed. E. Merriam.—MeS
Touching. From Songs for Nandu Bhende. N.
Ezekiel.—AgL
"Touch black, touch black". Unknown.—WiA
"Touch blue". Unknown.—ScA
Touchdown. Sharon Bell Mathis.—MaR
Touching. From Songs for Nandu Bhende. Nissim
Ezekiel.—AgL
"A tough kangaroo named Hopalong Brown". See
Kangaroo
"A tourist came in from Orbitville". See
Southbound on the freeway
Toward myself. Leah Goldberg, tr. by Robert
Friend.—GoT
Towns. See also Cities and city life; also names of
towns, as Jerusalem
My lost youth. H. W. Longfellow.—SuI
"Toy boat, toy boat, toy boat". Unknown.—WiA
"Toy boy". Bruce McMillan.—McP
Toys
Cat toys. V. Worth.—WoA
The coming of teddy bears. D. Lee.—KeT
"Cub tub". B. McMillan.—McP
"Duck truck". B. McMillan.—McP
J is for jack-in-the-box. W. J. Smith.—SmL
Jack in the box. W. J. Smith.—SmL
Jacks. V. Worth.—WoAl
Kaleidoscope. V. Worth.—WoAl
Magnet. V. Worth.—WoAl
"Smiling girls, rosy boys". Mother Goose.—WaM
Pedlar's song .—OpT
"Toy boy". B. McMillan.—McP
Where go the boats. R. L. Stevenson.—ElW—
KeT
"Tra-la-la-boom-de-ay". Unknown.—CoM
Tractor. Valerie Worth.—WoAl
"The tractor rests". See Tractor
Trade. See Markets and marketing; Peddlers and
vendors; Shops and shopkeepers; names of
occupations, as Cobbler;
Trading
The baseball card dealer. R. L. Harrison.—MoA
"I swapped me a horse and got me a cow".
Unknown.—ScA
Tradition. Eloise Greenfield.—GrU
Traffic
Thoughts. E. Greenfield.—GrU
"Traigo un ramillete". Unknown.—LoFh
Bouquet of roses ("A bouquet of roses").—LoFh
"A train is passing". Paul Borum.—NyT
Train tune. Louise Bogan.—MoR

Trees.—*Continued*
 The squirrel. S. Barakat.—NyT
 The telling tree. L. Peavy.—JaPr
 "There are some things I want to know about". J. Carson.—CaS
 There's an orange tree out there. A. Q. Urias.—NyT
 "They furnish shade to others". Unknown.—StP
 Thinking green. Earthworks Group.—LoFh
 "A tree". K. Koettner-Benigni.—NyT
 Tree ("If only I could stand"). F. Asch.—MoS
 The tree ("It graces our yard"). E. Greenfield.—GrU
 Tree at my window. R. Frost.—ElW
 Tree festival. D. Bateson.—FoLe
 Tree house. S. Silverstein.—DeS
 A tree within. O. Paz.—NyT
 Trees ("Of all the trees in England"). W. De La Mare.—DeR—MaP
 Trees ("Trees just stand around all day"). A. Fisher.—FiA
 Trees ("The trees share their shade with"). N. Dishman.—LoFh
 Under the Sunday tree. E. Greenfield.—GrU
 "When a big tree falls". Unknown.—ScA
 "Who has seen the wind". C. G. Rossetti.—BaW—DeS—KeT—LiDd—MoS—StP
 Windy tree. A. Fisher.—FiA
Trees ("Of all the trees in England"). Walter De La Mare.—DeR—MaP
Trees ("Trees just stand around all day"). Aileen Fisher.—FiA
Trees ("The trees share their shade with"). Nelda Dishman.—LoFh
"Trees just stand around all day". See Trees
"The trees share their shade with". See Trees
"Treetalk and windsong are". See Sugarfields
"Tremors of your network". See These yet to be United States
Trethewey, Eric
 Garbage ("We hauled trash that summer, the three of us").—JaM
 Rescue ("Sunday, beginning the week late").—JaPr
Triceratops. Jack Prelutsky.—PrT
"Triceratops had one short horn". See Triceratops
Trick or treating at age eight. Liz Rosenberg.—LiHp
Trifles. See Little things, importance of
"Trim, tran". Unknown.—OpI
Trimmed down tales. X. J. Kennedy.—KeGh
Tringress, Claire
 Five ("Five little children").—MoS
Trip to the seashore. Lois Simmie.—BoT
Tripp, Wallace
 "Going home with her books through the snow".—LiLo
 "Trit trot to market to buy a penny doll". Mother Goose.—WaM
 "Trois fois passera". Unknown.—YoS
 "Three times by she passes".—YoS
Trolls. See Monsters
Trophy. Sharon Bell Mathis.—MaR
Trouble. James Wright.—JaPr
Trouble with baby. X. J. Kennedy.—KeGh
Troupe, Quincy
 Fireflies ("Fireflies on night canvas").—SlM
 Flying kites.—SlM
 A poem for Magic.—SlM
The truants. Walter De La Mare.—DeR—MaP
Trucks
 "The horn on our pickup truck stayed stuck". X. J. Kennedy.—KeGh

True. Lilian Moore.—LaCc
A true account of talking to the sun at Fire Island. Frank O'Hara.—ElW
"True Mexicans or not, let's open our shirts". See Kearney Park
Truman, Harry S.
 Integration of the armed services of the United States.—SuC
The truth about the abominable footprint. Michael Baldwin.—PrFo
"Truth, truth, nobody's daughter". Unknown.—OpI
Truthfulness and falsehood
 All fool's day. J. Agard.—FoLe
 "As the guns thunder". E. Merriam.—MeS
 "Ask me no questions". Unknown.—WiA
 Between ebb and flow. F. Tuqan.—NyT
 "The boaster will make out someone else is the liar". From Jamaican Caribbean proverbs. Unknown.—BeW
 "Cross my heart and hope to die". Unknown.—ScA
 "Dear Lord, you are the Truth, when I keep". H. J. Nouwen.—StP
 The flattered flying fish. E. V. Rieu.—ElW
 How the rhinoceros got his nose. J. P. Lewis.—LeA
 "I am a man of peace, I believe in peace". M. Gandhi.—StP
 "I'll tell you the truth". Unknown.—WiA
 "It's not me". J. Carson.—CaS
 Jephson Gardens. D. J. Enright.—ElW
 "Liar, liar, lick spit". Unknown.—OpI
 "Liar, liar, pants on fire". Unknown.—CoM—ScA
 Marthe away (she is away). K. Rexroth.—GoU
 Not quite Kinsey. G. Hyland.—JaPr
 The nymph's reply to the shepherd. Sir W. Raleigh.—ElW
 On freedom. J. R. Lowell.—SuI
 The outlandish knight. Unknown.—ElW
 The pied piper of Hamelin, complete. R. Browning.—ElW
 Poetry ("I too, dislike it, there are things that are important"). M. Moore.—SuI
 A poison tree. W. Blake.—ElW
 Roscoe. P. B. Janeczko.—JaB
 A teacher's lament. K. Dakos.—DaI
 "There was a young lady named Ruth". Unknown.—LiLo
 They don't do math in Texas. K. Dakos.—DaI
 The tongue ("The tongue was the very first instrument"). L. Tafari.—AgL
 True. L. Moore.—LaCc
 "Truth, truth, nobody's daughter". Unknown.—OpI
 When I read the book. W. Whitman.—HoVo
"Try seeing through shoes' points of view". See How to treat shoes
Try, try again. T. H. Palmer.—SuI
Tube time. Eve Merriam.—KeT—MeS
Tubman, Harriet (about)
 Harriet Tubman. E. Greenfield.—SlM
 Mean to be free. Unknown.—SuC
Tueni, Nadia
 In the Lebanese mountains, tr. by Samuel Hazo.—NyT
Tulips
 The yellow tulip. G. Swede.—BoT
"Tuna turn". See A fishy square dance
Tuqan, Fadwa
 Behind bars, tr. by Hatem Hussaini.—NyT
 Between ebb and flow, tr. by Salma Khadra Jayyusi and Naomi Shihab Nye.—NyT

"Two small children in the Gardens on Sunday".
See Jephson Gardens
2195 In the arc of your mallet. Jalal-Ud-Din Rumi,
tr. by John Moyne and Coleman Barks.—GoU
2674 After being in love, the next responsibility.
Jalal-Ud-Din Rumi, tr. by John Moyne and
Coleman Barks.—GoU
"Two ugly toads were hopping about". See Kick and
live
Two ways to look at kites. Barbara Juster
Esbensen.—BaW
Two week car trip. X. J. Kennedy.—KeK
"Two worlds there are, one you think". See Cleaning
the well
Twogether. Eve Merriam.—MeCh
"Two's company". Unknown.—WiA
"Tyger, tyger, burning bright". See The tiger ("Tiger,
tiger, burning bright")
"Typewriter". See Ways of composing
The typewriter bird. William Jay Smith.—SmL
"The typewriter bird with the pitchfork beak". See
The typewriter bird
"A typical day in Mischief City". See Mischief City
Tyrannosaurus ("He strides onto the dance floor").
Jane Yolen.—YoDd
Tyrannosaurus ("Tyrannosaurus was a beast"). Jack
Prelutsky.—PrT
"Tyrannosaurus was a beast". See Tyrannosaurus

U

"U can be seen without a Q". See Quibble
U is for up. William Jay Smith.—SmL
"U R 2 good". Unknown.—WiA
Uchang, Kim
    Inside, tr.—NyT
"The ugly duckling's shoulders sag". See A misspent
youth
The ultimate product. Eve Merriam.—MeCh
Ululation. Eve Merriam.—MeS
"An umbrella". See Conversation
Umbrellas
    "Bella had a new umbrella". E. Merriam.—PrFo
    Conversation. Buson.—DeS
    "Stretch my ribs out wide and high". M. C.
    Livingston.—LiMh
Un-negative. Eve Merriam.—MeCh
"An unassuming owl". Jack Prelutsky.—LiIf
"Uncle Dick". Eve Merriam.—MeP
Uncle Fred. Max Fatchen.—FaCm
"Uncle Fred with glares and stitches". See Uncle
Fred
"Uncle Simon he". See Companions
Uncles
    Companions. Unknown.—OpT
    "Fame was a claim of Uncle Ed's". O. Nash.—
    PrFo
    Family genius. X. J. Kennedy.—KeGh
    "From the boat, while Uncle Sid". X. J.
    Kennedy.—KeFb
    "In Central Park I saw Uncle Jack". Unknown.—
    WiA
    Jim. J. Holden.—JaPr
    Kiph. W. De La Mare.—DeR
    Mechanical menagerie. X. J. Kennedy.—PrFo
    My great grand uncle. T. Ray.—NyT
    My uncle. M. A. Hoberman.—HoFa
    Night starvation or the biter bit. C. Blyton.—PrFo
    "Now just who, muses Uncle Bill Biddle". X. J.
    Kennedy.—KeGh—LiLo

"Uncle Dick". E. Merriam.—MeP
Uncle Fred. M. Fatchen.—FaCm
Visiting. Unknown.—OpT
"Under a maple tree". See Dog
"Under low black clouds". See Hurricane
"Under the bamboo, under the tree". Unknown.—
CoM
"Under the bed". See Scary things
"Under the full spring moon". See Holi
"Under the ground". See Rabbit and lark
"Under the linden in Sands". See Wolf-ancestry
Under the mistletoe. Countee Cullen.—SlM
Under the rose (the song of the wanderer). Walter
De La Mare.—DeR
Under the snow. Aileen Fisher.—FiH
Under the stairs. Daphne Lister.—BaH
"Under the stairs, a secret cave". See Closet
Under the Sunday tree. Eloise Greenfield.—GrU
Under the waterfall. Thomas Hardy.—ElW
"Under the willow". See Puppy
"Under this plum tree". See The black bull
Under this sky. Zia Hyder, tr. by Bhabani Sengupta
and Naomi Shihab Nye.—NyT
"Under this sod lies a great bucking horse".
Unknown.—ScA
"Underneath my belt". See When I was lost
"Underneath this pile of stones". Unknown.—BaH
Understanding. Myra Cohn Livingston.—LiDd
"The underwater wibbles". Jack Prelutsky.—JaP
Uneven parallel bars. Patricia Gary.—KnAs
Unexpected summer soup. Margaret Mahy.—MaN
The unfinished dream. Walter De La Mare.—DeR
Unfinished knews item. Eve Merriam.—MeCh
The unfortunate giraffe. Oliver Herford.—LiLo
The unicorn ("Oh this is the animal that never
was"). Rainer Maria Rilke.—WhDd
Unicorn ("Unicorn, unicorn"). Anne Corkett.—BoT
Unicorn ("The unicorn with the long white horn").
William Jay Smith.—SmL
"The unicorn". See What teacher said
"The unicorn I tried to paint". X. J. Kennedy.—
KeK
"Unicorn, unicorn". See Unicorn
"The unicorn with the long white horn". See
Unicorn
Unicorns
    "The lion and the unicorn". Mother Goose.—
    EdGl
    Narwhal. X. J. Kennedy.—WhAa
    The unicorn ("Oh this is the animal that never
    was"). R. M. Rilke.—WhDd
    Unicorn ("Unicorn, unicorn"). A. Corkett.—BoT
    Unicorn ("The unicorn with the long white
    horn"). W. J. Smith.—SmL
    "The unicorn I tried to paint". X. J. Kennedy.—
    KeK
    What teacher said. J. P. Lewis.—LeT
Unitas, Johnny (about)
    Unitas. E. Gold.—KnAs
Unitas. Edward Gold.—KnAs
United States
    Anthem. S. Vincent.—KnAs
    First flight. M. C. Livingston.—LiNe
    Flying west. M. C. Livingston.—LiNe
    Geography. E. Merriam.—MeS
    I hear America singing. W. Whitman.—HoVo
    Kansas visit. M. C. Livingston.—LiNe
    "Mississippi said to Missouri". Unknown.—WiA
    On journeys through the states. W. Whitman.—
    HoVo

V

"The **vacumn** cleaner's swallowed Will". X. J. Kennedy.—KeGh
Vagabonds. See Gypsies; Wayfaring life
Valentine for Ernest Mann. Naomi Shihab Nye.—JaP
Valentine hearts. Myra Cohn Livingston.—LiR
Valentines. Aileen Fisher.—FiA
Valentine's Day. See Saint Valentine's Day
Valentine's day. Aileen Fisher.—FiA
Valerie O'Neill. Mel Glenn.—GlBc
Valuables. X. J. Kennedy.—KeK
Vampires. See Monsters
Van Doren, Mark
    Dunce song 6.—DeT
    Merry-go-round ("Horses in front of me").—MoS
    Sleep, grandmother.—SuI
Van Laan, Nancy
    Rainbow crow.—WhDd
Van Toorn, Peter
    Mountain tambourine.—NyT
Van Walleghen, Michael
    The age of reason.—JaPr
    Bowling alley.—JaPr
"Vanilla, vanilla, vanilla for me". See A vote for vanilla
Vanity. See also Conceit
    Black hair. G. Soto.—JaP—SoA
    Combing the hair. Unknown.—OpT
    The coquette. W. De La Mare.—DeR
    The dog (as seen by the cat). O. Herford.—ElW
    The flattered flying fish. E. V. Rieu.—ElW
    Fox and crow. W. J. Smith.—SmL
    The mysterious cat. V. Lindsay.—DeS—LaCc
    "The peacock hides its leg when its tail gets praises". From Jamaican Caribbean proverbs. Unknown.—BeW
    Raccoon ("The raccoon wears a black mask"). K. Rexroth.—CoAz
    The toucan. P. Johnson.—CoAz
    Tyrannosaurus ("He strides onto the dance floor"). J. Yolen.—YoDd
Variety. From Animalimericks. Eve Merriam.—MeS
"Vaunts violoncello". See The egotistical orchestra
Vegetables. See also Food and eating; Gardens and gardening; also names of vegetables, as Potatoes
    Asparagus. V. Worth.—WoAl
    The cucumber. N. Hikmet.—NyT
    "Do you carrot all for me". Unknown.—WiA
    "Five tiny green peas, lying in a row". Unknown.—PrP
    Green with envy. E. Merriam.—MeCh
    Mr. Finney's turnip. Unknown.—HoS
    Raw carrots. V. Worth.—WoAl
    Spinach. F. P. Heide.—HeG
Vendors. See Peddlers and vendors
Verlaine, Paul
    Dusk ("The moon is red in the foggy sky"), tr. by C. F. MacIntyre.—GoT
    Muted, tr. by C. F. MacIntyre.—GoU
    VI, tr. by C. F. MacIntyre.—GoT
Vern. Gwendolyn Brooks.—LiDp
Verse. See Poets and poetry
Verse play. Eve Merriam.—MeS
"The **very** first rhino (from Tokyo)". See How the rhinoceros got his nose
Very much afraid. Unknown.—LiIf
"Very soon the Yankee teachers". See Learning to read
"A **very,** very old house I know". See The old house
"A **very** wise bird with a very long beak". Unknown.—PrP

The **vet.** Myra Cohn Livingston.—LiR
Veterans Day
    Remembrance Day ("Poppies, oh, miss"). J. Nicholls.—FoLe
    Remembrance Day ("To some"). J. Kitching.—FoLe
    When Johnny comes marching home again. Unknown.—LoFh
Victor Jeffreys. Mel Glenn.—GlBc
"Victor wore a velvet cape". Jack Prelutsky.—PrBe
A **victory.** R. T. Smith.—JaM
Victory banquet. Sharon Bell Mathis.—MaR
"Victory, union, faith, identity, time". From Starting from Paumanok. Walt Whitman.—HoVo
Viereck, Peter
    Twilight of the outward life, tr.—GoT
Village life
    "Ain't no hell on earth". J. Carson.—CaS
    Early country village morning. G. Nichols.—NiCo
    Johnny Spain's white heifer. H. Carruth.—JaM
    The lamplighter. W. De La Mare.—DeR
    The new lady barber at Ralph's Barber Shop. L. Dangel.—JaM
    The Paignton Christmas pudding. J. Yolen.—YoHa
    The royal visit. J. Reaney.—BoT
    Skating in Pleasant Hill, Ohio. K. Iddings.—KnAs
    Small town fireworks. X. J. Kennedy.—KeK
    Then. W. De La Mare.—DeR—MaP
    Village voices. A. Bryan.—BrS
    "When the tourists come to town". E. Greenfield.—GrU
    Why Rosalie did it. J. W. Miller.—JaM
    "You can always tell a tourist town". J. Carson.—CaS
Village voices. Ashley Bryan.—BrS
Vincent, Stephen
    Anthem.—KnAs
Vine leaves. Ashley Bryan.—BrS
Vinz, Mark
    Boys' night out.—JaPr
    Deserted farm.—JaP
    Spring thaw.—JaP
    What I remember about the 6th grade.—JaP
"Violet picks bluebells". Eve Merriam.—MeY
"Violets, daffodils". Elizabeth Coatsworth.—KeT
"Violetta is in the pantry". Unknown.—ScA
Violinists. See Fiddlers and fiddling
Viorst, Judith
    Goodbye, six, hello, seven.—LoFh
    Learning.—PrFo
    "Mother doesn't want a dog".—WhAa
    Night fun.—KeT
    Night scare.—BaH
    Since Hanna moved away.—LoFh
    Some things don't make any sense at all.—DeT
    Weird.—PrFo
    Wicked thoughts.—PrFo
The **vision** of Sir Launfal, sels. James Russell Lowell
    "And what is so rare as a day in June".—SuI
Visions. See also Dreams
    Crossing the park. H. Moss.—SuI
    Glass eye Harry Coote. P. B. Janeczko.—JaB
    "I never saw a moor". E. Dickinson.—SuI
    I watched an eagle soar. V. D. H. Sneve.—SnD
    "If we shadows have offended". From A midsummer night's dream. W. Shakespeare.—WhDd
    "To see a world in a grain of sand". From Auguries of innocence. W. Blake.—StP
A **visit** from St. Nicholas. Clement Clarke Moore.—ElW—HoS

W

Wake-up poems.—*Continued*
"There was a young pig who, in bed". A. Lobel.—LiLo
Time to rise. R. L. Stevenson.—DeT—PlW
"Wake up, Jacob". Unknown.—WiA
Waking. L. Moore.—MoS
Waking. Lilian Moore.—MoS
Waldrop, Keith
"My mouth is a horse's mouth", tr.—NyT
Wales
Saint David's Day. D. W. Price.—FoLe
St. David's Day ("The land returns from winter"). S. Cook.—FoLe
Welsh rabbit. Unknown.—OpT
"Walk good". See Goodbye now
"Walk together children". From Walk together children. Unknown.—SuC
Walk together children, sels. Unknown
"Walk together children".—SuC
"Walk with a bluebird in your heart". See Advice
Walker, Alice
In these dissenting times.—ElW
Walker, Kath
Corroboree ("Hot day dies, cook time comes").—FoLe
Walker, Margaret
For my people.—SuC
Lineage.—LiPg
Walker, Paul
Leaves.—BaW
Walker, Robbie
"I am young".—StP
Walker. Paul B. Janeczko.—JaB
"Walker was what everybody called him". See Walker
Walking
"Afoot and light-hearted I take to the open road". From Song of the open road. W. Whitman.—HoVo
Age four and my father. J. Cunningham.—LiPf
Alone in winter. J. P. Lewis.—LeT
"Anna Banana went out in the rain". J. Prelutsky.—PrBe
Around my room. W. J. Smith.—KeT—LiDd—SmL
As I did rove. W. De La Mare.—DeR
As Lucy went a-walking. W. De La Mare.—DeR
Cats ("Cats walk neatly"). R. Francis.—MoR
Christmas night. V. Worth.—WoA
City rain. V. Schonborg.—LaN
Close to home. F. Steele.—JaM
Coati-mundi. W. J. Smith.—SmL
Conversation. Buson.—DeS
Crabs. Seishi.—DeI
Daisies. V. Worth.—WoAl
Descent. E. Merriam.—MeCh
Evening walk. G. Soto.—SoA
Father and I in the meadow. D. McCord.—LiPf
Four generations. M. A. Hoberman.—HoFa
Galoshes. R. Bacmeister.—DeS
"Give me my scallop shell of quiet". Sir W. Raleigh.—StP
"Going home with her books through the snow". W. Tripp.—LiLo
"Hello, Bill". Unknown.—WiA
How to tell the wild animals. C. Wells.—CoAz
"I had a nickel and I walked around the block". Unknown.—WiA
"I kept on past". A. MacNeacail.—AgL
I meet sweet Sue for a walk on a cold and sunny afternoon. A. Adoff.—AdCh
I will hold your hand. A. Adoff.—AdCh

Ice-creepers. E. Merriam.—MeS
"In Central Park I saw Uncle Jack". Unknown.—WiA
Indian trail. B. Guernsey.—JaPr
It is late. A. Adoff.—AdIn
"Jack and Jill". Mother Goose.—EdGl—SuO—WaM
John's song. J. Aiken.—KeT
Just once. M. C. Livingston.—LiNe
Kick a little stone. D. Aldis.—KeT
Kicking up. J. Yolen.—YoBi
"Left, left". Unknown.—ScA
Master Rabbit. W. De La Mare.—DeR
Mr. Bickerstaff. Unknown.—OpT
Not I. W. De La Mare.—DeR—MaP
Old hound. V. Worth.—LiDp
On our way. E. Merriam.—DeS
"On the dewy trunk". Kyoshi.—CaR
On this winter after noon. A. Adoff.—AdCh
"One day a boy went walking". Unknown.—PrP—WiA
Oranges ("The first time I walked"). G. Soto.—JaM—SoA
Over the downs. W. De La Mare.—DeR
The path. W. De La Mare.—DeR
A path to the moon. B. P. Nichol.—BoT
Prayer ("Owl"). Unknown.—LiIf
"A rather polite man of Hawarden". Unknown.—LiLo
Sidewalks. V. Worth.—WoAl
"Step in a ditch". Unknown.—CoM—WiA
"Step in a hole". Unknown.—CoM
"Step on a crack". Unknown.—CoM—WiA
"Step on a line". Unknown.—CoM
Street song. M. C. Livingston.—MoS
The sun ("I told the sun that I was glad"). J. Drinkwater.—LiDd
The table and the chair. E. Lear.—LiDd
Tableau. K. Wilson.—JaPr
That kind of day. E. Greenfield.—GrU
"There was an old soldier of Bister". Unknown.—CII
"They strolled down the lane together". Unknown.—PrP
"Three young rats with black felt hats". Mother Goose.—PrP—SuO
Three young rats.—CII
To you. W. Whitman.—HoVo
Under the Sunday tree. E. Greenfield.—GrU
Unstooping. W. De La Mare.—DeR—MaP
Vern. G. Brooks.—LiDp
Visiting. Unknown.—OpT
"Walk together children". From Walk together children. Unknown.—SuC
Walking. A. Fisher.—FiA
Walking Big Bo. X. J. Kennedy.—KeK—LiDp
Walking-stick bird. W. J. Smith.—SmL
"When I walk through thy woods". M. Hakotun.—StP
Where we could go. G. Soto.—SoA
Winter walk in forest. G. Swede.—BoT
You are walking along eating. A. Adoff.—AdCh
Walking. Aileen Fisher.—FiA
Walking Big Bo. X. J. Kennedy.—KeK—LiDp
"The walking-stick bird". See Walking-stick bird
Walking-stick bird. William Jay Smith.—SmL
Walking with Jackie, sitting with a dog. Gary Soto.—JaPr
The wall. Tania Diaz Castro, tr. by Pablo Medina and Carolina Hospital.—NyT
"The wall is high". See The wall

Wallace, George
 Ode to a sneeze.—PrFo
Wallace, Robert
 Dog's song.—KeT
Wallace, Ronald
 Camp Calvary.—JaPr
 Constipation.—JaM
 A hot property.—JaP
Wallace, Susan J.
 Ilan' life.—LeCa
Wallace, William S.
 The song of Snohomish.—KnAs
Wallflower. Jane Yolen.—YoDd
Walls
 "Joshua fit the battle of Jericho, Jericho".
 Unknown.—StP
 Mending wall. R. Frost.—SuI
 The tickle rhyme. I. Serraillier.—MoS
 The wall. T. D. Castro.—NyT
Walnuts and walnut trees
 Daddy carries his empty basket on his head. A.
 Adoff.—AdIn
The **walrus.** Michael Flanders.—CaB—PrFo
The **walrus** and the carpenter. From Through the
 looking-glass. Lewis Carroll.—DeT—ElW—HoS
"The **walrus** lives on icy floes". See The walrus
Walruses
 The walrus. M. Flanders.—CaB—PrFo
 The walrus and the carpenter. From Through the
 looking-glass. L. Carroll.—DeT—ElW—HoS
Waltz, sels. Edith Sitwell
 "Daisy and Lily".—MoR
"**Waltzing** for leaves". From Riddle poems. James
 Berry.—BeW
Wamby or the nostalgic record book. Milton
 Bracker.—MoA
Wanderers. Walter De La Mare.—DeR—MaP
Wandering chorus. Eliezer Blum, tr. by Howard
 Schwartz.—GoT
Wandor, Michelene
 Heman.—AgL
Wang, Ping
 The mushroom river, tr.—NyT
"**Want** a penny". Unknown.—WiA
Wanted. Rose Fyleman.—LaM
"**Wanted,** a witch's cat". Shelagh McGee.—LaCc
Wanting to move. Vijaya Mukhopadhyay.—NyT
"**Wanton**". See A number of words
The **wapiti.** Ogden Nash.—KeT
War. See also Soldiers; also subdivisions under
 countries, as United States/History/Civil War
 Andy Battle's song. From The three royal
 monkeys. W. De La Mare.—DeR
 Around the campfire. A. Hudgins.—JaM
 "As the guns thunder". E. Merriam.—MeS
 The biggest questions. M. C. Livingston.—LiNe
 Captain Molly. W. Collins.—SuI
 Come up from the fields father. W. Whitman.—
 HoVo
 Dawn Weinberg. M. Glenn.—GlBc
 A dream of paradise in the shadow of war. M.
 Niazi.—NyT
 Enemies. C. Zolotow.—SaB
 "Father, may I go to war". Unknown.—WiA
 The game ("Plastic soldiers march on the floor").
 M. C. Livingston.—SaB
 The game ("Plastic soldiers on the floor").—
 LiNe
 "Gonna lay down my sword and shield".
 Unknown.—StP
 The huts at Esquimaux. N. Dubie.—JaM
 Illegitimate things. W. C. Williams.—MoR

Jerusalem. Y. Amichai.—NyT
Jim. J. Holden.—JaPr
Law of the great peace. Unknown.—SaB
Mine eyes have seen the glory. From Battle hymn
 of the republic. J. W. Howe.—SuC
O say. M. C. Livingston.—LiR
Remembrance Day ("To some"). J. Kitching.—
 FoLe
The song of soldiers. W. De La Mare.—DeR—
 MaP
Tending the garden. E. Pankey.—JaM
Wars. J. Little.—LiHe
"When howitzers began". H. Carruth.—MoR
When Johnny comes marching home again.
 Unknown.—LoFh
The white rose, Sophie Scholl, 1921-1943. E.
 Mumford.—JaM
"The winter they bombed Pearl Harbor". W.
 McDonald.—JaPr
A **war** baby looks back. Jonathan Holden.—JaPr
A **warbler.** Walter De La Mare.—DeR
Ward, David
 Hallowe'en ("It's a black plastic bin bag").—FoLe
 Remember.—FoLe
The **warlock's** cat. Jane Yolen.—YoBe
A **warning** ("I know a young girl who can speak").
 Mary A. Webber.—LiLo
A **warning** ("If you keep two angels in a cage").
 Adrian Mitchell.—AgL
Warnings
 Beware ("An ominous bird sang from its branch").
 W. De La Mare.—DeR
 A friendly warning. F. P. Heide.—HeG
 "I built my house, I built my walls". Unknown.—
 OpI
 "If any man should see this book". Unknown.—
 OpI
 The journey ("Heart-sick of his journey was the
 Wanderer"). W. De La Mare.—DeR
 "Ladybug, ladybug, fly away home". Mother
 Goose.—ScA—WiA
 "Ladybird, ladybird".—WaM
 To the ladybird ("Ladybird, ladybird").—OpI
 The magic house. J. Yolen.—LiHp—YoBe
 Mean song ("I'm warning you"). B. S. De
 Regniers.—DeW
 Milehigh Jeff the giant hare. N. Mellage.—SlM
 My brother Aaron runs outside to tell us there is
 a severe thunderstorm warning. A. Adoff.—
 AdIn
 Paul Revere's ride. H. W. Longfellow.—ElW—SuI
 The pedlar. W. De La Mare.—DeR
 "Rainbow at night, sailor's delight". Unknown.—
 WiA
 "See my pinky". Unknown.—ScA
 "See this finger". Unknown.—WiA
 "Skinny, skinny, run for your life". Unknown.—
 WiA
 Sorcery. W. De La Mare.—DeR
 "Tell tale tit". Unknown.—OpI
 The thief. D. Chandra.—LiIf
 "This book is one thing". Unknown.—OpI
 To the crow. Unknown.—OpI
 A warning ("If you keep two angels in a cage"). A.
 Mitchell.—AgL
 "Who folds a leaf down". Unknown.—OpI
Warren, Robert Penn
 Orphanage boy.—JaPr
 Swimming in the Pacific.—KnAs
Warren Christopher. Mel Glenn.—GlBc
Warrior nation trilogy, complete. Lance Henson
 "From the mountains we come".—SuI

"Great spirit".—SuI
"Oh ghost that follows me".—SuI
Wars. Jean Little.—LiHe
"Was invented by Sweet Irving Chaulkstein-Jones".
See The straw
"Was it there at all". See The bat in the bedroom
"Wash and wipe together". Unknown.—WiA
"Wash the dishes, wipe the dishes". Mother
Goose.—WaM
Washing. See Bathing; Laundry
Washington, D.C.
Potomac town in February. C. Sandburg.—LiDd
Washington, George (about)
Washington monument by night. C. Sandburg.—
SuI
Washington monument by night. Carl Sandburg.—
SuI
The **wasp.** William Sharp.—CaB
Wasps
"Big at each end and little in the middle".
Unknown.—WiA
The digger wasp. P. Fleischman.—FlJ
They had a point to make. J. Ciardi.—CiH
The wasp. W. Sharp.—CaB
A **wasted** journey. See "Hie to the market, Jenny
come trot"
The **watch** ("I wakened on my hot, hard bed").
Frances Cornford.—MoR
Watch ("The lamb baaed gently"). Juan Ramon
Jimenez, tr. by Eloise Roach.—LoFh
"Watch me juggle". See Arithmetrix
Watchdogs. Jim Thomas.—LiHp
Watches. See Clocks and watches
"Watching baseball". See Baseball canto
Watching football on TV, complete. Howard
Nemerov
"Each year brings rookies and makes veterans".—
KnAs
"It used to be only Sunday afternoons".—KnAs
"Passing and catching overcome the world".—
KnAs
"Priam on one side sending forth eleven".—KnAs
"To all this there are rules, the players must".—
KnAs
"Totemic scarabs, exoskeletal".—KnAs
"We watch all afternoon, we are enthralled".—
KnAs
"Watching from". See Angels
Watching gymnasts. Robert Francis.—MoR
"Watching the competition dancers at the Dakota
Wapici". See The ghost dance, August, 1976
Watching the Jets lose to Buffalo at Shea. May
Swenson.—KnAs
"Watching the moon". Izumi Shikibu, tr. by Jane
Hirschfield.—GoT
Water. See also Waterfalls; Wells; also names of
bodies of water, as Lakes
"All day I hear the noise of waters". J. Joyce.—
ElW
All wet. T. Johnston.—DeT
"Alla en la fuente". Unknown.—DeA
The fountain ("There in the fountain").—DeA
"Come morning". H. Yu.—GoT
Contingency. A. R. Ammons.—ElW
"Give me water". M. C. Livingston.—LiMh
Hose. V. Worth.—DeT—WoAl
"I washed my hands in water". Unknown.—WiA
Ice. W. De La Mare.—DeR
Jill, afterwards. P. Dacey.—JaM
Jump. J. Carson.—JaPr
The lifeguard. J. Dickey.—KnAs
Ode to the sprinkler. G. Soto.—SoNe

Old deep sing song. C. Sandburg.—MoR
Onomatopoeia. E. Merriam.—MoR
Open hydrant. M. Ridlon.—DeT
Pitcher. R. Ferrer de Arrellaga.—NyT
Rainbow making, magic. From Four poems for
Roy G Biv. B. J. Esbensen.—EsW
Wet. L. Moore.—MoR
Water boatmen. Paul Fleischman.—FlJ
Water buffalo. William Jay Smith.—SmL
"Water from the sprinkler". See Contingency
The **water** midden's song. From The three royal
monkeys. Walter De La Mare.—DeR
The **water-ousel.** Mary Webb.—ElW
"Water rushes up". See Open hydrant
"Water still flows". See Illegitimate things
Water striders. Paul Fleischman.—FlJ
The **waterbeetle.** Hilaire Belloc.—CaB
"The waterbeetle here shall teach". See The
waterbeetle
Waterfalls
"From its sources which well". From The cataract
of Lodore. R. Southey.—MoR
Mountain brook. E. Coatsworth.—FrS
Niagara, Canadian Horseshoe Falls. M. C.
Livingston.—LiNe
Under the waterfall. T. Hardy.—ElW
Watering trough. Maxine Kumin.—JaP
Watermelons
"Just plant a watermelon on my grave".
Unknown.—ScA
"Waters are loose, from Judith and the Larb". See
Schoolcrafts's diary, written on the Missouri,
1830
"The water's deep". Colin McNaughton.—PrFo
Watson, Clyde
"Dilly dilly piccalilli".—LiDd
"Oh my goodness, oh my dear".—LiDd
"Uptown, downtown".—LiDd
Watts, Isaac
Against idleness and mischief.—ElW
"Hush, my dear, lie still and slumber".—StP
The sluggard.—ElW
"Wave on wave". See Sea cliff
"Wave your hand, wave your hand". See "Kai
veesamma kai veesu"
Waves
"Gray and blue". M. C. Livingston.—LiMh
The hungry waves. D. Aldis.—DeT
The main deep. J. Stephens.—MoR
Sea wave. S. Liatsos.—HoS
"The waves are erasing the footprints". See At the
beach
"The waves washed in a mountain of shells". See
Remembering
"The way". See Jacks
"The way a crow". See Dust of snow
Way down south. See "Way down south where
bananas grow"
"Way down South in Grandma's lot". Unknown.—
WiA
"Way down south where bananas grow".
Unknown.—PrP—WiA
Way down south.—CII
"Way down South where I was born". See A long
time ago
"Way down yonder on the Piankatank".
Unknown.—WiA
"The way hands move around a clock". See Lines
for remembering about lids
"The way I must enter". Izumi Shikibu, tr. by Jane
Hirschfield.—GoT

Wealth.—*Continued*
"I should worry, I should care". Unknown.—WiA
    "Me no worry, me no care".—CoM
"If I'd as much money as I could spend". Mother Goose.—WaM
Kyle Quinn. M. Glenn.—GlBc
Louleen's feelings. X. J. Kennedy.—KeK
Mine. L. Moore.—MoS
My legacy. W. Whitman.—HoVo
"The rich and the poor do not meet". From Jamaican Caribbean proverbs. Unknown.—BeW
Sand dollar. B. J. Esbensen.—EsW
Tartary. W. De La Mare.—DeR
Then from a ruin. F.-U. Attar.—LiIf
"There is no frigate like a book". E. Dickinson.—DeT—ElW
The thief at Robin's castle. W. De La Mare.—DeR—MaP
Valuables. X. J. Kennedy.—KeK
"When land is gone and money spent". Mother Goose.—WaM
"Wear it". See Color
"Wear red suspenders, to get to the". See Why did the fireman
"Wearing my yellow straw hat". See My yellow straw hat
"Weary breeze through my window screen". See Windy work
"Weary of glare". See Tree lot
"Weary went the old witch". See The witch
Weasel. Buson, tr. by Tze-si Huang.—DeI
Weasels
"In art class I gasped at the easel". X. J. Kennedy.—KeGh
Weasel. Buson.—DeI
Weather. See also Clouds; Dew; Fog; Rain; Rainbows; Seasons; Snow; Storms; Wind
Granny's ninety-two-year-old legs. A. Adoff.—AdIn
Hail. S. Barry.—MoA
"If a rooster crows when he goes to bed". Unknown.—WhAa—WiA
"My learned friend and neighbor pig". Mother Goose.—WaM
"Often we are foolish". Unknown.—ScA
"Rain before seven". Unknown.—WiA
"Rainbow at night, sailor's delight". Unknown.—WiA
"Red sky at night". Mother Goose.—WaM
Saint Swithin's Day. A. Bonner.—FoLe
"Snow in the east". E. Merriam.—MeY—MoS
So long as there's weather. T. Kitt.—DeS
A song for England. A. Salkey.—AgL
"A sunshiny shower". Unknown.—WiA
That kind of day. E. Greenfield.—GrU
To the seagull. Unknown.—OpI
Tree at my window. R. Frost.—ElW
Understanding. M. C. Livingston.—LiDd
Weather ("Dot a dot dot, dot a dot dot"). E. Merriam.—DeS—KeT
Weather ("Weather is full"). A. Fisher.—FiA
Weather ("Whether the weather be fine"). Unknown.—SuI
"When a peacock loudly calls". Unknown.—WhAa
Weather ("Dot a dot dot, dot a dot dot"). Eve Merriam.—DeS—KeT
Weather ("It is a windy day"). Marchette Chute.—DeS
Weather ("Weather is full"). Aileen Fisher.—FiA

Weather ("Whether the weather be fine"). Unknown.—SuI
"Weather is full". See Weather
Weavers and weaving
"I see a star". A. Lopez.—LiPm
"O our mother the earth, O our father the sky". Unknown.—StP
What the gray cat sings. A. Guiterman.—LaCc
Webb, Charles Harper
Every chance we got.—JaPr
Of necessity, Weeb jokes about his height.—JaPr
Swinging the river.—JaPr
The time we cherry-bombed the toilet at the River Oaks.—JaPr
Webb, Mary
The water-ousel.—ElW
Webb, Thomas H. B.
"Give me a good digestion, Lord".—StP
Webber, Mary A.
A warning ("I know a young girl who can speak").—LiLo
Webster, Clive Herbert
Scraping the world away.—AgL
"Wed flowers bloob". See Llude sig kachoo
Wedding bears. J. Patrick Lewis.—LeT
Wedding day. Eloise Greenfield.—GrU
Weddings
"Bless you, bless you, burnie-bee". Mother Goose.—WaM
    The messenger.—OpT
A cat came fiddling. Mother Goose.—ClI
"Fiddle-de-dee, fiddle-de-dee". Mother Goose.—WaM
"Here comes the bride". Unknown.—ScA—WiA
Ode to weddings. G. Soto.—SoNe
"Oh, rare Harry Parry". Mother Goose.—WaM
"Pussicat, wussicat, with a white foot". Mother Goose.—WaM
Wedding bears. J. P. Lewis.—LeT
Wedding day. E. Greenfield.—GrU
Wee Willie Winkie. See "Wee Willie Winkie runs through the town"
"Wee Willie Winkie runs through the town". Mother Goose.—EdGl—SuO—WaM
Wee Willie Winkie.—HoS
Weeden, Craig
Right where he left off.—KnAs
Weeds. See also names of weeds, as Dandelions
Weeds. V. Worth.—WoAl
Weeds. Valerie Worth.—WoAl
A **week** to Christmas. John Cotton.—FoLe
Weems Ghastly's goodies. X. J. Kennedy.—KeGh
"Weep no more, nor grieve, nor sigh". See The playmate
Weights, in memory of my mother, Miriam Murray nee Arnall. Les Murray.—NyT
Weigl, Bruce
Killing chickens.—JaPr
Weinberger, Eliot
"At the horislope of the mountizon", tr.—NyT
"In his room the man watches", tr.—NyT
A tree within, tr.—NyT
Weird. Judith Viorst.—PrFo
Welch, Don
The chicken poem.—JaM
Welcome, Florence. Judith Steinbergh.—LiPg
Welcome here. Unknown.—GoA
"Welcome here, welcome here". See Welcome here
A **welcome** song for Laini Nzinga. Gwendolyn Brooks.—SlM
"Well". See Reading, spring
"Well I don't care, Denise". See The love nest

"A **well** known knavish knight with knobby knees".
See Unfinished knews item
"**We'll** play in the snow". See Snow
"**Well**, son, I'll tell you". See Mother to son
"**Well**, you can't say". See Sweet sixteen
Wells, Carolyn
How to tell the wild animals.—CoAz
Wells, Irene
"Dear God".—StP
"What are you, God".—StP
"When bad things happen to me, God".—StP
Wells
"As I went to the well-head". W. De La Mare.—
DeR
Cleaning the well. F. Chappell.—JaPr
"Ding dong bell". Mother Goose.—SuO—WaM
"Doctor Bell fell down the well". Unknown.—PrP
The grasshopper ("Down a deep well a
grasshopper fell"). D. McCord.—LiDd
Plans gone wrong. M. Mahy.—MaN
To a forgetful wishing well. X. J. Kennedy.—DeT
W is for well. W. J. Smith.—SmL
Welsh rabbit. Unknown.—OpT
"**Went** over to Heather's". See Others
"**Went** to the corner". See Things
"**We're** all dry with drinking on't". Mother Goose.—
WaM
"**We're** all jolly boys". Mother Goose.—WaM
"**We're** forty performing bananas". See Forty
performing bananas
"**We're** racing, racing down the walk". Phyllis
McGinley.—DeT
"**We're** related, you and I". See Brothers
"**We're** sending you this saucy card". See Wish you
were here
"**Were** those fine horses once white mice". See The
pantomime
"**We're** whirligig beetles". See Whirligig beetles
Were you ever fat like me. Kalli Dakos.—DaI
Wesley, Charles
"Hark, the herald angels sing".—YoHa
Wesley-Smith, Peter
The dodo ("The mournful dodo lay in bed").—
PrFo
The ombley-gombley.—PrFo
West, Colin
Adolphus.—PrFo
"Crocodile or alligator".—CoAz
Inquisitiveness.—AgL
Norman Norton's nostrils.—PrFo
The ogglewop.—PrFo
Samantha.—PrFo
Tiny Tony and his pony.—PrFo
The wherefore and the why.—AgL
"**West** is the springtime". See Points of the compass
West wind. Judith Nicholls.—LaN
Western wagons. Stephen Vincent Benet and
Rosemary Carr Benet.—SuI
Western wind. Unknown.—ElW
"**Westron** wind, when will thou blow". See Western
wind
Wet. Lilian Moore.—MoR
"**Wet** wet wet". See Wet
"**We've** a great big knocker". See Granny
"**We've** laughed until my cheeks are tight". See
Bursting
"**We've** ploughed our land". Mother Goose.—WaM
Wha me Mudder do. Grace Nichols.—NiCo
"**Wha** mek yu go Granny Yard". See Me go a
Granny Yard
"**Whai-o**, man, go-on o". See Diggin sing

The **whale** ("There was a most monstrous whale").
Theodore Roethke.—CoAz
The **whale** ("What could hold me"). Carmen Bernos
De Gasztold.—StP
Whale ("When I swam underwater I saw a blue
whale"). William Jay Smith.—SmL
Whalers. See Whales
Whales
"And God created great whales, and every living
creature that moveth". From Book of Genesis.
Bible/Old Testament.—WhAa
Blue whale knowledge. Z. Quobble.—AgL
Bluest whale. J. P. Lewis.—LeA
"Did you ever ever ever". Unknown.—WiA
Leviathan. From Book of Job. Bible/Old
Testament.—WhDd
Narwhal. X. J. Kennedy.—WhAa
The whale ("There was a most monstrous
whale"). T. Roethke.—CoAz
The whale ("What could hold me"). C. B. De
Gasztold.—StP
Whale ("When I swam underwater I saw a blue
whale"). W. J. Smith.—SmL
"**What** a moonstruck". Barbara Juster Esbensen.—
LiIf
What a wonderful bird. Unknown.—CII
"**What** a wonderful bird the frog are". See What a
wonderful bird
What all the owls know. John Hollander.—LiIf
What am I after all. Walt Whitman.—HoVo
"**What** am I after all but a child, pleas'd with the
sound of". See What am I after all
"**What** are all those rocks sticking up for, he says".
See You better be ready
What are heavy. Christina Georgina Rossetti.—ElW
"**What** are heavy, sea-sand and sorrow". See What
are heavy
"**What** are you, God". Irene Wells.—StP
"**What** can I give him". Christina Georgina
Rossetti.—StP
"**What** can we buy". See Sand dollar
"**What** can you do when you're six five". See Lanky
Hank Farrow
"**What** child is this". Unknown.—StP
What color is black. Barbara Mahone.—SlM
"**What** could hold me". See The whale
"**What** did the blackbird say to the crow".
Unknown.—ScA
"**What** difference did it make to Longfellow".
William Jay Smith.—SmL
"**What** do bunyips look like, asked the bunyip". See
Bunyip
"**What** do caterpillars do". See Caterpillars
"**What** do parents know anyhow". See Zip on "good
advice"
"**What** do people think about". See Aunt Roberta
"**What** do we do with a difference". See What do we
do with a variation
What do we do with a variation. James Berry.—
BeW
"**What** do you have for breakfast". See A little bird
"**What** do you minus". See Maths
"**What** do you seek so pensive and silent". From
Starting from Paumanok. Walt Whitman.—
HoVo
"**What** follows king walking, yet stays". From
Riddle poems. James Berry.—BeW
"**What** fun to be". Michael Flanders.—WhAa
"**What** fun to go riding like Santa". See Santa rides
What grandpa mouse said. Vachel Lindsay.—LiIf
What happens. Erich Fried.—AgL
"**What** happens to a dream deferred". See Harlem

"What happens to the colors". Jack Prelutsky.—PlW
"What has". Unknown.—WiA
What I like. Margaret Mahy.—MaN
"What I like for dinner when I'm on my own". See What I like
"What I remember about that day". See The 1st
What I remember about the 6th grade. Mark Vinz.—JaP
"What I remember most". See Winner
What I used to wonder. X. J. Kennedy.—KeK
"What if". Isabel Joshlin Glaser.—HoGo
"What if". Beatrice Schenk De Regniers.—DeW
"What in the world". Eve Merriam.—DeS
"What is a butterfly, at best". See Butterfly
"What is a family". Mary Ann Hoberman.—HoFa
"What is a llano". See Aa couple of doublles
What is Africa to me. From Heritage. Countee Cullen.—SuC
"What is it that upsets the volcanoes". Pablo Neruda, tr. by William O'Daly.—NyT
"What is it you always see". Unknown.—ScA
What is pink. Christina Georgina Rossetti.—DeS—ElW
"What is pink, a rose is pink". See What is pink
"What is poetry, who knows". See Poetry
"What is that bobbing". See Mr. and Mrs. Turtle
"What is the boy now, who has lost his ball". See The ball poem
"What is the difference". Unknown.—ScA
"What is the opposite of two". See The opposite of two
What is this here. Unknown.—WiA
"What is true for me and you". See Say nay
"What is vessel of gold sent off". From Riddle poems. James Berry.—BeW
What Johnny told me. John Ciardi.—KeT
"What kind of creature will you be". See Will you
"What kind of walk shall we take today". See On our way
"What luck, for lunch there's cream of leek". See Leek soup
"What price Goodens". See The baseball card dealer
What Saundra said about being short. Jim Hall.—JaM
"What shall I call". See The christening
What shall I pack in the box marked summer. Bobbi Katz.—LoFh
"What shall I tell about my life". See My life story
"What shall I wear for the Easter parade". See The Easter parade
"What shape is this in cowl of snow". See The snow-man
"What sight is this, on dazzling snow". See The ghost chase
What teacher said. J. Patrick Lewis.—LeT
What the diamond does is hold it all in. Jim LaVilla-Havelin.—MoA
What the engines said (the joining of the Union Pacific and Central Pacific Railroads, May 10, 1869). Bret Harte.—SuI
What the gray cat sings. Arthur Guiterman.—LaCc
What the little girl did. Roger McGough.—AgL
What the little girl said. Vachel Lindsay.—DeT
"The moon's the north wind's cooky".—LiDd
What they said. Unknown, tr. by Rose Fyleman.—DeS
"What throws you out is what drags you in". See Overboard
What Tomas said in a pub. James Stephens.—ElW
"What voice is that I hear". See Sorcery
"What was it like". See Interview with a winner

"What was it the engines said". See What the engines said (the joining of the Union Pacific and Central Pacific Railroads, May 10, 1869)
What we might be, what we are. X. J. Kennedy.—JaP—KeGh
What we said sitting making fantasies, complete. James Berry
"At last I have my anger breathalyser".—BeW
"I have a three-legged donkey".—BeW
"I want a talking dog wearing a cap".—BeW
"I'd like a great satellite-looking dish".—BeW
"I'd like a white bull with one horn only".—BeW
"I'd like to have a purple pigeon".—BeW
"I'd like to see cats with stubby wings".—BeW
"My first solo trial flight, you see".—BeW
"What were we doing up there". See Greenland's history, or the history of the Danes on Greenland
"What were we playing, was it prisoner's base". See Running
"What, what". Unknown.—OpI
"What words". See The new house
"What would I do forever in a big place, who". See An old Jamaican woman thinks about the hereafter
What you don't know about food. Florence Parry Heide.—HeG
"What you give me I cheerfully accept". See To rich givers
Whatnot. Eve Merriam.—MeS
"What's a howdah, a silk curtained shack". See How to live in a howdah
"What's hearty as a heart, round as a ring". From Riddle poems. James Berry.—BeW
"What's in the church". Unknown.—WiA
"What's the good of breathing". See The frost pane
"What's the hurry, the ship's not sailing till". See The ship's whistle
"What's the matter". See Dickery Dean
"What's your name". Unknown.—OpI
Wheat
The sheaves. E. A. Robinson.—SuI
Wheatley, Phillis
On being brought from Africa to America.—SuC
"Should you, my lord, while you pursue my song". See To the right honorable William, Earl of Dartmouth
To the right honorable William, Earl of Dartmouth, sels.
"Should you, my lord, while you pursue my song".—SuI
Wheels. Jim Daniels.—JaPr
"The wheels on the bus". Unknown.—CoE
When ("Once there was a little boy"). Unknown.—OpT
"When". See True
When ("When fire's freezing cold"). Eve Merriam.—MeS
When ("When tigers don't roar"). Yansan Agard.—AgL
"When a big tree falls". Unknown.—ScA
"When a cub, unaware being bare". See Beware
"When a jolly young fisher named Fisher". Unknown.—LiLo—PrP
"When a mermaid winks". See Rain coming
"When a peacock loudly calls". Unknown.—WhAa
"When a very little boy". See The genius
"When an archer is shooting for nothing". See The need to win
"When Andrew started coughing". See Don't you remember how sick you are
When angels came to Zimmer. Paul Zimmer.—JaM

"When I'd be at play in the smoky-breath cold". See Hot milk

"When I'm by myself". See By myself

"When I'm home, parsnips make me gag". See Parsnips

"When in our London gardens". See The London owl

"When it comes right down to it". See Regina Kelsey

"When it is snowing". Siv Cedering.—JaP

"When it spreads its wings and doffs its hat". See Cat whiskered Catbird

When it's snowing. Aileen Fisher.—FiH

When it's Thanksgiving. Aileen Fisher.—FiA

"When Joan had a birthday". From Birthday secrets. Myra Cohn Livingston.—LiBp

When Johnny comes marching home again. Unknown.—LoFh

"When Johnny comes marching home again, hurrah, hurrah". See When Johnny comes marching home again

"When kudzu seed the sower sows". See Kudzu

"When lakes grow too limber". See March thaw

"When land is gone and money spent". Mother Goose.—WaM

"When lilacs last in the dooryard bloom'd". Walt Whitman.—HoVo

"When Mare and Griffin meet and mate". See The hippogriff

When Mom plays just for me. April Halprin Wayland.—LiPm

"When monster mothers get together". See Monster mothers

"When morning comes". See Sparrow dreaming

When mother reads aloud. Unknown.—SuI

"When mother reads aloud, the past". See When mother reads aloud

"When music sounds, gone is the earth I know". See Music

"When my big brothers have a fight". See My big brothers

"When my brother". See Frankie Dempster

"When my brother hogs". See Blanket hog

"When my dad". See My dad

"When my daddy comes in from work". See My daddy is a cool dude

"When my dog had a birthday". From Birthday secrets. Myra Cohn Livingston.—LiBp

"When my friend Lessie runs she runs so fast". See Lessie

"When my friends all moved away". Steven Kroll.—JaP

"When my little dog is happy". See The tale of a dog

"When my mother fell from the cherry tree". See My mother and the touched old woman

"When my older sister Marilyn came for a visit". See Smart remark

"When my reading teacher". See Dancing on a rainbow

"When my silly little sister". See The little sister store

"When night is dark". See At night

"When night is o'er the wood". See The white owl

"When night means". See Before the end of this falling day

"When no one else". See Something strange

"When old Rocky Nelson shuffles up to the plate". See The ballad of old Rocky Nelson

"When on this page you look". Unknown.—WiA

"When once I walked out for a breath of fresh air". See Ballad of black and white

"When one of us hit". See The antelope

"When our old baby sitter quit". See Miss McGillicuddy

"When people call this beast to mind". See The elephant

"When people talk at me about God, I usually listen". See About God

"When Peter Lumpkin was a youth". See News story

"When Peter turned seven". See The hayride

"When Queen Djenira slumbers through". See Queen Djenira

"When rain stays, gray and unabating". See A different door

"When relatives come to visit us". See Relatives

"When safe into the fields Ann got". See Part VII: When safe in to the fields Ann got

"When Sallie with her pitcher goes". See Sallie

"When Sam goes back in memory". See Sam

"When she snoozes". See Lullaby for Suzanne

"When she was in her garden". See Part VIII: When she was in her garden

"When sheep can't sleep". See Sheep

"When sickly Jim Wilson's first wife died". See The courtship

"When skies are low and days are dark". N. M. Bodecker.—FrS

"When slim Sophia mounts her horse". See Reverie

"When someone I love is hurt". Jean Little.—LiHe

"When Spanky goes". See Basketball

"When spied on in a zoo, giraffe". See A giraffe's laughs last

"When spring comes round, our apple tree". See Our tree

"When stars get loosened". See Shooting stars

"When summer starts to fall". See Autumnal equinox

"When sun goes home". See Taking turns

"When the air is wine and the wind is free". See Song of the queen bee

"When the allosaurus". Jane Yolen.—YoDd

"When the banshees wail". See Forbidden sounds

"When the clouds". Mother Goose.—WaM

"When the dogstar is aglow". See Garden calendar

"When the donkey saw the zebra". Unknown.—WiA

"When the elders said she was too old". See Reverend Mona

"When the flowers". See Toad

"When the ground has softened and the sun is strong". See After the last hard freeze in early spring weather

"When the hackle bird". See Hackle bird

"When the high". See Crows

"When the high road". See The journey

"When the King and the Queen came to Stratford". See The royal visit

"When the last colours of the day". See The ruin

"When the last giant came out of his cave". See Magic story for falling asleep

"When the last of gloaming's gone". See The shadow

"When the leaves began to brown". See Mister October, Reggie Jackson

"When the light of day declineth". See The lamplighter

"When the lights went low". See Dinosaur dances

"When the neat white". See Duck

"When the pale moon hides and the wild wind wails". See The wolf

"When the Pilgrims". See The first Thanksgiving

"When the Robinsons gather". See Fambly time

"When the seller comes around". See The seller
"When the shoe strings break". See The blues
"When the tourists come to town". Eloise Greenfield.—GrU
"When the wind blows". See Wind song
"When they built the ship Titanic". See The Titanic
"When they pass the pink ice cream". Unknown.—WiA
"When they said the time to hide was mine". See The rabbit
"When they tried to take down the big trees in the park". See I was there
"When thou art as little as I am, Mother". See Full circle
"When tigers don't roar". See When
"When Tony was found dead in his". See Never be as fast as I have been, the jockey Tony DeSpirito dead at thirty-nine
"When Tonya's friends come to spend the night". Eloise Greenfield.—GrN
"When Too Tall Jim bends down to drink". See At the waterhole
"When Uncle Jim came back from World War II". See Jim
"When walking in a tiny rain". See Vern
"When we fired our rifles". See Target practice
"When we lived in a city". See Until we built a cabin
"When we two parted". Lord Byron.—ElW
"When we walk back from our healthy walk tonight". See It is late
"When we walk by". See Old hound
"When we were sixteen, summer nights in the suburbs sizzled". See Rites of passage
"When winter's o'er, the bear once more". See Who really
"When words grow jellylike". See Between ebb and flow
"When you are courting". Unknown.—WiA
When you are there at all, that is. John Ciardi.—CiH
"When you are walking by yourself". See Kick a little stone
"When you arrive in our town". See Salt and memory, a tribute to Marc Chagall
"When you get married and live on a hill". Unknown.—WiA
"When you get married and your husband gets cross". Unknown.—WiA
"When you get married and your wife has twins". Unknown.—WiA
"When you get old". Unknown.—WiA
"When you go away and I can't". See Distances of longing
"When you hear these words". See A friendly warning
"When you put me up on the elephant's back". See Elephant
"When you see a monkey up a tree". Unknown.—WiA
"When you see your neighbour's beard on fire, take some water and wet your own". From Jamaican Caribbean proverbs. Unknown.—BeW
"When you stand on the tip of your nose". N. M. Bodecker.—PrFo
"When you stand upon the stump". Unknown.—WiA
"When you talk to a monkey". Rowena Bennett.—DeS
"When you walk". See City rain
"When you walk that lonesome valley". Unknown.—StP

"When you want to go wherever you please". See The land of ho-ho-hum
"When you were a girl". See Woman
"When your boyfriend writes you a letter". See Song
"When you're hot, you're hot". See Hitting
"When you've had yourself accoutered". See Preparedness
"Whence come this rush of wings afar". See Carol of the birds
Whenever. Mary Ann Hoberman.—MoS
"Whenever a teacher announces a test". See Patricia Lampert
"Whenever he". See The man in red
"Whenever I". See Italian noodles
"Whenever I plunge my arm, like this". See Under the waterfall
"Whenever I stretch". See Obnoxious Nelly
"Whenever I want my room to move". See Whenever
"Whenever lightning strikes at night". See Bed mate
"Whenever the moon and stars are set". See Windy nights
"Whenever we're asked". See Water striders
Where ("Houses, houses, oh, I know"). Walter De La Mare.—DeR
Where ("Monkeys in a forest"). Walter De La Mare.—DeR
"Where are you going, child, so far away". See Going into dream
"Where can he be going". See Traveler
"Where can I go then from your spirit". From The book of psalms. Bible/Old Testament.—StP
"Where can the rabbits play". See Rabbits
Where do these words come from. Charlotte Pomerantz.—DeS
Where go the boats. Robert Louis Stevenson.—ElW—KeT
"Where have you gone". Mari Evans.—SuC
"Where is a poem". Eve Merriam.—MeS
"Where is beauty". See The song of the secret
"Where is the heart I am calling". Roberto Juarroz, tr. by William Stanley Merwin.—NyT
"Where is Thumbkin". Unknown.—CoE
"Where long the shadows of the wind had rolled". See The sheaves
Where mountain lion lay down with deer. Leslie Marmon Silko.—SuI
"Where mourning dove mother built her nest". See June, mourning doves
"Where my grandmother lived". See #4
"Where on the wrinkled stream the willows lean". See The water-ousel
"Where the barn stood". See Deserted farm
"Where the bluebells and the wind are". See Bluebells
"Where the dusty lane". See Daisies
"Where the open field is longest back to". See On Limestone Street
"Where the pools are bright and deep". See A boy's song
"Where the ripe pears droop heavily". See The wasp
"Where the sun shone white hot, Cass". X. J. Kennedy.—KeFb
"Where, there, scarlet needle-dart". See Ruby-throated hummingbird
"Where was Moses when the light went out, behind the door". Unknown.—WiA
"Where was Moses when the light went out, down in the cellar". Unknown.—WiA
"Where was Moses when the light went out, in the dark". Unknown.—WiA

"Where was Moses when the light went out, under the bed". Unknown.—WiA

Where we could go. Gary Soto.—SoA

"Where will we get married". Unknown.—WiA

Where would you be. Karla Kuskin.—LaN

"Where would you be on a night like this". See Where would you be

The **wherefore** and the why. Colin West.—AgL

"Where's the Queen of Sheba". See Gone

"Wherever I go, it also goes". See My body

"Whether it's cold". See So long as there's weather

"Whether the weather be fine". See Weather

"Which is more fleeting". See Time piece

"Which is the bow that has no arrow". See Riddling song

"Which the chicken has laid". See E is for egg

"Which to prefer". See Shoes

"While filling cones, Disgustus Goop". See Special flavor

"While I'd be at play in the smoky-breath cold". See Grandmother in winter

"While the school's star athletes". See High school

"While, unwatched, the soup pot boils". X. J. Kennedy.—KeFb

"While we". See Stars

While you were chasing a hat. Lilian Moore.—BaW

"The **whine** of our space-trolley along the wire". See Taking down the space-trolley

Whipple, Laura
  Basilisk/cockatrice.—WhDd

Whippoorwill. Patricia Hubbell.—LaN

"Whippoorwill this". Edward Estlin Cummings.—MoR

Whippoorwills
  A dream of paradise in the shadow of war. M. Niazi.—NyT
  Whippoorwill. P. Hubbell.—LaN
  "Whippoorwill this". E. E. Cummings.—MoR

Whirligig beetles. Paul Fleischman.—FlJ

A **whirring.** Daisy Aldan.—MoR

"A **whirring,** as of far-off music, not the stir". See A whirring

"Whirring as wound wires whir". See Humming bird

Whiskers meets Polly. Michael Stillman.—KeT

Whiskey
  "About them whiskey boys". J. Carson.—CaS
  My papa's waltz. T. Roethke.—ElW

"The **whiskey** on your breath". See My papa's waltz

"Whistle or wassail about the town". See Roistering

"The **whistler** on the whistle". See The little shop (for a picture)

Whistler's father. X. J. Kennedy.—KeGh

"Whistler's mother, she's world famous". See Whistler's father

Whistling
  "I bought a wooden whistle". Unknown.—WiA
  "One day a boy went walking". Unknown.—PrP—WiA
  "Whistling girls and crowing hens". Unknown.—WiA

"Whistling girls and crowing hens". Unknown.—WiA

White, Elwyn Brooks
  Song of the queen bee.—ElW
  The tennis.—KnAs

White (color)
  "A lady who lives there close to me". J. Carson.—CaS
  Silver. W. De La Mare.—DeR—LaN—MaP
  White ("Once a miller, and he would say"). W. De La Mare.—DeR

White on white. C. E. Hemp.—JaP

White ("1964 and I'm parked"). Christopher Buckley.—JaM

White ("Once a miller, and he would say"). Walter De La Mare.—DeR

"White bird featherless". Unknown.—OpT

The **white** birds. William Butler Yeats.—GoU

White bracelets. Colleen Thibaudeau.—NyT

White buffalo woman. John Bierhorst.—WhDd

The **white** city. Claude McKay.—SuC

"A white heron on the snow". See Ravens

"The white moonglow". See VI

White on white. Christine E. Hemp.—JaP

The **white** owl. F. J. Patmore.—LiIf

"White Rose is a quiet horse". See The four horses

The **white** rose, Sophie Scholl, 1921-1943. Erika Mumford.—JaM

"White sheep, white sheep". See Clouds

"White sun". See Zebra

"The white swan, swimming". See The swan

The **white** troops had their orders but the negroes looked like men, sels. Gwendolyn Brooks
  "They had supposed their formula was fixed".—SuC

The **white** wind. J. Patrick Lewis.—LeE

Whitfield, James M.
  "All hail, thou truly noble chief". See To Cinque
  To Cinque, sels.
    "All hail, thou truly noble chief".—SuC

Whitman, Ruth
  Beginning a new year means.—LoFh
  I hear my mother's.—LiPm

Whitman, Walt
  "Afoot and light-hearted I take to the open road". See Song of the open road
  After the dazzle of day.—HoVo
  "All this time and at all times wait the words of true poems". See Song of myself
  Beautiful women.—HoVo
  Cavalry crossing a ford.—ElW
  "A child said, what is the grass, fetching it".—StP
  A clear midnight.—HoVo
  Come up from the fields father.—HoVo
  Excelsior.—HoVo
  "A gigantic beauty of a stallion, fresh and responsive to my caresses". See Song of myself
  Gliding o'er all.—HoVo
  "Good-bye my fancy".—HoVo
  Great are the myths, sels.
    "Great is today, and beautiful".—HoVo
  "Great is today, and beautiful". See Great are the myths
  "Hast never come to thee an hour".—HoVo
  "I am of old and young, of the foolish as much as the wise". See Song of myself
  "I am the poet of the body and I am the poet of the soul". See Song of myself
  "I celebrate myself, and sing myself". See Song of myself
  I dream'd in a dream.—HoVo
  "I have heard what the talkers were talking, the talk of the". See Song of myself
  I hear America singing.—HoVo
  "I say whatever tastes sweet to the most perfect person, that". See Says
  "I see something of God each hour of the twenty four".—StP
  "I think I could turn and live with animals, they are so placid". See Song of myself
  "A leaf for hand in hand".—HoVo
  Locations and times.—HoVo
  Mannahatta.—HoVo

Whitman, Walt—*Continued*
Memories.—HoVo
Mother and babe.—HoVo
My legacy.—HoVo
My 71st year.—HoVo
"No labor-saving machine".—HoVo
Now lift me close.—HoVo
"O tan-faced prairie-boy".—HoVo
On journeys through the states.—HoVo
"One thought ever at the fore".—HoVo
"Out of the cradle endlessly rocking".—HoVo
Poets to come.—HoVo
Queries to my seventieth year.—HoVo
"The runaway slave came to my house and stopt
     outside". See Song of myself
The runner.—KnAs
Says, sels.
     "I say whatever tastes sweet to the most
          perfect person, that".—HoVo
"See, steamers steaming through my poems". See
     Starting from Paumanok
Shut not your doors.—HoVo
Song of myself, sels.
     "All this time and at all times wait the words
          of true poems".—HoVo
     "A gigantic beauty of a stallion, fresh and
          responsive to my caresses".—SuI
     Stallion.—KnAs
     "I am of old and young, of the foolish as
          much as the wise".—SuI
     "I am the poet of the body and I am the poet
          of the soul".—HoVo
     "I celebrate myself, and sing myself".—HoVo
     "I have heard what the talkers were talking,
          the talk of the".—HoVo
     "I think I could turn and live with animals,
          they are so placid".—HoVo
     "The runaway slave came to my house and
          stopt outside".—HoVo
     "You sea, I resign myself to you also, I guess
          what you".—HoVo
Song of the open road, sels.
     "Afoot and light-hearted I take to the open
          road".—HoVo
Stallion. See Song of myself—"A gigantic beauty
     of a stallion, fresh and responsive to my
     caresses"
"Starting from fish-shape Paumanok where I was
     born". See Starting from Paumanok
Starting from Paumanok, sels.
     "See, steamers steaming through my
          poems".—HoVo
     "Starting from fish-shape Paumanok where I
          was born".—HoVo
     "Victory, union, faith, identity, time".—
          HoVo
     "What do you seek so pensive and silent".—
          HoVo
Stronger lessons.—HoVo
Thou reader.—HoVo
Thought.—HoVo
"To get the final lilt of songs".—HoVo
To old age.—HoVo
To rich givers.—HoVo
To soar in freedom and in fullness of power.—
     HoVo
To you.—HoVo
What am I after all.—HoVo
"What do you seek so pensive and silent". See
     Starting from Paumanok

"When I heard the learn'd astronomer".—HoVo
When I read the book.—HoVo
"When lilacs last in the dooryard bloom'd".—
     HoVo
The words of the true poems.—SuI
"Would you hear of an old-time sea fight".—SuI
"Year that trembled and reel'd beneath me".—
     HoVo
"You sea, I resign myself to you also, I guess what
     you". See Song of myself
Whittemore, Reed
The tarantula.—ElW
Whittier, John Greenleaf
Barbara Frietchie.—ElW
The pumpkin ("Ah, on Thanksgiving day, when
     from east and from west").—SuI
Who. Lilian Moore.—LiDd
Who am I. Kali Grosvenor.—SlM
"Who am I, I am me". See "Elim, elim, ep elim"
"Who are you, a dirty old man". Mother Goose.—
     OpI—WaM
"Who called, I said, and the words". See Echo
"Who can be born black". Mari Evans.—SlM
"Who can open the door". See Overture
"Who comes here". Mother Goose.—WaM
"Who folds a leaf down". Unknown.—OpI
"Who has gone farthest, for I would go no further".
     See Excelsior
"Who has seen the wind". Christina Georgina
     Rossetti.—BaW—DeS—KeT—LiDd—MoS—
     StP
"Who I". See March bear
"Who is it calling by the darkened river". See
     Voices
"Who is it hides my sandals when I'm trying to get
     dressed". See Late for breakfast
"Who is it up there on top of the lodge". See It is
     I, the little owl
"Who is the East". See Yellow man, purple man
"Who knows if the moon's". Edward Estlin
     Cummings.—DeS
Who lived in a shoe. Beatrix Potter.—DeS
"Who needs". See February 14
"Who ooo". See Whooo
"Who put the overalls in Mrs. Murphy's chowder".
     Unknown.—ScA
     Endless chant.—WiA
Who really. Walter De La Mare.—DeR
"Who said, peacock pie". See The song of the mad
     prince
"Who says a mouse is timid". See Timid as a mouse
"Who tells the little deer mouse". See Deer mouse
"Who to trade stamps with". X. J. Kennedy.—KeK
"Who, who, who is it". Eve Merriam.—LiIf
Whoa. Max Fatchen.—FaCm
"Whoa, mule, whoa". Unknown.—WiA
"Whodunit". See Spilt milk, whodunit
Whodunnit. Eve Merriam.—MeCh
"Whoever egged our house on Halloween". See After
     Easter snow
"Whoever planned". See Wise
The wholly family. Eve Merriam.—MeS
"Whom shall I marry". Unknown.—WiA
Whooo. Lilian Moore.—LiIf
Whoopee ti yi yo, git along, little dogies.
     Unknown.—SuI
Whoops. See "A horse and a flea and three blind
     mice"
Whoops, Johnny. Unknown.—CoE
"Who's been". See Who
"Who's been squashing Billy Ray Smith". See Billy
     Ray Smith

Who's here. Eve Merriam.—MeS
"Who's sleepy". Aileen Fisher.—FiA
"Who's that tickling my back, said the wall". See The tickle rhyme
"Who's the one". See Snow stitches
Who's there. Max Fatchen.—FaCm
Whose boo is whose. X. J. Kennedy.—PrFo
Whose little pigs. Mother Goose.—CII
"Whose little pigs are these, these, these". See Whose little pigs
"Whose woods these are I think I know". See Stopping by woods on a snowy evening
"Whsst, and away, and over the green". See Nothing
Why ("Why do apricots look like eggs"). William Jay Smith.—SmL
Why ("Why do you weep, Mother, why do you weep"). Walter De La Mare.—DeR
Why are they happy people. Maya Angelou.—AnI
Why because. Brian MacKinnon.—BoT
Why can't a girl be the leader of the boys. Kalli Dakos.—DaI
"Why celebrate with bitter herbs". See Seder
"Why did I jump". See Why because
Why did the fireman. Arnold Adoff.—AdCh
Why dinosaurs disappeared. X. J. Kennedy.—KeGh
"Why do apricots look like eggs". See Why
"Why do you think". See Tell me
"Why do you weep, Mother, why do you weep". See Why
"Why does he still keep ticking". See The dunce
Why I always brush. Arnold Adoff.—AdCh
"Why lie abed when the sun's rising high". See Independence day
"Why oh why did an active volcano". See Backyard volcano
Why Rosalie did it. Jim Wayne Miller.—JaM
Why there are no cats in the forest. Simeon Dumdum.—NyT
"Why this child". See Poor grandma
"Why won't it snow in summer". See Wishing for winter in summer
Whyte, Jon
    Coyotes ("The coyotes are howling").—BoT
"Wi' decks awas'". See Nod's song
Wicked thoughts. Judith Viorst.—PrFo
Wicked witch's kitchen. X. J. Kennedy.—BaH—LiHp
Wicked witch's travels. X. J. Kennedy.—KeGh
"Widdicote, waddicote". Unknown.—OpT
"Wide are the meadows of night". See Wanderers
A widow's weeds. Walter De La Mare.—DeR—MaP
Wiggle waggle, wiggle waggle. Unknown.—CII
Wigs
    "Barber, barber, shave a pig". Mother Goose.—WaM
    "Gregory Griggs, Gregory Griggs". Mother Goose.—SuO
Wilbur, Richard
    Boy at the window.—ElW
    Digging for China.—SuI
    The opposite of two.—LoFh
    A prayer to go to paradise with the donkeys, tr.—CaB
    Running.—KnAs
    The writer.—SuI
Wild are the waves. Walter De La Mare.—DeR
"Wild are the waves when the wind blows". See Wild are the waves
Wild boars. Basho, tr. by Tze-si Huang.—DeI
Wild geese. Sandra Liatsos.—HoS
The wild goose. Misune, tr. by Tze-si Huang.—DeI

"Wild nights, wild nights". Emily Dickinson.—GoU
Wilde, Oscar
    The harlot's house.—ElW
Wildlife refuge. X. J. Kennedy.—KeGh
Wildpeace. Yehuda Amichai, tr. by Chana Bloch.—NyT
Wiley, Martyn, and McMillan, Ian
    My dad said.—FoLe
    Winter forest on Market Street.—FoLe
Wilhelm, Hoyt (about)
    For Hoyt Wilhelm. J. Oppenheimer.—KnAs
Wilkins, Alice
    The elephant's trunk.—SuI
Wilkinson, Anne
    Once upon a great holiday.—FoLe
Will ever. Walter De La Mare.—DeR—MaP
"Will he ever be weary of wandering". See Will ever
"Will-o'-the-wisp". Walter De La Mare.—DeR
Will you. Eve Merriam.—HoS
"Will you come". Edward Thomas.—MoR
"Will you walk a little faster, said a whiting to a snail". See The lobster quadrille
"Will you walk into my parlor, said the spider to the fly". See The spider and the fly
Willard, Nancy
    The games of night.—JaP
    A hardware store as proof of the existence of God.—JaP
    The king of cats sends a postcard to his wife.—LaCc
    Magic story for falling asleep.—HoSt—MoS
    One more time.—SaB
"Willful waste brings woeful want". Mother Goose.—WaM
"William Penn". William Jay Smith.—SmL
Williams, Dick
    "Our Father in heaven".—StP
Williams, Tennessee
    The Glass Menagerie, sels.
        "I didn't go to the moon, I went much further".—GoT
    "I didn't go to the moon, I went much further". See The Glass Menagerie
Williams, William Carlos
    Illegitimate things.—MoR
    The manoeuvre.—CaB
    Poem ("As the cat").—MoR
    The term.—BaW
    This is just to say.—ElW
Williams, Ted (about)
    The kid. K. Bezner.—KnAs
"Willie built a guillotine". William E. Engel.—PrFo
"Willie, Willie wheezer". Unknown.—ScA
"Willimae, she wouldn't, wouldn't". See Willimae's cornrows
Willimae's cornrows. Nanette Mellage.—SlM
Willis C. Sick. John Ciardi.—CiH
"Willis Comfort did not outlive". Jo Carson.—CaS
Willow cats. Aileen Fisher.—FiA
Willow trees
    Pussy willows. A. Fisher.—FiA
    Willow cats. A. Fisher.—FiA
Willy nilly. Eve Merriam.—MeP
"Willy nilly, round and round". See In a whirl
Wilson, Edward E.
    Autumnal equinox.—JaM
Wilson, Gina
    Jim-jam pyjamas.—CoAz
Wilson, J. F.
    Let X equal half.—LiLo
Wilson, Keith
    The dog poisoner.—JaM

"The **wind** has lots of noises". See Wind
"**Wind** has shaken autumn down". Tony Johnston.—FrS
"The **wind** has such a rainy sound". Christina Georgina Rossetti.—KeT
"**Wind** in the park". See Envoi, Washington Square Park
The **wind** in the willows, sels. Kenneth Grahame
The song of Mr. Toad.—CoAz
"**Wind** is a cat". Ethel Romig Fuller.—BaW
The **wind** is calling me away. Kalli Dakos.—DaI
The **wind** is from the north. Robert Hillyer.—GoT
Wind on the hill. Alan Alexander Milne.—BaW
Wind song. Lilian Moore.—DeS
"The **wind** stood up, and gave a shout". See The wind
"**Wind** takes the world". Eve Merriam.—MeY
"The **wind** that whirled your hat away". See While you were chasing a hat
"The **wind,** the wind". Unknown.—ScA
"The **wind** was throwing snowballs". See Snowball wind
"The **wind,** yes, I hear it, goes wandering by". See The wind
The **windhover**. Gerard Manley Hopkins.—CaB
"The **Windigo** is a spirit of the North, the Cree told us". See Windigo spirit
Windigo spirit. Ken Stange.—BoT
Windlady. James Reaney.—BoT
Windmills. See Millers and mills
The **window** ("Behind the blinds I sit and watch"). Walter De La Mare.—DeR—MaP
Window ("Night from a railroad car window"). Carl Sandburg.—DeT
The **window** cleaner. M. Long.—BaW
"**Window** window window pane". See Summer shower
Windows
"Flashing neon night". J. W. Hackett.—LaN
Frost. V. Worth.—WoAl
The frost pane. D. McCord.—MoS
Ginger. Unknown.—OpT
"Lift me up". M. C. Livingston.—LiMh
The little shop (for a picture). W. De La Mare.—DeR
News for the cafeteria. S. Fisher.—JaPr
Objectivity. M. Jamal.—AgL
The open shutter. K. Krolow.—NyT
Questioning faces. R. Frost.—LiIf
Summer shower. D. McCord.—KeT
Tree at my window. R. Frost.—ElW
The window ("Behind the blinds I sit and watch"). W. De La Mare.—DeR—MaP
Window ("Night from a railroad car window"). C. Sandburg.—DeT
The window cleaner. M. Long.—BaW
"**Windrush** down the timber chutes". See Mountain wind
Winds. See Wind
Wind's foam. Al Mahmud, tr. by Marian Maddern.—NyT
Windshield wiper. Eve Merriam.—MeCh
Windy nights. Robert Louis Stevenson.—DeS—DeT—MoR
Windy tree. Aileen Fisher.—FiA
Windy work. Max Fatchen.—FaCm
"**Wine** and cakes for gentlemen". Mother Goose.—WaM
Winner ("Mrs. Macey worked behind"). Paul B. Janeczko.—JaB
Winner ("What I remember most"). Gene Fehler.—MoA

Winnick, Karen B.
Snowstorm.—LiPf
"**Winograd's** a real jerk". See T. C. Tyler
Winston Hines. Mel Glenn.—GlBc
Winter. See also December; January; February; also Seasons; Snow
Alone in winter. J. P. Lewis.—LeT
Barn owl. M. Singer.—SiT
Beauty and the beast, an anniversary. J. Yolen.—YoFf
Betsy Robin. W. J. Smith.—SmL
Bird watcher. J. Yolen.—YoBi
The border bird. W. De La Mare.—DeR
A brief note to the bag lady, ma sister. Y. Eradam.—NyT
Bullhead in winter. M. Singer.—SiT
Buried treasure. A. Fisher.—FiA
The cat's eye. Yorie.—DeI
Caw. W. De La Mare.—DeR
Chrysalis diary. P. Fleischman.—FlJ
"Cold and raw the north winds blow". Mother Goose.—WaM
A commercial for spring. E. Merriam.—MeP
Coyotes ("The coyotes are howling"). J. Whyte.—BoT
Crows. V. Worth.—SuI—WoAl
Crumbs. W. De La Mare.—DeR
The cucumber. N. Hikmet.—NyT
Deer mouse ("Get get get get get"). M. Singer.—SiT
Dragon smoke. L. Moore.—DeS—DeT
The fire. W. De La Mare.—DeR
The first flakes are falling on our heads. A. Adoff.—AdIn
First sight. P. Larkin.—CaB—ElW
First snow ("When autumn stills"). A. Fisher.—FiH
First snowfall. A. Fisher.—FiH
Frost. V. Worth.—WoAl
A frosty night. R. Graves.—ElW
Furry bear. A. A. Milne.—DeS
Galoshes. R. Bacmeister.—DeS
The ghost chase. W. De La Mare.—DeR
"Good-by my winter suit". N. M. Bodecker.—MoS
Grandmother in winter. X. J. Kennedy.—LiPg
Grandpa bear's lullaby. J. Yolen.—DeS—HoS—MoS
Ground hog day. L. Moore.—DeT
Groundhog Day. M. Pomeroy.—CoAz
Hot milk. X. J. Kennedy.—KeK
"Hurry, hurry, Mary dear". N. M. Bodecker.—KeT
"I do not mind you, winter wind". J. Prelutsky.—BaW
I meet sweet Sue for a walk on a cold and sunny afternoon. A. Adoff.—AdCh
Ice. W. De La Mare.—DeR
Ice fishing. D. Pendleton.—KnAs
"In the valley in the vinter time". Unknown.—WiA
January. J. Updike.—FrS
January deer. M. Singer.—SiT
Joe. D. McCord.—MoS
Letter from my son. S. Sarkar.—NyT
Manhattan lullaby ("Now lighted windows climb the dark"). R. Field.—KeT
March hares. W. De La Mare.—DeR
March thaw. X. J. Kennedy.—KeK
The Milky Way. B. J. Esbensen.—LaN
Morning horses. Basho.—DeI
"Mother, we are cold". Unknown.—SnD

Writers and writing.—*Continued*

Catch ("Two boys uncoached are tossing a poem together"). R. Francis.—KnAs
Daybreak in Alabama. L. Hughes.—SuC
Everything in its place. F. McNeil.—BoT
The flying pen. E. Merriam.—MeS
The gatherer. A. Al-Mak.—NyT
Ghost story. R. Pack.—JaM
The gingerbread grandma. J. C. Thomas.—LiPg
Hen. W. J. Smith.—SmL
In the kitchen. J. Joubert.—NyT
The instruction manual. J. Ashbery.—ElW
Janet DeStasio. M. Glenn.—GlBc
Lamento. T. Transtromer.—NyT
Luanne Sheridan. M. Glenn.—GlBc
Mr. Smith. W. J. Smith.—SmL
"My head doth ache". Unknown.—OpI
Paperclips. X. J. Kennedy.—KeK
The pen. M. Al-Ghuzzi.—NyT
Pencils. B. J. Esbensen.—EsW
"Piping down the valleys wild". W. Blake.—DeT
Poetry ("What is poetry, who knows"). E. Farjeon.—ElW
Prose and poetry. E. Merriam.—MeS
Rainbow writing. E. Merriam.—MeS
Shut not your doors. W. Whitman.—HoVo
Sir John Mandeville's report on the griffin. J. Yolen.—LiDd
"Some write for pleasure". Unknown.—WiA
To the field goal kicker in a slump. L. Pastan.—KnAs
Ways of composing. E. Merriam.—MeS
When I read the book. W. Whitman.—HoVo
"When on this page you look". Unknown.—WiA
The writer. R. Wilbur.—SuI
"A wry smile cut your face". See There was a sound of airy seasons passing

Wu-ti, Liang

From the most distant time, tr. by Kenneth Rexroth.—GoT

Wynken, Blynken, and Nod. Eugene Field.—ElW

"**Wynken,** Blynken, and Nod one night". See Wynken, Blynken, and Nod

Wynne-Jones, Tim

Holes.—BoT

X

X is for x. William Jay Smith.—SmL
"**X,** x, x". See Eraser
"**Xiao** Ming, Xiao Ming". Unknown.—YoS
"Little Ming, Little Ming".—YoS
"**Xiao** pi qiu, xiang jiao li". Unknown.—YoS
"A little ball, a banana, a pear".—YoS

Y

Y is for yarn. William Jay Smith.—SmL
Yacht for sale. Archibald MacLeish.—KnAs
Yak ("The long haired yak has long black hair"). William Jay Smith.—SmL
The **yak** ("There was a most odious yak"). Theodore Roethke.—LiLo
Yak ("Yickity yackity, yickity yak"). Jack Prelutsky.—WhAa
"The **yak** is an old chatterbox of an ox". See The noise in the mountains

Yaks

Flight of the long-haired yak. W. J. Smith.—SmL
The noise in the mountains. J. P. Lewis.—LeA
Our yak. Unknown.—ClI
Yak ("The long haired yak has long black hair"). W. J. Smith.—SmL
The yak ("There was a most odious yak"). T. Roethke.—LiLo
Yak ("Yickity yackity, yickity yak"). J. Prelutsky.—WhAa

Yaku

"A discovery".—WhAa
Haiku.—DeT
Haiku. See "A discovery"

Yalim, O.

At the beach ("The waves are erasing the footprints"), tr.—NyT

Yamabe, Akahito

"I wish I were close".—GoU

Yanez, Ricardo

The penguin ("The penguin isn't meat, fish or bird"), tr. by Raul Aceves and Arturo Suarez and Jane Taylor.—NyT

"**Yankee** Doodle came to town". Mother Goose.—SuO
The **Yankees.** Robert Lord Keyes.—MoA
"The **Yankees** are in spring training". See The Yankees
"**Yankees,** Yankees". Unknown.—MoA
"**Yap** yawp palaver prattle". See Gab

Yaso

The winter cat, tr. by Tze-si Huang.—DeI
Yawn. Sean O. Huigan.—BoT
"**Yeah,** yeah, I know I was". See Hector Velasquez
Year. See Months; New Year; Seasons
"**Year** that trembled and reel'd beneath me". Walt Whitman.—HoVo
"**Year** we worked". See Sparrow
"**Yearn** thou may'st". See The coquette
"The **year's** at the spring". From Pippa passes. Robert Browning.—ElW—StP
"The **years** have made up my face". See Toward myself
"**Years** they mistook me for you". See Dodo

Yeats, William Butler

Down by the salley gardens.—ElW
He wishes for the cloths of heaven.—ElW
The mermaid.—AgL
The song of the old mother.—ElW
The song of wandering Aengus.—ElW—GoU
To a squirrel at Kyle-na-no.—DeS—LiDd
The white birds.—GoU

"**Yelling,** shouting, arguing". See Home

Yellow (color)

Duet. R. Krauss.—MoR
Yellow sonnet. P. Zimmer.—JaP
"**Yellow** cornmeal". Unknown.—ScA
Yellow man, purple man. Emily Dickinson.—KeT
Yellow sonnet. Paul Zimmer.—JaP
The **yellow** tulip. George Swede.—BoT
Yellow weed. Lilian Moore.—LiDd
Yeo ho. See Andy Battle's and Nod's song
The **yes** and the no, Redondo. Greg Pape.—JaPr
"**Yes** sir, no sir". Unknown.—WiA
Yesterday. Jean Little.—LiHe
"**Yesterday** I knew all the answers". See Yesterday
The **yeti.** John Gardner.—WhDd
"The **yeti** is a manlike beast". See The yeti
"The **yeti's** a beast". See The truth about the abominable footprint

"**You** don't have to go very far". See Some sights sometimes seen and seldom seen
"**You** don't have to insist on being yourself". See Agies's advice
"**You** go to church in England". See A different kind of Sunday
"**You** got a problem, kid". See Ms. Marilyn Lindowsky, counselor
"**You** have enslaved me with your lovely body". See The apple
"**You** have seen the world, you have seen the zoo". See Swan
"**You** hold the bat at eye-level". See Sacrifice bunt
"**You** in your shrunk-tight swimming suit". See Romping in the rain
"**You** keep our love hidden". See Love story (for Deirdre)
"**You** know". Jo Carson.—CaS
"**You** know I think". See Yawn
"**You** know, I'm a little ashamed". See Louleen's feelings
"**You** know Lou Beal". Jo Carson.—CaS
"**You** know my stupid parakeet". See My stupid parakeet named after you
"**You** know that old woman". See Who lived in a shoe
"**You** know the other day we went over at George's get some eggs". Jo Carson.—CaS
"**You** limb of a spider". Unknown.—OpI
"**You** little birds, I bring my crumbs". See Crumbs
"**You** live in de cement house, and no worry de hurricane". Unknown.—LeCa
"**You** make the cash-tills ring". See Pair of hands against football
"**You** may hang your hat on the nose of the Rhino". See Rhinoceros
"**You** may not believe it, for hardly could I". See The pumpkin
"**You** may not care at all for me". See Rebus Valentine
"**You** 'mind me of a man". See A southern circular saying
"**You**, neighbor God, if in the long night". Rainer Maria Rilke, tr. by Joan Erikson.—StP
"**You** never see a cow that kicks who doesn't produce a calf that kicks". From Jamaican Caribbean proverbs. Unknown.—BeW
"**You** never see me". Myra Cohn Livingston.—LiMh
"**You** never see them". See Coyotes
"**You** pleased with yourself". See You and yourself
You rang. Max Fatchen.—FaCm
"**You** ruined the Christmas tree". See On this, a holy night
"**You** said red hair made you". See Sister
"**You** sea, I resign myself to you also, I guess what you". From Song of myself. Walt Whitman.—HoVo
"**You** shouldn't meet, according to all rules". See Bird sighting
"**You** stand still in midair". See To a snowflake
"**You** step up to the platter". See Along came Ruth
"**You** stick out your tongue". See The tongue
You too lie down. Dennis Lee.—KeT
"**You** twist". See Football
"**You** wake me up, Father". Unknown.—StP
"**You** want me to go to the board". See Mallory Wade
"**You** were going to wear red". See Autumn with a daughter who's just catching on
"**You** will be running to the four corners of". See The four corners of the universe

"**You** will need a dozen assorted unlabeled cans of". See Hot and cold tin can surprise
"**You** won't believe it". See New Dad
"**You** wouldn't know". See The way I really am
"**You'll** find whenever the New Year comes". See Chinese New Year
"**You'll** never know a grosser grocer". See No grosser grocer
Young, Gary
To raise a chimney.—JaM
Young, Ree
Po's garden.—JaP
The storyteller ("I'll tell you what is real").—JaM
Young. Anne Sexton.—AgL—JaPr
Young calves. Banko, tr. by Tze-si Huang.—DeI
A **young** farmer of Leeds. See "There was a young farmer of Leeds"
"**Young** Frankenstein's robot invention". Berton Braley.—LiLo
A **young** lady from Glitch. Tamara Kitt.—DeS
A **young** lady of Crete. See "There was a young lady of Crete"
"A **young** man from old Terre Haute". William Jay Smith.—SmL
"**Young** radical Byron McNally". William Jay Smith.—SmL
"**Young** Roger came tapping at Dolly's window". Mother Goose.—WaM
Young soul. Imamu Amiri Baraka.—SuC
Young wrestlers. Grace Butcher.—KnAs
"**Younger** than they". See Sister
"**Youngling** fair, and dear delight". See Dear delight
"**Your** absent name at roll call was more present". See Anthony
"**Your** eyes, a searching yellow light". See The owl
"**Your** hand". See Love letters, unmailed
"**Your** hands lie open in the long fresh grass". See Silent noon
"**Your** intestines". See Pogoing
"**Your** moment, mayfly month". See Mayflies
"**Your** skin was blue". See Early love
"**Your** sore throat germ may say, heh heh.". See Things on a microscope slide
"**Your** street was named for berries". See Late
"**Your** voice sounds like a scorpion being pushed". See Sweet like a crow
Your world. Georgia Douglas Johnson.—SlM
"**Your** world is as big as you make it". See Your world
"**You're** a fat old man". See Another dad
"**You're** a poet". Unknown.—WiA
"**You're** in the mood for freaky food". See Wicked witch's kitchen
"**You're** my turtle". Eve Merriam.—MeY
"**You're** the one who called me down here, Mrs. L.". See Jimmy Zale
Youth. See Babies; Childhood recollections; Children and childhood; Youth and age
Youth and age
About angels and age. J. Little.—LiHe
About old people. J. Little.—LiHe
The admiration of Willie. G. Brooks.—PlW
Almost a madrigal. S. Quasimodo.—GoT
Aunt Roberta. E. Greenfield.—MoS
Babe and Lou. F. Douskey.—KnAs
"Baby's heart is lifted up". R. L. Gales.—StP
Beautiful women. W. Whitman.—HoVo
Beauty and the beast, an anniversary. J. Yolen.—YoFf
"Believe me, if all those endearing young charms". T. Moore.—ElW
"Beside a stone three". C. M. Krishnasami.—NyT

Z

DIRECTORY OF PUBLISHERS
AND DISTRIBUTORS

Abrams. Harry N. Abrams, Inc., Publisher, 120 Woodbine Avenue, Bergen-field, NJ 07621. 1-800-345-1359.

Atheneum. Atheneum Books, Macmillan Publishing Company, Inc., 866 Third Avenue, New York, NY 10022. 1-800-257-5755.

Bradbury. Bradbury Press, Macmillan Child Group, 866 Third Avenue, New York, NY 10022. 1-800-257-5755.

Candlewick. Candlewick Press, 207 Massachusets Avenue, Cambridge, MA 02140. 1-800-526-0275.

Checkerboard. Checkerboard Press, Inc., 30 Vesey Street, New York, NY 10007. 1-212-571-6300.

Clarion. Clarion Books, Houghton Mifflin Company, 222 Berkeley Street, Boston, MA 02116. 1-800-225-3362.

Dial. Dial Books for Young Readers, Penguin USA, 375 Hudson Street, New York, NY 10014-3657. 1-212-366-2000.

Dutton. Dutton Children's Books, Penguin USA, 375 Hudson Street, New York, NY 10014-3657. 1-212-366-2000.

Faber. Faber & Faber, Inc., 50 Cross Street, Winchester MA 01890. 1-800-666-2211.

Farrar. Farrar, Straus & Giroux, Inc., 19 Union Square West, New York, NY 10003. 1-212-741-6900.

Four Winds. Four Winds Press, Macmillan Children's Book Group, 866 Third Avenue, New York, NY 10022. 1-800-257-5755.

Greenwillow. Greenwillow Books, William Morrow & Co, Inc., 1350 Avenue of the Americas, New York, NY 10019. 1-800-843-9389.

Harcourt. Harcourt Brace & Company, 6277 Sea Harbor Drive, Orlando, FL 32887. 1-800-346-8648.

Harper. Harper & Row, HarperCollins Publishers, Inc., 10 East 53rd Street, New York, NY 10022-5299. 1-800-331-3761; 1-800-328-3443.

HarperCollins. HarperCollins Publishers, Inc., 10 East 53rd Street, New York, NY 10022-5299. 1-800-331-3761; 1-800-328-3443.

Holiday. Holiday House, Inc., 425 Madison Avenue, New York, NY 10017. 1-212-688-0085.

Holt. Henry Holt & Co., Inc., 115 West 18th Street, New York, NY 10011. 1-800-488-5233.

Houghton. Houghton Mifflin Company, 222 Berkeley Street, Boston, MA 02116. 1-800-225-3362.

Hyperion. Hyperion Books for Children, Disney Book Publishing, Inc., 114 Fifth Avenue, New York, NY 10011. 1-800-343-9204.

Joy Street. Joy Street Books. Little, Brown & Company, Time & Life Building, 1271 Avenue of the Americas, New York, NY 10020. 1-800-343-9204.

Knopf. Alfred A. Knopf, Inc., Random House, 201 East 50th Street, New York, NY 10022. 1-212-254-1600.

Lippincott. Lippincott Children's Books, HarperCollins, 10 East 53rd Street, New York, NY 10022-5299. 1-800-331-3761; 1-800-328-3443.

Little. Little, Brown & Company, Time Warner Libraries, Time & Life Building, 1271 Avenue of the Americas, New York, NY 10020. 1-800-343-9204.

Lothrop. Lothrop, Lee & Shepard Books, William Morrow & Company, Inc., 1350 Avenue of the Americas, New York, NY 10019. 1-800-237-0657.

Macmillan. Macmillan Publishing Company, Inc., 866 Third Avenue, New York, NY 10022. 1-800-257-5755.

McElderry. Margaret K. McElderry Books, Macmillan Children's Book Group, 866 Third Avenue, New York, NY 10022. 1-800-257-5755.

Morrow. William Morrow and Company, Inc., 1350 Avenue of the Americas, New York, NY 10019. 1-800-843-9389; 1-800-237-0657.

Orchard. Orchard Books, Inc., Franklin Watts, 95 Madison Avenue, 11th Floor, New York, NY 10016. 1-800-672-6672.

Oxford. Oxford University Press, Inc., 200 Madison Avenue, New York, NY 10016. 1-800-334-4249.

Philomel. Philomel Books, The Putnam Publishing Group, 200 Madison Avenue, New York, NY 10016. 1-800-631-8571.

Putnam. The Putnam Publishing Group, 200 Madison Avenue, New York, NY 10016. 1-800-631-8571.

Random. Random House Inc., 201 East 50th Street, New York, NY 10022. 1-800-733-3000; 1-800-726-0600.

Scholastic. Scholastic, Inc., 730 Broadway, 10th Floor, New York, NY 10003. 1-800-325-6149.

Simon. Simon & Schuster, Inc., 1230 Avenue of the Americas, New York, NY 10020. 1-212-698-7000.

Viking. Viking Penguin, Penguin USA, 375 Hudson Street, New York, NY 10014-3657. 1-800-331-4624.

Wordsong. Wordsong/Boyds Mills Press, 815 Church Street, Honesdale, PA 18431. 1-717-253-1164.